WE, THE TIKOPIA

A TIKOPIA ARISTOCRAT

Pa Fenuatara, heir to the chieftainship of Kafika, and an exceptionally intelligent man. He is here in dance array, with loose hair and fringed cordyline leaf and seaweed circlets at neck and brow.

WE, THE TIKOPIA

*A Sociological Study of Kinship
in Primitive Polynesia*

by

RAYMOND FIRTH

*Abridged by the author
with a new introduction*

Preface by BRONISLAW MALINOWSKI

First published in 1936 by George Allen & Unwin Ltd.
Second edition © 1957 by George Allen & Unwin Ltd.
First published as a Beacon Paperback in 1963
by arrangement with the original publisher
Printed in the United States of America

Beacon Press books are published under the auspices
of the Unitarian Universalist Association

Third printing, October 1966

TO

MY FATHER AND MOTHER

PREFACE

I AM writing these words in redemption of an old pledge, in memory of a long association, and in confirmation of that Durkheimian principle of solidarity personified in *l'Etre Moral*, the patron saint of joint work and of scientific ideals held in common. This certainly is not a genuine "functional" preface which functions as a preface properly should function. There is no need here to introduce a newcomer, to pat a novice on the back, or to put the *Imprimatur* on the book of an amateur in anthropology.

Dr Firth has already made his mark in the world of social science. His first book on *Primitive Economics of the New Zealand Maori* (1929), based on personal knowledge of the natives, but primarily a digest of older ethnographic records, has earned him a well-deserved reputation as a worker in ethnological theory. It is indeed a first-rate contribution in its soundness of judgment, lucidity of argument, and sincerity of style. These qualities, matured and refined, will be rediscovered by the reader of this book. Later on Dr Firth went for a year or so to one of the few remaining outposts of primeval Polynesia. The numerous articles which he has published on his little island, Tikopia, have been read and appreciated by the students of ethnography.

In the present book the Author deals with the social organization of the Tikopia, more especially with their kinship system, in a manner which is bound to place the book among the most important recent contributions to the science of man. I have no hesitation in describing the book as a model of anthropological research, both as regards the quality of field-work on which it is based and the theories which are implied in it. The thoroughgoing empirical spirit, the wealth of concrete documentation, bring before us living men and women. Their affairs become real to us although presented within a sane and sober theoretical framework.

A book like this is the more welcome just at this juncture when we are suffering from a surfeit of new anthropological theories. New standards are being hoisted every few months, and the reality of human life is being submitted to some queer and alarming manipulations. On the one hand, we have the application of mathematics, in fact calculus with integrals and differential equations, to facts as elusive and essentially unmathematical as belief, sentiment, or social organization. On the other hand, attempts are made to analyse cultures in terms of Schismogenesis, or to define the individual and singular "genius" of each particular society as Apollonian, Dionysiac, or Paranoid, and the like. Under the deft touch of another writer the women of one tribe appear masculine, while in another males develop feminine qualities almost to the verge of parturition. By contrast the present book is an unaffected piece of genuine scholarship, based on real experience of a culture and not on a few hypostasized impressions. The anthropologist who still believes that his work can be scientific will therefore breathe a sigh of relief and gratitude.

Dr Firth started his post-graduate anthropological training at my seminar exactly twelve years ago, in the autumn of 1924. I, on the other hand, began my teaching career with Dr Firth as chief arbiter of argument and catalyser of discussion. During that first year of academic collaboration we two, in company with some other students, argued and re-argued kinship nomenclatures and lines of descent ; the " principle of legitimacy " and the theory of unilateral stress in the counting of filiation ; the multiplicity of kinship groupings, and the two correlated processes of extension. We vindicated the theories of Westermarck and of E. Grosse ; we redemolished Morgan and Bachofen ; we learned from Rivers and Andrew Lang, without accepting their doctrines.

I dare say that the present book contains some echoes of these discussions, yet Dr Firth has done his work, in field and study alike, quite independent of anything but the evidence of facts. His results confirm my conviction that the best approach to kinship is through the functional method. The facts of family life and of territorial grouping ; the extension of kinship bonds beyond the household and their integration into the clan system follow in Tikopia the universal scheme of kinship which, with minor and major variations, obtains in every human society. Dr Firth's findings tally with the picture of kinship in the Trobriand Islands where I have done most of my field-work ; with what Dr Kroeber in his excellent monograph on *Zuni Kin and Clan* has established for that branch of the Pueblo Indians ; with the state of affairs which Dr Richards described among the Southern Bantu in her *Hunger and Work in a Savage Tribe* ; with what Dr Lowie has discovered among the Plains Indians and was able to develop from world-wide evidence as a universally valid theory of kinship in his excellent book *Primitive Society*.

Here and there Dr Firth underlines his disagreement with older views, in particular some of those previously expressed by myself. On the whole I would feel inclined to accept most of Dr Firth's new interpretations, and even some of his strictures. Sometimes, again, the divergence seems to me more apparent than real, and perhaps over-emphasized. Thus in one of the most important theoretical sections of the book (pp. 117-123), Dr Firth gives what to me appears an excellent and fully adequate survey of the " approaches to kinship " in field-work. After having listed several lines of attack, the " residential," " alimentary," and " linguistic," he continues :

" Somewhat different is the biographical approach, which concentrates attention on the study of kinship with the child, or later the maturing individual as the focal point. Problems of the development of the child's terms and behaviour, and its movement into the kinship configurations of later life occupy consideration here. This approach, which represents *a very specific* and *clearly formulated set of problems*, has proved of great value in the work of Professor Malinowski " (p. 119, the italics are mine).

Now I certainly agree with Dr Firth that " these different approaches are by no means mutually exclusive," but I should like to add that among all of them the " biographical approach " is the least specific of all. It is nothing else in fact but one of the possible ways of co-ordinating the other data : residential, alimentary, linguistic : one might also add : legal, magico-religious, and educational. But it is not " specific " in that the " biographical " approach in itself introduces no new subject-matter whatever. It does not yield any new data over and above those already collected in the study of the local setting, material aspects of household life, legal and customary rules of kinship, linguistic terminology, and whatnot. The " biographical " approach thus implies and embraces all the others. It adds to them only one new principle of correlation: the co-ordinate of time.

In my opinion, moreover, the biographical approach is not the only way of studying and presenting the data of kinship, though its use is indispensable. Of all the possible " histories " the life history of the representative, typical individual is the one which can be studied best empirically, and which gives us one of the most illuminating glimpses into the nature of kinship. Kinship is a process as well as a product, and where there is creative change the field-worker has to study it. The human being is conceived, born, suckled, and tended ; the infant develops into a child, a youth or maiden, and then matures into a man or woman. All this takes place within a material setting and a type of social organization. In its development the individual enters gradually widening groups, takes up increasingly heavier tasks and responsibilities, till he or she becomes a full citizen of the tribe.

But even then the biographical approach implies the study of society and culture as a whole : those aspects of organization and material setting, that is, which are relevant to the problem of personal bonds derived from propagation. I would always urge that while it has been fatal to most previous work on kinship that the study of process has been neglected, yet the product has often to be observed independently of process. Take the linguistic aspect of kinship. The neglect to work out the processes of extension in meaning has led to various misconceptions. Classificatory terms such as " father " and " mother," " brother " and " sister," " husband " and " wife " were assumed to lump together whole groups of relatives. To explain this really fictitious fact hypothesis upon hypothesis was piled.

In reality lumping terminologies are not to be found, for they cannot be found. The initial situation of kinship—to me a clumsy phrase of my own invention—appears to be universally the group consisting of child, father, mother, and a few brothers and sisters of the child ; a limited number of individuals, each giving a definite meaning to the initial uses of the term. This certainly is the case in Tikopia, when Dr Firth has found, studied, and in a masterly manner described the character of the family as the earliest social setting of the child.

Later on in life the Tikopian, as every other human being who ends with using " classificatory terms of kinship," learns to extend the initial meanings. This is not a process of lumping, in which the distinctions between the real mother and other " mothers," the real father and other " fathers," becomes obliterated. It is a series of steps in which new, frankly metaphorical uses are acquired, while the old ones remain in full vigour. The function of each such extension is in my opinion a *partial* assimilation of the person addressed as " father " to the primary individual, that is, the real father. Part of the expectations, emotional attitudes, and even legal claims are thus transferred—the linguistic usage running parallel to the formation of each new social tie.

Without the knowledge of this process one cannot understand the product. Yet the anthropologist has as a matter of routine invariably to study the product, that is, the finished classificatory nomenclature first, and then only follow the details of its gradual formation. The biographical approach is thus the indispensable complement of the cruder, preliminary study of linguistic products, but it is rather a fuller and more dynamically oriented type of linguistic research than a " specific approach."

And this is the case with all other aspects of kinship. In what I like to call the " concrete setting of kinship " and what Dr Firth refers to as the " residential approach," there is no doubt that genealogies, village plans and a census must be collected, at first without exclusive preoccupation with their relation to individual development. Later on, it is well, however, to introduce here also the time co-ordinate, as in fact Dr Firth has most competently done in the present work. In short, far from being able to disagree with him, I am prepared to endorse his starting-points, and I regard his conclusions as essentially sound and scientific.

All of them are based on a rich and fully presented material. The scientifically minded anthropologist, weary of the hasty, impressionistic, unsubstantiated " revelations " so fashionable in many modern writings, will rejoice in the clearly presented fullness of concrete data, well selected, told in convincing manner, and always carrying with them a theoretical lesson. The stories, anecdotes and incidents so abundantly given by the author are not one line too long ; they impart the true scientific character to the book. To the testimony of facts is also added that of native opinion in the rich collection of documentary texts.

Thus in every way the present work strengthens our conviction that cultural anthropology need not be a jumble of slogans or labels, a factory of impressionistic short-cuts, or guess-work reconstructions. Cultural anthropology is a social science—I almost feel tempted to say, the science among social studies. After all, science lives by inductive generalization, and this is only possible either by experiment or comparative study. The widest range of cultural fact makes the anthropologist the comparative student of societies *par excellence*. The longest span of evolutionary survey places at his disposal the collective experience of mankind, and thus ought to give him the fullest historical sense and the deepest insight into human nature. Finally, forced directly to resort to the living sources of human reality, the anthropologist was first to develop methods of sociological field-work. Field-worker in exotic humanity was only later followed by the empirical student of modern societies. Looked at from this angle, Dr Firth's book is a model of a scientific contribution to anthropology badly needed at the present moment.

B. MALINOWSKI

DIAGRAMS

PLANS

TABLES

GENEALOGIES

CONTENTS

ILLUSTRATIONS

INTRODUCTION

WHEN still a schoolboy I happened to wander into an Auckland bookshop where copies of Judge Maning's *Old New Zealand* were being remaindered cheaply. I bought one, and immediately fell under the spell of that vivid, amusing and subtly accurate narrative of native custom, written by an Irishman who arrived in the country in 1833 and who lived for many years with the Maori people. Delving further into the writings of Elsdon Best, of Colenso, of Gudgeon, of Percy Smith and of Te Rangi Hiroa, with quarryings in Mariner and Herman Melville, I began to nourish the faint hope that it might one day be my own fortune to see something at first hand of a Polynesian folk who had barely come into contact with civilization. Primitive Polynesians are rare nowadays—most of these islanders have taken to farming, to cricket, to politics, and a few even to anthropology, from which point of vantage they cast a quizzical eye on the solemnity of European values and institutions. But they still exist in isolated spots in the western Pacific, and this book is a record of some aspects of the life of those of Tikopia, whom I was finally able to study.

The Tikopia are a people without much interest in the elaborations of technology or of decorative art, but they have built up a complex system of social and religious activities, to which they attach great importance. They have a tradition of hospitality, a respect for birth and for wealth, a sensitiveness to public opinion, and a realistic attitude to social intercourse. They criticize in private and praise in public, they recognize norms of politeness which without the use of " please " or " thank you " maintain in elaborate style the smoothness of personal relations, but they insist on the frank building-up of friendship on a basis of material reciprocity. They have a lack of interest in small divisions of time, a concept of labour as being without special dignity but as obligatory upon every person, without distinction of rank or wealth, and they appreciate human life not as an end in itself but as contributory to social welfare. Intensely community-conscious, they are deeply attached to their tiny, ocean-girt island home and proud of the values that their culture holds. The title of this book, *We, The Tikopia*, is not fortuitous. The translation of a native expression which is constantly on the lips of the people themselves, it stands for that community of interest, that self-consciousness, that strongly marked individuality in physical appearance, dress, language and custom which they prize so highly.

This book is a sociological analysis of family life and kinship. The treatment is detailed, partly because in these days of rapid change of custom and break-down of ancient cultures it is essential to preserve as much as possible of the records of native institutions; partly because an anthropological study of kinship in primitive society needs much more than the summary account of the principles of organization which it usually receives.

In recent years the terminology of the kinship system of primitive people has been knit up with their social and ritual institutions, and correlated with their economic and political organization; classificatory kinship terms have been demonstrated to be not cumbrous mechanisms illustrating primitive man's incapacity to differentiate between his kinsfolk, but plastic social instruments with a useful function. The work of Malinowski, Radcliffe-Brown, Margaret Mead, Elkin, Lloyd Warner and Fortune has done much to rescue the sociology of kinship from hypotheses of origins and from the arid statement of rules without reference to the degree of observance of them. Vital studies of such phenomena have been in existence for a long time, though largely ignored by anthropologists. Lewis Morgan himself, founder of the school of kinship abstractions, in a work far less known than it deserves, the *League of the Iroquois*, published in 1851, shows clearly and explicitly how the kinship system of these Indians is fundamentally bound up with their political organization. And the best description that I know of the flesh and blood of a classificatory kinship terminology in use is given in an eighteenth-century Chinese novel by Tsao Hsueh-Chin, translated in an abridged form into English by Chi-Chen Wang under the title of *Dream of the Red Chamber*.

Yet much more remains to be done in order that comparative studies may be effective.

In writing this present book I have been conscious of the need in anthropology for an analytical study of kinship, with empirical generalizations founded on data presented as objectively as possible. I have been conscious also that, primarily due to the claims of teaching, this account represents not the field-work of yesterday but that of seven years ago. In the interim there has been a great advance in the use of systematic field methods, especially in the study of contact of cultures—an advance due in no small measure to the work of Professor Malinowski. There are then many problems in this book which nowadays, if I could return to Tikopia, I would treat much more intensively and from another angle—as, for example, the influence of Christianity on family cohesion.

This volume describes only one aspect of Tikopia sociology, and I hope to follow it shortly with an account of the political and religious organization of the people, including the seasonal cycle of ceremonies known by them as the "Work of the Gods," which is the crowning point of their social life. It will be realized that this division is simply a matter of convenience in presentation; the institutions in each case are interdependent. For simplicity this further material is referred to in the body of this book under the title of *Rank and Religion in Tikopia* or, specifically, *Work of the Gods*.

More than most scientists an anthropologist is indebted in his work to the interest and goodwill of others, and it is hardly possible to make adequate acknowledgment in all cases. I can mention here only some of those to whom I am grateful.

My thanks are due in the first place to Professor A. R. Radcliffe-Brown, who arranged my expedition to Tikopia, and to the Australian National Research Council, who financed it. The officials and staff of the Melanesian Mission, especially Bishop Steward and later Bishop Molyneux, facilitated my work greatly. I was allowed by the Mission to travel in their vessel the *Southern Cross*, which carried my stores, their members gave me hospitality at their various stations around the coasts of the Solomon Islands, and their schoolhouse, rarely used, was kindly placed at my disposal on my arrival in Tikopia. For the arduous self-sacrifice of the members of the Mission and their devotion to an ideal I have the highest admiration, even though, perhaps through a difference in premises, I am not able in all cases to share their conclusions. To Captain H. Burgess, then Master of the *Southern Cross*, a special word of thanks is due for his thoughtfulness, not least for his kindness in sharing his cabin with me for some weeks and allowing me to clutter it up with ethno-graphical specimens of unwieldy shape. From Major Hewitt of Gavutu and Mr J. C. Barley (now Resident Commissioner of the Gilbert and Ellice Islands) I received much assistance, as also from Mr F. Johnston, Treasurer of the Protectorate, who did much to facilitate my entry in his appreciation of the needs of science.

Before I left New Zealand the Reverend W. J. Durrad very generously placed at my disposal all the notes and photographs taken by him twenty years earlier, when he stayed for two months on Tikopia. These were very useful in giving me lines of enquiry and establishing my linguistic foothold, while the grammatical and lexico-graphical formulations of Mr Durrad's material by Mr S. H. Ray and Bishop Herbert Williams were also of service. The resemblance of Tikopia to Maori, of which I had some previous working knowledge, enabled me to exercise a certain fluency from the beginning. The material of Mr Durrad which was published by the late Dr Rivers in the *History of Melanesian Society* (in 1914) shows his keenness of observa-tion, and comparison of my work with it will show that I was able to substantiate most of his conclusions; in some things, naturally enough, he could give only a partial or approximate account.

Dr Rivers regarded the description of Tikopia custom in his book as of peculiar importance, and Oceanic scholars may wonder why I have made so little use of it in the following pages. On my travel through the Eastern Solomon Islands, when I spent seven weeks aboard the *Southern Cross* on the way to my field, I followed almost exactly in Rivers's footsteps, and while I admired the industry with which he had amassed so much of his data, from brief calls at villages and sessions with natives on the deck of the vessel I became increasingly convinced of the arid quality of this material, its superficiality and lack of perspective. This impression was confirmed by my stay in Tikopia. Rivers himself was there for only a single day and nearly the whole of his account, as he himself stresses, was derived from John Maresere, a native of Uvea who had lived for twenty years on the island. To this man's information Rivers attached an exaggerated value. Forgetful of the lessons of his own field-work among the Todas, which demonstrated the prime importance of lengthy personal contact with the people, he was content to reproduce the material of a single informant, a foreigner, collected in a *lingua franca*, without the possibility of check by direct observation. Hence the account is inaccurate in a great many details of custom and language, even in such simple matters as behaviour towards chiefs, and the picture of Tikopia life is over-simplified and distorted.

His presence on the deck of a Mission vessel may have accounted for Maresere's denial of the existence of polygyny, of which there were a number of cases, many more than now, while his own personal situation may have led him to state that adultery was rare. In particular " John was most emphatic in his statements that a married man would never offend with an unmarried woman " (Rivers, I. p. 310). One can perhaps understand the vigour of this when it is realized that it was precisely for this offence, committed with the sister of his " father " and protector the Ariki Tafua (then known as Pa Raŋifuri), that he had been banished from Tikopia.

So though Rivers's account was useful in providing me with many points for enquiry in my own field-work, it is unreliable as Tikopia ethnography. Rivers's assumption that the Tikopia are proto-Tongans, a hypothesis on which he based much of his reconstruction of Polynesian society, I believe to be also fallacious, but the evidence for this view must be adduced elsewhere.

For the assistance given in the preparation of the material of this book, and the collection of historical and comparative data not here published, I am especially grateful to Mrs Bosworth Goldman and

Miss Nina Cohen, as to the Committee of the Rockefeller Research Fund of the London School of Economics, through whom their services were made available.   To Mr R. A. Falla, Assistant-Director of the Auckland War Memorial Museum, I am indebted for the identification of species of birds recorded on Tikopia, and to Mr S. H. Beaver, my colleague at the London School of Economics, for patiently drawing the maps of the island from my scattered materials. To Professor Bronislaw Malinowski my debt is of a unique character. To him I owe my original systematic training in social anthropology and preparation for field-work, and to those familiar with his methods it will be obvious how greatly I have relied upon them.   Much of his kinship material is still unpublished, but his discussion of it some ten years ago gave me a very great stimulus in the study of this subject.

To my parents this book is dedicated as a small acknowledgment of their interest in anthropological research, their help to me in preparing my Tikopia expedition, and the warmth, consistency and wisdom of their application of the principles of kinship.

RAYMOND FIRTH

LONDON, *March* 1936

INTRODUCTION TO THIS EDITION

This edition of *We, The Tikopia* owes much to the encouragement of my colleague and friend, Douglas Oliver. The introduction replaces and incorporates the introduction to the second printing of the 1957 issue of the book. To keep the size of the book within bounds certain sections have been omitted from the original edition: some aspects of domestic life; food recipes and conduct at meals; some linguistic material on kinship speech and dirges; a chapter on the sociology of sex; and a section on comparative data on kinship in other Polynesian societies. (A number of the less important plates have also been omitted.) These excisions have inevitably meant a sacrifice of some detail of the social background, but the essential structure and functioning of the Tikopia kinship system has been preserved. The original preface by Bronislaw Malinowski has been retained since I wish still to acknowledge my debt to one to whom I owe so much. It also has some historical interest, since it is cited by Meyer Fortes in his essay on Malinowski and the study of kinship, published in *Man and Culture: an Evaluation of the Work of Bronislaw Malinowski,* (ed. Raymond Firth), London, 1957.

Almost unknown some twenty-five years ago, the little society of Tikopia has now obtained some recognition in anthropological circles. Given the changes in theoretical interest and in manner of presentation of data in the interim, obviously a different kind of book could be produced nowadays. But (apart from the omissions noted above) were I to write the book again I would not wish to change much of substance in it. The general emphasis upon the primary place of kinship in Tikopia social life still seems to me to be correct, and the general mode of treatment of the data still seems to me to represent one significant way of approaching the problem. If I did rewrite the book afresh now I would probably devote more detail to the kin groups and their residential distribution, but this would be more in order to conform to a modern trend of interest than because anything in the earlier treatment needs substantial alteration or recasting. I would however modify the expression in one respect. Instead of using the term "house" — the translation of the Tikopia term *paito* — for the patrilineal descent group, I would term it "lineage" in accordance with what has now become general usage. The term "ramage" which I tentatively applied to the "house" I would now reserve for other Polynesian descent groups which are not unilineal but in respect of which the factor of choice is built into their structural principle. I have discussed these questions in an article, "A Note on Descent Groups in Polynesia" (*Man,* 1957, No. 2).

The book makes reference optimistically to forthcoming publications on other aspects of Tikopia culture. The main ones which have appeared since this work was originally written include *Primitive Polynesian Economy* (London, 1939); *The Work of the Gods in Tikopia* (London School of Economics Monographs on Social Anthropology Nos. 1 and 2, London, 1940); and *History and Traditions of Tikopia* (New Plymouth, New Zealand, 1961). Various articles, e.g. on the sociology of "magic", authority and public opinion, succession to chieftainship, ceremonies for children, suicide, have given material on other aspects of Tikopia life.

In 1952, by arrangement with the Australian National University, when I was Acting Director of the Research School of Pacific Studies, I was able to spend another five months on Tikopia, assisted by James Spillius, who remained on the island for nearly a year after I left. Two articles of special interest in this connection are James Spillius's "Natural Disaster and Political Crisis in a Polynesian Society: an Exploration of Operational Research", (*Human Relations,* Vol. 10, pp. 3-27, 113-125, 1957); and W. D. Borrie, Raymond Firth and James Spillius, "The Population of Tikopia, 1929-1952", (*Population Studies,* Vol. X, pp. 229-52, 1957). I myself have published a general analysis of recent developments under the title of *Social Change in Tikopia* (London, 1959) which contains comparative tables on the social composition of the population, comparative village and land tenure plans, and other data showing the extent to which the society had been modified since my first visit a generation before.

RAYMOND FIRTH
London, March 1963.

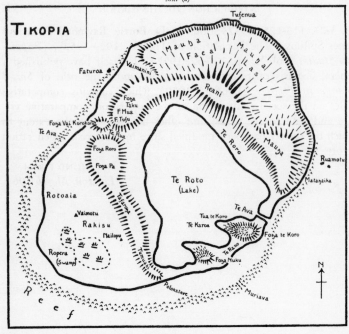

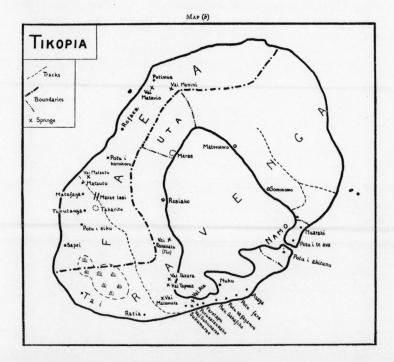

WE, THE TIKOPIA

CHAPTER I

IN PRIMITIVE POLYNESIA

In the cool of the early morning, just before sunrise, the bow of the *Southern Cross* headed towards the eastern horizon, on which a tiny dark blue outline was faintly visible. Slowly it grew into a rugged mountain mass, standing up sheer from the ocean; then as we approached within a few miles it revealed around its base a narrow ring of low, flat land, thick with vegetation. The sullen grey day with its lowering clouds strengthened my grim impression of a solitary peak, wild and stormy, upthrust in a waste of waters.

In an hour or so we were close inshore, and could see canoes coming round from the south, outside the reef, on which the tide was low. The outrigger-fitted craft drew near, the men in them bare to the waist, girdled with bark-cloth, large fans stuck in the backs of their belts, tortoise-shell rings or rolls of leaf in the ear-lobes and nose, bearded, and with long hair flowing loosely over their shoulders. Some plied the rough heavy paddles, some had finely plaited pandanus-leaf mats resting on the thwarts beside them, some had large clubs or spears in their hands. The ship anchored on a short cable in the open bay off the coral reef. Almost before the chain was down the natives began to scramble aboard, coming over the side by any means that offered, shouting fiercely to each other and to us in a tongue of which not a word was understood by the Mota-speaking folk of the mission vessel. I wondered how such turbulent human material could ever be induced to submit to scientific study.

Vahihaloa, my " boy," looked over the side from the upper deck. " My word, me fright too much," he said with a quavering laugh ; " me tink this fella man him he savvy kaikai me." *Kaikai* is the pidgin-English term for " eat." For the first time, perhaps, he began to doubt the wisdom of having left what was to him the civilization of Tulagi, the seat of Government four hundred miles away, in order to stay with me for a year in this far-off spot among such wild-looking savages. Feeling none too certain myself of the reception that awaited us—though I knew that it would stop short of cannibalism—I re-assured him, and we began to get out the stores. Later we went ashore in one of the canoes. As we came to the edge of the reef our craft halted on account of the falling tide. We slipped overboard on to the coral rock and began to wade ashore hand in hand with our hosts, like children at a party, exchanging smiles in lieu of

anything more intelligible or tangible at the moment. We were surrounded by crowds of naked chattering youngsters, with their pleasant
light-brown velvet skins and straight hair, so different from the
Melanesians we had left behind. They darted about splashing like
a shoal of fish, some of them falling bodily into pools in their enthusiasm. At last the long wade ended, we climbed up the steeply shelving
beach, crossed the soft, dry sand strewn with the brown needles of
the Casuarina trees—a home-like touch ; it was like a pine avenue—
and were led to an old chief, clad with great dignity in a white coat
and a loin-cloth, who awaited us on his stool under a large shady
tree.

Even with the pages of my diary before me it is difficult to recon-
struct the impressions of that first day ashore—to depersonalize the
people I later came to know so well and view them as merely a part
of the tawny surging crowd ; to put back again into that unreal
perspective, events which afterwards took on such different values.
In his early experiences in the field the anthropologist is constantly
grappling with the intangible. The reality of the native life is going
on all around him, but he himself is not yet in focus to see it. He
knows that most of what he records at first will be useless : it will
be either definitely incorrect, or so inadequate that it must later be
discarded. Yet he must make a beginning somewhere. He realizes
that at this stage he is incapable of separating the pattern of custom
from the accidentals of individual behaviour, he wonders if each
slight gesture does not hold some meaning which is hidden from him,
he aches to be able to catch and retain some of the flood of talk he
hears on all sides, and he is consumed with envy of the children who
are able to toss about so lightly that speech which he must so pain-
fully acquire. He is conscious of good material running to waste
before him moment by moment ; he is impressed by the vastness of
the task that lies before him and of his own feeble equipment for it ;
in the face of a language and custom to which he has not the key, he
feels that he is acting like a moron before the natives. At the same
time he is experiencing the delights of discovery, he is gaining an
inkling of what is in store ; like a gourmet walking round a feast
that is spread, he savours in anticipation the quality of what he will
later appreciate in full.

THE BACKGROUND TO ANTHROPOLOGICAL WORK

It is a matter of common agreement among modern anthropological
field-workers that an account of the institutions of a native people
should contain some description of the methods by which the

information was obtained. This is in accordance with the recognized logical position that even the simplest record of what purports to be the "facts" of a native culture has involved a considerable amount of interpretation, and every generalization about what the people do has meant a selection from the immeasurably wide field of their activity, a comparison of items of individual behaviour. The conditions of the selection—that is, the situation of the observer in regard to the material—should therefore be indicated. In terms of anthropology, it is desirable to make clear such points as : the relation of the investigator to other folk of his own culture, whether isolated from them or in daily contact ; the linguistic medium of communication with the natives, whether the vernacular, a " pidgin " or other *lingua franca*, or translation by interpreters ; the economic and social medium—payment, in money or kind, services rendered, goodwill, or simple gossip and conversational exchange ; the nature of the record, whether accounts of eye-witnesses, or hearsay evidence, or personal observation of the investigator himself ; whether what is described is current practice or is now obsolete ; and the range of instances relied upon for generalization. Elaborate documentation of every single statement is impossible in the space available, but some general reference is necessary. In the following pages details of this kind are given. They are not in tabular form but are set out as a running account, which is less of a tax on the reader's patience and allows of a realization of the flavour of scientific work in a remote community.

Rarely visited by Europeans and with no white residents, Tikopia lies in the extreme east of the British Solomon Islands Protectorate, and is inhabited by twelve hundred healthy and vigorous natives. Homogeneous in speech and culture, they are a unit of what may be termed the " Polynesian fringe " in Melanesia, their closest affinities being not with the people of the Solomons region but with those of Samoa, Tonga and even more distant groups to the east.

Almost untouched by the outside world the people of Tikopia manage their own affairs, are governed by their chiefs, and are proud of themselves and their culture. They are primitive in the sense that the level of their material technical achievement is not high and they have been affected in only a few externals by Western civilization ; at the same time they have an elaborate code of etiquette, a clear-cut systematic social organization, and they have developed very strongly the ceremonial side of their life. They still wear only their simple bark-cloth, they live in plain sago-leaf thatch huts, they carry out the traditional forms of mourning, marriage and initiation. *Mirabile dictu*, a large section of them still worship their ancient gods with full panoply of ritual, a condition almost unique in the Polynesia of to-day.

A brief reference to the religious condition of the people is necessary in order to give some idea of the setting in which my work was carried out.

A section of the Tikopia are ostensibly Christian, the mission vessel calls on the average once a year, and there is a native teacher from the Melanesian community of Motlav in the Banks group living on the island. He, however, is married to a Tikopia woman, and conforms in most respects to the customs of what has been for twenty years his home. He uses the Tikopia language alone, except in church services, he moves freely among the people, his children go through the normal ceremonies of youth, and he makes the appropriate exchanges at funerals and other social occasions. He has no ground of his own but works his wife's land in native style, and when a canoe is manned takes his place among the crew in the ordinary way. In so far as he conforms to native custom his position is that of a man of influence in Tikopia society. On the other hand he regulates church affairs with several Tikopia teachers under him, is strict regarding the observance of the *aso tapu*, the Sabbath, and endeavours to maintain morality by deprecating free sexual association of young people (an old Tikopia institution) urging marriage on those who sin, and debarring from church young men who attend the heathen festivals. He takes advantage of his position, too, to rally even the heathen among his wife's kin to assist him in large-scale gardening, initiation and other important affairs. A man of strong personality, he pursues the aims of the Church and his own advancement as parallel activities, and with equal zeal ; he is calculating but generous ; and he interprets the Christian teaching with force, in an essentially native manner.

The baptized Tikopia comprise about half the population, and though of the four churches two are on the eastern side of the island the majority of the Christians live in the district of Faea, on the western or lee side. Here is the only convenient anchorage for vessels. This has been one of the predisposing factors in the conversion of the local people. The traditional rivalry between the districts, the character of the chief of the dominant clan of Faea—a strong-willed old man with a distinct eye to the main chance—and the system of payment to mission teachers in European goods, which are greatly coveted by the natives, are other elements in the situation. The equivalent of even £1 or £1, 10s. per annum in calico, fish-hooks, knives and other articles—the salary of a Tikopia teacher—is a prodigious amount of wealth to a native family; the equivalent of the £7, 10s. which is given to the Motlav man each year contributes in a very large measure to his power and prestige. It has not been entirely accident that two of the teachers are sons of the old chief, and another is his brother's son, while the Motlav man is settled in the chief's village.

In many respects the Christianity of the Tikopia is only superficial. That the old gods still exist is never questioned by the chief or his people ; they are merely latent, and from time to time make their presence felt with startling effect. The old chief has abandoned the essence of his kava ritual—the pouring of libations to ancestors and gods with invocations for fruitfulness and health to the land. But he retains an emasculated version of it by throwing food offerings daily to his ancestors before meals. He also conducts the making of turmeric with most of the ancient ritual, especially in observance of taboos. When he fell ill during my stay, as the result of his dramatic attempt to coerce his old gods, it was by the intervention of a heathen chief with these deities that he was cured.

The heathen constitute the district of Raveŋa, and number among them three chiefs, including the principal of all, the Ariki Kafika. This man and his eldest son, Pa Fenuatara, were two of my most regular and valuable informants. Among others were the Christian chief, the Ariki Tafua, and his eldest son, Pa Raŋifuri, the Ariki Taumako, Pae Sao, Pa Teva, Seremata, Kavakiua, Pa Motuata, Pa Raŋimaseke, Pa Tekaumata, Pa Taraoro and Afirua. They were drawn without distinction from heathen and Christian, from all districts and clans, from married and unmarried, as will be seen in the course of the book.

As I moved about freely among the people of the whole island, however, most of my data were gathered not from selected individuals in set interviews but in the course of the ordinary affairs of their daily life. In particular I gained a great deal while reclining for hours at a time in the native houses during the intervals of ceremonies, or when food was cooking, when conversation flowed easily and without haste.

I spent just twelve months on Tikopia, from July 1928 to July 1929, and in that time received one visit from the mission vessel—an extra call by courtesy—in October 1928, bringing a second supply of stores and trade goods. For the ensuing nine months I saw no white man. The outer world seemed dim and far away, the only events of interest were those happening in Tikopia, and when the *Southern Cross* finally arrived I can honestly say that the colour of white faces seemed less pleasant than that of brown, and that my chief desire was for the letters of friends rather than for the company of Europeans as such. And this in no way is to impugn the hospitality of the Melanesian

Mission and the officers of the *Southern Cross*, from whom I received kindness much more than ordinary courtesy demanded, most generously given.

During practically all my stay I used only the native language, my initial medium of conversation—a mixture of Maori and pidgin-English—being abandoned entirely after the first three weeks. At no time did I have a regular interpreter. Naturally, I recorded as much material in the Tikopia tongue as possible. But apart from taking down the statements of informants in the ordinary way, I made a practice of jotting down verbatim on the spot scraps of what I overheard, conversations between people, comments on behaviour, observations made during the progress of work, and the like. These often give a more intimate insight into the human relationships involved than a long dictated text on the same theme, and I regard this type of material as among the most valuable of my records. The comparatively simple orthography needed for the language, and a fortunate rapidity of handwriting, enabled me to get down all such material immediately.

Of money I had no need, for the Tikopia do not understand its use. They know of the existence of this thing called *mane*, and that by its aid one may walk into a *fare koroa*, a house where goods are stored, and secure what one desires. From visiting vessels they have even received stray coins, but of their relative values they know nothing. Pa Fenuatara brought me a florin one day and said : " Friend, is this a pound ? "   " No," I said.

" What is its value ? "

" It is worth a knife, not a knife of the size for clearing the cultivations, but a knife so long——" (indicating a 10-inch blade).

" *A*, so that is it." And after deliberation he gave it to me as a keepsake, since, though he himself had no use for it, it was obviously a thing of value.

Another brought me a halfpenny, and said, " Friend, this is money ? "

" Yes."

" What is it ? "

I replied that it was worth five small fish-hooks for *api* and *nefunefu*, or two of the *tau kurakura* size—the only method of indicating its worth.

Others being given pence by sailors on board a warship in payment for coconuts and bananas threw them overboard on their way back to shore, exclaiming : " Useless bits of iron ! "

All my transactions took place through the medium of trade goods. Thus for the building of my house I paid Fakasiŋetevasa and his assistants the sum of one axe, two plane irons, five knives, six pipes, five sticks of tobacco and fifty fish-hooks, with douceur of rice, meat and tobacco to other people who helped to make the thatch. For the purchase and repair of my small canoe I handed over goods of about the same kind and amount, though they were received with rather bad grace, as an adze was desired instead.

This absence of money in Tikopia has a bearing on several situations. It is an index of the barrier that lies at present between the Tikopia and the economic forces which are at their door ; it was one of the conditioning factors in my relationship to my informants, since any equivalent which I gave them had to be in objects desired for their own sake, not as tokens of value ; it offers a point of comparison with the culture of other Polynesian peoples, practically all of whom now know and use money even among themselves.

At first I had the greatest difficulty in resisting the acceptance of presents, mainly of pandanus mats in exchange for my goods ; later these were implemented by invitations to meals, which it would have been discourteous to decline. Gradually, however, I made my would-be hosts understand that my goods were intended primarily not for purchase of specimens, but as gifts to those who assisted me in recording language and customs. And, in conformity with the native attitude, for the chiefs were reserved the choicest items, of which they early received a selection as an earnest. My system was to make good gifts to those who contributed valuable material and let this principle be known. In my experience the old anthropologist's maxim never to pay for information is not applicable in a community where individual or family privileges are jealously conserved. The only feasible method is to pay, but with discretion, and to rely on one's system of checks to ensure accuracy. As every field-worker who knows a native community well will probably agree, one can always find other people with some knowledge of the matter desired from the expert, and by cautious probing, by challenging his accuracy, by suggestion of his ignorance or of matters withheld by him, or by studied reticence oneself and implication of one's own foreknowledge, one may check very accurately the information given by the real authority. I myself knew for four months the secret name of the principal god of the Ariki Kafika and much subsidiary data before, his confidence won in the meanwhile, he whispered it to me himself, and unconsciously thus proved his own veracity. He never knew that I had forestalled him in this, though he suspected that some lesser " official secrets " were being disclosed by others of his clan. In such a closely knit community as that of Tikopia, where every chief and elder has links with the ritual of the others, it is comparatively simple, once one has made the first steps, to exercise fairly complete control even of esoteric material.

To make the first breach in the barrier, however, is no easy matter. When I arrived in the island my motives were of course suspect, and though outwardly very friendly and hospitable the people were really greatly disturbed. As I learnt much later, the chiefs gave orders that I was to be told nothing about their gods and ritual practices, and, such is still the solidarity against the stranger, Christian and heathen alike down to the smallest child continued to obey, and to preserve silence on such matters. Shortly after I settled in Matautu I had occasion to ask the sons of the Ariki Tafua, among whom were two Christian teachers, for the beginnings of the genealogy of their family. As one man they assured me with every appearance of sincerity that they did not remember the names of their ancestors, that even the old people did not know who their forefathers were. Surprised at finding such ignorance among a Polynesian folk, usually so proud of their descent, I let the matter pass for the time being. Months later of course they acknowledged their own deceit with a laugh, but when one realizes how in their belief the invocation of the names of their ancestors lies at the core of their safety and prosperity, one can well understand the attempt to mislead the stranger in the interests of the community. Gradually, however, I began to get an inkling of the facts. A fishing formula appealing to ancestors, the existence of the term *atua* (spirit), a disclosure by an informant who went further than he intended, a comparison with Maori custom, and the like all served to prise open the door. Even then, however, the majority remained aloof in such matters, and intensely suspicious of any people with whom I had private sessions. Even the man on whose ground I had built my house had incurred the anger of his fellow-villagers, and had been cursed by them for his acquiescence. In an atmosphere of distrust, spying, and reticence in all but overt social affairs I lived for some months, every step to establish a foothold being a struggle. Later I found that during the first few weeks of my stay a whole cycle of ceremonies of the " Work of the Gods " had taken place day after day in Raveŋa, and not a soul, not even the Motlav teacher, had told me a word about it. Men, women, and even children preserved absolute reticence. A canoe ceremony of the Ariki Taumako I indeed attended as a guest, by invitation, and also went through the ritual of the five days of the turmeric making of the Ariki Tafua, keeping its taboos, but in neither case was I allowed to realize that what I saw was merely a part of a long intricate scheme of systematic activities which marked the turn of the year. Towards the end of 1928, however, I had learned the significance of this cycle, and managed to make up the deficiency by attending the ritual of the following two seasons at the express invitation of the chiefs. And before this, mainly through the agency of one man of rank, a perversely honest rough-tongued elder, who after declaring on the beach on the day of my arrival his intention of boycotting me, later received me hospitably, performed for me his kava, and constituted himself one of my most trustworthy advisers and informants, I had obtained some insight into the real meaning of Tikopia ritual. Later again as I attended their ceremonies, behaved circumspectly, ate their food, conformed to the tapu, took part in the system of exchanges and, above all, spoke in approval of what I saw, chiefs and elders opened their stores of knowledge. Most of all, as an inmate of the houses of Kafika and Tafua, spending long days under their roofs, I began to feel the pulse of the real native life.

This was not without its reaction. When I fell ill after the ritual cycle of the monsoon season, gossip had it that the chiefs, fearful of my use of what they had disclosed, had sought my death through supernatural means. As I recovered it was said that, fearing vengeance from the white men if I died on Tikopia, they had changed their plan, and intended that I should go and die in my own land. Other responsibilities came too. The Ariki Kafika himself said to me : " Friend, I have told you the secrets of my kava ; my *ora* (life) and that of my people and this land Tikopia will go with you. I shall sit here and watch ; if evil comes to this land then I shall know that it is through your doing."

More than any other scientist the anthropologist is dependent on the confidence of his human material, and must be always faced by the quandary of how far he is betraying this trust by the publication of what he has learned. To withhold some sections of his data means distorting the picture he is trying to give.

Here I would like to express a personal feeling. What I have set down in this book, and what will appear in subsequent publications I have tried to make an exact and scientific record, keeping back nothing that I learned, and documenting opinions in order that as accurate an estimate as possible may be formed of the institutions and ways of life of these people. Much that was told me, especially in matters of religion, was given in confidence on the understanding that it would be made known only to *taŋata poto*, to adepts, to persons of wisdom. I publish it in the belief that this is being done. Should there be among the readers of this book any who may visit Tikopia, in a professional capacity or otherwise, I trust that the knowledge they may gain from it may give them an understanding and a respect for the native custom and belief, and that nothing which they find herein will be used to the discomfiture of the people or as a lever to disturb their mode of life, whatever be the motive. If this is observed I will have made no breach of faith.

As personal servant I took with me Vahihaloa, a lad of Ontong Java;[1] to secure a Tikopia who knew white men's ways was impossible. I had wished therefore for a boy who was trained, but a Polynesian, because of his ability to fit into the speech and culture of the Tikopia. Vahihaloa—Vasieloa, as they called him—was admirable in this role. With a native shrewdness was combined a quick wit and a capacity for making friends, and his flair for organizing the youth of the village to assist him in domestic duties and for attending to the proper distribution of the volume of food which flowed into our household was extremely useful to an anthropologist. His love story, a curious mixture of calculation and desire, of magic secretly practised and attraction openly disavowed, was an interesting and rather touching lesson to me in native mentality. I have since learned that tuberculosis has claimed him.

Vahihaloa soon recovered from his tremors on the day of our landing. After a month or so he began to consort with the young people, he became enamoured of the native dance, let his hair grow long and bleached it in Tikopia style. (See Plate II.)

For about a month we lived in the *fare sul*, the mission school hut kindly placed at my disposal by Bishop Steward. Then we moved to a house built for me near-by, and named Otara, after my New Zealand home. Midway through my stay I went over to Raveŋa to live, partly to become more closely acquainted with other sections of the people and partly to be near the scene of the season's religious ceremonies. There I occupied Tuaraŋi, an old house lent by the Resiake family, with father and grandfather of the owners lying buried beneath the floor, as is the common Tikopia practice. In both Faea and Raveŋa I lived in the villages, with neighbours within a few yards, so that I was able to observe a great deal of their domestic affairs with ease.

I give this somewhat egoistic recital not because I think that anthropology should be made light reading—though with a little more clarity of thought much of it might be made lighter than it is —but because some account of the relations of the anthropologist to his people is relevant to the nature of his results. It is an index

---

[1] He was transferred to my service for the time being through the kindness of Mr J. C. Barley, now His Honour the Resident Commissioner of the Gilbert and Ellice Islands.

to their social digestion—some folk cannot stomach an outsider, others absorb him easily. The student of human societies is in a different position from most scientists ; the active reactions of his material to him, the character of the association between them, determines to an important degree the quality of his data. The social or institutional digestion of the Tikopia, once induced to begin, is of a vigorous character. Conformity to their customs they take not so much as a compliment as a natural adaptation ; in a specific ceremony they can conceive only of participants, not of observers. At such a time one cannot be outside the group, one must be of it. There are limits, of course. One has a notebook, for writing is one's habit ; one does not wail at funerals, for it is recognized that Europeans are dry fountains ; but one must be of this party or that, one must keep the prescribed taboos of sitting or eating, one must make and receive the normal economic contributions.

At the same time the fact that one wears different clothing, usually sleeps in one's own house and normally takes at least the evening meal there, and acts in so many things as an independent unit, not as a member of a group, always prevents complete absorption into one's native surroundings.

Like most anthropologists I regard with scepticism the claim of any European writer that he has " been accepted by the natives as one of themselves." Leaving out of account the question of self-inflation, such a claim is usually founded upon a misapprehension of native politeness or of a momentary emotional verbal identification with themselves of a person who shares their sympathies. I myself have been assured a number of times that I was " just like a Tikopia " because I conformed in some particulars to the economic and social habits of their people, as in dancing with them and observing the etiquette of (pseudo-) kinship, or because I espoused their point of view on some problem of contact with civilization. But this I regarded as a compliment of much the same order as a reference to " our " canoe or " our " orchard (" yours and mine ") by one of my courtesy brothers, which did mean certain concrete privileges, but not a share in real ownership. This problem of identification with the native culture is not merely an academic one. Europeans who allege that they " have become a member of the tribe," or " are regarded by the natives as one of themselves," are prone to lay claim to knowing what the native thinks, to being qualified to represent the native point of view. On a particular issue this may be in substance true, but too often dogmatic statements about ideas are substituted for detailed evidence of observed behaviour.

The remaining sections of this chapter give a description of the

island of Tikopia and its people, to form a general introduction to
the study of their kinship system and social organization.

THE PEOPLE OF TIKOPIA

In my diary I jotted down my first impression of the people before
it had time to fade into the realm of accepted ideas. It was of wild-
looking men with bushy hair like a long and tawny mane, with fair
skin often stained yellow or saffron with turmeric. Their broad faces
seemed to have a strongly Mongoloid appearance, with prominent
cheek-bones and a tendency to slant in the eyes. In one or two
cases a slight Mongolian fold was present, and this impression of an
Oriental physiognomy was increased by their moustaches and short
chin beards. In stature they appeared to be very tall. With longer
residence I ceased to be so conscious of these features, especially as
the element of contrast provided by the memory of the dark, squat
Melanesians receded. The photographs (including Plates II, VII, and
XII) illustrate the variation in general type.

I made no detailed investigation of the physical anthropology of
the Tikopia, but give some data bearing on their most obvious characteristics. The idea of exceptional tallness which I have mentioned
has been put forward by other writers too, but in a more definite
sense. One indeed describes them as being none less than six feet,
and some he supposed to be well over seven feet six inches in height.[1]
Later I measured several men and found that Pa Nitini, the tallest
on the island, was 188·8 cm. (6 feet 2½ inches), Pa Taitai was 187·0 cm.,
and two others were 186·8 and 181·0 cm. respectively. These were
selected as the men acknowledged to be of greatest stature in the
island. Rimakoroa and Pa Fenuatara, who appeared to be of at
least normal height, were 177·2 cm. and 175·2 cm. respectively,
while Pa Tarairaki, who was not particularly short, was 173·0 cm.
It is doubtful then if the average height can be more than about
176·0 cm. (5 feet 9 inches), and it is possibly less.

The exaggeration by previous observers is probably due to their
sudden transition from the Melanesian environment and also, perhaps, to the coiffure of the men, their long hair rising well up above
the crown of the head. The women are big-boned and well built,
and, though I did not measure any of them, appeared to me to correspond to the men in height, the average being perhaps a couple of
inches less.

The physique of these people is magnificent. The men have

[1] W. Sinker, *By Reef and Shoal*, 59. Captain Sinker was Master of the *Southern
Cross* for many years.

brawny rounded limbs and I used to admire the musculature of the finely proportioned upper arm. There is no unshapely mass of bulging muscle ; its movement is seen under the smooth skin only when an object is grasped or lifted. The men in particular are remarkable for their upright carriage, which comports with their self-respect and their easy good manners. Their habit of getting food by climbing the steep mountain sides and descending with loads balanced on a pole over the shoulder probably assists their straight bearing. The women are apt to be more bent in later life, and this is probably to be related to their practice of carrying loads on the back. All the people bear themselves well, but the chiefs and their sons have the most dignity of all. This may be partly a reflex of the respect always accorded them.

Towards middle age there is a tendency for the figure to be spoiled by a baggy abdomen, not of the smooth paunchy type but loose and wrinkled behind the bark-cloth girdle. This seems to be due to the rapid consumption of the large masses of starchy food which form the staple of every meal. The healthy appearance of the people is the more interesting since fish alone has to supply the animal protein and so much of the other body-building constituents.

The Tikopia have no marked body odour, though the existence of " man-smell " (namu taŋata) is admitted by them and referred to in some of their traditional tales. They distinguish formally the odour of different regional groups of people, as Tongans, white people, etc. One day there was an amusing experience in which the tables were turned on the scientist. As I entered the house of the Ariki Faŋarere his old wife, nearly blind, said suddenly, " What a pungent smell of white man ! " I was rather disconcerted, and sat pondering on differences in sensory acuity till I remembered my oil of citronella, which I had smeared on liberally before leaving home as a protection against the mosquitoes.

The hands of many of the people are fine and shapely. Even in a big man like the Ariki Tafua they are well proportioned and move delicately, despite their size. The fingers are long and the palm is often small in comparison to the build of the person. The nails are not trimmed. The deftness of these people is remarkable, and I have often envied the skill with which an old man would tie a reef-knot with the smallest possible ends of string, without fumbling. The natives are very handy at tying things up. They can make a wrapping out of the most unpromising material—a few leaves, a bit of waste fibre, a piece stripped from the midrib of a coconut frond. Rarely does a man carry anything like betel or food or small articles which will not go into his belt folds, bare in his hand. He forages around till he finds a leaf and something to tie it with, and then neatly parcels up the article.

The feet of the natives are large, and the skin of the sole is very thick. It is usually deeply pitted, like a piece of crêpe rubber, from constant walking on the coral reef.

Physical strength is greatly admired. In the tales of an ancestor of the Ariki Tafua he is represented as having enormously broad shoulders—" a huge man " says the narrator, illustrating with about a fathom of arm stretch! And his power is stressed in accounts given of his wrestling matches and other combats. Pa Veterei, who died recently, is a kind of hero because of his strength. He is described as a little man, but very broad-shouldered, and the people never tire of telling how strong he was in the work of squeezing out coconut cream, or how he once broke a piece of iron in two between his hands. Strength and warlike prowess are thought to go together, and the term *toa* covers both qualities.

In bodily size the Tikopia distinctions are in accordance with ours : *taŋata lasi*, a big man, refers to breadth of body, especially shoulders ; *taŋata roa*, a long man, is a tall one ; *taŋata potulake* is a short man, and *viki taŋata* a small one. A person of normal height is *taŋata nofo maŋarie*, one who dwells evenly.

One of the most interesting features about the physical characters of the Tikopia is the curious shape of the head. This can be seen, for example, in the photograph of women fishing on the reef (Plate IV). In young children the back of the head looks quite flat. Soon after I arrived I heard Vahihaloa laughing in his queer cackle at the door of my house. I asked him what was the matter. He replied, " Back along head belong piccaninny alasame timber," pointing to the child of a neighbour. I measured a number of men, not as a serious contribution to physical anthropology, but simply to assure myself that my impressions were accurate. I give the data here in full recognition that they cannot pretend to represent an adequate series. Of the people mentioned above, Pa Nitini had a head length of 19·2 cm. and a head breadth of 15·2 cm. ; Pa Taitai, 18·3 cm. and 15·5 cm. ; Pa Fenuatara, 17·8 cm. and 16·3 cm. ; Pa Tarairaki, 17·4 cm. and 15·9 cm. ; Rimakoroa, 18·0 cm. and 15·8 cm. Others ranged from a head length of 19·1 cm. and a breadth of 15·2 cm. to a head length of 17·6 cm. and a breadth of 16·1 cm. with a fairly even distribution between. I made a number of these measurements twice in order to check the rather surprising results. A number of men apparently representative of the community with no cephalic index lower than 80 and with individuals reaching above 90 is striking. This is in accord, however, with the extreme brachycephaly found in Tonga,

Samoa, and certain other parts of Polynesia. I was assured that no artificial deformation of the skull was practised beyond the smoothing of it down by the mother soon after birth. Some people put forward the idea that the flatness of the back of the head was due to the babe lying continually on its back on a sheet of bark-cloth. This does not seem to be an adequate explanation. It may be that we are dealing here with an inherited physical character.

Apart from the fact that my main interest was not physical anthropology, I did not pursue my measurements very far for fear of prejudicing my other work. Though the *tapu* of the head common in many parts of Polynesia is not stringent in Tikopia, it is observed, and married men in particular were rather uneasy at submitting themselves to examination. Pae Sao indeed, though a good friend of mine, flatly refused to be measured, and if any piece of ill fortune had befallen one of my subjects soon afterwards it might have vitiated some aspects of my sociological enquiry, as I should certainly have been held responsible for having taken away his *ora*, his soul-substance. A significant point also was that I made the measurements at different times, and the later comers professed to be quite ignorant in each case of the nature of my instruments ; it seemed clear that they had not heard of the matter at all from the earlier subjects. Moreover, it was never discussed afterwards in my presence. The garrulity of the natives on new topics of interest was usually so marked that I could not but help being struck by this reticence, and accordingly discontinued the measurements.

The shape of the men's heads is usually concealed by their luxuriant hair, and on foraging about among it I was surprised to find how little back of the head there really was. In the majority of cases there was hardly any protuberance at all. With the older men I found irregular lumps and hollows in the surface, which they explained as being due to the use of the wooden head-rest. This may well be correct, since these irregularities appear to be lacking on the heads of women and young children, who use a soft pillow instead.

Because of the almost universal practice of chewing betel it is difficult to pronounce on the state of the teeth of the Tikopia. The juice stains the lips a brilliant red which gives the chewer a most sophisticated appearance to the European eye, but the teeth speedily become covered with black film which renders them practically invisible in the mouth. It is not possible to say whether dental caries is frequent or not, but I gather the latter. Seremata from personal choice often gave up chewing betel for a period, cleaned his teeth, and then presented a beautiful white set in a smile. The state of the teeth is used as an index of age. Pae Sao, in describing his dead brother, said, " Not a tooth had fallen ; he was only a young man." And soft foods are spoken of as " the food of the old people —because they have no teeth." The common practice of cracking a nut or other hard object with the teeth indicates their healthy state. Toothache appears to be rare. Teeth are not extracted by force, but if one becomes loose it is worked about until it comes out. The native expression is like ours—the tooth " falls."

The hair is wavy rather than crinkly. The photographs show the variation in type. The hair of some men falls into close curls when cut short, but usually it remains in wavy locks ; in some it presents a very bushy appearance. Baldness is rare, but in elderly men the hair is sometimes thin on top, and the Ariki Tafua has a bald patch on the back of his head. According to an ancient tale the sky in olden times was close down above the earth, and men became bald through their heads rubbing on it as they walked. The term for baldness is *kira* which is also the word used to describe the smooth, glassy surface of the sea on a day of flat calm. Body hair is usually not abundant. This is never removed, though some people now shave the cheeks roughly with a razor. Lice in the hair are common. They are removed by a mud-plaster (*v.* Ch. XIV) or by search. Lousing is often performed as a friendly act between young people, and in villages where Sabbath observance bars other work it is a great Sunday diversion.

There is considerable variation in the skin colour of the Tikopia, from a light warm brown, almost buff tint, to a rich chocolate. These differences may occur in a single family, the former tint being represented by Pa Fenuatara, and the latter by his father, the Ariki Kafika. The mother is of a medium shade. Whatever be the physical constitution of the Tikopia, in terms of intermixture of racial stocks, it seems to me to be unjustified to pick out the extremes of skin colour and speak of them as an index of former separate types, even though the natives allege that pale skin is a family trait. It is interesting to note, by the way, that in a number of individuals that I observed the skin normally concealed under the waist-cloth was somewhat lighter than that of the exposed surfaces of the body. The skin texture is fairly fine.

Albinism occurs and is regarded as an inherited character. Pa Fenuatara, discussing skin colour, said : " Pale skin is in families, it is not in the whole land ; it is in its families not only nowadays, but from of old. Look you ! some families are families of albinism, from of old also." Pae Avakofe the elder, perhaps the best-informed man in the island, stated that albinism first appeared in the house of Resiake, where four out of eight children were so born. Now it has appeared in the house of Raŋifau, where two children of Pa Raŋimatere are so affected. In this case, he said, it is held to have come from Resiake, whence a daughter of Pu Resiake, though herself not an albino, married Pa Raŋifau. The house of Siku is said to have had albinism among its members since ancient times. Recently the sister of Pa Ratia was an albino. It is interesting to observe that the grandmother of the albino family in Resiake was from Siku, though I was not given this statement in the present connection. It appears then as if albinism in this community really tends to emerge with greater frequency in members of the one kinship group—but the genetic material is obviously inadequate. The father of the Kafika chief, Tarotu, was an albino, but here the connection is obscure ; his mother was from Akitunu, and I have not been able to trace his more remote origin on the female side.

An albino is called *te moka*. The phenomenon is disliked. " It is not good. In this land an albino is bad ; he lives like that, then dies ; his span of life is not long." Such a person, it is said, may die soon after reaching maturity. He or she may marry, but usually not. People prefer as a rule to have intercourse with such people merely and not to marry them. Concerning the origin of albinism, as distinct from its transmission, ignorance is professed. " I do not know what it may be," said Pa Fenuatara ; " I know only that the spirits create it." The only albino I knew, a little boy of Raŋimatere family, was a rather unpleasant object with his white skin and pale eyes, always screwed up against the light. He was well treated by his companions and joined in their amusements, but seemed clumsy by comparison. He and his infant sister were the only two in the island when I was there.

A fact is worth noting that may surprise many people—namely, that a brown-skinned folk in a tropical climate can be susceptible to sunburn. In the hottest months the Tikopia not infrequently suffer from this, particularly after a day's fishing in the open sea. The skin of the back becomes a dusky red under the brown and is quite painful ; in some cases a crop of small blisters forms. The person has been " sunned," as the expression is. Incidentally, on days of flat calm fishermen often plait for themselves small eyeshades (*taumata*) from coconut leaf to give some protection from the glare on the water.

I prefer to allow the reader to make his own estimate of the mental qualities of the Tikopia from an examination of their behaviour as described in this book. But a reference to a few points may not be out of place. Psychologically, these natives would present an interesting set of problems. Verbally, they are sentimentalists ; in concrete transactions they are realists. They have many expressions for affection, friendship, and the like, which they use freely, but they demand that such expressions be implemented by action, and exact a material equivalent for services performed in the name of sentiment. At first this is disconcerting to the European reared in the literary idealism of personal relations, but soon he comes to recognize it as a frank acceptance of realities, an understanding of the value of courtesy and of solid contribution, each in its own place, without the distinction between them being blurred.

In observation and memory, without conducting any systematic tests, I found them very variable. On the one hand there were elders who mixed up the order of names in their ancestral lists and honestly could not remember all names in a set of a dozen or so. Such was Pa Farekofe who was known to have a *roto ŋaroŋaro*, " an inside that kept on losing," and who had to go to the Ariki Taumako to learn the names of his own gods afresh every time that he performed a kava ceremony. On the other were the attainments of Pa Panapa, who was an expert in reading footprints, and who was said, given the mark of a heel or a toe, to be able to identify the owner correctly. The Ariki Taumako asked him, " When you look, how is it done ? " He replied, " Oh ! When I look it is as if it were the face of the person." In describing this to me the chief said, " How does he do it ? Is it by spirits ? "

In general, within the limits of their experience, individual Tikopia may be said to have reached a fairly high level of intelligence, as can be seen from some of their comments on specific situations recorded in the body of this work.

THE LURE OF THE OUTSIDE WORLD

One of the characteristic sentiments of the Tikopia is their attachment to their island home. They are proud of the plentiful food supply which it affords and of their tradition of hospitality and peaceful conduct, and have no hesitation in naïvely asking the visitor for confirmation of these views. The young men display an extreme eagerness to see the world and numbers of them beg a passage of every vessel that calls. Some even try to stow away, but are usually discovered soon after the anchor is weighed and ignominiously hauled forth to be dropped off into canoes hovering near, or pushed overboard to swim to shore—a feat which presents no difficulty to them. This keenness to visit other lands and make a closer acquaintance in particular with the works of the white man is animated by a definite object. They want to become possessed of knowledge and property from which they can reap an advantage on their return—in social prestige as tellers of tales of breathless adventure which can be made to absorb the public interest in long hours of conversation ; in the possession of prized tools and ornaments ; in the acquisition of influence by acting as interpreters when a vessel calls ; or even by making profit as teachers of what they imagine to be the white man's language.

It is hard for anyone who has not actually lived on the island to realize its isolation from the rest of the world. It is so small that one is rarely out of sight or sound of the sea. The native concept of space bears a distinct relation to this. They find it almost impossible to conceive of any really large land mass, and if they were not by now accustomed to the fact that the things of the white man appear always to be in excess of their own, they would think that a visitor in his stories was deliberately drawing a long bow. I was once asked seriously by a group of them, " Friend, is there any land where the sound of the sea is not heard ? " Their confinement has another less obvious result. For all kinds of spatial reference they use the expressions *inland* and *to seawards*. Thus an axe lying on the floor of a house is localized in this way, and I have even heard a man direct the attention of another in saying : " There is a spot of mud on your seaward cheek."

Day by day, month after month, nothing breaks the level line of a clear horizon, and there is no faint haze to tell of the existence of any other land. Not more than once in a year as a rule does a faint stain of smoke or a slender thread of a mast tell of a ship somewhere below the rim of the ocean. Such a sight is greeted with the utmost excitement. The first announcement is usually the long melodious " *Iefu !* " from some keen-sighted worker on the mountain slope, and this is taken up and re-echoed around the hills by those who hear it before they can do more than speculate on its significance. Groups of people gather on the beach, straining their eyes and their imaginations for an hour or two, until the vessel—if such it be —comes sufficiently close inshore for it to be seen from the low land. Then the excitement is redoubled. Cries of " *Te vaka ! te vaka !* " " The ship ! the ship ! " ring through the villages, and messengers rush off to announce the fact to the other side of the island. If the vessel shows no signs of coming inshore canoes are hastily launched and go in pursuit, taking with them mats, coconuts, and other objects for purposes of trade. This is where a knowledge of nautical English comes in : some people are thought to know the words which, bawled out to the captain from the pursuing craft, cause him to take in sail and heave the ship to. As far as I could gather from the distorted phrases given me they represent the common orders to " put the helm over," " about ship," etc., but they are conceived as having a virtue in themselves, a kind of magic potency which compels the listening captain to stop. Part of the recent history of the islanders consists in the narration of long tales of vessels being sighted, and of their reception or pursuit, given with an intensity of interest and wealth of detail which brings home to the listener the importance of this breach in the round of the life of the people. If the vessel does drop anchor off shore the scene is one of extraordinary confusion. Children dash madly to and fro, shrieking and yelling without purpose, while folk begin to arrive from the other side of the island, some panting with heaving chests, having run all the way in their eagerness. Canoes put off with produce and domestic articles, the people swarm over the ship and eagerly seek knives, fish-hooks, tobacco and other things in barter. Lucky is the household which secures a large knife or a length of cloth in exchange for one of its fine mats. The poverty of the Tikopia in the most ordinary trade goods and their consequent greed to possess them is pathetic.

The people have been accused of theft by former visitors. All I can say is, that in the twelve months of my stay I lost two boxes of matches, a cube of washing blue, and three sheath knives, these last being the only planned theft. And yet my house was untenanted for days at a time, with nothing more than a few sheets of thatch to keep out intruders. It was not so much perhaps the absence of the will to steal as the vigilance of neighbours and the respect for public opinion which kept away would-be thieves.

The nearest land to Tikopia is Anuta, seventy miles away across the open ocean, and even smaller in size, being only half a mile across —a mere dot in the immensity of the waters. Yet to the Tikopia a visit to Anuta is a great adventure—almost as precious nowadays as a century ago, since the natives have largely given up going to and fro in their own canoes, but only rarely are allowed a trip in the mission vessel—the single regular caller.

Time and again I was approached quietly by young men with the request that when I left I should take them with me to see the lands overseas. These requests I had always to refuse. On one occasion my friend Tiforau, burly, black-bearded and good-natured, spoke to me in his rough deep voice as he followed me along the narrow path through the bush : " Friend, when you go I am going with you to the land of the white men."

" Oh no," I replied. " You will die, of the cold and of the white man's diseases. We two shall not go, I do not desire that you die."

" Oh yes," he urged, " we two shall go. What is man, a stone ?

If I go I die, if I stay here I die also. I am an unmarried man ; if I go and die it is good. I shall have looked on the white man's country."

The logic of this was irrefutable, so I took refuge in the edict of the authorities of Tulagi who represent to the Tikopia the last court of European appeal, to the effect that the Chief there had forbidden white men to take natives beyond the confines of the country of the dark-skinned folk. But many times the young men, impatient to see the world, said : " Why does not the Governor send us a ship, that we may be taken to other lands ? " And again a common response to the warning of danger of death from disease brought the response : " There are two lands, if one goes one dies ; if one stays one dies." The two lands are life and death, and one goes from one to the other no matter the place from which one starts.

The wish for foreign adventure is controlled, however, by the desire to return home. The wanderlust of the Tikopia is really guided by his appetite for a colourful narrative with which to impress other people when he comes back ; it is himself as the traveller against the background of an audience of stay-at-homes that fires his imagination. To realize the full truth of this one needs to understand the importance of conversation to a people practically devoid of any mechanical means of amusement. The Tikopia were very interested in hearing from me how many lands I had visited. At the end of one of these recitals the Ariki Taumako said, with an intensity of phrasing, " He goes travelling about, observing, while we sit here, we simply sit." And the way in which he prolonged the nasal sound of the word *nofo* (sit) gave an indication of his envy.

NATURAL RESOURCES OF THE ISLAND

Tikopia may best be described by the simile of a hollow bowl, old, battered, and moss-grown, with a broken irregular rim, one side of which is very much gapped and the interior partially full of water. As the ancient crater peak rises from the surface of the ocean its steep outer slopes with their rich volcanic soil are thickly clothed in vegetation, and its inner walls are scarred in many places by sheer rock cliffs which ring round the large dark lake. To the south of the crater wall lies a narrow expanse of light, sandy but fertile soil, the debris, as it were, accumulated in the lee of a sheltering mountain buttress.

The island is roughly elliptical in shape, the long axis running approximately north-east and south-west, and the mean dimensions

can hardly be more than three miles by a mile and a half.[1] As is to
be expected in such a rugged spot, there is considerable diversity of
scenery and from the point of view of landscape interest alone Tikopia
has considerable attractions. The coast-line is curved, not deeply
indented, and is protected from the ocean by a fringing reef, very
narrow on the northern side, which is left almost bare at low tide.
There is no lagoon and the small area of reef offers no shelter for
canoes, which are accordingly always drawn up on shore when not
in immediate use. Furthermore, the fishing is largely dependent on
the daily covering of the thin band of reef by the tide, and is therefore
very variable. Approach to the open sea is given both in Faea and
in Ravena by a narrow channel, in each case a mere fissure in the
coral rampart, that in Ravena being such a small cleft that it is
navigable only in good weather. Even in Faea, which is normally
on the lee side of the island, when a sea is running the break at the
channel mouth is sufficient to cause a canoe to ship a considerable
quantity of water. The natives, however, are expert seamen in a
rather rough kind of way, and manœuvre their outrigger craft with
some skill, riding a wave with down-pointed bow and light, swift
strokes of the paddle, and counteracting the drag on the float which
tends to pull the canoe round and capsize it. A considerable amount
of deep-sea fishing is done outside the reef in canoes, not always on
calm days, and the passage of the channel is a technical accomplishment in which every steersman worthy of the name of *tautai* (sea
expert) is deemed to be skilled. Failure means not only the spilling
out of the crew, which is not serious, but a grave risk of splitting
the hull of the vessel on the fangs of the reef around the entrance.

The shore consists of beaches of white sand, interspersed by
rocky bluffs reaching down to the water's edge ; coral boulders are
strewn in some parts, and along the northern coast stretches of
pebbles are found. In places the beach line is pleasantly bordered
by trees, but to the south shrubs are more frequent and the ubiquitous
goat's foot creeper (*Pes capri*) crawls over the sand. In parts of
Ravena and Tufenua the shore is bare of vegetation, and at no spot
in the island does the coconut palm actually reach the sea.

The characteristic trees of the coast-line are the *toa* (*Casuarina*)
with its pine-like needles, the *fetau* (*Callophyllum*) with its small
leaves, rough bark and hard green berries—its trunk provides the
canoe timber—the smooth-stemmed *puka* with a large deeply indented
leaf and soft pinkish berries, the *fara*, the pandanus with its bloated

[1] *The Pacific Islands Pilot*, 5th ed., 1918, gives the island as triangular in shape
and measuring two miles along each of the west and south sides, and three miles
from the east to the north-west point.

stem and blade-like leaves. Inland the same occur with an occasional *aoa* (banyan) or *voia* (*Canarium*) towering above, but they are set in a bewildering mass of breadfruit, paper mulberry, Tahitian chestnut and banana, interspersed with sago, coconut and areca palms. The natives recognize at least one hundred and fifty kinds of trees, shrubs, and plants of which some are represented by only a few individuals. Tree ferns, for example, are found only around the cliff head on Reani and Tumuaki, the bamboo can be obtained only from the mountain slopes, while plants such as the *tanetane*, a shrub with large reddish leaves, the *reva* and the *taratoto* grow on the mountain top alone. Practically all the trees and plants in the island are of utility to the inhabitants : even the common grass (*mauku*) is plucked and carried off to lay as a mulch around the taro crop.

The northern end of the island is extremely rugged. Short stretches of shingly beach are hemmed in by towering black cliffs, and on the reef which extends in narrow ribs for only a few yards beyond the shore the heaving Pacific swell is always breaking with a roar. At various spots around this coast there are caves, or rather rock shelters, termed *ana* by the natives and used by them as temporary dwellings, with heaps of dry coconut fronds as bedding. The largest of them, Te Ana Lasi, runs back under a side cliff in a little bay for a number of yards, and seepage from the roof provides drinking water. One of the most remarkable features of this part of the coast-line is a huge rock buttress jutting out into the sea in the form of a natural arch, through the portal of which the waves surge.

On the west side of the island is the bay known on the chart as Ringdove Anchorage, formed by a recession of the reef, and offering the only shelter, and that a slight one, for European vessels in the prevailing trade winds. Facing this a rocky bluff stands out from the cliff. On the eastern side the most prominent features are the massive isolated block of Foŋa te Koro, 200 feet high, with its cliff face falling sheer into the sea, and the pyramid of Foŋo i Nuku, lower but no less striking. Both are crowned with vegetation.

On the south, in the flat plain of alluvial soil, sandy as the coast is approached, stand the gardens of Rakisu and the orchards of Rotoaia. An area of this in Tai is taken up by a large swamp (*te ropera*), too water-logged to be used for cultivation and encircled by pandanus—a palm which in its nudity and angularity, supported in tripod fashion by multiple bare roots, seems like the inspiration of a modern artist.

A distinctive character is given to Tikopia by its lake, known as Te Roto, or more familiarly as Te Vai, a large open irregular sheet of brackish water, fringed by thick vegetation and set against a background of rugged hills. Its charm is enhanced by the flocks of grey duck which dot the surface and the occasional pied cormorant which emerges sleek and glistening after its dive for fish. From the beach of Namo the traveller goes inland through Te Roro, or Te Orooro in the older form, passing Somosomo, site of ancient ceremonies, the Oven of ŋa Raveŋa which once cooked a child, the stone slabs of Matorotoro, and other spots famous in tradition. In the inmost bay of the lake he arrives at Uta, where the most sacred temples stand. Leaving this, he rounds a rocky point where detritus of an age-old landslide has tumbled down to the water's edge, makes use of the roots of a gnarled and twisted banyan as steps, and comes to Raveŋa. This is a flat, almost marshy expanse where the sago palm grows thickly, and the swamp-loving giant taro is plentiful. Here the cliffs have receded, and the orchards are larger in extent. The track coils in and out, stones, logs and tree roots provide foothold in the mud and water, till finally the massif of the crater ring again draws nearer the lake shore, rocks appear in tumbled profusion, and past the spring of Vai Tekara, where the women of the Taumako village come to wash and fill their water-bottles, one debouches on to the beach of Tai Raveŋa. Far above, the mountain crest has broadened into a long flat tongue-like plateau, ending in the square-cut bluff of Tumuaki, from the lip of which a superb panorama of all Raveŋa is obtained.

There are two paths up to Tumuaki. The one is a simple trudge starting from Vai Teputa in Faea and following a stream up a steep gulley till, at the base of a huge Canarium almond tree, the wayfarer diverges to a scramble up over the lip of the plateau. Here, on emerging, shrubs of *Lasiandra* are to be seen, with purple flower and soft, woolly, rusty-green leaf, looking as if they have been transplanted from some suburban garden. The other path, from Raveŋa, a toilsome climb amid sharp stones, is crowned by a passage across a bulging rock face which needs a steady head and a sure foot to negotiate. This is Te Pikiaŋa, The Place Where One Hangs On, and it is the boast of Sukimataraŋa and two other young men that they alone of Raveŋa can come down it with loaded balance pole on shoulder. Others more cautious lower their burdens first and themselves after. Above this the slope is more gradual, and soon a minor track turns to Korofau, celebrated in song as the place of the sweet-scented *manoŋi* so much used as ornament. Here too grows a tawny variety of hibiscus blossom favoured by the youth of the district. The scented shrubs of Korofau are said to have been planted in ancient days, as also those of Tumuaki, when houses were inhabited on the plateau. Nowadays people visit it only to get food from their cultivations.

At the seaward end of the crest is a knife-edge lip from which there is a view appreciated even by the natives, normally not interested in such matters. To the right is a tumbled mass of rock ending in the promontory of Polokateve, boundary of Ratia and Sukumarae, while beneath and to the left are houses in groups among the trees. Farther out is the creamy band of beach, the shallow light-green waters of the reef and, sharply demarcated from them by a white line of surf, the dark blue of the open sea. A little to the north a slight gap in the tumbling line of foam marks the channel. And away beyond, like a cordon from which there is no escape, is the clean-cut line of the horizon, ringing in one's gaze with calm inevitability. Turning more to the north one sees the whole expanse of the lake laid open, its succession of little capes and bays with every landing-place clearly marked by a series of long curved lines running out for a hundred yards or so like the ribs of a fan beneath the shallow water. These curious lines are caused by the keels of canoes disturbing the loose mud. From above one can admire the widening ripples as a canoe moves slowly across the water and the graceful curve of its wake as it turns in towards the shore.

The whole of the Ravena coast-line from Polokateve to the cliffs of Nuaraki is in reality nothing else but a sand-bar between sea and lake, broken only by the rocky pinnacles of Fona te Koro and Nuku which stand up like pointed teeth. It appears as if originally they formed part of an eastern crater wall, but after a secondary explosion were left as sole guardians of the barrier. The sheet of water in the old crater is a lake and not a lagoon, but in exceptional gales when the wind presses on a spring tide the waters of the reef may break over. Then houses and trees are swept away. This happened about 1920, and again, I have heard, in 1930, in each case the natives having their own explanation of a supernatural order for the catastrophe. On the north side of Fona te Koro is a channel cut in ancient times through the sand ridge and known as Te Ava. Normally this is silted up, but at certain seasons of the year, notably in January, at the height of the monsoon, when the lake is full from rain and the tide is high, the channel is dug out by the people of the district. The excess lake waters flow down to the sea, taking with them numbers of fish, which are caught in long-handled nets. The channel is under the nominal control of the Ariki Tafua. The vegetation of this strip of coast-line is sparse, some pandanus, a few coconuts and weather-beaten shrubs forming the major part.

In the rear of Fono o Nuku is a tongue of land that runs far out into the lake and provides an easy means of access to the inner shore. When rains have not swelled the waters, by wading breast-high along a shelf, one can reach a point near Resiake far more quickly than by circling round the end of the lake. This is an area which is used on account of its shallowness for fish drives on foot ; elsewhere setting nets from canoes is the general method of securing a catch. The lake is populated by grey mullet (*kanae*) and *ika tapu*, which are edible, and by certain species of eel and the *ono*, which are not eaten. The chief fish is the *kiokio*, lordly as a salmon in his resounding leaps, and with most succulent pink firm flesh. Not being an ichthyologist I cannot say if this is really a member of the salmon family ; I imagine that its presence in an isolated Pacific crater might be somewhat of a puzzle in distribution. Like that other prized fish, the bonito, the *kiokio* is celebrated in song.

The shallowest part of the lake is at the southern end where the bottom is soft sand or mud, and slopes very gradually to the bank. In the north-eastern end there is a rock shelf which extends a long way into the lake and renders it fairly shallow there too. This is known as the *siku* and is named Te Siku o Namo and Te Siku o Raveŋa according to location. The depth of the lake is very well known to the natives because when they set nets below the surface for the *kiokio* they buoy them and anchor them to the bottom by weighted ropes of sinnet cord, which is measured in fathoms (*rofa*) of a double arm stretch, and tens of fathoms (*kumi*). On the *siku* shelf the water is only a single fathom deep or less, and the cowrie shells which weight the lower cord of the net rest on the bottom. The deeper parts of the lake are known generally as *te moana* (the ocean), and those of specifically greatest depth as *te mata o te vai*, the fore-part of the waters, and *te muri o te vai*, the rear-part of the waters respectively. The one is near Tua te Koro and is three *kumi*, that is thirty fathoms deep ; the other near the Raveŋa shore needs four *kumi*, forty fathoms of cord, to find bottom. According to Pa Fenuatara who told me this as we were paddling across, there are no parts deeper than these. They may represent vents of the extinct crater. Spots where a deep part, " the ocean," extends right up to the bank, are known as *te kaofaŋa*, and are two in number—at Te Karoa by the side of Tua te Koro, and at Soro in Te Roro.

The waters of the lake are not used for drinking since they are too murky, but for the people on the eastern side of the island in particular they provide an excellent bathing-ground, an easy medium of communication, and a valued source of food. They play, in fact, quite an important part in the life of the Tikopia.

Drinking water is obtained from a number of springs (*vai*), the location of which is shown on the map. Those flowing down from the hill-mass to the south of the lake are regarded as the material representation of the tentacles of the Octopus God Feke. It is of great utility for a village to have a spring near, and control over these waters is part of the privileges of the clan chiefs, being important for the seasonal manufacture of turmeric. In the dry season, about the end of the year, the flow from these springs is apt to diminish to a mere trickle. In most cases the water is carried out from the hill-slope in an aqueduct of areca palm trunks supported on poles.

Northward of the lake rises the peak of Reani, the crowning point of the island, from the sociological as well as from the topographical point of view. The crest itself is termed Te Uru o te Fenua, the Head of the Land, in acknowledgment of its physical superiority. More commonly it is spoken of as Te Uru Roŋoroŋo—the Cycas Head, from the fact that a cycad used in certain sacred ceremonies grows there. The climb to Reani is steep, though in no way difficult, and a native path of tolerable kind can be followed right up to the crest. There is a choice of ways for the ascent. One may start from Te Roro directly below the mountain and go up by a stiff scramble through Mara Tapu, the sacred taro cultivation on the north-eastern crater wall, or from Namo by the path through Keresa, or on a somewhat longer way up the cliff at Mataŋaika and over the plateau of Mauŋa. As one ascends the path sometimes runs close to the old crater lip, and a magnificent view is obtained over all Raveŋa and Namo. Far, far below the thatched villages lie amid the palms along the narrow sand bar, the canoe landing-places are clearly visible, and the craft themselves crawl like tiny water-beetles over the glassy surface.

The orientation of the Tikopia tends always towards the sea. Ever and again one comes to a halting-place on the climb, a few yards of level ground where one sits down to rest and chew betel. These halting-places are naturally situated on shoulders of the mountain. The last break in the contour before the upward sweep of the slope rises to the final peak is at an elevation of about a thousand feet above the sea. This is known as Te Uru Asia, and is one of the marks for the voyager. When a Tikopia sets out from his native land his first estimates of the distance he has travelled are based on the portion of the island still showing above the horizon. There are five principal points in the scale. The first is the *rauraro*, the lowland in the vicinity of the shore. When this disappears the voyager knows that he is some distance out. When the cliffs (*mato*) arising some 200 to 300 feet in various spots round the coast become lost, another point is reached ; then the *uru mauŋa*, the crests of the chain of hills ringing the lake, perhaps 500 to 800 feet in height, sink below the waves. When the *uru asia* goes down, then the voyager realizes that he is far out to sea ; and when at last he sees the *uru roŋoroŋo*, the tip of the mountain itself, vanish from sight, he greets the moment with sorrow. Many an ocean rover has expressed in song his feelings of the instant when Reani, the Head of the Land, is buried beneath the waves, or conversely when on his return it breaks once more into view, assuring him of his course and of an end to his wanderings. This interpretation of the horizontal scale of sea distances in terms of the vertical scale of Reani, together with the sentimental attachment to it as the symbol of the traveller's linkage with his home, are largely responsible for the interest which the mountain peak has in the eyes of this sea-faring people.

In the field of the supernatural, too, it plays its part : " It is held to be the place of descent of the gods, it is there that they first stand when they come down." Reani, as the projection nearest to their heavenly domain, is naturally the spot on which they choose to set foot when stepping down into the world of men. Though it is not *tapu* in the ordinary sense of the term, and people walk on it, sit down, and behave as anywhere else, a certain aura of the supernatural clings around the mountain crest. Cultivations of taro stretch nearly to the topmost peak, but the actual crest is a tangled mass of shrubbery, rarely cleared. Here are found certain types of plant wanting on the lower levels—because of human clearance it would seem, and not through a different natural environment. These peculiarities of the flora help to make Reani a place of special interest. The mountain possesses also certain stones with peculiar properties ; one is mentioned in a myth as being endowed with powers of locomotion.

The main way of communication in the island is along the beaches of Faea and Raveŋa ; other principal paths are shown on the map. The island is seamed with tracks which are regarded as public ways open to all, and from these minor tracks diverge into the cultivations. They are all not much more than a foot in width, so that travel in single file is imperative. In wet weather the vegetation on either hand makes walking unpleasant. Then in going between Faea and Raveŋa the people often take the long way through Tai, much of which lies along the open beach. Communication between these two districts can also be carried on when the tide suits by canoe journey round the south coast, inside the reef, and heavy loads are often carried in this way. One of the most interesting tracks is the short-cut from Rofaea to Uta up the path through Te Rua, a dip in the chain of hills. It is a steep rocky way which goes for some distance up the naked bed of a water-course. The wayfarer pants up the slope, and on reaching the saddle is glad to pause on the cleared space while he prepares a wad of betel. At some seasons he is surrounded by masses of the scarlet flowers of the *kalokalo*, the coral tree (*Erythrina*) which grows there in

great profusion.   From this spot looking eastward, down through the
fingered leaves of the breadfruit he sees the calm mirror of the lake
with the pyramid of Foŋo te Koro on the farther shore.   To the west,
over banana and paper mulberry trees, he looks on the reef where the
women are plying their hand-nets.

The rugged beauty of the Tikopia landscape is enhanced by the
magnificent play of colour at certain times of the day.   In the evening
the shades of the sea vary from a steely grey where the light is reflected
on it through a pale green of the reef waters inshore to a darker green
near the reef edge, and an indigo beyond.   Sometimes when the sky
is stormy the sea has leaden hues of the same tone.   On a lowering
evening the stark staring white of the surf-line is in forcible, almost
painful, contrast to the inky black of the sea, and then on a sunny day
the water has a brilliant ultramarine shade.   The sea in its myriad
aspects was a fascinating subject of study to me.   For the ear there
was always the sound of the surf, its constant noise varying with the
wind and the state of the tide.   One evening was especially remarkable.
It was a stormy sky and there was an impenetrably dense black band
of cloud just above the horizon, which itself was free.   The cloud hid
so completely the setting sun that it brought dusk before the sunset.
Then just when the sun was on the point of setting, it broke free, and
with the lower rim sinking below the horizon and the upper hidden
by the clouds, sent a lurid crimson colour on the sea, the walls of
houses and the trunks of trees, while the land already had begun to
take on the shades of darkness.   This weird conjunction of dusky
shadows and red sunset light with a fiery sky around the sun made
even the natives remark.   They stopped to stare, though they assigned
to it no especial significance.   As a rule the more subtle and really
more beautiful differentiation of shades escapes their notice.

Another evening I noted was of the quieter kind.   Beyond the
white shelving beach was the light green sea of the reef merging to a
dark blue-grey offshore.   To the right, looking along to Rofaea, rose
the olive-green steep bush-clad cliffs softened from the rather garish
tints of full day and backed by dove-coloured clouds.   The sun had
just set and the sky was still light ; there were no lurid cloud effects,
but only pastel tints, from steel grey on the horizon through cream
to white and then to steel grey again.   In the west there was light on
the water, though elsewhere it was dulled since overhead the clouds
threatened imminent rain.   On the beach was a solitary godwit, and
in the distance were the silhouettes of people doffing their garments
as they went to bathe.   In the curl of the beach at the water's edge
some debris was washing, a reminiscence of the heavy wind of the
few days before.   As I walked along the beach the colours changed

with the different angle of view. The sea at Rofaea took on a pale bird's-egg blue, but in the open it was almost black in reflection of the coming storm. And in the west came a weird gleam, of gilt more than of gold, which quickly faded as the dusk drew on.

The climate of Tikopia is comparatively pleasant, considering that it is only 8 degrees south of the equator. The temperature is usually between 80° F. and 85° F., and rarely goes much above 90° F., though the humidity renders even this somewhat trying. The principal climatic feature is the marked seasonal difference between the period of the trade winds, known to the natives as the *toŋa*, which blow steadily in the N.E.-S.E. quadrant from April till September, and that of the " monsoon," the time of variable northerly and westerly winds with long periods of calm, which rules from October till March. This is called the *raki*. In the *toŋa* the sky is frequently overcast for several days at a time, and the weather is often wet and even chilly. In the *raki* come the baking hot days, varied by torrential downpours, and about the end of the year, by fierce gales which at times assume almost hurricane force.

In this state of isolation from the outer world, in a home of great natural beauty, adequate in the staple materials for a simple but comfortable existence, the Tikopia have shaped their life.

CHAPTER II

ADJUSTMENT TO CIVILIZATION

THOUGH the Tikopia in common with the inhabitants of Mukava (Rennell) Island are unquestionably the most primitive of Polynesians, they have not remained altogether outside the orbit of European culture. For nearly a century and a half they have been subjected to various influences of the " civilizing " order, and these have left their mark. But the changes effected by the introduction of these foreign cultural elements, though seeming fairly considerable, when reviewed in total have really done very little to disturb the fundamental social structure of the people. The Tikopia have selected the items most relevant to their needs, have adapted them to their own social forms— sometimes in rather curious ways—have ingested them by the political organization, the kinship bonds, the religious system, and the linguistic apparatus of their own collective manner of life. The process so far has been one of inculturation rather than of acculturation ; the Tikopia, secure in their isolation, have been able to transform what they have received, rather than compelled to mould their own culture to it. Even of Christianity, the most powerful force they have yet encountered, they have made something which corresponds only in a few external features to the religion of monotheism, personal sacrifice, and universal brotherhood which has animated the bringers of that gospel.

Changes in church or government policy, the restrictions arising from a period of economic depression, and the knowledge that the island contains no resources worth the exploitation of the white man may hold back the forces of civilization for some time. But in the long run the Tikopia must come more and more under these influences, if only through increasing efficiency in means of communication. The " primitiveness " of the island must be then a condition that is passing —it is only to be hoped that the succeeding phases will not bring the cultural disruption and progressive decline of population that have been the tragic experience of other Polynesian peoples ; that intensified contact will not give the natives cause to lament the rapacity of the white man and to sigh for the times of their fathers.

For the comprehension of the native culture of to-day an account of the introduction of cultural elements from outside is relevant. This is a study in true culture-history, since the evidence is of a kind that can be verified. At the present the Tikopia are in an interesting phase of contact—they have some European tools but they have not adopted a money economy ; they recognize the shadowy existence of remote governmental authority, but their own chiefs are really responsible for law and order; half the people are ostensibly Christian, while the other half openly practise their ancient religion. The data of this chapter may then be of service if another sociologist should study this same people later. Comparative investigations on the vertical plane, in the same community at different periods of time, are much needed for the formulation of general principles of institutional change.

FOREIGN ELEMENTS OF CULTURE INTRODUCED

According to the native tradition the present population of Tikopia is the result of the commingling of a number of stocks—from Tonga, Samoa, Rotuma, Uvea and other Polynesian islands to the east, and from Melanesian islands in the Banks group to the south and Santa Cruz to the west.[1] It is only fair to assume that the culture of the people is likewise a mixed product, though explicit mention is made of the introduction of but a few types of material object, and not of customs and institutions. I do not propose here to attempt to separate Tikopia culture into its component parts from a comparative historical standpoint, but simply to indicate the most important recent acquisitions specifically referred to in native or European records.

The first European to touch at the island, as far as is known, was Quiros in 1606, but the results of the contact were negligible. Dillon visited Tikopia in 1813, in 1826 and in 1827, on each occasion leaving gifts of tools and other goods, and in 1828 Dumont D'Urville called there. By this time the natives had mastered the use of iron, and had learned the meaning of introduced epidemic disease. Later callers were mainly whalers and labour recruiters (" blackbirders "), of whom little record is available save the information handed down by the Tikopia themselves. Guns, fish-hooks, knives, calico and tobacco were among the principal items received. In 1857 the Melanesian Mission paid its first visit to the island, but it was over half a century before any converts resulted from the fleeting periodic calls. Perhaps most important from the point of view of culture contact have been the ocean wanderings of the Tikopia themselves. Fired by the lust for adventure and the desire to see new lands canoe after canoe set out and ranged the seas, and those members of the crews who returned contributed a great deal to such knowledge of the outside world as the islanders now possess. Fear of storms and shipwreck leaves them undeterred, and the reference in an ancient song to the loss of a man at sea as a " sweet burial " expresses very well the attitude of the Tikopia.

[1] It is hoped to publish shortly an account of *The History and Traditions of the Tikopia*.

From these foreign contacts, of one kind and another, a variety of objects have been introduced. European articles include knives, axes and fish-hooks, guns and swords (mostly in exchange for indentured labourers), beads, and cloth.[1] Tobacco is now grown, though in small quantities. Shell and turtle-shell ornaments have been brought from Vanikoro, as also the *Canarium* almond and a slender variety of coconut, which are established in Tikopia. One of the quaintest, though not the most important, of the efforts at acclimatization was the bringing in of cats. A couple of generations ago Tikopia was overrun with rats which ate food and clothing, and even gnawed the skin of the soles of the feet of the people as they slept. The grandfather of the present Ariki Tafua sent his son Pu Paiu abroad with instructions to observe how this pest was restrained in other lands. Seeing how useful the cats of the white people were, Pu Paiu said to them, " Give me your long-tails "—as he named them. So they gave him cats, male and female, which when brought back, multiplied, and have kept down the rats ever since. Such is the native story.

A number of plants have been introduced in recent times. Varieties of banana known as *takera* and *futi refu* (said to have sprung from ashes, hence its name) have been brought from Motlav by mission teachers ; that known as *futi mae* (falsely called *maea* by some people) from Maewo ; others were introduced earlier from Samoa, Rotuma and Asava (in Fiji), according to native record. Two introduced varieties of sugar-cane, the *toro peka* and *toro mea*, are distinguished from the *toro maori* which is said to be a Tikopia type from early times. Manioc (*manioka*) was introduced by Pa Paŋisi and others from Motlav, and is acknowledged to be a very useful addition to the food supply, particularly in a season of drought. The *naporo* (pawpaw) is also said to have been introduced. Rivers's statement that it is the only kind of food allowed in mourning, and is therefore remarkable for its prominent place in such ceremonies, needs some correction. The truth is it is not greatly liked by the Tikopia because of its watery quality, and so it is served to people who are debarred from the choicer kinds of food. It is by no means the only food taken at mourning.[2] A variety of turmeric known as *aŋo fakarotuma* was brought from Rotuma by Pu Tio and Pu Faraŋanoa, who went there in a European vessel.

[1] Most interesting to a historian, perhaps, is the native record of a gouge and other iron tools, and a glass decanter, brought over from Vanikoro in circumstances which leave no doubt that they were from the wreck of the La Pérouse expedition. The decanter, as I myself have seen, is still preserved in a temple of the Taumako clan. (Further details are given in *History and Traditions of Tikopia*.)

[2] Rivers, *History of Melanesian Society*, I, 1914, 333.

In the technological field there have been a number of acknowledged borrowings. It is recognized that the arrows of Tikopia
have been modelled on the type of the " Fiti "—Pileni, Taumako,
Fonofono, Vanikoro, etc. The people of Vanikoro, in particular,
brought these weapons on their frequent visits, and at the request
of the Tikopia left them behind when they returned. The feather
lure attached to the bonito-hook is described as being adapted from
Nanumea, in contrast to the hibiscus fibre lure—the old Tikopia
style. In olden days a canoe came from Nanumea (Ellice Islands)
to Anuta, where the crew were killed. Pu Niukapu, on one of his
voyages there, found the hooks, took them down, stripped them of
their lashing and lures and brought these back to Tikopia. They
were of no use to the people of Anuta, who are said not to practise
bonito-fishing. The chief of the Nanumea canoe was named Poranai.
According to the Ariki Kafika the present method of making thatch
in Tikopia was introduced by Tereiteata, the former Ariki Tafua,
from Vanikoro. It consists of removing the central rib from each
leaf and using it as a pin to fasten the leaves together. In former
days the practice was to join the leaves by inserting the thorn of the
sago palm and then breaking it off. This man is credited also with
bringing *kaifariki*, ringworm, with which many of the Tikopia are
now afflicted.

In the field of amusement foreign contacts have had an indirect
effect, being responsible for additions to the content more than
changes in the manner of amusement. This applies particularly to
dances, borrowed from Anuta and elsewhere, and to dance songs,
many of which have been composed with reference to other lands
and experiences abroad. A specific dance, the *mako fakaraka*, was
presented by Pa Mukava recently as an adaptation of a Raga dance
which he had seen in the Banks Islands.

I have not tried here to separate the cultural elements introduced
from native and from European sources, since the two have been so
closely inter-connected : the selection of items has usually been made
by the native, but the means of communication and transport more
often provided by the European.

The motives for the adoption of the new cultural elements have
been mainly the desire to secure economic advantage or enhancement
of the person. Mere imitation, as such, seems to have played little
part ; there has been in each case a set of ways of behaviour into
which the new item has fitted. It is the prior existence of this
general pattern that has given cultural value to the items introduced
by individuals, made them objects of general desire, and not merely
the unsupported whim of the introducer. This problem of the

translation of introduced items from the personal to the cultural sphere, the assignment of value to them, is important; it raises questions of the differential perception of individuals regarding gaps in the cultural equipment and the selection of materials to fill them. The conversion of tooth-brush handles into ear-rings, mentioned later, is a case in point.

Though grateful to Europeans for providing them with material things which have done much to lighten their labour, the Tikopia look upon the foreigners as essentially irresponsible people, where the welfare of the island is concerned. In the first place, they bring disease. " In this land in former times old people used to live until they crawled along the paths; they stayed thus a long while, then died, having arrived at senility. Nowadays it is not so; adults and children vanish, especially great being the death of children." This is the result of the coming of the white man.

The same influence is believed to operate towards the economic resources of the community; they are suddenly struck by drought, blight or hurricane, through the incalculable malevolence of white people. A former Bishop of the Melanesian Mission, for instance, resigned under pressure from his colleagues, since his health was not standing the strain. He used to be very generous to the Tikopia, but they aver that on his departure he cursed the islands of his charge, causing a hurricane and a tidal wave from which Tikopia suffered in common with other places. He sent also grubs which devoured the taro. " Stupid was the mind of Bishop, to cause the food to disappear," said one native. This idea is held by Christian and heathen alike, and they cannot be disabused of it. The news, in fact, came through the mission teachers, who alleged that the Bishop wrote from his home afterwards and announced what he had done. When I first began to display interest in the religious cere-monies the rumour went about—started by the spiritist mediums—that if I attended the kava ritual of the chiefs I would take away the *manu*, the power of the ritual, and in consequence the rain would not fall, the sea would not be smooth, and the crops would fail. Luckily favourable elements proved the inaccuracy of this prediction.

Talk also ran that photography was dangerous to its subjects : people whose photographs had been taken on former visits of the *Southern Cross* had died—chiefs of Tafua and Kafika, Pa Veterei and many others. Luckily again my contradiction of its ill effects was followed by no disaster. In any case, the Ariki Kafika said no, they died because of the Bishop.

The explanation of death and disaster by the vindictiveness or malevolence of the white man is a projection of Tikopia attitudes into the European sphere. It has this basis, that epidemics and European visits can be clearly correlated, though the precise nature of the correlation has not been correctly understood. It is not the first time that germs have been interpreted in terms of emotional force. A stanza of a well-known song puts the basic native attitude clearly enough :

> We here, great is the greed of our eyes
> For the valuables from abroad
> Which come with disaster.

THE PRESENT STATE OF TIKOPIA CULTURE

A review of Tikopia culture at the present time shows that it is in a peculiar state of divided allegiance. The mood of the people is one of mingled desire and apprehension. They want the material goods of the white man ; they do not want him to control their lives. They admire without stint his command of wealth, his mechanical devices ; they are largely ignorant of his institutions, but unhesitatingly prefer their own.

In former days the Tikopia used adze blades of clam shell and a few of black basalt. Nowadays these have been entirely discarded, and in their stead axes, tomahawks, and adzes with steel heads are used. A useful implement possessed by most families of importance is a small adze of which the blade is a plane iron. The Maori, it is interesting to note, have adapted this tool in the same way. The cutting instrument of former days was either a sliver of bamboo or a sharp bivalve shell called *kasi*. At the present time the shell is still used for minor work, such as scraping coconut, but European knives are in general use. This is not to say that they are plentiful ; the sole implement of a family may be a decrepit table-knife bartered from a passing vessel. The typical Polynesian implement is the adze, but in Tikopia European adzes are rare. They are highly prized, since they are the great canoe-builder's tool, and seem to be difficult to obtain. The absolute peak of interest in the presents which I gave during my stay was reached when I distributed half a dozen adzes among the chief men on the island, and the gifts created very great jealousy in other people of note. European fish-hooks are used and the older type of thorn-hook has been quite abandoned. Native fishing-gear (nets and lines) is, however, used in preference to European. The introduction of iron and steel has probably greatly increased the productive capacity of the people. The use of medium-sized fish-hooks, for instance, enables them to take a much greater range of fish than formerly from canoes, while a very small hook makes rod-fishing from the edge of the reef much simpler than before.

For clearing ground for cultivation a large knife is used, but for breaking it up the native digging-stick has not been replaced. A spade of European type does not seem to be appreciated; a light European crowbar is, however, liked by some people for this work. Thick plain fencing wire is used as a trace for shark-hooks, or for points to arrows or the multiple-pronged fish-spear. Both these latter, however, are still often made with slivers of areca palm heart. There are a few guns, mostly in the possession of the chiefs, and kept primarily for show, there being no powder or ammunition for them. They are all of an antique type, having been mostly acquired as part payment for labourers taken away in the blackbird days.

In everyday life clothing is of bark-cloth, but some women use strips of calico as sun-shields or scarves over their shoulders. For a large dance most men wear a piece of calico as a kilt in addition to their ordinary costume, though some, like Pa Fenuatara, wear a *kie* of native manufacture instead. This native kilt, plaited from fine pandanus and carefully ornamented, is not very common and the calico is usually its substitute. There is, however, a tendency for a piece of calico to be tied as a belt above the *kie* or worn as an under-kilt to it. One element in this is, I think, the desire of people to show that they possess calico. Cloth has also been incorporated into the religious system. Here it is allocated on the basis of colour. White calico is treated as equivalent to *mami*, the bark-cloth sheets offered to female deities, and red calico as equivalent to *marotafi*, the orange pieces offered to the most important male deities. On the advice of an important elder, I myself laid offerings of different kinds of calico at the canoe ceremonies of the Ariki Kafika and corresponding ritual of the other chiefs. The item that was most valued was a heavy red *pareo* with a white pattern, which went to the principal god in each case. The use of this cloth is a simple substitution in the field of material culture; it involves no change whatsoever in the ritual. There are scarcely any European clothes in Tikopia. The Melanesian teacher usually wears them, but no one else. At a dance a few shirts appear; the younger men tuck them in beneath their girdles, the older men let the tails fly loose with odd effect. But the sight of an old man dancing in shirt tails causes no amuse-ment—the point of interest and of envy is his possession of the garment.

Beads, both of European and of native manufacture, are worn by men and by women in dancing. Both kinds appear to have much the same value. A very few families, connected with the mission, have Dietz lanterns, but usually no kerosene or wicks. The families of the mission teachers again are centres of dispersion for occasional cooking-pots, bags of flour and sugar, and the like—as much as can be purchased with the salary of £1 per annum. There are practically no medical supplies on the island, but there is little occasion for them, and no one to administer them properly.

The adoption by the Tikopia of European goods can be properly described as a process of inculturation, since only those objects are adopted which serve their requirements, and they are transformed accordingly. My tooth-brushes may be given as an instance. They had handles of a transparent composition material, and for a long time attracted no attention. Then one day Pa Vainunu saw them, was struck by their likeness to tortoiseshell, and begged a couple. Working them in warm water, as the natives do with tortoiseshell, he made the handles into very presentable ear-rings, and they were greatly in demand afterwards. The reddish or light brown handles were much more highly thought of than the green or pale yellow, and this again is in correspondence with the native scheme of values.

The real vulnerability of the Tikopia to encroachment of European civilization is their desire for tools. They have learned the importance of steel, and they are helpless in the face of any visitors from the outside world who bring them tools to barter for even their most precious possession—their traditional institutions. They cannot receive what they want from traders as people in the other islands of the Solomons usually do, because the quantity of trochus, greensnail, tortoiseshell, and beche-de-mer is insufficient for commercial purposes, and the island is already under such intense cultivation that many more coconuts cannot be grown to supply copra. The natives easily consume all the product of the existing palms. They must depend, then, on casual visitors or on philanthropy to satisfy their needs. It is by means of this economic weapon that ultimately and inevitably their ancient culture will be forced to change its character. Even their enlistment as native labour would be ineffective, for reasons discussed later.

While a certain number of material elements of European origin have become incorporated into the Tikopia culture, the social structure has remained comparatively unchanged, with the exception of those aspects affected by the coming of Christianity, which are referred to a little later. The more responsible members of the community know that there is at Tulagi a *Kavemanu* (Government) which claims the right of punishing people who kill, and that such may be carried off and put into a place called *Karabusi* (calaboose). The nature of this place is rather vaguely known; it is viewed much in the way that Dante's contemporaries must have regarded his Inferno. Apart from this rather faint concession to authority, the polity of Tikopia is unaffected by its membership of the British Empire. The people at present pay no tax.

An interesting phase of the culture contact is the linguistic one. Two processes have been followed in dealing with the new situation created. A certain number of European objects are described by incorporating the closest approximation to the European name into the ordinary Tikopia sentence construction. A box of matches, or a tin are described respectively as *foi mashes* and *foi tini*, *foi* being the particle of individualization. Other words are *puni* (spoon), *kapu* (hat or cap), *poti* (boat), *suka* (sugar), *paipi* (pipe), *paka* (tobacco), *bokis* (box), *manuau* (man-o'-war), *laiti* (light, lantern). This comprises most of the European words ordinarily used in the native speech.

More common is the utilization of Tikopia words and phrases to describe the new objects which have come into these people's ken. A cup of china or metal is called *faŋoŋo*, the general term for coconut shells, qua substance as well as container. Any ship is *vaka*, the ordinary native word for canoe, and the captain is *te ariki te vaka*, " the chief of the craft." A smoke-stack is *pou afi*, " fire-post," tinned meat is *poi*, the word for pig. Biscuit is *kai pakupaku*, " dry food " which is not inappropriate for ship's hard tack. A European axe is *toki*, the general Polynesian word for adze. But a European adze curiously enough is *kamuro*. A tomahawk is *potu toki*, a little axe. A gimlet or a bit is *miri*, used in verbal form for " bore." Calico or clothing is *suru*, a word which I cannot trace ; a shirt is *suru tino*, " body clothing," and trousers *suru vae*, " leg clothing." Boots or shoes are just *vae*, " feet," and socks *a fao o a vae*, " enclosures for the feet." Similarly gloves are spoken of in the descriptive term as " enclosures for the fingers," or " enclosures for the hands." None of these latter items are of course worn by Tikopia. A cat is called *sukuroa*, " long-tail." A sword is *rautoro*, and I am not certain if this is not derived from the two words meaning sugar-cane leaf to which there is a resemblance in form. *Matini* is a flag. *Sinu*, the ordinary word for oil or fat, is used for kerosene, and *sinu kaifariki* is ringworm medicine, because it is a mixture with kerosene or petroleum jelly. The term for writing is *tusi*, which in ordinary Tikopia activity is used for making finger marks as with turmeric pigment on slabs for ritual purposes. To photograph is *tilo*, a word for which I cannot account, and the reduplicated form *tilotilo* is a photographic print. Iron or metal generally is described as *ŋatana*, a word again which is not used in ordinary Tikopia.

Copper and brass are called red *ŋatana*, and silver white *ŋatana*. The word is used also generically for all machinery. A necktie is termed *firifiri*, the name for necklets of the ritual kind used by the natives themselves. A handkerchief is regarded by them as an object of decoration for the head and is called accordingly *rafi suru*, hair-fillet of cloth. Recently words have had to be found for gramophone and for electric torch. The latter is termed *kamo*, " lightning," and the former *viko*, the native word for turning round and round because of the motion of the disc or the act of winding up the machine. The Tikopia have not seen an aeroplane, but have heard of it. They describe it ingeniously as " the vessel that flies in the sky." A motor-car on the other hand they refer to as *motoka*. A wheel is described by the terrific term of *fakarikarika*, which appears to suggest the act of revolution.

It is difficult to lay down any general principles as to the terminology in use for European objects. Where the most characteristic thing about the object is its peculiar type of activity, then it appears to be frequently described in purely native terms. On the other hand where it is immobile and its English name is easily convertible, then an adaptation of it is made. But there are a number of exceptions to this. The language as yet shows no trace of the phenomenon common in Maori of the grammatical structure having been affected, particularly among the young people, by contact with Europeans.

Reference has been made in the preceding chapter to the talismanic virtue attributed to English phrases. So much were they esteemed that in days past when Pu Raŋirikoi and others who had picked up a fair knowledge of " pidgin " returned from the sugar plantations in Queensland and Fiji, men would prepare food and go with a basket to the house of the traveller to be taught the rudiments of the subject. The language was not divulged to all and sundry, and except where exchanged for food, was jealously guarded for the benefit of the man's kinsfolk. When Pa Tekaumata asked me about English vocabulary of politeness I gave him the word " please." He said, " I know it, but I have not told it to all the people ; I alone know it. I was told by my ' father ' Pa Raŋirikoi, and I do not tell people because when a ship comes I can go aboard and her people will listen to me." This man gets gifts for acting as interpreter and go-between in exchanges, hence there is value to him in conserving his knowledge.

The mutilation this early phraseology has suffered in the process of transference is often great. " *Lipaf* " and " *nigres*," for instance, after much explanation I gathered to be " Keep off " and " niggerhead " (tobacco) respectively ; other words were absolutely unintelligible. After some time in the island I could understand Tikopia, but not Tikopia English.

The mission teachers, of whom there are about eight besides Pa Panisi, have been instructed in the elements of reading and writing in Mota, the *lingua franca* of the Melanesian Mission. They reserve their use of this tongue, however, for Church purposes only. Pa Panisi himself uses Tikopia in the bosom of his family and with his teachers, except in religious services. It was interesting, though, to hear " grace " said in Mota before meals during the turmeric-making ceremonies of the Ariki Tafua, and to see portions of the food thrown immediately afterwards as offerings to the ancient gods. This gives perhaps as good an index to the state of Christianity of the Tikopia of Faea as anything else. Two of the sons of the chief were teachers of the mission.

There has been but little incorporation of European ideas into the religious fabric of the Tikopia, apart from the bulk changes resulting from Christianity in the one district. But I was once told by Pae Sao, a heathen, a brief story purporting to describe the building of one of the sacred temples in the realm of the gods. As he proceeded it became clear that the tale bore the impress of culture contact, and was in fact an account of how white men came to be in possession of iron and the Tikopia to be without it. The story was genuine, in that it was told in all good faith as a piece of Tikopia ancient lore, and the narrator said that it had been transmitted to him by his father together with other data on sacred history. Whatever its origin it is at the present time a myth, being imbedded among the religious beliefs of the people as a justification of one of the greatest advantages which Europeans enjoy. This myth is merely auxiliary to the main Tikopia body of sacred lore, but is of interest as showing how additions come to be made to the traditional stock of recitals in response to new elements in the material environment.

THE TIKOPIA AND THE NATIVE LABOUR MARKET

The natives of the Tikopia, unlike the rest of the Solomon islanders, are not available in the labour market. By Government ordinance in common with the people of the other Polynesian communities in the Protectorate they are exempted from recruiting. With the wisdom of this policy I am quite in agreement. In the first place the island is practically free from disease so that when a Tikopia goes abroad into the malaria-infested islands to the west he is almost certain to contract fever. With his vitality reduced by this novel complaint the man is apt to be of very little use to his employer for some considerable time. He is exposed to chronic risk of infection from a variety of other diseases as well to which he has developed no immunity. In times past the mortality from this cause has been very heavy. Moreover those who survive and return home may act as carriers of disease particularly of an epidemic type, which may seriously affect the local population. The majority of the Tikopia themselves realize these facts, and I have been besought by elderly men, among them chiefs, to use my best efforts to prevent a recruiting vessel from removing their young relatives. With these the spirit of adventure is more to the fore, and some of them would welcome the opportunity of visiting other lands, though on the whole they are ignorant of the arduous conditions of work that they would encounter there.

Another factor of a less tangible kind is perhaps even more important. Living a comparatively contented existence on their own small island, with pleasant food, the Tikopia easily get into a state of nostalgic depression after some time abroad. The divergence from the conditions to which they are accustomed is great— for example, though all the natives ate eagerly of my biscuit, many of them refused to touch rice, and some who tried were actually made to vomit by it! Like Ratia of old, who went away with Dillon, to pine and die in a foreign land, they long for their own foods. Away from home they tend to sink into a state of psychological inertia from which it is difficult to rouse them, and in which they fall a ready prey to disease. This is no surmise, but has been observed to be the case. By Major Hewitt, of Gavutu, I was informed that some twenty-five years ago out of a score of Tikopia on Guadalcanal he succeeded in saving and returning only a single man, though he absolved them from plantation work and allowed them to go fishing all day in the hope of stimulating them into an active interest in the life about them.

By the natives themselves I was given details of the fate of groups of men who signed on labour vessels—one man returning out of fifteen who left; three returning out of twelve, and so on. It was for this reason that recruiting was prohibited in Tikopia and the other Polynesian communities.[1] The Melanesian Mission after some years of trial followed the same policy of not removing boys from the island, and an attempt to revive the training system in 1928–29 met with failure. Three boys were taken away to Vureas, but were returned on the next northward trip of the mission vessel long before the expiry of their term of schooling; they had been largely incapaci-

---

[1] *High Commissioner's Gazette*, Notice 99, Western Pacific, 24th September 1923. *Cf.* also Raymond Firth, *Oceania*, I, 1930, 107–8.

tated through fever and nostalgia. One in particular, Munakina, who went away a bright active lad, came back dull and sluggish, a pitiful semblance of his former self.

Consideration for the health of the people, the well-weighed opinion of the elder and more responsible men, and even the economic interests of the potential white employer indicates the wisdom of the non-recruitment policy.

EFFECTS OF MISSIONARY INFLUENCE

The greatest single force from the outside world which has been operating on the Tikopia in the last few decades has been the mission.

The effect of this contact has been in the first place to provide the Tikopia with a considerable quantity of European goods, especially tools, which they could not have obtained in any other way. To a considerable extent this has been philanthropy on the part of the mission, for they have not received or tried to receive an equivalent economic return. The productive power of the islanders has been increased in another way by the introduction of plants such as banana, *taumako* (a kind of yam) and manioc, which are especially useful in tiding over periods of scarcity between the regular crops.

The influence of the mission exerted through its teachers has also promoted the wearing of native clothing in children and youths, and has given a stimulus to the use of calico as a supplementary wrap for dancing.

In the sphere of the social life of the people it has caused certain changes to be made. Sabbath observance is enforced on all the people of Faea, and out of politeness many of the heathen of Raveŋa conform to this also. Little work is done during the day, though since the end of the period of the *aso tapu* is held to come at sunset, fishing is permissible at night and dancing too. Church attendance at some of the morning and evening services which are held daily is also obligatory on all Christians.

At certain seasons, as during Lent and just before Christmas, dancing is prohibited. This is felt as a severe deprivation by the young people, but they usually conform, and even the non-Christians from courtesy often follow suit. Young men of the Church group are expected also to keep their hair short. This is regarded as a distinct hardship, on account of the value of long hair in the dance, and there are private plaints about it.

In matters of sex the mission teachers naturally take up a definite attitude. Intercourse between unmarried men and girls is reprobated, and if pregnancy should occur marriage of the parties is insisted upon.

Occasionally this enthusiasm for morality has unlooked-for results, as in the case of the simulated pregnancy mentioned in Chapter XV. Any lad or girl who is found to have indulged in sex intercourse is banished from the Church for a time by the teacher. But detection is difficult, and this is probably the one rule which is consistently broken by the Christian youth. Polygyny is of course prohibited to a Christian, and several men, among them the Ariki Tafua and Pa Fenuaturaki, put away their secondary wives on entering the Church. In this sphere the effect of the mission action is not so marked since polygyny was by no means universal in the island. Infanticide is also reprobated, and the consequent effects on the population situation are discussed in Chapter XII.

All institutions connected with the ancient gods of the people are denounced. They are said to be evil. The Christians accept this judgment on the whole; the heathen are somewhat puzzled by it. They argue that the ritual is primarily performed in order to obtain food, secure fine weather, and promote the health of the people and the welfaȩe of the land. The Christian ritual, they say, seeks the same end; therefore they, the heathen, assist the Christians. Why, then, should they be stigmatized as " dark " (pouri), " evil " (pariki) and " Satan " ? This point was put to me over and over again by the Ariki Taumako and other people of Ravena. The intolerance of the Christian missionaries was in fact the one great complaint that they had to urge against them. " Look you, friend! Is it bad ? " the Taumako chief asked me forcibly after a religious rite that I attended. " It is made only for welfare," he argued. This man resented the epithets cast at him by the self-righteous converts, and composed several ironical songs on the matter. These were used as dance choruses by the young men of Ravena, in the usual Tikopia style. Here are two of them :

> Tafito : My dwelling is evil
> I dwell in darkness ;
> My mind is dark.
> Why don't I abandon it ?

> Kupu : It is good that I should die
> Die with the mind
> Of one who dwells in darkness.

> Safe : Stupid practices to which I have clung ;
> Let them be pulled down and caused to slip away.

The whole tone of this song is one of protest against what he considered unjustified rudeness and contempt in stigmatizing his kava rites as stupid, and him as evil. The other is :

Tafito: Let each think of his food
             And of his fish
             Gained at the side of the chiefs.

Kupu: We have heard ;
             Alas ! now we
             Are a land divided in two.
             When shall we be struck down from it ?

In the first stanza the converts are reminded that in turning to Christianity they are forsaking the chiefs under whose ægis they have been nourished.   In the second the chief voices his dismay at the splitting of the land into two factions, and his fear that the white man may come and expel the heathen in order that the Christians may succeed to their territory.   Exaggerated as this may seem, the record of the material assistance given in the past by Europeans to Christian chiefs in Tahiti and elsewhere to overcome their rivals shows that it is not altogether a fanciful idea.

By the Christians the major ceremonies have been abandoned, but the belief in the ancient gods is still very much alive.   They are regarded as simply staying quiescent, immobilized by the word of the Bishop and the mission.   But at times they enter again into the affairs of men.   This is the case mainly in the sphere of spirit possession. Dealing with the gods and spirits of the dead in this form is not countenanced by the mission, but here emotion and the influence of tradition are too strong.   Seances are commonly held, in Christian as well as heathen houses, when a person is ill, and assistance is asked from the *atua* of the family.   At least three prominent Christians are spirit mediums, and I have seen several Tikopia mission teachers assist in seances in their own families.   When one of these mediums was in a state of possession his " familiar " confessed to me that he, the spirit, had been baptized.   " Because I had entered my medium who had gone to be washed holy ; I desired the work of our Lord," he said.   In all probability this is the first time that a heathen ghost has been received into the bosom of the Church !   This was the same " familiar " who on another occasion described to me with gusto the delights of spirit intercourse with mortal women.

The seasonal cycles of ceremonies known as the " Work of the Gods " have been discontinued by the people of Faea, but the all-night dancing which takes place then sometimes proves too attractive to a few of the young men of Ravena who have ostensibly joined the Christian party.   They let their hair grow really long, go and dance, and are debarred from Church for a year in consequence.   One of these rebels was so treated when I was there.   The mechanism which allowed of his reception again was the carriage of a basket of food

to the chief mission teacher, with a prayer of forgiveness—the normal
Tikopia procedure to gain the favour of a man of rank again.   But
were it not for the reproaches they would receive, and the public
disgrace, many young people would gladly go.   The effect upon the
ceremonies themselves has been of course to remove about half the
available population from them, to mar their symmetry to some
extent by the absence of the Ariki Tafua, and to emphasize the divergence between the people of Faea and those of Raveŋa.   Did not the
Ariki Tafua believe that this ritual is evil, in conformity with what he
understands to be the opinion of white people on the matter, he would
probably revert to it.   His eldest son, in fact, implored me to confirm
the old man in his somewhat wavering view, lest he immediately seek
to re-institute his part of the ancient ritual, and the Bishop be angry
when the *Southern Cross* came.

A minor result of the conversion of a section of the people to
Christianity has been that " totemic " animals, where edible, as pigeon
and turtle, are now taken as food by some (though not all) of those
who formerly respected them.

Ceremonies such as initiation have been shortened through
missionary effort.   The attempted compression of the ritual into a
single day was resisted, by Christian as well as heathen Tikopia, as an
unwarranted interference with custom.   In native eyes this tendency
to interference has been most marked in the case of ceremonies involving gifts of food to the chiefs.   It is held by prominent Christians as
well as by heathen that the object is to depreciate the status of the
chiefs by taking away from them the privileges of the *muakai*, the
" first-fruits " and other offerings, and to elevate the mission teachers
at their expense.

The effects of mission activity have been most serious in the political
field, apart from the primary religious changes.   A general opinion is
that the mission teachers, especially their leader, from another island,
wish to exalt themselves at the expense of traditional authority.   The
practice of appointing local men as teachers on the basis of their
proficiency in reading and writing, or their support of the mission's
policy, without regard to their position in the native social structure,
tended to upset the normal balance.   Allegiance has been divided,
jealousy has arisen between the chiefs and the mission leaders, and
bewilderment and uneasiness has resulted among the people.

The influence of the mission is consistently exercised to restrain
breaches of the peace, and it is claimed that theft, brawling and adultery
have been greatly reduced since the coming of Christianity.   In so
far as this applies to theft from European visitors this is probably
true, but is due perhaps not so much to the restraining influence of the

mission as to the fact that the intensity of the anxiety of the natives to secure iron and other things has abated now to some extent, as these have become relatively more abundant. The only theft of my goods took place in Faea, and everybody accused a Christian ; in the time of shortage of food, theft was quite as common on the Christian as on the heathen side of the island. And the only case of adultery that occurred to my knowledge while I was there was between Christians in the village of the principal teacher. As far as the cruder forms of lying and greed were concerned heathen and Christian had to be classed alike.

Relations between the two parties are on the whole amicable enough. This is due to a considerable degree to the close kinship ties between them, which are too strongly riveted to be disregarded. One of the sons of the Ariki Kafika is a Christian, as is one of those of Pae Avakofe, and his daughter ; Pa Paŋisi himself, married to a woman of the Resiake house, is a son-in-law of the Ariki Taumako, who is a most uncompromising heathen, though personal relations are outwardly friendly between them. Occasionally the heathen feel that advantage is being taken of them, and accuse the mission teachers of misrepresenting the attitude of the white men of whom they purport to be the mouthpiece. " We are deceived by the missionaries (the native teachers)," said one chief ; " great is the lying of the missionaries."

But one effect of Christianity has been to accentuate the opposition between the districts of Faea and Raveŋa, between the chief of Tafua and his peers ; and in some cases to make a cleavage in groups where there was none before. A dance was held at Asaŋa in Raveŋa, and the Ariki Taumako refused to attend—it was a Church affair. The heathen Ariki Kafika, tolerant and always ready for co-operation, went to him and desired him to leave the decision to him—a common way of getting round an obstacle. The Ariki Taumako would not do so, and the Ariki Kafika returned hurt, his pride wounded, and depressed. " The chiefs have separated," he said bitterly afterwards. It is the tradition in Tikopia that the chiefs always act as a body in matters of public concern, each deferring to the opinion of the others, in spite of personal inclination and private disagreement. Here, as so often has happened in State affairs, they split on the rock of the Church. Even in families the divided religious allegiance is apt to make for disharmony. When a new net of the Ariki Tafua was being made a ceremony was performed which included an invocation to the old gods of the chief. All the sons were gathered together, except two who were mission teachers. They were missed, and comment was passed. " It is bad, that they are not here with us in the assembly," said Pa

Raŋifuri. Later he tried to cover their absence by saying to me that one of them was asleep and the other had a cold !

The aggressiveness of the mission teachers, feeling that they have behind them the power of the white man, and reinforced by their annual receipt of knives, calico and the like, is sometimes rather trying to the heathen, or even to the nominal Christians who are not on the teaching list.

The position of Christianity in Tikopia may be shown a little more clearly by considering the circumstances of its introduction. For many years teachers from the south lived there without any appreciable effect. Then the Ariki Tafua, primarily moved by the respect for the pronouncements of the only white men whom he met, those of the mission, and by the prospect of a closer relation with the source of wealth in European goods, announced his intention of becoming a Christian, and ordered his district of Faea to follow. His son, Pa Raŋifuri, according to his own account and that of others, implemented his father's decision. He stood up on the open beach with his club in his hand, and whooped in token of his warlike purpose. He said, " If there be a man of Faea who does not go to the *rotu* (Christian service) I will enter his house, seize him by the wrist and drag him there." He told me he thought it was the correct thing to do, to order the people to go ; he regarded himself as a benefactor to the mission, and was a little disgruntled that the teacher had not recognized his public services by the present of an adze. An honest, kindly soul, he was much surprised when I told him that it was not the fashion of the Church usually to secure converts thus.

At the time, it was held that all the gods of the chief had acquiesced in his conversion, except the Atua of the Vai—the eel-god. He was angry at the defection, and visited the chief's family with death. A son of the chief said to me, " That's all very well, but, on the last day, we shall be all right, but he will be consigned to the bad place."

The real test of the virtue of Christianity, in the eyes of the people of Faea, is that the crops have been good ever since that time. Economic prosperity is an index of the power of the gods to whom one's allegiance is given ; the new faith is thus justified. Pa Paŋisi, the Motlav teacher, is not backward in using this argument to reinforce his claims for the truth of the Church and the Gospel. On the other hand the heathen hold that the land has suffered to some extent by the change. In former days, it is said, when the Ariki Kafika performed ceremonies at Takarito in Faea, fish were extremely plentiful—as one shoal went another came. Nowadays the catches are not so good. " As soon as the *rotu* stood in this land, there were no fish. Were the gods angry ? We do not know."

In the early days of the conversion a number of the stones that formerly stood in the orchards as marking the resting-places of the ancient deities were removed and incorporated in the walls of the *fare sul*, the so-called schoolhouse. The susceptibilities of the heathen were wounded by interference with the stone which is the embodiment of the deity of Takarito, but they were satisfied when the teacher who was responsible developed an ulcerous affection of the arm which has persisted to this day. On the whole, however, there has been little active persecution of the heathen by the zealots of the new faith.

The most serious element in the situation, to my mind, is that the Tikopia, Christian and heathen alike, believe that the attitude of the mission, as expressed through its teachers, represents the official attitude of the European Government and white people in general. They are a docile people, and when informed by what they regard as a superior power that their customs are bad they endeavour to defend them, but with a tendency to yield to persistent pressure from quarters with such obviously greater experience. " We just go about urinating " is the deprecating way in which one man expressed their conviction of relative inefficiency.

This modest acceptance of their own ignorance while striving to preserve their ancient customs is pathetic to an outsider. The more intelligent of the heathen Tikopia realize their dilemma : they see the advance of the mission, the increase in the number of churches, teachers and converts, the success of its policy of inducing the children to attend its services ; they feel the weight of its economic power ; they bow to its claim to speak in the name of that vast white civilization which they respect so much. Yet they are convinced that their own institutions are good ; they are bound by strong emotional ties to belief in their gods and the spirits of their fathers ; they resent being labelled " the dark district," " Satan," and being told that they will go to a place of fire when they die. To me the spectacle of these people staunchly carrying on the traditions of their ancient faith, in the face of a pressure that is now being clearly felt, was disturbing. Their interest and pleasure to find that a white man, after seeing their ceremonies, could pronounce them to be in no way evil, was touching. " Friend, when you attended our doings and said that they were good, we started backwards in surprise," one of them said to me. And I cannot but regret that the urge to proselytization finds it necessary to disturb a people whose adjustment to life in their traditional institutions has been on the whole a satisfactory one. To make an unsophisticated, isolated, defenceless people bear a part of the burden of our own uneasy, restless spirit seems a pity. For the mission, it is true, no other course is possible : its followers

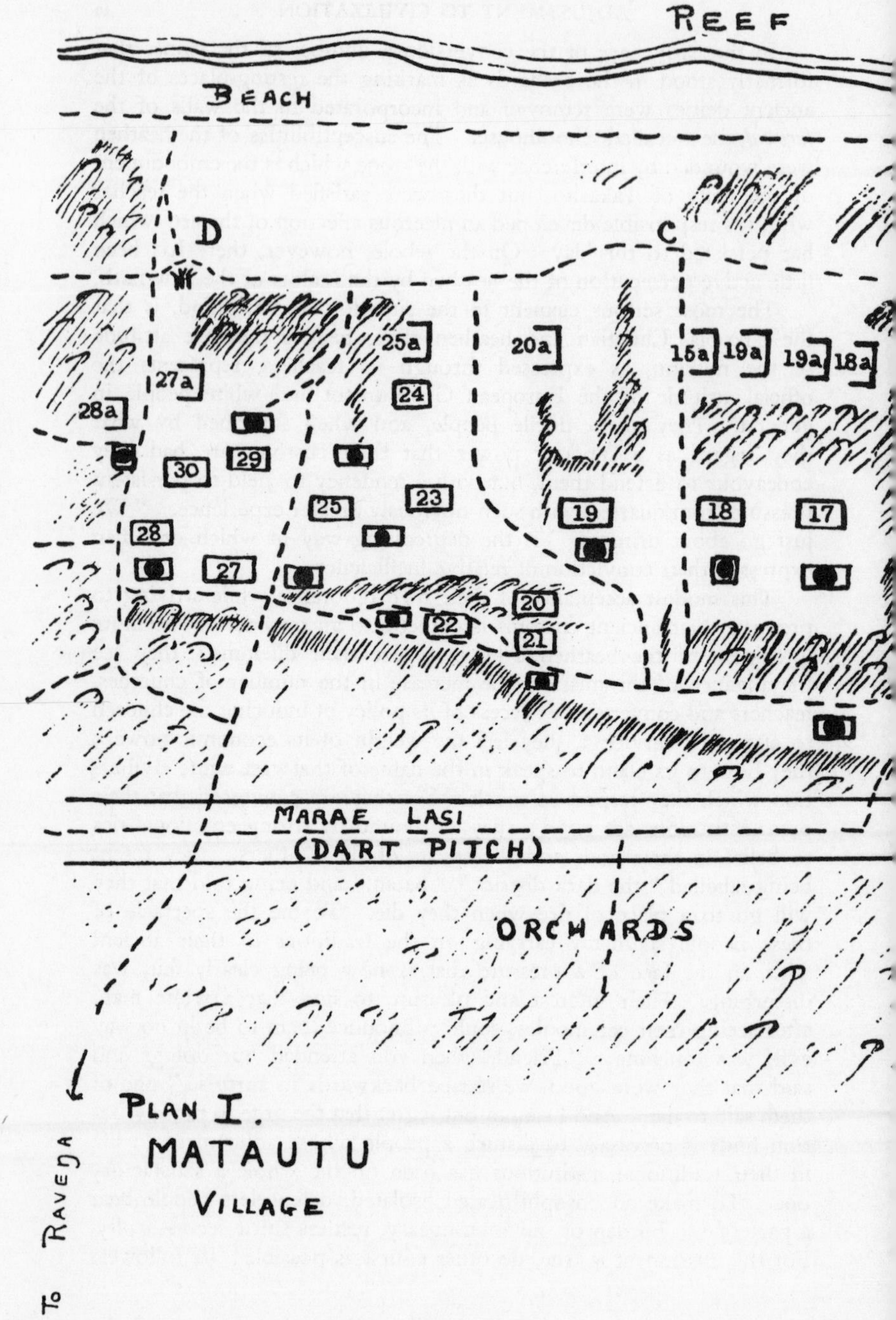

REEF

BEACH

D

C

25a

20a

27a

15a 19a 19a 18a

28a

24

30 29

25 23 19 18 17

28

27 1 20

22

21

MARAE LASI
(DART PITCH)

ORCHARDS

PLAN I.
MATAUTU
VILLAGE

To RAVEGA

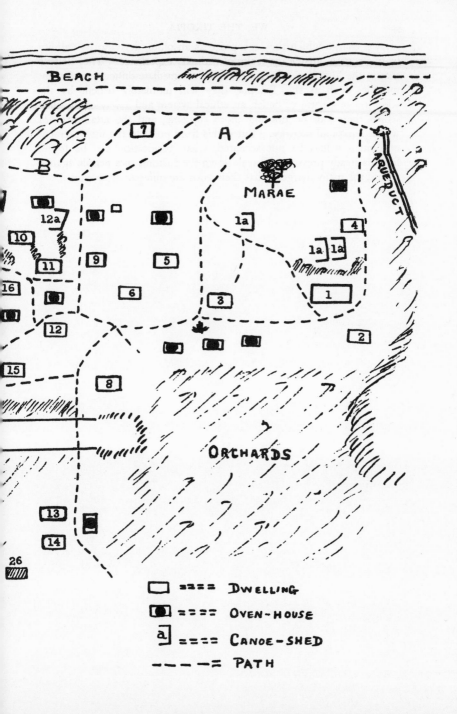

BEACH

B

A

7

MARAE

12a

1a

4

10

1a 1a

11

9

5

1

16

6

3

2

12

15

8

ORCHARDS

13

14

26

▭ ==== DWELLING

◼ ==== OVEN-HOUSE

a ==== CANOE-SHED

-----= PATH

AQUEDUCT

carry a charge which they recognize as absolute, deriving its validity from a source outside the realm of ordinary experience. They believe that in the long run, whatever be the intermediate difficulties of communities such as the Tikopia, they will ultimately benefit by the adoption of a form of belief, an ethical system and a way of life than which there can be nothing more supreme, and the attainment of which repays all sacrifice. But if this fixed point in the measurement of human values be not accepted, what justification can be found for this steady pressure to break down the customs of a people against whom the main charge is that their gods are different from ours?

CHAPTER III

VILLAGE LIFE

As the visitor wanders along the beach he sees before him at intervals a low huddle of leaf-thatch huts, primitive in workmanship and straggling in arrangement. These groups of houses are more pleasantly situated in Faea than in Raveŋa, since the hurricane which struck the island about fifteen years ago spent the greater part of its force on the windward side, and aided by the abnormally high seas swept away much of the vegetation which formerly lined the beach. Great Casuarina and Callophyllum trees adorn the bays of Faea, and fronted by a screen of undergrowth hide the houses from view off the coast. On the sea frontage of Raveŋa the first line of huts stands bleakly, with nothing but the rise of the beach itself to break the force of the steady trade winds, and with less convenient shade for the people during their leisure time.

Each group of huts may be termed a village since it is regarded by the natives as a distinct entity separated from its neighbours, however close they may be, by recognized boundaries and bearing a name of its own. This local separation is associated with differences of kinship grouping. Spatial divisions tend to become organized and explicit where the predominant interest of one social division gives place to that of another.

DAILY WORK AND RECREATION

Before discussing the constitution of the village in detail we may glance at the daily round of life of its inhabitants. This will give the setting of the economic, social and ritual activities discussed in full in subsequent chapters.

It is tempting to give a description in glowing terms of light and colour of the coming of the day in Tikopia. But banality about a tropic dawn is difficult to avoid when the scientist tries to range himself with the writers of fiction and belles-lettres, from whom, after all, a strict neutrality of observation and an accurately restrained delineation of the phenomenon are not expected. It is enough to say that the scene in the early morning when the dusk had lifted and the clouds over the shoulder of Mauŋa turned from smoky red to gold used to be more than compensation to me for the early rising I had to practise during the ritual season.

If one is still lying in the dimness of a hut with the thatch shutters drawn close one is given an index to the breaking of daylight by the change in sounds outside. The faint occasional noises of the darkness, the crack of a twig, the uneasy movement of a startled bird,

or the squeal of an exasperated bat, give way to something more
constant : the coo of stirring wood pigeons, the plaintive cry of
shore waders, the increasing rustle of the leaves as the morning breeze
begins to rise.   On the other hand the noise of the surf—on quiet
nights no more than a murmur, but filling the forefront of consciousness—now begins to sink back to its daily place of a pulsating, purring
undertone, a drone bass to all the melodies which man and the woods
may play.   At the same time the first hint is given that the cool
freshness of the darkness is about to recede before the awakening
heat of the morning.

Soon human sounds intrude upon the ear—the shouts of children
who, always more restless than their elders, are usually the first to
be abroad ; the conversation of returning fishermen, or the lively
beat of the bark-cloth pounder of some conscientious housewife.

The village wakes early.   On a normal day its people throw back
their bark-cloth blankets soon after sunrise, push aside their thatched
doors with a rustle and straggle out into the cool morning air.   They
stroll down the beach or to the lake shore to attend to the calls of
nature and to bathe, performing their toilet in full view, though at
some distance from each other.   The men, as a rule, bathe more
thoroughly than the women.   After the toilet they return up the
beach and chat about the night's fishing or exchange other gossip.
On going back to their houses they find the floor cleared of bedding
and the smouldering embers of the fire blown into a flame by someone
who has stayed behind—a child, an old person, or a woman nursing
a baby.   A kit of cold food, remnant of the meal of the day before,
is lifted down from its hook and anyone who wishes helps himself.
Ends of taro or slices of breadfruit are doled out to the children,
who run out munching.   Their elders eat indoors.   This food is
eaten quickly and without ceremony, and soon afterwards the able-
bodied members of the household scatter to their work.   This varies
according to season and to whim ; personal choice is allowed great
play so long as food is procured.   Fishing or work in the orchards
absorb the men and some of the womenfolk ; others stay behind to
look after young children, beat bark-cloth, or perform household
duties.   It may take an hour or more up to the cultivations on the
plateau or round the crests of the hills, so that the workers start early.
The morning passes in this way.

At midday the village is inactive and asleep in the hot glare of
the sun.   Most of its inhabitants are away.   Some are still in the
cultivations, from which they return home in the early afternoon
loaded with taro, breadfruit, or bananas.   Others, if the tide allows,
are out on the reef—the men with pronged spear or rod and line,

the women with their shell-bordered scoop hand-nets, sometimes combining in a large fish drive.   Children are in attendance or moving up and down in their own bands, with their own simple contrivances ; all are intent on garnering something from the harvest of the sea.

As the sun declines from the zenith the place begins to waken. People come in singly or in little groups, nearly everyone bearing some contribution to the forthcoming meal.   This preparation and consumption of their food is the chief point of the day's activities, the focus of the energies of each member of the community.   Two features of primitive life soon strike an observer who spends much time in close contact with its people.   One is the directness of the tie between a man and his food ; each day sees a fresh levy upon nature for the satisfaction of that day's needs, and the·individual himself must work and sweat to cull and transform the materials of his desire.   Co-operation, exchange and multiform obligations weave the quest for food into a complex social pattern, but the close contact of man with his primary natural resources remains an ever-recurring element.   The other feature is the manner in which the provision of food becomes the apex of the day's work.   In a civilized environment one is apt to look upon a meal as an interval in the real business of life : a pleasant social relaxation, a gastronomic indulgence or a conventional interruption for bodily refuelling.   In a primitive society it may be, as it is in Tikopia, the main daily business in itself.   To this the work of the fore part of the day leads up, and after it is over, the time of recreation has come.   People in this island community do not arrive home to snatch a meal and return to work ; the attainment of the meal itself is the fulfilment of their work.[1]   A man may go on with some piece of craftsmanship afterwards, but that is a concession to his personal interest, and is in no way socially dictated.   Only during specific tasks, such as the building of a house or a canoe, is the meal regarded as an interval in labour.

Shortly after the return of the people to the village thin columns of smoke waver up from the oven-houses as the fires are kindled, and in the vicinity of every household the processes of taro-scraping, coconut-grating, or breadfruit-splitting begin.   In this the young people take a prominent share.   A pause ensues after the leaf-covered, stone-lined ovens have been filled ; in this leisure space of an hour or so people go and bathe, chew betel or sleep.   Then the ovens disgorge their burden again, the food is sorted, repacked in

[1] Much the same is true at times of the peasant communities of Europe, and for the work of women in urban working-men's households, or on many Colonial farms.

leaf wrappings and in baskets, and the welcome sound of the pounding
of puddings in their wooden bowls is heard, a sign that the meal
will not now be long delayed. Instead of having communal ovens
as do some communities, each family in a Tikopia village cooks its
meal and consumes it independently of the others ; co-ordination
between them is represented by the occasional clubbing together of
neighbours when food has to be prepared for a formal presentation.
At last the most laggard household has completed its eating and
tidied away the remains, and its members begin to stroll off on their
various pursuits, or to while away the time before dusk in easy social
intercourse. This is when a craftsman can amuse himself with his
latest creation—a wooden bowl, a palm-leaf fan, a bow, a betel mortar,
or a fishing net.

In the cool of the afternoon as the sun is setting a Tikopia village
is a pleasant sight. Groups of men, their work over for the day,
are sitting on the sand, chatting, smoking and chewing betel. Any
visitor of note is accommodated with a baulk of wood or an upturned
bowl, or a floor-mat may even be brought out for him from an
adjoining house. Near by is a canoe drawn up under the trees,
roughly protected from the sun by a few boughs and a mat over
figurehead and stern. Nets are hanging out to dry, a woman is
seated in the background plaiting a fine pandanus mat, a foam of
silky strips around her knees ; from inland, if any ceremony is
toward, comes the ringing musical sound of the beating of bark-
cloth, with a rhythmic alternation of notes due to the different quality
of the beaters and slabs of the various workers. Everywhere are
the children, busy with their play in the dry sand of the upper beach,
running around the group of men, or dispersed among them listening
to their talk ; outside the circle of their elders the crackle of their
voices can be heard rising at times to explosive pitch as a quarrel
develops, then dying away again as their interest becomes reabsorbed
in the affair in hand.

As the afternoon wears towards evening the social side of the
village life becomes more evident. Gradually more and more people
stroll down from their houses towards the place where the crowd
is gathered on the beach, conversation becomes more general, games
start among the young men, wrestling, *fetāki* (a kind of single stick),
practice in the hurling of the *tika* dart, or in the tossing up and
enmeshing of chips of wood in their long-handled bag-nets in lieu
of the swift flying-fish. Dusk falls, and deepens quickly into night.
If there is no moon and the wind is right, the canoes which have
been got ready earlier are pushed out, equipped with torches, nets
and paddlers, and then begins the great nightly sweep for flying-

fish, partly sport but mostly hard work in grim earnest. Offshore the lights of the fleet begin to dance and move slowly up and down, in line along the reef, and inquiring eyes are directed on them from the shore, counting the torches, one to a canoe, and estimating their probable luck from the state of the wind, moon and tide. Much later, at moonrise or at dawn, the fishermen return, weary but full of their night's doings, ready with excuses and not backward with self-praise.

If the moon rides high and full or the surf forbids the launching of the canoes, then the dance is probably instituted, either on the village ground if there is one, or on the open beach, illuminated only by the light from the sky. Dancing does not occur in all the villages simultaneously, but the young people go over to one in the vicinity which has begun to beat its sounding board. There, however, they are accepted as visitors, not as entrants by right. Sometimes a dance is " set up " in a village and " carried " to another village, thus introducing a competitive atmosphere into what is usually an informal proceeding. Normally, married people do not take part in the dance and the field is left clear for the young and unattached. Here is the opportunity for flirtation and intrigue, and from time to time an individual drifts off with some flimsy excuse to join a lover in a canoe shed or empty dwelling. Other young people, losing energy, come back to the house, take food and floor-mats with them and go and sit on the sand, to gossip and joke or listen to the recital of some traditional tale. The delight of the Tikopia in *te arara*, yarning, is one of the most characteristic features of their social life, an amusement recognized and stressed by them.

Dancing, games and conversation on the beach may go on till any hour ; there is no conventionally appointed time for retiring, but people trickle off as the desire for sleep comes upon them. And so the day comes to an end.

CONSTITUTION OF THE VILLAGE

Some of the factors which give the village its character will have been gathered from this brief sketch—the sense of unity given by residence within a common boundary, under a common name ; the social intercourse at morning and evening ; the maintenance of the village individuality of the young people in their dancing ; the communal working of the reef and the setting out of the village fleet as a unit. In work, dancing and other social relations the intermingling of people from different villages constantly occurs, but it is done with a consciousness of their real provenance, a loyalty to their own local ties that does not allow the village independence to become submerged. Even when children play together those from the different sections of the same village mingle freely, but children from another village are apt to be treated as strangers, or to be admitted to the little group on sufferance. A child visitor, especially if he be not from an adjacent village, looks ill at ease, tends to keep by his father or the person with whom he comes ; if he joins the local children at play he is apt to find himself left on the fringe of the group ; other children call to him less frequently than they do to each other, and he may be reduced to sitting down by himself and watching the rest. It is fair to assume that these attitudes form a basis to some extent for analogous behaviour in adult life.

A closer investigation of the constitution of a village will show other factors : some are of a unifying kind, others tend to conflict with them in insistence upon a different allegiance. The local grouping of a people is most patent to initial observation, and the nature of the social bonds based upon it must be reckoned in estimating the forces regulating the life of the community. One difficulty, however, in the discussion of local organization is to isolate its workings ; it is not always possible to say where certain relations of friendliness and co-operation between fellow-villagers exist because they live in the same group or because they are kin to each other. Tests may be devised to estimate the power of residential affiliation as against that of kinship. One such test is given by economic contributions on ritual occasions. Some people bring food and other gifts explicitly because they are members of the same kin group as the person whom they assist, or are connected with him by marriage ; others give help primarily through neighbourliness.

This fundamental problem of the relation between the kinship system of the people of Tikopia and their local organization can be attacked from two sides. First an indication may be given of the kinship affiliations of the people as they are distributed in residential groups. Then conversely the spatial distribution of the members of the various major kinship groups can be given. These two processes of analysis taken together represent a superimposition of the genealogical record of the community upon a residential plan of it, and if carried out in entirety would fix as by a system of co-ordinates the position of every individual from the point of view of kinship and locality. For a population of twelve hundred it is manifestly impossible to do this, but a sample of the method may be given in the first place by the analysis of the composition of a village, Matautu in Faea, and comparing it with Potu sa Taumako in Raveŋa, both important groups ; then by tracing out the personnel of the " house " of Tafua (whose chief has his home in Matautu) in this and the other villages where its members live. A chart of the general distribution of clans between villages according to the number of households involved gives some further indication of the kind of relationship which obtains.

Such data are relevant to questions of comparative clan strength and wealth and their effect on political, economic and ritual activity, or of the respective claims of village and clan loyalty in cases of conflict between them. The actual distribution of a population in terms of residence and kinship is an important factor in the working of its institutions. And though it can only be empirically ascertained, in an anthropological description its effects are often assumed without enquiry, or are ignored. A record of the total population and its density is also of sociological import. It is only reasonable to assume, or at least it is a hypothesis which should be tested and disproved before being neglected, that all these are factors which have some bearing on the complexity of social relations, and give colour to institutions. I may in fact so far anticipate my conclusions here as to remark that in my opinion the high degree of interlocking of the economic and religious privileges of the different, frequently antagonistic kinship groups of Tikopia is to be correlated with the need for institutionalized co-operation of considerable sanction as a *modus vivendi* among the dense population of this small isolated island.

The village to be examined, Matautu, is the most important residential unit in the district of Faea. The accompanying diagram (Plan I), the original of which was drawn on the spot, shows the arrangement.

The bounds of the village are set on one side by the sea, with its strip of white sandy beach, and on the other by the fosse of the dart-pitch and the wall of trees marking the beginning of the orchards ; to the north rises the slope of the hill which climbs steeply up to the crest of Foŋapā, while to the south the main track from Raveŋa has its outlet on the open dancing-ground of Putafe ; at its side the Church of St Mary has been built in recent years. On the other side of Putafe begins the village of Matafaŋa. The north end—or more properly the north-east end—of Matautu is of interest for several reasons. In the first place there runs the *vai*, the gushing stream, the source of which is a spring some distance up the hill, and which is flumed down in an open aqueduct of areca palm trunks in the native fashion, to spout into a pool near the beach. The stream is one of the most important features in the life of the village : not only is it the source of household supplies, but it is used by the men to rinse themselves down after their sea bathing, and is the scene of much casual social inter-course in the morning and evening. All the larger villages have a *vai* within their confines or close at hand. This is also the most important section of Matuatu for another reason, namely that it is the residence of the chief, the Ariki Tafua. The stream in a sense is his, since it is controlled by one of his deities and enters into his ritual activities. The precise plot where a chief lives is called " *te noforaŋa ariki,*" the chiefly dwelling, and its name may, as in the case of Matautu, be taken over as that of the village as a whole. The actual dwelling of the Ariki Tafua, the large house Motuapi, stands a little inland, with its canoe-sheds in front (*v.* Plate III). It has no cook-house since those of the chief's sons nearby supply that need. Almost directly to seawards, and open to the beach is the *marae* of the chief, an open space used at rare intervals for dancing, but backed by a number of upright stone slabs which show its ritual function, since these are associated with his gods (*v.* Plate III). Further consultation of the plan reveals that the rest of the village is composed of a number of small clusters of huts not clearly defined, straggling along irregularly a little distance back from the beach. Each dwelling-house has adjacent or close to it a cook-house, and also in the vicinity, usually to seawards, a canoe-shed. Here, then, is an apparent nucleus—a family residence—the importance of which is very great in Tikopia life. The dwellings around the *marae* are occupied by the sons of the chief, their wives and children, and that whole section of the village is the *noforaŋa* of the chiefly family of Tafua, the hereditary residential site. In Motuapi itself lie the graves of the chief's father and other ancestors, thus acting as a visible link between the soil and the generations that have gone before. Mukava, Matautu (the house, at present used only as an occasional dwelling), Nukufuri, Roŋorei, Nukunefu and Te Uruŋ-amori (*v.* Plan and Genealogy of Tafua (II)) are all part of this group.

In the village of Matautu there appears at first sight to be a local unit of a simple type under the control of its chief, in this case of Tafua. But the residential situation in terms of kinship and clan grouping goes deeper. A reference to the progress of my own understanding of the matter may be of interest here.

When I arrived in Tikopia and settled in Matautu my enquiries as to the ownership and kinship status of the village were met with the answer, it was " all Tafua." This, it later appeared, was really a reference to the control exercised by the resident chief.[1] A little

---

[1] From the Rev. Durrad I had obtained the information which applies very well to Matautu, that " each village is not inhabited solely by one division but by people of all. The chief of one, however, has the sole right to the *tapu*, etc., there. Hence, to this division the village most truly belongs." But this could not be verified at once, and does not cover all cases.

while was sufficient for me to discover that men of Kafika and Taumako clans were also living there, leading to the hypothesis that they were settled in Tafua territory, possibly married to women of the place, or with some similar privilege of residence. But soon I found that not only were these people of other clans than Tafua but that they actually claimed to possess the land on which they were living, and that this claim was admitted by the chief and his family. It appeared moreover that this ownership was based on ancestral occupation, alleged to go back to a historical event of settlement some eight generations before. Here, then, consideration of the village constitution demanded investigation of clan relations, the rule of chiefs, historical data, and the manner of holding land.

The complexity of the territorial condition in this Tikopia village shows the difficulty in immediately appreciating what might appear to be one of the simplest of situations to investigate. It was, as a matter of fact, in my endeavours to obtain a site on which to build my own house that I was brought to realize all these circumstances and the nature of the principles working behind them. As my note-books and diary of the time show, I was puzzled by the fact that though the consent of the chief to my building in his village, which all agreed to be the essential factor, had been obtained, there yet seemed to be some invisible obstacle to beginning work on the site I had selected with his approval. I was then informed that the immediate house-holders in the vicinity would have to be consulted—it happened to be Pa Taitai and his neighbours—and they also agreed, after some debate. Still the work did not proceed. It then appeared that the builders, well-known experts from another locality, who were to provide the timber, refused to erect it at my request on the land of another family group, even of their own (Taumako) clan. This was a personal rather than a legal difficulty, a coolness springing from the ancient district feud and individual jealousies, but containing a kernel of customary behaviour. Finally, the dispute was settled by the builders consenting to erect the house on the site chosen, on condition that it was to be dismantled and the timber taken back by them, after my departure from the island. So the house "Otara" was built.

The reader may ask why I as an anthropologist trained to enquire into the subtleties of ownership should have been so blind at the outset to the realities of the situation. The reason lay in the difficulty of clarifying the principles of ownership from a mixture of conflicting statements, each representing one aspect of the truth, each motivated partly by the desire to profit from the situation, partly by a disinclination to explain what appeared to be obvious, and partly by the wish to conceal even innocuous information from a stranger. But later I was grateful for the trouble it caused, for the workings of such an institution cannot be perceived in the abstract. It was only by coming into conflict with such practical obstacles that I was brought to realize the complexity of the factors involved.

In Tikopia the ground on which the dwelling-house stands, and as a rule that where the subsidiary huts are too, is the hereditary property of a family group. Sometimes the dwelling-place (*noforaŋa*) is shared by several other householders who are relatives of the principal owner or are outsiders who have built there or occupied existing house-sites by his permission. A man who is not a close relative makes some gift to the person on whose land he has thus built. Some of these dwelling sites are separated from their neighbours by a clearly defined path or a screen of bushes ; many are not isolated by any such obvious barrier. Yet the extent of each family group's ground is known, and boundaries (*tuakoi*) are recognized as running between trees, marked off by stones or the like. Each little group of houses also has its own access to the beach, a narrow path termed the *riuafaŋa*, or more fully *te riuafaŋa ki ŋa tai*. *Riu* conveys the idea of a concave interior, and is commonly used for the inside of a bowl or a canoe hull ; here the idea seems to be that of a " channel to seawards," represented by the grooved path worn hollow by the treading of many feet. The attitude towards this is to treat it very much in the fashion of a right-of-way. As in the case of other paths it is difficult to say if actual ownership in it could be defended against the common use, but it is certainly an object of proprietary interest to the householders whom it serves primarily and whose claims to it are strong. At the seaward end of the *riuafaŋa* is the *matāra*, a space not marked off in any way ; this again is regarded as belonging to the family group whose dwellings stand inland. As the place of debouchement of the people and their canoes and a convenient lounging spot, it has a specific value for them. The whole complex system of native ownership will be discussed in a later context. What has been said here is sufficient to show that a village is not simply a commune of undifferentiated rights, but is an aggregation of smaller units, each preserving jealously the title to its own portion of ground, though co-operating with its neighbours on the larger issues.

Each little group of houses is often referred to in everyday speech as *te ŋaŋea sokotasi*, " the one place." The garden land lying immediately at the back is usually owned by the families concerned, as well as any breadfruit or nut trees, or banana plants in the vicinity. People of the same " place " help one another in such work as the building or repairing of a canoe-shed, or the dragging of a vessel down to the beach, and food portioned off from meals is handed over informally from one household to another. A child has a kit of smoking hot food thrust into its hand with such words as " Go and giv e this to your father in Sao "—or other dwelling near by.

The plan of Matautu indicates the actual residential divisions which obtain there, and their position in terms of kinship can be gauged from reference to Chapter X. There are four major sections of the village—the number has no special significance—known as Matautu, Raropuka, Marinoa and Raṇirikoi. They are not very often mentioned, the custom being to localize a reference by citing the specific house concerned.

Adjacent to Matautu proper are houses belonging to the Raropuka " house " of Kafika clan, some to the Nukuraro group, some to other branches, notably that of Reṇaru. Here live the brothers Pa Reṇaru and Pa Roṇotaono, whose long enmity is discussed later. Then comes a little oasis with two houses of Tafua, one of which is the dwelling of Pa Raṇifuri, eldest son of the chief, who is living near his mother's family of Marinoa. The other is occupied by an unmarried man and his sister, separated from her husband, these two being of the Fenutapu family group, distant relatives of the Tafua chief, with their ancestral home in Namo. Then comes a section of ground on which stand the houses of the principal men of the great Marinoa family group, also of Kafika clan, such as Nukuriaki, residence of the elder, Pa Fetauta. This area is sometimes spoken of as Potu i Motuaṇi, as if it were a village entity in itself, but the usage is rare.[1] The name is derived from the house-site Motuaṇi, where stands the dwelling occupied by Pa Motuaṇi ; he is the young son of the former elder, Pa Marinoa, and is a recent widower. A female relative is living with him to help with the care of the children. Lastly comes a section occupied by people of the Fasi family group of Taumako clan, the houses of Raroakau, Raṇirikoi (home of the present elder) and Roṇo-matini being in this group. This was where my own house stood.

Not only is the village divided up into dwelling-places specifically owned, but, broadly speaking, these are grouped on a clan basis. With this division is correlated the responsibility for use of the sites, and the right of decision on any fresh settlement. On the one hand authority for the conduct of affairs within any section is tacitly vested in the resident elder, or other senior man, on the other the consent of the owners immediately concerned is necessary before any change is carried into effect—as, for example, the erection of a house. It is as spokesman for the others rather than as the source of arbitrary decisions that such a headman acts. All the village inhabitants know in detail

[1] This is the " Potimatuang " of Rivers, H.M.S. I, 334, 335.

who are the persons entitled to speak in such matters, though there may be some difference of opinion as to which of them should have priority of judgment. In the area of the Fasi group, for example, the three householders Pu Raŋirikoi, Pa Taitai and Pa Roŋomatini all have a voice in any arrangements to be made. Pa Taitai claims that as the representative of the senior branch of the group he is the principal person to be consulted, but popular opinion is inclined to assign this position to Pu Raŋirikoi on account of his age, his fame as a traveller to the lands of the white man, and his rank as ritual elder.

The ownership of sets of dwelling-sites by family groups shows how the factor of kinship enters deeply into the village constitution. It is an element of strength since the family ties of the house-site owners usually help to bind them together, and further, where neighbouring families are members of the same clan there is an additional link. But where, as is sometimes the case, a section of the village is of a different clan from its neighbours, then the divided allegiance may make for tension and disunion. There is, however, another factor to be considered: the personal ties of members of the various clans through intermarriage. In Matautu, for instance, the folk of Marinoa are bound closely with those of Tafua; Pa Motuaŋi of the former group is the principal sister's child of the chief, and conversely through a reciprocal union the chief's sons stand in a similar relation to Pa Motuaŋi, Pa Fetauta and their kinsmen. On this account there is great freedom of social intercourse, and considerable friendship and economic assistance between these two groups. Pa Taitai and his relatives of Taumako again are also kinsfolk of the chief through Nau Raŋirikoi (v. Genealogy V and Chapter VII).

Matautu thus presents an interesting example of the commingling of multiple kinship and residential affiliations. Members of three clans, linked in part by intermarriage, have each a clear-cut interest in the soil, while acknowledging in everyday affairs the rule of the one resident chief and acting as an economic and social unit. The background for this state of affairs is given by the people themselves in the historical account of the settling of Faea. How this mixture of loyalties is resolved will be seen during the progress of our analysis.

KINSHIP AND RESIDENCE IN THE VILLAGE OF MATAUTU
(Key to Plan I)

Section A.—Matautu proper:

1. Motuapi (the chief's residence)
2. Mukava
3. Nukunefu
4. Matautu
5. Nukufuri
6. Roŋorei
7. Te Uruŋamori
8. Bachelors' house (unnamed)

Section B.—Raropuka:

9. Rarotoa	12. Roŋotaono
10. Nukuomanu	13. Nukutauriri
11. Reŋaru	14. Nukuraro

Section C.—Marinoa:

15. Rarofara	21. Tauŋa
16. Tarakifiri (Tafua)	22. Fenuatoa
17. Raŋifuri (Tafua)	23. Saumari
18. Motuaŋi	24. Farereu
19. Nukuriaki	25. Raŋimarepe
20. Feneitai	26. Marinoa (abandoned)

Section D.—Raŋirikoi:

27. Raŋirikoi	29. Roŋomatini
28. Raroakau	30. Otara (anthropologist)

An example of a more homogeneous kind of village is Potu sa Taumako. This, as its name suggests, is primarily the home of the Taumako clan. It is the residence of their chief, and most of its inhabitants are of the same kin group. In fact there are only two *noforaŋa* which shelter people of other groups, and both of these are occupied by members of the family of Sao, of the Tafua clan. Even here the ground itself is regarded as the property of the chief of Taumako, who could if the occasion arose drive off the occupants, though only the most extreme provocation would justify him in so doing. Like his compeer of Tafua in Matautu the Ariki Taumako lives a little apart from his clansfolk. His house, Motuata, stands with a few other buildings behind a thicket of bamboo, banana and other bushes. Next door stands its cook-house, while close in front is Raniniu, a sacred building no longer in permanent occupation but corresponding to Motuapi of Tafua in its esoteric significance.[1] Seawards again are two canoe-sheds, housing the sacred vessels of the chief, and opening out on to his canoe-yard, the scene of much important ritual. The beach in front is known as Maraniniu, a name associated with that of the house; formerly, before much of the sand was removed by a great hurricane, it was a noted dance ground. Immediately beyond the thicket boundary the houses of the remainder of the people begin.

Here again analysis would show the village as a group of family sites carefully demarcated and held in private ownership, though acknowledging the overlordship of the chief. In this case he is the

[1] See *Work of the Gods*. This was the village in which I lived for four months in the house Tuaraŋi.

head of the clan to which practically every member of the place belongs. One would imagine that there would tend to be more unity in a fairly homogeneous community of this type than in a village such as Matautu, composed of representatives of several major kinship groups distributed among different clans. Concrete evidence is difficult to adduce here ; I have the impression that personal relations were better and more intimate in Potu sa Taumako. But scandal and quarrelling occurred in both, and it must be remembered that the links created by intermarriage are a potent force in the creation of harmony between people of different clans, so that it is difficult to make comparison.

KINSHIP AND LOCAL ALIGNMENT

To sum up, in the Tikopia village we have several sets of forces at work. There is that of *local association*, village solidarity in everyday affairs, the tie created by common residence, co-operation in fishing, dancing together in the moonlight, and all the interchanges of courtesy and conversation which are found among people who live in close daily contact. Included in this is the bond through the chief in whose neighbourhood one lives. Then there is the *tie of descent*, comprising the bonds of family group membership, the ownership of house and ground, and the obligations due to the chief of the clan. In a village where the owners are divided among different clans this may be of course a factor of disunion. Lastly, ramifying through village and clan are the *general ties of kinship*, apart from those of descent, the result of ancient or recent intermarriages, linking group with group and tending to produce harmony between individuals otherwise opposed. It will become evident in later chapters that the behaviour of individuals can be fairly described in terms of these three categories.

The interlinkage produced by these intermarriages is shown in later genealogies. Meanwhile a chart of the distribution of the various clans among the villages, in terms of households, will help to place this analysis on a more objective basis. (See Table I.)

It may be pointed out to begin with that it is merely a coincidence that the relative strength of the different clans in terms of households is in accordance with the ritual precedence of their chiefs.

The most evenly distributed clan is that of Kafika, which has representatives in eighteen villages, nine in Raveŋa and Namo, and the same number in Faea. The greater number of households is in the latter district where the clan is represented in every village, though

WOMEN ON THE REEF

They are engaged in their daily work with the hand-net (*kuii*).

its principal concentration is in two. Their chief lives in Raveŋa. The greatest unit strength of each clan tends to be in the village where the chief resides. There is an exception in the case of Tafua, their most strongly populated village being next along the coast from their chief's, and partially in that of Kafika, whose chief spends most of the time in a smaller village of his clan. When his eldest son and heir succeeds him, however, the normal situation will obtain.

The strength of Tafua is concentrated in two areas—Faea, where it is the dominant clan, and Namo, its ancestral home ; it is very poorly represented in Raveŋa. Here, on the other hand, Taumako is well to the fore, being the dominant clan. It is less well represented in Faea where its strength is very much inferior to that of Tafua and Kafika. Faŋarere, which is small in numbers, is concentrated almost solely in a single village which it occupies to the exclusion of all other clans.

Reference to the historical account of the most recent settlement of the island would show how the distribution, here given, tends to corroborate that narrative. It is such as would naturally follow from such dispersion of ancestors.

Nearly every village shows a preponderance of households of one clan. This corresponds to the native attitude which regards a village as being primarily under the aegis of one group, though members of others may have land claims and possess full legal rights there. To give examples at random : Potu i Korokoro is regarded as a Tafua village with old Pa Korokoro, elder of the family group, as its principal man, while Potu i Rofaea is Kafika, with the Raropuka family group of that clan dominant there. Potu i Akitunu, despite its Tafua name (v. Genealogy II), is Taumako, with the Niumano family group and their resident elder possessing preponderating influence, while the neighbouring Potu i te Ava and Nuaraki are Tafua with offshoots of the chiefly family as principal members, but the elder of Fusi as leading man in the absence of a resident chief. Where a family is settled in a village peopled by members of another clan, historical causes, as a quarrel between brothers, a dividing of the inheritance, a friendly gift, or a preference for a different locality are given as explanation.

The impression of dominant or major influence is not, however, primarily a matter of numerical superiority, either in household or population, but is largely determined by the political and ritual organization in collaboration with the kinship system. A resident chief or elder may give the tone to the village despite the fact that his group members are not numerous there, though naturally, a leading man is found as a rule where the majority of his followers are residing.

TABLE I

CLAN DISTRIBUTION IN VILLAGES

Number of Households of Clan in Village or Settlement

Kinship Group

VILLAGE / CLAN	Number of villages in which clan members found	Tai	Ratia	Sukumarae	Potu sa Taumako	Faretapu	Potu sa Kafika	Potu sa Faŋarere	Potu i Fara	Asaŋa	Nuku	Raveŋa	Uta	RAVEŊA (total)	Potu i Akitunu	Potu i te Ava	Nuaraki	Te Roro	NAMO (total)	Potu i Siku	Sapei	Tukutauŋa	Mataŋga	Marauru	Potu i Korokoro	Potu i Faŋatafea	Potu i Rofaea	Potu i Mua	FAEA (total)	TIKOPIA (GRAND TOTAL)
Kafika	18	2	1	3	..	2	17	..	..	2	4	..	..	31	1	..	..	1	2	4	3	2	1	12	2	3	15	1	43	76
Tafua	14	..	1	..	3	..	..	..	..	..	..	..	..	4	3	6	5	2	16	..	1	5	4	8	18	4	3	3	46	66
Taumako	16	4	4	2	12	3	..	..	4	5	2	2	1	39	6	..	..	..	6	3	..	2	6	4	1	..	..	..	16	61
Faŋarere	4	..	..	..	..	..	..	10	..	..	..	..	..	10	3	..	..	..	3	1	1	..	..	..	..	..	..	..	2	15
Total	Total	6	6	5	15	5	17	10	4	7	6	2	1	84	13	6	5	3	27	8	5	9	11	24	21	7	18	4	107	218

NOTES.—(i) Bachelor's houses in constant residence are counted as households ; they are discussed later.

(ii) Unoccupied houses, or those used only occasionally, are not counted.

The problem of the broad relation between kinship groups and local groups may now be attacked from the other side, an indication being given of the spatial distribution of the members of one clan, that of Tafua. In detail this would demand consideration of genealogies, the census of the people, and historical data concerning the origination and settlement of the various divisions of the group. Much of this material will emerge later (see *e.g.* Genealogy II). Here will be shown merely the manner in which the various " houses " (*paito*) of a clan are scattered through the villages of the island. Since their kinship affiliations involve a constant interplay of gifts and services, particularly in relation to their chief, around whom they rally on important ritual and social occasions, their precise residence is important from the practical point of view. Contact between local groups which otherwise would be indifferent, or even hostile to each other, is generated and maintained by the existence of these kinship bonds.

The survey may start from the chief as the central point of the clan. He and the sons of his senior wife live close to each other at one end of the village of Matautu. The two sons of his second wife, separated from him since the advent of Christianity, live with their mother in the village of Matafaŋa. Of his two daughters, one lives with her husband of Taumako in Matafaŋa, the other, married to a man of Tafua, is some distance down the coast, but both come frequently to visit the old man and to help in the work of the household at special times. The chief had two brothers who married and produced children. The brothers are now dead but the offspring of the elder live in the house Aramera in the village of Potu i Korokoro, those of the other in Matafaŋa. The chief's elder sister, Nau Marinoa (now dead), lived close by, and her son Pa Motuaŋi has been mentioned already as being in close contact with him. A younger sister, married and living in Anuta, gives a *pied à terre* to any of the chief's family who visit that island.

The chief's father had three wives, the senior of whom was known as Nau Aramera. The second was known as Nau Matopo, and her son's wife, a woman of about fifty, and bearing the same name, lives now in the house Matopo in Potu i Korokoro. This woman's married son lives with his family next door. The third wife, Nau Mauŋarere, leaves as descendant her daughter Nau Raŋirikoi (wife of the elder mentioned above).

These folk comprise the more immediate relatives of the chief and co-operate with his household in many economic affairs. The repercussion of kinship and residence will be seen if one example is given. Pa Taitai goes to help the chief when the oven has to be made for ceremonial affairs. He does so officially because Nau Raŋirikoi is his "mother" (*see* Genealogy V) and the chief is thus his "mother's brother." This kinship linkage is rendered effective in economic terms largely because Pa Taitai lives in the chief's own village, whereas his own clan chief, the Ariki Taumako, is in Raveŋa. In actual practice it is very difficult to evaluate the relative strength of the ties of kinship and propinquity.

Of the other ramifications of the chiefly family of Tafua, one, the "house" of Atafu, is represented by descendants in Namo in the village of Potu i te Ava. Another, the "house" of Paiu, has representatives in Sapei and Tukutauŋa as well as in Namo. All the folk mentioned above are descendants of the present chief's grandfather. Another important branch of the chiefly family is represented by the group of Fenutapu, who spring from an earlier ancestor. Their importance is due to the fact that one of their number occupied the chieftainship during a kind of interregnum between the present chief and his father. The home of this group is in Namo, some living in Nuaraki and some in Potu i te Ava, though an exception exists in the family of Nukuariki, who live in Rofaea. Another branch of the line from a more remote ancestor is that of Akitunu, which lives in the house of that name in the village called after it. Three other groups of the chiefly family, sa Rarupe, Nukutauŋaru and Rotuma have their headquarters respectively in Rofaea, Tukutauŋa and Nuaraki.

These groups comprise the stem and all the offshoots of the chiefly line of Tafua. The rest of the clan is made up of "houses" only indirectly associated with this line, and controlled by elders of recognized ritual status. The principal home of the group of Fusi is in Namo with another centre in Rofaea, that of the group of Sao in Raveŋa with an offshoot in Rofaea; that of Notau in Matafaŋa; that of Samoa in Tukutauŋa; that of Korokoro in the village of the same name in Rofaea. The loyalty of these various groups of the clan to their kinship allegiance is demonstrated particularly in the manner in which they support their chief. Even though as residents in another district there is normally much suspicion and distrust between some of them and the chief's immediate helpers, they come along with their quota of provisions to assist at any important function which he initiates.

VILLAGE NAMES

In a society where proper names are of such importance those of the village are closely linked with other aspects of the social organization. The map gives their location, and a list of them is seen in Table I.

The generic term applied by the Tikopia to these residential units is *potu*.[1] This word forms a part of the actual village name in a number of cases : thus Potu i Siku, Potu i Fara, Potu i Korokoro, Potu i te Ava—pronounced " Potī Siku," " Potī Fara," " Potī Korokoro," " Potī te Ava "—and Potu sa Kafika, Potu sa Taumako and Potu sa Faŋarere.[2] All the village names may have the generic term introducing them. Instead of saying " Matautu " one may say " Potu i Matautu," and instead of Rofaea or Matafaŋa, Potu i Rofaea or Potu i Matafaŋa may be used, though this is not commonly done. The reason for the differentiation is that in the former case the proper names exist also as names for kinship groups or other important objects. Thus Kafika, Taumako and Faŋarere are clan names, Korokoro and Siku are the names of family groups, and, too, all apply to certain houses of great ritual interest. *Fara*, again, is the name of a common pandanus, and *te ava* is the name of the channel by which the particular village stands. Confusion might arise here if the bare proper name alone were used to indicate the village, whereas in the case of Matautu, Rofaea or Matafaŋa this is not the case. If a mere dwelling-house of the same name exists, the context alone is usually sufficient to make the meaning clear, and the descriptive label of *potu* can be dropped.

This generic term is also given a specific application, being employed in the sense of " the next village." A common answer to a question concerning a man's whereabouts is " *Ku poi ki potu*," literally " He has gone to the village," the name of the locality not being given, but being understood as being the one adjacent to that where the question was put. This linguistic convention depends for its efficacy upon the common ground of knowledge between enquirer and respondent as to the probable movements of the person concerned, his kinship affiliations, current events of the day and so on. Curiosity and free gossip supply this, so that very little explanation is needed to make the situation clear. In the same way the phrase *potu mai ko* indicates a further village, the one beyond the next, or beyond again. Thus if one finds the Ariki Kafika absent from his house in Sukumarae and receives the news that he is in *potu mai ko*, one knows that this is almost certain to be Potu sa Kafika, the

---

[1] *Pōtu*, meaning village, to be distinguished from *pŏtu*, meaning a short length of something ; as *potu fie*, a stick of firewood ; or *potu mami*, a short piece of bark-cloth.

[2] These are Rivers's " Posataumako," etc., which are incorrect renderings of the native rapid pronounciation ; the *tu* syllable is not elided before *sa* as the *u* is before *i* in such cases.

principal village of his clan and the home of his eldest son, several villages away, about a half a mile up the beach. If it were otherwise, then some indication of his purpose would be given, enough to establish the locality. This laconic form of expression does not indicate any desire of the Tikopia to avoid the use of the proper names of their residential groups, but is to be correlated with the small size of the island and consequent familiarity with details of events.

A village may also be referred to in a general way as *te noforaŋa*, a term which is also applied to any section of it ; it simply means " the dwelling-place." As a whole, it may be described more fully as the *noforaŋa lasi*, " the great dwelling-place " or settlement. Again, less commonly the word *kaiŋa* may be used for it. Pa Raŋifuri explained the *kaiŋa* as being *te noforaŋa katoa*—the whole dwelling-place—*i.e.* a complete village as against sections of it, and illustrated this by reference to specific examples. " That which stands in Tukutauŋa, the *kaiŋa* Tukutauŋa, that which stands in Matafaŋa, the *kaiŋa* Matafaŋa." Another statement illustrating the use of the term—taken down in Tikopia, and the first record to appear in my notebook after my arrival—was " the *kaiŋa* Matautu is the dwelling-place of the Ariki Tafua." In this book we shall have little concern with that unprofitable subject, the etymology of Polynesian words, but a comment on this term is not out of place in view of the existence of what is probably a cognate term in Maori, *kaiŋa*, which is the usual name for a village. There has been some mild discussion among scholars as to the possible derivation of the word from *kai*, to eat, when it would point to the importance of the village as the alimentary centre of the social life. The word in Tikopia, however, is pronounced *ka-iŋa*, indicating its affinity with *ka*, to burn, and thus its probable significance as the place where the fires are burning, implying the connection of the village with the hearth, that centre of home life which is so widely recognized in the ritual and lore of many peoples.

DISTRICT LOYALTY

Socially speaking Tikopia is divided into two districts, demarcated not by any clear-cut line, but by adopting as the approximate boundary the longer axis of the island, curving it where necessary to follow the sweep of the hill crest above the lake. The districts are known as *fasi*, " sides," or more rarely but more specifically, *fasi fenua*, " sides of the land," that on the east or weather side being Raveŋa, that to the west or lee being Faea. Raveŋa, much the

larger in superficial area, includes also in common parlance the sub-
districts of Tai and Uta, as also that of Namo ; this last is sufficiently
important to rank almost as a unit in itself. An essential point to
note about these districts is that although primarily geographical in
distinction they represent consciously separate social entities. Their
chief social feature is their rivalry, but despite the comparisons with
Melanesian or Australian dual organization which inevitably suggest
themselves, they are simply local divisions, not kinship moieties, and
they are not exogamous. The strength of the tie that binds the
members of each district together lies in their common residence,
with its consequent familiarity of intercourse ; it overpowers the
ordinary bond of clan membership and even that of family kinship,
unless this be very close.

For instance, Tiforau, a bachelor of the Raṇitisa house, goes
along to the residence of the Ariki Tafua when any function takes
place, bearing with him a contribution of food. He is of Taumako
clan, but as he himself says, he goes to assist the chief since he lives
in Faea. At the funeral of the chief's brother he presented a wooden
bowl, a roll of sinnet cord and a piece of bark-cloth to help the family
in their mortuary gifts ; for this he was repaid in food, as one of the
" home side." He goes over to Raveṇa to help the chief of his own
clan only on important ritual occasions—as at the rebuilding of the
oven-house of the temple Resiake. Similarly the elder Pae Sao, of
Tafua clan, but living in Potu sa Taumako, in Raveṇa, attends the
ritual of the Ariki Taumako, taking with him a contribution of green
food each time. He even takes an active part in the ceremonies of
the kava of this chief. This is facilitated because his own clan head
is nominally a Christian, but his father used to attend the ceremonies
of the former Ariki Taumako in the same way, and there is an
ancestral bond between the two families.

Meetings of groups of sa Faea and sa Raveṇa,[1] as the respective
inhabitants of each are collectively known, are apt to be characterized
by mutual suspicion and distrust ; each set of people tends to sit
apart in the common meeting-place, and a touch of formality creeps
into the exchange of opinions and news, and the inevitable handing
over of betel materials. In private conversation each district shows
a consistent attitude of criticism, even of contempt, for the other,
and with this is mingled an intense spirit of rivalry, which displays
itself in many unorganized ways. This attitude naturally enough is
reflected by the children, and is demonstrated even more strongly
than in the case of their village loyalties. In travelling with a child

---

[1] *Sa* is a collective particle which, used before a proper name, indicates the
group of people connected with it.

from one part of the island to another I have frequently noticed that as we arrived at a settlement and the local children began to hurry up in curiosity, my companion could usually be relied upon to exclaim contemptuously, " *Tamariki vare sa Namo,*" " Stupid children of Namo," or whatever the district might be.

The folk of one district are always eager for news from the other, on which they pass free comment, often of a sneering or ill-natured kind. Slander is common, including attributions of lying and theft in particular. In the course of my alternate residence in Faea and in Raveŋa my hosts for the time being always impressed upon me their own virtues in this respect and the bad character of their rivals, and were quick to seize any statement of mine and turn it to bolster up their arguments. Accuracy compels one to state that no material difference could be found between the districts on the score of moral attributes, despite the fact that the people of Faea are ostensibly Christian, while those of Raveŋa have remained heathen. This difference in religion is in itself an instance of the old rivalry, and in fact tends to intensify it as by tending to restrict freedom of marriage to an extra degree. The most important result of the introduction of the Christian ethic from this point of view has been to give to the folk of Faea not an extra measure of brotherly love, but an additional set of epithets to denote the benightedness of their heathen relatives. In giving his adherence to the *rotu*, the gospel, the chief of Tafua was undoubtedly stimulated greatly by the possibility of scoring off his compeers of Raveŋa.

Not long after my arrival in Tikopia I expressed the opinion that with a little effort of the imagination one could see in the inhabitants of each district characteristics corresponding to the nature of the coast on which they lived. The people of Faea appeared smoother in address, more peaceful, less boisterous, less wild in feature, conforming to their residence on a lee shore ; those of Raveŋa, as befitted their rougher weather coast, seemed more rugged and unkempt, louder voiced, excelling in manly sports. Later residence in Raveŋa itself caused me to reject this pathetic fallacy, and to attribute the difference, where it was still evident, to the personal characteristics of a few outstanding families, notably those of the chiefly line of Tafua on the one hand, and Taumako on the other.

A favourite habit of people in each district is to contrast their catch of flying-fish with that of the others, to the detriment of the latter if possible, and in the season the news of the night's work is most keenly awaited on the other side of the island the next morning. In other economic pursuits also the same spirit is shown. Once when sago was being made in Namo I saw Pa Fenuatara look at a

wooden bowl and say, " This was made by sa Faea." It was of poor
workmanship. He then claimed to me that the people of Ravena
could always tell the difference in bowls from Faea and those from
their own district, the former possessing no good craftsmen. This
was an exaggeration, though the standard in Ravena is probably
higher.

Each district boasts of its largeness of heart and makes sly remarks
at the expense of the other's hospitality to guests. Food is constantly
passing from one side of the island to the other in payment or
repayment of ceremonial obligations incurred through funerals, initia-
tions, marriages, visiting of children to relatives, and the like. From
villages close to each other in the same district a hand-kit (*loŋi*) of
food is sufficient ; for a village at some distance a larger basket (*popora*)
carried on a pole over the shoulder is usual ; if the gift is passing from
Faea to Ravena or vice versa then the donor always sends such a basket,
and sees to it that it is well filled, lest he be exposed to the contempt
of folk of the other district who meet him on the way. " The fool,
his basket is small," anyone would say who saw an inadequate burden
being carried. The first time I had a meal with Seremata at his house
Raŋiau in Tai two large fish were set before us. We ate a portion
of one only. When I rose to go he packed up the untouched fish
to be taken with me, and overruled my protest that it was far more
than could possibly be eaten in my house. He asked if I wished him
to be shamed by allowing the people of Faea to see a small food gift
from his house go with me along the path. He added some tubers
of taro, too, for good measure.

The rivalry between the districts finds formal expression particularly in the field of sport. Each side boasts of its prowess in the
dance, but apart from the acknowledged excellence of a few expert
performers, no conclusions are ever reached. From time to time a
kind of " field-day " in dancing is held, something in the nature of
a competitive display, but conducted with considerable formality and
strict adherence to traditional usages. Politeness rules, and there
are specific mechanisms for dissolving temporarily the strict district
solidarity. This *feasiŋa*, as it is called, has in part at least the effect
of canalizing the district rivalry, giving it opportunity for institutionalized expression, and also of subordinating it to the wider interests
of the community as a whole. Something similar occurs in the case
of the dart-match, the *tika*, the organized competition between two
sides, traditionally opposed, and arranged fundamentally on the basis
of district affiliations of family groups. This institution has already
been described in detail elsewhere,[1] and it is sufficient here to point

[1] *Oceania*, I, 1930, 64–96.

out that it is partly dependent upon the local organization. The different reasons given by either district for the abandonment of the game on the ancient ground of Marae lasi outside Matautu are interesting in this respect. The people of Faea say that the Ariki Tafua gave instructions to discontinue the sport because it attracted crowds from Raveŋa who on their way used to raid the local orchards and steal coconuts. The people of Raveŋa say that it was because their young men when competing with those of Faea were more virile and more skilful and carried off the *maro*, the prestige of victory, every time. Hence the Ariki in his chagrin stopped the matches from being held in his district. Both reasons advanced appear to contain some truth.

It should be observed that the animating factor in the district rivalry is not economic competition for subsistence. Each district has its own sources of supply, and there is hardly any sphere in which the food gains of one district mean a loss to the other. Such competition is always potentially active between the chiefly families and commoner families, but here it is not allowed to come to overt expression.

An indication of the antagonism between Faea and Raveŋa is given in the capturing of a bride (*v.* Chapter XV). The carrying-off of a woman from the other side of the island provokes a much more severe struggle than if she is taken from the side on which her groom lives. Local history, too, acts as witness and perpetuation of the feud. The narration of certain well-known conflicts, as in particular the killing of Kaitu, a man of rank of Faea, by people of Raveŋa, a story of which each party has its own version, helps to keep alive the spirit of resentment and to provide occasion for private boasting and for depreciation of the people of the other district.

In such spheres, however, it is difficult to separate the antagonism of clans from that of the districts. Table I shows how the members of Tafua clan are concentrated almost solely in Faea and Namo, and those of Taumako mainly in Raveŋa proper. The membership of Kafika clan is divided fairly evenly between the two districts. As may be expected, then, the district rivalry is focused particularly between Tafua and Taumako, since the bonds of clan cohesion tend to reinforce it. Kaitu and his slayers, for example, were of these respective groups. Identification of Faea district with Tafua clan is given point by the residence of its leader there as the only chief on that side of the island. As a man of Faea said, " Whatever it be that the Ariki Tafua speaks of, Faea which stands here goes in a body to him. He is the basis of this district." The tension and smouldering resentment of the people of the one side of the island towards those

on the other can then be translated from its basic terms of difference
of local interests into terms of rivalry between the three chiefs of
Raveŋa and the chief of Faea, and again into terms of opposition
between the major sections of Tuamako and Tafua clans, Kafika
having divided allegiance of residence, and Faŋarere being too small
to count as an effective protagonist.

Explanation of the situation from these different angles is necessary
in order to understand the diverse ways in which the social strain
presents itself in actual incidents.

Against this, on the other hand, there are various forces making
for some unity of sentiment and action in the community as a whole,
and tending to replace district loyalty by loyalty to other groups.
These factors are discussed individually in more detail elsewhere
and are summarized at the end of this chapter.

ARRANGEMENT OF THE NATIVE HOUSE

So far we have been considering the broader aspects of the local
grouping, taking a household as a given unit and observing the
various aggregations on this basis. Now we may investigate the
interior of a house itself, noting its material form and arrangements,
and the correspondence of these to details in the native social structure.

The external aspect of the Tikopia house has little to recommend
it. A low-pitched gable roof of sun-bleached thatch of sago palm
leaf reaches to within a foot or so of the ground, and end-walls and
sides of the same material complete the frail shelter. The doorways,
of which there are several, are openings large enough only to permit
of entry on hands and knees. The interior, except on a very bright
day, is dark and unprepossessing, the wooden rafters and ridge-pole,
as also the thatch, if it be an old house, are smoke-grimed, the supporting posts shiny with the friction of innumerable bare human backs.
The floor space is roughly rectangular, lacking in furniture, but
covered with mats of plaited coconut leaf, old and dry, and often
grimy in their turn.

And yet despite its simple appearance an analysis of the interior
arrangements of a Tikopia house will lead us immediately to some
of the most complex features of the native social organization (see
Ground Plan, Plan II). The explanation of certain linguistic expressions is perhaps the easiest method of approach. The house itself is
termed *te paito*,[1] and the ends and sides with the small amount of

[1] Cf. Mota *paito*, shed (Codrington, 44), or lean-to shelter in the forest as
temporary resting-place for cultivators (information received from Ellison

adjoining floor space are known as *potu paito* and *fasi paito* respectively.
The general floor space is divided into three rather amorphous sections,

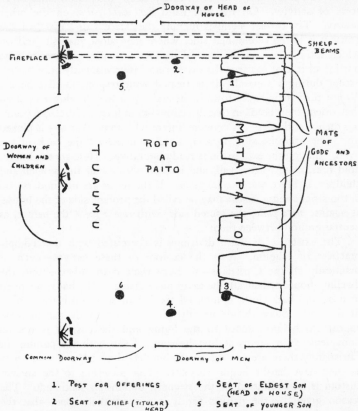

1. POST FOR OFFERINGS
2. SEAT OF CHIEF (TITULAR) HEAD
3. SEAT OF GUEST
4. SEAT OF ELDEST SON (HEAD OF HOUSE)
5. SEAT OF YOUNGER SON
6. SEAT OF SON OR GUEST

PLAN OF TIKOPIA HOUSE

without clearly defined boundaries. The central area is known
technically as *roto a paito*, or *roto tonu*, the middle of the house. It

Tergatok) ; also Samoa, *paito*, cooking-house. The distribution of this word is
an indication of the Polynesian-Melanesian relationship in this area of the Western
Pacific. The general term for house in Polynesia is some form of the word *fale*
(Maori, *whare* ; Uvea, *fale* ; Ontong Java, *hale* ; Samoa, *fale* ; cf. Fiji, *vale*). In
Tikopia, while ancestral temples are known as *fare*, cooking-houses are known as
fare umu. Curious differences in the application of such words appear in the
various Polynesian and allied Oceanic dialects.

is common ground to all the members of the household, objects brought in from outside are temporarily set down there, meals are spread out, and it is a kind of neutral area for the performance of all sorts of activity. On the one hand lies *matā paito*, on the other *tuaumu*. The former signifies literally the " face " or " eye " of the house ; it is the ceremonial side, where men alone may sit, and on which food is laid out in a ritual manner. In many houses a large portion of it, that towards the eaves, remains permanently unoccupied, except during a funeral. It is treated with respect, in that people do not turn their backs towards it, and when they lie down to sleep they orient their heads in that direction—or at least refrain from pointing their feet thither. A crawling infant who strays that way is picked up. The opposite side, *tuaumu*, signifies literally " the back of the oven," though the expression is really figurative. Here are the household fires, close to the wall, and in their vicinity sit the women and children, facing towards *mata paito*. If the terms are not understood in too strict a sense *tuaumu* may be called the profane side of the house, as against *mata paito*, the sacred side, with *roto a paito*, the centre, as neutral ground between them.

The existence of these divisions is correlated with the Tikopia practices of religion. It is the custom of these natives—even of practically all the Christians—to bury their dead either within the dwelling-house or beneath the eaves just outside. The body, wrapped in mats and bark-cloth, is interred six feet or so beneath the surface of the soil. Since this is usually of a porous, sandy nature there appears to be no offence to the living and the custom is not so unhygienic as it seems at first hearing. Even with the coming of Christianity there are few cases of churchyard burial, and cemeteries as such have hardly begun to exist. This adhesion to the ancient custom is an indication of the strength of kinship sentiment. The reason given by the natives for it is a sympathetic one—that the grave of the loved one may be the better protected from the force of the weather. Be that as it may, the side on which the interment takes place is *mata paito*. The visitor who enters a dwelling of any great age will see on one side of him a neat row of trapezoidal coconut-leaf mats, of the same type as those which cover the rest of the floor, only a trifle larger. They are arranged more carefully, and in some cases stand a little higher than the general level. Each marks the resting-place of a deceased member of the family, probably an ancestor of some note, and it is the presence of these dead forbears that is the basic reason for the respect paid to that side of the house.

Apart from the general deference paid to their burial-place, the presence of the dead is taken very much as a matter of course. I remember the dismay with which Vahihaloa came back to me after his first visit alone to the Ariki Tafua. The old man, wishing to be friendly and informative, waved his hand round and pointed out to him the grave-mats of his various relatives. When the lad understood that it was really dead men and not merely memorials that were with him in the house he was seized with fright and made a hurried excuse to leave. The custom seemed a horrifying one to him. But to the Tikopia it appears quite natural, and they wax sentimental over it in a sententious kind of way.

It is surprising how soon the anthropologist himself becomes accustomed to treating *mata paito* in native fashion. When I was introduced to Tuaraŋi, my home in Raveŋa, the two grave-mats of the father and grandfather of the present owners were shown to me and I was requested not to walk on them or use that portion of the floor—which of course I readily promised not to do. And though the graves were only a couple of feet from my table I observed the promise, skirting the mats punctiliously as I moved about the little dwelling. After a few weeks the habit of avoiding this portion of the floor was so far ingrained that it was no longer a conscious practice, and I remember that on one occasion it came as a slight shock to find how completely I had been ignoring the prohibited space and the company of the relics of the dead.

Mato paito is *tapu*, in the sense that it must be respected, but it can hardly be called sacred in itself ; the desire not to give offence to the dead lying there and to their living relatives is the motive for not using it. This brings about a simple habit of evasion. My neighbour Pae Sao dropped into Tuaraŋi one day and lay down to rest with his head on one of the grave-mats. I remonstrated with him, with some joke about having to pay for his bad manners in insulting the dead. " Oh ! " he replied with a chuckle, " I knew him in life ; he won't hurt me in death." Normally Pae Sao was rather a stickler for propriety, but we were alone at the time. Except in the case of one's own dead, on whom one is dependent in ritual, the respect for *mata paito* is as much a case of social as of religious observance. The only trouble I had was when one of the owners, a woman, called on me and said that the spirit of her dead father came to her in her sleep and threatened her with a club. I had been playing the gramophone to crowds of enthusiastic listeners, and their presence in the hut—some of them on *mata paito*—had disturbed the old man's rest. I promised to hold future concerts out in the open, and after this there were no more visitations.

The orientation of Tikopia dwellings varies somewhat, but most of them follow the same general scheme. The house lies with the

long axis parallel to the coast which is usually not far away, and *mata
paito* is the side facing the beach.   This arrangement is a very practical
one, since the slope of the roof and not the gable is thus presented to
the force of the wind from the sea, and with *tuaumu* side to the rear,
with the cook-house adjacent, some shelter is obtained for carrying
on domestic affairs.   On the other hand, the canoe-shed, with its
yard—the scene of sacred ritual—lies in front, so that it forms almost
a continuation of *mata paito*.   In an abstract schematic way one may
think of Tikopia as a circle of land bounded by the wastes of the
ocean, and just within the land edge a circle of houses, end to end,
their profane sides backed by cook-houses and leading inwards to the
orchards whence food comes, their sacred sides opening out on to the
canoe-yards, also sacred, and leading down to the beach, whence the
vessels set out for fish.   It is safe to say that no Tikopia thinks of the
situation in this diagrammatic way, but there is a consistency of this
kind about the general arrangement.

Exceptions occur, as in the case of the ancestral temples not used
as dwellings, which have no *mata paito*, strictly speaking.[1]

The use of the various doorways depends upon their position in
relation to *mata paito*.   This is always left blank of entrances, though
the sheets of thatch there may be taken down on hot days to admit as
much breeze as possible.   *Tuaumu* contains the side entrances used
normally by the women and children, and casually by neighbours
living on that side or by men going to the cook-house.   For more
ceremonious purposes men go in by a doorway at the end of the house,
near which the most obvious path runs.   Entering by this it is usual
to find that one has *mata paito* on one's right hand, *tuaumu* on one's left.
Opposite, at the other end of the building, is commonly another doorway which serves as a kind of private entrance for the head of the
house, particularly when he is a chief or man of high rank.

Another feature of the house demands attention.   As part of its
structure four stout posts stand some distance in from the corners.
The ordinary posture in a Tikopia house is for men to sit cross-legged
on the floor and for women to sit with legs stretched straight out in
front.   It is a mark of some consideration to be allowed to use a
house-post as a back-rest ; women do not share in this privilege, held
only by the senior male members of the household.   Here the usage
differs somewhat between commoners and persons of rank, and
between new houses and those of some age.   In new houses or those
of commoners there is no great cause for respect ; the living are of

---

[1] These are discussed in *The Work of the Gods*.   The only houses in Matautu
village which do not conform to the general plan of *mata paito* to seawards are
Matautu, Nukuomanu, Rarotoa, Nukufuri, Roŋotaono and Roŋomatini.

low status and there are no important dead buried there, so a fairly free use is made of the house-posts. In an old house or that of a man of rank a certain precedence is followed. One of the posts on *mata paito* is the private back-rest of the head of the house ; the others may be left vacant as posts for occasional visitors of importance, or for religious reasons may never be utilized at all. The posts on *tuaumu* will serve the resident brothers or married sons of the head of the house. Sometimes, if the building contains many important ancestors, then both posts on *mata paito* may be left free, from respect, and only those on the less sacred side of the house used. Plan II of the house Taramoa, showing its social arrangements, indicates the seating place of the head, Pa Fenuatara, his father the Ariki Kafika, who lives there from time to time, and his younger brother, Pa Fenuafuri.

It is clear that both rank and religious beliefs are reflected in the use made of the ordinary structural features of the house, its floor space and covering, posts and doorways.

There are few items of house furniture. At one end, usually above the head of the principal occupant, a pair of beams stretch across. These act as a shelf, *te fata*, on which is stored the most valuable property of the household : rolls of sinnet cord, pandanus leaf mats, sheets of bark-cloth, all carefully wrapped up, with a kit or two containing smaller articles. Nowadays the desire of every man is for a chest in which to store his private property, a *bokis* with a lock and key, but as yet comparatively few of these have found their way to the island. Hooks of branching wood are suspended from the rafters at intervals ; from one hangs a cluster of coconut water-bottles, from another the household food kit. A man of rank has a special peg and kit of his own.

The interior of a Tikopia house is so arranged that most activities take place on the floor ; the roof is low, and people move about generally on hands and knees. One stands up rarely, and then only to reach something down from the rafters. This is a habit which the visitor soon acquires. As one normally conducts one's life indoors so near the ground the proportions of a Tikopia dwelling take on a new meaning. It ceases to be felt as low ; with nearly a yard less roof-height there is the same head-room as in a European house. The desire to diminish resistance to the gales which sometimes sweep the island has no doubt been originally responsible for the squat appearance of the native huts, and for the small doorways, sufficient only to admit of a crouching body. On this the domestic habits of the people have been formed.

It is, by the way, the custom in Tikopia when entering a house to pause on the knees in the doorway and clap the feet vigorously together a couple of times to shake off adhering sand and so relieve the labours of the housewife.

HOUSE-NAMES AS TABLOID HISTORY

Houses in Tikopia bear names, and these are not mere casual appelations given for show, according to a rather stupid European habit, but are intimately related to the native social organization.[1] In fact the name belongs not so much to the building itself as to the site ; when one house decays and another is built in its place it bears the same name, even if several generations have elapsed in the interval. For this reason also subsidiary houses are assigned no distinct name ; they are described simply as " the cook-house of —," or " the bachelor house of —." The latter are small huts of no great permanence erected by young men with a feeling for independence, and serving as occasional sleeping quarters, or as rallying points for the unmarried youth of both sexes. There are several dozen of them altogether in Tikopia.

Many house-names are ancestral, used by the family groups for many generations, perhaps since their founding. Some of them are identical with the group name. In a study of kinship the name of a house then invites comparison with that of the residents, and of the family group, known also as the " house," to which they belong. Certain other house-names in the community are affiliated with this one, and examination of the reasons leads to ancestral linkage, family and clan history, and stories about the gods. Ancient house-sites are places of burial and are seasonally reconsecrated ; this involves a special kava ritual, co-operation with the clan chief, and esoteric connection with orchards associated with the house, and bearing the same or affiliated names. Any house-name in Tikopia thus represents a social situation of an individual kind, requiring an intimate knowledge of the organization of the people for its comprehension.

Here are the affiliations of some important house-names. In the Taumako clan the houses known as Ratia, Niukapu and ŋatotiu are at present occupied by the heads of the respective kinship groups so named. All these dwellings have been long in use. On some of the most ancient sites, though a house still stands there, it is no longer utilized for residence, but is reserved as a temple to the gods and ancestors of the group bearing its name. Tafua, Taumako and Kafika are names borne by the principal temples of those clans in Uta, while

---

[1] The Scottish custom of calling a landholder by the name of his holding has much in common with the Tikopia usage, v. for example " Grippy," " Plealands," etc., in John Galt's *Entail*.

Rarovi, Raropuka, Niumano, Fatumaru and Sao are the corresponding temples of the subsidiary kinship groups so named. Other house-names, though not borne by a major social group, are still connected therewith by ancient association. Such are Resiake (of Taumako), Notoa (of Sao), Veterei (of Taumako), Oa and Motuata (of Taumako), Fiora (of Tafua), Mapusaŋa (of Kafika). Still others may be of fairly recent coinage, as Raŋifuri (of Tafua), Avakofe (of Taumako), Fenu-mera (of Faŋarere). Many of these, indeed the majority, are com-pounds of Nuku (an archaic term for village), Fenua (land) or Raŋi (sky).

All the house-names mentioned so far are regarded as being of local origin. But the Tikopia show a very catholic spirit in their personal nomenclature : voyagers to other lands are prone to bring back foreign names to bestow on themselves and their dwellings ; stay-at-homes indulge their thirst for travel by taking over names which they hear from visitors or from their returned kinsfolk, and so endow themselves with at least the semblance of romance. For the desire to voyage overseas, to see strange countries, new lands, is the ambition of every youth or man in the little island, and rarely is it gratified. Preserved in the names of their houses and correlatively, of their married people, we find evidence of some of the external in-fluences with which the Tikopia have come into contact, fleeting as it has generally been, records of the ocean wanderings of the people themselves, or of the visits of strangers to their shores.

Mukava, the small dwelling of the youngest son of the Ariki Tafua, bears in memory the long voyage of the old chief's father, who touched at Rennell Island, which the Tikopia know from his accounts by the above name. Nukufetau has been derived from contact with the north-east, while Nitao is probably a rendering of Niutao also in the Ellice group. Panapa and Atafu, from the same area, are at present family names, the former borne by a member of the group sa Saŋa ; the latter not specificatory to any individual, though belonging to the chief's family of Tafua. These names are liable to be applied at any time to dwellings.

Pireni, a name borne by a famous voyager of the sa Saŋa group, commemorates Pileni in the Reef Islands, which he visited in his travels. A historical incident concerning this man may be given here as a digression to show the way in which material concerned with the doings of ancestors and preserving the names of foreign lands is handed down in tradition. Pu Pireni, who lived four generations ago, went off with four companions in a canoe and landed at a place known to the Tikopia as Averí. Up in the mountain of this island they were attacked by the local inhabitants. One member of the crew—a man of the Farekofe " house "—had lain down to sleep, murmuring as he did so in his pleasure at being on shore, " the sleep of a chief " (*te me ma se ariki*). He never woke again, but was killed as he lay. The rest roused themselves in time and ran for their canoe. As they fled, one of them, running blindly round a corner, struck his breast against a jutting rock and fell dead, pierced by a sharp spur. Pu Pireni, following close, came across the body of his friend lying in the path, snatched off his mat kilt as he ran, and threw it over the corpse, saying, " Yours there—mine lies before," *Ou tenei, kae oku tena ki mua*. By this he meant that his own death seemed close at hand. Then he ran on. As he went the enemy kept shooting arrows at him, but shot wildly. He kept stopping to bare his fundament at them in contempt, and, says the story, if he had not done this he would have survived. Several times he showed his silent scorn, and at last was pierced by an arrow through the back. In spite of his wound he succeeded in making his way to the vessel. Another of their company, Pu Tio, ran and jumped into a pool, diving down to hide. The enemy came and thrust spears into the water, probing about in every direction to find him, but he did not show himself. At last they went away, and jumping up he ran down to the shore and swam off to the canoe which was now stationed at some distance from the beach in the hope that he would reappear. Then the crew prepared to make their way back. They thought that their vessel would be lost and they would perish in the open ocean, so they asked Pu Pireni the way : " *Pa e ! Fenua tefea ?* " " Father, where is the land ? " Thereupon he pointed weakly with his hand to a star which stood in the heavens. " Set the bow of the canoe to the star which stands there." All this time the arrow was still sticking in his back. On they went, and again the question was asked, and the answer given. So they steered, the wounded man guiding them by his knowledge of the heavens, till at last they reached Tikopia. Soon afterwards he died from the effects of his wound ; he had been " pierced badly." He was buried in Asaŋa. To-day he has no direct descendants ; he was the *puna* (grandparent, classificatory) of the father of Pa Panapa now living. Another member of the crew, apart from those mentioned by name, was a man of the " house " of Rofaŋa.

The song which serves as the vehicle of transmission of this story is a dirge still sung on funeral occasions. It runs as follows :

> My canoe arrived at Averi
> Was carried up above
> Was slain.

The fight in the mountain makes us flee,
While I glance over my shoulder
To see who are coming to slay.

This thought also
" Pa is still behind "
So I wait, wait there
For him.

The poetic device of collectivizing the crew as " the canoe " may be noted in the first stanza. The last stanza refers to the thoughtfulness of Pu Pireni. His companions wanted to put out to sea without waiting for Pu Tio, who had hidden in the pool. Pu Pireni said, " Let us wait for father, he is coming down," and ignoring his own plight he had his way.

Other names, Matautu, Motuapi, Faoreu, are said to have been brought from Sikiana a long time ago, by Pu Maraetoto.

Names derived from modern contacts with European civilization are Niukaso, Potiakisi, Paŋisi, Melipani, Taone. The first two are expressions for Newcastle and Port Jackson, places visited by men of Tikopia when carried off on labour vessels. The third is the phonetic equivalent of Banks, the homeland of the native mission teacher, Ellison Tergatok, who is known under the name of Pa Paŋisi (Mr Banks). His former dwelling of this name in Raveŋa is now occupied by a relative of his wife's, Pa Teva. His own house is Taone, in other words Town, so named, probably, because he considered his residence to be the centre of civilization in an uncouth land. Melipani is an adaptation of the name of the cruiser *Melbourne* of the Australian squadron, which visited Tikopia about 1926. The name so attracted one man that he took it for himself and his dwelling without further ado.

The usual custom is for the married couple who live in a house to bear the house-name with the terms *Pa* and *Nau* preposed for husband and wife respectively. These correspond to the English usage of Mr and Mrs, though they are really kinship terms of address signifying father and mother. Once people have married they are given a house name immediately, and the general public, with the exception of their parents, brothers and sisters, ceases to use their former names. Together they are known as sa Nea,[1] " the So-and-sos," the name of the house being used in each case. Only in a few cases have bachelor men been assigned house-names with the usual prefix. This is decidedly exceptional, and occurs only when such a

[1] *Nea*, literally meaning " thing," or " person," is used by the Tikopia just as we use the expression " So-and-so."

man runs his own household instead of living with married relatives. Examples in former times were : Pae Otupua and Pa Raŋifuri (the first), brother and half-brother of the father of the present Ariki Tafua ; Pa Nukunefu (the first), brother of the Ariki. There are no instances of this at the present time.

The rule of bearing the same name as one's residence does not hold in all cases. Thus, Pa Fenuatara, eldest son of the Ariki Kafika, lives as head of the house Taramoa, while his younger brother Pa Taramoa lives with their father in the house Teve. At present there is no Pa Teve, this name having been borne by the present Ariki before he was elected to the chieftainship. It has not since been conferred on any of his sons, but will no doubt be revived at some future marriage, probably of one of his grandsons. The name was formerly that of an ancestor of the chief. In the Taumako clan the chief lives in Motuata, while his cousin Pa Motuata, his father's brother's son, lives in Avakofe. Pae Avakofe, father's brother to both of them, and the oldest and most well-informed man living in Tikopia in 1929, resided in Toa, a huge house standing alone in a clearing on the south-west side of the island. His eldest son Pa Tarikitoŋa lives in the village of Potu sa Taumako in the house Teva, while the younger Pa Roŋonafa lives in the house Oa near-by, the name borne formerly by an elder relative.

The general rule is coincidence of house-name and married name ; for the exceptions there is usually a specific reason. If two brothers both marry and live in the same house, one of them must obviously bear a distinct name. Again, the name of a man is changed very commonly if, on the death of his father, or other relative, he assumes the headship of a family. He then takes the family name as his own married name and may perhaps not change his residence. Thus, Pa Notoa living in the house of that name assumed the name of Pae Sao and the duties of the elder of the Sao family on the death of his brother some twenty years ago. He still continues to live with his wife and children, however, in Notoa, the original house. On being elected to the chieftainship of a clan the man is always known in familiar terms as Pa Kafika, Pa Tafua, or whatever it may be. Since the buildings bearing these names are now ancestral temples, unoccupied, there is always a lack of coincidence in such cases. Another reason for the change of a house-name, as indeed even of a dwelling itself, is the lack of children. A married pair who have produced no offspring after several years' residence in a house will often change their name lest the former one be unlucky and conducive to sterility. Change of name, it is said, often brings good results.

When a married pair have died, then their eldest son usually assumes the house-name if he has been living with them, or if he moves into the family dwelling, and this process is repeated with each generation. The name of the house (*iŋoa paito*) remains ; the names of individual men (*iŋoa taŋata*) disappear, the natives say. If a man dies and his widow is left with young children, it is common for her to retain her name while her eldest son at his wedding takes another married name (*iŋoa pure*). When his mother dies he is then free to take the house-name of his father. Thus, in the house Raroakau the widowed mother is still known as Nau Raroakau and her son has taken the name of Pa Taitai.

The device of giving permanent names to house-sites has provided the Tikopia with a most valuable mechanism for the preservation of social continuity. Houses decay, men perish, but the land goes on for ever. Hence whatever may be the vicissitudes of the human groups, the dwelling-site name furnishes always a basis of crystallization of kinship units in residential terms. Though the married pair who reside there may change their name in conformity with the needs of the political and religious organization, personal inclination, or the desire for children, the place is known as before. In European society it is the family name which tends to remain constant, whatever be the changes in the name of their house. In Tikopia the opposite obtains, a state of affairs apparently to be correlated with the small society which allows of an intimate personal knowledge of the kinship affiliations of everyone, no matter what name they bear. The permanency of dwelling names, combined with that of orchard names, tends to emphasize that feeling to which every Tikopia gives expression now and again, of the stability of land as compared with the human beings who inhabit it. It would be easy to over-emphasize the importance of this rather superficial native philosophical attitude, but it has its effect in such situations as a quarrel over lands between members of a clan (see Chapter XI).

That the system of house-site names provides a useful basis of social continuity is recognized by the custom that such names are borne (with rare exceptions) by married people only, *i.e.* by those who are in a position to provide the offspring who will tend to perpetuate the situation.

In Tikopia so strongly is the spatial referent developed that any ordinary mention of the more important ancestors of a group is usually done by specifying, not the personal name, but the place of burial. Thus the late Ariki Tafua Pukeŋa is referred to as " the chief who lies in Te Toka," this being a small and very sacred house of Tafua which used to stand in Uta. Taŋata o Namo is mentioned as

" grandfather who lies in Motuapi." This chief objected to the " wet grave " by the lake-side at Uta, and ordered that after his death he be carried to Faea and interred there. In the Marinoa family again, when anyone mentions "father who lies inland," Pa Marinoa, the father of Pa Motuani, is understood ; when it is " grandfather who lies by the beach" it is Pu Marinoa, the father of this man who is meant. The references are to the sacred houses of this family, standing in the orchard and by the shore respectively.

The habit of not mentioning the personal name of an ancestor is a deliberate avoidance, because of its ritual value. Though the house name may be mentioned without offence, it also is customarily avoided from association. The intimate knowledge of affairs current in a small community, and the general habit of spatial correlation, give a convenient mechanism of reference which can be used as a substitute.

PRINCIPLES OF LOCAL GROUPING

The account given of the Tikopia local organization and its relation to the kinship structure has been largely of an analytic character, and attention has been concentrated primarily on the adduction of detailed first-hand observations rather than on the presentation of broad generalizations from this material. Some indication of these may now be given.

Each of the various units discussed presents a very considerable degree of integration. The household is a compact little group with its own intimate life, preserving its secrets even from its neighbours and relatives elsewhere ; the village has a corporate unity expressed in economic and social co-operation, a unity which even the children recognize in their dealings with those of other villages ; the district has its own sphere of loyalties and presents a face of conventional politeness mingled with suspicion to persons from another area. But crossing these local ties are others which make for a wider loyalty. There are the bonds of kinship : on the one hand of actual group membership, and on the other of relationship engendered by marriage, particularly of brothers-in-law and mother's brother and sister's child. A set of strands akin to these, since their fundamental basis lies in a realization of ancestral kinship ties, are those resulting from the political organization under chiefs ; here clan ties and local ties sometimes coincide and sometimes are at variance. The so-called totemic structure whereby each chief controls one of the major vegetable foodstuffs, and through the religious system is responsible for its well-being, and the general system of worship of the clan gods on many ceremonial occasions, also necessitate co-operation of a very intricate kind between the chiefs and all their people, no matter where they may live.

A still further complicating factor is the recognition of two social strata, chiefs and commoners, which provides a measure of horizontal unity in the face of the vertical cleavage between clans and between districts. In former times there was even a feeling that marriage should take place only within the appropriate class. Important, again, are the intricate systems of reciprocal exchange spread like a network over the whole community, binding people of different villages and both sides of the island in close alliance. In ceremonial distributions of property, for instance, the traditional ethical principle is that as far as possible the goods should go to the opposite district. Yet whereas there is a strong moral imperative on the side of fulfilment of obligations to kindred, clan, chiefs and gods, the district and for that matter the village also have no such measure of protection. Loyalty to one's local group is a fact, not embodied in an injunction.

And then apart from these bases of specific organization there are the periodic assemblies such as the dart-match and the competitive dances already mentioned, and the religious gatherings of the " Work of the Gods," which involve the co-operation of both districts and all clans, enforce at least a show of amiability, and transcend a narrow parochialism. Then there is the distribution of land. The principles operating in this are discussed in Chapter XI. It is enough to point out that since the gardens and orchards of the chiefs and also of other members of their clans are not confined to the districts in which they reside, but are scattered fairly indiscriminately over the whole island, this renders inevitable a certain amount of contact in daily life between the members of these different localities. Still further are the cohesive factors of everyday operation, the use of a common language and sharing of a common culture, all that is implied by the natives when they speak of themselves as " tatou ŋa Tikopia," " We the Tikopia," and distinguish themselves from the folk of Tonga, of Samoa, or of Santa Cruz, or from that still more alien creature, the papalaŋi, the white man.

CHAPTER IV

HOUSEHOLD AND FAMILY

THE rhythm of the daily life of the Tikopia household varies according to the season of the year, the nature of the weather and the personal circumstances of its members at the time, but certain key events usually occur, their sequence forming a pattern with little variation. Waking, the toilet, a period of work in the forenoon to include the collection of raw food, a period of work round the oven culminating in the common meal, a more leisurely spending of the rest of the afternoon till darkness falls, and a final interval of recreation until sleep comes—such are the most significant divisions of the day. The general progress of daily affairs as seen in the village at large must now be analysed in detail on the more intimate household scale, the aim being to examine in particular the relations of the separate members of the household to one another.

Following the empirical method of presentation of data, the most adequate basis for generalization would be to give a series of observations, as complete as possible, of the conduct of several households, throughout a number of different days, setting down in the smallest detail the behaviour of each member. But it is manifestly not feasible for want of space to describe fully the minutiæ of the life of even a single household through a single day ; I give instead a few cross-sections of the position in several different houses at different times. These " slices of life " are not reconstructions ; they are taken practically verbatim from my notebooks, and are records of what was actually happening under my eyes, jotted down at the time while I was sitting in the houses of my native friends. As in each case I was well known there my presence was a minimal disturbing factor ; these can be taken therefore as typical excerpts, truly characteristic of the Tikopia mode of life.

These scenes are in no way spectacular ; they describe common everyday actions of what may seem a dull, trite kind, precisely what might be expected to happen in any household. Their interest lies in the fact that exact observations of how natives behave in their domestic existence are necessary before one is entitled to generalize regarding a number of important institutions, as for instance the family. Too often a certain pattern of domestic behaviour is simply taken for granted without investigation because it seems obvious, or it is inferred from a few dramatic incidents. On such assumptions far-reaching theories of primitive kinship are built up. Attempt is made here to document, however briefly, the conclusions later drawn as to the nature of kinship ties and their effects. The descriptions which follow are given in the present tense, as they appear in my notebooks.

It is early morning in the house of the Ariki Kafika in Uta, where he is living during the ceremonial season, together with some of his family, the remainder occupying the usual dwellings in the beach villages. The chief and his folk are sleeping, he with his own pandanus bed-mat on the *mata paito* side of the house, that facing the lake, towards which his head lies on its high-winged wooden rest. At his feet, on *tuaumu*, is stretched his wife, her head supported by the rectangular bundle of bark-cloth which is the woman's appropriate pillow. Next her are four youngsters in line, grandchildren of the chiefly pair, flanked by their unmarried daughter on the far side, and further away towards the back of the building are a couple of youths. In the dim light of the dawn they lie, curiously grotesque grey shapes under their bark-cloth sheets, and the heads of all, in accordance with correct etiquette, are oriented towards the chief. As the grey light of the early morning filters into the house, a child and a youth awake and in a few moments arouse the others. The chief, after a preliminary word or two, goes off down to the lake to bathe, while one of the little girls helps her grandmother to roll up the sheets and bed-mats into large bundles which are then stowed away in the unoccupied space in the gloom of the end of the house. Another small girl is told to go and fetch a fire-stick from the neighbouring hut. She dawdles about. " Run, don't sit and look ! " says her brother, a lad of about nine years of age, glaring at her but showing no disposition to perform the errand himself. Off she goes, while the others sit around, shivering occasionally in the cool air of the dawn.

The chief returns, his bare chocolate-coloured body damp, his straggly grey curls still dripping with moisture, and seats himself in his usual cross-legged posture under the eaves on his accustomed side of the hut. Savatau, a young relative of his, is still sleeping. The Ariki wants to get along with the business of the day, an important piece of ritual, so wakes him peremptorily. " Son ! Son ! Stand up ! " Then as Savatau stirs and sits up half-dozing still, with heavy-lidded eyes, the chief says to him, "Run and bathe." The young man quickly disappears and soon returns, with wet hair plastered down his back. Desultory conversation has been proceeding in the house meanwhile which the Ariki enlivens with characteristic quirks of humour, his lean cheeks, sensitive lips and hooked nose lending him the appearance of a primitive Mephistopheles. When the lad reappears the chief asks him if he has seen any signs of a canoe coming from the other shore—this meaning assistance and news—but he answers no. The two youths then go and uncover the oven which has been filled with food late the night before and left to cook slowly in preparation for the early morning ceremony. The chief prepares his betel mixture carefully, and continues to talk with his wife, daughter and others in the house as he pounds the paste in its little wooden mortar. After a short interval of pleasant mastication he goes off next door to the large house Kafika, the temple of his clan, to begin the rites of the kava. It is now a little after five o'clock, the day beginning rather earlier than usual because of the sacred task to be performed. When the ceremony is over the chief tells the youths to go and pluck some breadfruit, and then gives them other instructions for the morning's work.

This is an illustration of the collective life of a household in the early hours of the day. A common addition to what has been described above is the snack which is taken after the members return from bathing. This can hardly be called a meal: the children in particular are served, but the older members of the household often refrain.

After this the household breaks up for the rest of the morning; the folk disperse to their various pursuits, to assemble again for the preparation and consumption of the common meal in the early afternoon, and as often as not the dwelling is entirely deserted throughout the forenoon. Now if one seeks the inhabitants one must search their orchards, wander out among the groups on the reef, or attend where some ceremony is in progress. And since the household group is not necessarily coincident with the economic productive group, one may find members of other households intermingled with them, ties of kinship and neighbourliness being drawn upon to meet the demands of the moment. If food is sought from the cultivations, then husband and wife may go out to gather it together; if from the sea, then they will probably separate, the one taking his rod and line out to the edge of the reef or his deep-sea tackle in a canoe, the other going with her hand-net and fish-kit girded at her waist to sweep the pools. The younger people usually scatter, one or two perhaps remaining with either parent or some other adult member of the household, the rest wandering off on their own small food quests, joining in an organized game or ranging the village in search of casual amusement. The elderly folk also take their part in the day's work even to an advanced age, making their trip to the orchards or out on the reef, though in bad weather they usually stay indoors. Full description of the various activities mentioned here must be postponed till a later publication, where the technical apparatus and processes can be discussed in relation to the economic organization.

But let us follow a working party as they leave home on a fine morning, bound for the cultivations. They are going to dig turmeric, for it is August, the season for the preparation of this highly valued sacred dye. The group sets off from the village of Matautu, straggles along the beach to Rofaea and then turning inland begins to ascend the path running up to the crest of the hills. The turmeric plant, looking like a kind of canna, grows on the mountain-side and to reach the orchard where it has been planted involves a steep climb of several hundred feet up through the bush. The party consists of Pa Nukunefu and his wife, their young daughter, and three older girls, these latter having been co-opted from the households of friends and neighbours to assist in the work. For example, the Ariki Tafua, who is the father of Pa Nukunefu, asked Pa Paŋisi, the Motlav teacher, for one of his women-folk to lend a hand, and so his daughter Fakamaunuaŋa comes along. Soon after these people arrive they are joined by Vaitere, a youth whose family owns the neighbouring orchard; he is of the same clan as Nau Nukunefu and calls her his mother; his father's sister also is married to Pa Raŋifuri, the elder brother of Pa Nukunefu, so there are, as usual, bonds of kinship to provide a basis for co-operation. The work is of a very simple nature: the turmeric plants are dug out of their little shelves in the hillside with a digging stick, the clusters of roots are examined and broken up into separate nodules, most of which are set aside to be taken home, and a few having been exposed to the sun and rejected for technical reasons are dibbled in again to provide a crop for next year. Some cleaning of the roots also takes place. Pa Nukunefu and the women share the work fairly among them, he doing most of the clearing of vegetation and the digging, they some of the digging and replanting, and nearly all the cleaning and sorting. There is no strict division of labour, and the tempo of the work is an easy one. From time to time members of the party drop out for a rest, and to chew betel. To this end Vaitere, who takes no very active part in the work itself, climbs a near-by tree to collect some leaves of *pita*, the betel plant which twines its way luxuriantly up the trunk. About mid-morning the customary refreshment is provided in the shape of green coconuts, for which Vaitere is again sent to climb. Each nut is husked and the sparkling sweet milk is drunk through one of the eyes. It is then broken up by squeezing it between the hands or hammering it on a stone to extract the jelly-like white flesh. The husk is carefully packed at the base of a tree, not left lying about in disorder, which is the habit of thieves.

As the turmeric is being cleaned the young people pick out and chew an occasional root ; the small girl takes a special delight in this, not so much for its aromatic flavour as for the sight of the bright yellow saliva which she dribbles out into a little cup made from a roll of banana leaf. The whole atmosphere is one of labour diversified by recreation at will, and exhibits what even the cold-blooded objective scientist may be allowed to call touches of essential humanity, little humorous asides which, trivial in themselves, constitute nevertheless part of the flesh and blood of the native social relationships. Thus Pa Nukunefu as he digs the turmeric clears away the weeds before him and throws them to the side of the plot. Suddenly he takes a handful and tosses it out into the trees on the slope below him, so that the dirt from the roots sprinkles through the foliage on to the heads of his wife and daughter, who are working a little way down. They look up in some astonishment, see him grinning, and laugh too. Drawn out of their lairs by the hot sun, lizards dart about, the irridescent green *kalilisi* and the larger black *moko*. The latter comes inquisitively around, propping itself up on its forelegs to stare at the unusual disturbance of its quiet home. Every now and again one of the workers gives a flirt of the arm towards one of these creatures or tosses at it a clod of earth or a handful of pebbles, which results in a burst of flight and a tremendous scurry in the rustling leaves, eliciting a chuckle from the humans near. Vaitere, as the morning draws on, busies himself with the construction of a cap out of banana leaf, his own invention, and of no practical use. His self-conscious pleasure in it can be seen by the accompanying photograph (*v.* Plate V). When the turmeric roots have been dug and cleaned they are put into rough baskets that the women plait on the spot from coconut fronds and line with banana leaves. The handling of the coconut frond stimulates the girl Fakamaunuaŋa to make a plaited ball of the kind known as *patikitiki*, which is tossed in the air and hit up again and again by the palm of the hand. Her workmanship is not good, and Nau Nukunefu, resting near by, laughingly criticizes it. " She doesn't know how," she says to tease the girl, and quickly makes one in expert fashion herself. Her small daughter, Tokimata, goes to Fakamaunuaŋa and tries to take her ball from her to do the plaiting. At first she is not given it, but later the elder girl yields, and she tries her hand. Desire has outrun skill, however, and in a short time she has to run to her mother for assistance to complete it.

So between work and leisure the time passes, until as the sun declines perceptibly from the zenith the task of the party is done, and bearing their baskets of turmeric roots they go off down the mountain-side to their homes. There they take part in the preparation

of a meal for which in this case the others of their households have
collected the food.

Such is an example of the way in which a group of people behave
in the orchards ; it illustrates also how co-operation takes place
within a household, and between households.   Similar phenomena
on a wider scale are mentioned in the chapters describing food preparation at initiation and marriage.

Sleeping and eating are the activities which form the focal points
of household unity in Tikopia.   In this as in other Polynesian communities all food is usually cooked before being consumed, so that
the work of the oven is an important part of the household life, and
around it much of Tikopia sociology revolves.   It is well then to
give a description of the main processes involved before proceeding
with our sketches of family life.

AROUND THE OVEN

Most dwellings in Tikopia have adjacent to them an oven-house
used primarily for cooking, though occasionally a large hut of this
type is also used as a residence.   Men and women of the household
share in the work of getting food ready, most of the processes, as the
kindling of the oven fire, the preliminary scraping of tubers or peeling
of bananas being done by either.   In ordinary households there is a
tendency for the actual cooking to be left to the women, but as if in
compensation certain arduous details in the preparation, as grating
taro and expressing coconut cream, are specifically the charge of the
men.   The physical strain involved is the most potent reason why
these are not normally performed by women.   But nothing is more
common on public occasions than to see men and women together
around the oven.   So much is this co-operation regarded as a social
norm that a bachelor without close kin or a widower lacking mature
children will generally join forces with some elderly female relative
similarly situated ; there is no desire for sex relations here, but merely
the wish on both sides to have the complementary help in procuring
and cooking food.   At least half-a-dozen households in Tikopia are
of this composite kind.   Many " derelicts " with close kin usually
enter the household of a married brother or other relative, or live just
alongside.

The Tikopia oven (*umu*) is of general Polynesian type : it is a
shallow pit in the ground in which food is cooked by being laid on
hot stones and covered with leaves.   When a meal is to be prepared
the people responsible first clear out by hand the tumbled residue
of stones, ash and cinders.   When the bare earth is uncovered, dry

coconut frond, sago leaf or other light rubbish is laid down, a few sticks put on top, and the pile lit. The fire is started with embers or a glowing scrap of fibrous husk from the adjacent dwelling. If these are not available, then a neighbouring house or even a passer-by can usually supply the deficiency. The Tikopia is prone to carry about with him, even by canoe, a smouldering piece of wood, a torch of coconut leaf, or a section of the dry outer husk of the nut whereby he can start a fire whenever he requires. This tendency has been greatly stimulated in recent years by the natives' inveterate habit of smoking. In cases where no fire is obtainable it is generated by the *sika afi*, the plough method, at which the Tikopia are very adept, a small pointed stick (*sika afi*) being rubbed quickly up and down the groove in another piece of wood (*kauviroviro*) until the friction kindles the dust produced. It takes about a minute for a flame to be obtained. A pair of such sticks, which are of a fairly soft wood, commonly *varovaro*, are often kept in the oven-house or in rarely tenanted huts in the orchards.

When a flame has sprung up half shells of coconut, a waste product from former meals, are inverted and piled up on top while on them larger pieces of wood are laid. The lighting of the oven is described by the expression " *te umu ku pu.*" When the fire takes hold and begins to burn, the oven-stones are packed around and above it and wedged into all the interstices between the firewood until a fairly solid pyramid is built up. By now the oven has begun to burn —" *te umu ku ka.*" After a short time, as the fire attacks the heavier wood, often damp and decayed, dense volumes of smoke begin to pour out and fill the house, sometimes driving the people outside for relief.

Meanwhile the food is being got ready for cooking. Taro and yam tubers are scraped with the sharp edge of a *kasi* shell, a bivalve like a cockle, breadfruit are split open into halves or quarters, bananas are divided into small bunches. These when cooked constitute the *kai tao*, a term meaning literally baked food, but actually used to refer to tubers and other solid material as distinct from the *ŋarueŋa*, the mushy pudding which is the other basic vegetable part of a meal. There are many different ways of preparing and combining the native foods, constituting a set of recipes. Many of the dishes are very agreeable to the European palate. Pudding of one variety or another is the most prized food since it is a compound of coconut cream, but a meal is never destitute of *kai tao*, which is the equivalent of bread to these natives. The *ŋarueŋa* demands considerable preparation. Taro is grated on a spiked wooden slab over a bowl, wrapped up in small leaf packets and cooked in the oven, bananas are peeled and treated likewise, or breadfruit is roasted whole on the hot stones and then broken up. To the soft hot mass in each case the cream is added as it is pounded in a bowl. Of course it is not often that all these foods are prepared at the one time : in the breadfruit season this alone is utilised ; the banana is drawn upon as it bears, irregularly ; taro, the staple, and its giant cousin the *pulaka* (or *pilaka*), which last long when mature, are allowed to stay in the ground while other things are available. *Masi*, a fermented paste of taro or breadfruit kept in store-pits in the earth, is used to meet any deficiency. For an ordinary household meal one kind of pudding and a single bulk food is common, and on many occasions this is prepared only every second day or so, the people being content in the interim with the remnants of the meal of the day before, cold or reheated, supplemented by a roasted breadfruit or a few extra baked bananas or taro.

But by this time the wood has burned down and the stones are nearly red-hot, some of them indeed actually glowing. The oven now has to be spread—" *te umu ka toro*." With long sticks those who are tending the fire push the stones out towards the walls of the pit and bed them down, pulling out with tongs (*ukofi*) of coconut petiole any pieces of charred or burning wood still remaining. When the oven is a large one, as at some ceremonies to be described later (*v.* Chapter XIII), the spreading of the stones is a wildly exciting business ; people crowd in and shout and struggle, those in the foremost rank being protected from the fierce shimmering heat by leafy boughs held in front of them by supporters in the rear. When the oven is spread satisfactorily—and the work is done with care—some leaves of the giant taro or the like are thrown on the glowing stones, and the food, including the packets of grated taro or banana, is packed on top. More leaves are then arranged above, and finally the *repa*, thick brown slabs of leaf pinned together, matted and torn with constant use, are laid over the heap and gently tamped down. A few stones and logs of wood are set around the edges of the oven to keep the coverings in position. " The oven has been covered," " *te umu ku tao*." It may be noted that the Tikopia custom differs from that of the Maori and some other Polynesians in that no water is added to facilitate the steaming. The food is cooked entirely by its own moisture and that of the layer of green leaves protecting it from the stones. Nor is earth heaped on top of the oven after it is covered ; the *repa* supplies the place of this. The oven of Tikopia is covered with earth only when the contents are to be left in for a long time, as in case of turtle, which is cooked for twenty-four hours, or slabs of sago, for about five days.

In the ordinary way the food remains within the oven for an hour or two, the time depending on its quantity and on the initial temperature of the stones. Natives have a fairly good idea of the allowance which must be made for variation in these factors, though not infrequently hunger and digestive efficiency cause them to open the oven with the minimum of delay before the food is really done to satisfaction. Nevertheless well-cooked food is appreciated, and one of the commonest sayings to be heard uttered at a native gathering is " *Kai kai marie tatou, tatou ke umu ku moso.*" " Let us continue to eat quietly, our oven is cooked "—an encouragement to all present. There are a number of expressions which denote well-done or underdone food, and are used also to indicate the corresponding stage of the oven.

The Tikopia use no mechanical oven-indicator, as the Maori occasionally do by attaching a cord from the tip of a bent stick to a cooking tuber ; when the food is ready the tension on the cord pulls it away from the softened material and the stick straightens. They have, however, a rough guide in the progression of the subsidiary work, particularly in the preparation of the coconut cream, which takes long to get ready. A fragment of conversation illustrates this. A question was asked as to whether the food was cooked, and a reply was given telling of the long grating of the coconut after the food was put in the oven. The inference came swiftly, " The coconut had not been grated when the oven was covered ? It is cooked then ! " Thereupon the food was taken out. When there is a doubt as to whether food is properly done, and the oven should be uncovered, someone will often say, " O ! let it stay that it may be cooked."

These natives have no mechanical means of registering the flight of time in general. The sun, moon and stars do serve as their guides and the co-ordination of activities can be effected by reference to their position. But the period spent in bringing certain physical processes to completion—the period needed to convert raw food into cooked, to walk from one side of the island to the other, to take out a canoe, paddle the length of the reef and return, or sweep the bay with a seine net, to carry through half a dozen dances, also gives a useful measure of time. When a man is out fishing the length of his stay is governed not so much by the position of the sun but by the state of the tide, the amount of his catch and the degree of his interest in the pursuit. The conception of time as an infinite number of units of equal length, mathematically divisible and inexorably passing by is one that is quite foreign to the Tikopia. They allow their activity to be governed by their intrinsic requirements and not by any external regulator other than the alternation of day and night and of the seasons.   Even here the time factor is not so definite as one might expect.   Sleep and night, for example, are not correlated to the extent that they are in our society.   This must not be interpreted as meaning that the society is of an anarchical order ; common action is secured by group consultation which smooths out individual differences and controls behaviour.

The time of preparing the oven is known as *feraŋi o umu*, and is approximately midday.   But natives point out that there is considerable variation, which has become standardized as between Faea and Raveŋa.   In the latter district, it is said, the oven is uncovered, people eat, and then can go over to Faea to find the oven still covered, or perhaps only kindled.   The reason given is " because the sun is first in Raveŋa."   It is explained that the people of Raveŋa think that the sun is already in decline, but that when they get to Faea it seems to be still overhead.   This is put down to the fact that sa Raveŋa, who see the actual sunrise for the greater part of the year, are early abroad and out into the woods gathering food.   Sa Faea, for whom the sun is hidden for some time behind the mountain crest, are later astir.   So in mid-morning the sun does not seem so high for them as it does for sa Raveŋa.   Here is an interesting native view on the relativity of time !

The resulting lack of coincidence between the stages of the oven in the two districts serves as one of the many points of distinction which emphasize the individuality mentioned in the preceding chapter.

While the food is still cooking, if a pudding is to be made the coconut cream must be prepared.   This is the work of the men. The dry nuts are husked and cracked with a stone, splitting neatly in half, and the white flesh inside is grated into a bowl with quick rhythmic movements of the hands.   The operator sits on a three-legged stool to the head of which is lashed a serrated tongue of iron —in olden days a piece of coconut shell—which serves as the grater. This is known as *te tue*, the stool as *te rakau saro niu*.   The operation gives one of the very characteristic sounds of the Tikopia household, the short rasping *brr-brr-brr* on the grating iron, followed by a brief interval as the half-nut is turned in the hands, from left to right; then the triple rasp again.   At first in going round the circumference of the nut no return stroke is made, but as the operator approaches the middle he begins to take a return stroke each time, and every now and then alters the rhythm by making more than three strokes before the pause.   This phase of the work takes a long time. The process is shown in Plate VI.

The task of expressing the cream is done by means of the *vakai*, a mass of bark-fibre stripped from the *fau*, a variety of hibiscus which grows luxuriantly in all parts of the island. In ordinary domestic life the *vakai* is used several times, but for any public meal or occasion of importance it is freshly obtained. Its preparation is generally assigned to a lad. He cuts several long sticks or switches of the shrub, carries them down to the beach or the border of the lake and peels off the bark in strips. The outer coating is removed, the inner cortex is retained, and by slashing it again and again on the surface of the water it is cleansed and left as a white silky fibre, thin but very strong. The swishing of the fibre in the water gives another of the characteristic Tikopia meal-time sounds by which the appetite gauges how soon it is likely to be satisfied. At the same time the youth generally takes the opportunity of a bathe to refresh himself after his morning's work. The Tikopia are a very cleanly people with a penchant for bathing at all hours, and it is customary for members of a working party to slip down to the sea or the lake for a few minutes' immersion before a meal.

The *vakai* is shredded, rolled into a ball and brought back. A man then sits down to wring out the cream from the grated coconut. Usually the ethics of the division of labour ensure that this is a different person from the one who did the grating of the nuts. To express the cream properly is a task which requires a certain skill, besides strength of wrist and arm. The ball of fibre is placed on top of the grated coconut at the upper end of the bowl, spread out and the edges tucked in. It is then rolled up, enclosing a mass of flakes. The two ends of the roll are tightly grasped and twisted strongly until the cream trickles out and pours down over the hands into the bowl. The tension is increased until all the man's strength is being exerted, and the last drop has been wrung out of the grated material. This, termed *te ota*, is then discarded, being shaken into another bowl, the hands being clapped together to loosen the flakes. The process is then repeated as before. After a few twists of the *vakai* the breast of the operator begins to heave, the muscles stand out on shoulders and arms, globules of sweat break out on forehead, chest and back, and a grunt is emitted as the final turn is given. The work involves a considerable strain, and the fact of people having excelled in it is quite often remembered long after their death.

A small fire is kindled close at hand and leaves of the banana are scorched over it to render them soft and pliable as wrappings for the food when it is set out. Other leaves of the *pulaka* have a great part of the stiff midrib cut away for the same purpose, and are torn up into conveniently sized pieces. This is usually the work of the women.

By now the sun is high overhead and has probably begun to decline. It is generally about midday when the food is put in the oven, and about two o'clock or even later by our time when it is removed. *Te umu e fuke*, the oven is uncovered, is the description of this last stage. Men and women assemble, the *repa* drapings are whisked aside one by one and the prepared leaves of banana and *pulaka* are set near the pit. When the food is finally uncovered it is plucked out with the fingers and dropped hastily in a heap on the leaves, all hot and steaming. This is done by two or three people whose complaints on the score of burnt fingers usually fill the air. If the group of cooks is large other helpers attend to the pile and sort out tubers and other *kai tao* from the *papa*, the leaf packets. The former are put together in a heap, the latter are taken one by one, held on a coconut cup to protect the hand, and the leaf wrappings, now scorched and brown, are stripped off. Each lump of food is flung into a bowl, over which a man sits ready with a long pounder of palm leaf rib with which he mashes the sticky substance. The pounder, vigorously wielded, thumps on the sides and bottom of the wooden bowl, and this regular hollow beat gives another index of the stage which the preparation of the food has reached. Passers-by or people in houses near make comment : " The pudding is being pounded." After this mashing has been continued for some time— I have noted up to twenty minutes for breadfruit—and the food has been rendered as soft as possible, the bowl of coconut cream is drawn forward. Soaking the *vakai* in it like a sponge a helper holds it over the food in both hands, squeezing it gently so that the cream dribbles down and is mashed into the pudding. Care is taken to see that all portions of the food are creamed equally, and comment on this point is frequent among the workers. When the cream is exhausted, and a final squeeze of the *vakai* given, the hands of the operator pressed cursorily on top of the pudding transfer to it the last vestiges of the liquid. The bowl is then covered over with leaves, a half coconut shell wrapped in a limp banana leaf is put on top to serve as a ladle, and the vessel is pushed on one side to await the moment of distribution. By this time the *kai tao* has been sorted out and each kind placed separately into rough open-plaited coconut-leaf baskets (*popora*). As a rule these final preparations occupy about half an hour, and the food is apt to be cool when served.

A considerable amount of co-operation takes place among the members of a household at such time, and each plays a part in the division of labour. A couple of simple examples will illustrate this. Breadfruit pudding is being prepared in Nukutaukara, the house of

Pa Maniva (v. Genealogy III). The breadfruit are roasted on the oven-stones by two women, his unmarried daughters (his wife being dead), while in the dwelling-house a son, Rakeimuna, grates coconut and proceeds to express the cream. The breadfruit when cooked are peeled by the women in the oven-house and brought in steaming hot, wrapped in *pilaka* leaf. The father cuts them up and puts them into a wooden bowl, assisted by one of the daughters, while Mairuŋa, another son, cuts a pestle and begins to pound the food. After some minutes the father takes a spell at this work, and later the son takes the pestle back, the mashing of the fruit demanding considerable energy. Mairuŋa calls after a time, " Are the breadfruit ended ? " His sister in charge of them answers, " Yes." Then turning to the cream producer he asks, " Finished or not ? " " Wait a while," his brother replies. Soon both jobs are ended and the two men combine, the one squeezing his cream over the pudding while the other continues his pounding. The father meanwhile is tearing up *pilaka* leaf to hold the portions. A younger son, who has taken no part in the more energetic operations, passes him half a coconut shell, which he covers with banana leaf and then uses as a spoon to scoop out the food. Mairuŋa, his pounding over, now licks the pestle clean, while other members of the family hand round portions on their leaf platters. The meal is then begun.

Let us now watch the preparation of turmeric pudding (*sua tauo*) by the working party of the Ariki Tafua at the end of the season of manufacture of the sacred dye. The distribution of labour on this occasion illustrates incidentally how people temporarily resident in a household take part in its tasks as a normal procedure. The preparation of the food starts in the oven-house a little time before midday and continues for a couple of hours. The principal workers are the brothers Pa Nukunefu and Pa Nukufuri—the latter more obviously in charge— and their sister Nau Nukuarofi, who confines her attentions to the oven. Her husband and two young men, Rakeitino, son of Pa Fetauta, and Kavaika, son of Pa Nukutauriri, together with Nau Fetauta and a girl who is a " daughter " of Pa Nukuarofi complete the tale. These folk lend a hand spasmodically in all the precedent tasks of cooking the ordinary food which accompanies the *sua tauo*, but there are too many of them for all to co-operate effectively in each task. Nevertheless they remain in the oven-house as a token of their willingness to assist, leaving only their elders, the chief and his cronies, in the main dwelling. Their contribution lies in their presence and occasional assistance ; the bulk of the work falls on the ordinary members of the family.

The grating of the coconuts is done by Pa Nukunefu, whose

wife later enters with a basket of leaves to provide wrappings for the food. Turmeric flour is mixed with the coconut cream in a bowl and red-hot stones are then brought by the young men from the oven, using tongs of coconut rib. The stones are received by Pa Nukufuri on a stick and slid into the liquid, which soon begins to hiss and then to boil. Pa Nukunefu meanwhile has turned his energies to the extraction of more coconut cream. In about five minutes or so the *sua* begins to coagulate and solidify—it is cooked. Now it is stirred with a stick by Pa Nukuarofi, who has taken over the care of it from his brother-in-law. After some more stirring of the mixture Pa Nukunefu comes up with a bowl of cream and begins to squeeze it on to the *sua*. The stones are now lifted out on the stick by Pa Nukuarofi, lightly grasped by Pa Nukufuri and dropped on a leaf. He soon finds this method too hot for his fingers and calls out " give me the tongs." More cream is squeezed on, until the bowl is empty, when it is carefully wiped dry to get the last drops out. Pa Nukunefu then takes half a coconut shell, puts a piece of banana leaf over the top of it, and mashes the top of the pudding a little with this cup. Meanwhile Rakeitino, assisted later by Pa Nukuarofi, removes a coating of coagulated pudding from the surface of each stone ; this is eaten afterwards by the women. Pa Nukufuri carries in his arms the bowl of pudding covered with banana leaf to the dwelling-house, and then assists his brother to apportion out the contents. In the background one of the elders, father of Pa Nukuarofi, tears up banana leaves for wrappings. One of the lads carries round the portions of food, the chief receiving his first as a matter of course, and all then settle down to eat, after morsels have been nipped off and thrown out as offerings to the ancestors of the family.

These two sketches or vignettes give some idea of the co-operative economics of the ordinary Tikopia household in the work of food preparation.

Cooked food has a direct bearing on kinship in that so many obligations are fulfilled in terms of food, and to some extent the nature and quality of the dish are indices of the timbre, as it may be called, of the relationship. Comments made by the recipients as to composition and creamy texture of a dish reveal the importance of cooking in social relationships.

APPROACH TO THE STUDY OF KINSHIP

By kinship is meant that system of relationships between individuals in a society which is integrally connected with the recognition of biological connection by birth and procreation on the one hand, and of a legalized social union involving sex relations between two individuals on the other. Basically marriage and the production of children, themselves intimately related from the social point of view, are the two types of links in the kinship chain.

Before proceeding to the further analysis of Tikopia kinship some of the principal avenues of approach to the problem may be considered.

One of the obvious queries which the observer puts to himself at the beginning of his analysis is : " In what kind of groups do these people live—what are the essential principles of their local aggregation ? " This involves consideration of a number of related phenomena—the ownership of house-sites and their names, marriage arrangements, the claims of resident chiefs, and the like, the key to which is provided by the study of genealogical affiliation. The residential approach through spatial relations brings us to the recognition of kinship ties, of the expression of these ties in ownership, and the existence of large kinship units in which they are finally subsumed. And by reason of its accessibility to observation it is the residential approach that normally offers the easiest avenue to the initial understanding of kinship.

Closely related is the alimentary approach. Consideration of what people eat leads to the examination of the economic reciprocity between husband and wife, methods of wider co-operation in work, systems of land tenure, ritual offerings to ancestors and gods for fertility. From here one is led to family history, to political relations, especially those of chieftainship ; to the obligations and privileges of adoption, as reflected in food ; to bilateral kin relations in the utilization of family orchards by women and their children in other families ; to comparative wealth of kinship groups, in relation to population restriction on the one hand and social friction on the other. The full interrelation of these diverse phenomena will become apparent in succeeding chapters. The accompanying chart (Table II) gives, in diagrammatic form, an idea of the scope of the analysis.

Another approach is through material culture, the investigation of the actual objects that these people have and hold. This brings up problems of kinship in the field of production of implements, technical education, specialization and exchange, ownership and control of property, inheritance and so on.

The linguistic approach, considering what these people call each

TABLE II—FOOD AND KINSHIP

DEITIES OF CLAN

Ancestors to whom dedicated

Ancestral owners ; genealogies ; history ; marriages

LAND

SEA

Ancestral Orchards
Individual taro and family plots | Trees common to all owners
Use by women of house and by their children

Foreign plants and trees, coconuts, *voia*, brought from abroad by ancestors

Offering of *inaki* mat in clan temple ; division of mats among related houses

Fishing Canoes
Kinship in crew
Division of catch by owner

Knowledge of fishing banks, etc., passed on to kin

Canoe ritual : offerings by owner, anointing by clan chief

Household Meal
Common consumption in house ; aggregation of members

Ritual setting of food on *mata paito* ; throwing morsels to ancestors

Food brought by adopted child from its parents' orchard

Food brought by children from orchards of mother's house

Cook-house owned by family
Co-operation in work
Ownership of implements

Food received in ceremonial exchange, or by gift from chief, or other members of house other, their system of proper names and kinship terms, leads to examination of the behaviour appropriate to each term, and individual variations in such behaviour; of the correlation of kinship terminology and sex regulation, in particular that concerning marriage; the complex economic and ritual procedure at mourning and similar occasions. This approach from the side of kinship nomenclature has been most frequently employed in studies of kinship, but it can hardly be regarded as the most satisfactory, at least as a method of beginning the investigation.

Somewhat different is the biographical approach, which concentrates attention on the study of kinship with the child, or later the maturing individual as the focal point. Problems of the development of the child's terms and behaviour, and its movement into the kinship configurations of later life occupy consideration here. This approach, which represents a very specific and clearly formulated set of problems, has proved of great value in the work of Professor Malinowski.[1]

These different approaches are by no means mutually exclusive. Each in turn can be adopted as a starting-point for enquiry, and if the leads in each direction be systematically explored the result will be in each case the production of an institutional map covering the same set of facts in the native life, the same social configurations.

As the result of enquiry along such lines what we have is a number of projections of the kinship alignment in the society under analysis —the residential projection, the alimentary projection, etc.

Putting the matter another way, what we obtain is a number of different contextual situations of kinship by which we are enabled to give a closer definition of kinship phenomena, to clarify the relation of groups to each other and the relation of individuals to groups—in short, to visualize the kinship structure of the people. The requisite documentary evidence is provided by such material as house plans; village plans; maps illustrating holding of land; genealogies; historical records; charts of kinship terms; texts of kinship speech in conversation, as well as the records of ritual, economic and other daily life.

The residential approach has been used here to show how the spatial aggregation of the Tikopia in houses and villages is correlated closely with their kinship affiliations. By means of " slices of life " it has been demonstrated also how in daily conduct each household relies on principles of kinship, particularly family ties, to accomplish its economic and social ends. This approach is a useful one, since

---

[1] V. *Sexual Life of Savages*, 1929; *Man*, 1930, 17; article, " Kinship," *Encyc. Brit.* 14th ed.; " Parenthood as Basis of Social Structure," *New Generation*; article, " Culture," *American Encyc. Social Sciences*.

the data it relies upon is patent to observation and the inferences drawn can be easily checked.

The position of the individual family in the household, however, still remains to be analysed. Here the empirical method will still be followed : we shall take not a hypothetical household generalized from a number of instances entirely away from the control of the reader, but actual examples as far as space will allow. It will become clear that the examples chosen can be regarded as typical, *i.e.* similar configurations of persons, similar acts of behaviour occur in other households. The position of the individual family as a kinship unit in any society cannot be merely assumed. It cannot be taken for granted that a group of two parents and their children performs the same general functions in every case, nor can the presence of other relatives in immediate propinquity be ignored. Our problem—to be settled as the result of empirical enquiry—is threefold : to deter-mine the normal structure of the family in Tikopia ; to analyse its functions, particularly in regard to the position of the children ; to show how the family structure emerges into the broader social life, how it is correlated with other social institutions. The kinds of relationships to be studied are those between members of the family itself, between members of a family and others in the household, between the family as a unit and other families in the same position, between the family and kinship groups of which it is a component part, as the " house " and the clan.

The data now to be adduced are intended to show two things— the kinship relations of all persons comprising the households named, *i.e.* all folk who are normally resident in the dwelling ; and the residential position of persons immediately related by kinship to each household described. This information is important from the point of view of the ontogeny of kinship : it shows the variations in the configuration of family ties within which the individual Tikopia grows into the kinship structure ; and what effect, if any, this has upon his later response to the kinship system as he moves within it. More concretely, as an instance, the position of a family where a father's brother lives in the same house can be contrasted with one where the little group of parents and children dwells alone. There is a question as to how far such individual variations in the household pattern are relevant for the kinship system as a whole.

Towards the end of my stay, when I knew the people well, I made a sociological census of every household in the island. In this I set down the following data : name of the village ; name of the house ; clan and " house " affiliation of the members ; name, sex and approximate age of each resident ; and precise kinship between them in terms of relationship to a person taken as head of the household. I found this census, in combination with genealogies and other material, invaluable for the study of the social structure. The material given below is an example of it.

Of the four representative cases taken for examination, two are from the district of Raveŋa and two from Faea, and together they are distributed among three clans. Two are households of chief's sons, one of an elder, and one of an ordinary commoner. All of them were specially known to me personally.

PERSONNEL OF SAMPLE HOUSEHOLDS

Taramoa.—This may be described as a multiple family household. It is a large dwelling in the village of Potu sa Kafika, and is occupied by the eldest son of the Ariki Kafika, Pa Fenuatara, with his wife, two sons and three daughters, all children, the eldest, Rakeivave, being a boy. Pa Fenuafuri, third son of the chief, with his wife, son and daughter lives there also, and in addition Savatau, an " adhering child," a classificatory " son " of Pa Fenuatara, who adopted him soon after marriage. His real father, Pa Fenuatara's parallel cousin of the second degree, lives on the other side of the island.

Pa Fenuatara himself is a handsome man with almost an Arab profile, a splendid torso, careful of his personal appearance, particularly of his long golden hair. He is extremely intelligent. His portrait is given in Plates I and XV.

These two families share the house, each having its portion of floor space to itself, except on special ritual occasions such as net-making or the performance of kava after a night of thunder. Pa Fenuatara usually sits with the southern supporting post of the ridge-pole at his back, and his wife and children occupy *tuaumu* nearby, while sa Fenuafuri has the opposite *tuaumu* corner (*v.* Plan II). The chief himself often visits this house and sleeps there, having his own place at the base of the northern supporting post, which the others do not appropriate.

The chief's normal dwelling is in the village of Sukumarae down the beach, in Teve, the house in which he lived before assuming the chieftainship. Here he lives with his wife, Nau Kafika, and his second son, Pa Taramoa—whose name is derived from the house-site occupied by his elder brother—with wife, three boys and a girl. The chief's fourth son, a lad named Taupure, and his sister Roŋouvia, both unmarried, live also in Teve, though they spend a great deal of their time in Taramoa.

The inmates of these two houses comprise a closely-knit little group. They spend a considerable amount of time in each other's dwellings, taking meals there and joining in any work that is toward, they meet constantly in their orchards which are held jointly under the control of the chief, they assist each other as a matter of course in any ceremonial affairs, and the children of one brother are to be found in the company of any other. Rakeivave is in fact technically an "adhering child" of Pa Taramoa. The differentiation of the individual families in terms of precise relationship, however, is perfectly clear, and is given concrete expression by their occupation of the specified floor space in Taramoa, the separate movement of each married pair as a unit in changing domicile, or in going to the cultivations, and their separate ownership of bedding, betel apparatus, knives, and other property.

The immediate relatives of the chief's family are to be found in Potu sa Kafika, near Pa Fenuatara. Their precise degree of kinship will be seen from the genealogy (Gen. I); as far as Pa Fenuatara is concerned, for instance, they comprise a number of "fathers," "brothers," "sons," etc. One of the most important is Pa Siamano, who lives with his wife and children, Pa Niuaru his brother, this man's son, and Siasa his sister in the house Siamano. Somewhat less closely related, being the descendant of another chiefly branch, is Pa Vainunu, who lives in Maraetoto with his wife, married son (Pa Toŋarutu), daughter-in-law and their three boys; unmarried son, two unmarried daughters and an adopted lad from Motuata. This boy is a sister's son of Pa Tairaki, to be mentioned in a moment. Other married sons of Pa Vainunu live in houses round about. Both Pa Siamano and Pa Vainunu are men of influence in the councils of the "house" of Kafika; as classificatory brothers of the chief they are "fathers" to Pa Fenuatara and he shows them considerable deference. Members of the households of Siamano and Maraetoto are to be found fairly frequently in Taramoa, and they come at will, not by specific invitation. But they do not enter into such constant co-operation with the folk of Taramoa as do those of Teve, despite the fact that they are only a few yards apart instead of half a mile. Here is an instance where the bonds of close kinship between persons spatially distant are tighter than bonds between neighbours with more distant kinship. Another person who is frequently in Taramoa is Pa Tairaki. A son of the family of Mapusaŋa—really an elder branch of the chiefly house than the reigning Ariki—he is a man of some rank, and with his brothers Pa Ropeaukena and Pa Papaivaru comes frequently to assist the chief in economic and social affairs. The eldest brother, Pa Orokofe, lives apart from the others in Faea, and so is rarely seen in Raveŋa, but he is virtually represented by his son Savatau living with Pa Fenuatara. Pa Tarairaki himself is a small-boned but wiry, spare man, with curling black beard and young face, thin nose and sensitive lips, a whimsical soul always ready to crack a joke at someone's expense. He it was who at the sacred yam kava of his uncle instructed an innocent untutored youth in a whisper to go and pour a final cup over the heap of oven-coverings, a meaningless act which, solemnly performed, quite took the old man aback for a moment till he saw the humour of it. His restless personality and convivial leanings probably cause him to be more frequently in Taramoa than are his brothers. When any one of these comes, as he does perhaps several times a week, there is generally a child tagging along with him. Otherwise the children of these households do not spend much time in each other's dwellings, though they are very welcome there if they come with messages or in the course of their childish wanderings. Pa Nukumarere, cross-cousin to Pa Fenuatara, is often to be seen in Taramoa, but relatives by marriage do not seem to come so often as in the other households mentioned. A typical instance of the co-operation of the kin of the Ariki Kafika in economic affairs was given by their presence at the repairing of the sacred canoe, " Sapiniakau," to which reference is made elsewhere (v. Texts S.3 and S.4).

Notoa.—This may be termed an augmented family household. It consists of Pae Sao—head and *pure* of the " house " of that name, of the Tafua clan—his wife, three sons and four daughters, and Tanai-kava, a younger bachelor brother. In days past this man was known as Pa Notoa, after his residence, but in the epidemic of 1910 his elder half-brother Raŋitumera who then bore the title of Pae Sao died, and so the present holder succeeded to it. The sons of the dead man, Sia and Fakasarakau, who live in the house Vaitopu in the village of Ratia half a mile or so away round the bluff, come frequently to assist in the work of the household. Not very far from Notoa lives another younger brother of Pae Sao with his wife, son and daughter in the house Niata, the name of which he bears. The tale of relatives in close connection is completed by the offspring of the deceased Pa Raŋi-tauata, a man of the same " house " but of another branch. Three of his children live in the dwelling Raŋitauata in the same village as Pae Sao ; a fourth, a woman, shares with Sia and his brother their house in Ratia, where she helps them in the domestic arrangements.

All the kinsfolk mentioned come to Notoa from time to time, and co-operation with them is frequent, Sia and Fakasarakau being most often on the spot, since they have no children of their own to care for. Relations are close also with the households of Raŋimaseke and Nukufuti, the former being the family into which the sister of Pae Sao married, the latter that from which his own wife came. Moreover, though the tie of kinship is remote, and the people are of Taumako clan, the household of ŋatotiu which is next door has much to do with that of Sao, fitting in their oven arrangements to suit each other, borrowing coconuts, betel nuts and implements, helping each other whenever food gifts have to be prepared, making up canoe crews together, and assisting at each other's kava rites.

Raroakau.—This also is an augmented household, the constitution of which has already been indicated in the descriptions of daily life. It consists of Pa Taitai, his wife and son Tekila, and infant daughter, with his widowed mother Nau Raroakau and his two unmarried sisters. An elder brother also lives there periodically whenever he is home from Anuta, where he normally resides as a mission teacher. This little group has no very close kin in the male line, but in the adjacent house live families allied to it ancestrally as having been survivors from the expulsion of the former inhabitants of the district. These folk, though of Taumako clan, regard themselves as still constituting a group apart; they are the " house " of sa Fasi. They co-operate in all the major social affairs, regard the plot of ground where their houses stand as common property, and drop into each other's dwellings a good deal for casual conversation, to borrow betel materials and the like.

The relations of Pa Taitai with his brother-in-law and mother's brother are very friendly, in the manner indicated already, and his mother's brother's son, Uvia-i-te-raki, spends a considerable amount of time in Raroakau. Every few days one or other of the young men comes along and spends a night there, lending a hand in any work and taking meals with the household.

Raŋifuri.—This may be termed a diminished family household, since not all the members of the family are resident there. It consists of Pa Raŋifuri, his wife, three daughters and one son. There are no other people constantly living there. His eldest son was lost at sea the year before I arrived in Tikopia. Another daughter lives in the house Nukuomanu, a few yards to seaward, where she is the adopted child of Pa Nukuomanu and his wife, a childless couple who needed someone to fill the water-bottles for them and help in the work. Pa Nukuomanu is a classificatory " brother " of her own father. Pa Raŋifuri, as the eldest son and heir of the Ariki Tafua, is a man of great consequence throughout all Tikopia. His position in Faea corresponds to that of Pa Fenuatara in Raveŋa, and is even more favoured since there is, in his district, no rival family of great strength to challenge his prestige, as does that of Taumako stand over against Pa Fenuatara.

The location of the house Raŋifuri has already been shown in the village plan of Matautu, and a brief description has been given of the kinship affinities of its inmates. It will have been noted how four of the sons of the chief of Tafua, each with wife and children, live near their father, who divides his time between the chiefly dwelling Motuapi and the little house Mukava alongside it, where lives his youngest son Pa Mukava and his wife, with the old lady Nau Tafua. Co-operation between Pa Raŋifuri and his brothers is active in all matters such as combination for fishing crews, attendance at the old chief's ceremonies, contribution to family presentations, and utilization of the family orchards under the chief's direction. At the same time, as will be discussed later, relations between them are not of the best. Pa Raŋifuri himself has his house a little way from theirs, on the ground and near to the dwellings of his mother's family of Marinoa, with whom he is very familiar. Motuaŋi close by is the residence of his cross-cousin, the principal sister's son of the chief, with whom he is particularly intimate. In this latter household, by the way, the young man Mairuŋa is frequently to be seen, since the deceased wife of Pa Motuaŋi was his sister. This is but one of the many examples of how kinship ties bring people of the two districts together—Mairuŋa being a resident of Raveŋa.

To the house Raŋifuri comes fairly often Pa Niukapu, brother of Nau Raŋifuri, to visit his sister, nephews and nieces, and to assist his brother-in-law; relations are very friendly between them.

These four examples are typical of the majority of Tikopia households. Of the 218 dwellings in permanent occupation at the time of my stay in the island, 168 contained as their complement or part of it a married pair and their offspring with or without other dependents. The remainder comprise households : of childless couples ; where a breach has occurred in the original family circle, leaving one parent with the children, not having remarried ; where an elderly person or a young man lives alone in a hut, usually near the dwelling of a married brother or other close relative ; where several people of both sexes share a hut, with the tie of kinship between them being not very close. Examples of the first kind are Tarimataŋi, where the widowed Nau Tarimataŋi lives with her two sons and two daughters, all grown up or nearly so, and likely to marry soon ; and Raŋitisa, where lives Pa Raŋitisa with the young widow of his son (who died while I was in the island), her three little daughters, his other son and three daughters, all unmarried, and Nau Pereina, his sister, an aged childless widow. Here is a composite household where the various elements of it represent families broken down by death or nascent in young people ripe for marriage. Widows and widowers, who are distributed among the various types of household, are usually found living with their unmarried children, or with a married son or daughter, or sometimes in a small house close by. Apart from such bachelor's houses as are only occasionally tenanted and serve mainly as evening lounging-places, there are only about ten dwellings occupied by single persons, these being a couple of young orphaned men and several old bachelors and spinsters. In almost every case they live in close economic connection with a brother or other near relative. The need for co-operation in food-getting and cooking is the strongest motive towards association in the other type of household mentioned. For example, in the house Vaikava live two sisters, daughters of Pa Vaikava, deceased. Being lone women they have enlisted the help of Mairuŋa, a young man from the related family of Maniva, and Ariki-tauvia, their father's brother's son from Tekaumata. These are their "adhering sons" (Chapter VI). In Nukumanaia lives Muakinamo, his sister and his brother's son; in Mapusaŋa lives the old Nau Mapusaŋa with a son and two daughters, and with them a lad who is the child of the brother of one of her son's wives; in Raŋiau lives Seremata with his father's father's brother's wife Nau Resiake, her unmarried daughter, and a son of her married daughter as an "adhering child"; in Raŋimarepe lives Tauŋarakau with his "distant mother," a relative by marriage; in Fareumata the son of the house with the sister of Tauŋarakau, an "adhering sister" from the same general family group, though not closely connected; in Raŋikofe live two aged sisters with Vaniaraŋa, an "adhering son" from another family and clan, but from the same district and the village of their chief. It will be noted that all these associations are given in terms of kinship by the natives.

Comparison of the four households described in detail and the other quantitative data given shows an evident crystallization of simple family in the ordinary Tikopia dwelling; the nuclear structure is the little group of parents and children. There is no need to enlarge this statement here, since the material of the subsequent chapters will bring it out even more clearly.

Already, too, it can be seen how certain ties of kinship outside this sphere come to the front, how out of a circle of relatives some in particular are more closely associated with the family. Either they share a dwelling with the family or they are in constant communication with it, in which case the ties of consanguinity are effective over a considerable distance. This does not of course rule out the ties of neighbourliness.

The description of sample households in terms of kinship, correlating residence with genealogies, has demonstrated some of the most important structural features of Tikopia society. The working of this mechanism will be further indicated by analysing the character of the behaviour between the various types of kin mentioned. This preliminary account of families and households may also be of use to the reader in plotting the social position of many individuals he will meet in his excursion through these pages.

HOUSEHOLD VARIATION AS A PROBLEM IN KINSHIP STRUCTURE

There is one problem raised by the analysis of household constitution which is of importance to the study of kinship. Despite the partial isolation of the simple family as an element in the life of the household, there are in the examples mentioned different configurations of kin with whom the members are in immediate contact. Examine the position of the children in these houses. They are of different ages and so are in different degrees of dependence upon their parents. And again a child in one of these households is in daily intimate contact with different types of close kin than is its confrère in another.

Rakeivave, a young boy, is the eldest son of Pa Fenuatara. He is the adopted child of Pa Taramoa, so ostensibly lives in Teve, but he is very attached to his own father, goes about with him a great deal, and spends most of his time in the house Taramoa. Katoarara is the second son of Pae Sao, and while the eldest is away at Vureas for a year, deputizes for him with great success, being a manly, sturdy little fellow. He has his father's bachelor brother Tanaikava in the same house. Tekila, the eldest child of Pa Taitai, is only an infant, not yet able to talk. He has many nurses, including in addition to his parents, his father's sisters, who live in the house, his mother's brother and his father's mother's brother's son who come there often. Seteraki is a small boy, heir to Pa Raŋifuri owing to the untimely death of his elder brother. Because of his position he is spoiled a good deal, ordinary people not caring to thwart him. He has no father's brothers or father's sisters resident in the same house, but sees these relatives frequently.

Is there not the possibility that the patterns of kinship generated in the most impressionable years will vary considerably in each case? The actual care of the child, the feeding of it, carrying of it, issuing commands to it, punishing it and educating it is performed in different cases, partially at least by different sets of relatives; one might expect then that different types of behaviour would arise towards relatives of the same kind according as they lived under the same roof as the child or not. It seems that this is largely obviated through the adoption by the child of generalized modes of behaviour to all persons within its orbit in its early contacts. One difficulty exists here —that of studying the real development of kinship in any case, of tracing the behaviour of a person through a long period of years. Resort must always be made to abstraction—to the comparison of episodes in the lives of a number of persons at different stages, and to the postulate of a unity in the development of each to allow of a fusion of the results. Even the " biographical method " of Professor Malinowski is based on this process, and only to a limited extent is the result of an observed ontogeny. But to proceed with our analysis.

First let us distinguish between *formal* and *informal* behaviour towards relatives. By formal is meant that which is expressed in explicit formulation—the use of specific terms, speech avoidances, obligations of gifts and services, the performance of customary acts such as wailing. By informal is meant the acts which are not a matter of obligation, but take place more or less spontaneously between the persons concerned. As alternative terms " prescribed " and " non-prescribed " behaviour may be used, or " compulsive " and " voluntary."

The character of family life in Tikopia, as in other communities, can be described much more in terms of informal than of formal behaviour—of caresses, food handed over without pretension, glances of eye, tone of voice, bodily protection sought and accorded, as when the babe runs to its father—in short, a multitude of small services not falling under any social stipulation. It is this informal behaviour, these almost infinitesimal actions, which are so difficult to describe in words, though they can be readily appreciated by a careful observer, that I propose to group together under the term *sentiment*. A fuller discussion of the subject, detailing the relations between parent and child in this sphere, is given in the following chapter. But it can be stated at once here that the difference in the relation of a person to his or her real classificatory kin, to near and distant kin, to kin with whom social intercourse is frequent and those with whom it is not, to kin who live in the same house and those who live elsewhere, is largely a matter of variation in informal behaviour. The response to formal obligations in all these different cases is of the same general order, though it may fade away according to circumstances.

This distinction allows us to enlarge somewhat the common view of kinship structure. At worst, this has been taken to mean simply the system of terminology as it can be set out on a chart, and from a more theoretical standpoint it does not appear to have gone far beyond the inclusion of certain codified obligations. But by the structure of a kinship system is not meant simply the summation of the formal or prescribed behaviour. It involves the norm of the informal, non-prescribed elements as well. Such aspects of behaviour in family life as the consumption of a common meal, or the cleansing of a child by its mother are a part of the kinship structure of the community, as much as the legally enforceable gifts made by a mother's brother to a sister's son at a funeral.

The question which immediately obtrudes itself at this juncture is—are all reactions of individuals a part of the structure? Here the distinction can be drawn between elements of kinship behaviour which persist from one generation to another, which provide the factors of continuity in the social institutions, and those which have no such persistence. The kinship structure, empirically regarded, is the set of items of individual behaviour which have continuity in the social life, which are repeated over and over again in the existence of the same person, and through the generations. For various reasons the behaviour may become inappropriate to the given situation, out of harmony with it, and may change, thus introducing a variation in the structure.

In all social affairs the child does not create its manner of life *de novo*; it emerges into a world where certain types of behaviour are already established, though they may not be necessarily backed up by any explicit legal or moral sanction. Personal relations in kinship then tend to express themselves within this pre-existing framework. Where the act of an individual diverges from the structural norm it may be regarded with approval, it may be ignored or it may be counteracted by a mechanism serving the express function of handling such breach of continuity.

Study of the variation in the residential grouping of specific kinds of kinsfolk may be significant in amplifying our conception of the norms of the social structure. Kinship, in the last resort, is always a set of relations between individual persons, and from a summation of individual behaviour one sees what is common practice, and what is the personal interpretation of this. I regret that in this direction my material is scanty, since I hardly realized the interest of the problem when I was in the field. But I did not notice any perceptible difference in the behaviour of boys towards resident and non-resident kin— except in the case of actual parents. My general impression is that the socially approved norm of formal behaviour is affected by little difference in residential situation, since the crystallization of precise relationships takes time, and contact with other kin outside the home circle is so frequent. But closer study might reveal a difference. It would seem, though, that the intimacy of behaviour formed with kin living in the same house tends to spread outwards and to lessen the degree of possible difference in the treatment of immediate and classificatory relatives. It has been said that the pattern of the latter is derived from the former. It appears, however, that not only the parents, but other kin resident in the house act as a bridge mechanism, a conveyor of kinship attitudes. It is only reasonable after all to expect residence under a common roof to have its effect. (Compare also the linguistic data of Chapter VII.)

HUSBAND AND WIFE IN THE FAMILY

One of the cardinal features which emerged from the analysis of the Tikopia households was the common character they showed wherever there were still immature persons. This was the separation to some degree of the simple or individual family. The data may be briefly recapitulated here before proceeding further to examine the position of the members.

There are a number of different situations where the position of the family as a separate entity is clear.

A house is frequently occupied by a group of parents and children alone ; if by more than these then there is a spatial separation on the house floor. Husband and wife have a portion of the floor to themselves ; their children move about during the day but commonly return to sleep with the parents at night. When visits are paid to other households it is this little group that moves together. Such practices are not exclusive, but are certainly normal. In the nominal or linguistic sphere one of the signs of the individual family is the common name given to the married pair, a name usually correlated with that of the house in which they live. And when two married brothers share a dwelling each has a separate name ; the families are thus clearly delimited within the household. Husband and wife are known by the collective term *sa — Nea*, and it is significant that a child whose personal name is not used is called *tama i Nea*, " child of So-and-so," the name, not of the dwelling, but of its parents being employed for specification. Added to this specialization, the kinship terms *matua* and *nofine* are used exclusively for husband and wife respectively. Terms for parents and for children are shared with other persons inside the household and outside it, but there are specificatory phrases to make the distinction clear. At meals the separation of the family is not so marked ; they are frequently of a communal character, though husband and wife usually partake of food on the same occasion.

Husband and wife are also united in respect of their children. What Professor Malinowski has described as the *initial situation of kinship* is important in Tikopia, as elsewhere. In later chapters the beliefs regarding procreation, the postulate of legitimacy, the relation between pregnancy and marriage, and the sanctity of the marriage bond, will be discussed in detail; here it is sufficient merely to indicate their relevance as part of the institutional paraphernalia with which the Tikopia family is equipped for its defence and maintenance. The pregnancy of a woman is often a stimulus to a permanent union in marriage; her pregnancy as a wife affects her husband, who does not keep taboos, but is sympathetically weakened from reaping the fruits of his labour; in the economic aspect of the pregnancy ritual for the first child—the foundation of a family—the husband takes a prominent part. The ritual of birth finds the husband aligned with the wife and on the other hand, in the recital of the Fire formula at this time, the child is specifically enjoined to acquire economic proficiency in order to assist its parents. In infant nutrition, education, discipline and ritual of adolescence a father is closely associated with his child—there is a specific seat for him to occupy; he is responsible for food exchanges in the child's interest; he is expected to be emotionally concerned in its welfare, and he has a special relationship with his wife's people in virtue of being the father of her child.

Citation of these phenomena, which are perceptible in each household, irrespective of its precise constitution, is enough to demonstrate that the individual family is one of the structural units of Tikopia kinship, and to indicate the kind of social situation in which its individuality becomes most manifest. And these family relations are based not merely on the immediate situation in each case, but on a deferred or potential situation.

Integration in the activities of husband and wife is partly enjoined by the social code and partly follows logically from the general character of their association. When one partner is ill the other stays near by—during the turmeric-making of Tafua the youngest son of the chief did not participate because he was with his sick wife who had gone to stay at the house of her parents in the next village.

Between a married pair there is theoretically sexual exclusiveness, and jealous behaviour assists in the reduction of theory to practice. Polygyny is quite permissible—nowadays on the heathen side of the island only—and there are several polygynous households, though such marriages seem to be less stable than ordinary unions, which rarely dissolve. But some have been recently severed owing to Christianity. In olden times, as the genealogies show, polygyny was frequent in circles of rank. Discussion is given of these cases together with those of the present day in Chapter XV. The existence of these polygynous households complicates the Tikopia family relationships, but does not alter their essentially personal nature. As the assigning of separate marital names to polygynous wives shows, they and their children are regarded as separate family entities, each simply happening to have a husband and father in common. In the case of the children, each is cared for in life and in death by his own mother's relatives ; there is never any confusion or aggregation. As far as my records indicate there has never been an instance of true polyandry in Tikopia. Since the mechanism of divorce is not clearly defined there are cases of women while still legally attached to one husband in his eyes, living with another man and being regarded as his wife, the mark of this being the assumption of his house-name. But in such a case all sex relations with the first husband cease.

Adultery by a married woman is stated in reply to casual enquiry never to occur, and in actual fact does seem to be very rare ; only one case became public during my stay in Tikopia, though I have notes of a few others. This and other deviations from the sexual norms are discussed in later chapters. It is said " the married woman is *tapu*," " marriage is weighty for the woman," and severe punishment is liable to be visited upon her by her husband or brothers if her breach is discovered. A married man, however, has not to suffer this restriction to the same degree. Convention allows him to go among the unmarried girls without suffering any real stigma. He may be chaffed or sneered at by other men for his lecherous conduct, but the only check that is liable to be put on his amorous exploits is that applied by the jealousy of his wife. Fear of a nagging tongue and sharp female nails are probably the most potent deterrents in keeping many husbands faithful. Jealousy is a definitely recognized type of behaviour in Tikopia, characterized by a special linguistic expression, *masaro*. It is particularly evident in newly-married people, the natives say, and they regard it as a kind of accompaniment to the recently-wedded state. One of the young pair excites the jealousy of the other by standing near a person of the opposite sex, or by talking or glancing in what is interpreted as a suggestive manner. A quarrel ensues and bystanders are later questioned by those who have heard the gossip. " The married couple of So-and-so fought over what ? " " We don't know ; there it is ; the co-habitation of a newly married pair. They dwell together, they become jealous." [1]

In such case, if the husband goes out alone at night the wife does not sleep but watches for him anxiously. When time draws on and it is near morning, then she knows " he has gone to the women " (the conventional Tikopia expression for lechery). When he returns, he thinks she is asleep, but no, she is waiting for him. She has a stick, with which she bangs him on the back and legs—the head is taboo—and she pinches his flesh until the skin is broken. This he must suffer as quietly as he can, in order not to arouse the whole household.

Quarrels in which accusations of impropriety or infidelity are prominent may, however, be merely symptomatic of a more radical state of domestic friction. With my neighbour Pa Taitai and his wife things did not always go smoothly. He was a tall young fellow, generally easy-going and good natured to outsiders, but capable of selfish, domineering behaviour in his own household. Since my servant Vahihaloa lived there, I had his frequent commentary to add to my own observations. Rows in the dwelling were frequent, mainly over betel, tobacco or food. Pa Taitai would come back from fishing or from working in his garden and would find the women chewing betel. If none were left for him he would make a scene. Or his wife having netted a few small fish on the reef would cook them for herself and her child, and he considering that they should have been left till he returned, would be angry. On one occasion she accused him in somewhat indirect terms of infidelity. She said, " I know; I have heard the talk." Pa Taitai demanded of what, and from whom. She then accused him more plainly, and after some bitter recriminations said that they would separate, she would take the younger child and go to live with her parents at Rofaea, and they—*i.e.* her husband and his people—might have the elder. Pa Taitai was angry. He clenched his fist and struck his wife repeatedly on the head, he and his mother holding her by the arms to make her divulge the source of her information, if she was telling the truth or was merely inventing the story. When she stuck to her asseveration then he hit her. Once he struck her so that she bumped heavily against his mother who was sitting near the house-post and the old woman knocked her head. " May your father eat filth ! " she said crossly to her son. Finally both parties calmed down and Nau Taitai stayed on.

---

[1] On one occasion a pair of fruit bats entwined in a tree began to squeal and nip each other. I asked what was the matter. A cynic replied, " *Taunoso peka e featu* "—" Married bats who are fighting."

Another occasion was even more dramatic. As I was sitting in my house after the evening meal Vahihaloa came rushing in and gasped, " Come quick ! Ata (Pa Taitai) is killing his wife ! " Hastily I grabbed up a torch—for the moon had not risen—and ran next door. I bent down at the low doorway, whence came sounds of sobbing and the heavy struggling of human bodies. But Vahihaloa was before me. " Ata ! " he cried, and knelt to enter. Suddenly there was a terrific crash on the thatch above his head, and he jumped back as a wooden pillow fell. Pa Taitai had hurled it at the intruder. Thereupon I flashed my torch up through the doorway and silence immediately fell inside. No further missile followed ; Ata was evidently not willing to risk his friendship with me, however furious he might be at this intrusion. As I crept in the little entrance I saw in the beam of light the man sitting in front of his wife, grasping her tightly by her wrists, while she silently writhed to be free. At her back rose a house-post picked out of the surrounding gloom by the shaft of light. Both of them spoke almost simultaneously. Pa Taitai said, " This wretched woman has been trying to kill herself ; she has been dashing her head against the post, and I have hardly been able to restrain her." His wife said, " He struck me ; he desires that I should be dead." I was in an awkward position, since it was none of my business to interfere in a marital difference, and yet at the same time there was a possibility of serious hurt being done to the woman. I therefore took the line that eminent persons in Tikopia take—that any disturbance in their neighbourhood is an affront to their dignity—gave some counsel about the advisability of husband and wife agreeing, and an intimation that if I heard any further noise I should come in again. I carefully left unstated what I should do in that case, fervently hoping that the warning in itself would be enough. Then I left, and heard no more. Later I gathered that Nau Taitai had become suspicious of her husband and an unmarried woman in the adjacent village, hearing that he had made gifts of tobacco and betel nut to her, and had taxed him with it. He had replied angrily and she had wanted the last word. After this episode, if I remember rightly, the wife went home to her parents and stayed there for several days with her infant daughter, till her husband sent a gift of food and a request for her return, as the custom is in such cases. Sometimes, however, a woman will not wait to be solicited back by her husband, but returns of her own accord.

In general, amicable relations exist between a married couple in Tikopia. There are no open signs of affection between them : no public caresses, no use of terms corresponding to " dear," or of those diminutive suffixes which so delight the heart of Teuton or

Slav. A blunt mode of address is usual. A meal was being prepared in the household of the Ariki Kafika. Nau Kafika, in the oven-hut, called out to her husband, " Hey ! the oven (*i.e.* the food) is cooked." The chief, sitting in the dwelling-house, called back without stirring, " It is cooked ? Why don't you go and uncover it ? " Again, Nau Kafika was making a wad of betel. " A bit of betel for me ! " she demanded of the house at large. Her husband without a word tossed her a packet of the leaf, which she took silently, without even a gesture of acknowledgment. Such is in accord with the ordinary norms of informal address between persons who are not husband and wife ; actions, not words, are the index to the marital relationship.

Wife and husband do not use each other's personal names at all, but only the house-name, with the appropriate prefix *Pa* or *Nau*. Occasionally a woman may call to her husband by the term of equality, *Pe*, as I have heard Nau Kafika address the chief : " Pe Kafika ! " And though the chief and others such as Pa Tarairaki frequently spoke of Pa Fenuatara as Taurono, the name he bore before he was married, I never heard his wife use it, nor could she have done so without committing a grave breach of etiquette. This is part of the native theory of domestic relations : husband and wife should show respect to each other, and avoidance of the personal name is one feature of this attitude. Another is the procedure which is held up as the ideal in case of difference of opinion. The man is held to be the head of the house, but mutual deference is the norm aimed at. Each partner issues orders in his or her own sphere, orders which the other is free to ignore or object to if desired. If the husband scolds the wife, then she should bow her head to the words, not contradict and exasperate him. But conversely, if she should scold him he should bow likewise ; it is right, the natives say, that each party should " listen to " the other when rebuked. The husband is of course in a superior position since the house usually stands on the ground owned by his family ; it is then " his " house rather than hers in the last resort. The strength of the wife lies in her ability to return at any time to her own family, and this she can use as a weapon, the mere threat of which may be sufficient to make a querulous or unjust husband see reason.

A married woman in general is regarded as *tapu*, and her position is seen in the deference paid to her by people other than her husband. Her active intervention quells the more active aspects of a fight (an illustration is given in Chapter XI). If a man is going to brawl, and his wife is with him, she goes over to the other man and grasps his arm, thus immobilizing him. As it is said, " the wife is the shelter

of her husband." In after days the opponent may jeer and boast,
" That one was saved only through his wife ; if he had come on alone
I would have cut his throat." If perchance the wife should be hit
in the struggle, then it is said the husband will throw all caution away
and rush in furiously, striking down the offender at once. This
rarely occurs. The theory of the sanctity of a married woman is a
convention by which the Tikopia abide, and which acts as a legal
mechanism for the preservation of social order.

The convention of respect for the spouse tends to eliminate much
in the way of domestic joking of a personal kind ; this is reserved for
relatives specifically licit. The group " totem " of the one partner
is also respected by the other, though this demands little observance,
since it amounts to hardly more than refraining from eating something
which would rarely appear in any case on the bill of fare. The animals
and birds concerned thus tend to become household totems.

The character of the sex relations between husband and wife is
important, particularly in the matter of control of child-bearing, but
this can be more appropriately discussed in the chapter on sex matters
in general.

When a man is away from home and a visitor calls it is proper
for the woman to receive him. She says to the husband on his return,
" So-and-so came, you were absent, but I gave him food to eat ;
after he had eaten and drunk from the water-bottle he went out and
departed to his house." [1]

The relation of husband and wife is of greatest social importance
in their co-operation in the economic sphere on the one hand, and
in the rearing of their children on the other. As will be apparent
from examples given subsequently in many contexts, they perform
a number of essential tasks jointly, and supplement each other's
activities directly in many others. They commonly go out to their
orchards together in the morning to plant, and to gather materials
for the midday meal, and they usually combine in the preparation
and cooking of the food. On the other hand the husband makes all
the nets for the household—or gets them made by some other man—
even the *kuti* which his wife uses ; he fells the trees for her to make
the bark-cloth for them both, cuts the coconut fronds from which
she makes baskets and floor-mats, and catches fish in the open sea
for the common meal. All manner of woodwork, too, is his care, as
well as such tasks as the building or re-thatching of their dwelling.
She is responsible for sweeping the house out and keeping it in order—
a duty very imperfectly conceived in some cases—for plaiting the

[1] Rivers's statement that a visitor goes away if only the wife is at home is not
correct.

floor-mats and bed-mats and beating and dyeing the bark-cloth of the family, and airing this property from time to time to stop it from being mildewed ; [1] she goes out with the hand-net each day on the reef and obtains a most valuable contribution to the larder therewith. She is also primarily responsible for seeing that the family water-bottles are kept filled and that there is food in the kit on the hook to dispense hospitality to any visitor who may drop in. In all these things skill and industry are much esteemed, and a family take them into account before approving their son's choice of a wife. Close co-operation also takes place between the married pair on any occasion when ritual which affects either of them is performed. If it be a matter of a husband's " house " or clan, the wife accompanies him, bearing her back-load of raw taro or other food as part of the ordinary household contribution ; if it be of the wife's group the husband takes part in fulfilment of his specific duty as cook.

A married couple are expected by custom to share such things as areca nut and tobacco, and refusal or evasion is apt to cause a quarrel. Conduct in such matters depends of course upon the temperament of individuals. Food, too, should be shared, though some latitude is given to the claims of differential appetite. The effect of this rule is seen most clearly outside the household. Whenever a visitor calls at another house he is usually offered food, and at meal time such an invitation is never omitted. A close kinsman may eat, but another man, if married, will commonly decline with a " *Makona*," " satisfied." This he will say whether he has eaten or not, since he fears the tongue of slander, which will murmur behind his back, " Ah ! There he sits and eats, but what of his wife and children, hungry at home ? " An unmarried person may eat without fear, since he has no such responsibilities. Property which is not specifically linked with one sex is shared by husband and wife, or used indifferently by them both. A gift of a string of beads which I made to the Ariki Kafika—beads are highly valued and worn by men as well as women —was calmly appropriated by his wife, who took charge of them at once with the word " Mine," eliciting merely a joking remark from the Ariki.

In bringing up their children the husband and wife are in the closest association, but description of their roles here deserves a separate chapter.

---

[1] Some women of Tikopia are careful and thrifty housewives. I remember after I had been there some months being called to order by Nau Paŋisi for allowing my stores of bark-cloth and pandanus mats to lie in bundles in my house without sunning them. After scolding me for my carelessness, she came over several times with her daughters and attended to them while I was away.

CHAPTER V

PERSONAL RELATIONS IN THE FAMILY CIRCLE

THE family situation in Tikopia might be expected to conform to the general scheme of such relations in other Polynesian communities and therefore to need no elaborate discussion. But in spite of the voluminous literature of Polynesian ethnography there is as yet little systematic material which can be utilized for a general formulation of the character of the bases of the kinship system in this area. This study of Tikopia family life, in addition to being an integral part of the description of the culture of these isolated primitive natives, will afford comparative material and challenge enquiry into the institutions of other islands.

The nuclear social group in Tikopia is the family of parents and children. Every " house " (*paito*) and clan (*kainaŋa*) traces its ultimate origin to an individual family circle and from that centre spread the ramifications of the native culture. The contribution of the individual to the ends of the society and its participation in all its most important events are aligned on this basis.

It is necessary to give concrete detail about small points of behaviour in order to indicate the contours of the Tikopia family. In practice its ties and obligations neither receive nor require explicit formulation : they are not expressed in such definite sets of rules as those which govern the relations of kinsfolk in the wider social sphere. The native usually prefers to point to some striking obligatory gifts and services as the fundamental aspect of any relationship. But it is not in these specified duties performed only on occasions of note that the essence of the family bond lies. It lies in the daily help and protection of interests, in the apparently trivial contacts of everyday life. In ethnographic lists of the " functions of kin " the reciprocal relations between parents and children are usually most ill-defined. They are more difficult to classify and enumerate than are the periodic devoirs to be rendered by kin outside this circle. Here, above all, the investigator's personal observation of behaviour must supplement and give perspective to the statements received from his informants, since from them it is impossible to obtain any adequate explicit formulation of the actual conditions. For accuracy of presentation, it is necessary to give actual examples of what seem to be trivial incidents, but which in reality form the substance of the kinship pattern.

CARE OF THE YOUNG CHILD

The entrance of a child into a family circle which has previously contained only husband and wife naturally causes a considerable change in the habits of both. After the ritual connected with the birth and consecration of the child is over, the babe is taken in charge by the mother aided by her own and her husband's female relatives, who devote themselves to its welfare. A child in Tikopia can never be said to be neglected—in the early stages of its life at all events. The infant is not bound with swaddling clothes but is laid on a length of bark-cloth. It is handled with extreme care, and while it is very young only adult women experienced in nursing are allowed to interfere with it. Children of the household who come to touch or look at the new arrival are warned away lest they damage its fragility, and it is treated as a delicate object by all the family. Seated on the floor, the mother or its temporary nurse holds it in her arms, bending over it in caressing fashion. When it cries it is rocked very gently to and fro, with its face pressed against the woman's cheek, while she makes soft pulsating little " br-r-r-r " noises with the lips to soothe it. It is laid to sleep on a bed of bark-cloth, padded with many thicknesses, in the middle of the floor, and a little sheet of the same soft material is laid over the top to protect it from flies or dust. Whenever it is lifted its head is carefully supported with the nurse's left hand while she raises its body with her right, its legs being held against her forearm and breast. From time to time its fundament is gently lifted to examine the condition of the bark-cloth beneath. A short supplementary piece of this stuff is kept underneath its body, and changed when necessary. Both this and the other material on which the child is laid is of the kind called *mami*, of great softness.

Persistent crying or coughing of the babe is usually followed by an attempt at feeding, and it is either given the breast by the mother, or fed artificially by her or an assistant nurse. The woman takes a mouthful of taro or yam, masticates it well so that it is thoroughly mixed with saliva, then places her lips to those of the child and extrudes a little of the liquid mass so that it sucks.[1] For drink the mouth of the nurse is filled with water, which is swilled round well, and then administered in the same way. The impression given is that of a bird feeding its young.

The mother, as is natural, plays the principal part in the nursing and feeding of the babe, but other members of the household share

---

[1] The natives do not assign a scientific basis to this custom, but it may be noted that the preliminary salivation in the mouth of the mother means that the process of digestion is actually started for the child.

the labour with her. If the child cries constantly and disturbs the family it is taken out, if old enough, by some female relative and walked up and down to pacify it. At the mother's instance a sister of the father, unmarried and therefore still residing in the house, may take on many of the duties of nurse, or the mother may request one of her own sisters to come and live with the family for some time in order to assist her with the tending of the child. Cases of polygynous marriage, according to the natives, frequently arise in this latter way, since the husband, seeing this girl constantly in the house desires her and obtains her as his wife, often after sexual relations have occurred between them.

The father also is expected to take his turn at looking after the child, and usually does this with apparent interest and pride. He does not take charge of the infant in its very earliest days, but later he is frequently to be found holding it in his arms. His first essays in this direction are of a tentative character: when his first-born is laid in his lap he acts very gingerly and with the greatest caution, the wife and other female relatives watching him carefully and giving instructions and criticism of his efforts. He is told to put his arms further underneath it, not to let its head droop back, and similar points, all of which he obeys meekly, conscious of his ignorance in this sphere of female knowledge. Such a scene takes place of course *en famille*. As the child grows older the father may be called upon to mind it in the absence of its mother, and responds to the duty as a matter of course, if not with alacrity. I was sitting one day in my house Tuaraŋi, talking with a group of men, when a messenger came and spoke to my principal informant of the moment, Pa Teva, a great black-bearded fellow with a fierce eye, but of much good nature, who rose with a muttered excuse and crept out. The rest of the company explained with gravity that he had been summoned to go and mind the baby, since his wife wanted to go fishing. " If the woman goes on to the reef she leaves the little child to its father to look after," the natives say. Co-operation of this kind between husband and wife is common, and the tending of their children is regarded as an obligation to be shared between them. But the father is summoned to tend the babe only when it is of age to walk or to crawl about freely. While it is still in arms or barely able to move itself around (*koi pariki*), a woman with some experience of children is always obtained to come and sit with it ; a mere man could not be left in charge alone.

As the child grows and its body gains strength it is carried round in the arms of the women of the household, or of its elder brothers or sisters. A sling of bark-cloth is used for an infant old enough to be held upright but unable to support itself, and in this it is set and carried on the back or at the side of its nurse. A broader piece of bark-cloth is also usually held as a shield over the head and side of the babe to protect it from the sun (*v.* Plate V), since at this stage its skin is pale and delicate. Older children are held on the hip without the sling or carried pick-a-back fashion, and one of the common sights of the village in the early morning or evening is to see quite young boys and girls, from about four years of age upwards, acting as carriers for younger brothers and sisters in this way, neither of the pair wearing a stitch of clothing. It is amusing to see one naked babe staggering along under the weight of another almost as big, and also to notice how passively the latter lies in all kinds of contorted positions, as if fully conscious of the good intentions of its nurse. Firimori, a grandson of the Ariki Tafua, a lad of six or seven, frequently acted as nurse in this way. During the first day of the turmeric-making, when his family were very busy, he carried a child around throughout the whole day, and took the first opportunity of telling me that it was his brother. From time to time he would caress the babe by passing his lips gently over its ear.

By the women of the house, who of course are clothed in the bark-cloth skirt, a curious method of supporting the child is in vogue : it stands upright at the back of its nurse, using her waistbelt as a foothold, digging in its small toes and grasping her shoulders with its hands. Thus perched a child reminds one forcibly of the young of an anthropoid. Though apparently so insecure it is in reality quite safe ; at least I saw no casualties therefrom. The woman of course takes care to move very steadily. The mother in particular carries the child in this manner when away from the house and encumbered with burdens, as in carrying food to some other section of the village or water-bottles up from the spring.

Different terms are in use to describe these methods of carrying : *rukuruku* is to bear in the arms ; *pepe* on the back. The latter term is also used to indicate the action of carrying in a sling, but is qualified by reference to the *tau*, the name of this article.

As soon as the child can crawl and becomes more of a tax upon the watchfulness of the household, to a mother occupied in preparing food or in plaiting a pandanus mat it is almost obligatory to have someone to keep an eye on her babe. It is surprising how fast and how often a determined human infant can get away on voyages of exploration in the course of a few hours. Since my house was next door to that of Pa Taitai, father of the babe Tekila, born a few months before I arrived in the island, I had excellent opportunities for observing—and suffering from—this infant curiosity and urge to exercise. Shortly after he could crawl Tekila developed a strong impulse to investigate the interior of my house, and as soon as released made as fast as he could on all fours in this direction. Sometimes he attained his objective undiscovered, and spent blissful minutes there until his absence was noted ; more often he was pursued and captured, some relative or youthful visitor bearing him off. Different people, by the way, have their own methods of picking up children, the result, as far as I know, of personal habit rather than conscious theory. Nau Taitai, for example, in picking up Tekila, usually caught him round the breast with one hand and between the legs with the other; his father normally gathered him up under the armpits.

To guard against his constant intrusion I set up a barricade across the doorway, but as soon as he could toddle he used to come and hang on this, especially at meal times, when he would whine for food like a little dog (not in imitation, since there were none of these animals on the island). Biscuit he appreciated with a chuckle, but his special delight was a partially exhausted coconut, with which he would stagger off with a gurgle of joy, raising it to his lips and drinking, but spilling more than half the milk down his naked little body. He was a charming child, with a soft velvety light-brown skin, silky hair, and one of the most attractive smiles that I have come across in babies of any colour. He was the object of great care on the part of his household—his grandmother, his father's sister and male cousins, and his mother's brothers frequently nursing him, in addition to the attention given him by his parents (*v.* Plate XIV). On one occasion I heard more noise than usual at the barrier, mingled with laughter from outside, and looked up from my meal to see not one but two infants there. Tekila had brought along, by the mere force of association apparently, since neither could speak a coherent word, a baby girl from a neighbouring house, and there the two naked morsels stood, nodding and chuckling at each other amid the amusement and suggestive jokes of the adults. A biscuit apiece sent them away contented, mumbling with evident enjoyment.

After a child can walk, or at least crawl, the father enters more into his own, and especially in the early morning and in the evening he is to be seen with his child between his knees or in his arms, or toddling along by his side, its hand in his. If it has ventured away from him and becomes frightened it does not try to hide but retreats to him, clinging to his leg if he is standing, or tumbling over his knees if he is seated, seeking the intimacy of bodily contact which demonstrates the reliance it places upon him as a shield against the world.

From this account it will be clear how the care of a child is essentially a household affair, in which both parents play their part, but in which other persons who live there also assist. Actual kinship to the child is practically immaterial in the latter case ; one cannot say that in Tikopia the personal care which a woman lavishes upon her brother's child is any different from that which she bestows upon her sister's child. It is largely a result of the residential situation. As far as one can judge, the child's parents appear to have charge of it more constantly than other people—it usually sleeps between them, for example—but in a large household with several unmarried young folk they are relieved of their duties to a much greater extent than in a small household where they are the only adults. In general the care of children rests essentially on a kinship basis, but not solely thereon, and residence, whether permanent or temporary, and common courtesy and pleasure are responsible for considerable tending.

Natives, as a whole, are fond of taking children around, and it is common to find a child, on the beach or with a group in the shade of the trees, in the arms of someone not of its household or immediate circle of kin. It is not customary to take such infants far away from their homes, but they are handed on from one person to another as a call of domestic duty summons their nurses of the moment. Young men as well as girls take part in this, and it is no rare sight to see a lad of sixteen or seventeen years bearing a child in his arms. Even when such an infant belongs to a distant relative [1] it is nursed as a matter of course, and is treated with gentleness and consideration, if with no special display of affection. In Tikopia no young person is ever teased for nursing a child, as sometimes happens in our own society.

Young children in Tikopia are rarely left unattended, and in the absence of parents and other adults an elder child is left with instructions to watch the young one carefully. Occasionally this surveillance fails, or in the night when all the household are sleeping the infant crawls away and is lost. A great hubbub ensues, search-parties set out in all directions looking among bushes, in cook-houses and canoe-sheds, till the missing one is finally discovered. One evening the youngest child of Pae Sao was lost. A sickly little thing, with solemn black eyes, tiny thin legs and several large uncomfortable lesions of yaws, it could crawl but could not walk, despite its couple of years. The parents returned from a distant trip and found that it was missing. It had been heard by neighbours crying in the dark, while its eldest sister, deputed to watch over it, slept, and it was surmised that it had crawled away out into the open in

---

[1] There are no " strangers " in Tikopia, or entirely unrelated persons.

search of its parents.   Search was made in the vicinity by the anxious relatives, and as the time went on and no trace of the babe was found they began to grow really alarmed.   With the aid of torches and of lanterns, borrowed from my house, the hunt continued, while stories were told of other infants such as the first-born girl of Pa Nukumanaia, who had crawled down on to the beach, where she vanished altogether. The furrow of her going had been traced down to the water's edge, but there all sign of her was lost, and she was never seen again. " Snatched away by a spirit " was the conclusion to which everyone ·had come.   Memory of this and like events must have tortured the unhappy Pae Sao and his wife.   At last there came the welcome shout that the child had been found.   She had crawled off till she reached the house of some neighbours who, hearing her crying under the eaves, had taken her in, fed her and put her to sleep, while they themselves, having followed suit, had heard nothing of the initial stir.

Young children are frequently taken by their parents to the scene of their work in the garden or orchard and are set down to sleep or play.   In the case of a very young infant a shelter of boughs is sometimes erected in order to shield it from the direct rays of the sun, which are recognized as being too strong for it.   Children who can stagger about are carried to the place of work and then set free, while those who can walk frequently trot along after their parents. This early association with the economic life acts as a very important educational mechanism, since the child comes gradually to participate in the task of the moment, and is almost imperceptibly inducted into one of the major spheres of its future activity.   There is also in consequence little real breach in the tenor of life.   The infant play period, the childhood and adolescent educational period, and the adult working period are not sharply demarcated as in modern urban communities.

Here begins the first real differentiation of the sexes.   Male children tend to be taken by the father, female children by the mother to their separate tasks, and this separation begins to widen from about the age of one year onwards.

As the child finds its feet, socially as well as literally, and begins to walk alone outside the house, it joins up with neighbouring children, and a little group of youngsters of varying ages forms on a basis of adjacent residence.   Even before they can talk these infants begin to foregather.   On one occasion I saw Tekila and Noarima, naked little urchins about fifteen months and twenty months respectively, sons of my neighbours, standing side by side and imitating the movements of a dance which had recently taken place.

They held short sticks in their right hands, and together they stamped the foot and raised the arm after the fashion of their elders, uttering at the same time a shrill cry for which as yet they had no words to give. This sort of thing amuses the natives very much, and they stimulate the babes with encouraging phrases.

When somewhat older, children begin to go about in independent little bands. Thus one day I watched three small girls—two as yet too young for clothing—each with her hand-net and tiny fish-basket, working along the reef. At the same time three little boys were gathering *Conus* shells for dart heads. The groups joined forces for a time, with much chatter, showing of prizes, laughing, and cursing of one another in trifling disagreement. At last the girls went off singing, and the boys, after hanging about for a while, went off along the beach in another direction.

In these early years boys and girls associate together fairly freely. In a community where small children wear no clothing, however, the difference of sex is patent even to the most casual observer, and their elders are at pains to emphasize the distinction. No matter how young, a female child is always a female, and there are certain aspects of the social life, especially in ritual affairs, from which females are excluded. In religious ceremonies, for example, a boy, no matter how tiny, is always admitted, whereas a little girl is prevented from following her father if she makes this attempt, as sometimes happens. If a female child enters the sacred place she is removed as soon as possible, though not forcibly. When the canoe-house of the sacred craft " *Peru i te vai* " of the Ariki Kafika was being renovated Mataŋore, the small daughter of Pa Fenuatara, strayed among the foundations in search of her father. He did not treat her harshly, but going up to her put his arm around her and speaking quietly and persuasively said, " Go away ! you see women do not come here, it is *tapu* ! " She pouted and did not move at first, but after a little more gentle reasoning of this kind, and a slight push, she trotted away.

Children are often spoken to quite gravely by adults, as if they were fully responsible and competent beings, though the language used is somewhat simpler than in ordinary free conversation. As an example—a fishing ceremony had just been performed in Kafika, with several male children present. One of them remained afterwards and ate of the common meal. When his elders had finished he was told, " Wrap up your pudding, friend ! go and eat it in your house. The talk of men is going to begin." " The talk of men " is the stock phrase for the long yarning conversations which while away the time and have a dignified status as recreation. Small boys are often allowed to be present, but it is not regarded as their proper sphere.

There is no use of " baby talk " on the part of grown-ups towards children, though it is recognized that children have their own curious abbreviations and malformations in names for things, which the parents and members of the household alone understand.

I took down some samples of the sounds made by Tekila when he was about a year old. A frequent expression was a shout of " du ē," which he uttered, apparently without specific reference, as he staggered happily about, " Ge gu ga " and " gǎ gǎ gǎ gǎ " were other collections of sounds often used in the same way. When he pointed to an object he said " di dai dó," and on seeing some coconut being eaten he said " mama." These vocables correspond in only one particular with specific sounds of Tikopia speech. Mama means " chew " and Tekila had apparently gathered the association in this case. Elsewhere he was making sounds primarily adapted to the passage of breath through larynx, mouth and lips, with modification by the tongue, and not yet moulded into the specific sounds of meaning within the culture. Children a little older get closer to the current speech forms of their elders. A youngster was told to go and get a fire-stick. After a moment of investigation it called out, " Ku maŋi," an attempt at " Ku mate," " It is dead."

" Each child has its own names for food—and fish," I was told. Some children use a whine or grunt to express other words than " mother " and " father "—an action described by the term ŋu. One small boy used to say, " Pa E ! Pa ! ŋ— mau ! " He could not say maku, " for me," properly. Saupuke, when he was thirsty, said, " ŋ . . . . Inu a ! Inu a ! " Inu is the word for " drink " and a a meaningless vocable ; his words were equivalent to " drinky, drinky." Most of these whining sounds are accompanied by pointing with the finger. One youngster used to say " koko " when he wanted fish, instead of ika. " Pa E ! Pa ! koko maku " means literally " Father, father, some sago flour for me." But his parents and close relatives, such as his father's cousin, knew what he wanted and gave him fish. Sometimes a child unknowingly uses an obscene expression. Thus one boy used to say " mimi mau," meaning " mei maku," " breadfruit for me." Mimi refers to the female genitalia. Apart from food, there are other childish abbreviations. One infant when it wished to excrete used to call to its mother, " Nana ! nana ! ka to ! ka to ! " which is literally " Mother ! mother ! it is going to fall, it is going to fall." But to here is probably an attempt at tiko, to excrete. In personal names the same kind of abbreviations occur. Mataŋore at one stage used to talk of her brother Rakeivave by the correct kinship term " *toku kave*," but addressed him as "Keivave E! Keivave."

EDUCATION AND KINSHIP

The cardinal points of education in a native society such as Tikopia are its continuity in both a temporal and a social sense, its position as an activity of kinsfolk, its practicality—not in the sense of being directed to economic ends, but as arising from actual situations in daily life—and its non-disciplinary character. A certain subordination to authority is required and is sometimes impressed by forcible and dramatic methods, but these are sporadic and the individual is a fairly free agent to come and go as he likes, to refuse to heed what is being taught him. All this is in direct contrast to a system of education for native children wherever it is carried out under European tutelage. Such consists usually of periodic instruction with segregation, intermitted by intervals of relaxation and rejoining of the normal village life, and imparted not by kinsfolk of the children but by strangers, often from another area, even when non-Europeans. This instruction is given not in connection with practical situations of life as they occur, but in accord with general principles, the utility of which is only vaguely perceived by the pupils. Moreover, it is disciplinary, the pupils are under some degree of direct restraint and may even suffer punishment for neglect of appointed tasks.

The divorce from the reality of the native social life, the staccato rhythm of instruction and the alien methods of restraint undoubtedly are potent factors in retarding the achievement of the aims of so much of what is rather falsely termed " native education."

In Tikopia we have an example of a people largely free from European influence, where education is not an imagined preparation for social life but is actually a vital part of it, hinging upon the participation of the child in all ordinary activities from early years, and arising out of the inevitable lacunæ in its knowledge when called upon to face practical situations. The observer is impressed almost immediately by the absence of any institutionalized education. The training of children is a private affair, and is very largely a function of the kinship situation, the parents of a child playing the most important part as instructors. The residential factor must by no means be left out of account however, as in the case of orphans, or of " adhering children " (*v.* later), for much of whose teaching the elder members of the household where they live are responsible.

Since education may be considered to include all social processes which serve to fit the human individual more adequately for his social environment, it is clear that much of the descriptive part of this book may be comprised under this head. What is desired here, however, is merely to indicate some of the more obvious fields of education in Tikopia, and particularly by means of examples to show the mechanism of the social processes involved. Specific spheres in the education of a child are instruction in the manners and moral rules of the society, training in arts and crafts and imparting knowledge of traditional lore and ritual formulæ. Formal lessons are rarely given in these departments, but advice, explanation and commands tend to cluster around the performance of any activity, or the onset of any social situation.

The kinship factor in education is extremely important, and by the natives themselves it is continually stressed. Tuition in points of etiquette is frequently given by parents, and they are held responsible for breaches of manners on the part of their children. Discipline, especially in the field of obedience to the authority of father and of clan chief, is inculcated by them as a moral duty but is not apt to be insisted upon in ordinary affairs. In the economic sphere too they severally play leading parts. The training of a boy, however, is often due to the interest of one of his mother's brothers in him. If this man is an expert in any branch of knowledge he will probably see to it that his nephew receives some of the results of his experience. If he is a noted canoe-voyager and fisherman he will pass on his store of information in the finer points of his craft to the lad : especially will he show him the location of fishing-banks, a prized set of data not possessed by all fishermen. In dirges composed to the memory of mothers' brothers reference is not infrequently made to this sort of assistance. A grandfather may take a great interest in a child's upbringing and may provide him with traditional lore, names of family ancestors and their history, tales of ancient fights and immigrations, of the origins of the land and the doings of the gods. The transmission of details of family ritual and more esoteric information concerning the family religious life is essentially the role of the father, and not infrequently does the head of a house lament the fact of his own comparative ignorance due to his father's early death. Individual circumstances vary considerably in this respect, but as a rule in such cases the gap is filled more or less adequately by a father's brother or even a father's sister, who will be acquainted in some degree with the requisite information. A mother's brother is of little use here, since family ritual and religious formulæ are secret property, jealously conserved, and transmitted essentially through the male line.

Education of the last type applies particularly to the heirs of family headships.

This brief outline of the educational system of the Tikopia will allow the detailed descriptive material which follows to be set in perspective.

Even before the child is of an age to comprehend properly what is being said to it, it is addressed quite solemnly by its elders, with a view to promoting its understanding and education. The Ariki Kafika, for example, shows quite an interest in Arikifakasaupuke, his young grandson, a light-skinned plump youngster with a round face and a seriously determined expression. The old chief gets the child to bring him little things which he requires, and gives him directions carefully. In preparing his betel mixture he splits the areca nuts with the butt end of his spatula, puts them down in front of him in a row and gets Saupuke to pick them up one by one, take out each kernel in turn and hand it to him. He speaks to him solemnly all the while, then sits and looks at him steadily for a space. If the infant does not do as he is told the chief sometimes says to him calmly without the least spark of annoyance, " May your father eat filth," the conventional curse of Tikopia. Saupuke is treated with considerable indulgencce in the house of the chief ; perhaps because he is the offspring of a younger son, he is by way of being the old man's favourite. His gluttony and bursts of ill-temper are indulged, so long as they do not interfere too much with the peace of the household, or imperil the dignity of his grandsire. And even such a disgraceful exhibition as his beating the end of the house with a stick while he shrieked with rage at being stopped from entering called forth no more than a mild remonstrance from his grandmother. His education, however, is not altogether neglected. His father, his father's brothers and cousins reprove him as they do each other's children, and he is taught, like all other junior members of the household to respect the interior of the dwelling and in particular the presence of his grandfather the chief. His elder cousins, children of six to nine, take a considerable hand in his upbringing, and the little girls in particular give him severe commands as to how to conduct himself. Here is one instance. He sits and eats food that has been given him, then goes and gets the coconut water-bottle, taking off an empty bottle from the hook first, then the full one, and then carefully replacing the empty one again. He raises the nut with both hands to his lips and drinks. As he goes to put back the plug his cousin intervenes, " Give the plug here," then " Run and hang it up " she says, sticking in the plug firmly and giving him the bottle. Then as he quietly complies, " Go to the back," an injunction to retire to the rear of the house away from people of importance, and finally as a parting shot the order comes, " Don't go walking about on the mats "—all of which he obeys without a murmur and sinks down in obscurity.   This is a sample of the way in which children are continually ordered about by their elders, a process in which a few years gives an immense advantage, so that the Tikopia kingdom of youth tends to be one which is ruled on the basis of seniority.   Girls rather than boys tend to act as mentors of the young.

Instruction in Tikopia in matters of etiquette and decorum in the house begins at a very early age, almost before the child can fully understand what is required of it, but as the essence of the system for the young is quietness and self-effacement, the general lesson is soon learnt—though apparently as soon forgotten, or disregarded, per- haps as the result of over-repetition.   As always, instruction is given in relation to concrete situations, rather than to abstract principles. For instance, to *pe tua*, " throw the back " to people of superior status is bad manners.   Firimori was sitting thus in Motuapi, facing away from his grandfather the chief.   Nau Nukunefu, his father's brother's wife, spoke to him sharply, " Do not turn your back on your grand- father," whereupon he shifted round slightly.   So children learn.

The child soon comes to take part in the work of the community, and so useful is it that a household without one is at a distinct loss. At first it goes out with a relative to the cultivations and intersperses its play with fetching and carrying things.   Gradually most of the economic minutiæ are allotted to it by its elders, including others than the parents, and its performances, small in themselves, act as the emollient which allows the household machinery to run smoothly. Girls go and fill the water-bottles, carrying them in kits on their backs at morning and evening ; it may be for a considerable distance.   They bring back loads of firewood from the orchards, they go and pluck the yellow leaves of *ti* from which the family decorations are made for the dance.   At some part of the day, according to the state of the tide, they are to be found accompanying their mother or their father's unmarried sister in her scoop-net fishing on the reef.   Boys also go fishing on the reef, but with them this is apt to be more a matter of personal sport than actual work, since the obligation of combing the reef daily is primarily a woman's task.   But they too have their place in the economic scheme.   They are sent on errands, as to fetch a fire-stick, to borrow betel leaf, or some lime, to return a net to its owner, or to take a message about fishing.   They accompany older brothers to the orchards to pluck breadfruit or green coconuts or to cut a bunch of bananas.   Anything to be carried to another house is given to a child, and the injunction " *Feti o sau mai . . .*" " Run and fetch me . . ." is one of the commonest phrases heard addressed to young children in Tikopia.

The little one is speedily made aware of its subordination to authority and its function as an element in a larger group. These limitations on its freedom of action are not always kindly received, and sternness, threats or even physical coercion may be necessary to exact obedience. On one occasion a group of men sat yarning under the trees at the head of the beach and began as usual to chew betel. Lime was wanting, and Mosese, a chubby little three-year-old, was sent by his father to get it from their house some fifty yards inland. He got some yards off, then stood still, wriggled, whined and objected to going any farther. " He wants to listen to the talk of the men," said his father with a smile. But he insisted, speaking sharply to the child, who after some urging disappeared, to return as commanded.

Another scene in illustration may be given from the house of Pa Niukaso, a Christian teacher newly returned from Anuta with his wife and small son, Allen. This is a chubby child with a soft chocolate brown skin, darker than most, and an attractively solemn expression in repose—which is not, however, his constant state. His only vesture consists of a string round his neck, suspending a bone of a phalange type, said to be that of a turtle, and worn not as an amulet but for ornament. While his mother and father are inside the house Allen is ranging up and down outside with a stick, battering the walls and roof, to his evident pleasure. A small girl—a naked little urchin like himself —begins to crawl out of the doorway, and he turns to lunge at her a couple of times, for which he is reproved by his mother. She draws back, then attempts to emerge again a little later. This time Allen's aim is more accurate, to judge from her cries as she re-enters. Frightened by the success of his exploit he begins to yell too, but soon quietens down. A short time afterwards he comes in and is given some ends of taro, which he passes to his father, saying, " *Dudi, dudi*," meaning " *tutia, tutia*," " Cut, cut." This is done. Then he gets hold of the knife, and when it is taken from him he lies on his back on the floor and yells, then kicks and screams. Gradually he is pacified by his father and mother, frequent references being made, since I am there, to what the *papalaŋi* (white man) will think. When we leave he comes too, and howls on being ordered to go back. He is appeased only by being carried along on his father's back, and from this point of vantage prattles away cheerfully with many questions, all of which his father answers patiently and seriously.

The cleanliness of the child in its early years is the care of the mother ; later it is supposed to have learned to look after itself.

Native peoples may be classified into two types—those who wash and those who do not. The Tikopia must be put most distinctly into the former category. Frequent washing by children is encouraged by the parents, and those who are reluctant may soon find themselves the object of derisive remarks from their companions or elders. Such is Kapolo of Matautu, a poor half-wit with a cleft palate who was continually being mocked by his fellows for his dirty state. In the south-east trade wind season the air in the early morning is sometimes decidedly chilly, and children may then have to be driven to wash. Scenes such as the following, which I noted, are common in the village soon after sunrise. A woman approaches the aqueduct mouth carrying a child on her arm and leading another by the hand. The latter—a three-year-old—is urged to get under the spouting water and wash. He grumbles and refuses to stir. " Jump into the water, friend ! " says his mother. Still he hesitates, upon which she takes him firmly, stands him under the stream and rubs his face and body hastily with her hand. " There ! you are wet ! " she says rather unnecessarily. Then he is released, to stump off up the path, still querulously grunting. The younger child is treated with more care. Towels are unknown on the island, so that such of the moisture as is not stripped off by the fingers must evaporate from the body surface, leaving a chilly feeling for some time.

It is a canon of the society that parents are most fitted to coach their offspring in manners and customs and that the obligation of so doing lies on them. Of a child which is a nuisance at public gatherings, which wilfully misbehaves itself, or shows itself to be lacking in some of the elementary notions of decorum, people say, " Why do not its parents instruct it ? Why is it not told by its parents not to act thus ? " In a family which cares for the proper upbringing of its children—and such families exist in Tikopia society and can be distinguished from others of a more slovenly habit—considerable attention is paid to the child's ways of speech. It is taught by mother and father two main principles.

The first is to avoid rude and indecent expressions. They listen to its talk, and hearing objectionable words say to it, " Your speech that is made is bad speech, give it up ! But use good speech," or again they say, " When you go out, do not call out to people ; you hear, is the speech of the land made thus ? " " Ea ? " replies the child in wonderment. " These words that you use are evil speech ; abandon them," the parents answer. The child is thus early taught to distinguish two categories of expressions : *taraŋa laui* and *taraŋa pariki*—good speech and bad speech. It soon learns that the latter is not permissible in public, or in the presence of certain relatives, or of members of the opposite sex, though regarded as amusing, and even allowable among groups of its own kind and status. The distinction between these two types of speech is further elaborated in Chapter IX. It is well known that children of three or four years of age pick up expressions relating, for instance, to the sexual act, as *fekoni*, " copulate," which are not used in polite conversation. When they repeat them in the home parents take this opportunity for correction. Some children are said to " grow up foolishly," *somo vare*; they do not listen to any instruction from their parents, but repeat every new phrase they hear, calling it out to strangers, to the amusement of the vulgar and the shame of their relatives. Young folk draw attention to these lapses with a laugh, chiding the child, yet turning the matter to a point of humour. I noted once a child babbling meaningless syllables to itself, " La—la—la—la." It was overheard by a group of unmarried people. " May its father eat filth ! It utters evil speech—the *lala* ! " cried a girl (*lala* signifies female genitalia, in particular the clitoris). This was with an affectation of disapproval but a giggle at the end for the benefit of the boys near.

The second rule which is impressed on a child, with rather less success, is that it must refrain from calling out to passers-by, strangers, or people at large. The mere fact of shouting out to them implies some degree of ill-breeding on the part of the child, and moreover, there is always the likelihood of its using some objectionable remarks. In this as in other cases the parents are concerned not so much with abstract rules of conduct as with the possibility of offending other people, and even bringing down the wrath of an insulted chief on their heads. Instruction in good manners has a distinctly practical side.

PUNISHMENT AND OBEDIENCE

The sanction for good manners in Tikopia is the fear of social disapproval rather than that of physical retaliation. The attitude of the community towards the punishment of children for offences may be summarized as one full of promises but rather empty of performance. In any case where direct action is taken corporal punishment of a mild type is adopted ; more subtle methods of inflicting discomfort on an offender, such as restriction of liberty or deprivation of food, are never practised. Execution is always immediate, and there is nothing comparable to the refinement of mental torture practised in some European families of leaving a sentence hanging over the child's head till the return of the male parent to act as vehicle of chastisement. The punishment, it may be noted, is to be interpreted as a reaction of anger on the part of a parent or other elder, not as retribution for an offence. It is regarded as deterrent in that promises of its infliction are held out as warnings, threats to strike, but it appears to be actually inflicted as a result of the emotions aroused to an explosive point. Again, it is the act of beating rather than the severity of the punishment which is regarded as being so serious. Often the blows are delivered with a fan, the result being that the spirit rather than the body is bruised. When the daughter of Pa Paŋisi was suspected of an intrigue with a boy of whom she was obviously enamoured, her mother threw her down, made uncomplimentary remarks about her morals and beat her in this way. The girl escaped, crying, and went off to Raveŋa to other relations where she stayed for a few days. The whole village talked about the incident. It is the affront to self-esteem that is the greatest wound. The argument that such punishment is really immaterial because it is so light would not appeal to a Tikopia. Young children are not often struck, and are not thrashed by successive blows. Occasionally a child is hit with a stick, but, light or hard, a single blow normally suffices.

In later years, when there is a likelihood of its being punished, the child takes care to avoid the issue by discreet absence and stays with relatives elsewhere till the storm has blown over. This is rendered extremely simple by the ramifications of the kinship system, and by the ordinary habit of the natives of spending a night or so away from home for casual reasons of work or pleasure. The final resort of the adolescent or young adult who wishes to avoid punishment or wipe out its stigma is, of course, suicide at sea. It is with this in mind that the father—presuming that he is the responsible parent—sometimes goes in search of his child, from *arofa*, affection, as the natives say, and brings it back with harmony restored.

To strike a child or to threaten to strike it is frequently done, not in punishment for any specifically wrong action committed but merely to induce it to go away, the offence consisting in its obstruction or inquisitiveness. A couple of samples show the type of action. Seteraki, son of Pa Raŋifuri, was making a nuisance of himself in the house. " *Taia ke poi ki fafo !* " " Strike him so that he goes outside," said his father fiercely to one of the daughters. As his sister moved towards him, however, the little boy fled. Another child continued to play with a wooden bowl after being told not to. " You want to cry, eh ? You don't listen." " *Ke fia taŋi ne ? Ke se roŋo,*" its parent said, announcing what was in store if it persisted. So it stopped.

There are various expressions in the native vocabulary to denote the different modes of action in getting rid of the encumbrance of unwelcome youth. The general term is *fue*, meaning to drive away, while *fakarei* and *fakakiro* have a similar meaning. These describe the uttering of injunctions to go, accompanied by a toss of the head or a wave of the arm, the usual way of shooing children off. " *Oro kese ŋa tamariki,*" " Go away, children," is an injunction uttered continually and almost automatically by people at public gatherings— and hardly heeded by the objects of it. " *Fakareia ke poi,*" " Let them be driven away," it is said. *Fakakiro* may represent rather more vigorous methods. Thus " *Fakakiro tau soa ke kiro,*" a command addressed to someone to chase away a persistent child, may be freely translated as " Quieten our friend ; hit him with a stick." *Teteŋe* is used of striking with a stick, " *te rakau ke teŋe.*" Any light piece of wood is used and the blow is often very mild. I once observed Nau Taitai, my neighbour's wife, getting angry with her little child for his obstinacy, catch up a stalk of the betel creeper, a pliant green twig not more than six inches long, and strike him on the hand. The blow was the merest tap, but the child broke into a roar and stamped the ground in his indignation.

" I talk, talk ; you do not listen to me," she explained to him and to the world at large, in part anger, part extenuation, as she lifted him up and bore him off. Such incidents of petty punishment are frequent and instructive to the observer in the light they throw on family relations and the guardianship exercised by elders. Thus a lad who struck a younger child with what appeared to be insufficient provocation was promptly smacked by his grandmother, half-smiling as she did so. The commonest method of punishing a child or clearing it out of the way is a light smack on the head, the term for this action, *patu*, meaning to hit with the hand. A person who is driving a child away may give it one clout on the back of the head to send it off, or more leisurely and in playful mood may strike it on the temple, the forehead, the other temple and the back of the head, counting as he does so, " One, two, three, four ! " Having thus " boxed the compass," as it were, he tells it to go. If an adult is in a callous frame of mind he tells another, " *Fakanimo ko a mata o tau soa,*" " Make the eyes of our friend swim "—a command to bang the unfortunate intruder on the head without ceremony. I have seen a child which tried to enter a house in which adults were busy, given a resounding smack on the arm with the flat of a paddle. It withdrew without a cry, but with an extremely hurt expression.

Another method of punishing a child or dissuading it from some act is to pinch its cheek just at the corner of the mouth with some force. This is termed *umoumo*. On one occasion the treatment of Saupuke by his mother's father, Pa Porima, provoked the whole household of Kafika to discussion. The child, it was said, insisted on following his elder down to the sea and would not go back when spoken to. Pa Porima was reputed to have struck him—actually it was only a pinch, which had however broken the skin, since examination established a slight scratch. This caused quite a hubbub for a few minutes and called forth a scornful remark from Nau Kafika, " What kind of a grandparent is he ? " During the washing operations connected with the manufacture of turmeric a child was taken down to bathe by one of the workers. A wave came up and soused them, some water going up the child's nose. It yelled, and was pinched by its angry parent, at which it yelled the more. Finally it was pacified by being told to help in cleaning the turmeric roots, the spot that had been pinched was rubbed and peace was restored.

The subject here has departed somewhat from the immediate sphere of family relations, but the treatment of children when outside the household circle by parents and by outsiders in the matter of punishment is very much the same. The use of the word friend, soa, in the linguistic example given above implies that the child stands in no very close kinship relation to the speaker.

Since promises of punishment are much more frequent than the act itself children, knowing this, are apt to stand their ground despite all commands made to them. Though these be uttered in most peremptory tones the youngsters merely smile. Repetition is necessary to produce any effect, and so much is this a habit that most orders are given automatically three times over at the start ! Much talk and little obedience is the impression gained of family discipline in questions of ordinary restraint. The most blood-curdling threats may be used to make children go away, the object being merely to frighten them. Thus to generalize an incident often witnessed—a band of children on mischief bent come to the side of a dwelling-house and stamp on the ground, peer in, or make objectionable noises, to the irritation of people within. A man inside calls to them to go away, but without effect. He says then, " I shall come out to you, take a stick and split open your heads ! " but no notice is taken. Or he curses them, saying, " May your fathers eat filth ! If I come out, you will die on the spot ! " (Text S. 13). This horrific threat may silence them for a short space, but a recrudescence of their efforts by the bolder spirits begins almost at once and now it produces no effect whatever. Finally he has to crawl out of the door to disperse them. As soon as he is perceived a general stampede ensues, the sound of running feet is heard in all directions, and he stands there to pursue them with words alone.

In addition to the performance of small services and the observance of good manners, the child must also conform to the rules of *tapu*. These are manifold, consisting of a set of prohibitions that can only be learned after long experience. A few of the most obvious, however, speedily come within the infant's comprehension. It soon comes to mingle mainly in the affairs conducted by people of its own sex, to keep clear of the elders and people of rank in its neighbourhood, and be moderately quiet in their presence. It learns also to avoid touching large canoes, certain house-posts and spears or clubs hung up, and to refrain from walking on the *mata paito* side of the house. Here constant instruction from its parents when a breach of *tapu* has been made or seems impending speedily impresses on it its duties, and the verbal restraint in such case is usually translated into physical terms more rapidly than with the ordinary social rules discussed above. " It is prohibited, do not grasp it " is a frequent warning, which the child learns to accept, with wide eyes, sensing something strange beyond its ken, but recognizing from the solemn tone that here are matters to be heeded, things to be avoided. If it does not obey immediately, then it is grabbed and shaken. Such habits of avoidance inculcated in early years when no reason is understood, save the command of a parent, form the basis of the system of rules to which such attention is paid in later life.

Thus the child Mataŋore inquired of her father regarding articles belonging to her grandfather, the Ariki Kafika. " Things of your *puna*; do not go and interefere with them," he said. " *Toku puna, te Ariki Kafika?* My grandfather the chief of Kafika?" "Yes, don't speak of him, it is *tapu*." "It is *tapu*?" "Yes." "My grandfather the chief of Kafika," she repeated. Here the prohibition does not represent a definite social regulation—children are permitted to speak of their grandparents, even by name—but the anxiety of a man as chief's son and as parent lest his small daughter wander further in speech and unwittingly infringe the bounds of propriety. In wide-eyed acquiescence Mataŋore subsided and soon began to prattle of other things.

Even in matters of *tapu* the obedience of the child is not always so easily procured. A father brought his small son to a kava rite of ordinary type in Kafika lasi, one of the sacred houses in Uta, and tucked it between his knees. Children are welcome at these functions —much as children in European God-fearing families are encouraged to go to church—so long as they remain decorous. This child, however, began to grizzle, and the father's efforts to pacify it were useless. The child's complaint swelled to a roar, when suddenly the father, abandoning his soothing words and gestures, shook it roughly and shouted, " May your father eat filth ! The house is *tapu* ! " At the moment this had no effect, but soon the cries subsided to a whimper. No one else present paid any attention.

A couple more examples of the disobedience of children may be given. Seteraki, walking with some older people, climbed up on a rock. " Come down," he was sternly ordered. But he stayed where he was and nothing was done to him. Some days before his initiation Munakina was wanted. His mother's brother ordered him to go. He adopted a policy of passive resistance and did not budge. Various people told him, " Go when your uncle tells you." He still sat tight, until laughingly holding back he was dragged to his feet and led off struggling. As he went he grasped the waistband of another boy, to the latter's discomfiture and the general amusement. On this occasion Munakina's sister took a leading part in the chiding.

Usually little action is taken to compel obedience. The individuality of the child is respected and its freedom allowed, even when this freedom involves discomfort or additional work on the part of its elders. Conformity to the will of a senior is regarded as a concession to be granted, not a right to be expected ; an adult behaves to a child as one free spirit to another, and gives an order to another adult in just as peremptory a fashion. Indifference to commands, as indicated above, is common on the part of children and persists in adult years. Often children answer angrily to an order, or make no reply at all. The father in turn speaks angrily, but rarely takes direct steps to enforce his will. In spite of the recognition of the general obligation of filial obedience, moreover, practically no specific moral instruction is given to children on the point.

Children are apt to react petulantly if thwarted and to commit violent actions, till they get their way and allow themselves to be pacified. From my seat in Taramoa, during the ritual celebrations of the fishing season, I watched a small child attempt to enter. It tried to crawl in at the seaward door, but since this is the men's entrance, it was rebuffed by those sitting there. It began to cry, then petulantly threw away the taro tuber which it had just been given to eat. Pa Fenuatara, observing it, said angrily—the gift was from his house—" May its father eat filth ! It has cast away its food ! " Soon afterwards the child was allowed to enter and then quietened down.

Children are kept in control by the near relatives of their parents as well as by these latter. Here is an incident of common type. Saupuke, the small grandson of the Ariki Kafika, stands up in the dwelling-house and begins to wander about. He is immediately grabbed by a cousin of his father's with the exclamation, " Whither ? the house is sacred, sit down ! " The immediate factor here is the presence of the chief, who is lying asleep, and who must be respected.

In the ordinary domestic life a child is constantly being reproved for shouting, for rattling a stick, for standing up in front of its elders. "*A mata tou mana !*" "*A mata tou puna !*" literally "Face of your father !" "Face of your grandfather !" *i.e.* colloquially, "Mind your father !" etc., are commands frequently given and enforced. By this means the child gradually learns the rules of etiquette proper to a house, and how to behave in front of people.

Of specific instruction in technology I saw very little ; the child is usually told how to carry out a process only when the article itself is required for practical purposes. I did see, however, a cross-piece of wood, lashed together with sinnet braid in a complex style, specially prepared. This was a model of the *sumu*, the lashing used to fasten the roof-tree of a house to the supporting posts. The prevalence of gales, rising at times to a hurricane, makes a secure lashing important, especially for the large ancestral temples. When I asked the maker, Pa Niukapu, what the model was he said that it was for his son—" that he may know how it is done." The process needs knowledge and considerable skill, and few men are adepts, hence the unusual care.

Craft instruction is normally given by parents. "Boys are taught by their fathers. When men plait sinnet, they are instructed by their fathers." The first piece of work, it is said, is often poor ; the second is better. But some boys and girls do good work from the beginning ; of such people the expression is used " they have grown up as experts " (*e somo tufuŋa*). So also in the dance. When a person masters the complicated movements of hands and feet known as the *auŋa* while still a child, then it is said " *e somo purotu.*"

In a great deal of the economic co-operation between parents and children the latter can hardly fail to absorb knowledge of technical processes. For instance, a little group consisting of a man, his wife and children, is to be seen in the angle formed by two stone walls of a fish corral. The man, armed with a long-handled net, stands at the junction of the walls, and blocks the exit of the fish, while the other members of the family, with scoop-nets in their hands, half-walking, half-running, sweep inwards from the open water. Small fish are thus caught, and the children by shouted commands are taught how to perform their part.

THE REALITY OF PARENTAL AFFECTION

Modern anthropology has so far freed itself from the incubus of travellers' tales as to recognize that the " savage " parent is just as capable of affection towards his children as a father in a contemporary European community. This information, however, still needs to be

conveyed to the popular mind, which is astonished to find that naked-
ness and savagery of disposition are not always synonymous, and that
even cannibals may be kind-hearted in their own family circle. The
statements of early writers alleging an absence of sentiment on the part
of natives for their children, or that this sentiment is so diffused that
close kin and distant kin are treated alike, are now regarded by the
scientist with scepticism, as being based on superficial observation or
on a misconception of the nature of social obligations. The following
section will show that in Tikopia parental and filial sentiments certainly
exist, of a kind that may be compared very closely with those recognized
in our own society.

But the use of the term " sentiment " in this book implies not a
psychological reality but a cultural reality ; it describes a type of
behaviour which can be observed, not a state of mind which must be
inferred. Inflexions in the voice, the look of the eyes and carriage
of the head, intimate little movements of the hands and arms, reactions
to complex situations affecting the welfare of parent or child, utter-
ances describing the imagined state of the internal organs—such are
the phenomena which are classed together under the head of sentiment, the qualifying terms of " affection," " sadness," etc., being given
on the basis of distinctions recognized by the natives themselves and
embodied in their terminology. Such distinctions, broadly speaking,
correspond to those distinguished in our own society.

One point must be made clear at the outset, and that is that family
sentiment is not everywhere the same in Tikopia culture. There are
individual differences, as between parents, and also a differential
attitude on the part of the same parent as between his or her elder and
younger children, male or female. Moreover, changes in the sentiment are said to take place with the passage of time. This variation
is important to bear in mind if a general theory of kinship is based on
the postulate of sentiments of universal validity. A study of individual households in Tikopia will indicate the general character of the
relationship of father and child and also the lack of uniformity which
exists. It will be seen that the attitude varies from apparent indifference on the one hand to an easy affection on the other, this latter
capable of rising in times of crisis to a vivid and unashamed display of
emotion. The " bad " father who is harsh with his children, beats
them, is careless about their safety and their food, is not unknown in
Tikopia, at least in popular description. On personal acquaintance,
however, some " bad " fathers turned out to be men of somewhat
gruff habit of speech and eccentric personality like my friend Pae Sao
who—with surprising fidelity to the best traditions—concealed a very
kindly heart beneath a somewhat unprepossessing exterior.

Ugly of feature and unpleasant of body—he is covered with ringworm—Pae Sao is blunt and harsh in speech, and is apt to be the object of mingled derision and fear to the people. As an elder of high status he is a storehouse of traditional knowledge, and his god, who is one of those responsible for thunder and storms, gives him great power in sorcery. He speaks roughly to his children and others in his rasping tones, but he is courteous to guests; sharp-tongued, he is at the same time capable of many kindly actions. He strikes his children more often than is usual, even for slight misdemeanours, hence his reputation as a bad father. For instance, as he sat on the beach one evening yarning with his neighbours his youngest child— a yaws-afflicted morsel—began to cry. Where another man would have picked it up and comforted it, he beat it with his fan and ordered it inside. He used to beat his eldest son, Pureseiroa, a harmless youth, because, according to his own story, the lad kept on giving away the possessions of the house to comparative strangers. But all his beating had apparently little success.

Yet in spite of this public record he still displays affection for his children. He looks on them with pride while he castigates them with his tongue. In the tone that people reserve for things they like, he said to me with a smile as he watched his youngest crawl out of a doorway, "*Te vare!*" "The stupid!" Much against his wish—for he worships the gods of his land—he allowed Pureseiroa to be carried off in a proselytizing campaign to Vureas in the Banks Islands by the Mission. He feared lest his son might die there, and was careful to do all he could to ensure his safe return. He was unwilling to give me the final residue of his sacred lore lest it imperil the boy's spiritual defences; he implored me to use my supernatural powers to bring him back in health. A few weeks before I left the island he explained to me regretfully that he would not be able to come down to the vessel to bid me farewell. This was the trip on which Pureseiroa was expected to return and according to Tikopia custom he would wait in his house till the news arrived. If he came to see me off and the boy had died he would have to face the bad news in public, an ordeal too great for him to bear; he must stop in his house, where he could weep in private if the blow fell. In all this he displayed considerable emotion. Again, he told me, he had his eye on a tree in his woods which he was going to fell on the boy's return to make a canoe for him, as a sort of home-coming gift. He took considerable pains to equip his second son Katoara with clothing, ornaments and a plentiful supply of food for his novitiate entry into the dances of Marae. When someone suggested that the lad was too young he replied fiercely, " His oven has been kindled," that is, he had passed through the superincision ritual and was therefore technically eligible.

Pa Taitai is a different type of parent. A much younger man, large of body, and good-natured, he is of the sheepishly affectionate kind. Of his children he is distinctly proud. I was able, as mentioned, to observe his family life constantly and in great detail, from the days when he began to be allowed by the womenfolk to nurse his unconscious first-born to the time when this child was able to walk alone. It was interesting to observe his smiling pleasure as he watched the infant stagger about, his quick care to pick him up and fondle him if he tumbled over, and his annoyance with his sister or his wife if he thought that harm was likely to come to the child during their household activities. When he sat on the beach to talk the child was nearly always face upwards in his lap or between his knees. A sister of his had one of her periodic fits of lunacy while I was there, and this continued after the birth of Pa Taitai's second child. Thinking she might interfere with mother and babe, with inventive spirit he laced a web of sinnet cord across one end of the house every night in order to protect them.

Pa Raŋifuri, the simple honest heir of the Ariki Tafua, lost his own eldest son Noakena at sea—a suicide expedition. He and his wife were stricken with grief. For months afterwards the voice of the bereaved mother carried a falling inflexion of sadness, pitiful to hear, and the father's face worked with emotion as he spoke of the dead boy. Though the night of his tragic escapade was one of fierce wind, while he was in a tiny canoe, and all outsiders agreed that he must have perished within a few hundred yards of the shore, both parents clung pathetically to the faint hope that he might have fetched up on some island to the westward—the nearest being at least one hundred and twenty miles away! In great detail the father gave me instructions as to how to enquire for him in foreign lands. In his description he alternated between characterizing him as a fine big lad, almost grown up, keen on dance and sport, in which he excelled, and on the other hand, in reference to the fatal night as " only a child unable to battle against wind, and the waves." The manly or the infantile character of his son was uppermost according to the situation which he had before his mind. A year after the death of the boy a vivid dream of the lad's return stirred his emotions deeply, and led to a most dramatic event in the life of the village.

As the loss of children is generally deeply felt by parents, so also is the want of children felt by a married couple. Pa Nukunefu, brother of Pa Raŋifuri, has only one child, a girl. As I asked in the first days of our acquaintanceship about the size of his family he sadly informed me—" a single fruit." His wife, it was known, desired more children. Barrenness, usually, though not inevitably attributed to the wife, is not a matter of shame, but for commiseration. Other people speak with pity of such a couple, and they themselves display their disappointment. Pa Nukuomanu, one of the few childless husbands on the island, asked me hopefully if there was no medicine by which the *ara tama*, the pathway of children, of his wife could be opened, and they could have offspring. All Tikopia remedies had been tried and had failed.

The old picture of the savage father, brutal and unfeeling towards his young, has then no place in the gallery of Tikopia types. To give one further instance—at the time of an incision ceremony in Rofaea, Pa Niukapu made a double journey to Matafaŋa and back after dark in pouring rain to see how his children were. He knew they were sleeping with their grandmother, in no discomfort, but he wished to be assured of their well-being. As he was a mother's brother of one of the initiates he had to return again to Rofaea to sleep. Such things are frequently done by parents, at the price of considerable bodily discomfiture, and with no prompting of specific social obligations, merely for the satisfaction of their own personal inclinations. They are not done by other kin. It is on this level of extra degree of voluntary personal effort that one can most clearly distinguish the behaviour of true parents from that of other people included in the same kinship category. The criterion of distinction is normally one of degree and frequency of performance rather than of the type of action performed.

The strength and range of any sentiment in a society, particularly when not one's own, is difficult to estimate, and one can judge only by that variable standard, behaviour. In Tikopia the norm of behaviour between parent and child as a specific relationship may be expressed as an interchange of many friendly amenities not comprised in the social pattern, and less frequently indulged in by other kin. As already indicated in the examples given, this conduct is apparently backed by much real feeling, especially on the part of the parent. Anyone who has observed a mother or father playing with her or his infant will have no doubt on this point. Small demonstrations of affection are exceedingly common in the contacts of everyday life, especially when the child is young. Coming round the corner of a house near mine one day, I was able to watch unnoticed the wife of one of my neighbours as she sat playing with her babe. She held it on her knees and looked at it with fond smiling eyes, then caught it up to her with a sudden movement, and began to press her nose in a greeting of affection to its nose, its cheeks, its ears, its breast and the hollow of its neck and limbs, with swift but soft caresses in an abandon of obvious pleasure. As far as she knew, she was alone with her child. Such passionate displays are rare in public, but in the tones of the voice, the protective curve of her hand, the look of pride in the eye and many other lesser ways, one may note the average mother's regard.

The father also may give way to such affectionate demonstrations. He holds his young child in his arms or lays it on a piece of bark-cloth on the floor, and bending over it nuzzles it and makes pretended bites at its nose and cheeks. The caress of Tikopia is either that of the nose—the common type—or the soft nibbling with the lips drawn over the teeth that is playfully bestowed on infants.

A brief analysis may be made of the linguistic expressions used to indicate the emotional state of affairs in general. In accordance with the character of the language as one of the Polynesian group, the term in most common use is found to be *arofa*.[1] This word describes a wide range of sentiments including those of friendship and sympathy as well as of family affection. These are distinguished clearly from sexual love, which is broadly termed *fifia*, " desire." An example may be given. During a ceremony the Ariki Kafika said, " *Kuou e arofa ki Pa Faŋarere* "; he had watched the old man carry round a wooden bowl to assist in the work. The nearest equivalent here is, " I appreciate what he has done " or " I am grateful to him." In a different sense a father may speak of his child. One morning Pa Reŋaru, whose little son, a poor wasted frail thing, was near death, came to me to enquire if there was no medicine which could cure it. " *Kuou e arofa ki taku tama, soa E!* " he said in tones of deep feeling. " I have love for my son, friend." When I went he took the child from its mother, placed it between his knees, and tried in coaxing tones to induce it to drink the medicine I gave him. But nothing could be done for the child, which died the next day.

Arofa in Tikopia may describe emotion of any intensity, but certain other terms are also in use to indicate reactions of a strong affective order. The etymology of these shows the recognition of a certain correlation between emotional and physiological states. For deep grief, for instance, *fakakaiate* may be used. " *Matea na fakakaiate ki tana tama*," " Great is his grief for his son." This term analysed signifies " causing to eat the liver." Other terms of similar import are *fakamotumotumanava*, etymologically a compound of *motu*, " to part " or " to break," and *manava*, belly, hence " belly breaking "; *fakareremanava* or *fakarerereremanava*, compounded of *rere*,

[1] Cf. Maori *aroha*; Hawaii *aloha*; Samoa *alofa*.

to fly, with causitive prefix giving *fakarere*, to startle, hence "belly start-ling"; *fakakaikaimanava*, from *kai*, to eat, hence "belly consuming." These terms, though concrete in origin, all imply a strong positive sentiment for an object. They may be applied to affection for a lover. " *Matea te motu toku manava ki ei*," " great is the breaking of my belly for him." " *Matae te fakakaikai toku manava ki ei*," " great is the consuming of my belly for him." Affection between parent and child, or grief at the death of one of these, also calls forth the use of these terms, which represent *arofa* in the highest degree.

There are numerous other expressions also. " My *arofa* is intense ; I am moved in my belly ; my heart is hot ; the tears drip down," a person may say. Most of the terms here, such as heart (*fatu manava*) and hot (*vera*), have quite a concrete reference in other contexts. That translated by " moved " (*afu*) [1] is used only for situa-tions of emotional disturbance, as in personal loss ; it apparently corresponds to an organic disturbance. " A man sits, and is moved in his belly ; his son has died," the natives say, for instance (cf. also Texts S. 15 and S. 16).

It is interesting to note the concept of destruction of bodily organs in use by the Tikopia as a metaphor for acute emotion of attachment, much as in our own society.[2] This terminology for the expression of emotion may be based upon a reference to those actual organic phenomena in the body which are apparently the product of change in the sympathetic nervous system.

FAVOURITISM IN THE FAMILY

The affection of parent for child is not indiscriminate, but is strongly directed toward its specific individual object. It is not merely a social requirement following blindly a behaviour pattern set by society, it is a personal attitude which is dependent in each separate case upon factors of individual temperament and status.

This is indicated by the fact that it is well recognized by the natives that the sentiment of a parent is not identical in the case of each child. A younger child tends to be regarded with more affection than an elder, a daughter than a son. A native statement on this point from Pa Vainunu, the father of a numerous family, is interesting : " The married pair who have many children, great is the affection for their youngest, and for the girls, but as for the eldest, there is not affection— they are affectionate to him, but lightly, because he is the eldest, the

---

[1] *Afu* in the sense of a kinship relation is a homophone (*v.* Chapter VI).
[2] Cf. the rough equivalents : " My heart is broken " ; " My heart bleeds " ; " My heart sank."

household has begun to obey him. Therefore affectionate are the parents to the youngest. In this land the youngest, last appearing, great is the affection for him. They spoil their youngest."

The term *fakapere*, which I have translated as " spoil," has a more general meaning—to honour, exalt or respect. The reason given for the lessened affection bestowed on the eldest son, namely, because of his authority in the household, is based on sociological factors of real weight which operate in many families. With the growth in executive ability and importance of the eldest son, friction with the parents is apt to arise, while apart from this the junior position of the youngest and his tender years tend to evoke sympathy. That this is not a partisan point of view is shown by the fact that this informant was on quite good terms with his own eldest son. Such friction appears to be more apparent in families of rank where the economic and social possessions involved are of more importance. With this is perhaps to be correlated also the fact that men of rank usually delay imparting the final elements of their sacerdotal knowledge to their heirs until they think they are not far from death—though I have no native assurance of this.

A differentiation in family sentiment of an even stronger kind is recognized by the Tikopia as existing on a sexual basis. The affection of a father for his daughter is stated to be often greater than that for his sons. " Great is his favour to his female child." Pa Fenuatara, very capable in framing generalizations of Tikopia custom, explained as follows : " In this land a man makes a necklet of his female child. The female child is termed ' the necklet ' ; the mind of a man is jealous for his female child. He alone may scold her. Here I who sit here, my speech is not bad to my sister, to Roŋouvia. For should I scold her, and my father hear me doing evil to my sister, he would be angry."

The comparison of the daughter with the necklet is with an ornament, something prized, something personal. A man feels a peculiar interest in his daughter as in a decoration of himself. It is the father's place to rebuke her if she offends. " If the doings of his daughter are bad, he only may touch her." And if demanded, punishment is administered by him. Such is to some extent an idealization of the situation ; in actual fact a father does not always show more favour to his daughters than to his sons, and chastisement is apparently given by the mother about as often as by the father. But the existence of a native generalization is indicative of a real situation in the sense that there is at least a wish to believe in this favour.

This special bond of attachment of father to daughter is significant. It fits in with the psycho-analytic expectation of resolution of family sympathies and antipathies along the lines of the Œdipus complex, and in this respect it is supported to some extent by the attitude of mother to son. Some months after making the statement given above, Pa Fenuatara returned to the subject, in each case our conversation arising out of the concrete matter of the disposal of property by parents. Native opinion is quite clear on this point —that parents tend to show greater favour to their children of the opposite sex. Pa Fenuatara put the situation quite lucidly in his usual balanced style :

" In this land the man favours his female children, the mother favours her male children. The woman, great is her affection for her male children, the man, great his affection for his female children; it is done from affection. When a man in this land dies, he divides his goods, he gives a small portion to his male children and a large portion to his female children. The woman marries, she secretly takes away her goods from the relatives and gives them to her husband. The point of her taking these things secretly is because her brothers object to her having gone and married." After the daughter's marriage, if the father is still living, he makes her presents from time to time, of food, or more durable family property, such as ornaments, even prized heirlooms, somewhat to the disgust of her brothers. They may object in private to this, but they dare not oppose their father's wishes actively, owing to their personal respect for his authority and anger, and the social doctrine of filial obedience.

The Tikopia easily formulate a statement regarding this relation of father and daughter, the property aspect being uppermost in their mind. Pa Vainunu said :

" Now, I who am sitting here, I have desire only for my female child, to give my goods to her. I do not desire my male child. As for my male children, I do not say to leave property for them because their own wives come hither from other families. They go to their fathers and speak for something for themselves to be given hither by their fathers. Thereupon these give it, because they have affection for their daughters. Tikopia which stands here, such are its customs —the mind of Tikopia."

The request of a daughter to her father is backed by mention of the fact that anything so given is really for the *makopuna*, the grandchild, for whom the grandparent has usually a special affection. On one occasion Pa Vainunu gave his ear-rings of turtleshell, on her request, to his daughter, who was married to a man of another clan. His sons objected—verbally only—and as he admits, were annoyed that he should thus have given them away, as they might have formed part of their legitimate inheritance. Tobacco, small knives and other similar objects are also given away to the daughter. " And food. One sees that she is hungry, one takes food and gives it to her."

It may be mentioned that these observations of Pa Vainunu came unsolicited, arising out of an enquiry as to the reason for the transfer of certain sacred adzes from one clan to another; the explanation lay along these lines and prompted the general statement.

This more emphatic affection between parent and child of the opposite sex is thus well known to the Tikopia. They do not correlate it, however, with any specific sexual attraction in the Freudian sense. They are interested not in its cause but in its effects, and discuss it as it determines the distribution of goods. To them the chief point of comment is that the father's especial affection for his daughter, something for which there is no provision by the society, expresses itself in concrete terms and means the loss of property to a family on the girl's marriage. The Tikopia view the soft-hearted behaviour of fathers as a melancholy fact, not as a psychological problem. It must be stated also that there is little direct evidence to support a Freudian point of view. Cases of mother-son incest are extremely rare, and I could obtain no hint of incest between father and daughter. It looks, in fact, as if the Tikopia, by openly admitting a heterosexual predilection between parent and child, have managed to avoid repression and crime.

The protective attitude of the father towards the daughter is to be correlated with the relation of brothers to their sisters, which is discussed later. In Tikopia a brother is definitely restrained in his conduct towards his sister by fear of his father's authority.

In substantiation of the recognized affection of a father for his daughters, it is found that the presence of girl children in a family is welcomed as much as that of boys. Some families are composed solely of boys—the married couple " set up males " (fakatu taŋata); others have produced girls only, they " set up females " (fakatu fafine).

The personal predilections of the parents vary of course in each case, but in general a mixed family is desired, boys to go out in the canoes and fish, girls to cultivate taro, carry water, and perform other domestic duties. A family which has no girls is really in a more awkward position than one which has no boys, since by convention the tasks of filling the water-bottles, plaiting mats and beating bark-cloth are essentially those of females. Both Pa Teva and Pa Tarikitoŋa, brothers with several sons, each keenly desire a daughter; never a girl has been born to either of them. Their cousin the Ariki Taumako, with four sons and two daughters to his credit, wants more girls in his family. During my stay in Tikopia Pa Fenuatara, boasting at

first of a boy and four girls, had another child born to him.   On my
enquiry as to its sex he answered that it was a boy, and, somewhat to
my surprise, added that though this was good he was sorry it was
not a girl.   Other families, other wishes, he intimated, but such was
his preference.   Even in a family comprised almost solely of girls
the birth of another girl is not unwelcome.   In the question of the
proportion of the sexes in a family as apart from the individual children
concerned, the emphasis is laid on the economic advantages involved
rather than on any factors of sentiment.   The smaller number of
females in the Tikopia family, which represents the actual state of
things on the average, is certainly not due to infanticide as might be
thought at first.   Females are sometimes put out of the way, but so
also are males, and apparently as often—statistics are naturally hard to
obtain.   This point is taken up again in Chapters XII and XIV.

The attitude towards an only child appears much the same as in
our own society.   A special term is used, *te fuatasi*, "the single fruit,"
to describe the child, and from genealogies such a condition seems to
have been fairly common in Tikopia in former times—though how
far due to infanticide and other methods of control of family, it is
impossible to say.   Considerable affection is usually lavished on an
only child, though I regret that I made no special investigation of this
point, nor of any possible comparison between the treatment of
youngest and only children.   Tokumata, only daughter of Pa Nukunefu, certainly had more than the average freedom.   It is the habit of
the Tikopia to speak of an only son by this term *fuatasi* when there are
daughters as well ; this is to be correlated with the role of a son as
heir to the family possessions, and in particular as a vehicle of transmission of the family name and performer of the group ritual.
Seteraki of Raŋifuri was in this position after the death of his elder
brother, and was thoroughly spoiled in consequence.

FILIAL SENTIMENT

It is clear now how the sentiment of parent for child operates in the
Tikopia family, and how there are considerable spheres where specific
social regulation is not paramount, and where individual temperament
and bias, founded on personal association, hold sway.   The sentiment of a child towards its parent in Tikopia cannot be regarded as a
directly reciprocal attitude.   As far as my observations went it does
not appear to be so deep nor so clearly defined, and consists more in
a manifestation of the desire for protective contact and a display of
friendly feeling than in any express statements of attachment, or in
caresses of a manual, labial or other type.   Among the Tikopia, it

may be noted, there is none of that sentimentalism which in our own society finds pleasure in attempting to extract from the child purely verbal expressions of affection. The native infant is not taught to say " I love you " to its parents or others, nor is it encouraged to caress them.

A boy or girl in this native society, however, is by no means devoid of feeling for its parents, feeling based originally on selective interest in the two persons who have been chiefly concerned in its feeding and upbringing. As the first item of evidence native opinion may be adduced which distinctly corroborates this point of vew. According to Pa Fenuatara a child recognizes its mother and father at a very early age, being familiar with their faces from the constancy with which they attend it. To a question as to whether a young child knows its parents, he replied by a concrete observation, " It knows, and when it looks on a person who is different, it does not go and speak to him." Some other remarks which he made to me on this point are also worthy of record :

" The child knows its own mother and its own father also by tokens—it looks constantly on them. The infant recognizes its parents while yet it cannot speak. Faces only are recognized ; therefore when it looks then on faces which are different, the infant cries. The babe which has not yet made speech (*i.e.* begun to speak properly), if its father be absent, be he gone to the woods or whither for a stroll, it seeks then for its father, cries, cries, cries, cries, calling ' *Pa !* ' (Father) then wails ' *Pa E ! Pa E ! Pa, pa, pa, pa !* ' That is, it knows the relatives, but it weeps for its father. When they listen to it crying ' *Pa, pa, pa, pa,*' thereupon someone goes out to look for him. When the father is found he asks, ' What ? ' ' Come to the child who has cried and cried for you ; cried *Pa* awfully ! ' Thereon its father goes over, lifts it up in his arms, and so looking at its father it stops and does not cry. And the infant scolds its father, ' You—went—went—went ! ' "

This admirable description of a domestic scene is representative of countless such incidents in everyday life, illustrating the peculiar bond which exists between a small child and its parent—a bond freely admitted by the rest of the family.

Pa Fenuatara reverted to the same topic on another occasion, being anxious to resolve by practical evidence what he conceived to be my scepticism. Again he described a similar situation of an absent father, a crying child, and the final search by the impotent relatives. His account of the incident varied little from his former version, the only change being in the form of the dialogue. The father on his arrival is given as saying to the child, " What are you crying for, friend ? " The child, which cannot yet speak properly, says between its sobs only " *Ko—ke ! ko—ke !* " " You ! You ! " in broken words. The description was clearly drawn from life. The accounts of Pa Fenuatara and others show that these natives have a definite conviction that the child shows a selective interest in its parents and a special affection for them, even when it is still very young. This opinion they formulate in clear fashion. It is of course true that such opinions may not represent the facts, that the parents generalize in terms of what they *wish to believe* is the child's attitude—in other words, that such statements really embody the parents' desire for affection and not the child's practice of it. If we had to rely on these formulations alone, then an argument of this kind might have weight ; as already noted, though, the observer can himself see numbers of small incidents which prove that the intimacy of which parents speak does actually occur.

Small native children cry for their father, are quieted at his coming, try to follow him when he goes abroad, prattle to him of their childish interests, and fly to him if danger threatens. More sophisticated attitudes are taken up by older children, but they indicate their interest in other ways. Boys, especially, accompany him to work in the cultivations, fetch and carry for him, act as his messengers, and deputize for him in household affairs. " My father tells me . . .," " my father begs . . .," " my father has gone . . .," such phrases are continually on the lips of his sons and daughters, indicating a knowledge of his affairs, retailing his opinions, defending his actions. It is in the study of such minutiæ of detail that the observer sees the reality of a kinship system at work.

There are many little incidents which illustrate the sense of deprivation of children at their father's absence.

Thus Mataŋore, a chubby little thing of about four years, interrogates her father on his return from an afternoon's meal and talk in the village.

She comes to him, " Father, whither did you go ? "

" To such and such a house."

" You ate your fish ? "—a delicacy much prized by children.

" O no ! "

" Turn up your hands."

She takes his hands and smells his fingers one by one. If she finds traces of fish thereon, she says in tones of deep reproach : " And you deserted me ! You ate your fish and deserted me ! "

Here are elements of " cupboard love " strongly indicated, but the terms used show clearly that it is her father's neglect of her as much as the loss of titbits that lies behind her plaint. The relation between this pair is one of friendly companionship. The daughter comes up and clings to the father's shoulder or his knee, and they exchange whispered confidences—the usual subjects being the destination of the child and the prospects of food. He treats her with gentle consideration even when she becomes obstructive. I observed him one day cutting out an axe handle, when Mataŋore climbed on to the baulk of timber on which he was sitting and hung on his shoulder. Quietly he told her to get down and go. Instead, she suddenly grasped his working arm and made the tool slip. He gave a sharp exclamation, shook her off, and methodically went on with his task. Persistent, she again clutched his arm, and the same result occurred. Put out at being rebuffed, she slapped him on the shoulder smartly. In spite of the fact that this was a breach of taboo on her part, he did not resent it actively, though he frowned at her till she subsided—after which he glared around to see if anyone was laughing at his expense. Such is the Tikopia father in his milder moods.

The relations of Pa Fenuatara with his son Rakeivave are of the same equable, pleasantly affectionate type.

In any general consideration of kinship behaviour the time factor should be borne in mind. The sentiments of childish days abate by time and the intimate personal relationship gradually fades. But they do not vanish completely, and men of mature years may display a considerable degree of affection for their parents, caring for them, fulfilling their wishes with gentleness and consideration, and after their death speaking of them with respect and admiration in a spontaneous tribute not demanded of them by the social code. I was once discussing with Pa Vaŋatau, a man of over sixty years of age, the doings of his father, a canoe voyager, who was lost at sea many decades before. Suddenly he said to me in a demonstration of affectionate memory, " Friend ! I who dwell here, the face of my father is never lost to me."

A couple of days after my arrival I showed Nau Paŋisi a photograph which was identified as that of Pa Maneve, her " father " (her father's first cousin), who had died some years before. She pressed it to her nose in greeting, and I saw tears come, which were wiped away once or twice with the back of her hand. This was no formal demonstration. Affection may go beyond immediate family ties.

TABOOS AND OBLIGATIONS BETWEEN PARENT AND CHILD

The family life of the child in its early years, the care of it by mother and father, and the degree of reciprocal affection between the parents and children constitutes the more personal aspect of the kinship relation. This varies from individual to individual, but presents a fairly constant pattern which can be taken as a social norm of the less formal relations of life. In addition there is the more formal structure of the family, the obligations on which the society sets especial store, the fulfilment of which it regards as the final test of efficiency in the performance of kinship functions. Every society concerns itself primarily with the external tokens of relationship, with adequate observance of rules of behaviour. No amount of evident sentiment can excuse the neglect of a parent to provide food for his child ; no plea of silent affection can extenuate the failure of a child to mourn audibly for its parent. Concrete performance of duty is demanded to avoid social disapproval.

In addition to the attitudes illustrated above, then, which are to some extent personal and optional, there are other rules of family behaviour which are enjoined upon each member by the social tradition.

As far as the parent-child bonds are concerned there are few formal economic obligations to be observed, because they are subsumed under the events of everyday domestic life.

The specific duties of the parents are of a type which can be fulfilled only by constant effort, usually unnoticed, rarely by any spectacular performance on a stated occasion. It is the primary duty of a father to provide food and shelter for his children in their youth. Shame attaches to a man if it be said of him, " His children are crying from their want of food." A man will say in excusing himself from attendance on any particular occasion, " I must go to our orchards to get food, lest our children cry in their hunger." Failure in this direction will be made a matter of specific reproach by other relatives. They say, " You are lazing about there, but are you not a man who has children ? What shall your children be fed with ? Will you go and steal for the feeding of your children ? " Family obligations involve work, particularly in planting taro, since the claims of hungry children are no excuse for theft. This situation is further recognized by incorporating a reference to it in a precise formal injunction which used to be recited annually in a ritual manner during the seasonal religious ceremonies.[1]

The comment on a man's laziness is often, " What shall his children eat ? Shall the children of the common crowd eat taro and his children eat any rubbish ? " In other situations, too, the referent is the children. When the Ariki Kafika was going to Uta to impose the customary *tapu* of the sacred season which would prevent tree-cutting or other loud noise, he called in on his way to see Pae Sao

[1] *Work of the Gods*, " The Fono at Rarokoka."

and advise him of the fact. He said, " Go and fell a sago palm for food for your children ; the land is going to be made *tapu*."

It is the duty of a mother to assist in feeding the children, to keep them clean, and to efface their infant indiscretions. Both parents, again, should train their offspring in habits of courteous and restrained speech. Outsiders are quick to comment on failure in these matters, but no premium is put on attending to them adequately.

Peculiarly incumbent upon the mother and other women of the household is the duty of removing the child's faeces when such happen to be deposited in a public place ; carelessness in this respect is a matter for deep reproach. This is illustrated in a mythological tale where a father in going out from his house finds his foot defiled from the act of one of his children. In disgust he flings a curse at his wife, who thereupon weeping leaves him. A domestic incident I myself witnessed shows the frankness employed in such affairs. The small son of my next-door neighbour had relieved himself in the path ; observing this, a youth who frequented the house called out to the child's grandmother, " Mother ! Tekila has defecated in the place there." " Where has he defecated ? " " In the path leading to the beach." " In the path ? " she replied anxiously, and hastened with a bunch of leaves to remove the offence. They conducted this conversation some fifty yards apart, and in loud tones, without embarrassment to themselves or to the audience (Text S. 1).

The provision of bark-cloth for the child's garments, though a light responsibility, is a matter for the parents ; more weighty are the obligations which lie upon them to provide the food and property wherewith the child may be passed through the various rites of youth. In the case of a boy in particular, his father must take thought for the lad's reputation, plant taro, store coconuts and accumulate the necessary pandanus mats and bark-cloth in order that his initiation ceremony may be held soon after puberty has been reached—or even before. Assistance of a material kind at marriage is also taken for granted from the parents, though the immediate initiative in such cases does not lie so directly in their hands. Such provision is complementary to the help which the child is expected to give in the work of the household from the earliest years, help which comes to assume such importance that fathers in Tikopia are credited with a distinct disinclination to sanction the marriage and consequent removal of their daughters. Should the child's death be untimely, the principal duty of mourning falls upon the parents.

A point of special interest here is the conduct required of a widow and its bearing on the unity of the family. If a woman loses her husband, and still has young children about her, then it is her duty in the eyes of her husband's relatives and of the village as a whole to stay and look after them. She herself may desire to remarry, but this involves departing to another household, and is not deemed right. The custom of breaking the lobe of the ear of a widow is in part an expression of the intention not to take another spouse. Even sexual relations with her are not regarded as correct. As the natives say, " Because she is *tapu*, when a woman's husband dies no man goes to her. Some men are foolish, they go to her, but when they go to her they are termed persons who make sport." They are belittling her state. The net effect of this rule is the acknowledgment of patrilineal primacy, the maintenance of the claims of the male parent's " house " as paramount in the offspring of their dead son. The levirate does not exist in Tikopia, but this feeling against the re-marriage of widows supplies to a great extent the same mechanism for conserving the interests of the man's kinship group in his children.

Public opinion emerges most clearly in the case of a breach of this principle. If a widow with a young family makes up her mind to take a new husband, then she will leave her children in their father's house, in charge of his people, and go her way. She will not return to visit them—officially at all events—since the relatives of her late husband are angry at her desertion and will greet her with hot words or even blows. It is said, " She has abandoned us, has gone as a child of the crowd " (*Ku tiakina ko tatou, ku poi te tama a faoa*), a classic expression which conveys the offended pride of the speakers and a suggestion of vulgarity on the part of the deserter.

When the child of such a mother grows up, and is of an age to understand her defection, she may attempt to draw closer again the bonds of relationship. She goes up to him with a cry of " *Aue ! taku tama*," " Alas, my child ! " and tries to greet him with the *soŋi* of the pressed nose. If he is kind-hearted, and still has affection for her, he may return the greeting ; if not, he turns his head aside and pretends not to recognize her. If she persists, he may even strike her in his scorn and go his way. I have not observed a case of this kind, but such is the native account. Making allowances for the native flair for extracting all the dramatic interest possible out of a situation, one may hazard a guess that such unfilial conduct—as we should regard it—is not so frequent after all. But at all events affection of a child for the mother is regarded by the Tikopia as a tender plant which needs the watering of constant care to bring it to full growth. The natives are realists in this matter. They recognize no unvarying moral obligation ; they do not subscribe to the opinion that a son is bound to remain attached to his mother by any filial sentiment *per se*. Reference to genealogies supports the general situation indicated here; remarriage of widows is rare, and seems to have occurred mainly in cases where there was no issue at the husband's death. This takes away most of the sting from her departure. In any event the second husband's family seem to raise no objection to the union.

A widower is on an entirely different footing. The same forces which tend to inhibit the further interest of a widow in sex and marriage stimulate him towards it. Consequently we find that bereaved husbands frequently remarry. This is not invariable, however, as witness nowadays Pa Maniva, Pa Mataŋi, Pa Faŋatauriki, Pa Motuaŋi, Pa Raŋitisa, all men of middle age or under, who are widowers. All, however, have either adult daughters or other female relatives who take the responsibility of caring for their young children.

The behaviour of a child towards its parents is fairly clearly defined—to the father in particular respect is the keynote of the attitude. He is the acknowledged master of the household, to whom all the children render obedience. The native term for this is *fakaroŋo*, of which the primary meaning is "to listen," but which has acquired the more technical significance of acknowledgment of authority. The child "listens" to the commands of its father just as he in his turn "listens" to the wishes of his chief. The suggestion called up by *fakaroŋo* is that of a person seated, with head slightly bowed, listening in silence to what is being said to him.[1] Instances of the obedience of children have already been given. Even when the sons are quite grown up their father issues commands to them in a peremptory tone, and they usually obey with little demur. I have heard the Ariki Tafua say testily to his sons when food was needed for the oven. "Here! you brethren go and pluck breadfruit. Don't sit here!" And off they went quietly.

The Tikopia father is termed the "head" (*pokouru*) of the son, indicating his superiority of relationship. The respect shown by child to father is a matter of social injunction, not mere personal choice, and is backed by the moral sanction of strong disapproval in cases of breach, and even, it is believed, in extreme cases by the intervention of the gods. A man who lifts his hand against his father would be worse than a criminal, he would be committing sacrilege, and a parricide would be looked upon with the greatest horror. In the situation described above, where a father makes gifts to his daughters, in spite of the disapproval of his sons, not one of these would dare to stretch out a hand and pull the article away. Such would be outraging all the canons of filial behaviour. The comment

[1] Cf. our English expression "to listen to someone," often equated with "to obey."

of Pa Fenuatara was, " They are not afraid—and yet they are, because this land which stands here listens to the father. Now a man who would do that to his father, would have done wrong. The gods would be angry." The word *sara* in the original, which I have translated as " done wrong," is used adjectively as the opposite of " correct." As a verb it conveys something more, the idea of conduct not in accord with the social harmonies, and therefore subject to super- natural sanction. Wherever it is said of a person, " *ku sara*," as in this instance, it implies that he has sinned and misfortune may be expected to follow from the outraged ancestors and deities. When the relations of father and son are discussed, natives assure one that a son is never angry with his father—that is, openly. If enquiry is made whether bad men do not transgress, it is admitted that some men are evil enough to show anger against their father. If a person struck his father, however, that would be too much. He would be expected to take a canoe and go out to sea, there to be lost—the favourite method of suicide. The father would wail for his son, then go out in search of him. If he found him, he would bring him back. If not, he might go on himself to meet death, or turn back to weep in his house and dwell there.

This is a hypothetical procedure, advanced by my informants in reply to questioning, and not tested by observation, since I did not witness such a scene, nor could anyone tell me of an instance. The striking of father by son is indeed almost out of the realm of native social behaviour, since a violent reaction of the son against the father would lead him to suicide direct, as not infrequently happens. This is in fact the son's remedy against injustice, and the knowledge of it acts as a check upon temperamental fathers.

On the only occasion that I saw an instance of strong opposition between father and son—it was the Ariki Tafua and Pa Raŋifuri—the latter withdrew immediately from the scene. As he said afterwards, and all agreed, what else could he do ? " The father is weighty "— he was in a cleft stick. In this case an adjustment was soon made.

One case only was quoted to me of a person having struck his mother. The man was Pa Nukuomanu, who at present suffers from what is apparently a type of framboesia, a pustular affection of the arm and leg which keeps breaking down into large open lesions of angry colouration. He has sought for a cure for years without success. His illness was attributed by the people at large to his wrong conduct, he having taken a stick in a fit of anger and hit his mother with it. She did not die at that time, but wept bitterly. After her death she is conceived as having returned to her son in spirit form, bringing the illness which she presented to him, as one hands over a material object.   The procedure employed by the mother is held to have followed a definite form usual in such cases of unfilial conduct. I transcribe from the native account.   The mother goes and announces to her ancestors : " My son has not spoken properly to me.   I have been struck by him."   Her ancestors grow angry ; they speak : " It is good that you return to men to work sickness upon your son."   She does so and the thing is done.

It is important to notice how the sanction for filial conduct is thus ultimately a supernatural one, and that the full weight of the ancestral line is set behind it.   The parent does not take action without having consulted the forbears and received their approval.   This obviates action from purely personal pique or hard-heartedness, and gives the sanction a universal validity.

The position of the father in the Tikopia household is not so autocratic as appears at first sight.   In theory he is the head of the family ; in practice he agrees to the wishes of the rest of the household to a very large degree.   In domestic matters in Tikopia father, mother and children commonly act as an informal family council, constituting a unit much as in our own society.   The father assumes the initiative and voices decisions, the mother assents, contradicts, qualifies, moulds her man's opinions, the children listen greedily and comment sagely and often inopportunely on what is said.   The little group, conscious of its own interests, has its own secrets, and presents a united front to the community.   In later life the parents recede more into the background though their opinions are received with respect, and sons and daughters take upon themselves more of the responsibility of the family affairs.   More deference is shown on the one hand by the children, but also more energy in directing the family policy and maintaining their own point of view.   On any important matter a conclave takes place, when opinions are freely given and as freely rebutted by any member of the circle, male or female.   More deference is certainly paid to the head than to other members.   "*E tonu ko Pa !*" "Father is right" is a statement very frequently heard, while dissent from his view is tactful and courteous.   Nevertheless his opinions may be swayed to accord with those of his children.

In discussions of this kind the eldest son has a prominent place.   In the kinship terminology there is a special word for eldest, *te urumatua*, shortened to *te uru*.   This latter is an ordinary word for " head," hence the eldest child may also be referred to as *te uru o fanau*, the head of the family.   The terms *tanata* or *fafine* may be added to *urumatua* to indicate sex, but when used alone it signifies the eldest son.   This person, especially after he has reached adult years, has the deciding voice in the family councils.   He defers to his father, but so also by traditional rule does his father defer to him. The native theory is a situation of mutual respect and deference between father and eldest son, each supporting the other in the family interest.

As Pa Raŋifuri put it, " If I speak to my father, my father listens to me ; if my father speaks to me, I listen to him. We two, he and I, are one speech "—that is, they present a united front.

This ideal is usually approximately realized, but the harmony may be merely external, the result of obedience to the social code. Friction between father and eldest son is not unknown, and though hardly evident in public affairs is apparent to one who sees the inner life of the family. Since I knew several families very well, and stayed with them for days on end, I had excellent opportunities of observing this discrepancy between the ideal and the actual relations. The case of Pa Raŋifuri himself is a good illustration. Living apart in a small house of his own about fifty yards from the dwelling of the old chief, he harboured suspicions, usually well-founded, that his younger brothers—and their wives—who lived closer, had the ear of his father, and turned their advantage to good use. Small articles of value disappeared from the old man's hut and rested in the thatch of his brothers' houses ; baskets of food came to them more frequently, and they received more 'consideration in regard to work in the orchards. Pa Raŋifuri and his father were quite friendly, but spatial distance in this case was an index of emotional distance also.

The dwelling of the eldest son apart from the father is not an uncommon situation. Houses in Tikopia are not very large, so that as the children grow up and marry they must move on. The eldest son is usually the first to go, and he builds himself a house ; it may be quite near to that of his parents, or it may be on his father's ground in another village, or another part of the village. The next son in order does the same, till by the time the youngest is ready to marry the parental house is nearly empty, and at the desire of the old people he and his wife stay with them. He then provides his father with food, working his father's immediate orchards for this purpose. The eldest son may use these too, or may have been assigned certain other lands. The friction between the father and the eldest son is apt to be stimulated by the tacit division of authority between them, a division which has the sanction of tradition. With the younger sons, where there is no such formal obligation on the father's part, relations are easier. This intimacy of relation with the youngest son and mild alienation from the eldest can be correlated also with the declared opinion of the natives as given above, that the parents lavish much more affection on the former than the latter.

There is, however, a counteracting tendency. In families of rank, in particular, it is not uncommon for the eldest son to take over the ancestral house on his father's death, and to assume the family name borne by its occupier. This is prompted to a considerable degree by the fact that the dead forbears to whom appeals are made in the kava are buried there. Such a contingency is occasionally anticipated by the eldest son remaining in the house of his parents after marriage and devoting himself to the charge of affairs, while his younger brothers in turn move off and build for themselves as they acquire wives. After the death of their parents they continue to live with him until they marry.

Generalization on this point must not be pushed too far, as there is no uniformity of practice in this matter. It is difficult to say how far the correlation of residence and amity in family relations goes, but reference to a few concrete illustrations will show at least the divergences that exist. The cases of Pa Raŋifuri and Pa Fenuatara have been discussed already. In contrast to these is the family situation of the Ariki Faŋarere, who lives with his elder son, Pa Nukumaro, while the younger, Pa Raŋateatua, lives next door in the closest co-operative relationship, the two households being run as one. In Maneve, formerly the residence of the late Pa Maneve, lives his eldest son, Pa Nukureŋa, with the unmarried youngest, Sukuŋataraŋa, while the others dwell elsewhere. All the married sons of the aged Pae Ava-kofe live in separate dwellings away from him, but maintain relations of the greatest cordiality with their father and with each other.

Further light is thrown on the continuity of the family and the nature of the sentiments between its members by the customs of inheritance. On the death of the head of a household, the family property—mats, sinnet cord, bark-cloth, paddles, bowls, fish-hooks and tobacco—is largely absorbed in the various ritual payments to the mother's family of the deceased and other mourners. Apart from this, goods go to his daughters in other households, since their children are the *tama tapu* of him and his sons. Land interests may also be transferred. Some other goods remain with the sons, especially sinnet belts, clubs, spears, and ornaments which have been the property of the family ancestors. These are *tauarofa*, heirlooms, of which the history is known and which are not lightly given away. Sometimes after a man's death his son or daughter may decide to have his wooden head-rest as a neck ornament. It is slung round the neck and worn on the back—much as a tooth is ordinarily kept as a relic. It is usually a woman who does this. When she dies she may direct that the head-rest shall be buried with her, in order that her father may see that it comes with her on her arrival into the spirit world. A betel mortar may also be an heirloom. Sometimes a

man orders it to be buried with him at his death, but he frequently
hands it on to his son instead.

Often before his death a man will give final instructions to his
sons and other relatives regarding the disposal of the property. In
these last words he is said to *toŋi*. Pa Fenuatara described to me the
fashion in which he expected his father, the Ariki Kafika, to instruct
him.

" Now, my father living here, as he lives on and becomes old, he
will divide the property, he will do it himself. He will speak to me.
He will say thus, ' Come and sit here ! Come and sit and look at
your things which are going to be divided by me.' Then it's a matter
of whom he announces first, us or the chiefs. If the latter, he speaks
to me so, ' Look at them, at your things which I am going to divide.
That is for the chiefs. When I am gone, that is the property of Pa
Tafua, that is the property of Pa Taumako, that the property of Pa
Faŋarere.' Then he puts aside another set. ' That is the property of
the *tama tapu*. When I am gone, that will be the completion of the
valuables given to my nephews and nieces.' As his solemn instructions he tells me to hand over the goods properly to his ' sacred
children.' ' When you succeed, you can care for your own nephews
and nieces.' Now the instructions regarding the *tama tapu* and the
chiefs are finished. Then he takes up another piece of property.
' That is my burial payment,' and adds to it a wooden bowl or whatever may be his wish. Then he speaks about it too, ' Now, this is
my burial payment.' Then he speaks to me, ' Here ! Look at the
things for you and your brothers ; I am going to apportion them.'
Then he takes up and apportions several things. ' Now, your things
are there, the property of Rakeivave.' He bequeathes them to me,
but announces them as the property of his grandchild. Then he
says, ' The things of Rakeimuruki (Pa Fenuafuri, a younger brother of
Pa Fenuatara) are there. They remain with him, but they are the things
of Fakasaupuke. I shall be gone, but my grandchildren will not be
poor.' Then he takes up another piece of property and leaves it to
Fuamau (Pa Taramoa). And his last word is this, ' I am properly
present then in your sons.' "

This last sentence needs some explanation. The idea is that the
person himself will be dead, but he is as one living constantly in the
presence of his sons through his property that is in the possession of
them and their children. Throughout this account there is patent
the attitude of interest in the family continuity, the old man charging
his sons to be trustees for his grandchildren. And it is an index to
the position of the eldest son that he is normally the one selected as
the father's confidant and executor. As Pa Fenuatara said, " My

father announces things to me, ' Those are your things '—all kinds of things, the house, a canoe, and orchards. Then he charges me, ' When you succeed me, always treat your brothers properly.' "

A general principle of bequest is that when the goods are divided a proportion larger than that of his brothers goes to the eldest son. But, it is said, " the daughter is treated just the same as the eldest male."

Some further data may now be given regarding the attitude of child to parent. Towards the father a mingling of affection and respect appears to be the norm, each component being a matter of social injunction as well as of individual feeling. In the code of behaviour which the child must observe certain prohibitions speedily come to notice. Despite the great familiarity which so often exists and the close personal contact, particularly in youth, certain actions must be avoided as too intimate. The child must not use his father's personal name, though the man may freely use that of the child ; the kinship term alone is permissible in the former case, with a descriptive expression added if necessary. The name of the mother also is *tapu*. This name avoidance is carried so far that a native may actually be prepared to declare with every appearance of truth that he is ignorant of his father's name. His house name (*iŋoa paito*) is of course known, but his personal name (*iŋoa taŋata*), that which he bore before marriage and by which he is still called by persons who stand in a sibling relationship to him, is alleged to be unknown. This assertion, it may be judged, is usually a fiction composed to avoid the possibility of being pressed to speak that which it is not proper to utter. As a rule a boy sooner or later hears the name of the father spoken in his presence by some " brother " of the father's, though it is really not etiquette to mention it when the son is near, especially in company. If the name is really required, as in establishing a genealogy for an inquisitive ethnographer, the correct thing is for the son to get up and go out for a stroll. The question then to ask is : " What is the name of the father of that one who has gone ? " and it will be supplied. It is said that people really know the names of their father and mother though they may not utter them. This prohibition against speaking the name of the parent is in force primarily while they live ; the *tapu* is lifted on their death, and many a son or daughter utters for the first time the name of father or mother in the *taŋi soa*, the funeral dirge which is sung over the corpse. Asked if some people did not utter the name of the father by chance or when cross, natives reply in the negative, with a rider that a person is never cross with his father. This, as indicated above, is an overstatement, but it is unlikely that in any event the use of the personal name would accompany any demonstration of anger. No case of this breach of *tapu* in regard to the real father ever came to my knowledge. One should never, of course, curse one's own father.

The conventional attitude of respect to the father which is evidenced by the avoidance of the use of his personal name shows itself also in certain bodily avoidances. The system of personal *tapu* is not highly developed in Tikopia—there is nothing approaching the complexity of the Maori regulations, for example—and in its field of operation it appears to be largely a function of the kinship situation. For instance a man's head is not *tapu per se*, but it is *tapu* to his children. His brother or mother's brother may touch it without breach of rule. The result is that intimate personal services, such as cutting the hair at mourning, or de-lousing it, are not usually performed by a man's son or daughter. The child will not touch the hair of his parent of his own accord, though if called upon to do so he may. A man may say, " Son ! Step here and forage in my head." It is quite correct for the son to comply, and the lousing is done openly. But if the son should even accidentally put hand to his father's head without instructions, the latter would be angry. A chief, however, may not under any circumstances invite his child to assist him in his toilet. It is also forbidden to stand immediately in front of one's father when he is seated or to take objects from above his head. He is asked to reach up and hand them down himself.

Accidental contact with the father's body, such as brushing him in the course of work, is not seriously regarded, but to lay hands on him with intent is definitely *tapu*. On one occasion the Ariki Kafika strained his back when lifting a canoe, and complained of pain. I compounded an ointment and gave it to the family, absent-mindedly suggesting that one of his sons could rub it on the old man's back. No enthusiasm was displayed by anyone ; finally one of the sons mentioned the *tapu* and another masseur had to be found. Again, the *fetaki* game, a kind of singlestick, is not played with one's own father, as to strike him would be a grievous breach of etiquette. The personal *tapu* of the father extends also to articles of his more intimate property. His *uruŋa*, the wooden stand on which he lays his head, is *tapu*. " It is sacrosanct to his child, the prop of the countenance of his father," said Pa Raŋifuri. If a small child should seize the head-rest to sit on, it is hastily taken away from it. If an infant is crawling about on the floor and the pillow of its father is lying within reach, someone calls to its elder brother or sister. " That is the pillow of your father there. Take it away ! " In like fashion the bed-mat of the father is *tapu* to the son. Awkward incidents in the family are usually avoided by having all the bedding rolled up individually and stowed away under the eaves of the house during the day. Other items of personal property, such as knife, axe and pipe are prohibited from casual use by the son or daughter. They may be taken with the father's express permission, but ought not to be touched otherwise. Careless sons infringe this rule, to their father's annoyance. These regulations of personal *tapu* are particularly strict in the case of chiefs, to whom a considerable degree of sacredness attaches by virtue of their relation to the gods. Nau Fenuatara once cut her hand in slicing Tahitian chestnuts. Her husband explained, " She did wrong, she took my father's knife to do it."

A compensatory reaction to the rules of *tapu* relating to the person and property of the father is that while such things are prohibited to the child in his lifetime, they form memorial tokens and heirlooms after his death. Hair of the dead, his waistcloth, and even his pillow may be worn as ornaments by his children. Such things are *tauarofa*, which can be translated as " links of affection."

The sentiment of attachment to close kinsfolk expresses itself in a number of actions, one of the most common being the wearing of tokens. Apart from relics or heirlooms of the dead, symbols of the living person may be worn. In every case they have some peculiar bodily association with the person held in regard. Hair and teeth are most frequently utilized, and not only from parents. The women of a family bind the hair of their male relatives—sons, brothers, husbands or fathers—shorn during funerals into circlets (*fau rauuru*) which they wear upon their heads. Indoors the circlet is often hung upon a hook, but when the woman goes outside she reaches it down and claps it on her head just as her civilized sister pulls on a hat—though with considerably less adjustment. There seems to be, too, a feeling on the part of a woman that she is not properly dressed in public unless she is wearing her hair circlet. Great affection is displayed for these objects as symbols of the relatives, especially when they are no longer living. Hair of women is not worn in this way.

A dropped tooth is frequently worn as a token of affection, being bored and suspended on a cord round the neck. The photograph of Pa Raŋifuri (Plate VII) shows him wearing the tooth of his father. A grandparent may also be thus remembered. The grandchild of Pa Nukuraro carries the back tooth of his *puna* in this way, as does a grand-daughter of Nau Kafika. If the elder should be dead, the relic is described sentimentally as " an heirloom of one's grandparent, because his face has become hidden." Incidentally it may be mentioned that when a tooth of a chief falls, the wail of the dirge is raised by his family, an oven is kindled and his sons gash their foreheads in mourning—this is a conventional tribute of affection to the ageing man for the food that he will now be unable to consume. A woman wears the tooth of a female relative ; a man that of a male only.

Another rule of *tapu* which is observed with considerable stringency is that which forbids the utterance of any " bad speech " in the presence of the parent. Obscene expressions, risqué stories, lewd jokes are barred, a ritual sanction thus operating to fortify the guidance of good taste. The expression is " to observe gravity towards the father ; not to go and make sport with him." The native term means literally " to make weighty," and is used in a metaphorical sense as are similar words in English. On one occasion I was taking down from the lips of Pa Fenuatara a traditional tale told by young men for purposes of amusement, and containing some rather frank anatomical details, when the Ariki Kafika crawled in through the further doorway. " My father has come ; we will finish it another time," he murmured, adding in parenthesis, " In this land father and son do not talk thus." This regulation operates in other spheres of kinship, as that of affinal relationship, with even more severity.

The behaviour of a person to his mother conforms to much the same rules as in the case of the father, though not with the same stringency. The *tapu* between them is less severe, and the assumption of authority in the household by the eldest son, when he is of mature years, makes the mother defer to him rather than he to her. While he is a child, for instance, she handles him freely, but once he is adult she does not do so, refraining especially from touching his head. Her daughter's head she may touch. Warmth of affection from the mother and authority on the part of the father are conventional norms of behaviour from parent to child, though as like as not they may be blended or reversed in any particular family. Consideration and respect for her opinion, small gifts of tobacco and betel, care to see that she gets her portion of food, usually mark the attitude of grown-up children to their mother.

It is interesting to note that, as will be shown later in the discussion of terms of kinship, children in Tikopia are credited with recognizing the mother first of all relatives, because of her constant association with them in infancy ; moreover they are apt to salute other kinsfolk, even males, as " mother " when they are first learning to use the terminology.

In concluding this account of the type of behaviour imposed by the society on a child with regard to its parent, several duties of importance must be mentioned. One is that of providing food for the parent in his or her old age. This is referred to in formulæ recited over the infant a few hours after birth, ensuring that this obligation is inculcated as early as possible.   Another obligation, one of the most definite of all, is that of mourning the parent in the appropriate manner at his or her death.   Here the social group takes charge, and the child has no option but to express these sentiments of *arofa* which as we have shown are usually felt in actuality, and which the society has determined shall be demonstrated.   Again the children, particularly those with whom the parents reside, are expected to have supplies of bark-cloth and pandanus mats ready against the time of their death, so that the family can withstand the drain of such goods at their burial.   Improvidence in this respect is censured by observant outsiders, who even if they are not of close kinship may mention the matter to the young people concerned.

FREEDOM BETWEEN BROTHERS

As far as the immediate family circle is concerned the relations of the children, brothers and sisters, now remain to be considered. Without going into details of the terminology of these relationships, which will be discussed in Chapter VII, it may be simply noted here that siblings of the same sex refer to and address each other by one term, while they use another term for those of opposite sex.   Differences of age are not made apparent in the ordinary kinship expressions, but there are descriptive terms to indicate birth order.   The eldest, a child from the middle of the family, and the youngest can be singled out for mention in simple terms, but further distinction needs more elaborate phraseology.   This is of practical use, since the eldest male is acknowledged as their leader and spokesman in public affairs, a sharer to a large extent with the father in the responsibility for the family welfare.   Deference is usually given to him by the rest.   They live together in a fair degree of amity, broken only by occasional clashes of opinion in minor matters, when the elder may have to yield to sound reasons advanced by his junior.   The strength of the family tie is considerable, and jealousy when it occurs is normally not allowed to mar the symmetry of the attitude of the group to the outside world.

There are of course exceptions to this.   Sometimes a pair of brothers are known as *tau fanau pariki*, evil brethren, with bad blood between them.   Such were Pa Roŋotaono and Pa Reŋaru, sons of the same father and mother.   They fought about some land and each destroyed food that the other had planted—a sign that the quarrel was serious, and developing into a feud.   Then the child of Pa Reŋaru died, as far as I could see as the result of malnutrition following on weakliness at birth, but in native opinion as the result of its having been bewitched by Pa Roŋotaono.   Later a child of this man died in turn—bewitched by Pa Reŋaru.   In the latter case it was thought that the curse had been directed against the brother, but he being a strong man it fell on the child, who succumbed.   That the deaths were due to sorcery was a view given credence by the people at large, and this view was a deduction from the enmity, an expression of the friction actually existing.   Brothers in harmony do not resort to such practices.   In other words an attribution of sorcery in such circumstances springs from the realization of a pre-existing situation of conflict; it is rarely if ever the primary cause of such a condition—a point which might give food for thought to colonial administrators trying to enforce anti-sorcery regulations.   The place of sorcery in relation to the legal system of the Tikopia will be dealt with in a succeeding volume.

When brothers are young the attitude between them is marked on the part of the senior by a compound of protective interest and affection, good-natured toleration, disregard, patronizing deprecation and sharp instruction, the precise element which is uppermost depending upon circumstances.   The junior varies imitation and obedience with self-assertion; quarrels occur over the division of food, playthings and childish privileges, but the prevailing spirit is one of cameraderie.   The interests of the younger may be ignored with fraternal superiority.   I was standing by once when a group of lads announced their intention of going round the reef by canoe instead of by the path, to get food.   They recited to their elders a list of who were going in the usual meticulous native style.   " So-and-so, and so-and-so and so-and-so. . . ."—" and me," added a small brother of one of them.   But his interruption passed unheeded. Again, a small boy asked a very obvious question.   His elder brother commented in a tone of good-natured contempt, " The fool enquires ! "

Such examples have no point beyond demonstrating the informality of the relationship in these youthful groups.

Sentiment for a brother as for other relatives is shown in funeral dirges which commemorate his death or separation from him.   Though the songs are of a formal type and often embody much trite phraseology, they indicate what is conceived to be the appropriate attitude of affection in such circumstances.   One such example may be given here ; others will be found in Chapter VIII.

This is a dirge which Fetasi, the father of the present Ariki Kafika, composed to his father and brothers, who were lost at sea on a tragic voyage to Anuta when some of the finest Tikopia seamen went down.

The song is unusual in having three extra intermediate stanzas. In the original it runs :

Tafito : Te matayi fakatiu e tatara
Moria o kave

Kupu : E oku taina
E tatāyi i te foŋāvaka

Kupu : Furi o fetaŋisi ki taumuri
Oro ki oi E!

Kupu : I ei nānā ki te riu
Manu vare ka tau mai

Kupu : Ne riele riele
Ki foŋa te peau
Ka tu mai

Safe : Vaea moi se foe
Ma fakatu mai o te ra mau.

Translation :

The wind of the south is fierce
The canoe is driven, carrying

My brothers who
Are wailing on the deck of the vessel.

They turn to weep together towards the stern
They go to him (their father) O!

O! There they bow their heads into the hull
Floating birds who will be cast up.

Riele, riele
On the crest of the foam
They will stand.

Separate me a paddle
And set up the sail firm.

The general sense of the dirge is clear, though it is difficult without long explanation to convey the exact shade of meaning given by the choice of such words as *tatara* and *manu vare*. The last stanza needs some interpretation. It is really *tauaŋutu*, a taunt, to the vessels of sa Taumako, who were on the same voyage. They did not go and pick up the crew of the foundered vessel, but returned to shore in fear of their own lives. The composer asks ironically that one paddle at least should be picked out for him—that is, sa Taumako might have saved one of his brothers ! Each member of a crew may be referred to as a paddle, much as we speak of a " good oar " in a boat. Reference to the sail being set up firm carries on the same idea. It is the Tikopia custom, if the fleet returns with its full complement, to come in with all sail set. If there is bad news aboard—*te roŋo pariki*—the sail is set, then lowered, set up again, lowered again, and so on, as the vessels approach shore. By this primitive signalling device the watching relatives are warned to prepare for the worst.

Between classificatory brothers who are fairly close kin the bond is very real. Mutual confidence and assistance are given, as between the sons of two actual brothers, or with equal weight, between the sons of two sisters. Whether correctly or not, such ties are frequently invoked as a reason for action which seems to want some justification. During the ceremonies of Uta at one season the Ariki Kafika was annoyed because none of his elders came to stay with him, as was their duty. They all had excuses. Among others Pa Porima refused to go ostensibly because the chief had spoken crossly about his *taina*, Pae Sao, the mothers of these two being related. The excuse may have been used partly as a cover for disinclination to face the solitude and mosquitoes of Uta, but the fact that it was adduced shows that such kinship ties are held in repute. In ordinary life Pa Porima and Pae Sao see a great deal of each other, exchange confidences, seek each other's aid in co-operative activities, and make frequent gifts of food to each other's households. When Pa Porima revealed to me his kava ritual, it was Pae Sao whom he invited to assist him, and not his own relatives on the male side. This is of the more significance since the former is of Kafika clan and the latter of Tafua ; their religious affiliations are different and might be expected to act as a barrier to such familiarity.

One characteristic feature of the relation of " brothers " is their freedom of conversation. Par excellence, they are the persons who may joke together and make obscene remarks to each other. The *faifakakata*, the jest, is regarded as eminently proper between persons of this standing, no matter how close or how distant their kinship may be. The bond of terminological brotherhood stretches even across the gulf which separates chief and commoner, and the two of them may crack a lewd joke together without constraint. On one occasion I was walking with the Ariki Kafika from Uta back over the path up to Te Rua to his hut in Toŋa, when we passed the orchard of Pae Sao. He and some of his kinsfolk were sitting there after their work. All the principals present were brothers through various ties, and with one accord they fell upon each other with obscene chaff. Epithets

of " Big testicles !"   " You are the enormous testicles ! " flew back
and forth to the accompaniment of hilarious laughter. I was
somewhat surprised at the vigour of the badinage, for the Ariki
Kafika, as the most respected chief of the island, has a good deal
of sanctity attaching to him, even in everyday life. However,
this did not save him, and he took it in good part, adopting
the *tu quoque* method of reply. A point of interest was that the
laughter seemed almost hysterical and probably covered a certain
strain, since Pae Sao and the chief regarded each other with some
suspicion at the time.

This incident appears to suggest that their conduct may be
properly interpreted as evidence of a joking relationship which,
as in some Amerindian tribes, involves a definite obligation to
jest with specified relatives. The relationship of brothers, however,
is not of this type. The joking, even on this occasion, was quite
optional ; it is a socially recognized permission, not a prescription,
and there is no sense of duty involved. Rough jesting may be the
best means of tiding over a tense or delicate situation, as in this
case, but that does not constitute it a norm of behaviour. Brothers
often meet socially without introducing any spice of humour into
their conversation.

An excellent treatment of " jesting relationships " has been given
by Dr Margaret Mead on the basis of her work in Manus.[1]   In
particular she shows how the degree of familiarity differs between
various types of kin, and in accordance with the nearness of relationship, seniority and other factors. Her inclusion of a very wide range
of behaviour in the " jesting " category, and her formal definition of
the phenomenon seem, however, to be open to certain objections.
To quote : " the jesting relationship may be defined as a relationship
within which are permitted words and actions which, performed in
any other relationship, would arouse the anger of the person with
whom one jested, the parents or spouse of that person, or the spirits."
The citation of absence of anger as the criterion of classification would
seem somewhat inadequate were it not based explicitly on the Manus
point of view. In other societies such as Tikopia shame may be the
criterion, and in fact the permissibility of anger between kinsfolk
may be one of the elements in their freedom of intercourse. Even in
Manus itself anger does appear to rise at times within the jesting sphere
(*op. cit.* 251, 255). Logically, by definition, the relationship in
such cases ceases then to be of the jesting order, which would mean
that it was governed by personal fluctuating considerations, not by

[1] " Kinship in the Admiralty Islands," *American Museum of Natural History,
Anthropological Papers*, XXXIV, 1934, 243-255.

social rule, as it certainly is. Again, to use simply *permissibility* to jest without reference to the *social expectation* or even tinge of compulsion which obtains as the criterion for classification, means that all phenomena on the neutral ground of general familiarity or lack of constraint are included ; the real distinction between this and the exercise of specific privileges is then obscured.

What has been said regarding the attitude of brothers to each other applies also very much to the case of sisters, though here my information is scanty. In childhood and adolescence the elder is guide, guardian and censor to the younger, and there are no restraints on their conversation. A frequent topic of interest and badinage between them is their sexual life, and accusations of loss of virginity or of being common to all the young men of the place are hurled at each other in quarrels.

FAMILIARITY BETWEEN BROTHER AND SISTER

In domestic affairs brother and sister co-operate. Each fulfils the tasks in his or her particular sphere, but they meet in the common work of the household, as in the handling of food around the oven. Critical comments and peremptory orders fly from one to the other, but these are in the general spirit of Tikopia conversation and indicate neither animus or attempt at enforcing subordination. Either party shows a sturdy independence of thought and action, and it is as common to hear a sister call her brother a fool as contrariwise. For instance, the Tikopia pay great attention to the minutiae of apportioning gifts, as on the occasion of incision or funeral ceremonies, and a person of standing in the family is put in charge of the arrangements. After the death of Pa Maevetau came the distribution of fish-hooks and other goods for services rendered to the mourners. Pa Raŋifuri, as eldest son of the Ariki Tafua, who was brother to the dead man, was carefully handing out the shares to each person with much pondering, when his sister, disliking his style of doing it, commented in tones quite audible through the crowded house, " Look at the simpleton distributing there." No one took any special notice of her remark, which was a normal kind of criticism.

When they are young, children are much given to supplementing the commands of their elders. If a small girl is sent to fetch a fire-stick, or to fill the water-bottles, her elder brother or sister is apt to reinforce the order. " Mind father ! " or " Mind grandfather " is a warning frequently given by one child to another who is in danger of infringing the proprieties by standing in front of its elders.

The relation of brother to sister stands to some degree in contrast to that of brothers or sisters alone. Ordinary conversation is easy enough between siblings of the opposite sex, but it is supposed to avoid any obscene or sexual reference. When the young folk meet on the beach in the evening and gather in groups to talk, no stories of a suggestive kind should be told in the presence of a brother and sister; one or the other should go away. In practice, however, this rule is often overlooked, and so long as the language is not too specific, public opinion is not really outraged. It is said by the natives that in olden times brothers and sisters were more careful than nowadays, but it is possible that this statement represents only an idealization of *le temps perdu* and an attempt to condone the incompatibility between practice and theory. The term " avoidance " can be used only in its widest sociological sense to describe the brother-sister relationship in Tikopia, and the rules governing their social intercourse are certainly much less stringent than those in Tonga or Ontong Java on the one hand, or in the Banks Islands on the other. This is where individual temperament enters; some people are more delicate-minded than others, and walk away at the first hint of impropriety; others wait on and listen greedily in the presence of their sex-opposite until someone reminds the party of these incongruous elements and the conversation is turned into safer channels.

The love affairs of a sister are likewise supposed to be outside the purview of a brother and vice versa. A brother is the guardian of his sister's morals to the extent that if she conceives as the result of an intrigue, he will generally try to take some action. It is usually more practical for him to do so than the father. But apart from this he keeps clear of his sister's sweethearting, as she of his, and refrains from taking notice of that which he may accidentally observe. Into a house placed at the disposal of lovers came Mairuŋa one evening. He found there his friend Koroamanoŋi with a girl by his side. "Who is that?" he asked, but received only a giggle in reply. Recognizing the voice of his sister he cursed her—" May your father eat filth " and hastily withdrew. The tale was spread as an amusing incident through the youth of the village, from whom I heard it.

This avoidance of sex matters in conversation between brother and sister is not associated with equal bodily avoidance. Brother and sister may take part freely in all joint household affairs, tend the oven together, eat together, sit together, and even more strange, sleep side by side, covered by the one blanket. When the wife of my neighbour Pa Taitai was soon to have a child, she slept some distance away from him, while his sister lay next to him on the floor of the house. This evokes no comment from the Tikopia; it is quite normal. In Tonga and some other Oceanic groups such behaviour would be most distasteful, even savouring of incest.[1]

Pa Teva advanced a practical explanation for this proximity of brother and sister at night. They sleep side by side he said in order that a strange man, wishing to have relations with the girl, will be afraid of disturbing her brother, and so will not come near her. In some cases this precaution may be advisable, but it can hardly be of general necessity. The custom of outsiders stealing sexual intercourse, as in the *moe totolo* of Samoa, hardly obtains in Tikopia, and interference from men in the household is unlikely without some degree of connivance on the girl's part. And if she is willing, she can meet her lover in the usual way in a canoe-house or an old clearing in the forest.

In Tikopia incest between brother and sister is abhorred, and often stated to be impossible ; its occurrence is denied point-blank by most people. Sometimes, however, an informant will admit that the temptation may be too much for a man, and that he may yield to an overpowering urge for sexual satisfaction. Such conduct is always represented as the fruit of his momentary sex passion, not the attainment of a long-cherished desire. It is the presence of an accessible female that is held to be the cause of the incest, not the wish to embrace the sister as such. A characteristic statement on this whole matter is that given by Pa Teva. He began by denying that a man would have relations with his sister. Then he went on to qualify this, first by saying, " An occasional man only, when his sister is different (*i.e.* classificatory), sleeps, sleeps, and does it to her." Then he allowed the breach with the real sister. " For true brother and sister to live together is not good ; if they marry (a euphemism here for ' copulate,' they are never allowed actually to marry) they will go off to sea (in suicide). But brother and sister who are different, it is good, and yet bad." Further discussion of this problem, including analysis of the meaning of the " goodness and badness " of the marriage of close kin is given in the latter part of Chapter IX.

Cases of real incest appear to be very rare. The freedom of social intercourse has apparently some effect in moderating the incidence of sex intercourse. The native assumption is that sex relations being impossible, or nearly so, there need be no objection to ordinary intimacy. The same point of view is brought out in another way, namely, in the practice of changing garments when they get wet during the day's work. Women show more delicacy in this than do men,

---

[1] *E.g.* Mead, *Manu'a*, 138-9 ; Gifford, *Tonga*, 21-2 ; Hogbin, *Law and Order in Polynesia* (Ontong Java), 105 ; Codrington, *Melanesians* (New Hebrides), 232 ; Malinowski, *Sexual Life of Savages* (Trobriands), 437-40.

retiring into the oven-house or the adjacent bush for the purpose, whereas the latter change in the presence of female relatives. If a man has been fishing, for instance, he comes up to his house, removes his wet waistcloth, and covering his genitalia with his hand—a practice in which the Tikopia are peculiarly expert in preserving their modesty —hands the garment with no trace of embarrassment to his sister to wring it out for him and lay it on the sand in the sun to dry. Upon request also she brings him a fresh cloth, with no discomposure. All this takes place irrespective of whether there are other people in the house or not. In the presence of affinal relatives only would such an act be proscribed.

The curious thing is that more freedom in this matter exists between a man and his own sister than between classificatory kin. Native opinion differs on the point, some men stating that it is improper to hand one's waistcloth to a distant " sister," " *e tapu*," it is prohibited ; others holding that it is correct enough to do so occasionally, but not habitually. If such a service were desired regularly, then it would be thought that the man desired sexual relations with the woman. The diversity of behaviour and comment indicates that latitude in personal interpretation of the standards of etiquette which is found in respect of all the less rigid moral rules of the society. The fact of whether the woman is from one's own village or is a stranger, whether she happens to be an adoptive daughter residing in the family, and the like, influences the particular line of conduct which a man takes towards her in such matters. The freedom towards the real sister is shown in the following statement by Kavakiua, a young bachelor and a very intelligent informant.

" When a man is undressing and his true sister is sitting at his side, it is proper, after he is undressed, to give his waistcloth to her to go and spread it out. As for his distant sister, whatever she may be, it may be given to her to go and spread out ; or if not he goes then to hang it up himself. If he goes and gives it continually, gives it continually to her, then his evil mind climbs up, they two copulate. As to his true sister, his evil mind does not climb up, because they two were born from their one mother."

The generalization of the Tikopia that the closeness of blood relationship is a barrier to sex intimacy is then no idle theory, but is acted upon in very practical fashion. An interesting corollary to this proposition is found in the use of terms of kinship as symbols of a sexual relationship. By emphasizing the kinship tie it is implied that intercourse is not possible or desired. This occurs as between distant relatives, where there are no incest prohibitions to be regarded. Thus if a man has as a classificatory " mother," a girl of about his own age, he will normally address her by the *taraŋa fakaepa* (respectful speech) of " *Nau E !* " " Mother ! " If he uses her personal name then it is an indication that he is not averse to sex relations with her, or may be thinking of approaching her with a view to marriage. She may rebuke him, saying in derision, " Let the two of us, mother and son unite." This shames the man, who will then drop the less formal mode of address unless he is really in love with the girl, when he will persist in spite of all rebuffs.

In one of the most sacred myths of the Tikopia an incident of a similar type occurs, but with the initiative coming from the female. The tale relates how a lad went down to surf at Namo, leaving his *maro*, his waistcloth, near a canoe-house. When he returned from the beach it had disappeared. Peering round he located it in the possession of a woman at the back of the shed. He called out to her :

" Bring me, mother, my *maro*."

" Come and take it away," she replied.

" Bring me, grandmother, my *maro*."

" Come and take it away."

" Bring me, aunt (unmarried mother), my *maro*."

" Come and take it away."

" Bring me, sister, my *maro*."

" Come and take it away."

" Bring me, friend, my *maro*."

" Now that's it then ! "

She brought him his waistcloth, he put it on, took her by the wrist—the formal manner of leading a person, as a bride—and off they went to his house, where they married. The woman had thus forced him through the safe range of kinship terms where services of such intimate kind were without significance, out into the open plain of strangerhood where the sexual factor in their contact became of paramount importance. The fetching of the waistcloth became incorporated into another sphere of reference.

The native correlation between closeness of relationship, freedom of social intercourse and absence of sex disturbance is obviously not complete. It is inconsistent to disregard the sexual aspect in the bodily contacts or proximity of assisting in change of garments or sleeping side by side, which are allowed, while emphasizing it in amusing tales and bawdy conversation, which are prohibited. The consciousness of sex, and sense of shame in that consciousness are kept awake in one direction while they are allowed to lie dormant in another. Is it because the household bodily contacts involve only the immediate persons, the brother and sister, between whom

the presumption is that sex relations are not possible, whereas speech
may quite conceivably bear upon the outside sex life of either of the
parties ?

A reference is sometimes made by a brother to the sex life of his
sister, but only upon provocation. The one case which came to
my notice refers to not a true sister but to a father's brother's daughter.
It concerns a song composed by Kavakiua. His *kave* by pretending
sickness had induced his own bond-friend to visit her and had then
persuaded him to sexual relations with her. The affair became
notorious, since the girl conceived and the status of the several parties
concerned was high. The man in fact was a mission teacher. The
song which is *tauaŋutu*, a song of derision, is as follows :—

> *Tafito :* *Te fofine taka*
> *Fai tokaroto ra*
> *Faufau-ki-o-tane*
> *Fakamate ma te fakaroiroi.*

> *Kupu :* *Uvio mai ko te roŋo*
> *Te vaka o Aro*
> *Ku o ifo ko nau taka*
> *Ne mate ku ŋasue*
> *Ko nau taka ne mate ku mosike.*

The song was made ostensibly about a *kai*, a legendary tale. This
concerns a woman Faufau-ki-o-tane and her husband Aro. The man
went on a voyage, leaving her pregnant. People soon began to tell
her she had been deserted, though he had told her he would return.
At last, finding her life made a burden by clacking tongues she pretended to be ill and refused all food, though in fact she was fed
secretly by her sister at night. At last she " died." The funeral
arrangements were put in hand, but her sister objected to the burial
the next day as is the custom and told the people to wait ten days.
To this they gave assent, and each night the " corpse " was fed. The
sixth day came and with it came the canoe of Aro. When the vessel
was sighted, the sister climbed on the roof of the house where the
mourning was in progress and sang :

> *Ka te taŋata ko Aro*
> *Ka te fafine ko*
> *Faufau-ki-o-tane*
> *Nea ne mate kove na.*

> Now the man is Aro
> And the woman is
> Faufau-ki-o-tane
> Thou—that which hast died there.

People reproached her for singing a composition not of the dirge type while the wailing for the dead was proceeding, but she continued. And as she sang the toes of the " corpse " moved. She sang more and the foot moved, then the fingers, then the hand. By this time the crowd had observed the phenomenon and told her to sing on. Then the eyes of the " dead " woman opened and at last she rose up. By this time the canoe of Aro was close inshore. His wife went down to the beach, jumped aboard and off they went. The people by this time had understood the deception. They said to each other, " *Ku fakaroiroi*," She has been pretending."

We can now comprehend the point of the song of Kavakiua.

> The unmarried woman
> Made herself secretly then a
> Faufau-ki-o-tane
> And in pretence caused herself to die.
>
> When the news was brought to her
> That the canoe of Aro
> Had come over, the spinster aunt
> Who died now stirred
> The spinster aunt who died now rose up.

The term *nau taka*, which is ordinarily applied to an unmarried woman of one kinship grade higher than the speaker, equivalent to a mother's sister, I have translated here as " spinster aunt," since the use of it by Kavakiua for his own " sister " conveys a suggestion of derision. After the girl had initiated the intrigue in this fashion, he saw that she had been shamming, and so cast his dance song in this form. Like her prototype of old she rose up from her bed at the entry of a man ! When questioned by people as to what his composition referred, he always answered from policy that it was simply a versification of the ancestral tale. The girl herself, however, knew his meaning, while many others suspected it.

If an unmarried girl becomes pregnant and is not taken in wedlock to her lover's house, then it will probably be her brothers who will take action against him. They force her to divulge his name and then publicly demonstrate against him or offer him violence if they meet him. He on his part endeavours to avoid them. When Kasoaveteiteraki was got with child by Pa Faiaki, her brother Pa Nukureŋa, catching sight of the man in the village one morning, hurled a coral rock at him and hit him on the shoulder. There was no retaliation, since the lover recognized that he was in the wrong and would receive no public support. The girl in such case is not driven out of her parents' or brother's house, but remains a member of the family.

Her child may be reared by them, as was that of Tosara, or quietly put out of the way at birth, as happened in the case mentioned immediately above.

The further position of brother and sister in sexual affairs will be demonstrated later in Chapters VI and IX in connection with marriage, and the status of mother's brother and father's sister; their relations in later life will be gathered from other chapters.

Sentiment between brother and sister appears to consist not in verbal demonstrations or caresses—rather the opposite seems to be common practice—but in small gifts and services exchanged, assistance against external opposition or criticism and visits to each other when separated. And as with other relationships there are dirges which express their sentiments, canalize them and indicate at least the formal propriety of brotherly and sisterly affection.

CHAPTER VI

THE KIN OF FATHER AND MOTHER

IN a small native community it would be impossible to follow the advice given to Henry de Montherlant by an aristocratic old lady of his family, " *Surtout, ne pas se faire de relations*." A person cannot escape the ties of consanguinity, and primitive kinship is notable for the range of its recognition of these ties and the variety and intensity of the obligations borne by them. Tikopia is no exception to this rule, and it is with relatives outside the immediate family circle that a person goes through some of the most important experiences of his life. So far-flung are the ties of kinship that, as the natives themselves say, the whole island is " one group of relatives."

In discussing the nuclear structure of Tikopia kinship—the group of children and their parents—a certain amount of incidental material relating to other kin has been included, since their presence is a conditioning factor in actual life. Since also the type of behaviour to persons outside the immediate family circle is so definitely connected with that towards those within the family, I have considered from this point onwards the position of classificatory kin in conjunction with that of closer corresponding kin.

There are two approaches to the study of such phenomena. One, the synchronic, consists in starting from an individual at a given moment and tracing out his or her recognition of kin, the terms in use and the behaviour to each person included within the kinship range. The other, of the diachronic kind, considers in greater detail the process by which this recognition comes into being. Starting with an individual at an early age a record is made of the manner in which kinsfolk come into the orbit of the child, the steps involved in acquiring one kind of relationship after another, until the social equipment is complete. Obviously, these are not separate branches of study; a complete diachronic observation would be simply a synthesis of a great number of synchronic ones. From the comparatively short space of time available to the anthropologist in the field, and the ordinary limitations of human observation, a systematic record of the kinship behaviour of any individual over an adequate period has not been made. The valuable material recorded by Malinowski [1] and by Margaret Mead [2] covers a relatively brief time in the social evolution of their subjects, and is necessarily fragmentary, consisting of sections of the social milieu taken as opportunity offered.

---

[1] B. Malinowski, *Psychology of Kinship* (unpublished).
[2] M. Mead, *Coming of Age in Samoa* ; *Kinship in the Admiralty Islands* ; *The Changing Culture of an Indian Tribe*.

My own record in this direction is no more systematic. It consists partly of observations made on the spot, partly of native statements about the behaviour of their children. I concentrated my attention not on the associations of any particular individual, but on securing a selection of examples from a wide field. The material of the following chapters consists of a synthetic record, the fusion of the results of extensive rather than intensive enquiry.

CLASSIFICATORY PARENTS

Tikopia kinship is of course of the type known as classificatory. The material relations between a child and his or her " fathers " who are near kindred depend to a great extent upon factors of residence and the social contacts that this implies. If, as is frequent, they happen to live as neighbours or in adjacent villages, they visit each other often, and the child learns to include its father's brothers and male cousins generously in its economic scheme. It runs errands for them, helps them in its small way in gardening and fishing, shins up palms to pluck green coconuts for drinking, and performs many other little services. As an example, Soakimaru, a lad of seven years or so, is going to fill the family water-bottles. " Reach me the water-bottle of Father," he calls, and takes it away with the rest. Here, as it happens, he is speaking of Pa Teva, his father's father's brother's son, though one could not tell either from his actions or the inflexions in his voice that it was not his own father. The context of persons and property supplies the clue.

Instances of the disobedience of children may be compared in this connection. The native dictum is that a child obeys its father—" listens to him," as the people express it. Yet this is a rule to which many exceptions are found, and the frequency of non-compliance appears to be much the same in the case of classificatory as of real parents. Some material has been given already in Chapter V, but here are two more small incidents. A father told his young son to help carry a food bowl down to the sea to clean it. The child frowned and grunted. The father tried to insist, whereon the child trotted off along the beach without doing what he was bid. " What is this thing, may its father eat filth, that continues to dodge off ? May its father eat filth ! " bawled its parent after it. This was uttered in exasperation but with no sign of real anger (Text S. 14). The other instance occurred in the house of Pa Nukuomanu, where dwelt his classificatory child, Foraurakei, daughter of Pa Raŋifuri. As they were preparing food the man said to her, " Go and get me the pounder," which was in the cook-house close by. " I don't want to," she said dispassionately, and did not move. Finally someone else fetched it.

Obedience is not a strictly codified obligation in Tikopia, as it is in some communities. Passive resistance is the method generally adopted when a command is not obeyed; the code of respect to a "father" renders active opposition out of the question. Even in small things a man is usually careful to "speak fair" to a classificatory parent. Pa Fenuatara asked Pa Siamano, his father's cousin, if there was enough coconut cream in a pudding just put in the oven. "Was it made by children? The Ariki and I made it," he answered angrily. "*E laui*," answered Pa Fenuatara soothingly, the equivalent of "That's all right."

All men spoken of as "father" are treated with formal respect. Their personal names are not mentioned and contact with their heads is avoided. In playing *fetaki*, a duelling game somewhat akin to singlesticks, a man is careful, if opposed to one who is a "father" of his, even in the widest classificatory sense, not to tap him on the head with his sago-leaf shaft weapon—the normal aim of the contestants. Instead, if he penetrates his guard, he taps him in the ribs. With one's true father one does not play such a game at all.

In conformity with the usual rule, conversation is restrained in the presence of such relatives, though age, rank and degree of everyday association have much to do with the stringency with which this is observed. Even persons connected merely by a courtesy bond are in the same category. Since I was nominally a son in the houses of the two principal chiefs of the island, I was addressed by appropriate kinship terms by the members of their families. One evening I met at the watering-place of Matautu a man whom I did not know well but who was a classificatory son of Pa Raŋifuri. Unthinking, I tossed a common joke at him in greeting. A serious-minded individual, he was perturbed. He reminded me of our respective status. "Friend, do not speak thus. We two are *tau mana* (in the father-son relationship)." But considerable variation occurred, primarily because I was a white man. Another young man of similar standing used to treat me with much more levity, and with but a formal protest would discuss with relish the intimate personal affairs of the youth of the village. Again one day, when endeavouring to establish a point of family relationship, I pressed Mairuŋa to tell me the name of an old man who lived in his household. At first he would not say, but finally gave me the name, and then, laughing in a shamefaced way, turned to a friend who was with him and cried, "I have spoken the name of my father." As it was on a trip round the lonely northern end of the island, and the three of us were far away from any dwellings, he gave himself more than usual latitude. Then the old man was from Anuta, and by no means closely connected, so this really made the matter one of comparatively small moment. He certainly would not have uttered the name of his own father, even under these conditions. On the few occasions on which I recorded the personal name of a man from the lips of his son, it was when the father was dead and the name formed part of a ritual series for invocation. Such a name is usually given softly, with a hesitant air.

As far as the codified obligations are concerned, it is difficult to see any difference between the way in which a boy treats his own father and that in which he treats his father's brothers. He seems to observe the rules of personal *tapu* as strictly in the one case as in the other, in speech he maintains the same discretion, he obeys with equal alacrity or dilatoriness. Where the differences are to be found are in the intimacies of the domestic life, the greater frequency of conversation with the father, the appeal to him first in a group of men of equal status, the tendency when young to keep by him in any gathering, the direct assumption of responsibility for his support in old age, and the more rigid interpretation of the rules of mourning at his death. No generalization can be absolute in this field; the personal equation enters so largely into the situation. As pointed out long ago by Radcliffe-Brown,[1] and by Malinowski,[2] the intensity of behaviour tends to vary with the nearness of relationship. When a man dies, his " sons " will wail the appropriate dirge for him, tear the cheeks, beat the breast and exhibit the other conventional signs of mourning. The real son remains in seclusion for many weeks, bathes only at night, cuts his hair, observes stringent food taboos and for a very long time does not dance. A brother's son will do all these things too, but his period of abstinence will be shorter and his list of permissible foods longer. A classificatory son may perhaps do none of these things ; if of distant relationship, he will go off to work the next morning in complete cheerfulness. In each case their conduct is approved by the community because, as the natives themselves say, their relationship to the dead is not identical; the society itself recognizes a gradation of duty. But the variation of behaviour according to propinquity of kinship is not a complete statement of the position : family conditions differ, as do individual temperament and residential arrangements. Moreover, the differences in informal behaviour increase with the remoteness of the kinship tie in much greater proportion than do those in formal behaviour. The personal,

---

[1] " Three Tribes of Western Australia," *J.R.A.I.*, xliii, 1913, 150, 159.

[2] *Sexual Life of Savages*, 1929, 431-444.

non-codified aspect varies greatly with nearness or distance of the kinship bond, proximity of residence or number of persons involved in the kinship situation.

A native kinship system of the Tikopia type—perhaps of any type—does not provide a final classification of relatives ; in so far as it purports to do so it is inconsistent. It groups relatives of varying genealogical status together under single terms ; it insists that they be treated on a basis of equality ; then it allows of the relaxation or breach of some obligations when the tie is weak, and actually provides for release in other cases where such is imperative. The kinship system, being one attempt at social regulation, has to co-ordinate theory with practice.

THE ADHERING CHILD

The behaviour of a child in the family is apt to be influenced considerably by mechanisms which detach it from its parents and attach it to other members of the wider kinship group. The first of these is the practice on the part of these elders of tutoring it in infancy to have regard for them and to turn towards them (*fakarata*) rather than towards its father and mother. The object of this in particular is that the babe may not cry constantly when its parents are absent. While the child is still unable to walk or speak, a brother of its father, maybe, bends over it as it lies on the floor of the house, and fondling and nuzzling it, speaks to it thus : " You remember me. I am your father. When I go away you come and seek for me. Do not cry for your parents, cry for me . . ." and so on. This action of murmuring instruction to the babe in an intimate manner has a term of its own. It is known as *fakasanisani*. The native theory, based upon practical observation, is that familiarity breeds attachment. " The child desires its father to look constantly upon it, its true father only," said Pa Fenuatara. By the term " true father " (*mana maori*) he meant, as he explained, not only the male parent, but also brothers and unmarried cousins of close kinship in the male line (*mana maroa*), who constantly play with the child and thus become the objects of its affection. But at the same time the primary interest still tends to lie in the original foci of sentiment. " The chief desire of the babe— its own parents " (*Te matuā fifia te memea ; ona ke mātua*) is the *leitmotiv* of the discussion of these kinship attitudes.

Two social forces are thus in opposition within the family group. The one, as the natives themselves recognize, is the major desire of the child for its own parents ; the other is the artificial barrier raised against this by the other male members of the family who endeavour, by rendering themselves familiar and necessary to the babe, to seduce a portion of its affection. The interest of this to the anthropologist is the conscious realization of the Tikopia of the factors involved, and their power of formulating the issues—for the situation which I have represented here was given to me in native statements as well as observed in operation.

The other mechanism which has the effect of breaking apart the individual family is the custom whereby some member of the wider group of relatives—the *kano a paito*—bears off a child from the married pair and brings it up in his own household. This is not adoption in the true sense, since the child retains its own family titles and rights to inheritance—the opposite of a Maori practice, where by adoption the child gains land rights in its new family and loses them in the old. There is nothing in Tikopia resembling the *ahi ka* of the Maori whereby an ancestral land interest is revived by the migration of the child adopted. In this community it is merely a severance for ordinary social and economic purposes, and the child goes frequently to its own family lands to bring back food to its residence. The child so taken is known as a *tama fakapiki* in its new household, literally an " adhering child." " It is held that I adhere to my father," said one lad; the person to whom he was attached being in this case his true father's elder brother. Altogether I recorded eighteen cases of children clearly seconded for services in this way and living apart from their parents, but there are a number of borderline cases where the separation is not so marked. Rakeivave, for instance, son of Pa Fenuatara, was supposed to belong to the household of Pa Taramoa, but he spent quite as much time with his own father. There is much gradation in the degree of " adherence," and only a proportion of children, as a rule the elder ones, are so treated. The child is normally removed from its parents as soon as it is weaned. The relative who takes it is usually a " brother " of the husband or, more rarely, of the wife, and not a very distant connection. In some cases a child is brought up in the household of a different clan, this being the result of neighbourliness or bond-friendship. When a man loses a son, it is common for a son of a near relative to come and live in his house. After the death of Noakena, a son of Pa Nukuone came and stayed for a time in the dwelling of Pa Raŋifuri, though he did not remain there. Childless couples frequently provide themselves with a boy and a girl, desolate women with a lad.

The relationship is not always of the parent-child order. *Kave fakapiki* (adhering sisters or brothers) and *makopuna fakapiki* (adhering grandchildren) are also known. The late Ariki Taumako was an " adhering grandchild " of the famous Pu Niukapu, the fishing expert, who taught him the lore of the sea banks.   At present in the house Fareumata lives Fuarua, the surviving resident member of the family, with Tarimuna, his "adhering sister" from Raŋimarepe; both are of the great "house" of Raropuka, but not close relatives.   They are unmarried, approaching middle age, and are affirmed to lead a blameless life.

This institution of the *tama fakapiki* has the effect of providing a child in a house where otherwise there is none to help in the work, but the natives do not always regard it primarily as a device for assisting barren couples or increasing the household strength.   This is shown by the fact that though a man's eldest child is often taken by his younger brother who has as yet no offspring of his own, in other cases the child is added to an already existing set.   It has no inferiority in the family to the real children.   On the contrary the natives describe the custom as the *fakapere* of the child—a mark of respect to it and its parents.   Moreover it is not practised in the case of a man who is not liked, who deals badly by his relatives, quarrels continually with them, and the like ; people do not come and take the children of such an one to their homes.   But if he is generous and feeds his *kano a paito*, then his children are sought by his kinsfolk.   At the back of this is the idea, quite clearly expressed in frequent statements to me by natives, that it is bad for a child to adhere only to its parents ; it belongs to the larger group, the *kano a paito*, and must stand in an equal relation to all therein.

The native point of view in regard to the relation of individual family to wider family group may then be put in the form of three propositions :

In the first place, there is a definite preference of a child for its own parents—they are its " chief desire."

Secondly, this affection, based upon intimate association, should be to some extent alienated in favour of the wider group of relatives. Two mechanisms are employed to part the child from its parents, both depending for their success upon the principle which gives the parents their place in the child's regard—namely, constant association. The child may be severed from the household of its father and mother at an early age and attached to another ; failing this, or supplemented by this, its interest is attracted by other members of its family circle who thus seduce its budding affections.   The parents, it may be noted, regard this with approval, and the *tama fakapiki* custom is even erected into a mark of confidence in them and honour to their offspring.

Finally, the basic social motive in this is to preserve as far as possible uniformity of conduct and attitudes within the larger social group and not allow the bonds of the individual family to become so strong as to threaten the wider harmony.   This idea is put in practical form by the Tikopia in such statements as that it is bad for the child to be attached to its parents alone, since when they are away from the house—in the cultivations or out on the reef—it cries and will not be comforted by anyone else. This is a nuisance to the relatives, and to the parents themselves, who are always liable to be disturbed at their work or rest. They approve then that the child shall undergo a *social weaning* as well as a physiological one.

Here we have a realistic attitude towards kinship, a practical analysis and synthesis of elements, an appreciation of the bases of family sentiment which have not often been remarked among a primitive people.

Incidentally, the facts just adduced bear on the hypothesis of communism in children which has been put forward by Rivers and later by Briffault. It seems at first sight that in Tikopia the individual family is not a real entity, that it is replaced by a wider social unit. This is not the case. The wider kinship group is not self-sufficient and stable ; it has to be bolstered up by conscious means which wrench aside the most intimate ties and sever parent and child. The natives use the term *motu*, meaning " to part," as a rope does, strand by strand, when speaking of this disorientation. In this sense of a conscious detachment from parental ties for the sake of practical ends one might speak of a communistic attitude, but this is a different conception from that of Rivers. The affiliation of the child to the larger group is not the only, nor even the predominant feature in its group alignment, and its attachment to the members of this group is still individual and personal, not vague and undifferentiated to them as a whole. To the Tikopia, affection for parents is a fact, and one which should not be allowed to dominate the social life.

THE KINDNESS OF GRANDPARENTS

Other relatives also have their interest in the children of a household. The habit of " patrilocal " residence means that the father's parents usually see more of a child than do its mother's parents, though both have equal claims upon it. In the early days, if the young people are living either in the house of the man's father or adjacent to it, the paternal grandmother keeps a watchful eye on the infant and is free with advice to her daughter-in-law upon the best methods of child-rearing. The interest of the maternal grandparents in the child is acknowledged by frequent visiting. The young couple take the child and go to stay with the wife's people, or she may go herself and leave the husband at home, or one or other of the grandparents may visit them. For example, when Tekila was young his mother's father, Pa Nukutai, came and stayed in Raroakau for a week or so.

A considerable degree of affection for a grandchild is displayed by the Tikopia. They treat it with indulgence, caress it and make it little gifts of food and the like. During a ceremony I saw Pa Fetu nursing his daughter's baby. From time to time the mother bent forward and chucked it under the chin. The father was sitting by, but taking no part in this. As the child began to cry the grandparent, holding it in his arms, bent over and pretended affectionately to bite its cheek. It settled down for a time, but soon started to cry again. This time the mother took it and gave it the breast, which effectually pacified it.

At times this affection acquires a possessive tenor and the grandparents contend with the parents to keep the child in their house. When Nau Taitai had her second confinement, she lived in her mother's house at Rofaea. One day she came to Matautu to visit her son Tekila and wanted to take him back with her. Nau Raroakau, her mother-in-law objected, saying that she would wail if he were taken away. The child himself cried because he wanted to go with his mother, but he was finally left behind. On the whole he was happy enough during her absence : he could neither walk nor talk properly, so was dependent on adult support, and appeared quite content to be carried about by his father's sister and a brother of his mother's who was staying there. The mother was not away for long. She returned permanently a couple of days after her former visit. On the same topic the Ariki Kafika said, " In this land great is the affection for the grandchild, indeed. One dwells, and does not look upon the grandchild, one does not eat ; but one dwells, and looks upon the grandchild, one reaches hither food and eats." This is not pretence on his own part. Whenever he is away from his home on ceremonial business, as happens for a long period twice a year, he always tries to have a grandchild or two about the dwelling. The young things are company and can be useful in fetching water or fire-sticks or taking messages. But it is more than their services that he desires ; he is genuinely fond of them. Sometimes argument occurs with the parents over his wish to keep them by him. The father wants to take a child home, the grandfather objects, and puts a decided negative to all his son's pleadings. After one such succession of appeals by Pa Taramoa I returned to find the child still there. I asked if the father did not cry for the boy, after the native fashion. " He cries, but I refuse, that the child may stop, " the old man said stoutly.

Friction between parents and grandparents over the children is never really acute. Several reasons tend to prevent this. Firstly, the respect enjoined upon the father and mother towards their own parents, and still more towards their parents-in-law, means that the latter will probably get their way ; this is reinforced by the idea that parent and child should not be too closely bound, and that after all grandparents have some rights in their childrens' offspring.

Formal relations with grandparents on both sides are allowed to be considerably freer than with parents. This is particularly the case in the sphere of conversation, where the proscription on lewd joking and the mention of sexual matters does not hold with the same force. The avoidance of personal names and of bodily contact is also lighter, though some decorum has still to be observed. It may be suggested that the freedom between grandparent and grandchild is to some extent a reflex of the constraint between parent and child. The latter is to be correlated with the authoritarian position of the parent and his or her capacity for active control of affairs. With the waning energies of the grandparent there is a tendency for authority in practical affairs to be resigned, and so there is no hindrance to the growth of an easy familiar relationship with the grandchildren. The difference in age and status does still of course play a part in putting the social weight on the side of the grandparent. In the ordinary Tikopia household a phrase continually addressed to young children is "*A mata tou puna*," " Mind your grandparent," cautioning them not to stand in front of such a relative, crawl about him or wave objects before his face. When the grandfather is a chief, then the child is always made to behave circumspectly to him.

Grandparents usually take some share in regulating the conduct of children in the household, giving advice in ordinary affairs. For instance, two youngsters in Kafika were proposing to go out on a stormy day. Their grandmother said to them sarcastically, " Where are you two going ? The sky is bad ; are you going to look for a house for the two of you ? " The grandfather said, " The path is muddy." Again, the old man spoke to his grandchild Saupuke about personal matters. " When you feel that your belly wishes to excrete, run then to the lake to deposit." The chief was anxious, moreover, about the safety of this child, lest he be drowned in the lake. Once before, on going to bathe, he had come across him in difficulties and pulled him out. Consequently, during the stay of the party in Uta, he gave the child orders to remain on shore. Incidentally, children do sometimes drown in Tikopia, though they learn to swim early. In recent years a girl and a boy lost their lives in the lake, and two boys were drowned in the sea. These were all small children who could not swim properly. The body of one of those in the lake was found by a man who was going to set his nets.

A certain amount of practical and esoteric knowledge may also be imparted by grandparents. Pa Tarairaki once told me how as a boy he asked a *puna* of his (in this case not his own grandfather but a collateral kinsman) for a shark-fishing formula : " Grandfather, where is the formula of the *penu toki* (the clam shell) ? " The old man was pounding his betel in his little mortar, and he continued pounding up and down, then said, " What ? " " I want you to tell me the spell of the *penu toki*." The old man began to pound again. Then he replied, " It is not known to me." After a few moments he said, " But this is it as I have heard it from an old man in Faea. Listen ! "— and he began to recite to the lad.

THE SACREDNESS OF THE FATHER'S SISTER

The sisters of the father stand in a unique position among a child's female kindred. On the one hand, like secondary mothers, they may act as nurses, protectors and mentors, give it food and drink and attend to its other bodily needs ; on the other they are the object of special taboos which stress not the warm intimacy of motherly contacts but authority and the possession of ritual powers akin to those of a father. As far as can be observed, without the practice of a special technique of analysis, the elements of conflict which might be expected to result from this divided attitude find no expression in the ordinary behaviour patterns.

The actual relation of a child to his or her father's sisters depends a great deal upon casual factors of marriage and residence. The younger children tend to see less of the father's sister in her role of substitute mother and more of her, relatively, in that of participant in economic and ritual affairs than do their elder brothers and sisters. While she is young and unmarried she will probably be living in the same house as the child or just next door, and she will be free to devote a great deal of time and solicitude to nursing it. But as she marries and moves away to a house of her own, perhaps in a distant village, and begins to accumulate family cares of her own, her brother's children see her less as domestic guardian and nurse. She is now a frequent visitor, not a resident of the household, and though the intimacy of their relationship does not appear to suffer much in quality, it necessarily diminishes in quantity.

The formal observances remain the same whatever loss the accidents of time may bring to the informal relations. They consist on the part of the child of a series of avoidances—prohibition on the use of the personal name of the father's sister, on indecent conversation in her presence, and most particularly on striking her, or on cursing her by any of those full-mouthed oaths by which the Tikopia are only too prone to express even their lightest emotions. One will not say to her, for example, "May your father eat filth," as one does without much restraint to most of one's blood kin. One would commit a wrong in so doing ; the father's sister is *tapu*, and the family ancestors would see to it that one suffered, probably in the extreme of physical pain.

She partakes indeed of some of the qualities of the father in that, apart from being a representative of his group in social affairs, she also to some extent personifies authority over family property, and may even act as a repository of sacerdotal knowledge. If a man of rank, a chief or elder, sees that his son is young and that he himself is likely to die, then he may decide to make known to his sister the *kava*, the names of his ancestors and gods, that she may tell the lad when he is old enough. She holds it in trust for him ; no case is on record of her having passed it on to her own son in lieu of the rightful heir. The present Ariki Tafua is said to have been instructed in such lore by his father's sister Pufine i Tavi. This of course introduces again the personal factor of differentiation. Only in families of rank does this happen, and normally only the eldest sister would be entrusted with such a sacred duty.

In more ordinary affairs, however, a father's sister may act *in statu patris*. By the Tikopia themselves this dual role is expressed explicitly in their kinship usages. The normal word for father's sister is *masikitaŋa*, and by this she is usually addressed. But on occasion she may be called " *Nau E*," " Mother," or even " *Pa E*," " Father," according to the feeling of her nephew or niece at the time. This last term is apt to be applied particularly if she happens to be the sole remaining representative in her generation of the father's family. As one man said, " There am I here—because no father of mine is still alive, and since my father's sister is living, the only one remaining, then I go and address her as ' Father.' " It was this man, Pa Motuaŋi, who described the father's sister as " the double of the father," " just the same as the father." [1]

This respect for a father's sister and the control she is apt to exercise over the children of her brother are obviously related to an attitude widespread in Western Polynesia and parts of Melanesia.[2]

[1] For a further statement see my article, " Marriage and the Classificatory System of Relationship," *J.R.A.I.*, LX, 242, 1930.

[2] E.g. Rivers, "Father's Sister in Samoa," *Folklore*, XIII, 1902 ; *idem*, "Father's Sister in Oceania," *ibid.* XXI, 1910 ; *idem*, *H.M.S.*, I, 38-40, 204, 222, etc. ; A. B. Deacon, *Malekula*, 83 ; Fortune, *Sorcerers of Dobu*, 20-21 ; Gifford, *Tongan Society*, 17, etc. ; Mead, *Manu'a*, 136-138. Cf. the Trobriands (Malinowski, *Sexual Life of Savages*, 450-451, etc.), where the father's sister is the prototype of " lawful woman." This relative has no special functions among the Maori.

Its sociological implications will be discussed towards the end of this chapter.

PROTECTION BY THE MOTHER'S FAMILY

The major portion of this study so far has been concerned with relatives on the father's side of the house.   This has been a matter of convenience in treatment, since owing to the general habit of a person of living on the ground of his father's people—patrilocal residence in the strict sense—he is apt to see more of them in daily life.   Moreover, apart from a few historic individual exceptions descent, *i.e.* acknowledged membership of the named social groups on a kinship basis, is patrilineal, succession always and inheritance mainly so.   But as has been made abundantly clear by Malinowski, Lowie, Radcliffe-Brown and others, a specific inclination of a society towards one line of transmission of its cultural forms does not mean that others are ignored.   The system of descent in Polynesia is usually described as patrilineal, but everywhere affiliation through females of one kind or another is important.   The Tikopia draw the distinction very sharply : never is a person reckoned in the personnel of his mother's kinship group, and therefore, it is impossible for a title ever to pass outside the male line.   Even where a title is held by a female it passes on her death to her brother's daughter or equivalent relative, not to her own daughter.   In the practically complete genealogical record which I have of the line of succession of the score or so major " houses," there is not a single case of departure from this rule.   Compared with this the Samoan usage, whereby a man from the distaff side of a house can incorporate himself into the group and under favourable circumstances may insinuate himself into the leadership of it as *matai*, seems extremely loose.

Yet in Tikopia the family of one's mother is just as important as that of one's father.   Apart from the informal hospitality and social contacts, one receives from it protection in case of need, assistance both practical and ritual in the crucial public events of one's emergence into maturity, and extensive formal gifts from time to time as long as any member of that group is living.   At death one's body is buried by the mother's folk and the soul taken in charge by her ancestors, purified and conducted to its appropriate heaven.   If one is a man of rank, then some of the mother's family gods are at disposal on earth for one's ritual appeals.

The linkage with the maternal kindred is manifested in certain linguistic expressions, which are analysed later.   This social bond begins even before birth.   Indeed, all unknowing, a child is indebted to some of these folk for a complete reversal of his nascent state, since it is alleged, by physical manipulation on the part of the mother's female relatives, the babe is turned over in her womb. As far as is known it emerges into the world with no grudge against them for this upsetting process ; it might be argued perhaps that the sensations of this pre-natal revolution help to lay the foundation of those amicable relations which ever after mark their reciprocal intercourse. This, however, I must leave to psycho-analysts to determine.

The cordiality between a person and his mother's family is considerable, and is developed by initiative on both sides. Soon after the infant's arrival, if it is not born at her parent's house, the mother takes it on a visit there, and such visits are repeated at frequent intervals until the child is old enough to go alone. The others seek it, too. A grandfather comes to stay with his daughter expressly to satisfy his affection by the sight of his grandchild ; a sister or a brother of the mother comes and bears it off for a night. One of them says, " I have felt affection for my nephew ; I will go now and bring him here that we two may sleep together to-night, and return on the morrow." As the child grows up it becomes accustomed to the freedom of the household in this family. It goes and dwells there from time to time, and will run there for refuge when offended or threatened with punishment at home. This is a mode of behaviour which imitates that of its mother in any disagreement with her husband or his family. There are no acute taboos to be observed in this circle ; intercourse can be easy, with joking unrestrained. This social feature must not be exaggerated, but one may contrast to a considerable extent the type of behaviour between, say, son and father, with that of nephew and mother's brother. The relationship of the former is characterized by socially enjoined respect, avoidance of the personal name, restrictions in bodily contact and associations, as bathing, and in speech, particularly as regards jesting of a risqué order. That of the latter is marked by customarily sanctioned freedom, both in bodily contact and speech, reciprocal use of personal names and lewd jesting.

The position of some of the individual relatives, mother's sisters and parents has already been described. The main social interest of the mother's group tends to centre in the *tuatina*, the mother's brothers and her less immediate relatives of the same status. The mother's brother has become a classic figure in anthropology. But it should be remembered that though for convenience it is customary to speak of him in the singular, there is in reality no collective abstract personality, as some accounts of native life, and even some textbooks, seem to suggest. There are a number of " mother's brothers " of varying degrees of propinquity, and they do not form a single undifferentiated group, but tend to play a greater part in the life of their nephew or niece the closer their actual blood kinship.   In some societies, it is true, as that of Dobu,[1] there is a special bond between a person and some one brother of his or her mother for the transmission of cultural values, but even here one is usually left to imagine what happens when Nature has not provided equivalent numbers on both sides.   In Tikopia there is no special alignment of persons in this way ; there is a grading of responsibility.   For convenience I shall often speak of " the mother's brother," but everyone who is a *kave* of the mother comes in this category, and each of her children is a charge upon the sympathy and wealth of this whole group.   A nephew or niece is known for ceremonial purposes as a *tama tapu*, sacred child, and the transmission of gifts from *tuatina* to *tama tapu* is one of the most important economic phenomena in Tikopia.

As with *tuatina*, so also with *tama tapu*—they are graded in importance according to their propinquity of relationship.   In the " house " of Tafua, for instance, the principal, *te matua tama tapu*, is Pa Motuaŋi, son of the chief's full sister.   Next in order come Tofiariki and the other children of the chief's daughter, Nau Tekaumata, with Afirua and his brethren, children of Nau Raŋirikoi, who is the chief's half-sister (their mothers being different).   Nau Nukuarofi, another daughter of the chief, and her husband usually receive gifts too when a distribution is made to *tama tapu*.   They are childless, but as the natives say, " they are not rejected " on that account ; the gift is really made to the family in which the *tama tapu* are born, and is in part a recognition of the services of the son-in-law.   Of lesser account are the children of the daughters of the chief's brothers and the children of the daughters of the chief's sisters, though in any large distribution they are not omitted.   Strictly speaking, the former are the *tama tapu* of the chief and the latter of his sons, but this distinction is largely immaterial ; the " house " normally counts its *tama tapu* as a whole.   Children of more distant female cousins of the chief could be included too, but normally the tie in such case is too weak to be actively maintained in terms of economic reciprocity.

The duties of mother's brothers begin at the birth of a child.   One of their representatives must attend, take the babe in his arms and recite a formula which purports to imprint on its mind the requisite economic and social duties to be observed towards its relatives and other members of the community.   At the initial torchlight fishing of a boy, a mother's brother takes charge of him in the canoe, formally introduces him to the work, and on the return of the party to shore is rewarded with food by the lad's father for his trouble.   At times the youth of a village get up a sightseeing party for the purpose of walking

[1] R. F. Fortune, *Sorcerers of Dobu*, 16, 64, etc.

round the crest of the hills encircling the lake, and on their way they visit two rocky spurs which jut out from the inner crater wall. This excursion is done according to traditional form, and in scrambling out to these spurs along a narrow track, it is necessary for every novice to have a mother's brother alongside to proffer a helping hand. For this customary service the oven is made below in the village by the parents of the youth or maiden, and a large basket of food carried to the house of the *tuatina* who officiated. This is reciprocated in due course.

Every boy in Tikopia undergoes the operation of super-incision before reaching manhood. Here, too, it is the obligation of the mother's brothers to take the chief part. They assemble in force and take charge of their sacred child. They prepare him with advice for what is to come, seize him and bring him to the place selected outside the house-eaves, strip him and support him while the most expert of their number performs the actual operation. For this rich gifts are made them by the father's family, gifts which are reciprocated in part, though not in full. And for weeks afterwards the boy travels round from the house of one *tuatina* to another, being fed richly and entertained for a couple of days in each place, while his parents at home toil at the oven to fill the baskets of food which must be provided in acknowledgment. These too must be returned in kind.

Again when a person appears for the first time at the sacred religious dances of Marae, it is the duty of *tuatina* to look after the novice, the *koromata* as he or she is called—particularly if a certain dance known as the *tau* is performed. The *tuatina* support their *tama tapu*, standing in front of him to shield him from the curious gaze of the crowd, holding up his arms and going through the motions of the dance with him, so that through ignorance or shyness he does not fall over nor is otherwise put to shame. Such behaviour is termed " *a pereperena o te tama pa tonu*," " an honouring of the assured child," a demonstration that he is well looked after. The conventional expression used by people who are watching is, " That person there is an assured child ; he does not fall down," conveying the suggestion that his uncles are many and his future well-guarded. The *tau* is made for girls in the same way, except that they dance at the rear of the main body of the men, not in the midst of it.

At marriage the mother's family does not play such an important part, but let sickness, accident or death overtake their " sacred child," and they rally round in full force to show their sympathy and to take an active part in the proceedings. When a man is ill it is his chief *tuatina* who uncomplainingly offers his back as a support or holds his nephew in his arms, and later, when recovery seems assured, brings along the *maro* of bark-cloth, turmeric-dyed and plain, as a token of assurance from the family deities. Again the father and his own relatives prepare food in acknowledgment of these good offices. When a person returns from a sojourn outside the island he is smeared with turmeric by his mother's brother as a mark of distinction, and a basket of food is brought to him from this family. At death a division of labour occurs between the kin. It is for the father and his people to mourn, and for the mother's family, led by the mother's brother, to attend to the burial. The separation is largely a formal one, but such an arrangement certainly does free the immediate relatives of the deceased from what might otherwise be a heavy strain, and allows them time to recover from the first onset of their grief. The services of the mother's kin are reciprocated by heavy gifts of food and property, only part of which are returned in kind. And using the occasion for the reinforcement of further social bonds, the father's family frequently make other gifts to their own *tama tapu*, the children of the women of their own group. A death thus gives a pretext for emphasizing maternal kinship ties within a wide sphere.

Sometimes in the latter case a differentiation may be made in favour of the senior " sacred children." Pa Fenuatara explained how a chief may say to his sons, " Let your *tama tapu* be left on one side, and you do things only for my own *tama tapu*, but only while my eyes are open. When I die, and you live on, do things for your own nephews." This means first preference to the chief's nephews and nieces as against his grandchildren. When he dies the sons decide for themselves what is to be done. Usually, it is said, they continue to make the customary gifts to the principal *tama tapu* of their dead father, in addition to those to their own sisters' children.

In some cases even with the death of the *tama tapu* material interest in him is not entirely dropped. One day I met Tuila, young relative of the Ariki Kafika, going along with a basket of food and a bundle of areca nut. When I accosted him and asked what he had, he replied, " The betel of Pa Veterei." Further enquiry revealed that the Ariki had held a little ceremony that afternoon. He had said that he felt *arofa*, affection, to his dead nephew Pa Veterei and had sent an invitation to Pa Nukurotoi, who acted as medium for this particular spirit, to call upon him at Teve. The man came in a state of possession, or, as the people said, the spirit came ; he and the Ariki greeted each other by the pressing of noses and conversed together, and the " spirit " chewed betel. At the conclusion of the visit food and areca were carried to the medium's home, as I saw. Such is a custom of chiefs and other folk when they desire to commune with the dead.

The converse may also take place, the spirit assuming the initiative and from affection to its kinsfolk appearing to them.

This last indicates another most important aspect of kinship—the ties which the living feel to the dead, and express concretely in ritual offerings, appeals for welfare, and summonses to manifest themselves in human mediums ; and the beliefs that ancestors and relatives have a persistent interest in their surviving kinsfolk, which they are held to exhibit in songs, advice on debatable points, assistance in fishing, agriculture and the like. Recognition of kinship as transcending mortality forms a large part of the religious practices of the Tikopia.[1]

The mother's group has then a complementary function to the father's group. In brief, members of the former supply protection and personal active assistance in the critical affairs of life ; members of the latter stand by as witnesses, and supply the material economic provision so necessary to successful accomplishment. Reciprocity is a leading principle. Services are performed for a person by his mother's group and repaid accordingly with food by his father's group. But reversing this one-sided transfer of material property, on other occasions goods are given in large measure to a person by his mother's group. So the social pendulum swings in never-ceasing alternation.

Apart from the ceremonial obligations of assistance, a real mother's brother does much to help his sister's child, and the latter regards him as a great standby in time of trouble. The sympathy between them is expressed in a picturesque way by an old custom told me by the Ariki Tafua. If uncle and nephew form part of a crew at sea together and meet with misfortune—their food and water fail—then the uncle takes the *sukuŋa titara*, the end of his waistcloth, and binds a wrist of each with it. Then both jump overboard. "They perish in one grave. In this land in times past the brother of the mother and his sister's son die in the one grave at sea—comparable to the grave on shore." It is even said that a man preferred to die with his mother's brother than with his own father. In an ancient tale, the killing of Pu Kefu, a lad sides with his mother's brother against his father and so brings about the latter's death. The Tikopia display no horror at this indirect parricide ; the boy's action seems to them an obvious corollary of his close association with the mother's brother.

The mutual trust between these two rests on a solid foundation of intimacy. In infancy the child soon comes to recognize its mother's brothers. Says Pa Fenuatara, " It knows its true mother's brother, because he comes constantly to it, he looks constantly on it, therefore it also marks him." This statement, like so many others of the

---

[1] See *Rank and Religion in Tikopia*.

Tikopia, expresses their pragmatic point of view in kinship. Just as they acknowledge no obligation on the part of a son to have anything to do with a mother who has deserted him in infancy, so they hold that the tie between mother's brother and sister's son is a function of the degree of their reciprocal social intercourse. The concept of " natural " feelings between kin does not enter the Tikopia scheme of values, though it has not wholly disappeared from our own sociological analyses.

In the normal way the father and the mother's brother of a child live in amity, the mother being the initial link between them, but the child forming the really vital social tie. Instances of what are called *tau ma pariki*, brothers-in-law in an evil relationship, are not unknown but are rare. Disagreement over some economic transaction is usually the cause. Two cases came to my notice through failure in the performance of the normal mother's brother obligations. One was in the case of the super-incision ceremonies of the boys of the Nukuafua family. Their *tuatina maori*, their true mother's brother, Pa Faŋatoto, had quarrelled with their father, Pa Nukuafua, and so did not come to the gathering. He was not entirely divorced from the proceedings, for a gift was sent from the household of his parents which by courtesy could be held to represent his interest. There were of course plenty of other *tuatina*, of more distant relationship, who filled the practical and ceremonial roles demanded. The other instance occurred at the funeral of a child of Pa Roŋotaono. Its true mother's brother, Pa Raŋitafuri, of the Rarupe family, was at enmity with the father who bore a bad reputation, as witnessed by his feud with his own brother, described earlier. Before the obsequies people were saying that he probably would not come, and were speculating as to who would perform the burial. Later it was learnt that Pa Raŋifatua, a more distant mother's brother of a different family altogether, that of Sao, though of the same village, had come to wrap the child up and see to its interment. In both cases the situation was accepted by the respective fathers and by the people at large. In such cases of non-fulfilment of kinship obligation no compulsion of any kind is put upon the defaulter, either by other relatives or by other people in the community. Emotional situations are given great weight by the Tikopia, and the sacrifice of personal feelings to an abstract sense of duty is a form of ethical ideal which they do not recognize. To the community as a whole an active feud between two individuals may seem much less preferable than a harmonious relationship which allows of a normal response to obligations, but to them as to the person who has to take the initiative the sentiments of antagonism are just as valid factors in the situation as the obligations, and ethically are no worse.   General opinion is summed up in a realistic point of view which, while agreeing with the futility of strife between kinsfolk, sees no moral imperative in kinship obligations to override the emotional tension.   Hence the net result—nothing is done.

It may be noted here, however, that the friction which led to the discarding or neglect of the ordinary duties of a mother's brother to his sister's son lay not in the relation of these two individuals to each other, but in that of the lad's father to the latter's brother-in-law. The rebound upon the sister's son was a secondary, one might almost say incidental, phenomenon.   This illustrates how impossible it is to separate completely the discussion of one set of kinship ties from that of others in the same system ; they are like a set of forces in delicately poised equilibrium ; if one is disturbed, others must respond in adjustment also.

Co-operation between *tuatina* and *iramutu* is common in many walks of life.   In obtaining and preparing food, in accumulating goods for a ceremonial distribution they help each other ; in social affairs they sit by each other for company and moral support.   At the initiation ceremony of Nukuafua Pa Raŋifuri took part as one of the parental group of the boys " in order to sit with his mother's brother."   Pa Nukuafua, father of the lads, was not his immediate *tuatina*, but on this public occasion of great moment to his family he merited support.

Uncle and nephew have frequent contact in daily life.   For instance, Pa Motuaŋi, principal sister's son of the Ariki Tafua, enters the old man's house often with a casual air.   He unties the chief's food bundle, and when the old man has finished mumbling his wad of betel and removes it, the young man stretches out his hand without a word, takes it and pops it into his own mouth.   In such interchange of small services, not premeditated or prescribed, the nephew is in very much the position of a son, except that convention allows him rather more laxity of speech and behaviour.

In common with other relatives the mother's brother becomes the subject of dirges, funeral compositions which express, if not always the true individual sentiment of singer or composer, at least the approved social attitude in the circumstances.   These dirges are many, and form a very valuable body of material for the study of the native kinship ; much of their interest lies in the fact they often refer to personal experiences in a way which illuminates the working of the actual relationships.

The following, for example, indicates that the bond between mother's brother and sister's son can be so close as to lead to a reversal of the usual obligations.   The song runs :

Tafito :   I weep as I walk ; I used to go
             When uncle was alive and dwelling there

Kupu :   I arise from the middle of Faŋarere
             From the middle of Vaisakiri
             To go

Safe :   Vetepavao has heard the news
             To come
             That Father may be buried in the earth.

This is a dirge composed by a man whose mother's people were of Faŋarere clan.   He is named Vetepavao—he introduces his own name into the song, which is unusual—and he is lamenting his uncle's death.   The *leitmotiv* commonly found in such dirges is given in the first stanza : one goes to the kinsman (for food, help or comfort is the implication) while he is alive ; now that he is dead one can no longer do so, therefore one weeps.   Vaisakiri is a well-known ancestral orchard of Faŋarere clan in which stands a sacred house of the same name, and symbolizes again the kinship bond.   In the last stanza the reference to the man's going to bury his uncle is interesting.   This departure from the usual order of ritual (whereby a person is buried by his mother's brother or this person's representative) was explained as due to the prevalence of an epidemic at that time.   " *Fenua pariki,*" the land was in a bad state.   The absence of correct relatives made it an act of piety on the composer's part to perform the last obsequies.[1] As usual the text of the song refers obliquely to the actual details of the case.

An interesting point of terminology in the last stanza is the use of the word " Father " (*Pa*), which is not ordinarily applied to a mother's brother, and here is even a term of address, not of reference.   Its introduction is possibly due to the composer's infertility of invention —he could find no other word to suit the rhythm—or is simply the result of a quirk of his fancy.   Poetic licence in Tikopia is extremely free, even where grammar is concerned.

Other examples of such songs are given in Chapter VIII.

---

[1] In this case it appears that the brunt of the actual burial fell on Vetepavao. Attendance at the funeral is usual.   On one occasion I enquired about someone who was engaged in helping to dig a grave for a man just dead.   The answer came, " He has gone to jump into the grave of his mother's brother—from affection." This too was a voluntary act.

THE RESTRAINT BETWEEN CROSS-COUSINS

To ordinary observation the relations between cross-cousins are the same as between brothers and sisters. The kinship terms used in addressing each other are identical, and there are no obvious taboos in operation. There is, however, a difference in the attitude towards the children of one's father's sister or of one's mother's brother compared with that towards members of one's own family, one's father's brother's or mother's sister's children. This difference is expressed when necessary in the kinship terminology by adding the words *fakalaui* or *fakapariki* to the ordinary terms of reference. The former signifies an attitude devoid of restraint and applies to parallel cousins ; the latter an attitude of restraint and applies to cross-cousins. The restraint consists particularly, as is usual in Tikopia, in avoidance of certain forms of cursing and a prohibition against striking the other person. It is said by some natives that these restrictions apply equally to both sides, by others that they lie with greatest force upon the children of the brother, while those of the sister can be more free in return. There appears to be no clear-cut rule on the matter of the reciprocity of obligation ; what is very certain is that the children of a sister of one's father must always be respected. The sanction for this is held to be the same as in the case of the father's sister, and to be derived directly from this—namely, the fear of supernatural vengeance through her influence with the family ancestors after her death. " *E tapu i toku masikitaŋa*," " sacred through my father's sister," is the phrase used.

An explanation given by Pa Raŋifuri shows the underlying factors which the natives themselves hold to be responsible for this attitude. He said, " My cross-cousin is weighty indeed. I do not speak evilly to him. He also does not speak evilly to me. Because he is the son of the father's sister. One does not strike the father's sister, one does not speak evilly to her. Good speech only is made to her. The basis of the father's sister is the father. I do not speak evilly to my father, nor do I speak evilly to his sister, my aunt. I again do not speak evilly to the child of my father's sister. It is done in this fashion because she is of weight. Should I speak evilly to my father and my father's sister, when my father's sister dies, and I have spoken evilly to her, then it reacts and I become ill. That is its basis. The oven is fired, and when her oven-firing (final rite for the dead) is finished, the father's sister goes then to her ancestors and returns hither again to bring sickness upon her child who spoke evilly."

The procedure of bringing illness (*fakafua*) is described as that of personal appeal to the ancestors to avenge the wrong committed ;

they approve of the punishment, and direct it. This power of calling down a visitation of illness upon an errant child is not, be it noted, the sole prerogative of the father's sister. That power lies also in the hands of a father, and even in that of a mother, through her own ancestors, as exemplified in the case of Pa Nukuomanu quoted above. Naturally the exercise of it is less frequent in the case of parents. (But action in the case of incestuous unions may be noted.)

Towards the cross-cousin who is the child of the mother's brother there is not the same tradition of restraint. Since the mother's brother is himself a licit relative for freedom of conduct, there is less hindrance towards his children. An illustration given by Pa Fenuatara brings out this point. His *taina fakapariki*, Pa Nukumarere, can throw at him the curse, " May your father eat filth," since the Ariki Kafika is this man's mother's brother and the excremental oath is thereby robbed of offence. Conversely, said Pa Fenuatara, " I may not use this expression to Pa Nukumarere; it would be a breach of the *tapu* of my father's sister; I would have done wrong." Normally, however, both parties in such a relationship behave with a fair amount of freedom towards each other, and with equal circumspection as regards unseemly language. Such restraint from the cross-cousins on the female side appears to be due to parallelism—a tendency to exhibit towards a relative the same type of conduct as he exhibits towards oneself, granted of course the existence of a certain similarity in age and social status.

I have quoted native statement in regard to the constraint of this relationship here, because in actual fact it was difficult to find noticeable instances of its exercise. The differentiation between cross-cousin and parallel cousin is certainly not one of the outstanding features of the Tikopia kinship system. The personal name, for instance, is not *tapu*: Pa Raŋifuri often spoke to me of Pa Motuaŋi as Moritaurua. Domestic relations are of an easy amicable kind, though here a certain formality exists in theory regarding rights of entry. For example, the mother of Pa Taitai is of the family of Faraŋanoa. While she lives any of the children of her brother, Pa Faraŋanoa, enter her house, that is the house of her son, since she is a widow, unannounced. When she dies that person will no longer be able to do this by privilege, though in actual fact he probably will do so. The correct thing for him to do is to stand outside the doorway and his cousin, seeing him standing there, will call out, " Why don't you come in ? " whereupon he enters. So Pa Taitai told me.

Marriage with cross-cousins is not common in Tikopia and is not favoured, being placed on exactly the same footing as the union of parallel cousins. The element of nearness of kinship is that to which specific objection is raised, and it is immaterial what the family or clan affiliation of the parties may be. Here is a situation in which relationship through male or female is counted equally. Cases of cross-cousin marriage that have occurred in recent years, with the invidious statements made about them, have been quoted in a previous publication,[1] and are discussed further in Chapter IX.

The special features of the cross-cousin relationship, both in behaviour and terminology, are given up after the first generation, and there is a reversion to the ordinary brother-sister pattern. " If brother and sister dwell together, and she goes and marries another man, producing children by him, when they come to the children that her brother has produced, they are all called *tau fanau fakapariki*. But that is the end. When they produce their children in turn these are called *tau fanau maori*."

SPECIAL KINSHIP TIES OF A WOMAN

The role of father's sister, mother's brother and the children of each will be seen in detail in the different aspects of the social and ritual life of these natives described later. The salient characteristic in this network of relationships is their contrast. The dominant note in the attitude towards the sister of the father is respect, and this persists in the behaviour towards her children. In the attitude of these latter toward the reciprocal kin, their mother's brother and his children, familiarity and dependence are the ruling elements. What basic social factor tends to promote the growth of such contrasted types of behaviour and to keep them so strongly operative? It is clear that each of these relationships is part of one system, having as its nucleus the relationship of brother and sister. It might be possible to suggest, as does Margaret Mead for Samoa, and indeed for the whole of Western Polynesia and parts of Melanesia as well, that the key to many features of the kinship structure is to be found in the dominant positions of the sister over the brother, due to her possession of a power of a peculiar kind. He is held at a disadvantage by the " fear of the sister's curse," which in native theory is conceived to be effective by virtue of her power with the family gods or ancestors. In her fieldwork accounts Dr Mead states clearly what she regards as the clue to the situation, namely, the expression of an ancestral ghost cult.[2] Is this argument sound? The Tikopia data fall fairly well into

[1] *J.R.A.I.*, *loc. cit.*

[2] *Social Organization of Manu'a*, 146, etc., 1930. "Perhaps the greatest historical interest of the Manus kinship system lies in the completeness and explicitness with which the sanctions, which support the power of the father's sister's line, are pre-

line with those of these other areas, but there are factors which make it difficult to accept such a conclusion.   In the first place, as a matter of ethnographic fact, while the Tikopia have what may be called an ancestral ghost cult, it is of a different type from that in Manus, is manipulated primarily by men and is not duplex.   Women exercise merely a general power of pleading with the family ancestors, have no special ghostly reservoir of their own to draw upon, and are believed to render their antagonism effective only after death, when for the first time they are really in touch with the ancestral line.   But the Tikopia relationships between brother and sister and their children are a dynamic, well-integrated system.   Since there is an entire absence of a cult of the Manus *tandritanitani* type, invoked by descendants of the female line against those of the male line, in what way can the sanctions of Manus make intelligible the present institutions of Tikopia ?

Moreover, why, one may ask, is the sister conceived to possess this peculiar power over her brother and his children ?   Dr Mead takes this belief as a primary factor in the situation, and bases the operation of the other factors upon it.   To me the more feasible explanation is that any supernatural sanction with which the influence of the sister over the brother is endowed comes as a secondary phenomenon, a reinforcement of practical value to the economic and social situation.   The fundamental elements of sociological interest, I think, are to be found in the increased security given by this form of relationship to a woman after marriage, and, more important still, to the children of her marriage, and in the effect it has of conserving their ties with the group from which she came.   The possession of superior rank to her brother, as in Tonga ; of power with the ancestors, as in Samoa or Manus ; the respect which is her due in Tikopia and elsewhere, give her a *point d'appui*, a weapon over her own family which she can use if she needs help against her husband's people, or in the interests of her children.   These latter, too, are provided with a double basis of support in life.   In Tikopia all the drift of the kinship institutions that we have been considering goes this way.   The favouritism of the father for the daughter, often expressly directed to her children, the obligations laid upon a mother's brother towards his *tama tapu*, the respect due to a father's sister from her brother's children, and finally the co-operation enjoined upon

served.   An institution which is found in Samoa, Tonga, Fiji, Tikopia, New Caledonia, and undoubtedly in many other parts of Oceania also, is illuminated and made intelligible, shown to be an expression of a well-integrated ancestral ghost cult."   *Kinship in the Admiralty Islands*, Anthropological Papers of the American Museum of Natural History, XXXIV, Part II, 356   1934.

brothers-in-law (discussed presently) all point in definite, explicit terms to this fact. The belief in an ancestral ghost cult wielded by women, in the power of the sister's curse, and the rest, are safeguards, strengthening agencies; they represent the utilization of a supernatural sanction as a means of buttressing acquiescence in a culturally valuable situation.

In Tikopia the situation is very clear. The emphasis upon the primary importance of acknowledging the children of women married out of the family is a reality which colours a great deal of the institutional activity. In a society with patrilineal descent so strongly marked and patrilocal residence also in vogue, without such institutional mechanisms there would be a danger that the children of the women of the family would become dissipated through other groups and lose close touch with a unit of great cultural advantage to them. Moreover, if they were let go, the brothers' family would suffer too. They provide an important channel for economic co-operation and the execution of social affairs; linkage with them is advantageous even in the religious sphere.

The vital things in society are the forces which keep it in action, which draw and hold groups together, and allow of the functioning of institutions, of sets of human relationships. These forces come to expression in different ways in different societies, and once having taken one form of expression, a kind of institutional efflorescence sometimes takes place, an over-development which, like the complex system of kava etiquette in Samoa, amounts to an aesthetic elaboration of the basic forms. In the sociological phenomenon we have just been studying, the provision of a dual kinship foundation for the individual, such diverse institutional mechanisms as the power of a sister's curse in Polynesia, the obligation of a brother to fill his sister's yam-house in the Trobriands, the *Légitime* in Belgium and other parts of Europe all play their part. Some societies provide a firmer foundation than others, and in this respect the tiny primitive community of Tikopia is as well endowed as any.

The function of these sets of obligations is to enforce on the descendants on the male side an attitude of assistance and protection towards the children of women from their house. Such an interpretation of behaviour patterns assumes that social well-being is served by the creation and maintenance of kinship ties.

In Tikopia, moreover, there are possibilities of friction between the offspring of the men of a group and those of the women, their sisters. An indication of this has already been given in discussing the division of property by a man among his children. Parental sentiment, not to be restrained by formal principles of descent and inheritance, which emphasize the male side at the expense of the female, attempts to express itself in gifts to daughters and to their children. This is liable to be resented by their sons and sons' sons. But here the obligations to *tama tapu* and respect for sister and father's sister respectively and their children point the way, inculcating sentiments of friendliness and stifling resentment at its source. There is a conversion by social insistence of a potentially negative

TABLE III

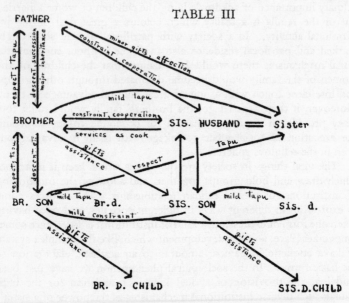

sentiment into a positive sentiment—of approval, even affection, of acknowledgment of the call for assistance and protection.

The result is that a social principle of continuous transmission from mother's brother to sister's child is at work which, if expressed in diagrammatic form, could be represented as diagonal in operation, as contrasted with the vertical principle of transmission from father to son (*v.* Table III). In either case the junior generation receives more than it gives in return. There is reciprocity between mother's brother and sister's son, just as there is between father and son, but on balance the sister's son gains. But in his turn he expends his wealth and still more important his time and his energies in sustaining his own sister's son when the day comes. So the society moves on, each individual drawing sustenance, both literal and metaphorical, from two sources, and when the time comes pouring it out again through two channels. And while for some purposes there is separation of interests between mother's brother and sister's son, father and son, for others there is identification of interests between them : *tau tua-tina*, to give them their native designation, may sit together in public ceremonial and supplement each other's gifts ; *tau mana* act as one in matters affecting their family group as a whole.

THE GENERAL BODY OF KINSFOLK

At times of stress or congratulation in a person's life, it is the duty of his or her relatives on both the mother's and the father's side to assemble and play their part in condoling or rejoicing. The collective term used for them is " *te kano a paito*." This can be most nearly translated as " the collected families " or " the whole of the families," and may be compared with *te kano fenua*, " the whole land," that is, the total population or *te kano ariki*, " the chiefs as a whole." These relatives, despite their separate " house " affiliations, are conceived as a body, existing through the common relation to the single individual concerned.

A *kano a paito*, being formed of kinsfolk on both sides of the house, is not in itself an autonomous unit of the Tikopia social structure, separate from other units of the same type. Each such group is constituted with reference to a single person, its membership is not exclusive but interleaved, the group is amorphous, forming and reforming even from parent to child. In this, such aggregations differ from the ordinary *paito*, the " houses " described in Chapter X, which are patrilineal kinship groups of exclusive membership. The *paito* is a clear-cut, named unit to which a person either does or does not belong ; the *kano a paito*, unnamed except by reference to its personal focus, has its borders vaguely defined, fading away into the broad plain where classificatory kinship needs the spur of economic interest, neighbourliness or the touch of rank to make it effective.

I have emphasized the functional aspects of this distinction since there has been some confusion as to the part which such collective bodies of kinsfolk play in native social life. Rivers has described for Eddystone Island in the Western Solomons, the *taviti*, which he calls a " bilateral kinship group," and which he insists is the one important social unit recognized by the natives. Descent and marriage are alleged to be regulated on this basis, though no attempt is made to deal with the complications which the complete observance of such a bilateral principle would entail in practice after a few generations. Further, the characterization of the *taviti* has been incorporated into a theoretical discussion of kinship [1] in which it has obscured the real

---

[1] Rivers, *Social Organization*, 13-14, 42, 104, 115.

nature of descent. Following Rivers in uncritical fashion, Ivens describes in much the same terms the *komu* of Southern Malaita in the Eastern Solomons.[1]   But again, while maintaining that land rights are held by such groups, that marriage is not allowed with anyone with whom blood relationship can be traced, on the male or female side, he entirely fails to demonstrate how in such a small community (the total population of Sa'a a few years ago was only 250) recognizing kinship to the fourth generation, it is possible to have bilateral units of this type carrying out such exclusive functions.   The lack of information makes it difficult to see from internal evidence what the true situation is, but it seems fairly clear that both *taviti* and *komu* are not really structural kinship units of the native society, parallel and with exclusive membership—except on a basis of local affiliation—but are composite, amorphous groups of the *kano a paito* order, based on reference to specific individuals in each case.   They are certainly composed on a bilateral basis, but there is probably a more clearly defined set of kinship units, organized on the unilateral principle, which form the true skeletal structure of the society, in which descent is traced.   In the case of the material of Ivens, for example, it is specifically stated that patrilineal groups of this type do obtain in one portion of the community ;   the " families " of the chiefs, as I myself was able to corroborate in a brief visit to that area, are composed of their relatives in the male line.

One effect of the operation of the *kano a paito* groups is to give that weight to kinship linkage through females which is ignored in the ordinary transmission of *paito* membership.   The accompanying diagram, Table IV, illustrates how greatly this enlarges the effective circle of social relations.   If A[3] falls ill, his *kano a paito* assemble.   They comprise all the men and women of his own " house " A, and those also of the " house " of his mother and his mother's brother, B, to whom he is *tama tapu*.   From the " house " into which his sister has married, X, will come her children, who are his own *tama tapu*, and her husband, because of the bond between brothers-in-law.   From T and S will also come T[4] and S[4], his *tama tapu* too, because they are children of his female cross-cousins, and T[3] and S[3], his " brothers-in-law."   From W will come his female cross-cousin w[3], his male cross-cousin W[3], and this man's son W[4].   The two former are his father's *tama tapu*, and therefore his also ;   W[4] is his " son."   From E will come his wife's brother, and this man's son, the latter because A[3] is " my father, the husband of my father's sister."   Considering merely a bare skeletal arrangement within three generations, there are already a

---

[1] W. G. Ivens, *Melanesians of the South-East Solomons*, 1927, 60-61, 65, 69.   Cf. also C. Daryll Forde, *Habitat, Economy and Society*, 1934, 180-181.

TABLE IV

THE KIN GROUP, KANO A PAITO

				$a^1 = V^1$			
	D		$A = d$			$a^2 = W^2$	
		C^1	$A^1 = c^1$		$W^3 = r^3$	$w^3 = S^3$	
	P^1	$B^1 = p^1$	$A^2 = b^2$		W^4	S^4	
	$B^2 = y^2$		$A^3 = e^3$	$a^3 = X^3$			
$T^3 = b^3$	$B^3 = z^3$	E^3	A^4	a^4	X^4	x^4	
T^4	B^4	E^4					
T	B	A	E	X	W	S	

score of people gathered, embracing six patrilineal groups in addition
to that of the sick man himself. On any actual occasion there would
be considerably more, since families are larger than the diagram can
show, wives go with their husbands, and brothers recognize an
obligation towards a family into which one of their number has
married. The ties also reach beyond the first ascending generation.
In the family P of the mother's mother's brother of A³, P² will regard
A³ as one of his *tama tapu*, and even if he be dead his son P³ will
represent the family interest by going to the place where his " brother "
lies. Folk from D and V houses may also be present.

The *kano a paito* embraces relatives even wider afield. A typical
example is given by Pa Raŋifuri and Pa Nukura. The mother of the
latter is the sister of Pa Nukuofo, of the *paito* sa Rarupe, descended
from Mataŋa, brother of Niupani, an Ariki Tafua of eight generations
ago (*v.* Genealogy II). Pa Nukuofo and the present Ariki Tafua
are " brothers " by this. Hence Pa Nukura's mother is a "father's
sister " of Pa Raŋifuri and Pa Nukura is of his *kano a paito*, " he belongs
to my body of kinsfolk—the family into which my father's sister
married. I dwell then, I call him my brother," said Pa Raŋifuri.

This instance illustrates well the principle of the classificatory
system which Morgan expressed so many years ago—the manner
in which by this terminology the collateral line is continually merged
with the "lineal" line. What he did not recognize clearly enough was
that this merging is primarily terminological, that there is a grading in
behaviour on the basis of propinquity in kinship, and that there is
always a system of secondary terminology to indicate the differences.
The linguistic aspect of the matter is dealt with in the following
chapter.

It must not be thought that the relationship involved in the term
kano a paito is effective only on more dramatic occasions in the social
life. These see a full assemblage of kindred, but continually such
ties are relied upon for co-operation in ordinary economic affairs.

An example may be taken from the turmeric making of the Ariki
Tafua in 1928. The activities of the working party engaged in
digging the root have been described in Chapter IV. The ownership
of the ground illustrates a common practice. The root was dug from
land belonging to the Mapusaŋa family of Kafika. Pa Mapusaŋa
(deceased) was own mother's brother to Nau Nukunefu (herself of
Taumako clan) who had planted the turmeric there. So by bonds of
kinship and marriage the territory of Kafika supplied material for the
dye manufacture of Tafua.

In the actual preparation of the dye the working party were also
kano a paito, and one heard few personal names, but nearly always

terms of kinship. The men engaged were of Tafua and Kafika clans. There were the chief of Tafua and his sons, together with a son-in-law of the chief and this man's father, Pa Nukuofo. There was also Satapuaki of the allied group of Paiu. " Our son; he assists us," said the Tafua folk. Then there was the eldest son of Pa Fetauta of the Marinoa group, related to the Tafua family by the brother-sister marriage exchange of the chief and Pa Marinoa. There was also Kavaika of the Nukuraro group of Kafika. Pa Nukuraro was a classificatory mother's brother of the Ariki Tafua, and Kavaika, the former's grandson, was therefore a " brother" of the chief's sons. There was also a cross relationship between Pa Nukuofo and Kavaika, since the former was the husband of the latter's grandfather's sister. There were other cross relationships too, but these are sufficient to show how the purely economic contacts at every stage of the task were liable to be affected by the kinship status of the various parties in regard to each other. For example, the issuing of working orders, the discussion of the division of the product, the contribution of food supplies during the work, and the apportionment of food at meals were all conditioned by the existence of kinship taboos. The interplay between economics and kinship, which is such a character-istic feature of the Tikopia social structure, thus involves certain limitations upon co-operative activity, although in itself it strengthens both factors.

The appeal for co-operation beteeen kin is not always effective. As I was sitting with Pa Raŋifuri in his house one morning, one of his brothers' sons came in and said, " My father wants you to make up a crew to go fishing." He replied, " My shoulders are sore from yesterday. Tell your father to go and look for a crew for himself."

METAPHORS FOR KINSHIP

The Tikopia are not content to use a single set of kinship terms with unvarying monotony. They have allowed the system to effloresce, grafting upon it descriptive and metaphorical expressions. Such secondary terminology, though making for variety and delicacy in social situations, is usually not so precise in its definition; it tends to indicate general types of relationship rather than specify exact ties with individuals. Here are some terms used among *kano a paito*.

Linkage with kindred of past generations is expressed in a number of linguistic usages. The word *tafito*, for instance, signifies in general situations " base," " beginning," " origin," " source," " cause." One talks of the *tafito* of a tree, meaning that portion of the trunk in the region of its emergence from the ground, that on which its stability depends ; one talks of the *tafito* of a song, meaning the first stanza, which gives the clue to the others, and one asks for the *tafito* of an action, meaning the causes which led to it. This is one of the terms used to refer to the family group either on the father's or on the mother's side. Another term is *afu*, the connotation of which is restricted to social linkage, but which is a synonym of *tafito* in this sphere. It may be translated as " sprung from." Some examples will show the sense in which these are used.

Seremata, who was always desirous of explaining social forms, discussed these terms. He said, " *E afu mai mai te paito te fafine, mai te tuatina. Kuou e afu mai sa Raropuka, toku tafito sa Raropuka ; a kuou te Taumako ; tera tukutukuŋa o fenua tera.*" " One springs from the family of the woman, from the mother's brother. I spring from sa Raropuka ; my origin is sa Raropuka ; and yet I am Taumako ; that is the custom of this land." As he said again, "*E rua oku tafito ; tafito foki toku mana foki.*" " My origins are two ; I originate also from my father too." A person usually speaks of the family group of his father as " *toku paito,*" " my house," and that of his mother as " *te paito kuou ne afu mai i ei,*" " the house from which I sprang." So Pa Motuaŋi, sister's child of the Ariki Tafua, said, " *Kuou ne afu mai mai paito ariki,*" " I have sprung from a chiefly house." And during the incision ceremony of a boy in Nukuafua family it was said of his true mother's brother, Pa Faŋatoto, " *Na afu tau tonu tera Pa Faŋatoto,*" " His absolutely correct *afu*, that is Pa Faŋatoto," contrasting him with more distant relatives on the mother's side. Again, if natives are questioned casually regarding the origin of the unfortunate Faŋarere clan, they nearly always reply " *ne afu mai Toŋa,*" " they sprung from Tonga," referring to the fact that the ancestral marriage which was responsible for the emergence of the present-day group was of a Tongan woman with the son of a local chief.

It might be gathered from this that *afu* is a term used to refer to the specific linkage of a person with his mother's kin. It is certainly used most commonly in this connection, but not exclusively. The following examples show that it has a wider interpretation. A man said, " *Kuou ka nofonofo lavaki, aku tama tera oku afu. E afuafu i a kuou,*" " I shall dwell on then and die, but my children, there are my descendants. They have sprung from me." Pae Sao too, to be relied upon for correct usage, in speaking of his ancestors said to me, " *Kuou e nofo e afu mai a Pono, taŋata mai Uvea, te manu te ariki Tafua, ne au o nofo,*" " I who dwell here am sprung from Pono, a man of Uvea, the protégé of the Ariki Tafua who came to settle." Again he explained that this man Pono was taken as a son by Fakaofotau, the representative of the Sao group, " who sprang from the earth."

After stating that the autochthones of the various " houses " were of different origin, he also pointed out that each present " house " is really of immigrant stock.   " We who dwell here *afu* one and all from foreign skies," he said.[1]   Here *afu* refers definitely to filiation in the male line.   When the Ariki Taumako, referring to a well-known ancestor, Perurua of ŋa Faea, said, " *na afu, Pa Raŋirikoi*," he meant the same thing, the latter being a direct descendant of the former through males.   The term may be used in an extended sense, as by Pa Korokoro in speaking of Vahihaloa.   " My own *afu*," he said.   His ancestor traditionally came from Luaŋiua, the home of Vahihaloa.

The word *afu*, it may be noted, is not equivalent to " being born " in the ordinary sense ; it is a concept of social and not physiological nativity.   Though in common with *tafito*, it is used to describe the connection with either the father's or the mother's kinship group the use of such terms of origination in respect of the latter, in a society where recognition of physiological paternity is combined with patrilineal filiation, indicates again the importance which these natives place upon the preservation of the matrilineal tie.   An elaboration of *afu* is *maafuafu*, a term used mainly in ritual formulae.   It signifies " to breed, to have descendants."

A word allied in meaning to those just described, but the reverse of them, is *rafuŋa*, which is used for descendants, representatives in following generations.   One man explained it thus : " *Siei se tama mau, tera tou taina e nofo ana tama tera mau rafuŋa.   Te tama, te makopuna, e poi katoa*."   " If you have no child, and there is your brother with children living, there are your descendants.   The child, the grandchild, it operates everywhere."   The term *rafuŋa* of course means descendants in general ; the speaker is merely concerned to point out here that even if one has no offspring oneself, those of one's brother count as one's own.   Such is the native theory.   An iterative form of this word is *rafurafuŋa*.

The above expressions involve no very obvious metaphors.   But there are a number of these.   One's children or descendants may be described, for example, as *oku fua*, my fruit.   A man may speak of such an one again as *tatou fosa*, our root.   This last appears to reverse the physiological relation, but the word in ordinary speech denotes a tuber of taro or yam, that is, the product of those plants, so the logic of the situation is not violated.   These expressions recall the Biblical use of the term " seed " for children.

Another figure of speech is contained in the term *va* or *vava*, used

---

[1] A discussion of the term " Afukere," referring to autochthonous groups, will be given in *History and Traditions of Tikopia*.

to indicate the relationship of cousins. Pa Taitai said of Faŋotavave, son of his mother's brother, Pa Faraŋanoa, "*Toku va tena; toku nana ne au mai i Faraŋanoa*," "That one is my *va*; my mother came hither from Faraŋanoa." The term is reciprocal and covers ortho-cousins as well as cross-cousins. A common phrase heard to describe two persons is, "*tau fanau maori; vava i rau nana.*" A neat translation of this expression is difficult, but the best rendering of it is, "they are first cousins, closely related through their mothers." Thus Pa Fenuatara said of himself and Pa Rarovai, "*e vava i mau nana.*" His mother and that of the latter were sisters. The term *va* or *vava* is used only for reference; such a person is addressed as *taina* or *kave* in the ordinary way. The word is an application of that for umbilicus and conveys metaphorically the idea of birth from the same stock.

As a collective term for a group of relatives *kano a paito* is generally used. But I once heard the Ariki Taumako describe the group (including himself) who came to support a woman thus, "*Konei na faoa*," "Here are her people." This usage is the same as in English.

Inclusion in the *kano a paito* rests primarily on consanguinity. If two men marry two sisters, they will not consider themselves to be *kano a paito* on these grounds alone. But wives are regarded as of the *kano a paito* of their husbands, since they come and live in the house, so the usage is not quite parallel here. The bond of consanguinity may in some circumstances be simulated. When the ancestor of the Sao group immigrated to Tikopia, he was taken under the protection of the Ariki Tafua. Said Pa Raŋifuri, "Being left with the chief, he dwelt as the *kano a paito* of the chief; he became a ritual elder, he made kava for the chief, he became a son (*fakatama*) to the chief." In the ordinary way the bond of blood is traced far. In the olden days a woman of the "house" of ŋa Fiti married into the "house" of Faraŋanoa. Hence all persons of these two houses regard themselves as related, as constituting *kano a paito*, and when a woman of the latter group died during my stay, representatives of the former attended the funeral on this explicit basis.

Groups of the *kano a paito* order, though not of unitary character, may be of extreme importance in the social life. They assemble around their focus for birth, incision, marriage, death or other striking occasion. When Pa Paiu was afflicted with swollen glands in the neck, which gave promise of a serious dénouement, he was surrounded by these kin who cheered him, propped him up and attended to him in his pain. When food was brought his first thought was for them. "*Inu se vai motou, toku kano a paito*," "Take some nourishment for yourselves, my body of kinsfolk," he croaked. His use of the possessive indicates the personal reference that such a gathering always has. When a mourning feast was made for the relatives of Noakena, drowned son of Pa Raŋifuri, the father addressed the gathering, " My *kano a paito*, you eat your fish from our canoe which was dragged down to secure fish from the sea." It was the first time the canoes had been out since the boy was lost. Apostrophe to the assembled kin in this form is frequently made.

Membership of such a group is of course reciprocal, and a person spends much of his time rendering service in recognition of these claims. The bounds of the *kano a paito* are in fact set not by the inability to trace kinship further, but by the practical difficulties of close economic and social co-operation with a great number of people. The chiefly families, naturally, have larger active *kano a paito* than do the commoners. As in most Polynesian communities the political system and the kinship structure are closely interdependent.

The possibility of counting kinship on both sides, apart from matters of descent and succession, has meant in Tikopia that every person of ordinary competency can ultimately trace connection with every other person in the community of over twelve hundred souls. As it is said, " the whole land is a single body of kinsfolk ; or, " the land which stands here, it makes a body of kinsfolk throughout." The recognition of this is of importance in promoting the unity of the various autonomous groups of the patrilineal order, by providing them with numerous cross-ties which couple them firmly together for common action. The law and government of the community and the integrity of its religious institutions rest largely upon this basis, and it is probably accurate to say that the social health of the Tikopia community, one of the most prosperous in the Western Pacific, is dependent upon this kinship system, with its associations, being maintained unimpaired.

CHAPTER VII

THE LANGUAGE OF KINSHIP

THE classificatory system of relationship has been often enough described, so that its general features are familiar. What has not so often been realized, though, is the function of such a system as a stabilizing mechanism in a society. It forms a most useful mode of grouping people, it establishes their relations to one another. Looked at from this point of view, the old contrast with systems of the descriptive type is meaningless; within a classificatory system it is perfectly possible to describe individuals by modification or qualification of terms, or by additional terms for special relatives—all of which phenomena are frequent in primitive kinship. Moreover, a so-called " descriptive " system is also a means of classifying persons, though its range may not be so extensive.

COMMONSENSE IN PRIMITIVE CATEGORIES

The question then is not whether a kinship term classifies or describes, but whether it has a single or a multiple referent. And in a small society where individuals are well known to each other, it is probably more convenient to allow kinship terms to have a multiple referent and to make further personal distinctions within this framework than to have a separate term for each individual who is of social interest. Moreover, in primitive societies, where other modes of classifying and grouping persons are not highly elaborated—by absence of economic specialization or a manifold differentiation in rank—the classificatory system offers a useful mechanism for fitting in strangers with the minimum of trouble. All visitors to the shores of Tikopia soon find themselves embraced within the kinship scheme. In olden times immigrants were *fakatama*, " made sons " to the chiefs; Maresere, the informant of Rivers, in more recent years was received into the family of the Ariki Tafua, and played his part accordingly. When it became apparent to the Tikopia that I was taking a considerable interest in their more complex institutions, the two chiefs with whom I associated a great deal, the Ariki Kafika and the Ariki Tafua, brought me within their kinship range. The Ariki Tafua, in his usual authoritative style, addressed me without question as *tama*, son; the Ariki Kafika debated for a while, then courteously said, speaking to one of his family, " I don't know whether the two of us are *tau mana* (father and son) or *tau fanau* (brothers)." It was pointed out that on grounds of relative age the former was more appropriate. " *Kaia rei !* " " So be it ! " he said. This immediately gave a lead to a great many other people, who adjusted themselves accordingly, and I dropped as it were into a slot of the kinship machine. This determined my position on the floor of the house when I attended funerals and other ceremonies, and the gifts I made and received; some young men called me " brother " and told me lewd jests, teased me and helped me in difficulties, others called me " father " and treated me with respect, and—what might have been embarrassing in other circumstances—small children took me confidingly by the hand and addressed me as " unmarried father," as is the custom with bachelor uncles.

Personal contact with the classificatory system of a Polynesian community shows its utility and smooth working; it certainly appears to be no more cumbrous than our own way of handling the relationships of kin. In some respects it is more convenient, as reference to the *tau* terminology of linkage will prove (see p. 254).

In an empirical study of a language each speech situation in which a word occurs presents a specific connotation of it. The problem of translation consists in finding by comparison and abstraction the most suitable equivalent by which to render this indefinite number of connotations. In practice what is done is to take the statistical mode of a number of speech situations and by reference to this to construct a general or basic equivalent, which is commonly called the " meaning " of the word. In speech situations where the connotation of the word diverges widely from the mode, it is convenient to employ also one or more special equivalents, leaving aside the question of their genetic relation to the modal usage. Thus in Tikopia the general equivalent of *fenua* is " land " in the sense of a certain circumscribed territory. *Toku fenua ko Tikopia*—my land, it is Tikopia, a person says in describing his provenance. *Ko Tikopia te viki fenua*, Tikopia is a small land. In the greater number of speech configurations in which this word is used, it bears this connotation. But there are divergent uses. To translate the expression *fenua ku fai taraŋa* by the general equivalent, " land has made speech," would be too indeterminate. The specific reference is to occupiers of the land; using the special equivalent, a more adequate rendering is " people have been talking "—there has been gossip, or exchange of opinion. In the slighting expression *fenua vare*, the word has much the same force, though here the reference is usually intended as a reflection upon definite persons. " You stupid people " gives the meaning (*v.* also Text 6).

The imperfections of the average dictionary of a native language, with its assumption of identical connotation for the same word in different speech situations, are obvious.

The same principle applies to homophones. An entirely different set of connotations is found in differing speech situations for the same set of sounds, and other groups of equivalents altogether must be provided. Thus the set of phonemes *fenua* is found in a set of speech situations widely divergent from those mentioned above, the connotation being the placenta. The use of *mana* in Tikopia also illustrates this. One modal equivalent, as will be clear from the foregoing kinship analysis, is " father " ; another is " effectiveness." In the expression " *na mana ku sau e ŋa atua*," " his *mana* has been taken away by the spirits," either equivalent is ostensibly applicable, and context is necessary to give the clue. Whether or not there is a genetic connection between the use of the same set of phonemes in such different contexts is a question which it is impossible to decide in the absence of historical evidence.

In the translation of native phrases in this book the basic equivalent is generally given, but sometimes where necessary for a more accurate rendering of the sense of the original a special equivalent has been used. The foregoing brief explanation gives the justification for what may otherwise seem an inconsistency. Though I have used on occasion the terms " literal " and " free " to describe translation, I do so for convenience, not because I regard them as accurate. A word-for-word rendering from one language into another is not a literal or exact translation any more than the absence of such rendering means a loss of exactness. In any particular speech situation a special equivalent may be more exact than the basic one, and the number of words involved is irrelevant.

It is unnecessary to traverse further any part of the theoretical exposition of the empirical, functional study of language so admirably and definitively given by Bronislaw Malinowski.[1]

This chapter is primarily a section of the study of kinship, not an essay in linguistics. The problem is that of defining as accurately as possible the meaning of what may be called items of verbal behaviour towards kin in Tikopia, in particular the behaviour involved in the use of kinship terms. These latter are words of special function. They refer to a relationship at the same time as they denote an individual. Where practically every term has a multiple referent, in order that the same set of vocables may serve with some precision to induce a desired reaction in the social life, the clue to their meaning must be given by the situation in which they are used.

[1] B. Malinowski, " The Problem of Meaning in Primitive Languages " in *The Meaning of Meaning*, by Ogden and Richards, 1923, 451-510 ; idem, *Coral Gardens and their Magic*, 1935, vol. ii. Useful observations of the same general type are given by J. R. Firth, *Speech*, 1930.

Different types of kinship situation have been recorded and analysed in the preceding chapters, and some of the linguistic data bearing upon them is discussed below.

BEARING OFF THE GIFTS

The girls are taking these heavy baskets of cooked food, topped with *maro* of bark-cloth, as presents to the maternal kinfolk of the boy.

STRUCTURAL ASPECT OF TIKOPIA KINSHIP TERMINOLOGY

It will be clear from this analysis that kinship is fundamentally a social mechanism for the handling of situations between persons and not simply a restatement of the facts of procreation.

Granted a semantic definition of kinship terms, the body of terminology in use in a society has in itself a certain order and arrangement. The labels of descriptive and classificatory applied by Morgan to distinguish his primary types of kinship system are admittedly inadequate, even from the linguistic aspect of the phenomena, but while his typology erected on this basis is unsatisfactory, nevertheless Morgan drew attention to two fundamental elements in kinship usage—the specification of relatives as individuals and the grouping of them. Both practices are to be found in any kinship system ; they are not mutually exclusive, and the presence of them in association is no indication of a historical movement from one to the other. But the scope of either element varies according to the constitution of the society in which the kinship system functions, though the extent of the correlation has not yet been generally established. The specification of individual kinsfolk in terminology, the linguistic mechanism by which such specification is made precise, the kinds of kinsfolk grouped and separated show great variation in different societies. The formal bases of this grouping and separation have been analysed by Kroeber, Rivers, Lowie, Kirchoff,[1] and categories have been distinguished by which the kinship systems of different societies can be compared. Such comparison will, in time, undoubtedly lead to the creation of a sounder typology, but work of this taxonomic character is at present mainly effective only in so far as it is productive of further investigation of the social conditions in which these types have emerged and persist. This has been the case for instance in the field of aboriginal Australian sociology, where the stimulus given through the systematic studies of kinship by A. R. Radcliffe-Brown has resulted in a number of intensive institutional analyses.[2]

The central problem for the student is to see his kinship terminologies as a definite part of the dynamism of kinship relations, to determine how far the separation and combination of relatives under linguistic labels can be correlated with other sociological phenomena.

---

[1] E.g. Kroeber, "Classificatory Systems of Relationship," J.R.A.I., XXXIX, 1909, 77-84. Rivers, Kinship and Social Organization, London, 1914. Lowie, "A Note on Relationship Terminologies, Amer. Anthropologist, XXX, 1928, 263-267 ; "Relationship Terms," Encyc. Brit., 14th ed. Kirchoff, "Verwandtschaftsbezeichnungen und Verwandtenheirat," Z. f. Ethnologie, Band 64.

[2] See especially papers by Elkin, Lloyd Warner, Ursula H. McConnel, Hart, Piddington, Stanner and others in Oceania.

In trying to explain the observed variations from one society to another it seems best from the methodological standpoint to take a group of societies of the same general type of culture, as Radcliffe-Brown has done in Australia. Since this is primarily a descriptive study, only incidental comparisons are made with other Polynesian communities.

In discussing kinship terminology it is convenient to draw a distinction between *generation* and *kinship grade*. The former implies a biological classification, based upon birth; the latter is of the sociological order, based upon genealogical ranking. The two are normally coincident—as when a person called " father " is a score or more years the senior. At times, however, especially when the classificatory terminology is in use, there may be considerable divergence between them. Hence clarity is maintained by speaking of kinship grades rather than of generations. The same duality of meaning as is expressed ordinarily in our word generation is given by the Tikopia word *tupuraŋa*. This signifies primarily " growth," being the substantival form of *tupu*, to grow, but it has also come to convey the idea of stage or status. It is said of two men, they are of the *tupuraŋa sokotasi*, the one growth-stage, implying that they are of approximately the same age. Since this normally means an equivalence in kinship status, the term is also used to signify kinship grade.

The general configuration of the kinship system of Tikopia is simple, though the vocabulary employed is rich. In brief, these people distinguish by separate terms fourteen main kinds of relatives (see Table V), omitting a number of clearly derivative terms and also terms of address, which are dealt with later.

PRINCIPAL TERMS OF REFERENCE

The distinction of kin in ordinary terms of reference, apart from individual description in detail, does not go further back than the second ascending kinship grade—the grandparent level. All persons of this grade, and also of anterior grades, are grouped together under the name of *tupuna*, or in abbreviated and more common form, *puna*. There is a tendency for the latter form to be used to refer to the immediate grade of grandparents and for the former to be applied to more remote ancestors. The relative concerned is distinguished by sex only when addressed (*v.* Table VI), but no distinction is drawn between the maternal and paternal grandparents.

Consanguineous relatives of the first ascending kinship grade are grouped terminologically into four types, broadly as male and female

of the male parent's and female parent's side respectively. Affinal
relationship is indicated when direct by adding a qualifying term,
foŋovai, to the ordinary words for father and mother; when indirect
(*e.g.* the husband of one's father's sister) by incorporating within the
nomenclature of consanguinity, using the parental terms alone. Thus
the term *tamana*, more commonly found in its abbreviated form *mana*,
refers not only to the father and his male siblings but also to the
husband of a father's sister; the term *tinana*, generally used as *nana*,
refers to the wife of a mother's brother as well as to the mother and

TABLE V

SCHEMATIC LIST OF TIKOPIA KINSHIP TERMS OF REFERENCE

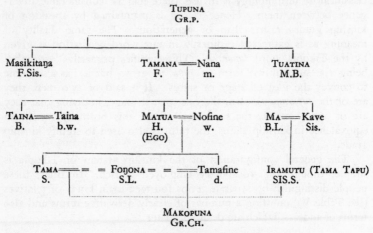

NOTE.—Terms for males, or for males and females, in capitals.
Terms for females only, in small type.

her female siblings, while *mana foŋovai* and *nana foŋovai* refer to the
father-in-law and mother-in-law. *Matua* is also used for the father-
in-law (*v.* Text S. 10) as a term of reference, without any possessive
adjunct (cf. p. 251).

Most important in the scheme of relationship is the separation of
the family group of the mother from that of the father. It is true
that in the kinship grade of the grandparents both sides of the house
are classed together and treated much alike. But the social alignment expressed particularly by the two relationships, *tuatina* and
masikitaŋa, as has been shown, is of nuclear importance for the grouping of kin and the ordering of the social life, especially in its ceremonial
aspect. The phenomenon of distinguishing mother's brother and

father's sister terminologically from their cognates, while omitting to draw such a distinction between mother's parents and father's parents, can obviously be correlated with the more active part which persons of the junior kinship grade play in the drama of practical affairs. These are people in the prime of life, and in their hands the destinies of the society basically lie, as guiding, ruling and advising, they influence the conduct of its individuals. This is one more illustration of the general proposition that kinship terminology is a correlate of social function, though not necessarily always a perfect reflection of it.

For consanguineous relatives of one's own kinship grade there are two principal terms which are capable of some modification. In their primary meanings they distinguish basically between siblings of the same sex (*taina*) and those of opposite sex (*kave*). The brother of a man is regarded, terminologically, the same as the sister of a woman, and distinguished from the man's sister and the woman's brother. The emphasis is thus placed not on the sex of the person to whom reference is made, but to the similarity or difference of sex of the two persons concerned. A further division of a subsidiary kind is made between the children of male or female siblings on the one hand, and the children of a male and of a female sibling on the other, *taina* or *kave fakalaui*, and *taina* or *kave fakapariki*. The differentiation which is begun by the heterosexual relationship in one generation is thus carried through to the next. It vanishes, however, in the case of a portion of the third generation, the children of *taina*—siblings of the same sex—who use towards each other's parents the ordinary parent terms and among their own ranks the " good " brother-sister terminology, involving no restraint between persons of the same sex. The process of differentiation may then begin again. There is thus a mechanism inherent in the kinship system itself for the continual conversion of certain restrained into free relationships. This process represents in effect, a delayed equation of the sister's son with the brother's son and is, terminologically at least, a negation or nullification of that differentiation of brother and sister and their respective offspring which is so fundamental to the Tikopia polity. We have thus the balanced application of a principle, the imposition of a stress and the correction for it, which makes for a well organized smoothly functioning society. To set the matter in its sociological perspective, one can see in this successive splitting and re-combining of kindred with regard to sex-alignment in the prior kinship grade the means whereby extremely important functional groupings are preserved in their fullest extension. The social security of an individual depends upon having groups of *tuatina*, *masikitaŋa*, *mana* and *nana* to play different parts in the ceremonial by which he is enabled to enter life, pass through its stages and depart from it in the appropriate manner. These groups are formed mainly from his immediate relatives in his mother's and his father's *paito*, but are not confined to these. The mechanism just discussed spreads their membership throughout the community, so that failing one's own family ties, there are always more distant relatives to whom one may turn. " No-one in Tikopia is left relationless," it is said, and this terminological mechanism does not allow the relationship to become blurred, but keeps it sharp and distinct, in keeping with social and ritual needs. People are not " just relatives " to others, no matter how distant; they are always a definite species of relative ready to assume appropriate reciprocal functions to others in respect of their common kinsman.

The terms for wife and for husband in Tikopia are specific and individual in their application. They are the only ones that are. A man speaks of no other woman as " *toku nofine*," and she of no other man as *toku matua*. These are the terms in common use, but occasionally the general words for male and female are employed instead, the possessive pronoun making the meaning clear. Thus a man to indicate his wife to me from among the other members of the household said " *Fafine aku*." The literal translation, " woman of mine," is more colloquial and derogatory than the original. The corresponding *ma femme* in French, like the German usage of *mein Mann* by a wife, is of the same order as the Tikopia expression.

Affinal relatives of one's own kinship grade, apart from the spouse, are separated into two classes, according to whether they are of the same sex as oneself or of the opposite sex. The former are referred to as *ma*, sisters-in-law being termed *ma fafine* and brothers-in-law *ma tanata*. A relative by marriage of the opposite sex is known as *taina*. It is of interest to note that this is the same term used for a relative by blood of the same kinship grade and *of the same sex* as oneself. A man thus uses for a woman a word basically applied to his own brother. Here is an instance of the economy of the Tikopia kinship system. Refusing the creation of an entirely new term the people have pressed into service a term of consanguinity, but robbed it of the significance of blood relationship by causing it to suffer a change of sex. The reason for this is obvious. It might have been expected that a man would describe his sister-in-law as his *kave* (sister); but this would mean that if the logical implications of the term were followed out, her children would stand in a special relationship to him, would be the recipient of gifts and ritual services, would call him *tuatina* (mother's brother), and be called by him *iramutu* (nephew or niece) and *tama tapu* (sacred child). This would conflict with the normal patterns of behaviour, since they are really his brother's children and regard him as a secondary father (*tamana*) in quite a different category from that just mentioned. The whole system would be thrown into confusion. The term *taina* is consequently employed with a neutral significance, and since the children of any *taina*, unlike those of a *kave*, are in the same general category of formal behaviour patterns as one's own and one's brother's children, the logical integrity of the system is preserved. As is often the case, the native reason given for the usage is less consistent than the usage itself. The people themselves in explaining this application of the term stress the identity of husband and wife. A man's brother is his *taina*, therefore the brother's wife should also be termed *taina*—this is the native idea. Similar also are the cases of a wife's sister, a husband's brother and a woman's sister's husband. The general principle is that anyone whom the spouse knows as *kave* is known to oneself as *ma*; anyone whom the spouse knows as *taina* is known to oneself as *taina*. Needless to say, this coalescence of terminology due to marriage found in the one case is by no means operative in all aspects of Tikopia kinship.

The use of the term *taina* under such conditions is not a device to block sexual connection between relatives by marriage. *A priori*, one might expect that for a man to call a woman by what is primarily a " brother " term and vice versa would place a barrier between them, but such is not the case. Freedom of behaviour, casual sexual relations and even marriage between affinal *taina* occur, and are governed merely by the normal rules of social intercourse. In a case known to me where a man begot a child by one of his *taina* without marrying her, the social interest centred in the stigma of illegitimacy applying to the child and the minor scandal of the father's avoidance of responsibility, not in the prior kinship status of the pair. The woman was the sister of his brother's wife, who was Nau Nitini, hence in the native phrase the two persons were *tau fanau i Nau Nitini*, *taina* linked through her.

In the kinship grade below one's own the commonest term is *tama*, child, employed by any person for his or her own children and for the children of *taina* (a man's brother's children or a woman's sister's children). This word covers both sexes, but is used freely without qualification to describe males as the equivalent of " son," while for females the secondary form *tamafine*, obviously a contraction for *tama fafine*, female child, is commonly employed. The parallel form to the latter, *tama tanata*, male child, is used only as a descriptive phrase in specific explanation, as in answer to a question, " What is the sex of the child ? " This fusion of the particular and the general in the Tikopia terms for son and child—a usage common elsewhere in Polynesia—smacks of a superiority of male status which would not satisfy a modern feminist. The native women take it calmly enough.

As usual, the context is sufficient to supply the meaning.

Following the ruling principle, a terminological distinction might be expected between the children of *taina* and of *kave*. There is, however, only a partial one, since though a brother refers to his sister's children as *iramutu*, she uses the word *tama* for his as for her own. Both use the ordinary terms of address to children. But in behaviour the differentiation is clear ; the separate linguistic category enters where the weight of social differentiation is greatest.

In the kinship grade below one's own a special term is used for affinal relatives. Persons who marry one's children are designated, irrespective of sex, as *foŋona*, a word clearly related in derivation with its reciprocal *foŋovai* (or *foŋoai*), though the latter is not used independently, but as an appendage to the ordinary parental terms.

To persons a double kinship grade below one's own there is only one term applied—*makopuna*, meaning primarily a grandchild, but covering offspring of son or daughter in the widest sense. Etymologically there is evident affiliation of this term with its reciprocal *puna*, though the exact semantic significance of this is no longer ascertainable. This is not the principle of equivalence of alternate generations ; the grandfather's father is called *tupuna*, not *tamana*, and the great-grandchild *makopuna*, not *tama*. There are no affinal terms in the grandchild kinship grade ; persons married to one's *makopuna* are simply called by the same term as their spouses.

Reviewing the general structure of the Tikopia system, one can point to its essential symmetry. Ten major categories of relatives by blood are recognized, each comprising a set of near and distant kin under a specific term and a definite set of ways of behaviour, without of course attempting to identify the propinquity of such kin or to fuse the individual personal relationships involved. One category in the grandparents' grade ; four in the parents' grade ; two in one's own ; two in that of one's children ; and one in the grade of the grandchildren—such is the scheme. Of kin by marriage there are four new categories—one of the grade above one's own, two of the same grade, and one of the grade below, not counting the differentiation on a sex basis.

This division of relatives, though so simple, is extraordinarily effective in operation, being plastic enough to meet the needs of the elaborate social organization, where it serves as a basis for much of the economic, ritual, aesthetic and religious life of the people.

ELABORATIONS OF THE STRUCTURAL SCHEME

So far the essential structure of the linguistic mechanism of the kinship system has been presented, an analysis of the form and nature of the grouping recognized and the cardinal principles which underlie it. In several directions, however, the system has developed features which, whatever be their origin, serve to modify its real simplicity and thereby render it a richer medium for the expression of social relationships, facilitating the freer use of the linguistic categories in ordinary life.

LINKED RELATIONSHIP TERMS

A convenient usage in Tikopia enables one to address or describe two or more kinsfolk in a short phrase containing only a single kinship term. In English this usage is very limited, more so even than in other European languages. We can talk about " brothers " but we have no single term to include both brothers and sisters, as in the German Geschwister. And both languages can refer only in full to a father and son, or uncle and nephew. In Tikopia the term of linkage, *tau*, allows this to be neatly done. *Tau* may be described as a relational particle, not altogether of the possessive order, but indicating the existence of a bond between the objects mentioned. The phrase *taŋata tau vaka* signifies the owner of a canoe (most nearly : " man linked with canoe ") ; *tau arofa* (" linked with affection ") is the term used for an heirloom, an object taken over from the dead, and therefore fraught with emotional associations.

By placing *tau* before one term of kinship, the existence of the other term or terms may be inferred, and a dual or plural reciprocal significance given to the concept. *Tau kave* means brother and sister ; *tau ma*, a pair of brothers-in-law, or of sisters-in-law. In the latter case the adjuncts *taŋata* or *fafine* will indicate the sex of the parties. When it is a case of more than one kinship grade, then the superior term of relationship is given; the inferior follows from it. *Tau mana* means then father and child ; *tau nana*, mother and child ; *tau tuatina*, mother's brother and sister's child ; *tau masikitaŋa*, father's sister and brother's child ; *tau tamana maroa*, father's bachelor brother and his brother's child.[1] Here, too, sex can be indicated when that

[1] A similar usage occurs in parts of Melanesia and Western Polynesia. In Eddystone Island the prefix *tama* is used with a kinship term to denote a reciprocal relationship (Rivers, *H.M.S.*, I, 253) ; in San Cristoval the prefix *wa* is used with the reciprocal *hagi*, followed by the kinship term and the third personal pronominal suffix *ta* (Fox, *Threshold of the Pacific*, 1924, 51) ; in New Ireland various particles are used to the same effect (P. G. Peckel, *Anthropos*, iii, 1908, 456-481) ; in Ontong Java the particle *hai* is used (Hogbin, *Oceania*, I, 1931, 413). See also my article, *J.R.A.I.*, LX, 1930.

of both parties is the same. An ancient tale begins, " *Tau puna fafine e nofo o reo ufi*," literally " Linked grandparent female dwelt and guarded yams," that is, a grandmother and her granddaughter performed the office. Again the adjuncts *laui* and *pariki*, good and bad, indicate the state of feeling between the parties. A pair of brothers-in-law who have fallen out over a matter of land are described as " *tau ma pariki*," " brothers-in-law in evil relationship." Plurality is given to these phrases by beginning them with the ordinary plural particle *ŋa*. Thus " *ŋa tau nana e nofo i ŋa uta* " means " the mother and her children living inland " (*v.* also Text S. 3). As a native explained it, " One father's sister and brethren, maybe two, collectively they are *ŋa tan masikitaŋa*." Such an expression can be collectivized around the kinship term still further by introducing it with the particle *te* (the), thus converting it into the singular and emphasizing its unitary nature. " *Te ŋa tau mana i Tafua*"—an expression often heard—means the Ariki Tafua and his sons.

These phrases, a convenient part of the ordinary idiom, are woven into the fabric of the language by extending their meaning by the ordinary processes. It was by this means that I stumbled on the usage early in my stay. Seeing a couple of women going along a path I asked idly who they were. The answer came, " *te tau masikitaŋa anea tokarua e oro*," which after some puzzled enquiry I discovered to mean, " It's a father's sister and her niece, those two persons who are proceeding there." The ensuing explanation included the following actual instances of such relationship. " Nau Terara, who is living in the house Motuaŋi, went to her ' son ' to dwell with him to stabilize their position. I can say to you, ' *Te tau masikitaŋa* are Moritaurua (Pa Motuaŋi) and Nau Terara.' Pa Taitai and Pa Faraŋanoa when together are *te tau tuatina*. A man may ask, ' Who are they ? ' I can say, ' *Tau tuatina* in Faraŋanoa.' " The ordinary extensions of usage apply to such expressions. The father's sister of Afirua married the brother of Pa Raŋipaea. Hence Afirua and the daughters of Pa Raŋipaea are *ŋa tau kave*. The house-name is frequently subjoined to give specification. Thus I have heard a child refer to *ŋa tau mana maroa i Maneve*, " the bachelor uncles and their brothers' children in Maneve." A casual comment is made in the domestic circle of the chief of Kafika. " *Tau puna i Tavi e nofo*," " Grandparent and grandchild in Tavi are at home." " *Ma ai ?* " comes the question, literally " With whom ? " This is an enquiry as to who is the grandchild ; the grandparent is known.

An exception to the general rule of compounding such phrases is in the case of siblings of the same sex. Instead of retaining the word *taina* a new term is introduced, and brothers or sisters are spoken of as *tau fanau*. I found no reason for this anomaly in sibling terminology. But the term may include half-brothers and half-sisters also —" *te fanauŋa sokotasi, te mana sokotasi, nana kesekese*," " the single family ; the one father, different mothers " was a phrase often used in describing to me sibling relationship. *Fanau* as an independent verb means " to give birth " ; this phrase then signifies rather vaguely " persons linked by the giving of birth." *Fanauŋa* is applied to the children of a family—*te fanauŋa sokotasi*—it is said, to indicate that they have the same parents (the one birth-group).

The particle *tau* is used also outside the range of kinship with similar meaning. *Tau soa* means a pair of bond-friends, *te ŋa tau soa*, a group of bond-friends ; while the two great categories of persons between whom there is restraint of conduct and those between whom there is not are distinguished as *tautau pariki* and *tautau laui*—those badly and those well linked.[1]

In ordinary domestic conversation personal names are not used a great deal, but the terms of linked relationship or analogous expressions, such as numerical couplings, are utilized much more. One reason for this, no doubt, is that adherence to the rule of avoidance of the names of relatives by marriage is rendered easier by the employment of such a mechanism. Again, the scale of Tikopia society is so small that participants in a conversation can usually gather from, say, a coupling of a kinship term and a reference to locality, who are the persons mentioned.

TERMS OF ADDRESS

An elaboration of which the observer soon becomes conscious is the use of special terms for relatives who are being addressed, as against the terms used for referring to them. This phenomenon is not very common in Polynesian communities where the practice of using the personal name of the relative instead of any kinship classification is more usual. In Tikopia, however, the use of the personal name is a sign of superiority on the part of the user or of freedom of behaviour between the two persons concerned. There are a number of cases where this should not be. A grandparent or parent may call their grandchild or child by his or her name, but not conversely, and the name of a father's sister should not be uttered by her brother's children. Mother's brother and sister's child may call each other by name, as may brothers and sisters indifferently ; between all affinal relatives, however, the use of the personal name is rigidly barred. It

[1] For discussion of bond-friendship, see my contribution to a Festschrift in honour of R. R. Marett, 1936 ; for *tautau laui* and *tautau pariki*, see Chapter IX.

is just in these cases where the prohibition of the use of the personal name impels resort to the kinship term that special terms of address exist. In the other cases, where either name or kinship term may be used at will, the term of reference also serves for that of address. Moreover, in the former case the term of address quite frequently represents a bifurcation of the term of reference, the distinction of sex being introduced by a modification or an adjunct. These points

TABLE VI

SCHEMATIC LIST OF TIKOPIA KINSHIP TERMS OF ADDRESS

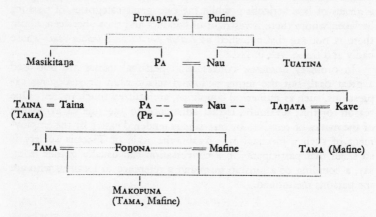

illustrate the closeness of the connection between the use of terminology and other behaviour in kinship—that vital plastic interdependence which cannot be rendered by any mere cataloguing of the " functions of kin."

As a rule in Tikopia the vocative particle " E " follows the personal name or kinship term used in addressing someone, the speech sequence being so close that one might almost regard the particle as an affix. As, however, the speech habit of these natives is of a nervous, iterative kind in address or command, it is customary (apparently as the result of the native feeling for balance of diction) for such a word when repeated to be uttered without the particle, or for the word to be first called out alone and then repeated with the particle added. For instance, one hears a cry of " *Nau E ! Nau !* " or " *Pa ! Pa E !* "[1] Colour and force can be given to speech by

[1] The Maori custom is to precede the kinship term or proper name with the particle " E " under similar conditions. I know no reason that can be assigned for this difference of idiom.

this habit of variation in repetition, which appears also in many other linguistic situations.

The terms of address to grandparents (referred to as *puna*) retain the root *pu* which with slight modification is common to many Oceanic languages in this significance. The grandfather is addressed as " *Putaŋata*," the grandmother as " *Pufine*." [1] For mother's brother and father's sister the terms of reference are retained as terms of address, though as noted already the latter may be called by substitute terms. The call to a mother, *Nau*, and to a father, *Pa*, are different from their respective terms of reference, *nana* and *mana*, but in the true Tikopia spirit of economy are employed again in another sense as the titles for married people preceding their house-name.[2] In this form they are used between husband and wife, though relations between them are not so stiff as this might be thought to imply. The wife can address the husband also as *Pe* ——, while for him there is another term, *Fine*, to be compounded with the wife's house-name. *Fine* is apparently an abbreviation from the term of reference for wife, *nofine*, and it is used also as a term of address between sisters-in-law. As in the case of the term for grandmother, *pufine*, and that for daughter, *tamafine*, there is an affiliation with the general term *fafine*, female ; the idea of " femaleness " is brought out fully in the kinship terminology of these folk.

The term *Pe* is significant as used towards a husband. The title of a married man has a range of vowel change which is an index of social status. *Pu* indicates primarily age, sometimes ancestral dignity, sometimes a grandfather's position ; *Pa* indicates general married status and is the common title, and connotes also fatherhood ; *Pe* indicates essentially a married man of equivalent kinship status as the speaker, as a brother, or brother-in-law ; more rarely it is used for a son. Pa Tarikitoŋa in introducing me to the members of his family pointed out his wife, then added, " *Na kave tena, Pe Maniva*," " That is her brother," giving his house-name with the brotherly prefix. The Ariki Tafua calls the elder of Korokoro " Pe Korokoro," and

---

[1] It is difficult to decide on grounds of consistency whether *putaŋata* should be written as one word or two. *Taŋata* is ordinarily used as a separate word and *fine* is not, except in quite a different significance ; on the other hand *Pu fafine*, the form strictly parallel to *putaŋata*, is used only as the formal title of a female deity. This bifurcation of form with frequent shift of meaning is an interesting feature of Tikopia linguistics, albeit exasperating to the recorder who strives for uniformity. In a clearly exoteric context such as ordinary kinship I therefore use the form *putaŋata*, analogous to its sex opposite.

[2] Similar, though not precisely the same usages may be compared in the Andaman Islands on the one hand (A. R. Brown, *Andaman Islanders*, 54), and in European culture, e.g. *Monsieur, Madame*, on the other.

I have heard him speak of his youngest son as " Pe Mukava." The terms used for the various chiefs may be taken by way of further illustration, since their rank tends to make the terms of address towards them be on the highest plane. The point to be noted is that it is the relative age and kinship status that determines the precise term used.

All deceased chiefs are spoken of as *Pu*, irrespective of their position in the genealogical tree ; the names Pu Kafika, Pu Tafua, etc., cover a long range of ancestors. The present chief of Faŋarere is usually spoken of as Pu Faŋarere, since he is an old man, though the Ariki Kafika calls upon him at religious ceremonies as Pa Faŋarere and his peers in kinship grade occasionally call him Pe Faŋarere. The Ariki Tafua comes in the same category. The Ariki Kafika, a man of middle age, is commonly addressed or spoken of as Pa Kafika or Pae Kafika. (The second form is more euphonious to the native ear and conveys a suggestion of greater courtesy ; it is used mostly for elders, and Pae Sao was nearly always so called.) I have heard one of his elders, however, as well as his wife, address him as Pe Kafika. Neither he nor the Ariki Taumako are ever called Pu Kafika or Pu Taumako ; if either of these titles were to be used at present people would think that reference was being made to one of their ancestors. But the usage may vary according to circumstances. The Ariki Tafua and the Ariki Taumako are classificatory brothers. The latter normally refers to the former as Pu Tafua because of the difference in years between them ; when it is the kinship bond that is prominent between them, then he calls him Pe Tafua, as I have heard. It may be noted that the particle *pe* cannot stand alone as a kinship term.[1]

Terms for address to gods too partake of a kinship character. All deities are put in the kinship grade at least twice removed from the speaker, thus indicating their seniority. In spite of the fact that father and mother are the relationships of greater codified respect, it is as " Grandfather " and " Grandmother " that the deities stand in the heavens. *Putaŋata* or *Pu*, and *Pufine* are the ordinary ways of invoking them ; Pu Fafine, Pufine Ma, Pu Lasi are individual titles.

Between brothers and sisters terms of address and reference are the same. Men, however, commonly substitute a word of the lower kinship grade, *tama*, which is less formal. Women have no parallel usage, but more frequently call each other by their personal names. Even chiefs may be thus informally addressed. I was sitting one evening beside the lake with Seremata and talking with the Ariki Taumako who had come to dress his hair with mud in the native

[1] Between this and the self-sufficient homophone *pe*, meaning an over-ripe breadfruit, there appears to be no obvious connection

fashion. After a pause in the conversation, as darkness was drawing near, my companion said, " *Tama E, maua ka oro.*" "Son! he and I are going." "Go," replied the chief politely. He and Seremata were *taina*, not true brothers, but ancestrally connected (*v.* also Texts S. 4, S. 5 and S. 6).

Relatives by marriage of opposite sex address each other as *taina* when they do not use the house-name. For those of the same sex there are special terms of address. Brothers-in-law call each other *taŋata* [1] (*v.* Text S. 9), sisters-in-law call each other *fine.*

For the kinship grades lower than one's own the only difference between the terminology of reference and of address is that *tamafine*, daughter, is abbreviated to " *mafine*," and that a grandchild is often addressed by the term for son or daughter—as generally used for a child, in fact.

One interesting idiom may be noticed here—the use of terms of address in referring to people. This is parallel to the English custom in family life. Thus a Tikopia will say, " Hand me the water-bottle of Father " (*Pa*), not " of my father " (*toku mana*). The old Ariki Faŋarere is wanted for a ceremony. " Call to grandfather to come " (*Karaŋa ki a putaŋata ke au*) cry the young men ; and the Ariki Kafika, his son-in-law, enquires, " Father has come ? " (*Ku au Pae ?*). The Ariki Tafua lays down the law in his usual cryptic authoritative tone. " Father is right " (*E tonu ko Pa*) the sons and daughters say. The use of these forms argues a greater intimacy than is conveyed by the corresponding terms of reference. The sentence " Our father is right " (*E tonu ko tatou mana*) is frequently also heard, but in open gatherings where more distant relatives are present, and usually uttered by one of them. Naturally there is no sharp dividing line regulating the choice of terms, and it is difficult to convey these more delicate flavours of differentiation without giving them a misleading harshness and definiteness. Yet it is in the subtle choice and blending of these differences that the polite native brings out the full richness of his kinship terminology and adapts himself gracefully and efficiently to the variety of his social contacts.

It may be noted that it is only in songs, where licence is permissible, that the kinship terms of address are used with the possessive pronoun, and thus really deputize for the terms of reference. " *Toku*

---

[1] Pronounced *ta:ŋa:ta* or when spoken quickly, *taŋa:ta*, as distinct from the ordinary word *taŋata*, meaning " man," and its plural *ta:ŋata*, " men," " people." If one were to venture on an etymological reconstruction one would say that the term for brother-in-law has probably been derived from a specific application of that for man, as giving a colourless term correlated with the name-avoidance taboo, and that the sound-shift is then a secondary phenomenon to assist clarity.

nau" a person may wail in a dirge, " my mother," instead of the correct " *toku nana.*" The anomaly of this is quite recognized by the natives themselves, but justified on grounds of preservation of rhythm (*v.* Chapter VIII).

THE MEANING OF KINSHIP TERMS

Since in a classificatory system each term has a multiple referent, it is necessary to consider how differentiation of kin is managed. No modern anthropologist would deny that there is such differentiation, a selection on a personal basis. That there is a source of confusion present may be illustrated by an incident which I witnessed. Pakikiterena, a son of the Ariki Taumako, called out to a group of men, " *Pa E! Pa!* " The chief replied, " What ? " " *Pa i Faitoka,*" called the boy, ignoring his own father, but mentioning the house-name of the " father " he wanted—in this case his father's sister's husband. " What ? " answered this man in turn. Here there was a lack of coincidence in meaning between speaker and hearer, and an elucidatory phrase had to be added. Malinowski describes such a method of giving clarity to classificatory terms as an *index of circum-locution*; I should prefer to describe it, if a name is wanted, as an *index of precision* or of *specification*, since it does not go round the point, but makes it more precise.

These indices are numerous. Important among them is the index of ocular precision, when the speaker looks at the person he wants, the manual index (the selection of a person by pointing or beckoning), the tonal index, and the verbal index. The first three are used particularly by young children to give precision to their kinship statements. I must say that I could not find any differentiation in emotional tone corresponding to difference in propinquity of kinship when the same term was used in varying context, such as Malinowski describes.[1] In Tikopia general situation was apparently the only guide to meaning. As the example above shows, the natives themselves were often uncertain, and even confused the reference when the circumstances were not clear.

One method of specifying a given relative is of course to supple-ment the reference to him by the mention of his personal name. This, however, is not frequently done in Tikopia, where name barriers between kin are common. Among the Maori it is much more general. The most usual method of giving precision to a kinship reference in Tikopia is by addition of the house-name to the term, as in the example of Pakikiterena quoted above. It is most frequently

[1] B. Malinowski, " Culture," *op. cit.*

done when it is not the most immediate relative that is being spoken of. Thus Katoarara, son of Pae Sao, if conveying an invitation from his own father would probably simply say, "*Toku mana e kafi mai ki a ke.*" If, however, it was on behalf of his father's brother, he would most likely put it, "*Toku mana i Niata e kafi mai ki a ke,*" or, if on behalf of the Ariki Taumako, he would say, "*Toku mana te ariki. . .,*" "my 'father' the chief." But such a reference is often introduced in order to specify the person, and not to clarify the kinship situation, which is taken for granted.

PROPINQUITY OF RELATIONSHIP

There are a number of terms which can be subjoined to those of kinship and, without specifying the precise genealogical position of a relative, place him or her in the category of near or distant kin. A combination of categories is used for this purpose. A relative may be :

maori,	literally " true," " correct "	*i.e.*	close
fakatafatafa	„ " set aside "	„	distant
i take ŋaŋea	„ " in another place "	„	„
kesekese (or ke)	„ " different "	„	„

Maori ordinarily in Tikopia means true.[1] " *E maori, pe te loi ?* " one asks of a piece of news. " Is it true, or is it false ? " " *Aku maori soa E,*" a man will say if you doubt his word. " My truth, friend." " *Te atua maori soa E,*" " It was really a ghost, friend," and so on. But in the kinship sphere *maori* can be opposed only by a negative and not by its general opposite *loi*. As in English, one can say, " he is not my true brother " (*Ko ia sise toku taina maori*), but one may not say, " he is my false brother."

There is the further anomaly, that in the positive sense, *maori*, truth, is set against the criteria of spatial separation on the one hand and difference on the other. As if that which is distant cannot be true ; that which is true cannot be distant, or different. But to place weight on this contrast as evidence for a certain psychological or philosophical attitude would be to wrench these terms from their immediate setting, an unjustifiable proceeding. Whatever be the etymological grounds for this usage, they are beyond our power to recapture here. The terms must be taken in their specific not in their general (literal) sense.

Of interest is the tendency to render the sociological category of kinship in terms of the spatial category. There is some grounds for equating them since the kin of more remote consanguinity tend to be living at a distance, whereas those of near relationship tend to be next

[1] *Maori* bears different meanings in other Polynesian dialects.

door, or close at hand. But the correlation is by no means a very definite one; " distant " fathers and sons may well be living in the same village. We also have of course in English the same use of metaphor.

What may be called the vice of the classificatory system may also be noted—the tendency to expand not its terminology, but its referents, to convert an expression of limited range into one of wider application. The term *maori*, for instance, from its general usage might be supposed to refer to immediate kin only. But by *taina maori* is not meant necessarily one's own brother of the same father and mother; the term includes also what we call first cousins—though normally not the children of these. If one wishes to be precise, then other descriptive phrases must be used, of the type of *te fanauŋa sokotasi*, " of the one birth group," or one goes still further and says, " the one father, the one mother." In the work of collecting genealogies and census material this is the only safe guide for the anthropologist.

The extent to which the use of the term *maori* may go is seen in

GENEALOGY IV.

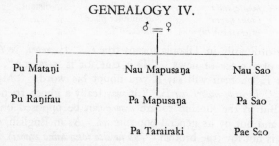

Here, Pu Raŋifau, who was the *taina maori, taina fakapariki* of the fathers of Pae Sao and Pa Tarairaki, is spoken of as their *mana maori* by them; he is their father's mother's brother's son. It may be noted that the characterization of him as a " true " father has no relation to the fact that the fathers of both these men are dead; he is not a sub-stitute parent, but was called such when they were alive.

A few examples will show how the *fakatafatafa* relationship is derived.

Pa Fenuatara and Vaetauraro, wife of Pa Paŋisi, are *tau kave fakatafatafa*. The *puna* of Vaetauraro, her father's mother, was the sister of Tarotu, former Ariki Kafika. This man's son, Pa Vainunu, is *tau fanau* with the present chief; hence the chief and the father of Vaetauraro are also *tau fanau* and their children *tau kave*, but of distant relationship (*v.* Genealogies I and III).

Pa Motuaŋi and Pa Taitai are *tau fanau fakatafatafa*, distant brothers (*v.* Genealogy V). The father's father's mother of Pa Taitai married

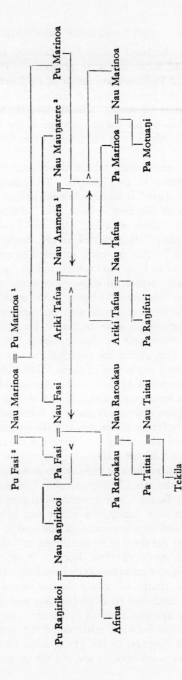

GENEALOGY V

RELATIONSHIPS OF PA TAITAI

twice, her first husband being Pu Marinoa, her second Pu Fasi. Grandchildren of these men were respectively Pa Marinoa, father of Pa Motuaŋi, and Pa Raroakau, father of Pa Taitai. Incidentally Nau Tafua, wife of the present chief, is the *masikitaŋa* of Pa Taitai, hence the Ariki Tafua is his *mana*. Kinship and the village tie (the latter being responsible for the initial marriage at the basis of the kinship) thus give the loyalty to the chief which the difference of clans fails to do.

The social distinctions which these terms express are of the greatest importance to the Tikopia. Thus marriage with the *kave maori*, the " real sister," is, if not abhorred, at least strongly reprobated, whereas that with the *kave kesekese*, the " different sister," the *kave fakatafatafa*, the " sister set aside," the *kave i take ŋaŋea*, the " sister from another place," is regarded as the proper union. At death, again, the " true " father or son is expected to mourn in seclusion for a long period and to keep food taboos rigidly ; a " different " relative of the same status tapers off these expressions of grief according to the distance of his relationship. *Taina maori*, whether brothers or cousins, keep in close touch with one another and co-operate in many ways ; *taina* who have become " set aside " by the passage of generations meet only as chance serves. At the super-incision ceremony of a boy, again, the principal man is the *tuatina maori*, or if there are several, the senior of them. His privilege and duty is to invite the co-operation of the various *tuatina fakatafatafa*, called for this purpose the *kerekere*, the soil, a term which, without being directly derogatory, implies their lower status in this connection. They must wait individually for an invitation, and do not attend without it ; he goes by right and takes charge. " Is he not the true mother's brother of the boy ? " (*v.* Chapter XIII).

The immediate nephew or niece as the *matua tama tapu*, the principal sacred child, is the most important object of the care and attention of the mother's family. For general social purposes, when there are several children in a family, the eldest son is usually taken as the representative, and gifts are made to him and in his name, though it is not infrequent for them to be consigned to " the brothers in . . .," mentioning the name of their house. It is the business of the principal sister's son on important ceremonial occasions, if he be old enough, to take charge of certain aspects of the organization of the work. He oversees the food preparation and directs any activities which the *tama tapu* may conduct as a body.

The distinction between relatives of the same nominal class on the basis of the closeness of the genealogical tie is then very clear in Tikopia. There is no need to amplify the point further here, since it will emerge incidentally in later chapters dealing with kinship in the ceremonial life. It will be remembered, however, that the correlation between terminology and functional relationship is by no means complete ; the kinship nomenclature has to be supplemented by other devices in order to make the situation clear.

ADJUSTMENT OF KINSHIP

In any community where kinship is traced bilaterally the question of limits set to the recognition of the tie is important. Several factors may enter here. The capacity of the mechanism for recording kinship is one. The instruction in genealogies provided among the best families in Polynesia—not to mention the more specific memorizing of *fa'alupeŋa* by the *tulafale* of Samoa, or of the *kauae raro* knowledge in the House of Learning by the Maori *tohuŋa*—makes for a wide range of effective kinship, as compared with many of the societies of Melanesia. The existence of this mechanism is of course itself to be correlated with a form of social structure where the attainment or possession of rank, power and religious privilege is bound up with the fact of seniority by birth. Locality also is a factor of moment in conditioning the recognition of kinship ties. Residence may give tacit admission in the first instance to a kinship group, as in Samoa, or more important, non-residence tends to cut people off from their kinship affiliations, as among the Maori. The fact that spatial aggregation can so be a determinant of kinship grouping indicates again how the survival of kinship bonds is dependent upon active social contact between the persons concerned.

Tikopia is too small a community for kinship ties to be entirely lost in this way. Here there are no strangers ; there are merely peripheral kinsfolk. But the ties of consanguinity are continually being interfered with by those of affinity, and adjustment is necessary. I have already given examples of this in a previous publication [1] ; it is of interest here simply to point out the implications. Such apparently inconsistent terminology at first puzzles the investigator. In Tikopia a lad may be " son " to a certain man and " nephew " to that man's father. Two persons who are " grand-daughter " and " son " respectively to a third, may be " sister " and " brother " to each other. There is no real confusion, but merely an adjustment of the general categories to specific cases. Reference to Genealogy V will show how this is done in the case of Pa Taitai. He is *tau puna* with Pa (Pu) Raŋirikoi and *tau fanau* with this man's son Afirua. His father Pa Raroakau and Pa Raŋirikoi were *tau mana*, in a parental relation-

[1] Marriage and the Classificatory System of Relationship, *op. cit.*

ship, but his father's mother and the mother of Nau Raŋirikoi were blood sisters; hence his father and Nau Raŋirikoi were *tau kave maori*, and he is a "brother" of Afirua. It is more convenient for this latter relationship to be traced through the female line, since Pa Taitai and Afirua are much of an age, and brotherhood is therefore most appropriate for them. Where there are several lines from which a person may select his kinship to another, the basis of selection is one of comparative age and rank, coupled with personal interest. What I have termed the *significant relationship*, the one primarily acted upon, tends to be that which involves the greatest incidence of reciprocal obligations and services.

The marriage of people of approximately the same age but of disparate kinship grades tends to level out such discrepancies in terminology. Cases of union between "father" and "daughter," "son" and "mother," "nephew" and "father's sister," all in the classificatory sense, are by no means uncommon in Tikopia. Pa Taitai and his wife were *tau masikitaŋa* before marriage, since Pa Nukutai, the woman's father, is the *mana* (classificatory father) of Nau Raroakau by an ancient kinship tie. Thus, before this union Nau Taitai and Nau Raroakau were *tau fanau*; now they are *tautau pariki*. Pa Fenutapu married his *iramutu fakatafatafa* (classificatory niece). His mother, who was from Anuta, was *tau fanau fakatafatafa* with the mother of Nau Nukuone, the girl's mother. Pa Niukapu, whose mother came from Anuta, was *tau fanau* with Pa Fenutapu before the marriage; now he is *tau mana foŋovai*. These are "anomalous" marriages actually occurring, but on the basis of personal choice, not institutional arrangement. The adjustments which follow on them illustrate very well how the terminology of a classificatory kinship system is the servant, not the master, of the social relationships which it portrays.

In this connection Rivers's suggestion that marriages which are anomalous in terms of the kinship status of the parties who unite are necessarily between persons of disparate age as well is not borne out. Incidentally, it has been shown already by Malinowski and by Fortune that the "correspondences" in terminology which Rivers uses as evidence for such marriages are explicable on economic or other bases apart from that of sex union.

The Tikopia themselves recognize the verbal inconsistency of marriages between "brother" and "sister," "father" and "daughter," etc., and chuckle about it when the point is put to them. Pae Sao was one day amused at my earnestness in following up this line of enquiry. After we had been discussing it together some other men came in, whereupon he said to them quaintly, "While we were talking, he and I, I wanted to laugh, but I did not laugh, because he and I were talking." Respect for the act of conversation restrained him.

REPRESENTATIVE STATUS IN TIKOPIA KINSHIP

An important sociological phenomenon in Tikopia is the frequent occurrence of what may be called representative status in kinship. Certain relationships, certain configurations of units are fundamental to the particular social structure, and the position of individual persons is deliberately subordinated to them. This involves the transference of obligations, both vertically and laterally, from one generation to another, and from one group to an allied group in the same generation. It has been shown how in Tikopia one of the basic elements in the social structure is the tie between a person and his mother's family, focused as the relationship of sister's child and mother's brother. As story, song and the observation of the daily life have proved, this is a bond which arouses the deepest feelings in the natives. Unhappy indeed is the man who has no mother's brother; it is a deprivation quite equal to that of being bereft of parents; it is an orphaning fraught with dire terror for the passage through this world and into the next. Or rather it would be if society did not supply the lack. If one's real *tuatina*, the true brothers of one's mother die, then other brothers of more distant relationship must fill the gap—substitution on the lateral principle, as it may be termed. It is one of the points that can be adduced as evidence for the efficiency of a classificatory system, since it allows of this substitution with the minimum of friction. Terminologically there is no change in the relationship; the new succourer simply moves one step nearer on the social chessboard. But when in the course of time all the men who can fill that position have passed away this is not the end. The vertical principle is in operation, whereby the duties of the mother's brother have been taken over by his son, and if the object of their care still continues to outlive him, then the grandson in turn carries out the task. This operates in conjunction with the lateral principle, so that in concrete terms, when an old man or woman comes to die, all their closer kinsfolk may have long since preceded them, and the person who takes charge of the burial may be the grandson of some distant cousin on the mother's side. But the aged one is still called the *tama tapu*, the sacred child of that person, despite all discrepancies in generation. Kinship in Tikopia is the rod on which one leans throughout life; even in death one is propped up by it. No one can be relationless while the community itself exists.

A few examples will indicate the working of this representative status.

On the occasion of a death it is the custom to include among the gifts brought to the mourning relatives a piece of bark-cloth, later followed by a basket of food, and known as the *kupukupu*. This is specifically a present to the man in charge of the funeral arrangements from his own mother's family. It is a formal expression of sympathy with their *tama tapu*. On the death of the child of Pa Reŋaru he himself was naturally the " basis " of the funeral. As the child was being wrapped up for burial the young man Afirua, who had entered some little time previously and had been watching, went quickly forward and girdled the weeping father with an orange cloth, saying as he did so, " *Tou kupukupu.*" Afirua explained his action by saying, " He is my brother, my sacred child." By this he meant that though they were of the same kinship grade he himself stood *in statu avunculi* to the man ; he was acting for his father, Pu Raŋirikoi, the proper *tuatina*, who was bed-ridden. But the Raŋirikoi family itself was not the real mother's family of Pa Reŋaru ; this was the family of Siku, from which the true mother's brother, Pa Siku, was long since dead, and his son, for private reasons, had not come to the funeral. Hence Afirua played the part of *tuatina* as a deputy for his father who was in turn deputy for an allied group.

A native comment on the situation shows how the absence of a *tuatina* is regarded. " It is the custom of this land from of old because the mother's brother looks after his sister's child. If there is not a *kupukupu* for one then folk will say, ' A person without a *tuatina*,' because his *tuatina* has died. And the man is ashamed. Because in this land while the mother's brother is living his sister's child is rich : when the mother's brother dies he is made poor " (literally a " commoner " or an " orphan "). It is interesting to note how a state of kinlessness becomes a matter of shame. This is the sequence : *amour propre* is retained on public occasions by having due regard to what is conceived to be one's social status ; social status is measured at funerals largely in material terms, by the amount of wailing expended on one's behalf, and the quantity of gifts received; few kinsfolk means sparseness in gifts, hence one is made to feel ashamed for their absence. Incidentally this is one of the reasons why none but foolish and perverse people cultivate enmity with their brothers-in-law. If it be only for the sake of the children, their own or their sister's, most men remain on good terms.

A further example of the way in which the *tuatina* bonds are carried by someone as long as the *tama tapu* who is the object of them is alive is given by the conduct of our friend Pae Sao. He is reckoned as the mother's brother of the children of Nau Mea, Nau Nukura and Nau Nitini. They are women of the family of Toŋatapu, which separated from Sao long ago, but since all the males of it are dead, Pae Sao acts as administrator of ritual and protector to the children, by whom he is called *tuatina* (the women are his classificatory *kave*). At the birth of an infant in one of these families the initial food present known as the *kava makariri* is sent to him, and he expects to be called to sit on the ceremonial side of the house at their incision rites. Some time ago he gave Nau Mea and her husband permission to build their dwelling in one of his orchards, Fakafenuatau, with usufruct of the land, telling them merely not to use the site of an ancient house there.

Attendance at ceremonies and provision of ritual services is practically obligatory on the nearest surviving mother's brother, but the gift of a dwelling-site and the use of land is a voluntary act of kindness. It was done in this case because of his kinship tie with the woman, in whom and whose offspring he feels a protective interest.

Another illustration may be taken from the relationships of the Tafua family. The principal *tama tapu* of the Ariki Tafua, the person who receives the lion's share of gifts and attention from the chief and his household, is the chief's sister's son Moritaurua, known by the house-name of Pa Motuaŋi. To all the Tafua family he is *matou tama tapu*, "our sacred child." As Pa Raŋifuri explained, he and Moritaurua are *taina*, but the latter is also his *tama tapu*; in time his son Seteraki, a "son" (*tama*) to Moritaurua too, will take on the same relation and may be called by him *tuatina* for formal purposes. *Tama tapu* and *tuatina* then, though applying to immediate individual relationships, receive a broader connotation, and stand not for a simple genealogical expression, but for a kinship tie of a certain general type, namely, that between a person and his maternal kindred. The personal relationship is not lost—a man will say of another, "he is actually my *taina* as well as my *tama tapu*"—but for some social purposes it is subordinated. The component elements of the system are submerged for the preservation of the harmony and symmetry of the structural principles. It is the relationship that matters first and the precise position of the individual in it that is secondary.

Fluidity in the use of kinship terms between people is a characteristic feature of the Tikopia method of handling their system. They run up and down the scale with great freedom, picking out the kinship note that is appropriate to the occasion. They can call an aunt a father, a cousin an uncle, with the utmost unconcern, quite untramelled by what appear to us to be biological limitations of these words.

THE KINSHIP TERM AS SYMBOL

This point may be expressed in another way by saying that a kinship term often acts as a piece of verbal compression, a symbol for a set of ideas and attitudes, a guide to a norm of behaviour, not only of the institutionalized type, but also of less rigidly enjoined habits. It may be of course much more than this : as Malinowski has shown in his theoretical studies of primitive language, a word is essentially a mode of expressing and inducing action. But in Tikopia, where social circumstances render a change in relationship imperative or advisable, it is the adoption of a different kinship term which first ushers in the change. The term is an index to the type of behaviour now to be current between the persons concerned.[1] This is particularly the case beyond the bounds of the *paito*, where the relations between the individuals concerned are not already resting upon a strong basis of personal sentiment and close social contacts.

A traditional tale of Puremato and his son Asoaso[2] is an illustration of how, when circumstances render necessary a radical change in behaviour, this may be symbolized—though not determined—by an alteration in the terms employed. A former mistress greeted her returned lover, who happened to be the father of the man whom she had since married, with a song beginning " *Pa E !* " This immediately put their relationship into the parent-child category ; it showed that a completely different set of kinship attitudes had been established, and led the wanderer to hit at once upon the correct explanation.

The Tikopia are fairly well conscious of this symbolic aspect of their kinship terminology, and conversely, are not above turning it to a point of humour by using terms in an incongruous situation. The word for grandfather, or its associates, for instance, conveys the idea of respect to be observed towards the aged ; consequently to call a lusty youth of one's own age by this term may be quite amusing. There is no need to act towards him as if he were this relative ; in fact, to call him such and treat him otherwise gives savour to the jest. Thus his peers on one occasion insisted on addressing Pa Teva as Pu Teva, as if he were an ancient, and got great hilarity therefrom. On another occasion a man wanted a light for his pipe. " The fire— Grandfather ! Father ! Grandson ! " said he. His first call brought no response, hence he jokingly ran through the kinship terms to secure attention. It must be noted that this free play is conducted within the framework of the kinship system itself. The persons

[1] For evidence of this, see my article, *J.R.A.I.*, *op. cit.* ; also Chapter IX of this book.

[2] Given in *History and Traditions of Tikopia*.

whom one addresses with such licence are of the correct status for jesting ; in the case just quoted, the man was a brother.

THE KINSHIP SPEECH OF YOUNG CHILDREN

An indication may now be given of the way in which the young child attempts to formulate in speech its identification of the relatives which comprise its little world.   The child in Tikopia, as elsewhere, does not start off in life with a full set of kinship names and attitudes ready made ; these have gradually to be imposed upon it by tuition, and not without difficulty does it fit itself into the framework which its elders seek to provide for it.   In its earliest years the infant has of course no conception of the nature and scope of its kinship ties, and behaves to its kin on the basis of personal selection according to their association with it.   At first it does not distinguish the kinship terms at all clearly.   It is liable to apply them indiscriminately, irrespective of the type of behaviour appropriate to each, and disregarding the factor of sex.   It distinguishes the persons, but not their relationship.

The first speech of the young child, the natives say, is " *Nau E !* " normally meaning mother. This it learns before all else. Once mastered, this term is apt to be applied indiscriminately to all members of the household, irrespective of their sex or status.   Pa Fenuatara, an interested observer of his children's habits, mentioned the behaviour of his youngest daughter.   He said, " I here am ' Mother.' It will enter from outside and call hither to me, ' *Nau E.*' Thereupon I reply to it, ' What ? '   Now Mataŋore (the next youngest) used to say to me, ' Mother ! Father,' doubling with the word father.   She said first, ' Mother,' thereupon thought, because she knew the speech, therefore said ' Father ' to me afterwards " (Text S. 2).

Here we see the most intimate term coming first as the generic index, and the specific term following, as she recollected what she had been taught. Just as a father of a child may be included in a linguistic category which should be properly confined only to mothers, so are other members of the family group called indiscriminately by these terms, the first to cross the speech threshold of the child. Having once learnt them, it applies them with exuberance.   " The relatives are ' Mother ' throughout and ' Father ' throughout ; its grandparents are ' Father ' throughout and ' Mother ' throughout to it," said Pa Fenuatara.   In other words the connotation of these terms is not one of kinship but of persons known to the infant.

The errors displayed by the child in the application of even the closest terms of kinship are paralleled by mistakes made in the pro-

nunciation of the words themselves, and also in a frequent confusion
between the use of the terms of address and those of reference. Thus,
as I was seated one day in talk with Pa Fenuatara, we heard a neighbour's child outside calling for its mother, but saying, " *Nana, nana !* "
instead of " *Nau,*" a substitution which made my visitor chuckle.
Thereupon he gave me some further examples of the speech of
children. His youngest child said " *Pa E,*" Father, correctly from
the beginning, but " *Nau E* " was at first only " *Au E.*" The
parents recognize the intention of such abbreviations and answer to
them, though from time to time they try to correct the child and
enlarge its vocabulary. " The child which is skilled in the speech,
that is one which has been instructed by its parents," said Pa Fenuatara. He drew an interesting distinction between children who know
the application of the terms and speak them badly, and those who
speak the terms properly but apply them stupidly. He said, " The
speech which is first is ' *Pa* ' (father) and ' *Nau* ' (mother). The
first speech is ' *pa, pa, pa, pa !* ' Next to it comes the speech, ' *Pa
E !* ' Some children are competent in the speech, but their minds
are foolish. They want to speak to their mother. They do not
say ' *Nau E !* ' They go calling out ' *Toku nana E ! Toku
nana E !* ' (' my mother '—a reference term). Another will be able
in the speech, but inept in the uttering of the speech. Thereupon it
says to its *tuatina* (mother's brother), ' *Tatina, tatina.*' And the
masikitaŋa (father's sister) becomes ' *Titāŋa, Titāŋa.*' " Similar unsuccessful attempts are made to grasp the terminology for grandparents (*puna,* in referring to them, and *putaŋata* or *pufine,* according to
sex, in addressing them). " The child may speak foolishly, ' *Puna E,
puna E,*' or speak then, ' *Pūna, pūna.*' And to its grandfather, instead
of *putaŋata,* it calls, ' *Pu E, pu ! Pu E, pu !* ' " This last term is peculiarly inappropriate, since it is essentially the manner of addressing
revered ancestors long dead. Mataŋore, daughter of Pa Fenuatara,
calls her grandmother Nau Kafika, " *Punafine i Kafika,*" which is a
mixture of the two forms of address and reference. And a bachelor
brother of the father, properly designated *mana maroa,* has his title
abbreviated to *mamaroa.*

With these last we have passed of course beyond the sphere of the
first speech of the infant child : the separation of grandparents from
parents, of bachelor from married uncles, of father's sister and
mother's brother from the general knot of elder male and female kin
represents a stage in linguistic development reached only at about
three or four years of age. And children differ greatly in the terminological competency which they have attained by that period. With
the enlargement of vocabulary comes *pari passu,* an increasing verbal

differentiation between persons previously called by the same term, a differentiation which follows that made much earlier in other aspects of the daily life.

The data of Tikopia, scanty as they are, supplement and to some extent contrast with the observations of Professor Malinowski in the Trobriands. He has noted as the result of his work in this region that there takes place an expansion by clear-cut stages in the child's development of kinship terminology and attitudes. As part of this expansion appears the extension to the father's brother and mother's sister of terms used for the parents, and it is suggested that these terms are used by the child not only secondarily in point of time, but also in a figurative way. In a general analysis of the role of kinship in native life Malinowski says, " The first meaning acquired by the child is always individual. It is based on personal relations to the father and mother, to brothers and sisters. A full outfit of family terms with well determined individual meaning is always acquired before any further linguistic developments. But then a series of extensions of meaning takes place. The words mother and father come to be applied first to the mother's sister and father's brother respectively, but they are applied to these people in a frankly metaphorical manner." [1] If the last statement is to be taken literally and the term " family " to be interpreted as meaning the little group of father, mother and children only, then this generalization is hardly likely to be of universal application.

It will be agreed, I think, that the first meaning attached by the child to its kinship speech is individual, based on personal relations to those who surround it. In Tikopia it is clear that the focal point of the child's interest and kinship nomenclature is its own parents, but also that this is to be regarded purely as a function of the proportionately greater care and attention bestowed by them upon it than by other relatives. Some of these, however, do not enter any later upon the scene. Very frequently, as our analysis of the composition of households has shown, there is a father's brother or sister, or both, living under the same roof as the babe and devoting much time to tending and feeding it. The bodily activity of the child towards them is not secondary, derived from that expressed towards the father and mother, but primary, directed towards its specific object from the beginning, only of a slightly different order than that towards the parents whose contact with it is even more intimate and frequent. So also with the verbal activity—the terminology of kinship. As far as could be ascertained, the infant begins to talk no sooner to its father under such conditions than to its father's brother.

[1] Article, " Culture " in *American Encyclopedia of Social Sciences*, 1932.

Here the factor of the transmission of speech forms comes in. The members of the household directly or indirectly train the child to use towards all of them—irrespective of whether true parents or not—its first efforts at identificatory speech. The result is as I have shown— the child broadcasts the terms to all and sundry who enter the house. This is not to deny that the term has a personal application in each case, but the differentiation in meaning which undoubtedly exists does not seem to be given linguistic expression at this stage.

From the Tikopia evidence then, the suggestion of a time lag in the application of terms to specific close relatives cannot be sub- stantiated. Common residence makes for parallel recognition, and the word " Pa " addressed to the father's bachelor brother is no more delayed nor more metaphorical than when addressed to the father himself. The same may apply to those other relatives who may come within the child's kinship horizon and share in the largesse of its nascent speech. The examples of terminological confusion illustrate this from another angle ; the child does not confuse the persons, it merely applies a single term to them. It seems too that the meta- phorical aspect of the ' father ' and ' mother ' terms comes only with the increasing sophistication of the child, long after the terms themselves are in current use.

The processes of growth of kinship terminology in Tikopia are of a multiple character. As the child's circle of acquaintance widens, its response to tuition becomes more conscious and its understanding of relationship deepens, it certainly extends the little budget of terms it possesses to novel individuals who come within cognisance and are presented to it in the known categories. But there is another process at work. With more appreciation of personalities and their status comes an increasing definition, a narrowing down of the parental terms to certain persons only within the kinship range, and an applica- tion of new terms to the others thus eliminated. To the broad undifferentiated use of terms (with clear personal distinction in bodily action between those thus aggregated) succeeds the attribution of differential connotations to each term. This involves the relation of it to a primary source. In other words the linguistic development of the child at this period is not to be equated with its perceptive development ; the former demands much more institutionalized con- formity. It clings to some persons in preference to others, but calls them all " Pa " or " Nau " with no notion that it is extending these words from their primary meaning of " Father " and " Mother." The mother's sister or father's sister does not become a substitute " Nau " ; the mother comes to be treated linguistically as the basic " Nau." The father's sister, for instance, is first called " Nau " by the child, then placed in a different category and called " *Titaŋa*," in an attempt to cope with her difficult title. Finally, she is given her full designation of *masikitaŋa* as the child's speech becomes more supple.

In ordinary speech in later years there is no explicit differentiation in terminology between one's own father or mother and "fathers" or "mothers" of more distant relationship. This suggests that the latter is a metaphorical usage. Linguistically, in fact, it is a specifying usage, a phraseology of precision and narrowing down that is employed to indicate true parents.

That the regular development of a terminology is not identical in all cases the use of the term *tama* shows. The basic significance of this word is "son," but for every man till he is married its primary sense must be "brother's son" or "cousin's son." With the progress of time, as he gets children of his own, then the primary sense of the term will alter for him. But for the society as a whole its place in the structure of the kinship system remains always the same.

With regard to the processes of education of the child in kinship terminology I have little concrete material. Specific instruction does not often obtain—I observed no cases. The child learns far more by hearing its kinsfolk addressed by each other, or by being spoken to itself. Commands such as "Mind your *mana*," "Don't hit your *kave*" and the like are given to it from a very early age. Pa Taitai, before Tekila could walk or talk, gently picked him up under the armpits and lifted him over to his grandmother, with the words, "Go to your *puna*." The frequent hearing of the term of reference often leads a child to use this instead of the term of address, as "*Puna E !*" instead of "*Putaŋata E !*" A similar instance is of Noarima calling "*Nana*" instead of "*Nau E.*"

It is clear that consideration of the linguistic aspect of kinship must be separated to some degree from that of other aspects of infant kinship behaviour, since the speech habit is learned much more slowly than the responses involved in obtaining nourishment and general bodily comfort. Kinship terms, like any other pieces of the social mechanism, are a matter of gradual acquisition, and children have to be taught how to use them, to grow into them.

In different societies the processes involved appear to me to be largely a function of the type of residence in vogue and the degree of intimacy of contact between the child and its various kinsfolk in its earliest months. The thesis here put forward in no way gainsays, of course, the general sociological principle of the primacy of the individual family in the formation of kinship terminologies. It points out simply that social process and individual behaviour are not necessarily coincident, that ontogeny in kinship need not always recapitulate phylogeny.

A TOKEN OF FILIAL SENTIMENT
Pa Ranifuri wearing a tooth of his father, the Ariki Tafua.

CHAPTER VIII

CO-OPERATION AND CONSTRAINT IN MARRIAGE
RELATIONSHIPS

It is often forgotten in anthropological studies of kinship that relationships by marriage can be profitably discussed only against the background of the position of the children of the marriage. As a man's father-in-law and mother-in-law are the grandparents of his child the affinal relationship is inevitably conditioned by this. A man's brother-in-law, except in the few childless unions, is either the father of his own *tama tapu*, or the *tuatina* of his own child, and as such has calls upon him additional to those involved in the immediate bond through his sister or his wife. Since the mother's brother-sister's child situation is of fundamental importance in Tikopia society the two sets of bonds, the affinal and the consanguineous, obviously reinforce each other.

HOW CHILDREN BIND AFFINAL KIN

The natives themselves say that brothers-in-law should stand well with each other because of the children. Thus the Ariki Kafika : " Because the *tuatina* comes and carries the son to the head of the house to fire his oven, because he comes to bury the child, therefore a man behaves well to his brother-in-law. If they fight, who will come ? Will the man carry his son to the head of the house ? Will he bury his son ? No, because he has sat down to wail." This puts the case quite succinctly. At the initiation or burial ceremonies of his child it is a father's place to remain seated and raise the mourning lament ; in theory he is incapable of carrying out the practical duties required. For these he must rely on the mother's brother of the boy. A native saying is, " The brother-in-law comes to see his nephew (or niece), his brother-in-law and his sister." This expresses clearly his joint position.

Another native saying is, " The brother-in-law goes to seek his brother-in-law," that is, the pair mutually help each other. Said Pae Sao when the family of Nukufuti were paying for a canoe built for them, " Anything done in the house of brother-in-law, I rise and go to look after it." On this occasion he had brought a contribution of food and bark-cloth, for which he did not expect repayment.

When they are on friendly terms brothers-in-law are known as *tau ma laui* ; they are in a good relationship. There are, however, some who do not conform to the norm of conduct. From a quarrel-some temperament or some specific clash of interests they have become *tau ma pariki*, brothers-in-law in a bad relationship. Such are Pa Roŋotaono and Pa Raŋitafuri, Pa Reŋaru and Pa Faŋatoto (see above), and also Pa Nukura and Pa Faioa, the latter being brother to the former's second wife, Nau Nukutaofia. These form notable exceptions to the general amity of such relatives by marriage, socially disturbing since their normal obligations are often not fulfilled, and adjustments have to be made by other people.

It is understood that brothers-in-law in the ordinary way render each other assistance in economic undertakings. If one wants help in breaking up ground for a cultivation, felling a tree, setting a net or building a house; if he wishes to borrow some article or to augment his food supplies he calls upon the other, and the call is rarely denied; indeed it is often anticipated. If the wife's brother is a bachelor he may spend quite a lot of time at his sister's house, working and having his meals there, the one service cancelling out the other. Naturally when each brother-in-law has his own family cares the same symbiotic relationship cannot obtain, though the sentiment appears just as friendly, and the reciprocal visiting is frequent. As regards the multiplicity of bonds, the interest is stronger on the side of the wife's brother, since he has a triple tie with the other family—the sister, the sister's children and the sister's husband. But as far as ordinary informal services to that little group are concerned it is practically impossible to distinguish the elements involved. Even in the formal sphere, though gifts are named as being to and from one or other of the individual parties, yet the sum total of relations involved is usually taken into consideration.

Even when the affinal bond is not immediate a brother-in-law is expected to render assistance where needed. On one occasion when Pa Rarovi had to prepare food for a presentation to Kafika he tended the oven alone, until one of his neighbours, seeing the smoke, came along and lent a hand. When the Ariki Kafika heard of this he commented volubly on the work having to be done single-handed. "Where were you brothers-in-law?" he asked angrily of his sons. The relationship was only classificatory, since Nau Rarovi was from the house of Porima. But considering the co-operation in religious ceremonial that was proceeding at the time, and the absence of the true brothers-in-law from Uta, it was the duty of these men to have seen that assistance was provided.

COOKS AFTER MARRIAGE

On the husband's side an obligation of special weight is to come and assist his wife's relatives when, as a group, they have to provide food for some ceremonial occasion. Every man who has married a woman of the family should come along with his bundle of firewood on his shoulder and his bunch of coconuts, while his contribution of taro, breadfruit or bananas is carried by his wife, following behind. If the man cannot come in person he sends as substitute his brother or his son. Since chiefs do not attend in such menial capacity, at the marriage of Pa Roŋoifo the Ariki Taumako, whose wife was a daughter of Pa Niumano, head of that family, was represented, in his absence, by his eldest son Rimakoroa. On important occasions the bonds of relationship are interpreted very widely. At the incision ceremony of the sons of Pa Nukuafua and Pa Nukuone (*v.* Chapter XIII), apart from the immediate brothers-in-law of the two men, there was Pa Matatai, who was married to the daughter of Pa Fetauta, head of an entirely different branch of the family. Pa Mauŋakena was present in a dual role. He was married to the sister of Pa Nukuafua, who in turn was married to his sister. As the natives said therefore, " There he goes, a cook and a mother's brother."

These men constitute the band known as *a soko*, cooks, whose primary function is to be responsible for the tending of the oven, the preparation and serving of the food. They are also termed *rafie*, firewood, or *fatu umu*, oven-stones, terms bluntly descriptive of their duties. This institution has a clear practical significance. The work of the oven is heavy and continuous throughout the day, and also unpleasant from the heat. By putting it traditionally as a definite kinship obligation incumbent upon all sons-in-law, which for the sake of their reputation they do not try to escape, the most essential factor in the organization of the day's ceremonies is made secure. Moreover, the same mechanism secures an adequate supply of firewood. The natives say " Unpleasant work is that of the oven ; all things are got ready by the cooks. When the ordinary crowd come they simply sit down but the cook walks about, he goes and looks at all things. The man whose feast it is does not speak to the crowd, he speaks only to the cook, he speaks to the cook to look to things. He doesn't scold the crowd, he scolds the cook." This shows clearly the unenviable position of this functionary.

The members of the family itself are comparatively free to concentrate upon the provision of the major supplies and on arranging the details of the actual ceremony. The institution has also a secondary convenience in that it allows the women of the family, who have married and gone to live elsewhere, to return automatically to assist their men-folk on these occasions and so retain their family ties unimpaired.

In the native belief even gods are pressed into service in this way. When a male deity of one clan is regarded as married to a female deity of another, he is conceived as being bound by his kinship duties and obliged to come along in intangible spirit form to attend the most sacred ritual of the latter clan, bearing his firewood and his food gifts—also intangible, but none the less real, with him. Failure in food supplies from orchard or fishing grounds at the critical time may be put down, half in jest but half in earnest, to slackness on the part of such deities, who are adjured to bestir themselves accordingly.

Among men the obligations of the *soko* are not entirely without recompense. Not only have they so to speak been " paid in advance " by the reception of the women in marriage, but their performance on certain occasions, as at initiation ceremonies, entitles them to gifts and food. Here as elsewhere the principle of individual distinction on the basis of primacy of kinship bonds is in operation. The principal cook is distinguished from those of more distant connection and rewarded accordingly. Thus in anything that the Tafua family does the *rafie e mua*, literally the " foremost firewood," is Pa Motuaŋi. It will be remembered that he is also the principal *tama tapu* of those people. Here is another instance of representative status, for he is acting in this capacity of cook for his father, long since dead, who was the true brother-in-law of the chief. Seconding him come Pa Tekaumata and Pa Nukuarofi who have married the chief's daughters. Later in status come members of the family of Raŋirikoi, since Nau Raŋirikoi, though a *kave* of the chief, is but a half-sister, and her mother was secondary (*fakamurimuri*) to his in the polygynous household. All these people are *soko*, but the distinction between them is very clear—further proof, if need be, of the recognition of the personal factor in classificatory kinship usage. The persistence of such ties is seen in the case of Pa Motuaŋi, who still comes to play his part at the oven though his father and his mother, the basis of the obligation, are both dead.

Over against this essential co-operation in such affairs on the part of brothers-in-law is to be set the sharp separation that occurs in ceremonial matters connected with their respective child and sister's child. On these occasions they part company and head two camps, one representing the parents, the other the mother's family or her male relatives, and strict formal exchange, not informal assistance, becomes the order of the day. So frequently, however, does this process of crystallization and recrystallization of groups take place that it is done without strain. Moreover, when a person happens through some accident of marriage to fill two roles, as those of sister's husband and wife's brother to another, as in the case of Pa Mauŋakena mentioned above, then he may play a double part on the occasion, bringing direct contributions on the one side and making formal presentations for exchange on the other. Often he will choose that relationship which seems to him most significant and reject the others, but if not he may cope with several obligations. What he may not do is to pretend to occupy more than one role and then not fulfil it. He may act in character or abandon the part for the time being, even though he take it up again later. Examples of such behaviour will be adduced in other sections of this work. The Tikopia are entirely realistic in such matters. They are perfectly capable of conceiving of the division of activity on the basis of social function.

FREEDOM AND RESTRAINT IN KINSHIP

Side by side with this high degree of reciprocal assistance and exchange of goods goes a distinct reserve between relatives by marriage. The Tikopia distinguish two categories of kinsfolk of the highest importance in the regulation of the social life. These are *tautau laui* and *tautau pariki*, in literal terms, the categories of good relationship and bad relationship, but implying here not a moral judgment as to the character of the relationships themselves but a distinction between the type of behaviour permissible in conducting them. Freedom in the first case, restraint in the second, are the watchwords. To the first category belong the relationships of brothers, of mother's brother and sister's child, and, to some extent, of grandparent and grandchild. Details of these have already been given. To the second category belong the relationships of parent and child, especially father and son, father's sister and her brother's children, and above all, affinal relatives. Constraint between father and son, and between father's sister and her brother's son has been dealt with earlier. The rules applying in those cases operate for relatives by marriage also, but in more detail and with greater stringency, and when the term *tautau pariki* is used by Tikopia of two people, or several, without qualification, it is understood that their relation is of this type.

Such people must avoid the use of each other's personal names and use kinship terms instead, and by convention those terms are usually oriented towards the affinal relative. Thus a person asks after his brother-in-law from that man's son. " *Ko taŋata tefea ?* " "Where is brother-in-law?" he enquires. " *Ku poi tou ma ki potu mai ko."* " Your brother-in-law has gone to the next village but one," is the reply. At a funeral the Ariki Kafika, the Ariki Tafua and the latter's son were present. I heard the son say to the Ariki Kafika, who was his classificatory mother's brother, " *Tuatina E !* Tell your brother-in-law to eat." The chief then said to the Ariki Tafua, " Brother-in-law ! Eat ! " [1] In neither case do the speakers make use of the term " father." This, however, is a custom and not a rigid rule. The house-name (*iŋoa paito*) of the brother-in-law may be used, and nowadays with such of the natives who have adopted the externals of Christianity, the baptismal name (*iŋoa fakaokutapu*) is allowed. It is indeed very useful in the case of unmarried men, since they have no house-name and ordinarily can be referred to only by indirect means.

Occasionally the rule of name-avoidance may be broken, through accident or carelessness when the people so concerned are but distantly related, or by design as an affront. One instance of this displays considerable subtlety. As is not infrequent, a man composed a song in praise of his brother-in-law. In it he expressed his admiration for this relative, but alluded to him by name, thus conveying an insult under the cloak of a gesture of respect. The song runs :

> *Tafito :* E ka toku ma e au na
> Mai toku kave
> Mai te Roki
> Au rei ki te oro o Namo
> Ara kito ki te Mouŋo roto Raveŋa
>
> *Kupu :* A kokove na e au na
> Se taraŋa e roŋo kove ki oi pe sioi
> A faoa o te tu moŋorie
>
> *Kupu :* E fenoke kove mo te viki ti
> Kanoi ki oi toku monovo
>
> *Safe :* Ko Taŋatalei toku ma E !
> Kau fakaepa na ki a kokove.

Translation :

> O ! It's my brother-in-law who comes there
> From my sister
> From the West
> Comes then in the path to Namo
> While I wake and go to the Mountain in the midst of Raveŋa.

[1] Rivers's statement quoted from John Maresere (*H.M.S.* I, 308) that should a man wish to talk to his brother-in-law, he would do so only from a distance is quite incorrect.

O it's you there who are coming
Have you heard any news or no ?
People of the double face.

You arrive with the little package of *ti*
Therewith to fill my belly
O Taŋatalei my brother-in-law
I do honour now to you.

The song was composed by Pu ŋarapu about Pu Manarua, whose personal name was Taŋatalei. " People of the double face " is an insult to the folk of Faea, accusing them of backbiting and slander, the constant burden of mutual complaint between districts and other lesser groups. The reference to the small package of food sounds very much like another jibe.

Occasionally the house-name of the brother-in-law is used in preference to the kinship term, but always for a special reason. Thus Kavakiua had a *kave* (now dead) in the allied family of Resiake, who married Pa Raŋifau. The latter is now a white-haired old man, one of the " ancients " of the village, whereas the former is still a young bachelor. In spite of the fact that they are titular brothers-in-law, Kavakiua does not address the other as " *taŋata*." " I am shy," he said. " Such a venerable old benedict. I say, ' Pa Raŋifau ' only." The old man on the other hand insists on addressing him correctly as " brother-in-law."

In accordance with normal classificatory usage the application of the affinal terms of relationship is valid throughout the entire range of traceable kinship. Own and distant brothers-in-law are addressed in the same way. At times, however, for precision a person may employ more strictly descriptive terms. Thus I noted on one occasion Pa Raŋateatua refer to Tanaikava, brother of Pae Sao, as " the brother of brother-in-law who sits there." He could equally well have used the latter term alone, but he wanted to make a personal distinction, Pae Sao being the head of the family and closely associated as an individual with the speaker in his domestic affairs. Here, of course, it is not a question of separating relatives on a basis of comparative nearness of kinship, but on criteria of purely personal interest.

If the name-avoidance is fairly exacting in the case of brothers-in-law or sisters-in-law, it may be said to be complete between affinal relatives of different kinship grades. Etiquette demands that there shall be no suspicion of brusqueness or familiarity in address. The ordinary kinship term for son-in-law or daughter-in-law is *foŋona*, and this is used by the elders once the union of the young people has become an established fact. Some days after the bride is carried off to her husband, she returns to visit her parents, and then her father becomes socially conscious for the first time of the existence of his son-in-law. He says to a son of the house, "Go and invite *foŋona* to come," using the new appelation. The lad goes and delivers the invitation, addressing the husband himself as *taŋata* for the first time also. The man rises and goes to the house of his parents-in-law. Seeing him at the door, the father calls to him, "Enter, *foŋona E*," and he goes in. He has taken tobacco and areca nut with him, and with these in the fold of his waistcloth, he goes up to his father-in-law and the two press noses in the *soŋi* of greeting. Then he offers his gifts and retires to sit on one side. The food-basket is taken down from its hook and all eat together; the new bonds of relationship are ratified. "Now it has been made correct by food," the natives say. Much show is made by the parents-in-law of the newly acquired kinship term. Children crawling round are sharply caught up. "Have respect to *foŋona*," they are commanded. All join in courteous acknowledgment of the husband, and he displays equal deference to them. It is probably the most trying time in a man's life. Conversation is carried on, of a kind which the natives call "crooked discussion" (*te arara fakapikopiko*): talk of the state of food in the orchards, the weather, fishing and other neutral subjects, marriage and other equally emotional events being by tacit consent omitted. For it must be remembered that in Tikopia a father is not asked for his consent to his daughter's union, but she is reft from him, in theory and often in practice very much against his will, secretly and suddenly. Prescribed terms of address and conventional topics of conversation have then a definite value in tiding over the period of initial strain till all parties have adjusted themselves satisfactorily to the new situation and the ravisher is acknowledged as a kinsman.

Night comes on. The man, out of politeness, "to make his face good," makes a show of going, but is pressed to stay and sleep with the family. He does so. The next morning, without any word of command from his parents-in-law, he takes the family knife and he and his wife go off to the orchard of the elders to bring back food. This is a sign that he is assuming the ordinary responsibilities of his relationship. He and his wife work away till their task is done and then return to the village. If he is not accustomed to the ways of the house and is shy, he goes off to bathe and to change in his own dwelling, sending his wife on with the load of food. She arrives, and her parents ask, "Where is father? where is son-in-law?" She tells them that he will come later. And so gradually the bonds of the new relationship settle into place.

All this free use of kinship terms is to "lift up" the son-in-law, as the natives put it, to honour him (*ke sau ki ruŋa, ke fakaepa ki ei*). An analysis of the various forms of reference and address between such affinal relatives shows how these are designed to offer each other mutual courtesy. Let us take the case of Pa Tekaumata and the Ariki Tafua. In addition to calling his son-in-law by the ordinary term of *foŋona*, the father-in-law refers to him by the softened form of his house-name, as Pae Tekaumata, the particle *e* having the effect of a polite modification, or he addresses him as " *Pa*," giving him the term for " father." Or both parties refer to each other as Matua i Tekaumata and Matua i Tafua respectively, the word *matua* conveying the sense of a married man, a husband, an elder, and indicating status of respect. This term may be used alone (cf. Text S. 10). The most usual, since the easiest mode of address, is for each to call the other " *Pa*," " Father," thus tacitly acknowledging superiority on both sides. " *E fetau Pa*," " they ' Father ' each other," the natives say.

Another usage which is somewhat curious is the form of pronouns current between them. In many languages (French and German for instance, and formerly English also) a courtesy differentiation is made between the singular and plural forms of the personal pronouns. In Tikopia there is also a dual form, commonly used for situations involving two people, but employed by affinal relatives in addressing each other singly. This may be termed the " polite dual." [1] The person in question is spoken to as if he were two people instead of one. " Where are you two going ? " would be the literal translation of a polite query addressed to one's father-in-law or son-in-law. To say " Where art thou going ? " in the ordinary way is distinctly " bad form," a conception of which the Tikopia have a very clear idea. " *Sise laui*," they say, " It is not good." The use of the " polite dual " is not imperative in the same sense as is avoidance of the personal name, but it is rarely forgotten. In all the intercourse between Pa Rarovi and the Ariki Kafika at which I was present, I do not remember a single instance of this omission. The Tikopia recognize, however, the existence of louts, persons not " adept in speech and ways," as they say, and such may be expected sometimes to disregard the niceties of convention.

A series of statements by Pa Tekaumata illustrate how clearly an intelligent native recognizes the points of etiquette involved. " One calls out to the father-in-law, ' *Tau puna E*.' He hears, and calls, ' What ? ' The speech ' *Tau puna E* ' is based upon the children, though they may be anywhere at all, or absent. . . . One does not call out thus, ' Where didst thou go ? ' but calls ' Where did you

---

[1] Codrington (*Melanesians*, 45) gives similar examples for the Banks Islands and the New Hebrides.

(two) go ? ' The single man, the *tautau pariki*. This is the base of
the speech indeed to the father-in-law. . . . One calls out, ' Call out
to my father-in-law to come ' ; one does not call, ' Call out to So-
and-so to come.' It is tapu, it is weighty indeed ; one does not do
thus. The father-in-law calls out to the son-in-law, ' Come hither
and enter here, son-in-law. Take up and eat something for you two,
tau ma E.' When he speaks to that person does he mean two ? O !
it is a single man ; he makes it weighty for the *tautau pariki*. Because
he calls upon their own children ; he makes a brother-in-law for him.
I here am one alone, but am two ; am provided with a brother-in-law
from their sons."

The quotations given above give the linked kinship term, which
is a variant or refinement of the polite dual. The expression *tau
puna* may be addressed to one's wife's father. Meaning literally
" grandfather and grandchild," this, so the natives say, is based upon
the fiction that there is a grandchild present, though in actual fact
this is not so, and such offspring may not even exist. A similar feat
of terminological doubling occurs in the case of the son-in-law, who
may be spoken to by his father-in-law as " *tau ma E*," " brothers-in-
law." Here the elder is tacitly including his own son in the situation,
though again his presence or existence are not necessarily involved
in reality. The determination of the exact psychological basis of
why it is considered more polite to address a single individual as if
he were two or more I am content to leave to others. The analysis
will have to go deeper than attributing it to the puff to self-esteem
by thus being as it were effortlessly multiplied, but the wide prevalence of this linguistic usage demands a sociological explanation.

There is, however, one principle of far more general application
which appears to be illustrated by this practice. That is the principle
of explaining the unknown in terms of the known, the novel in terms
of the familiar, of expressing a more distant relationship in terms of a
nearer one. The linkage of the less familiar element with that which
is more so implies that it is an indispensible correlate of the latter,
and in the present case in addition to any effect of inflation of self-
esteem that it may have, tends also to reduce social tension by seeming
to put the person addressed on a closer footing of intimacy. Here
the link between son-in-law and father-in-law is expressed, not in
terms of marriage, but in terms of blood ; it passes through the
man's own child who is the descendant of the elder also. Affinal
bonds are thus translated into consanguineous bonds, with *prima facie*
at least, a gain in social unity. Even when the link is hypothetical, and
there is no child, the assumption of one tends in the same direction.
The basis of this argument might be broadened by considering such

data as, for example, our own society provides in the known frequent increase in the cordiality of relations between a person and his or her parents-in-law which follows on the birth of a child to the young pair. Grandparents and parents are linked together by a common interest, a centre from which direct ties of kinship go out. In Tikopia this appears also to be the case, though not so consciously realized as in our own communities, and to its advantage the society has been able to incorporate a terminology expressing this into its social mechanism. The citation of the son-in-law as a pair of brothers-in-law indicates the same feature ; the father-in-law approaches the relationship through his own son.

Other rules governing the social intercourse of affinal relatives are concerned with bodily avoidance. Taking things from above the head of a relative-in-law is barred, as also is passing directly in front of him as he sits. A person entering a house and seeing his father-in-law or son-in-law seated there will not crawl up the floor but will seat himself near the door. Again, in such case, he will not *toko te kamu*, that is, put betel leaf into lime preparatory to chewing while standing up, but will sit down before beginning this nearly automatic reaction of all Tikopia at rest. In modern times he does not smoke a pipe while standing in the presence of such relatives ; he sits down first. When he rises to go he takes the pipe out of his mouth and does not put it in again till he is well away.

These things are not done with ostentation, but so quietly and naturally that unless the observer is aware of the situation he can easily conclude that they are the ordinary general habits of the people under all conditions. Such indeed they tend to become, unless there is a strong pull in the contrary direction, since if a course of action is likely to offend a number of people with whom one is closely connected and very frequently in contact, one is apt to modify it in general intercourse. So one avoids unwittingly transgressing and wounding the susceptibilities of persons present but unnoticed. The Tikopia certainly follow this principle in the education of their children. They inculcate certain types of behaviour for general use in order that the child shall not make mistakes in the presence of that category of people in whose company a breach of decorum would cause real shame. Thus a command constantly given to young children in any company is *"Nofo fakalaui,"* " Sit properly," that is for boys with legs neatly crossed, for girls with legs tucked away at the side or stretched straight out in front. Squatting, hunched-up or kneeling postures are not encouraged. A strong reason for this is that such positions are not proper in the presence of *tautau pariki*, of whom one has always to think.

Exposure of the person in the presence of a relative-in-law is regarded as unseemly. Hence children are taught from their earliest years to avoid attitudes which display the genitalia or fundament too prominently. At a later age when they wear clothing and understand the obligations of affinal relationship, they can discriminate between the occasions on which the proprieties must be kept and those on which they may be relaxed. *Tautau pariki* do not bathe together for this reason. If a man sees his brother-in-law going down to bathe, or still more important, his father-in-law or his mother-in-law, he goes off on a different path.

It will have doubtless been noticed that there has not been much sexual discrimination in the account of these customs. This is not necessary in Tikopia, where the rules are at least as stringent in the case of male relatives by marriage as in that of male and female. There is one situation where the conduct of a mother-in-law or a daughter-in-law attracts special attention. When meeting her male *tautau pariki* in the path she draws clear and goes on a wide circuit round him. This is, however, not a peculiar observance for those alone but merely a special form of the general *tapu* on bodily contact. Here it is conditioned by the factor of male superiority, ordinarily not very marked, but a recognized social norm of wide application. The " mother-in-law taboo " in Tikopia has no particular validity of its own ; it is simply a part and not the most important part of the whole set of regulations governing the behaviour of affinal kin. As will be evident, the term " avoidance," now established in anthropological literature to describe such customs, must be understood to apply to the Tikopia in a not too literal sense. For some of the customs it is a fitting term, but for others, as those of decorous behaviour, it is too strong. I have used therefore the expression " constraint of conduct " as being more accurate to cover this aspect of kinship as a whole.

OBSCENITY AND KINSHIP

The part of the code which is most troublesome to keep is undoubtedly that which prescribes " good speech " only in the presence of one's affinal relatives. The Tikopia is of a cheerful disposition ; his definition of a good man is a man who laughs, and his humour like that of most people, savage or civilized, is apt to draw easily upon what we may call for the nonce the indecent, principally in the sexual and the scatalogical spheres. Expressions of his anger draw also upon the same material.

A stock type of joke is " Where is the fool going ? " coupled with an attribution of association with someone of the opposite sex. With or without basis of probability such is accepted as a good joke, and provokes general laughter, in which there may be a spice of malice if a real assignation is suspected. Even on ceremonial occasions the same theme may creep in. On one occasion the Ariki Kafika, commenting on a ritual gift of food sent in to him from the Ariki Taumako, said laughingly, " Why doesn't the chief send in some women with it as wives for us ? "

The *tausua*, the cursing joke, is regarded as proper behaviour between persons who stand in the relationship of " brother." Examples of this have already been given ; they show how faint in many cases is the line between curse and jest, and how frequently reference to excreta is embodied in them. To give one more instance—a man asked a woman to pass him the lime for his betel mixture. She threw it over in such a fashion that some of it spilled on the floor. " That which is poured out will be pounded up with our excrement ? " he demanded testily. This was the common sort of abusive language which obtains between *tautau laui* when small mishaps and annoyances occur, and evokes no resentment or embarrassment. It may be ignored ; it may receive an equally pungent reply.

One general sociological function of obscenity appears to lie in the titillation of the sex interest of the people concerned ; if it does not act as a verbal aphrodisiac, it provides at least a substitute sexual reaction. Now the obligations laid upon affinal relatives involve abstention from such expressions. In contrast to other norms of conduct this necessitates conscious conformity to a rule, since outside the prohibited limits there is a definite satisfaction to be had. But the Tikopia are very scrupulous in the observance of the prohibition. How careful they are the following incident will show. I took with me to the island a gramophone which, though intended primarily for my own edification, proved ultimately to be more for that of the people. They enjoyed it extremely, especially in its reproductions of the human voice, though I regret to say that the finest notes of our most famous European tenors and sopranos appealed to them merely as efforts at humour. That a voice should be modulated in this exaggerated fashion seemed to them to be merely comic. However, the most popular items were a few records of allegedly humorous songs, in which the artist himself laughed. These I had imported specially for their benefit, and they were an immense success. The first night I gave a recital in Raveŋa I invited the resident chiefs, and they rocked with mirth—so much so that the Ariki Kafika held his ribs and complained to me, " Friend, it hurts with the laughing." On the second occasion I invited some other men of rank, including Pa Fenuatara, Pa Vaŋatau and a few others of Kafika and Taumako. To my surprise, though all listened carefully and smiled politely at the singing, there was no such uproarious scene as had occurred previously. Enlightenment came when one of the audience leaned forward and asked, " Friend, these jokes that we hear, are they good jokes ? " His query applied of course not to the quality of the wit, but to the nature of the subject matter. I then realized that among those present were *tautau pariki* and humour, it might be on sexual themes, even in a foreign language, could not be lightly responded to, lest with explanation come shame. On my assurance that the matters handled were innocent of all evil, they began to chuckle freely and soon abandoned themselves to the same ecstasies as did their predecessors.

The speech observance demands much more care than the other types of regulation ; it involves a deliberate selection of subject and modification in form of expression. To facilitate the correct behaviour in the presence of one's affinal relatives, certain terms have come into use as synonyms for others which might savour of sex or things obscene. For instance, an ordinary name for one type of areca nut is *kalemata*. The first half of this word however is suggestive of the term for testes, *fatu kala*, so that in the company of women or relatives by marriage this areca nut is usually called *fuariki* or *kaula mata*. I was advised of this by Pa Rarovi after I had made such a blunder in his presence and that of the Ariki Kafika. Again, the behaviour of little children is sometimes unconsciously offensive. One does not bluntly refer to the actions or organs of the child, but draws its mother's attention by the phrase " *a taukupu te tama*," a neutral expression vaguely indicating its genitalia. Instead of using the plain descriptive word *tiko* when a child has excreted in the presence of the *kano a paito*, a person says, " The child there has ' *maru* ' in the place " or has " *peka*." The ordinary connotation of these words is far removed from excretion (*peka* is a bat; *maru* means shady or soft), and here they might be broadly translated as " loosened." The problem of euphemism in this connection is an interesting one. It seems as if a word can act in this way only when normally it is used in an entirely different context. This divides the attention of the listener, presents him with a double meaning and so mitigates the directness of the allusion. Some of these euphemistic synonyms are a part of the everyday speech. A person does not normally say, " *Kuou ka poi o mimi* " or " *Kuou e fiatiko*," " I am going to urinate " or " I wish to defecate." He uses instead the expression *fakaaŋavare*, meaning literally " to face idly about," or *fakato ki ŋa tai*, " to descend to the shore," the latter being the place where the natural functions are most commonly performed. Terms for copulation and details of genital anatomy are likewise avoided in ordinary speech, but especially between *tautau pariki*. Lewd jesting again is *tapu*, and participation in two classes of well-recognized social amusement, the narration of obscene tales—some of high antiquity—and the competitive chanting of obscene songs at dances is likewise forbidden to affinal relatives.

Even ordinary laughter is not regarded as good when *tautau pariki* are eating together—perhaps because it might engender a suspicion of some concealed obscenity.

The obscene in Tikopia is a category defined primarily by relation to situations of constraint in kinship. It is delimited by the recognition of the essential incongruity of a certain type of behaviour—sex reference or exposure—in a situation where a sex bond has been the fundamental factor of association. It can be termed a moral category since its obligations are accepted as binding, not through such influences as political authority or religious fear, but through their own virtue ; they are not questioned in their own sphere. A breach of these obligations does sometimes occur but evokes a strong emotional attitude. The reaction to a presentation of the obscene is what may be called behaviour of disorder—symptoms of uneasiness, a tendency to escape, to avoid the situation, maybe in the more extreme cases a strong verbal reaction, as anger. These comprise what the Tikopia subsume under the term *fakama*, which in this connection signifies shame. The citation or admission of obscenity (*taraŋa pariki*) even in contact between relatives in free relationship means that the category is given autonomy outside its own immediate sphere—it is carried over from situations of constraint to those where the incompatibility exists to a much less degree. Then, too, the curse or indecent expression which associates excrement with a father makes use of a relationship of restraint as an implement of action.

The restraints of *taraŋa pariki* are wider than the purely sex sphere : they include also scatalogical references, mainly of the objurgative kind. For this no doubt the close association of the organs of excretion and sex in the human anatomy is responsible. Certain well-recognized forms of cursing by kinship in this way occur, and are licit between persons not under constraint of *tautau pariki*. The most frequent is what is termed the *kau ki te mana*, the " command to the father "—to eat ordure. " *Kai te mo te mana*," " May your father eat filth " is an expression used with all grades of vehemence, from a merely conventional exclamation of good-humoured repartee, to a fling of annoyance or a full-mouthed curse in a blaze of anger (cf. Texts S. 8, S. 13, S. 14 and S. 16). The reaction on the part of the listener or recipient is in corresponding fashion ; if he takes umbrage, it will be at the tone and circumstances, not at the exclamation itself. The expression is common as a verbal reflex of astonishment. I showed some lads a picture of a horse, an animal of which they had heard but had never seen. " May its grandfather eat filth," said one of them in surprise when he took it in—the equivalent of " Well I'm damned " in our more religiously minded community. A photograph of white people in ordinary garments provoked a similar expletive, in which there was no intention of rudeness or insult. Another expression frequently used is " Food of your parents is there on the tide-mark." This amounts to the same thing ; the native habit is to defecate on the beach near the water's edge. Another variety of curse is " *Kau tiko i ou ŋakau*," " I excrete in your gullet."

The value attached to these expressions varies according to circumstances—if used in anger or jest ; between kinsfolk in constrained or free relationship. Used mildly, when there is no formal bar of kinship, such a curse is termed *tausua*, a word which includes practical jokes as well, and is quite proper. It is " good speech." But in anger, or between affinal relatives, it is " bad speech." Except in the case of incestuous imputation, it is the immediate context of situation which determines in which class the utterance falls ; though the categories of speech are fixed and fairly well defined, their content in each case is not an invariable and exclusive set of items.

Care has to be exercised in the pronouns employed with such expressions. One night, soon after I went to live in Raveŋa, I was annoyed very much by some of the youths of the village while I was developing photographs. I lost my temper, went to the door of my house and cursed them roundly as they fled, imitating the ordinary native phraseology which I had heard. People seated in the shadow of the trees above the beach listened quietly. No word was said and I went inside, pleased with the impression I had made. The next morning Seremata came in and said after a while, " Friend, it is good that you should learn to speak our tongue correctly. When one curses, one does it thus ——" and he proceeded to illustrate. The point he made was that to folk at a distance one should say " *Kai te mo ratou mana*," " May their fathers eat filth," not use *te mana*, " the father " as ordinarily. " Friend," he said, " it was us whom you were cursing last night."

Such types of curse are usually not taken literally. A father uses them frequently towards his child, and in effect, as the Tikopia point out, he is in reality objurgating himself. Thus, they say, no harm is done.

But conventional phraseology has its inconsistencies, and when used between brothers, as is quite allowable, it involves their father, a *tapu* relative. In this case the natives ignore the referent and consider only the motive of the expletive. But I once heard an old lady tutoring a child regarding its expressions towards another : " Do you know that his father is a chief ? You know. Then do not say to him, ' May your father eat filth.' Speak like this, ' May your mother eat filth ' " !

Pa Raŋifuri, in discussing these matters with me, drew a distinction between the mere invitation to eat excrement in its various forms and cursing by spiritual beings. The former he characterized as " good speech " by contrast with the latter. " May your father eat filth " can be light banter, but if one subjoins to it a phrase thus, " May your father and your deity eat filth " (*Kai te te mana ma tou atua* "), then " it has run over into evil speech." It is a sign that the speaker is really angry.

Incestuous allusions are rare and are employed only as grave insults when a dispute has reached extreme heat. If two men are arguing over a piece of land, and one of them loses his temper entirely, he may burst out, " Why don't you embrace your mother ? " or " Go you and marry your own mother and your own sister," or " Go to your own mother and your own sister to take them as your wives," or " Married couple, you and your mother." It is the suggestion of sex intercourse that is the sting here, and the wound is made more severe by specifying precisely the person's closest kin. The result of the flinging of such an insult is that the men at once take to fighting with sticks or other weapons until they are separated by the crowd— " They fight to kill " as it is said. At no time did I myself hear such expressions actually used.

Most forms of cursing are forbidden to relatives by marriage. " May your father eat filth " is not allowed. According to Pa Raŋifuri, a man careful in matters of etiquette, forms of speech which are licit to brothers-in-law are " *Te fare matua o ŋa atua*," " The house of husbands of the deities " or " *A matua o ŋa atua ki a taŋata ma*," " Husbands of the deities to brothers-in-law," which are roughly equivalent in strength and sense to " Bad cess to them." The more precise and therefore more noxious " *Matua te nofine*," " Husband of the female deity," is not regarded as a permissible form of expletive to a brother-in-law. One must not consign such relatives directly to the devil—" *sori ki a ŋa atua*," as the natives put it, implying a handing-over process.

Yet there are, as we have noted already, *tau ma pariki*, brothers-in-law in a bad relationship, and these do not abide by the ordinary norms. Indeed the start of their real quarrel may have been signified

by the use by one of them of such an insulting expresson. Thus, I
was told, Pa Roŋotaone and Pa Raŋitafuri aforementioned constantly
speak of each other in such terms as these : " The family may its
father eat filth which lives by here " or " May his father eat filth who
lives there." This speech is shocking to all normal right-thinking
people ; it is not good. *Tau ma laui* (brothers-in-law on good terms)
avoid such expressions. But relatives by marriage do occasionally get
in sly digs at each other without absolutely transgressing the bounds
of good manners. Pa Raŋifuri told me with great glee of how the
Ariki Taumako spoke to him of his classificatory son-in-law Pa
Paŋisi as " *Matua i te sosipani* "—*sosipani* being the native pronuncia-
tion of *saucepan*, of which sooty vessel this man was as far as I recollect
the only possessor in the island.[1] As a dark-skinned foreigner he
was slightly sneered at (behind his back) by the Tikopia. Scolding,
I was told, though not permitted by convention directly, may take
place at a distance, " where the other person cannot hear." So there
is some relief for wounded feelings after all.

So far the social intercourse of affinal relatives has been spoken of
as if it were regulated with equal stringency, despite the precise genealogical relationship of the persons concerned. As might be expected,
this is not the case. Where the tie of kinship is weak there is much
less scrupulousness in the observance of the code of behaviour, and
it is in the field of loose conversation that breaches most commonly
occur. The inducements here are so much greater : there is little
temptation to touch another person's head ; there may be a strong
one to tell him a joke with a spice in it. And so the Tikopia recognize
a distinction, as far as jesting goes, between different kinds of relatives
by marriage on the grounds of their nearness. They say, " True
brothers-in-law alone are bad, are in a bad relationship, but the brother-
in-law from another settlement (*i.e.* distant in kinship) is good ; to
give cause for laughter with him is good ; he has separated differently
away."

Somewhat amusing situations arise when in a company of men of
more or less the same age, some are *tautau laui* and others are *tautau
pariki*. The former with no restraints of relationship to hold them
carry on a bright conversation with indecent joking and suggestive
laughter. The latter have to observe the mutual decorum due to the
presence of relatives-in-law and sit there with composed faces, trying
hard not to laugh, cursing those who are joking. They tell them they
are acting like children, like fools, and the like, and their embarrassment only adds to the enjoyment of the others. Taking advantage of

---

[1] The nearest equivalent in sense is something like " Father of Saucepans,"
after the Arab style of invective.

the discomfiture of affinal relatives in this way is done only to a limited extent, among men of like standing and not very close relationship. If an actual father-in-law and son-in-law were present, then no one would act thus, nor perhaps if one of the company were a chief, though I seem to remember the Ariki Taumako smilingly protesting against Pae Sao for this.

The obligations of *tautau pariki* never wear off, but it is possible for them to diminish. As the years go by, between son-in-law and father-in-law, for example, on whom the incidence of the *tapu* falls most heavily, an easier attitude begins to obtain. This is brought about partly by the relative approximation of the younger to the elder in seniority—when both are grey-haired their difference of years is not so obvious—and partly by the birth of children, who according to the natives themselves, render the rules " light " or " mild." A factor of importance here is undoubtedly the tie of sentiment between the grandparents and their grandchildren which, by expressing itself in concrete kindnesses to their household, tends to ameliorate any harshness between the elders and the children's parents. Again a social occasion of festivity is regarded as freeing a person to some extent from the more onerous observances of the *tautau pariki* ; to jokes and frivolous conversation in particular no exception should be taken. One informant expressed the matter thus. " The man who has married, at that time, before he has yet created children for himself, great is the weight of *tautau pariki*. But as he dwells and dwells, and his children become many, then the *tautau pariki* become mild. Since he has produced children in plenty, it is held that it has become good.

" And when he has applied aromatic leaves to his body, then it has become good ; he has become adorned for the dance ; it is regarded as good ; no objection may be made."

Not only married persons are involved in the obligations of relatives-in-law ; the unmarried are also drawn in through their brothers and sisters. " The bachelors have *tautau pariki* too, from their brothers who have married." The father and mother of a girl, for example, call their son-in-law's unmarried brother " Pae maroa " or " Foŋona tamaroa," including in the term a qualification indicating his bachelor state. He on his part addresses them as might be expected, as *Pa foŋovai* and *Nau foŋovai* or simply as *Pa* and *Nau*.

GENERAL FEATURES OF "AVOIDANCE"

We may now attempt to sum up the general features of this detailed account of the relationships of constraint in Tikopia, and endeavour to indicate their place in the working scheme of kinship arrangements. In the first place there is no doubt of the importance of this type of kinship bond in this community. "Great is its weight, *tautau pariki*," natives say, and the inclusion of the unmarried in the system throws a net over the whole population through the meshes of which only young children are small enough to escape. The *tautau pariki tapu* prescribes a code of behaviour on the part of every adult towards great sections of the people, a code which it is true is flexible in its application according to closeness of kinship, and leaves room for individual selection according to conflicting claims.

It is clear that the basis of the regulations is social and not sexual in the limited sense. They restrict freedom of social intercourse and not merely place a barrier before the possibilities of sexual intercourse as at one time was suggested as the motivating factor behind such "avoidances." In Tikopia men observe the same restraints towards each other as they do towards women; and the greatest burden of the *tapu* is if anything on father-in-law and son-in-law, since their contacts in social and economic life are so much more constant and intimate than those of son-in-law and mother-in-law, or father-in-law and daughter-in-law. And even those aspects of the *tapu* which deal with sexual matters apply equally between males and are considered by the natives themselves from the point of view of their effect upon social sentiments and not upon the primary sexual functions. The point which the Tikopia stress continually is the need for such observances to avoid "shame," and this seems to me to be the keynote of the harmony of relationships involved.

The most important elements concerned may be grouped, for ease of definition, under three heads : the avoidance of familiarity in speech, gesture and bodily contact; the avoidance of sexual suggestion by word or act ; the avoidance of the appearance of anger by word or act. But the term avoidance does not adequately describe the situation, since the actual conduct of a person to his affinal relatives does not consist in a series of negatives. It may be defined and hemmed in by proscriptions, but in actuality it is comprised of a multiplicity of positive acts, which in themselves constitute the relationship. To put it crudely and somewhat loosely, behaviour of people consists in what they do, not in what they do not do. Thus a description of what is observed to happen in Tikopia must be in such terms as—a person uses expressions of respect, as the "polite dual" to his affinal relatives ; he speaks courteously to them, on a plane of seriousness, or jokes with them about the ordinary misadventures of life. He assists them in their work and helps them to meet their commitments, and counts on them for similar services. Keeping out of their way and refraining from using their names is only one aspect of the phenomenon. Co-operation and mutual respect in the relations of such people is the attitude that impresses the observer.

The negative aspect, the constraint, the avoidance is seen to be the reverse side of the shield of which the obverse for the most part represents the things actually done. The prohibitory regulations have as their great function the provision and delimitation of channels for the maintenance of friendly relations between the parties connected by marriage. The double question arises : of what nature is the basic situation that there should be room for such a stimulus to friendly relations ; and what value is there in this development ?

The answer to the first question lies in a study of the initial situation at marriage. A new sexual and social relationship has been contracted, and the partners to this are thereby confronted with persons who heretofore have stood alone in another sexual and social relationship to the spouse, equally intimate, though of a different order. The son-in-law has become on peculiarly intimate terms with the woman who has been so closely associated with his father-in-law and mother-in-law, in a different sphere. There are certain subjects then in which the sentiments of all parties are too nearly concerned to admit of entire absence of reserve. As far as the Tikopia are concerned this reserve is fortified by the mode of obtaining a wife which could easily tend to create a certain estrangement between the woman's father and her husband (see Chapter XV). But the prescribed line of conduct for *tautau pariki* rules out sex, obviates situations of embarrassment and other emotional disorder, enforces calm, even discussion, frowns on any open breach no matter what the feelings may be, and in general prevents overt social strain.

As far as the second question is concerned it can, I think, be shown that in at least two ways this prevention of strain is culturally valuable—for the efficiency of the social life as a whole, and for the welfare of the children of the marriage. It will be readily admitted that the efficiency of a society is likely to be promoted by the smoothing out of friction between its members, and a code of behaviour which blocks potential feuds and insists on co-operation needs no further defence. The value of the widespread application of the code, even to the unmarried, has this effect, that it deals with the crystallization of sentiments in family groups, which is a common social phenomenon. As far as the children are concerned the obligation to friendly relations between their parents and the affinals of these means a greater chance of security for them in maintaining a working set of links with both the mother's and the father's kin. The lessening of the obligations towards distant relatives, and towards close relatives as the years go on, confirms the interpretation that the "avoidance" of affinal kindred is a product of a family situation in which a configuration of relationships is involved. Restraint between father and son, or between brother and sister, appear to be essentially of the same type, and to be explicable on similar general principles.

An explanation of this kind gives little support to the hypothesis of Rivers on the subject, backed up as it is by no evidence. He suggests that such a combination of avoidance and co-operation may possibly be explained as having grown out of the relations which arise when marriage habitually takes place between hostile tribes, or it may be the result of marriages which form part of the process of fusion of two peoples.[1] As the material of this Chapter has shown, there may be an element of hostility, but there is no need to invoke more than one community to account for it.

The next group of problems for examination is concerned with the manner in which sex relations in general and marriage in particular are affected by the kinship status of the persons involved.

THE PROBLEM OF INCEST

The problem of incest has acquired in sociology a kind of mystic aura which is partly due to the fact that, instead of being remote from us like so many of the customs studied, it is part of our own cultural institutions as well as of those of primitive tribes. It is difficult, therefore, to view it with that detachment necessary to an objective enquiry. It is for this reason, probably, that the reaction to incest has been assigned to an instinctive foundation. Attention has been concentrated on the fear and horror, the repulsion aroused by the idea of sexual connection with a close kinsman, and it is argued as being innate. As a first step it seems necessary to remove the problem from the field of psychology, and to consider it as one of sociological interest; to examine it in terms of observed behaviour in social situations. As a general definition it may be said that incest consists in sexual relations between persons related by kinship, the tie being of such kind that sexual connection between them is legally prohibited. This means of course interpreting "legally" in a wide sense as applying to conscious institutional action. Investigation

[1] Article, "Marriage," Hastings' *Encyclopaedia of Religion and Ethics.*

soon makes it apparent that in different societies different types of kin are involved in such regulation ; in other words, what the native in one particular community regards as incest may not be so regarded in another.   The sociological definition of incest should refer then, not to union with specific relatives, since these vary according to the culture, but to legal prohibition of union with kin and to the reaction which follows the breach of such prohibition.   The habit of characterizing sex relations between brothers and sisters as incestuous, and of describing those between distant cousins or more remote relatives, such as clan members, in terms of breach of exogamous rule, is really to carry over the norm of our own society into our scientific analysis.   Malinowski, in *The Sexual Life of Savages*, quite rightly lists exogamy under the heading of " Clan Incest." Just as the concept of marriage has been altered to include the practices of peoples who make no religious union or formal pronouncement beyond the tacit recognition accorded to two people who live together, so also that of incest should be widened to cover the institutionalized behaviour of communities who draw no generic line between the union of brother and sister and that, say, of second cousins.   It can probably be shown that as the degree of propinquity within the incest sphere increases, so an increasing reaction is provoked by a breach of the rule.

What is necessary for the study of incest is an observational basis —a careful analysis of the phenomenon in a number of societies, considering it in relation to other institutions, such as the place of the mother's brother, the relation between brothers-in-law, and so on.   Quantitative data must be provided to show the frequency of the phenomenon, its differential occurrence as between different types of relatives, and any difference in the reaction of the community in such cases.   The work of Malinowski in the Trobriands provides almost the only example of such method.   Too often theories of incest are based upon consideration of a hypothetical society or of general statements regarding actual societies, but not supported by evidence of frequency or any attempt at examining the phenomenon in relation to its social background.

First, it is necessary to explain how incest is conceived in the particular society, how it is dealt with, and what effect the mechanism for dealing with it produces.   In view of the paucity of such studies a functional analysis of incest in the island community of Tikopia may be of interest.   The institutional correlations which exist there will not be universally valid, but they will at least give some indication of the kind of data necessary for the construction of an adequate general theory.

THE REACTION TO INCEST IN TIKOPIA

There are in Tikopia no rules prescribed for the marriage of kin, nothing resembling the cross-cousin marriage which was favoured by some of the ruling families of Tonga and is so common in parts of Melanesia. There is, on the other hand, a proscription on the union of close kin, which may be termed a rule against incest.

The recognition of an incest prohibition involves the consideration of three features—sex relations, a bond of kinship uniting the persons concerned in such relation, and an attitude of moral disapproval on the part of the community in general. The " incest situation " differs considerably from one society to another, the factors mentioned varying in their incidence. The group of persons whose kinship is reckoned as significant from this standpoint is sometimes small—in all societies it appears to include the individual family ; in some it is interpreted a little more widely, on a bilateral basis to include first cousins, or even second cousins ; in others it is interpreted much more sweepingly, but on a unilateral basis, and comprises all persons within the clan or similar group, even though genealogical relationship between them cannot be traced. This is the reverse or negative side of the rule of exogamy, by which a person is obliged to marry out of his or her kinship group. Sometimes the prohibition is double, and extends to the kinship group of the other parent than the one through whom descent is reckoned. Different communities again take different attitudes towards a breach of the rule : in some mere sex relations are visited with the utmost rigours of punishment ; in others sex relations which are contrary to the rule are tolerated or winked at while marriage is never allowed ; in others still marriage between the guilty parties may be even allowed to take place, though unwillingly, and in the face of the disapproval of the major portion of the community. This indicates also the variation in the type of sanction involved, and in the individual response to it. Law, morality and religion may all be invoked, but in varying degree in different communities, or even in the same community, and personal respect for them, as evidenced in obedience to or breach of the rule, is subject to a considerable range of variation.

This lack of any general pattern of universal procedure is emphasized in order to bring out the necessity of analyzing the " incest situation " in detail in the community studied, since its relation to the problems of kinship can by no means be taken for granted. Our central point of interest, as elsewhere in this book, is not the teleology of the institution—the cultural design which may have given rise to the prohibition—nor the bare description of the reasons which the natives themselves give for its existence, but the effects which conformity to the rule, or breach of it, have upon the life of the people.

One may say at once that to the Tikopia the idea of incest seems to evoke disgust rather than horror—their comments suggest æsthetic repugnance rather than religious fear, though, as will be seen, there is a definite religious element in the sanction which backs up the prohibition. It is in this light that the more extreme forms of incestuous relationship, those between parent and child, are viewed—extreme because there can be no possible question of marriage eventuating as a result of the relationship being legalized by society.

There is no specific regulation forbidding sex intercourse of parent and child, because the general prohibition between close kin covers this also ; discussion of its possibility is regarded as somewhat absurd, and its occurrence is usually categorically denied. In this sphere my material is very scanty, and I have reason to believe that this is a fair reflection of an existing rarity of incident. The natives themselves in fact display little interest in the topic. Though father-daughter incest probably occasionally takes place, I did not manage to collect any records of it, and of mother-son incest only a rather scandalous statement from the gossip Pa Tekaumata, which I regret to say I did not verify from other sources. He began by scouting the notion entirely, and then after a moment's reflection admitted of his own volition that under cover of darkness anything might happen. " The mother, no absolutely ! Yet we do not know if when the land is night a mother and son do not embrace each other, they two." Then he went on to cite the only case he knew. It concerned the family of my neighbours, my informant alleging that " The father of Pa Taitai turned to his mother ; they two, mother and son, copulated. I heard in the conversation of Pa Raŋirikoi (the respected elder who lived in the house adjacent) by whom they were discovered. They two copulated, copulated, upon which his mother lost her reason. Then was begun the *mara* in their family." The *mara*, to which reference will be made later, can be translated here as " bad luck " or " ill fortune " ; it refers to the fits of periodic lunacy which afflict members of this family.

It would be surprising if incestuous relations between mother and son did not occur at times ; but the difficulty in obtaining evidence makes it impossible to ascertain its frequency. However, I am of the opinion that it is not at all common, certainly much less so than brother-sister incest, for which there are more facilities, more ostensible temptation—youth to youth—and a great deal more data available.

THE INCEST-DREAM

Dreams of sexual connection with the mother are apparently not uncommon, and for convenience other types of incestuous dreams will also be considered here in conjunction with them.[1] A few native statements may be first quoted. Said Pa Tekaumata, after a discussion of dreams in general, " The spirit comes to a man, comes, takes on the semblance then of his true sister, then they two, own brother and sister, copulate in the realm of spirits. That person wakes up and says, ' As I am sleeping now there comes a spirit of the marrying kind, takes on the appearance of my sister, and we two then have intercourse.' His member has ejaculated on to his waist-cloth. His mind was excited by the spirits, he copulated wrongly then with his sister. . . . The dream is made also to the mother. Another person sleeps, sleeps, sees the spirit in the semblance of his mother, it comes, they two copulate, they two copulate, copulate, then the man wakes with a start. ' May the father of the spirit eat filth ! It impersonated my mother, came, and we two then copulated.' He feels down on his waistcloth, and it is damp ; his member has ejaculated. Another man hears him yell and curse, thereupon he asks him. He does not conceal it from the people in the house, even if his mother or sister is present." Seremata, in discussing dreams of intercourse with women, said, " As a man sleeps a spirit impersonates his mother or it may be his sister, the spirit of the marrying kind comes, and the man is overcome. Thereupon the man who is having his dream wakes with a start and ponders ; it is not good."

The analysis of these statements shows that the key to the under-standing of the incest-dream is the explanation in terms of spiritual agencies. The act is not incest at all, but plain seduction from the other world. And even here no blame is attachable to the dreamer, since his lewd desires are not held to be the product of his own volition, but to be formed by the spirits or at least on the spirit plane. To the question why does a man not refuse to copulate in the dream with a woman who appears to be his mother or sister the answer given is, " He does not object because his mind is made up among the spirits." The Tikopia have thus evolved for themselves a splendid mechanism for removing all sense of responsibility from the human actor in an incest-dream. The really serious matter to the natives is not the simulation of incest, but the possible physical effects upon the dreamer. To be " overcome "—tōa in Tikopia—is a significant

---

[1] For further discussion of this subject see " The Meaning of Dreams in Tikopia," one of the *Essays Presented to C. G. Seligman*, 1934, *pp.* 63-74.

expression with a complex connotation, which must be discussed elsewhere.[1]   In brief it means the loss of vitality, with the prospect of illness or even death supervening, unless the action of the spirit can be countered.   For a spirit to trick a man by causing him to copulate with her and at the same time to feign to be his close relative is, literally, to add insult to injury.   Hence the reaction upon waking is not one of shame, but of anger mingled with fear—a man does not conceal such a dream, he curses aloud.

The incest-dream is thus arbitrarily divorced by the natives from what we would regard as its sociological reality in waking life, owing to their ideas of the diversity of powers which they believe spirits to possess.   They readily admit, however, the existence of incest in the flesh.   I regret that I did not endeavour with any pertinacity in the field to link up the two sets of phenomena for them and test their views.   I am inclined to think that they would have summarily rejected any formulation which would place the incest-dream on a footing of real desire, since their theory of spirit impersonation enters so deeply into many of their institutions.[2]

MARRIAGE WITHIN THE PROHIBITED DEGREE

Even apart from casual opinions expressed in public conversation, there is a tendency on the part of the Tikopia to deny that incestuous relations occur between brother and sister.   The habits of the people by implication exclude the possibility of such a thing happening ; brother and sister have much to do with each other in ordinary life, sleep side by side at night, and, as already mentioned, may even share the same blanket without odium or suspicion being aroused.   Normally it appears that sex relations do not take place ; the inhibiting force of custom is effective (see Chapter V).   But occasionally it is admitted the sexual interest of the brother finds its object in the sister and then the two may copulate secretly.   As they sleep close together they " adhere " (fakapiki).   The ease with which this may be accomplished at night as they lie side by side makes detection very difficult ; it is not surprising, perhaps, then that I have no actual cases to record. True brother and sister can of course never marry, and for a girl to become pregnant by her brother would be a scandalous proceeding. It is said that the pair would be made to put off to sea (fakaforau), with small chance of survival, as a punishment.   In consequence, it is alleged that they practise the crude method of contraception described in Chapter XIV.

[1] Rank and Religion in Tikopia, in which the native ideas of health and sickness are analyzed.

[2] See, for example, the writer's " Totemism in Polynesia," Oceania, I, 1930-1.

The prohibition of sex relations and *a fortiori* of marriage between closely related kin applies in Tikopia in common ruling as far as first cousins—the children of these people are free to do as they wish. This, however, is not a fiat of equal weight everywhere within the sphere cited. The prohibition of incest is rather a series of bans of decreasing intensity, the prospect of breaking the rule and substantiating one's conduct becoming the greater as the kinship tie becomes less close. Parent and child, true brother and sister would not be allowed to marry, and sexual intercourse between them is viewed with extreme repugnance, to such extent that if persisted in, and a matter of common knowledge, they would probably be banished or driven to suicide. Half-brother and half-sister also come within the prohibited degree, but here at least two cases are on record of marriage between them being permitted. One was the couple sa Toŋarei, both now dead, and leaving no issue, their father being the former Ariki Kafika Fetasi, their mothers being from different families, of the man from sa Te Roro (or Te Kavamotu) and of the woman from Rimanu. This union brought forth great disapproval from the people at large, but it was not prevented. If they had been children of the one mother as well, it would not have been allowed to occur. " True brother and sister, the one mother, the one father, have intercourse with each other only, they copulate secretly, and then they two go ; they do not dwell," said Pa Tekaumata, meaning that they could not live together as husband and wife. The other case is that of sa Fetauta, whom I knew very well. This pair had the same mother, but separate fathers. The woman married first Pu Korokoro, by whom she bore Nau Fetauta, and later, whether having left him or after his death I do not know, she married Pu Fetauta, by whom she had the present bearer of the title. This couple lived together in the village of Matautu, with a healthy family of children around them, held in honour and esteem by all. The husband, Pa Fetauta (Plate V), is the head of the important " house " of Marinoa and has performed all the appropriate duties of an elder. In this position he is also one of the principal mother's brothers of the sons of the Ariki Tafua, is treated with the greatest courtesy accordingly, and gives and is given all the usual presents associated with this status. In short, no open stigma now attaches to his incestuous union, however much it did at a former time. In discussing the matter of this marriage, my informants said, " We do not call out ' brother and sister ' because it causes to quiver in shame "—politeness forbids that they should be ridiculed by mention of their prior kinship. Thus in the case of a *fait accompli* the norms of etiquette are of more regard than the expression of the moral rule. In the case of sa Fetauta the mouths of folk are kept closed, partly by the rank of the married pair, but even more by the very fact of the extreme nearness of their blood relationship. The time for objection is past and courtesy dictates silence.

A number of cases also exist of marriages within the generally recognized proscribed degree—first cousins of various kinds. When I was in Tikopia there were six unions in which men had married their parallel cousins—four being with the father's brother's daughter and two with the mother's sister's daughter—and two in which men had married their cross-cousins—one being with the father's sister's daughter and the other with the mother's brother's daughter.[1]

It is interesting to note that six of these cases occurred within two families, four in one and two in the other, the practice of brother-sister exchange, which does take place at times in Tikopia, being apparently accentuated under conditions where a social bar is being disregarded. Both sides give and receive women, thus sharing the onus equally. In some of these cases the disapproval of the community has been expressed by jests and sneering remarks. One man who married his father's brother's daughter, Pa Nukupuia, was known in his bachelor days by the name (*iŋoa tamaroa*) of Tulai. Nowadays, by way of a joke, people liken one another to him. " Where are you going, Tulai ? " one person may call out to another, accusing him in fun of being an incestuous lover. This is merely a variant on the old theme, the charge of womanizing, freely flung around by men at each other. Pa Nukupuia and his wife lived in the same house Nukuraro before marriage, and there had intercourse. " The man went to treat his sister as a wife," it was said, the expression used, *fai nofine*, signifying desire for sexual relations rather than actual marriage. When the two of them wished to marry, their families objected, but after a time gave way. (The marriage took place, it may be noted, before the coming of Christianity to Tikopia.) More generally, a person who marries his cross-cousin, or his parallel cousin, is compared with the family of sa Raropuka, to which Tulai belongs, and in which so many of these unions have taken place that the name has become notorious in this connection.

Such unions of first cousins, though not actually prevented, are viewed with disgust by the people at large, as a few comments show.

A crystallization of the native point of view is given in the following statement, quoted in the original. " *Tera e laui, ke avaŋa ki te kave i take ŋaŋea, te kave fakatafatafa ; kae avaŋa ki te kave maori, e pariki, sise laui.*" " That is good, to marry the sister from another

[1] For genealogies see " Marriage and the Classificatory System of Relationship," *op. cit.*

place, the sister set to one side; but to marry the true sister is bad, is not good." As already noted, first cousins are included in the ring of close kin, and are termed *tau kave maori*, true brother and sister. It is important to observe that the restriction is of a bilateral type; it is just the same whether the *tau kave maori* trace relationship through father or mother, and belong to the same or to different *kainaya*, major kinship groups. The popular attitude is expressed in another way. "It is good to go and marry into another family (*paito*); to come back again is not good." And Pa Fenuatara said, "The person who marries his *kave maori* is termed one who eats *soi*," this being a fruit which is edible, but is exceedingly bitter until it has been steeped for some time. Afirua referred to such a marriage as "the one flesh joined within itself; it is not good, it is bad. It's an old idea in Tikopia." More simply, as in the case of Tulai, these persons are said "to commit foolishness together" (*fevareaki*). Afirua also said, "Some persons have married their cross-cousins (*kave fakapariki*); it is not good, but it is their own idea." In another statement he expanded the same point of view, "Because the father's sister has gone to another house, then the brother and sister standpoint is adopted throughout (as between her children and those of her brother). That is its custom in this land. Now if a man is wise, he will keep clear of his near relatives, and then they are called brothers and sisters. But if not, he abandons the brotherhood and sisterhood which used to obtain, adopts then the brother-in-law relationship, and then he has gone foolishly." Two expressions of criticism are used in this connection. Of such a man it will be said, "*Se iroa ki ona va maori*" or "*Sise masara ki ona va maori*." *Va maori* are his close or "true" relatives, as his first cousins; these expressions mean "he does not recognize his near relatives" or, in a practically literal translation of the Tikopia idiom, "he does not keep clear of his near relatives." This action is condemned; as Afirua said, it involves the conversion of "brothers" into brothers-in-law, to the irritation of his family.

The marriage of persons less closely connected, as of second cousins, is regarded with more equanimity. According to Pa Fenuatara, while the union of first cousins is barred, that of their children is permissible—they have "gone aside" (*fakatafa atu*). In such case it is said that "their families have entered into each other" or that "their families have determined to dwell together." Such a state of affairs does not provoke the expressions of disgust applied to closer unions, but a mild kind of censure may be passed. I have heard such a marriage described as "bitter." It is difficult to generalize when it comes to this sphere. It is a broad principle of

Tikopia sociology that to marry a close relative is bad ; it is good to marry a relative who is " distant," both by blood and residence (the two tending to be coincident). But when it comes to the third generation from a common ancestor—second cousins—there have been so many marriages that few families can afford to throw stones lest they injure their own reputations. As was admitted on this point, a great proportion of the people have married near relatives. " In this land they stand divided into parts : a great part have commonsense, a great part are foolish," said Kavakiua.

The usual attitude of natives on the point is to express a kind of qualified approval, the idiom being in such cases to call the thing both good and bad. Though a licit act, it is not wholly welcome. Thus Pa Teva said, " When true brother and sister dwell together it is not good ; if they marry, they are sent off to sea. But when they are distant brother and sister, it is good, and yet bad. Indeed in this land it is the sister (or brother) from another place who is married." And Kavakiua characterized marriage within the immediate group of relatives, the *kano a paito*, in the same terms. " *E fai ; e laui kae pariki.*"

The general attitude of the Tikopia in this matter will now be clear. Apart from individual divergences, it is held that while consanguinity and affinity are not all incompatible, the closer the blood relationship the less the approbation of marriage, until when it comes to real brother and sister a permanent union between them is intolerable. If we were to define incest in current phraseology as sex relations between kin between whom legal marriage is not permitted,[1] then the only true incest in Tikopia would be intercourse between parent and child and true brother and sister. Such a rigid interpretation, however, by ignoring the gradation in reprobation and the difference between forcible restraint and public evaluation as factors of prevention, would distort the real nature of the Tikopia phenomena.

THE SUPERNATURAL SANCTION

At first sight it is puzzling to understand why the disapproval of unions of close kin is carried no further than verbally, and why the marriage of even half-brother and half-sister does not provoke the community to more vigorous action. The clue lies in the supernatural sanction which is believed to operate in such cases. The idea is firmly held that unions of close kin bear with them their own doom, their *mara*. This concept is the opposite of that of *manu* (the

[1] " Incest," *Encyclopaedia Britannica*, 11th ed. ; cf. *Notes and Queries in Anthropology*, 5th ed. 93.

Tikopia form of the better known *mana*), the best translation of which is efficacy, success. *Mara* may be rendered therefore as failure, or as ill-luck, misfortune. The idea essentially concerns barrenness. A chief is *mara* when his ritual is non-productive ; when the breadfruit does not bud, when the fish do not come, his invocations are lacking in power. The peculiar barrenness of an incestuous union consists not in the absence of children, but in their illness or death, or some other mishap, as the periodic lunacy believed to result from the incest of mother and son mentioned above. The idea that the offspring of a marriage between near kin are weakly and likely to die young is stoutly held by these natives and examples are adduced to prove it. When we heard the news of the death of the child of Pa Fenuafara my neighbour, Nau Raroakau, an old lady of kindly but firm opinions, remarked to me briefly, " *Rau mara* " " their barrenness." Then she explained that the parents were the children of two sisters.

This generalization is not of the nature of a biological theory that inbreeding is injurious *per se*, but is a belief in the operation of super-natural forces. These are an expression of the resentment of the parents of the guilty pair, who in life have suffered the union, but after death vent their accumulated spleen on the offspring. Thus sa Toŋarei, cited above, were left without issue. " Their children died ; died when big. They died because this was their barrenness, true brother and sister ; their parents came hither and bewitched them, to hurt their children." Such malicious action on the part of the parents is represented by a special linguistic term ; it is known as *fakakinaue*, a term equivalent to the more ordinary *fakafua*, bewitch-ing. To my objection that sa Fetauta have a flourishing family the reply came that these are all recent ; their elder children are all dead, and with this the vengeance of the parents was presumably slaked. These parents, the woman and her two husbands, died much about the same time, and going together to the realm of spirits, set their anger in motion. As a native statement puts it, "Among men they keep it within themselves, but when they have departed (after death) they think upon it, look at the children which have been begotten, and come then to strike, to bewitch them, because for true brother and sister to dwell together, it is not good."

In a conversation which I had with Pa Tekaumata on the subject of incest he brought up the matter of the supernatural sanction as follows. " Some brothers and sisters," he said, " who have the one father but different mothers, will join together, will embrace each other. When such brother and sister have begotten their children, these keep on dying, dying, dying, and the labour is of wailing, wailing, wailing for the children who do not exist long, but die off."

" How do you mean ? " I asked him.   " Well, of course, it's terrific,
because of the true brother and sister who have copulated evilly.   It
is a spirit who has come to work sickness, to do its *feao*, that is, a
spirit of the family of those two coming in another medium."   The
feao here is equivalent to the *mara* described above, and means a
sterility actively imposed.   That the offspring of such incestuous
marriages do die in this way he was prepared to support by definite
evidence, like other informants.   " The observation of it in this land
is finished," he said, meaning that there were cases to hand, known
to everyone, which formed the empirical basis for the common opinion.
To these reference has already been made.

Another longer statement throwing some light on the kind of
motivation which actuates the spirits of parents in thus harming their
own children has been quoted elsewhere, in a literal translation.
Here I give it in a freer rendering which perhaps brings out the
meaning more clearly.

" The children of true brother and sister are not good ; they are
diseased and weakly.   When true brother and sister marry their
children live only while the fathers of the married pair remain alive.
But when their fathers die, then evil befalls their children.   Their
fathers come and bewitch the offspring of the married pair.   When
their fathers die they go to the realm of the spirits, they go to take
part in what the spirits are doing, that is they go to dance among
them (dancing being the one great amusement in the spirit world).
As they go and join in the dance, dancing away, the spirits call
out to them, ' Yes !   Come and dance !   What about your notoriety
because of your children who are living together ? '   That is those
who have united as a married pair.   Thereupon the parents are
ashamed.   In their shame they turn round, and strike down the offspring of the marriage."   According to this version it is by the
taunts of their peers in a realm where they are at once freer from
responsibility and less open to reproach by their children that the
parents of the guilty pair are stimulated to take action.   It is clear
also from this, the general Tikopia opinion, that while supernatural
punishment is part of the sanction for the prohibition of incest, it
does not, even for the natives, provide the ultimate basis for the rule
itself.   The spirits, just as men, respond to a norm of conduct of an
external character.   The moral law exists in the absolute, independent
of the gods.

The belief in the supernatural consequence which will follow
incest, however, helps to explain why the Tikopia seem so apathetic
about taking action in regard to it.   They disapprove, they sneer,
but they put no other physical barrier in the way of the union of

closely related lovers.   Even the objections of the family seem to be
fairly easily overruled.   For sooner or later the incestuous pair will
have to pay for their disregard of custom.

SOCIOLOGICAL BASIS OF THE INCEST BAN

Before discussing the fundamental basis of the incest disapproval
in Tikopia, it will be well to recall some of the changes which result
from marriage.

In the normal way, since all of Tikopia are kinsfolk and a person
usually marries his " distant " sister, marriage means the conversion
of remote consanguineous relatives into close affinal relatives.   A
brother of distant status becomes an immediate brother-in-law, for
instance, a classificatory father or mother's brother an immediate
father-in-law.   This involves the adoption of a novel restraint in
speech and other behaviour, with the creation of definite formal
reciprocal obligations and much informal co-operation.   The people
concerned become *tautau pariki* to each other.   But the previous
distance of the relationship allows the change to take place with the
minimum of friction.   Moreover, the newly married pair and their
future offspring have the double co-operation of the husband's group
and the wife's, drawn together through the union.

The marriage of close kin on the other hand fails to secure this
harmony.   In the first place, if it occurs between first cousins the
husband has as his brothers-in-law men whom he has previously
considered among his nearest blood kin, his *tau fanau maori*, with
whom he has been on terms of greatest intimacy, in economic and
social affairs.   Now he can no longer joke with them, use their
personal names or treat them with real freedom.   His own brothers,
too, find themselves in a dilemma.   If they follow the ordinary
Tikopia principle and adopt the same terminology and behaviour
towards the husband's relatives by marriage as he does, they will be
putting a barrier between themselves and their closest kin, members
of their own " house."   If they do not, then they abandon their
brother to bear his social burdens as best he may.   Either way, the
ranks of a closely-knit band of brethren are split.   The latter course
is frequently the one chosen.   If a man insists on marrying his near
sister, then his own brothers say to him, " You make your own
brothers-in-law yourself singly and alone, but our own band of
brothers is already formed."   This means that they refuse to align
themselves with him ; they do not wish to be differentiated from
those men who have been their closest blood kin for so many years,
to have to avoid the use of their names, never to pass a suggestive

joke with them, to be separated from them officially whenever it comes to any ceremonial concerning the household of the married pair. Where marriage occurs within the small circle of kin, as between first cousins, the person immediately concerned is the only one to alter his ties to his wife's relatives ; his brothers remain as before. " His *tautau pariki* are formed by him singly ; they are left to him alone " ; " The man who marries thus makes his brother-in-law links himself alone," are typical expressions of the situation by natives. Such a person has not " kept clear of his *va maori* " as custom and common sense enjoin, and must expect to suffer accordingly. Furthermore, he is placing any children he may have at a distinct disadvantage. They normally look to the males of their father's " house," his ortho-cousins, to act as secondary fathers to them, and to sit on the parent's side of the house at their initiation and other ritual affairs ; and on the other hand to their mother's brothers and cousins, a very different set of people, to provide them with other important services. A marriage between close kin causes these two groups to overlap, from the child's point of view, and deprives him of a full normal set of relatives. Such has been the case in the family of Pa Roŋonafa, married to his *kave maori* of Aneve (Genealogy III ; cf. Genealogy I of *J.R.A.I.* article) ; the groups have to split where they should be united.

Thus in converting absence of restraint between near kin into a formalized restrained set of attitudes, in splitting up a group of brothers in their behaviour towards these kin, in cutting down the number of kinsfolk available to the offspring, a marriage of the type described creates difficulties in the working of the kinship group. These are accentuated in the case of unions of a more incestuous kind, as between half-brother and half-sister. Here not only must brothers in a family break their united front in adopting different attitudes towards some third parties, but a fundamental rift is made in their own ranks. Choice is allowed to a husband's brothers as to whether they will adopt affinal relationship with his wife's kin or not, but the husband himself has no option. Here his own mother's or father's sons, as the case may be, must become his brothers-in-law, and the maternal uncles of his children. As can be imagined, this hampers the normal working of the exchange system in the kinship sphere very much. In all cases of marriage between close kin indeed, the Tikopia practice is to omit some of the exchanges of food and valuables ; the people say that it is good that these things should go out to another group, but not that they should circulate within the family. Such attitudes are of course connected with ideas of generosity and the correlation of gift-making with social status.

As far as Tikopia is concerned, then, one can point out how the operation of the rule against incest does in fact tend to avoid the creation of incompatible relationships, the life-long split of close kin, the reduction of co-operation in marriage and institutional care of children from a double to a single group affair. These, it may be noted, are sociological, not psychological considerations. Whatever be the mental reactions of the persons concerned, they are too difficult of study and, it may be, too variable in individual manifestation to be used as evidence by the anthropologist. In most explanations of the incest rule the tendency has been to correlate it primarily with the function of the avoidance of sex relations within the family. Such a narrow interpretation seems unnecessary. Far more important is its function in securing the harmonious working of social relationships which, if opposed within the same kinship group, would be difficult if not virtually impossible to exercise. It is the permanent social union, not the temporary sex relation alone, that is of the most importance ; the latter is included in the ban because in ordinary life it is part of such union, and tends to lead to the formation of a permanent association.

These conclusions, it seems to me, may well have a more general application. It is obvious that this analysis has been dependent upon the recognition of gradation in the classificatory system of relationship—it presupposes the existence of a clear distinction between near and distant consanguineous kin, and the consequent possibility of the harmonious conversion of the latter into close affinals.

The Tikopia are not an exogamous community, but the point of view here put forward would seem to apply to such a case also. Where the rule of marriage outside the clan is in force it would appear to assist clarity in distinguishing these groups in the society, and to remove a potential factor of incompatibility, of disharmony in social relations. This regulation does not necessarily eliminate sex from the clan ; breaches of exogamy between clan members usually seem to occur. But it does tend to prevent such liaisons from becoming permanent, to eliminate the clash of interests of an economic and social kind. The clan members can act all on the one side in a marriage of one of their number, can form a solid group towards the child of the marriage, can stand together in a feud. Hence one line in society is strengthened, that which is followed for the continuity of cultural forms, as in descent, or succession. The rule of exogamy makes for social simplification. It is the prohibition of a division by marriage among persons whose interests are already bound up in other ways.

But there are also the advantages of external co-operation to be considered, as has been pointed out by Fortune and by F. E. Williams.[1] This is in some ways the reverse aspect of the situation just discussed, though the factor of interest in women as a commodity might be an important motive. Despite the fact of the non-exogamy of the Tikopia, I met a number of times the opinion that intra-clan marriage was not proper. Two men of Taumako, discussing on separate occasions the marriages of the Ariki Taumako, Pa Tarikitoŋa and Pa Roŋonafa, leading men of their own clan, who had made such unions, put this view. One of them said, " E! It is correct; it is wrong; it is not good," meaning that though lawful it was in bad taste. He said that exogamy was the old custom, and gave as the reason that in such case when the marriage feast was made the gifts for the bride were carried to another clan and another chief from those of the husband. Actually as genealogies show, the Tikopia have never followed any clear-cut rule in the matter. It is significant that those who held this brief for exogamy had themselves married out of their own clan. But other people, some having made intra-clan and other extra-clan marriages, held that the former custom was not as just stated, and that of old folk married whom they chose, as at present. The feeling in favour of exogamy seemed in fact to be simply an extension among some people—rendered virtuous by their own situation—of the sentiment against the union of close kin, and the recognition of the advantages of applying to marriage the general principle that economic exchange should have as wide a sphere of operation as possible. The element of external pressure must not be regarded as primary in all cases, and I cannot accept the suggestion of Fortune that the prohibition of incest is simply the internal application of a rule of exogamy dictated from outside the group concerned. This suggestion does not account for the situation where there is no exogamous rule, and where it is immaterial into what specific group the marriage takes place—so long as it is extra-familial. Not only is this true of Tikopia, but also of other Polynesian communities, where though our information is scanty it points to the same condition. Such is the Maori state of affairs,[2] where the incest situation is clearly defined, but so far from there being exogamy, marriage was usually favoured within the tribe, leading Best to use the term endogamy in this connection.

In the heap of theories that have accumulated around the problems of the incest barrier and the regulations of exogamy, there is hardly one which is based upon an empirical analysis of conditions in a

---

[1] R. F. Fortune, article, " Incest," *American Encyclopædia Social Sciences*, 1932 ; F. E. Williams, " Exchange Marriage and Exogamy," *Man*, 131, 1934.

[2] See Elsdon Best, *The Maori*, I, 447.

specified community—the behaviour of actual persons and groups.   In
this chapter I have tried to give some material of this kind, to define
the incest situation in one community, to give the native objections
to it, and to show how the mechanism works in concrete cases.   When
more data has been adduced from other communities it may be found
that the incest-exogamy attitudes may not be reducible to a simple
formula.   I am prepared to see it shown that the incest situation varies
according to the social structure of each community, that it has little
to do with the prevention of sex relations as such, but that its real
correlation is to be found in the maintenance of institutional forms
in the society as a whole, and of the specific interest of groups in
particular.   Where these latter demand it for the preservation of
their privileges, the union permitted between kin may be the closest
possible.

In the ruling families of Hawaii, Egypt and Peru, as is well known,
marriage between brother and sister occurred.   In Tonga the cross-
cousin marriage, normally a violation of the brother-sister taboo, was
approved by kinsfolk of the pair for political and economic reasons.   It
was common among chiefs and was used as a mechanism to strengthen
the relation of Tui Tonga to Tui Kanokupolu.[1]   In Raratonga one of
the Makea family married his full-blood sister.[2]   In Tahiti marriage
of near kin occurred among people of rank when political interest
made it necessary.[3]   Here maintenance of rank dictated unions which
normally would be regarded as incestuous.   In ancient Egypt of the
XIIth Dynasty also, it seems that among the lower middle classes the
marriage of father and daughter and other close kin was not infrequent,
the object being apparently the conservation of property.[4]   The ortho-
cousin marriage of Arab communities too seems to have an economic
basis.

Thus where interest of rank or property steps in, the incest prohibition is likely to melt away ; its basis is to be sought in sociological
conditions, not in instinctive or other psychological foundations.   In
general the harmony of group interests is maintained better by keeping
the body solid and undifferentiated from the affinal point of view.   The
" horror of incest " then falls into place as one of those supernatural
sanctions, the aura of which gives weight to so many useful social
attitudes.

Allowance must of course always be made for the efflorescence of

---

[1] Gifford, *op. cit.* 22, 60-61, 189, 281.

[2] Te Rangi Hiroa, *Mangaian Society*, 91-92.

[3] Moerenhout, *Voyages*, II, 67.

[4] Margaret Murray, *Congres Internationale des Sciences Anthropologiques*, etc.
Compte-rendu, 1934, 282.

an institution—the tendency for it to develop logical extensions within the premises of its own system, to acquire an autonomy in which its rules are kept for their own sake, with no wider function to serve than the perpetuation of the existing form.

It is difficult to substantiate this particular theory of the sociological nature of the incest prohibition by reference to other societies. As the work of Westermarck and others has shown there is a great deal of data which indicate the objections which native peoples have to incest, the strong measures they take to prevent or punish it, but there is hardly any material to demonstrate the disintegrating effect of such unions on the family group, nor to show what kind of equilibrium is arrived at between the various social forces when such unions actually take place. My generalization from Tikopia remains then a hypothesis for other societies, though there is at least a suggestion that analogous social forces are at work elsewhere.

From the general sociological standpoint it seems to me also that the attitude towards incest has something in common with a popular, uninformed view about union of the sexes in the " colour problem." Here one meets with a comparable repugnance to the idea, the same tendency to put the objection on a " natural " or " instinctive " foundation. Close family sentiment is even invoked as the clinching argument in favour of the impossibility of the admission of such unions—in the well-known formula, " Would you like to see your sister marry. . . ." This is adduced to prove the instinctive revulsion from the idea. It is often held that the very fibres of the being rebel against such a union, and that this rebellion is not the result of social conditioning but of innate biological constitution. Here, as in the case of the prohibition of the union of very close kin, is an irrational emotional attitude, developing from a set of powerful complex social institutions. That there is no really instinctive repugnance to sex union between persons of different skin colour is shown by the frequency with which such unions have taken place, and still take place, sometimes within the bond of marriage, more often, for various social reasons, outside it. The social practice here varies, from one country to another—France contrasted with the United States of America ; according to the " racial " affinities of the persons concerned—negro, Polynesian, Hindu ; the relative numbers of each group in the total population, their economic condition and the like. The colour problem takes on a different *facies* in each community ; the colour situation must be defined in terms of economic and social factors superimposed upon the recognition of skin shade. Variation in economic status or political status (nationality) may entirely change the character of a judgment passed on individuals of the same " race."

Barriers to social intercourse which do not exist for the Maori in New Zealand apply to Polynesians of other parts of the Pacific; in a situation of race difficulty in the United States a negro who is not an American citizen may be free from many disabilities.[1] Religious interests may also complicate the situation. Under Islam there is no colour bar either in theory or in practice, whereas under Christianity the concept of the brotherhood of man often stops short at men of colour.

Difference of skin shade is a physical fact aesthetically and ethically as neutral as difference of hair colour or eye colour. The citation of skin colour as an index of cultural discrimination, the placing of it on a genealogical basis, so that it becomes potential and not actual shade (for the term " coloured " in the United States has come to have that significance), can be explained only by analysis of sociological factors. The position of individuals who are the product of race-crossing can be interpreted only in this way. In some cases an individual of mixed blood is attributed for social purposes to one of the component " races," even when he or she does not show any of the external physical traits proper to that parent stock. The outstanding example is the classification as a negro of a person who has sufficient of the external physical characters of the people among whom he lives to " pass " ordinarily as white. How can there be an instinctive repugnance to a " negro " who can normally mix undetected in white society ? The stress here laid upon the purely genetic position of the individual is the result of the social evaluation of the large number of negroes of ordinarily recognized physical character. No doubt early conditioning may result in some aversion to skin contacts and the like between persons of different colour. But ultimately this discrimination rests on a cleavage of social interests, largely but by no means wholly of the economic order. And on this foundation has been erected an enormous superstructure of social codes of behaviour, legislative enactments, sentiments and beliefs, conformity to which on the part of any individual is the result of subjection to the influence of the cultural tradition. Difference of social interests may give rise to cleavage which it is difficult to avoid, but at least it should be made clear that the factors involved in the " colour problem " have no deeper basis, and that to treat the accumulated prejudices as having any real innate validity is absurd.

The rules against incest, though operating in quite a different milieu, are also of social creation. They vary from one community to another, and where there is no cleavage of interest, but a positive

[1] See the dispassionate and illuminating analysis by James Weldon Johnson, *Along this Way*, 1934, 88-89, *et passim*.

social gain to be had from the union of close kin, the union takes place with full approbation, and the phenomenon of incest does not exist. The widespread occurrence of the incest prohibition simply goes to show that the constitution of the individual family, and the personal needs of its members for a wider support and co-operation than the family itself affords, render it difficult as a rule for close consanguinity and affinity to coincide.   With the colour bar of course the situation is not analogous, in that there is no basic correlation with the structure of the individual family as such.

CHAPTER IX

"HOUSE" AND CLAN

In previous chapters the salient principles of Tikopia kinship have been considered primarily with reference to the way they work in the lives of individuals, especially in the immediate family circle. Many of the activities of people, however, are phrased in terms of their relationship to each other in larger groups. Analysis of these is of interest not only to a descriptive account of Tikopia culture but also to a general theory of kinship aggregations, since they exhibit structural forms more amorphous than those usually referred to in textbooks under the name of joint family, clan and the like, but just as efficient as a basis of social co-operation.

PATRILINEAL AND MATRILINEAL GROUPS

The classification of societies into patrilineal and matrilineal would have no meaning if by that were implied an exclusive concentration in all social affairs on one or other line to the total neglect or rigid repression of the other. It is now recognized that in all communities the kin of the mother and those of the father have each a role to play. They supplement each other, sometimes occupying reverse positions in different cases, but always forming a necessary integral part of the social mechanism.[1] At times the interlocking is very patent, as when membership of kinship groups is traced through the mother in the female line while succession to chieftainship or other social privileges goes in the male line, the father being the transmitting agent.[2] Again, the division of property may employ both these principles, the possessions of a father going to his sons and those of a woman to her daughters. In more subtle ways also, even where the chief weight is ostensibly laid on one side of the house, the other comes in for a share of attention. In the performance of less codified services for individuals, as the provision of hospitality, protection, defence against slander, it facilitates their progress through life.

At the same time, simplification of choice in transmission of social privileges is aided by adherence to one or other side of the family. A society in which no such selection of principle had been made would find it difficult to avoid a chaotic dispersion of its most valued and most unique rights, and would multiply the potentialities of

---

[1] v. A. I. Richards, "Mother Right Among the Central Bantu," *Essays Presented to C. G. Seligman*, 267-279, 1934, for an interesting recent essay on this theme.

[2] Codrington, *Melanesians*, 55, 61, illustrates this well.

social disturbance through conflicting ambitions and jealousies. The designation of a community as patrilineal or matrilineal means no more, therefore, than that the most formal and basic criterion of social status, membership of a kinship group, is determined through the male or the female line respectively. In general the native societies of Polynesia may be spoken of as belonging to the patrilineal order, since for the most part a person traces his incorporation in a named kinship group through his father and his father's male forbears. Affiliation with the mother's group is regarded, if anything, as important as that with the father's, but it is of a different type. One does not take one's family name therefrom, and again the position of the mother in that group is determined through her father and his male forbears in turn; this too is a patrilineal group. Nowhere in Polynesia is the basic social unit a group for which the fundamental tie is kinship through women. Even in Ontong Java, where a person may belong to the joint family of his mother's brother, this joint family is basically patrilineal. In the Maori *hapu*, though relationship may be traced through a female ancestor as an alternative to a male, the male connection is more primary and the most esteemed. In Maŋaia where the custom of contracting a child out into its mother's group seems to have been very frequent on account of the incidence of human sacrifice, the existence of this formal mechanism of adoption indicates that the primary principle of filiation is patrilineal.

In Tikopia the kinship unit is definitely of the patrilineal type. Every individual family of father, mother and children is part of a larger group known as the *paito* and composed of similar families, tracing their relationship ultimately to a common male ancestor through male forbears in each case. Each *paito* bears a proper name. The head of the *paito* is, in theory, the senior male descendant of this ancestor, though circumstances may have introduced a representative from a junior branch for the time being. The *paito* as the incorporation of a number of individual families is itself the outgrowth of such a single family in past time; there is, in fact, a continuous process of fission at work in Tikopia society, a proliferation which, unless checked by other social and economic causes, leads to an ever increasing multiplication of kinship groups. The factors which lead to the development of autonomy in these *paito* will be considered later.

The position of an individual as a member of a *paito* is one of the most crucial factors in his social status. From it, through his father he receives guardianship from others of the group in his young days, rights to the produce of lands and later a share in them and other property, a house-site and an associated name when he marries,

economic and ritual assistance on the necessary occasions, and privileges in the use of religious formulae and in appeal to the principal
ancestral deities.   Wealth, rank and clan membership are all primarily
determined by the *paito* into which he may be born.   With the people
of this family group he lives, works and appears on public occasions,
and his kinship ties with them are recognized specifically as being
of a strong and close kind.

The Tikopia have a predilection for using a word with a wide
variation in meaning in different contexts, a contrast between a general
and a specific significance being particularly common.   The term
paito in the most concrete sense indicates a house, a building in
which people live.   By a fairly obvious transference of meaning it
may also refer to the family living therein.   But in another sense it
is the recognized designation for the kinship unit constituted by a
number of households living under different roofs.   Unless otherwise indicated the native word is used in this book to indicate this
kinship group; alternatively, the term " house " is used as its
equivalent.

The influence of the patrilineal principle is extremely strong in the
overt legal sphere of Tikopia social relations.   Descent is patrilineal
and under no circumstances can a person belong to the " house "
of his mother as against that of his father.   Succession is as strictly
in the male line.   In the very numerous genealogies which I have
collected there is not a single instance where a person in the female
line has succeeded.   The " house " goes to the farthest limits of male
descent and explores the collaterals to the utmost to find an heir to
a chief or elder, while all the time the immediate sister's son is never
considered.   He is excluded automatically from the succession by
the fact of his mother's marriage into another " house."   The
" house " may die out, it cannot be carried on through the distaff
line.   Even where the sister's son lives as an adopted child in the
dwelling of the mother's brother who is childless, he may play the
part of a son so far as the ordinary economic and social life is concerned, and may even inherit the possessions of his maternal uncle,
but it is impossible for him to take on this man's official status.   At
the present time Pa Saukirima and Pa Nukusaukava, the son of his
sister Nau Raŋipaea, are in this position.

Inheritance is patrilineal in the main, but as might be expected,
there is economic provision made for the females of the family.   After
the lapse of a generation, however, landed property reverts to the
male line.   Special cases of entail to the descendants of females are
mentioned below, and occur nearly always through definite injunction
on the part of the father.

GENEALOGY I

CHIEFLY HOUSE OF KAFIKA
(In Historic Times)

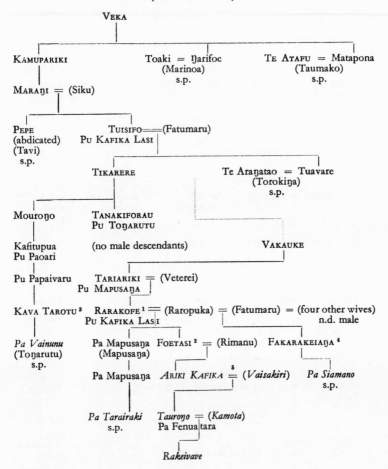

EXPLANATION :

These genealogies are skeletal, omitting many polygynous marriages, offspring
   without modern descendants, junior members of families, etc.

Chiefs in capitals, thus : TUISIFO.

Numbers indicate order of succession in the last few generations.

Houses (ramages) in brackets thus : (Siku).

s.p.—still proceeding.

n.d.—no descendants.

Names of living persons italicized.

GENEALOGY II

CHIEFLY HOUSE OF TAFUA

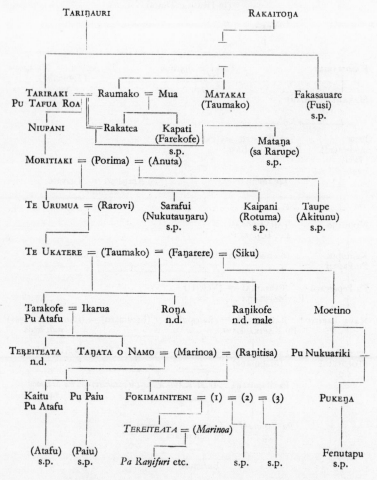

CONSTITUTION OF THE " HOUSE " IN TIKOPIA

Let us consider first the constitution of a " house " from an actual example, seeing the manner in which by traditional account such a group originates, and the kind of relations which obtain between branches of a single stock. Historically considered *paito* are of three types: offshoots from some chiefly house, descendants from immigrants landing in Tikopia and marrying into the local people, or the descendants from single local individuals who for one reason or another have been able to start a line. The branching-off of subsidiary houses from the parent stem of Tafua will serve as an instance of the former kind. For this reference will be necessary to the genealogy (Genealogy II).

The tradition of the original ancestor of this group is given elsewhere ; [1] the location of the modern representatives is described in Chapter II. The most remote historical person who interests us here is Tariŋauri, who lived nine generations ago. Of his two sons one, Tariraki, known as Pu Tafua Roa from his great height, succeeded him as chief. He it was who made the voyage to Luaŋiua. His younger brother Fakasauare was the founder of the great house of Fusi, whose latest representative is the elder Pa Saukirima. Tariraki married a mother and daughter (in somewhat peculiar circumstances) ; the son of the elder woman became chief in turn. Mataŋa, the son of the younger, married a sister of Perurua, the warrior of the autochthonous ŋa Faea, but had no child by her. A son by another wife was the progenitor of the "house" of Sa Rarupe. Niupani, his chiefly brother, was succeeded by his son Moritiaki whose sons in turn founded several well-known houses of to-day. The eldest, Te Urumua, became chief. The next two founded the houses of Nuku-tauŋaru and Rotuma respectively. These were all sons of a woman from Porima. From a woman of Anuta, the second wife, was born Taupe, who founded the house of Akitunu. Accounts differ concerning the precise status which this man attained. According to Pa Sukuporu, the present representative of his descendants, Taupe actually became head of the clan on his father's death. This, however, is denied by the Ariki Tafua, whose statement probably is the more accurate. But the two versions agree in all other essentials. Taupe, being a junior son, had not the right of succession, but Moritiaki wished him to have the *kasoa*, i.e. the chiefly necklet, with all its privileges. The reason was that since his mother was from another island Taupe had no standing in Tikopia apart from his father, whereas his half-brothers had firm provision through their mother's family. On hearing their father's intention the other brothers were very angry, and all deserted the family home at Uta, abandoning their father. Seeing this Taupe became ashamed and went alone to live in Namo, where he stayed for a long time catching fish and cooking them himself, eating and sleeping in solitude. At last the father gave way. He summoned Taupe to Uta, and when he came gave him a kit containing a number of sacred adze blades of clam shell of

[1] *History and Traditions of Tikopia.*

the small type known as *pipi*. He then accompanied him to Mauŋafaea and there buried the blades in various parts of the orchards. Here they served as barriers (*pīpī*) to secure the land to him in perpetuity and to ward off any possible encroachment by his brothers or their descendants. At the same time Moritiaki said to his son that he and his seed should not *paru te tau kava*, infuse the kava, that is, that they should not at any future time hold position as chiefs of the clan. Thus his descendants, though normally they would be among the potential heirs if the direct succession failed, were forever placed among the ranks of the commoners. The pronouncement was also made that this house should send its gifts of food only occasionally to the Tafua chief instead of regularly, as is the duty of commoners. This singled Akitunu out as being in a special relation to the chiefly line, analogous to that which Tavi and Torokiŋa bear to the chiefs of Kafika.[1]

The burial of the adze blades in the orchards had the effect of making the land " bitter " (*kona*). If chiefs or their families in later generations attempted to take food from the orchards of Akitunu the presence of these sacred objects would make this food not unpalatable, but bitter in the deeper sense of rendering them ill. Compensation in the form of a permanent insurance was thus provided to Taupe and his descendants for the deprivation of their rights of succession and the absence of initial maternal kindred in the land. The barrier then set up has been observed down to the present day, and to my knowledge its efficacy has never been tested, since the power of the sacred adze wielded spiritually, as it were, by a tutelary deity is greatly feared by these natives. The present Ariki, who is accused not unjustly of encroaching upon the lands of members of his clan, has made no attempt in this direction. The principal god of Akitunu is Taŋaroa, whom Taupe took with him to Namo ; a list of the others and their qualities will be given in a later publication.

Consequent on this act, the successor to Moritiaki was Te Urumua. He was followed by his son Te Ukatere, the child of his second wife, his sons by the first having died without issue. This man had three wives from two of whom sprang " houses," offshoots of the chiefly line. The house of Raŋikofe is represented to-day only by two unmarried women, and in a few more years will be extinct. The other, the house of Fenutapu, had as its ancestor Moetino, and includes the present families of Nukuariki, Fenutapu proper and Tekaukena. This house provided the last chief of Tafua, by name Pukeŋa, as a substitute while the present chief was still a child. The first wife of Te Ukatere bore him three sons. The eldest, the famous

[1] See *History and Traditions*.

Tarakofe who married the bewitching Ikarua, did not succeed, but his son in turn, Tereiteata, came next in the line of chiefs. He was a bachelor chief, which is unusual, and being lost at sea on a voyage to Vanikoro, left no descendants. He is known colloquially as Pu Tafua Lasi on account of his size, and is the "familiar" of his brother's grandson, the present chief. After him the succession reverted to his father's brother Roŋa, who also left no descendants, and the chieftainship then fell upon Taŋata o Namo, brother of Terei·eata.

By his first wife, a woman of the Marinoa house, this man had five sons and two daughters, but of the former three have left no descendants. They died, either in foreign lands or in the ocean wastes while voyaging. Another founded the *paito* of Paiu, recognized as being closely allied to the chiefly house proper of Tafua. The eldest son was distinguished for various exploits. He was married to five wives and, not content with this, engaged in amorous exploits throughout the island. His virility, his size and his ferocity made him hated of husbands and feared by all. He is frequently spoken of by his house-name Pu Atafu, which is borne by his descendants, but his personal name was Kaitu. His death was one of the many dramatic incidents in the recent history of Tikopia; he was killed by two men of the house of Resiake (*v.* Genealogy III).

Taŋata o Namo lived to an advanced age, and was followed in the chieftainship by the eldest son of his second wife, known usually as Foki mai Niteni. The wanderings of this man are almost an epic in themselves; even his name, "Returned from Ntendi" (Santa Cruz), is an allusion to his arrival, like that of Odysseus, long after he had been given up for lost in his native home.

Foki mai Niteni was succeeded by his eldest son, now reigning, whose personal name (never uttered in public) is Tereiteata, in memory of his grandfather's brother. The family of the chief and those of his brothers, Pa Maevetau and Pa Tarimataŋi, form what is known in ordinary conversation as Paito i Tafua. This group comprises something over fifty people located, as already explained, in three villages. The houses of Paiu and Atafu are included in the designation for important social affairs; that of Fenutapu is regarded simply as an allied branch, but on the occasion, for example, of the death or marriage of any member of rank in either, the two houses unite as one, in distinction from the other chiefly houses of Kafika, Taumako and Faŋarere.

In the course of time certain *paito* have come to possess an individuality, to be credited with a set of traits peculiar to their members, which has been acquired through generations of achievement or habit. Thus the house of Taumako are recognized as *toa*, men of strong personality, and virile, ready to fight and to command. In the traditional account of Tikopia history this reputation has been fairly consistently upheld throughout the centuries. Present members of this house are recognized as keepers of the peace in the island, and exercise considerable authority of a personal kind for which no allowance is made in the social structure. They are also a house of craftsmen, particularly as workers in wood. The house of Niukapu are renowned particularly as *tautai*, sea-experts. Various ancestors of theirs in the past have been noted sea-voyagers and navigators, a reputation which the folk of Taumako also share to some degree. The house of Tafua, which has had noted voyagers in its time, is known at the present time principally for its prowess in fishing, and also in the dance. This is due in no small measure to the ability of the present chief, a man of strong personality, albeit of somewhat uncertain temper. The house of Sao has some distinction, not so much from the personality of its leaders as from the potency of its principal god, who can control storms and other destructive agencies; this is even more the case with the chiefs of Kafika. The folk of Raropuka house have an unenviable reputation for incestuous conduct, though this is of modern origin. Most other houses have no distinguishing traits of character.

This brief account shows, from the point of view of a present-day Tikopia, the basis for the existence of the set of houses known by the names of "*paito i Tafua*," "*paito i Akitunu*," "*paito sa Rarupe*," etc. The reference to their founding has necessarily been of skeletal order, for want of space; an amplified analysis would give in each case a description of how the ancestral founder married, settled on lands assigned to him by his father or elder brother, produced male children who lived, married and had male offspring in their turn, until the group of descendants came to represent an appreciable fraction of the clan and of the total population, to be ranked as a major house. With this process goes the designation by a collective name, the assumption of some autonomy, the acknowledgment of definite allegiance to the senior of the group, the exercise of privileges as against other groups, the concentration of ritual appeals upon exclusive ancestors. But it is impossible to specify the exact moment at which all these features become precise and overtly recognized. There is no constitution of a new kinship group by enactment or by public agreement, nor does the attainment of a certain size automatically qualify a set of people for characterization as a house. In native explanations the cardinal points usually stressed are the reasons for the separation of the original ancestor from his brethren, and the grant to him of lands or ritual

RAKING THE OVEN

Hot stones are being spread preparatory to a renewal of cooking during the repair of a canoe of the Ariki Kafika. His son Pa Taramoa, with hair down his back, is giving instructions, his principal elder Pa Rarovi is guiding the pole and Nau Rarovi is using the tongs. This is a typical working group. Baskets of cooked food, to be used as offerings to the gods, rest on the coconut-leaf mat.

privileges by the chief ; the growth in size, the attribution of a common name are treated as incidental. And it is true that once a group is recognized as a *paito* it retains that individuality so long as any member of it remains to represent it. With the death of the last member the house ceases to exist, unless it is expedient for the continuance of some ritual practices to revive it by a process of grafting. The houses of Nuŋa and Rofaŋa are extinct, with no representatives on the patrilineal side ; the houses of Sao and Taumako, according to tradition, were reconstituted in ancient times from immigrant sources, and a similar allegation is made against certain other houses of prime importance to the ceremonial life of the people.

It will become clear in the course of this book how the formation and continued existence of these kinship groups is associated with and dependent upon the exercise of specific social functions—exclusive relationships towards certain lands and the buildings which stand thereon, specialization in ritual, isolation in spiritual affairs.

Succession by seniority in the *paito* is the theory, but is liable to be abrogated by circumstances, and the descendants of the eldest branch may be left aside. There is always a tendency to revert to them if the offspring of the reigning head be not adequate, if there be a gap in the succession, or if they are fit to take up office when a collateral headman has died. For example, the present Ariki Tafua succeeded his father after a representative of the Namo branch of the chiefly house (the family of Fenutapu) had held the chieftainship. The present Ariki Kafika came to the chieftainship in like circumstances after an interval of two reigns. In both cases their fathers were lost at sea when they were mere children unable to take on the responsibility of office. But when one line has held the chieftainship for several generations, then an elder branch ceases to be considered as the most appropriate for the succession, except under very special circumstances. The house of Mapusaŋa is senior in point of descent to that of the reigning chief of Kafika, but their ancestor did not himself ever act as chief and so, as the natives say, they have " gone to one side " from the succession. In such a case descendants of this line exert a somewhat greater influence than those in junior non-regnant branches, because, should the reigning line fail, they would probably be called upon to provide the chief.

In some cases the succession goes almost indifferently from one branch to another. This is the case with Fetauta and Marinoa proper, which form a kind of duplex unit though they separated in name several generations ago. The representative of either may act as elder for the group as a whole. It is purely a matter of choice. " If the elder is lifted from the house of Fetauta then he will dwell as Pa Fetauta. If he is taken from the house of Marinoa then he will dwell as Pa Marinoa." Either title is valid. This flexibility of succession is to be correlated with a recognition of the principle of branching as leading to the creation of new kinship groups, independent yet linked with those from which they sprang.

The constitution of the " house " has now become clear; it is obvious that its cohesion depends primarily on the tie of recognized descent from common ancestors. The degree of corporate unity of this group varies considerably. The general principle is that the immediacy of the occasion determines how far the branches of a house shall assemble together and whether all the constituent individual families shall be present. In small affairs such as the ritual following the first night torchlight fishing of a boy, or the first sightseeing expedition of a girl, only the immediate members of the household usually take part. At marriage, initiation, or death the bonds of kinship become effective over a much wider range and the several branches of the parent stem unite in virtue of their common ancestor for the economic and ritual services to be performed. The presence of a clan as a whole on a ceremonial occasion may be viewed, as the natives themselves indicate, as an extension of this kinship principle. Frequently when all the members of the house do not come to participate in the transaction of their group, each branch of a family sends representatives—a chief, for instance, often arranges for his eldest son to act for him, or out of a family of several brothers two only may attend. This principle of representation is well recognized and works in an interesting fashion on important ceremonial occasions of reciprocity between groups, when through kinship affiliation the house may have ties with both sides. Some members of it will then go on each side so that none of the group bonds are ignored.

Our earlier analysis showed that the *paito* is not a residential unit; its members may be scattered throughout several villages. However, its group existence is expressed in residential terms by named housesites. The house-name of the common ancestor frequently forms the name for his group of descendants, and his original dwelling commonly serves as a temple for ritual services to ancestors and gods. Other principal buildings of the group bear hereditary names carried also by men of the group and as a result the kinship unit has a strong local focus of interest.

In ordinary economic affairs the house does not bother to come together as a whole; the branches of it act as separate units. For instance, when the flying fish were rising on the western coast one evening two canoes from the chief's family of Tafua went out. In one, Tereiteata, bearing the same ancestral name as the chief himself, the crew consisted of Pa Raŋifuri, his younger brother Pa Roŋorei, Satapuaki, a young man of the Atafu branch of Tafua, who frequently lives in the household of the chief because his father is dead; a young man of the house of Faraŋanoa, who joined because he was staying in the village with his cousin, Pa Taitai, and another man of the village. In the other canoe, Tafeunu, were Pa Nukunefu and Pa Paiu, sons of the chief, their brother-in-law Pa Tekaumata from an adjoining village, a lad from the house of Nukuone of Rofaea, and Fakasarakau from the house of Sao in Raveŋa. Here we have the vessels provided by the chief, the direction of affairs by four of his sons, and the enlisting of other men to assist either because of kinship association or local availability. An ordinary party in the taro gardens on another day consisted of the Ariki Kafika, his wife, his son Pa Taramoa, his grandson Rakeivave (son of Pa Fenuatara), Nau Taramoa, and Nau Motuata, who is a daughter of the allied house of Mapusaŋa. These people collaborated in their work, dove-tailing the respective portions of their task.

Since the *paito* is a kinship group which is formed by a process of branching, it is sometimes difficult to draw the line clearly between separate units. For some things a branch considers itself inde-pendent of the parent stem, for others the two combine. Related *paito* frequently speak of themselves as one. For example, the houses of Maniva, Raŋifau and Fetu talk of " *matou paito sokotasi*," that is, " our one house." Their common ancestor Ataro split off from the chiefly stock of Taumako six generations ago; three genera-tions ago the group-ancestor of Fetu and Maniva was differentiated from the ancestor of Raŋifau. The present descendants of the former number about thirty people, and of the latter about fifteen. This is a house of moderate size. The names of Fetauta, Motuaŋi, Tauŋa, Tarafaŋa, and Saumari refer to small units ancestrally related. To-gether, however, they are known as " the one house, clustered together, Marinoa." They go fishing, or to the cultivations, separately, but when it comes to any ceremonial proceeding, as for example attendance on the house of Tafua, with which they are re-lated by marriage, the whole group assembles or sends representa-tives. The number of people in a group, the extent to which they are scattered through the villages, and the personal relations between the heads of households largely determine when a separation shall occur. No rule of general application can be laid down. In the chiefly house of Kafika there is a division between the branch headed by the Ariki himself and that headed by Pa Vainunu. The latter's father, though not in the direct line of descent, was elected chief, owing to the absence of nearer heirs, and so his descendants have a

GENEALOGY III
CHIEFLY HOUSE OF TAUMAKO

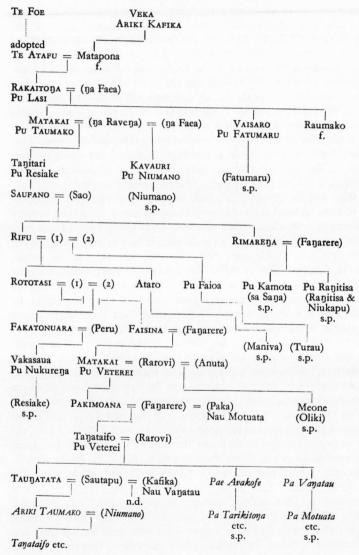

special position. They are spoken of as a " chiefly family separated off nowadays " (*paito ariki mavae atu iasonei*). This branch consists of over thirty people.

After some time representatives of junior branches of the chiefly stock cease to be considered as chiefly families (*paito ariki*). They are counted among the commoners. For instance, eight generations ago there lived Te Orofana, who was known by his house-name of Pu Faioa. He was the son of Rifu, the Ariki Taumako. He had two grandsons, one known as Pu Turau and the other as Pu Faone. The descendants of the former are the present-day house of Faioa, known alternatively as the house of Turau. The descendants of the latter, the younger, are the present house of Aneve or Faone, names which are borne by two men at the present time. Of these folk it is said, " they are termed commoners, they separated off from Taumako, they went to dwell at the back, but they are from the one stem." The same is the case with the houses of Maniva, and of Raŋitisa. " They have separated from the chiefly house."

The relationship of *paito* goes off in a new direction owing to the communication with the neighbouring island of Anuta, seventy miles away. In olden times many canoe voyages between them took place, but nowadays most of the contact is by the yearly visit of the *Southern Cross*. Each important house in Tikopia has its special link in Anuta. This is called the *tauraŋa*, a word which suggests derivation from *taura*, an anchor rope, which is what these folk are in a foreign land. When a man goes from one island to another, he usually stays with his *tauraŋa*, reciprocating their hospitality in time by similar service to them, or it may be to their descendants. No exact forms of reciprocity are pursued between them. The people of the *tauraŋa* group are alternatively described as *kano a paito*, " relatives," though the kinship tie with them may not be very clear. An example may be given. Long ago Pu Raŋitisa, grandson of the then Ariki Taumako, went to Anuta, married a girl from there, and on his return had a son, Pu Niukapu. In this way the present bearer of the name Niukapu has ancestral connection with Anuta. Again, the mother's mother of this man and the mother's mother of Ti Anuta, the present principal chief, were sisters. Hence Ti Anuta and Pa Niukapu reckon themselves as " brothers," and Niukapu is the dwelling of the Anuta chief when he comes to Tikopia. This is described as " the linkage through women of old." Pa Niukapu said, " Ti Anuta is the post of this house." The present Anuta chief and his wife lived for a year with their host in Tikopia, and on another occasion Pa Niukapu took his wife to live for a time in Anuta with the chief. Their son was left with the brothers of Pa

Niukapu in Tikopia. The chiefs of Tafua have their kinsfolk in Anuta, and Taŋata o Namo, grandfather of the present Ariki, used to go there from time to time. In 1924 a party of youths came from Anuta in a canoe, the name of which was Te Aravave (the swift path), which they left with their hosts of Tafua. A portion of it now is the large slab forming the side wall of the dwelling Mukava. This system has also another use in the case of intermarriage between the two islands, which means that one of the spouses is deprived of close kin in the place of residence. This gap is supplied by the *tauraŋa*, who fulfil all important ritual obligations. Thus the mother of Pa Rarovi of Tikopia was from Anuta. His *tuatina* in Tikopia then are the house of Aneve, who happen to be the *tauraŋa* of his mother's Anuta house. Such a system of affiliation ensures that a person shall never suffer the fate of being kinless in a strange land.

Some names of houses as Taumako, Raropuko, Avakofe are identical in the two islands ; most are quite different.

RANK, WEALTH AND KINSHIP

Paito in Tikopia are differentiated by a system of rank based primarily upon traditional ritual privileges and obligations associated with the beliefs in the native gods. It must be emphasized that it is not primarily an alignment on the basis of wealth. As the outcome of these ritual divisions, three social classes are distinguished : firstly chiefly families (*paito ariki*), and secondly commoner families (*paito fakaarofa*) ; these latter are divided again into those which have a ritual elder as their head (*paito pure*) and those whose headmen have no ritual privileges of any note. Some of the *paito pure* are originally of chiefly stock, for example, Maniva, Niumano, Fusi. Others had an immigrant as their first ancestor. He, like the prince in a fairy tale, usually married the daughter of a chief, and so began the *pure* house. Marinoa, Farekofe, Sao, ŋatotiu are all examples of this.

The differences in the ordinary social position of chiefly and commoner families are not great. They all own lands, they mingle freely, exchanges take place between them on a basis of general reciprocity, there is no " chief's language," as in Samoa or in Java, kinship terms are used between them, and nowadays intermarriage takes place freely between their members (see Chapter XV). The discrimination is mainly in the sphere of authority. A person of a chiefly family, particularly if closely related to the chief himself, is more apt to give than to receive orders. Again, if a commoner strikes a member of a chiefly family, he will probably have to expiate his offence by going off to sea ; the reverse can occur with impunity.

In general, persons from a chiefly house conduct themselves with more pride than do commoners. In a quarrel a woman of such a house rushes in without fear, brandishing a weapon, where a woman of common stock remains in the background. It must be said that I am simply quoting native statements here, for I have not observed a fight between two such people. I have, however, frequently seen deference paid by commoners to members of chiefly families, which has been explained on such grounds. There is also the statement of one informant who was describing the abasement made by men who have carried off a bride from the house of her father. As they crawl in to atone for the ravishment they are pommelled by the woman's male relatives. But, as it was rather naively explained : " If they are sons of chiefs, we do not hit them hard, lest they rise up and strike us back." Normally the rough treatment should be endured without retaliation. The relations of commoners to the families of chiefs cannot be fully dealt with here ; in a later volume the import of the distinction between them in social and economic terms will then be made more precise. The interest of the class distinction here is in comparing the position of families with their wealth, a matter which will be dealt with below.

In religious affairs the difference in position of certain families is extremely marked. Some are in close relation with important gods, others are dependent upon these for their contact with the higher supernatural powers. Each family has its representative or channel of communication with the gods and ancestors, be he chief, elder, or ordinary headman. The principle of appointment is seniority of descent ; the oldest man does not succeed, as in Ontong Java.[1] In addition most families have a spiritistic medium, who acts as the direct mouthpiece of one or other of their prime supernatural beings. He is often not the head of the family, but his younger brother or other close kinsman.

The class distinction between houses in Tikopia is not made on the basis of wealth, but at the same time the distribution of wealth has a bearing on it. The Tikopia, like other more civilized communities, have a great respect for the possessor of material goods, and are apt to accord him privileges normally above those of his formal station. A poor man is described as "a bat " ; like that animal he is devoid of possessions and must live upon the bounty of others. He has no stores of his own upon which to rely. A rich man is known by the term *taufenua*, literally " owning the country," a metaphorical exaggeration of his command over material things. In general, chiefly families in Tikopia are wealthy in comparison with commoner

[1] H. I. Hogbin, *Law and Order in Polynesia*, 127-9.

families.   An exception is the house of Faŋarere which, for historical reasons, occupies a position different from the others.   The major wealth of Tikopia consists in land, and here one of the principal objects of consideration is the coconut.   The chiefs of Taumako and Tafua are particularly rich in coconut palms and the Ariki Kafika rather less so.   Though he is the premier chief by virtue of his ritual privileges, he is apt to be at a disadvantage when it comes to the fulfilment of his economic obligations.   His principal elder, Pa Rarovi, too, is wealthier than he is.   I had occasion to witness his resentment during the sacred ceremonies of Somosomo.   There was a shortage of coconut in the land, and the chief had issued orders that the customary ritual presentations were to be on a moderate scale— " to be made corresponding to the food supplies which are scanty," he said.   Pa Rarovi disregarded these instructions, and when his time came to take the initiative sent in the usual large mass of baskets, the sight of which exasperated the old chief.   His resources were slender, and yet for his good name he had to reciprocate in the same style.   This lack of correspondence between his wealth and his leading ritual and social position was a source of irritation to him, and in time of stringency threatened to engender friction between him and other important members of the community who were better situated. In normal times the discrepancy, which is not a great one, is of little moment.

This is an instance of how differences in the personal situation of individuals or groups which are not an explicit part of the formal structure of a community can nevertheless affect its social institutions, and even become embodied in the structural arrangements.

The causes of the differential wealth of *paito* must be sought in the traditional data relating to landholding.   The chiefs of Kafika, for instance, have in past generations undoubtedly tended to impoverish themselves and their descendants by grants of orchards to immigrants, and to destitute persons.   In this way they have maintained their reputation for beneficence and care for the welfare of the population as a whole at the expense of their own economic interests.   This attitude of responsibility for the general prosperity is no figment of the imagination, but is expressed by the Kafika chief himself and expected by the people at large.   It is bound up to a considerable extent with his position as religious head of the community and representative of its supreme god.

The wealth of a kinship group as a whole is at the disposal of its head, but the individual share of it which each member can command depends of course upon the size of the group.   The wealth of Pa Rarovi on the one hand and of the Ariki Taumako on the other is to a considerable degree due to the fact that both of them are the only surviving sons. The question of population in relation to lands then is of importance for our enquiry. The absence of any great discrepancy in the landholdings between even the richest and the poorest houses means that in normal times every group has enough food to meet its daily requirements and fulfil its economic exchanges or presentations. It is only in times of shortage that the matter becomes acute ; it takes the form not of a revolt of the poorer against the richer groups, but of another kind of strain due to the particular social cleavage which exists between chiefs and commoners. It is the comparatively wealthy who exert the pressure, and the comparatively poor who with some complaint resist. To be more accurate, the men of rank in virtue of the maintenance of their ritual obligations endeavour to enlarge their resources at the expense of those lower in the social rather than the economic scale. This position is demonstrated at the present time in the island. In Chapter XII the population question of Tikopia as a whole is discussed ; it is the threat of a general expansion rather than of any differential group change that is the sociological factor of most weight.

It has been shown how the *paito* or " house " in Tikopia is a most important element in the social structure. It is not a unified local group, but has strong local affiliations ; its members are linked in kinship by ties of descent from a common ancestor ; it has a definite social status correlated with the rank of its head, and this in turn is dependent upon his ritual functions. It is, moreover, a property-owning unit of considerable importance, its members having a common interest in canoes, especially sacred vessels, and in tracts of land bearing ancestral names.

The constitution of another type of social group which is primarily of a kinship character may now be considered.

AN ANOMALOUS FORM OF THE CLAN

The largest social group in the island is that called *kainaŋa*, a word which unlike *paito* has no other referent. There are four of these groups, Kafika, Tafua, Taumako and Faŋarere, each headed by a chief, an *Ariki*, whose rank, as to some degree that of his group, is represented in the foregoing order of precedence. The *kainaŋa* is an aggregate of *paito*, that of the chief in each case giving the name to the *kainaŋa* as a whole. As membership of a *paito* is patrilineal, so also is that of a *kainaŋa*. Only in the case of marriage between persons of the same group does a man belong to the same *kainaŋa* as his mother, but as there is no bar against unions of this type all the members of a family are frequently found to be of the same clan allegiance. At the end of this chapter the propriety of using the term " clan " for a group of such a kind is discussed.

On my first enquiry into Tikopia social structure I pursued the question as to whether a wife could be said to belong to the clan of her husband. A few informants maintained that she changed her allegiance on marriage, " *Ku avaŋa, ku kese,*" " Has married, has become different," as it was put. Later I found that this was an academic problem. The woman enters her husband's household, assists him in all his ritual exchanges as well as in ordinary matters, and attends the religious ceremonies of his clan in a domestic capacity. But she still retains all her old privileges in her father's house, returns there to help in important matters, and in times of crisis is succoured by members of his clan and that of her own mother's brother. She has then a double allegiance, each with its own type of obligation and recompense. As I learnt later, the best way of expressing her position is to say that on the one hand for formal privileges she remains a member of her clan, but on the other for economic and social co-operation she is included in the group of relatives (*kano a paito*) of her husband.

The majority of the members of each *kainaŋa* are of common descent, their *paito* being offshoots in various generations from the original stock of their chief. As it is explained in tabloid form " the chief dwells and dwells, then dies. His sons separate off to the rear and dwell as the *kainaŋa*, while the eldest lives as chief." So also comes the analogy " the chief is the head of the *kainaŋa* " where in the Tikopia tongue the same word is used as for the part of the physical body—exactly as in English. Other *paito* have been incorporated into the clan by assimilation, usually through the marriage of an orphan or an immigrant from another island with a daughter of the reigning chief. There are many examples of this in the traditional records. Thus Pa Farekofe said of his primary ancestor, " He was a protégé (*manu*) of the Ariki Taumako who set him down to dwell ; hence I adhere to the chief of Taumako." The constitution of any clan shows this process. The clan Kafika consists of the major houses of Kafika proper, Raropuka and Rarovi (said to be of autochthonous origin), Marinoa (descended from Toaki who married ŋarifoe, daughter of Pu Veka, and received lands with her), Porima (whose ancestor came in the original Kafika canoe), Tavi (offspring of Pepe, diseased chief who abdicated), and Torokiŋa (descended from a protégé of the Ariki Kafika after the expulsion of ŋa Faea). The clan Taumako consists of the major houses of Taumako proper, Niumano, Fatumaru and Maniva (offshoots from the chiefly stock), Farekofe (descended from a Samoan survivor of a Tongan invasion), ŋatotiu (whose ancestor came from Anuta), Siku and Fasi (descended from two lads who were left behind at the expulsion of ŋa Faea), Niukapu (Raŋitisa) and sa Saŋa (offshoots from the chiefly stock, but without *pure* privileges). Owing to past intermarriages all the houses of a clan are connected now in some way or other, and classificatory terms of relationship are used between their members. This, however, is not purely a clan phenomenon, since such kinship operates over the community as a whole. But if no other kinship tie can be called to mind, the fact that two people belong to the same clan is sufficient for them to regard themselves as kin.

The Tikopia " clan " is not exogamous. " If a man wishes to marry into his own *kainaŋa*, he marries " is a typical formulation of the position. When I first began to make enquiries on this matter I was assured by some informants that such marriages were not good, but I speedily found that this opinion was not general, and was in fact put forward in order to make a cheap impression of superiority. As the genealogies show, there has always been a very large proportion of intra-clan unions, and nowadays one of the chiefs and a number of other leading men have wives taken from their own group. Propinquity of kinship is the only true guide, and when casual disapproval of an intra-clan marriage is expressed it is found to be really on the actual closeness of kinship between the parties. A union of first cousins of different clans is looked on with disfavour where that between clansfolk who are distantly related is approved. This absence of exogamy, which is general in Polynesia (with the exception of the Gilbert Islands), indicates that the adoption of divergent attitudes between members of a large kinship unit does not present so great a disharmony as in the case of the individual family, where some rule of incest always exists.

The accompanying chart shows how through one single set of lines the four chiefs of Tikopia are kinsfolk, and so bound in the network of appropriate conduct (Genealogy VI).

The Ariki Faŋarere is really the senior, but he and the Ariki Tafua are *tau fanau* through his mother's mother who came from the house of Tafua ; the Ariki Faŋarere and the Ariki Taumako were formerly *tau mana* ; now they are *tautau pariki* because of the latter's marriage to the woman of Niumano ; the same relationship holds with the Ariki Kafika, since Pa Vaisakiri and the Ariki Faŋarere are *tau fanau*. The other three chiefs are all *tau fanau* through various lines (Tanimua and Sautapu, for instance, are branches of the house of Fusi), with the exception of the Ariki Kafika and the Ariki Tafua, who are *tau ma*. The Ariki Kafika said of himself and the Ariki Tafua : " He and I were brothers before, as bachelors, we married.

When he married and his wife went to him, we became brothers-in-law, because she was my *kave*." Of himself and the Ariki Taumako he said, " We are brothers *fakapariki*; he is the son of my father's sister; her mother was from Raropuka and my father was from Raropuka, and they were brother and sister."

This kind of intermarriage has been going on for generations, and has resulted in the fact that unofficially but in reality the most important ancestors of each clan have become to some degree common to all; they are spoken of individually in ordinary conversation as " our ancestor," and their memory is treated with respect. Each of them impinges sooner or later on the maternal line of every chief. It is only, however, where such ancestor is a *tama tapu* of a group that his name can be invoked in the kava. Rakaitoŋa, primary ancestor of Taumako clan, for instance, is spoken of by sa Kafika as " *tatou puna*," since his mother came from them.

The functions of the clans are primarily political and religious, and in this latter sphere their number, four, lends itself to a symmetrical arrangement, as in economic exchange between pairs of clans. The clan is not a residentially compact unit by any means ; there are, however, certain nuclei of clan members, usually in the vicinity of their chief, as shown in Chapter III. The result is that there is often a dual linkage : a man assists the chief of the village and district where he happens to live in ordinary economic and social affairs, and goes over periodically with a basket of food to pay his respects to his clan chief, or attends on ritual occasions of importance. Individual practice varies considerably in such matters, and the estimate that a chief gives of a man's character is apt to vary accordingly.

The unity of a clan is considerable. Not only are many of its component groups offshoots from the one stem, but its members are bound in service to their chief, they have common traditions, a common god bearing the clan name and associated with special objects, a clan temple, corporate ritual performances, and the same " totemic " taboos. In religious ceremonies attended by the whole island each clan plays its part as a separate body ; its contribution is often distinguished by appending the clan name to the title of this ceremony. Thus in the sacred " Work of the Gods " the presentation of areca nut, *te aso*, is marked off as " *te aso sa Kafika* " etc., while later each clan has a night for the chanting of its own songs to which the whole assembly dances—" *te po sa Kafika*," " *te po sa Tafua*," and so on.

In the economic sphere the clan as an undifferentiated whole owns no property, but the possessions of its component houses are subsumed under its name, as for instance the sacred canoes or the lands. A question about the ownership of an orchard frequently obtains the answer that it is, say, Kafika ground. This is by virtue of the function of the chief as supreme holder of the jurisdiction.

Clan pride is quite high, and boasting of clan prowess in fishing, dart throwing or fighting is not uncommon. Thus in travelling round the northern coast with two young men they took great pains to point out to me the lands of Taumako, their clan. Later one of them remarked, " In Tikopia which stands here sa Taumako are great." When I was taking the census of the people I was assisted by Pa Tarairaki, with whom I had a laughing argument, he asserting that his clan Kafika was the greatest in numbers and I questioning this. His boast in this case later proved to be correct. In the historical field pride of clanship is frequent. Thus sa Tafua allege that they were responsible for the expulsion of ŋa Faea eight generations ago, but this the Ariki Kafika denies, attributing greater weight to the prior magical activity of folk of Kafika. With children the local unit is more of a referent than the kinship unit, but gradually they too assume the phraseology of clan solidarity. They are assisted into this by attendance at ritual performances where the fact of clan membership is impressed upon them by deed if not by word. For instance, at the ceremony which is known as the " Freeing of the Land " [1] a crowd of lads, their kinship affiliations being immaterial, have to march from Tai to Uta with shouts and yells to celebrate the breaking of the *tapu*. On the occasion that I saw this happen, when the ritual was over the Ariki Kafika, director of the proceedings, remarked, " Great was the number of the children of sa Taumako," a commendation which indicates how the lines of the clan division always tend to be present in the minds of responsible people, and how also they can become inculcated into children.

The very fact of a strong clan individuality has given rise to mechanisms to bring the clans together. These mechanisms are very largely of a ritual kind and so must be discussed in detail in a later volume, but mention of a few points may be made here in illustration. Thus in the ceremonial season known as the Work of the Gods, to which reference has already been made, there is continual interplay of ritual and ecomonic obligations between the clans. One example is given by the *loŋi*. Large baskets of food are prepared and exchanged, between Kafika and Taumako on the one hand, and Tafua and Faŋarere on the other. The actual passage of food takes place between individual families or households, but the whole transaction is regarded in being in clan terms. As it is said, " The clan sa Kafika is bound to sa Taumako," the word used, *noa*, being that denoting an

To be described in *Work of the Gods*.

ordinary tie with rope. Twice the exchange takes place, the first time between the women, the second between the men. Other food presentations are made on behalf of the clan as a whole. Of this kind is that called " The Path of Pu," a sacred gift made from sa Taumako to sa Kafika in commemoration of the great ancestor of the former clan, whose mother was a daughter of the Kafika chief Veka. This gift is of course reciprocated by sa Kafika, and all the houses of both clans rally to assist in the preparation of the vast mass of food required. When I witnessed the ceremony sa Taumako had excelled themselves, and drew from the Kafika chief and his followers considerable praise, which was of more than a purely courtesy character. Pa Torokiŋa said, with great emphasis on the initial word, " Great is the beauty of anything sa Taumako do." Such ritual affairs, with their supernatural sanction, are a great factor of consolidation in the Tikopia community.

The strength of three of the clans, Kafika, Tafua and Taumako is roughly comparable, the number of their members in 1929 being 443, 365 and 384 respectively. Faŋarere, through the accident of history, numbers few people, then only 89, and for certain ritual purposes joins forces with Kafika, under the protection of whose chief their original ancestor was placed at the slaying of their forbears. Thus, for the *fakavaetoru*, a special form of dance contest which takes place at Matautu, Kafika and Faŋarere are treated as one clan. In the re-carpeting of the sacred house Nukuora again, the chiefs of the two clans both take part, a unique occurrence.

It has been already mentioned how the bonds of kinship formed on the basis of marriage and matrilineal ties cut across the unilateral patrilineal house and clan alignment. Not only does this bind members of different clans together in ordinary social intercourse and mitigate friction between them, but it also has its place in the sphere of ritual. Normally only clan members attend the religious affairs of their chief. Others are welcome, but they do not go without a reason. Apart from residents in the same locality and close kinsfolk, anyone feels himself free to participate in the ceremonies of a chief from whose clan his mother or his wife has come. He makes a basket of food—no one would think in such circumstances of going without—and sets off. He is treated as an ordinary participant, except that after the ceremony is over his contribution is not repaid by the rough equivalence of the *taumafa*, but a special parcel of food is made up for him. His gift is *toŋoi*, specifically reciprocated, by the chief " because indeed he has come from another clan."

To give a complete account of inter-clan relations would mean a description of such institutions as competitive dances and dart

GENEALOGY VI

KINSHIP OF CHIEFS OF TIKOPIA

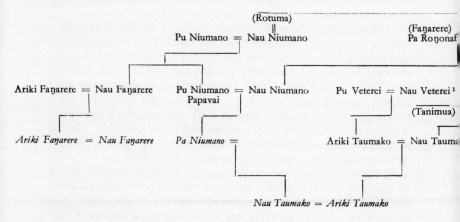

NOTE.—Dotted lines represent distant kinship by ancestral connection;

parallel vertical lines a tie with a woman's (patrilineal) house.

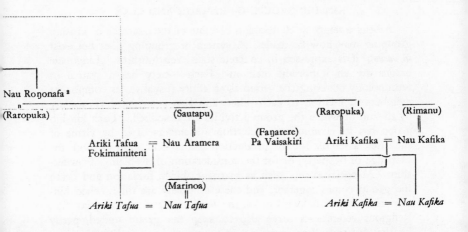

matches,[1] the election, the progressive feasts, and the funeral rites of chiefs, cases of illness, outstanding breach of the law, rivalry in fishing and agriculture, the marriage of persons of rank, and the acquisition of European goods. This is in addition to the whole religious structure, which is closely linked with the clan structure. The affiliation of each clan, through its gods, with one of the most important vegetable foodstuffs in the island has already been described.[2] The increase ceremonies performed in each case by the single clan chief are intended to benefit the community as a whole.

The frequent use of the clan names in different context throughout this book will make perfectly clear how important an element these groups are in the native social organization.

KINSHIP GROUPING—RAMAGE AND CLAN

A brief attempt at clarification of some of the concepts of kinship grouping may now be made. A system of grouping does not exist *in vacuo*; it is expressed in concrete social relationships. Linguistic usages are an important medium. Each society has a system of terminology covering the group as an entity (usually), its component members in relation to each other, and also a technical vocabulary by the aid of which the group activities are described. Each kinship group has its economic organization. Members of it, by virtue of such ties, assemble for the production and consumption of food, the exchange of property, or for the consideration of problems of owner-ship. At social events such as marriage, birth, initiation and death the group comes together, and these especially are times when kin-ship ties can crystallize out of the fluid material of everyday life. Religious ceremonies serve also to keep the group united, partly by the demands they make on collective activity and partly since ritual as in ancestor worship so often recalls past members of the group. Political organization represented especially in the headship gives the group other functions, and in the transmission of cultural goods, tradition, rank, property, and—of extreme importance—group membership itself, the kinship unit plays an indispensable part in culture.

These concrete social relationships do not always necessitate the complete assembly of the group members. Some affairs involve a temporary local unity, others not, and even from the meetings of the group as a body there may be absent members.

What is the principle of definition of a kinship group, what

[1] A Dart Match in Tikopia, *op. cit.*
[2] Totemism in Polynesia, *op. cit.*

constitutes it a unit? It is clear that it cannot be defined by any of the above elements alone—they are the means for expressing the existence of the group, they reinforce its unity. Economic situations, for instance, supply in part the *raison d'etre* for a kinship group, but the essential binding factor is not this economic co-operation. Though there may be members of a kinship unit who do not co-operate, do not fulfil commonly recognized obligations, do not take advantage of available privileges, yet still they are part of the group. The basic element is the recognition of people that they do constitute a unit through genealogical ties, real or assumed.

Kinship groups have to do with two primary spheres of interest: *personal situations*, where the people concerned meet together in orientation to a single individual, as in the crises of life; and *the promotion of the continuity of group interests*, as by the transmission of property, material or immaterial. For personal situations the kinship aggregation is essentially temporary, lasting in all very little longer than the life-span of the individual (sufficient to ensure the disposal of his body and perhaps the safe entry of his soul into the future life). The reproduction of culture, the handing on of tradition and knowledge from one generation to the next, is fundamental to the existence of a society, and this the kinship unit performs in a higher degree than any other social group.

The maintenance of the continuity of culture endows the group with an identity which transcends the generations of its component individuals, changing its personnel almost imperceptibly through substitution, through replacement, through the loss and gain of single individuals. In the former case the birth or death of a person creates or dissolves a whole aggregation; he or she is the pivotal component. In the latter, individuals contribute their mite to the sum of the group's activities and then pass on. Here each individual is only a marginal component.

The term " grouping " has been used to describe kinship aggregations of the first type; the term " group " those of the second type.[1] But there does not really seem to be much need for separate terms, especially since a " grouping " is usually composed of two or more groups.

The distinction of spheres of interest is, however, important because of the principle of group formation. When it is a question of orientation to a particular individual, the bilateral principle of organization is usually followed: the kin of both the mother and the father are involved in promoting the interests of their child. The continuity of this combined group is limited by the lifetime of the

[1] E. W. Armstrong, *Rossel Island*, 1928, 31-34.

individual pivotal component and so there is no confusion. But to carry on the continuity of group interests over the generations to allow for the most efficient reproduction of culture, the unilateral principle is most valid. Through one line alone the transmission of property and privilege is best accomplished. Empirical enquiry shows that the virtue of limitation in this respect is practised by most human societies, whether or no by conscious design.

An indication of the contrast between unilateral groups concerned with the transmission of cultural interests and the recognition of bilateral kinship is provided by the Tikopia. They themselves say that all the people of the island are akin to one another, and on investigation one can find lines of connection which do relate them all. Bilaterally, the whole population forms one group. Except in the most general situations, however, it would be impossible for all these people to work together, and we find accordingly that they are divided into the many " houses," independent groups, in each of which membership is traced along one line only to the exclusion of the other. There are about thirty major units of this type.

In a similar way one suspects that the *taviti* of Eddystone Island and the *komu* of South Malaita would be impossible in operation if the definition given of them were strictly true.

If such groups are bilateral to some degree, the local affiliations must be the defining factor, setting bounds to the active recognition of kinship.

A very common type of unilateral group, the clan, has provoked much discussion. Some agreement has now been reached on what shall be included under this term, but still the fallacy of nominalism persists, and the problem is apt to be stated as " what is a clan ? " not, more correctly, as " what shall we mean by a clan ? " It is unnecessary here to contrast the exclusive and inclusive points of view—that of Rivers who would define the clan boundary rigidly by a marriage prescription of exogamy or endogamy, but admit either type of parent as transmitter of the line, with the usage of some American writers who would restrict the term to matrilineal groups alone and use " gens " for patrilineal groups. Nor need any critical attitude be adopted towards Lowie's attempt to avoid confusion by the use of the term " sib," which was also utilized for a time by Radcliffe-Brown. The problem of what kinship group in the variation of social reality shall be included under the term clan concerns us particularly from another point of view.

The element of common agreement which seems most important has been the use of the term clan (or gens) for that type of kinship group of which the membership is exclusive—not duplicatory or merging—exogamy providing the usual though not invariable factor of delimitation.

But in many African and Polynesian societies it is the *unilateral recognition of common descent* which has primary emphasis as the factor of kinship group unity. Delimitation by exogamy and usually by totemism too is wanting. The terminology in current use to describe such kinship groups is not systematic; " joint family," " extended family," " family group " have all been employed, and more recently the word " lineage " has been used, as by Radcliffe-Brown (in unpublished work), E. W. Gifford, R. H. Lowie and Evans-Pritchard.[1] H. I. Hogbin has recently announced his adoption of the Maori word *hapu* to describe primarily patrilineal groups of this character which he has investigated in North Malaita.[2] As I have already pointed out, the Maori group to which this term refers is really ambilateral, either father or mother or both being eligible as criterion for membership.[3] But Dr Hogbin specifically states that in North Malaita the group is not ambilateral, on the grounds of the greater frequency of affiliation with the father's kin. If the cases are not parallel, then considering the specific sociological implications of the term *hapu*, it would be better to retain it to describe groups of this Maori character alone.[4]

The term " joint family " relates to the economic or residential factor of commonalty and, like " extended family " and " family group," points to a factor of emergence which is of considerable importance to the theory of social grouping. But included in it are members of other agnatic groups as wives. The term " lineage " normally refers to a single line of ancestors, though it has the authority of the *Oxford Dictionary* behind it for use to indicate a group of people. To my mind, however, the emphasis which it appears to lay upon individual linkage hardly does credit to one of the most important factors in such kinship groups, that is the principle of fission and dispersion in the creation of them. As a rule by historical tradition, and presumably in actual social process, they have arisen through

[1] E. W. Gifford, *Tongan Society*, 1929, 29 *et seq.* ; R. H. Lowie, *Amer. Anthrop.*, XXXV, 1933, 547 ; E. E. Evans-Pritchard, " The Nuer : Tribe and Clan," *Sudan Notes and Records*, XVI, 1933, 28 *et seq.* In Polynesia the word " tribe " has been commonly used by Elsdon Best, Te Rangi Hiroa and others, with the connotation of a kinship group as well as a local group. In literature on the Maori the native word *hapu* has usually been retained.

[2] *Oceania*, V, 1933-4, 254.

[3] *Primitive Economics*, 1929, 97-100.

[4] Moreover the introduction of a native word for general use presents difficulties ; Africanists, for example, may not unjustifiably object to employing an Oceanic term. *Mana* has given trouble enough already !

the branching and re-branching of the family structure, acquiring greater autonomy and independence the further they move away from the parent stem.   The tree metaphor is actually used by some native peoples in describing their social organization.   Here, very often, great importance is attached to seniority as a principle of social differentiation.   One term which might be employed to characterize such kinship groups is " ramage," for which there is literary authority, though it has now fallen out of use.   This term has the advantage of suggesting immediately by its etymology the branching process by which these groups attain individuality and yet keep their connection with the parent stem.   It is also consistent in metaphor with the expression " genealogical tree."   The process can be correctly described as one of ramification.

The term " house " is used in the body of this work to describe the Tikopia kinship unit, *paito*, as it is a direct translation of the native word.   But it might be called in a more general way a " ramage " ; I have used this term in the final chapter to indicate the common character of the groups there discussed by different writers under a variety of names.

The term " clan " as normally used is in contrast to those mentioned above, since according to most anthropologists an essential part of the definition is the exogamy of such a group.   Yet the difference between groups of the expanded family type and those of the clan type is often very slight.   The former lay emphasis on the genealogical aspect of their kinship, the latter on the codification of conduct between unilateral kin.   As far as Tikopia is concerned, apart from the " ramage " (*paito*), there is the more comprehensive form of grouping, the *kainaŋa*, of which the primary tie is also one of kinship.   I have adopted the term " clan " for this major unit in spite of its non-exogamous character, a usage in accordance with a view given in a previous publication.[1]   If the precise nature of such a group is explained, no confusion need arise, and it seems advisable now that the diversity of kinship groups is coming to be better realized as a result of intensive functional studies, to adopt a comprehensive rather than a narrow definition of the term.

The concept of descent means the membership of a kinship group by birth in a socially regulated manner.   Membership of a group is constituted by the formal legal recognition that a person is an integral part of it, that he is entitled to share in the specific activities which are the aim of the group association, in such privileges as the bearing of the group name, and in such obligations as the regulation of conduct by the group limits and in its interests.   The constitution of the kinship

[1] *Primitive Economics*, 98.

group is associated with the native beliefs in procreation which are usually in part elementary science and in part religious tenets. These find expression in linguistic terms, as in Tikopia the words *tafito* and *afu*, which have already been discussed in Chapter VI.

It is obvious that in any society the ties of bilateral kinship cut across the unilateral groupings on the basis of descent. The terminology of kinship stretches across from one clan or " house " to another, and so do other social ties. Thus in a " patrilineal " community such as Tikopia a man " belongs " to his father's group, is closely linked with his mother's brothers' group, co-operates with his wife's brothers' group, and owes other obligations to his sister's husband's group, that is, his sister's son's group. Here the man is enmeshed in a web of which the strands are four independent patrilineal kinship units. A network of intertwined privileges, obligations and personal arrangements covers the whole community, fastening group to group through the individual ties of the members that comprise them.

Looking at the matter from another angle, it may be said that in each generation complete bilaterality is attained for each individual, since the houses of his father and his mother are united around him. But from generation to generation these bilateral alignments are constantly shifting, a process of focal substitution takes place, with a fresh individual family as nucleus each time. These changing bilateral groupings cross and interweave with the unilateral groups, which persist throughout the generations, changing their personnel almost imperceptibly by a process of unitary substitution. The point of this distinction is that certain institutions are most appropriately performed by one set of groups, or the other, as they are of primary interest to the individual *per se*, or concern him mainly as a mechanism of cultural continuity ; as for instance funeral rites in the first case, or inheritance in the second.

CHAPTER X

PRINCIPLES OF LAND TENURE

LAND is the greatest source of wealth in Tikopia. Some of the terms for a wealthy person are really references to control over land and therefore over food. *Taŋata kai kai lasi*, " man who eats greatly " ; *taŋata kai kai rau fenua*, " man who eats from the breadth of the land " ; *tau fenua*, " owner of the land "—these are all common expressions for wealthy men. One of the correlates of the power of chiefs is their relative superiority in food resources as exemplified by their greater command of territory. In a burst of confidence Pa Paŋisi, the Motlav missionary teacher, once told me, " in a few years, friend, I shall be like a chief. I am planting all my wife's land with coconut trees, and when they begin to bear I shall be as wealthy as any man in Tikopia." The natives themselves emphasize how the desire for land is a potential cause of dissension. In olden times it even gave rise to fratricide. In former days, it is said, brothers did not go out fishing in canoes or diving for shellfish together, the reason being that their thirst for land might tempt one to kill the other and so inherit the lot. " He plots for food-sites in order that he may eat alone." The general principle of patrilineal inheritance rendered it safe for a man to go out with his mother's brother or his brother-in-law in a canoe. There was no incentive to murder here.

THE SOCIAL BACKGROUND TO LAND OWNERSHIP

In spite of the interest of the Tikopia in land and its products, it is not a community where the differential possession of wealth is an overt feature in the social structure. A wealthy man or a family having large cultivations and many coconut trees—a particular sign of riches—is not by virtue of this endowed with any formal status. In marriage the comparative wealth of the parties is not a factor to be debated by the prospective spouse or by his or her parents. Formerly there was a barrier on marriage between chiefs and commoners, but this was regulated by descent and not by wealth. Industry, temperament (or more strictly temper) are factors taken into consideration, but I have never heard orchards or coconuts enter into the conversation. The fortune-hunter is not a type in Tikopia society, even to the extent to which he appears to exist in Ontong Java or the Trobriands.[1]

[1] H. I. Hogbin, *op. cit.* 140, *J.P.S.*, XXXIX, 1930, 96 ; B. Malinowski, *Sexual Life of Savages*, 107. The restriction on marriage between chiefly families and commoners does, however, act as an artificial barrier on fortune-hunting. My friend Pa Tekaumata is the only man I know who really makes capital out of his wife's family, and I am not sure how far this is with intent.

Land does not enter into the philosophy and sentiment of the Tikopia in the way in which it does in Maori society.[1] No Tikopia ever wept over his soil or died in battle in defence of the sanctity of his orchards. And yet the natives have a feeling for the permanency of land as opposed to the fleeting presence of man who draws his sustenance from it. If two people fight over the possession of an orchard, the chief may send a message to them, " Do not go and fight. Each man go and plant food for himself. The land is laughing at us." As it is said, " the land stands, but man dies ; he weakens and is buried down below. We dwell for but a little while, but the land stands in its abiding-place." In other words, " How futile are the struggles of men compared with the permanency of the soil." But as usual in native life one finds that it is not entirely a pure philosophy which dictates their expression. To a considerable extent the respect for the soil which does form a real part of the Tikopia attitude is due to the belief that the ancestors, who in generations past owned and cultivated the land, still keep watch and ward over it. Their descendants must walk carefully lest they offend the powerful spirits on whose goodwill the fertility of crops depends. As usual the factor of kinship is strong. The ancestors do not take an undifferentiated interest in all the lands of the community, but exercise their powers on the territory of their descendants alone. For this interest gratitude is shown partly in ritual formulae and partly by material expressions of acknowledgment. As the natives say : the cultivations must be regularly " bought " from the ancestors, and every season a ceremony takes place, the re-carpeting of the sacred houses, whereby a man renders due return to his forbears. The mats which are used to lay on the floor of the temple and the sheets of thatch to repair it are termed *inaki,* a word which recalls the Tongan *inasi,* and are said specifically to be the recompense for the food obtained from the family orchards. Point is given to this idea when it is remembered that these mats and pieces of thatch cover the individual graves or memorial resting-places of the dead ancestors. Moreover they are made from coconut and sago leaf, cut from the very orchards which the ancestors themselves used to cultivate.[2]

As one comes in to the Tikopia coast from the sea one thinks that it is very much like any other of the Solomon Islands, heavily wooded with small and infrequent patches of cultivation in the neighbourhood of scattered villages. This impression is apt to persist for

[1] Raymond Firth, *op. cit.* 1929, 361-366.
[2] Details of the ceremony will be given in the publication, *Work of the Gods.*

some time after taking up residence on the island. Gradually, however, as one wanders abroad, ascends the ring of hills that encircles
the lake, climbs the peak of Reani or skirts the rugged northern
shore, it becomes evident that the whole place is in a high state of
economic utilization, that gardens are made right up the mountain,
and that what appears to be bush is really a collection of trees and
shrubs, each having its own value to the people, either for its food or
in their material arts. It is difficult, except on a cliff face, to discover
in the apparently wild forest any plant of any size which is not utilized
in one way or another. It can be well understood then that the
whole territory is held in strict ownership. Even the lake is property. It is under the jurisdiction of the four chiefs, particularly the
Ariki Kafika, and though anyone may set net therein, it is in virtue of
his relationship to the chief and not as one who resorts to a waste
area. The reef is also under a broad jurisdiction. The principle of
fishing the lake or the sea coast is, in fact, much the same as that
which operates in the case of taro planting (v. *infra*).

The ordinary land is divided in native terminology into several
kinds. There are the *tofi*, areas of mixed woodland and clearing of
varying size, averaging perhaps ten acres each. For these the best
translation seems to be " orchard." Then there are the *vao*, open
stretches of ground which are planted in taro. The most important
of these is Rakisu. They may be referred to as " gardens." The
larger of these areas are termed *mara*, and some of them have more
than an ordinary significance, since they are used for sacred crops,
from which first-fruit offerings are taken. They are termed *mara
tapu*. Included in this scheme of division is the *ropera*, a word of
which the etymology is alleged to be *roto pela*, literally " middle mud,"
or perhaps " the mud lake." This is the swampy area, of which one
stretch lies to the south of Rakisu and another on the inner shore of
the lake in Raveŋa. Patches of taro, *pulaka*, and other food plants
are set on any exposed portion of ground, and the pandanus used
for floor-mats and other material grows freely here. Here it is in
particular that the swamp-hen, terror of the cultivator, has his haunt,
stalking about with white rump flicking, as if in derision at man, of
the fruits of whose energies he takes such toll. Each *tofi* or section
of *vao* is divided off by boundary marks (*tuakoi*) consisting of rough
low hedges (*saesae*) made by slashing and laying the undergrowth in
a line between trees, or of a stone or two at the corners. Paths
run freely along the edge and through the orchards and gardens,
frequently not impeded on either side, but in the case of the chief
highways (*ara matua*) being closed in on either hand by hedges
man-high. Walking along between these leafy walls gives one a

curious feeling of an old-world civilization, utterly alien to one's conception of the crude agriculture of half-naked savages.

Enquiries as to land ownership in Tikopia elicit a description in one of four different ways. An orchard is described as being the land of a certain clan, the land of the chief of that clan, the land of one of the component houses, or the land of an individual in it. Each attribution is correct and it depends on the point of view of questioner and informant what reply is given. In Tikopia as in other native communities one meets on first enquiry the same puzzle of chief and people, of individual and community as owners. And as elsewhere the puzzle is to be solved only after consideration of the respective privileges and claims of each party to the situation. The relationship of clan and *paito* has already been considered, so it is clear that land owned by a *paito* must by definition be part of the clan territory. The problem before us lies primarily in the definition of the interests of chief and people, of an individual and the house of which he is a member.

OVERLORDSHIP OF THE CHIEF

Let us first examine the position of the chief. The cardinal principle of Tikopia land tenure is that all the land held by any members of the clan is at the chief's disposal. The reason for this is simple. The chief is the head of the clan, its representative with the gods, mediator for his people in regard to the fertility of their crops. Hence his control of supernatural forces in the interests of his people on the one hand should be matched by control of their material resources on the other. So we get the proposition frequently expressed by chief and commoner alike that the orchards of the people are the orchards of their leader. A native expression is, " They stand in the clan but they are the orchards of the chief." This is no idle statement. For not only in economic matters is the chief the ultimate authority. If a man insults or offends him, he must pay the penalty. Sooner or later to avoid exile on the face of the ocean and almost certain death, he must abase himself, and with food and gifts atone for his insubordination. A man cannot live without lands or without a chief. So in the last resort the power is in the chief's hands. It must be said in justice to the chiefs of Tikopia that each as I knew him was fully cognisant of his duty to his people ; though in theory and in fact their lands were under his jurisdiction, he regarded himself as the guardian of their common interests and rarely attempted to misuse his undoubted authority. Only in one case, described below, did something resembling oppression take place.

Exercise of authority by the chief in order to guide the utilization

of economic resources by his people is seen particularly in the imposition of a *tapu*. Each of the four chiefs has under control one of the
major foodstuffs, the sanction for this lying in the religious sphere.[1]
This allows him from time to time to institute a " close season " for
the product in question, and the restriction is obeyed not only by his
own clansmen but by all people who have an interest in lands where
the *tapu* operates. About a year before I arrived in Tikopia the Ariki
Tafua judged that the supply of coconuts was getting scarce, so put
up a mark of *tapu* in Rofaea. This was removed shortly after I came,
and the occasion was celebrated by a feast. The sons of the Ariki
collected food from his orchards, Pa Saukirima and Pa Fenutapu
brought contributions from Namo, Pa Tekaumata his son-in-law and
Pa Motuaŋi his sister's son also assisted, and other people of his
clan and his district. Before the food was prepared, the chief said to
the assembled company, " the *tapu* is lifted," which gave freedom to
all to utilize the coconuts from that area once again. A period of
several years usually elapses before any such large-scale restriction
is imposed once more. The Ariki Faŋarere controls the breadfruit
in the same way, the Ariki Kafika the yam, and the Ariki Taumako
the taro, though since the latter two crops are planted seasonally there
is little point in attempting to conserve them by restriction, and these
chiefs are concerned with harvest ritual instead.

A conservation *tapu* is not inviolable. If a man's orchards happen
to be concentrated in a single area affected by the restriction, then he
may take his coconuts, prepare a portion of food for the chief and go
to him. When the chief has finished eating, the man says, " I have
taken coconuts from . . . for food." The chief usually then replies,
" It is good." The act of notification does away with any offence.
Sometimes, however, the *tapu* is broken secretly, without attempt at
advising the chief. This does not represent a denial of his right to
impose the restriction, but a recognition that the case for breach is
not a good one, and that he would probably not approve. To avoid
censure and shame the owner has resort to furtive action.

Sidelights on the position of the chief were seen not long before
I left the island. Food was becoming rather scarce and the supply
of mature coconuts in particular was running short. The breadfruit
was not yet ripe and the taro of the previous season not mature.
When people went to work in their orchards or gardens they were
in the habit of taking green coconuts from their trees to supply them
with their usual midday refreshment. In Uta particularly this left
a scarcity of coconut which showed itself in the poor quality of the
puddings made for ceremonial occasions. The Ariki Kafika was

---

[1] " Totemism in Polynesia," *Oceania*, I, 1930-1.

very annoyed and day after day expressed his displeasure, though he pronounced no express fiat on the subject. His point was that the orchards of the commoners were at the chief's disposal and that when he wanted supplies for the kava ceremony his people should respect his wishes. Another factor also complicated the situation. The Ariki Tafua had announced his intention of making the *aŋa*, a large feast which is one of the three or four ceremonial high-water marks of a chief's reign. The anxiety of the Ariki Kafika, his sons and elders on the score of food supplies was not because of possible hunger—unlikely, since the new crops were coming forward—but because of the obligations involved when the feast would take place. The Ariki Tafua was rich in food, especially in coconuts, and the trouble was to know where to get these in order to make the customary return gifts. This point was touched upon over and over again in the last few weeks of my stay, when I was spending long hours in the company of the Kafika folk. They would go over the possible sources of supply, realize that these were very scanty, and bemoan the fact that they did not know where the coconuts could come from. " Shan't we return the presents then ? " was the rhetorical question frequently asked. People pointed out to each other that the Ariki Taumako and the allied family of Pa Vaŋatau alone had plenty of coconut, but that in the land in general it was scarce, and the re-cipients of the bounty of the Tafua chief would be at a very awkward disadvantage.

While listening to the conversations at the time I jotted down in my notebook several points which emerged as a result of the scarcity. In the first place signs of *tapu* were very plentiful. Few orchards did not bear a garland of young coconut frond (*sakilo*) on the palm stems to denote a prohibition on the taking of nuts by any but the rightful owner. In the second place theft became common, despite the *tapu* and the threat of supernatural punishment implied by the signs. This took place in Raveŋa as well as in Faea. Hardly a day went by without my hearing a *forua*, a series of whoops, somewhere or other, which was an expression of anger on the part of some orchard owner at having been robbed. People were not content to stay on short commons and respect the thrift of others, but stole to satisfy their desire for pleasant food. Very naturally too owners began to pluck their own property rather than lose all the fruits of their saving. The married men and elders, the *pure*, criticized the conduct of the young bachelors, the *tamaroa*, who were collectively accused of eating coconut when they went to work in the orchards, and of doing so beyond all moderation in view of the scarcity. This charge the *tamaroa* denied, but since they did not have the same responsibilities

as the married men there was probably considerable truth in it.   On
the part of the more important of the *pure*—senior elders such as Pa
Porima, Pa Rarovi or Pae Sao—there was constant grumbling, mostly
in private, about the commoners in general, who *would* eat coconut,
and about those in particular who went and took the fruit surreptitiously from orchards.   The main point of the diatribe was that they
ought to leave the coconut for the use of the chief in the coming
feast.   This point was stressed over and over again in the discussions.
" A man may die, but he should allow his food to stand for the service
of his chief."   This was the most extreme form of statements, but
there were milder kinds to the same effect.   " A man should leave
his coconuts and other food for ' *a roŋo o ŋa ariki*,' or ' *a roŋo o fenua* '
—' reputation of the chiefs,' or ' reputation of the land,' " that is,
for public ceremonial events.

Another instance of friction will show the theoretical place of
the chief in regard to the cultivable land of his clan.   It was planting
time for taro at the turn of the season to the *toŋa*, and Pa Rarovi had
a nice piece of ground in Rakisu.   As soon as the digging began
this was rushed by folk who wanted to plant, and the owner, who
had thought to keep it for his own *paito* and that of Kafika, was somewhat annoyed, though etiquette did not allow him to protest.   The
Ariki also was rather piqued.   He said that he was waiting till the
breaking up began, and he meant to ask Pa Rarovi to leave him a
plot to cultivate.   " I would have said to you to leave a cut of it for
me."   Then he woke up one morning to find that all had been appropriated.   Pa Rarovi agreed with him ; the ordinary people should
have given the chief a chance to indicate his choice.   He said, " The
gardens which stand there are our (exclusive) gardens, but indeed
they are the gardens of the chief."

The instances just given have shown the chief in a quiescent
mood ; he and his following made no more than a verbal protest
against the infringement of his right, and the fact that the infringement occurred shows that there is by no means automatic conformity
to the chief's suzerainty.   But in these cases there was no specific
individual denial of privilege ; there was simply a general slackness
in observing the rule, which any of the negligent persons would have
acknowledged in the abstract to be correct.   Normally the chief
does not interfere with the conduct of the members of his clan ; he
expresses his displeasure in private grumbling, and this acts as a
check upon too excessive a disregard of his authority and wishes.
The mechanism of Tikopia society, like that of many another, is apt
to emit creaks and groans as it works.   There may come a time,
however, when the chief thinks that his wishes have been flouted

far enough. Then the situation changes with amazing rapidity. The lightning of his anger flashes, and all abase themselves before it. The easy carelessness of his people is replaced by a vivid concern, and with anxious demeanour they hasten to do his bidding, or try with soft words to pacify him. As one sees his fury and hears the thunder of his voice, notices the solemn faces and hushed tones of those who discuss the situation, one is left in no doubt as to who in the last resort rules the clan ! Several times I have witnessed such a scene, and these were among the most dramatic moments of my residence in the island, revealing human passions of a depth one would not normally suspect among this quiet, easy-going Polynesian folk.

Two of these cases were the direct result of contravention of the chief's orders regarding land. One was a complex situation wherein the Ariki Tafua vented his spleen on account of the cutting of trees for bark-cloth, and my friend Pa Raŋifuri became innocently involved. The other case concerned the Ariki Taumako, Pa Faitoka and a *mara taro* which the chief wanted to reserve for planting later in the season. He had in mind to have it cleared but stated that he did not want it touched for the time being. The piece of ground was named Te Koko. Pa Faitoka, presuming on his relationship—he was the brother-in-law of the chief, having married his sister—went off without announcing his intention and in company with Fakaseŋafa, a young man of the house of Faioa, began to prepare the ground. The Ariki Taumako went down to the lake shore at the back of his house to bathe, as his custom was, and heard the sound of scrub being felled in the reserved area. He was angry, since his permission had not been asked and in fact his express wish had been disregarded. Suddenly the village was startled by terrific yells, five in number, the " *Iefu* " whoops of offended dignity. The people tumbled out in alarm, to see their chief stalking back to his house. He asked curtly who was responsible and was told. En route he met his sister and cursed her in a fury, as if she had been to blame. " May your father eat excrement. Filthy house. Who told you to go and dig ? May your father eat filth," and more to the same effect, all of which was rather shocking. She went off weeping. Then he spoke to Pa Rarovi, who lived near by, and to Pa Teva, his cousin ; he gave them orders to go as his messengers and tell the leaders of the party to go off to the woods. This was a form of banishment. They were told to hurry, and in fear of the wrath of the chief went off at a smart pace. He ordered them also to go " *forua saere*," whooping as they strode, a sign to all at large of his urgent displeasure, and a threat of disturbing consequences to the offenders. Being of a peacable turn of mind, however, Pa Rarovi, the senior of the pair,

whooped twice only, and that when well on his way, at Asaŋa, to
save rousing the land unduly. When the messengers arrived they
cursed the culprits for fools and told them either to flee to Faea or
to take to the woods. Off they went, Pa Faitoka wailing as he proceeded on his way. He went to Faea where he took refuge with Pa
Papaivaru. The same afternoon a party went over with the cognisance, though not at the express wish of the chief, to persuade him
to return. This is called the " seeking." They were unsuccessful
at that time, but on the next day but one he came back, and after
abasing himself before the chief and making the customary gift of
food was received back into favour again.

The point of interest to our present enquiry is the attitude taken
up by the people in general. I discussed the matter with numbers
of them, including Pa Fenuatara. " Who has the right of it ? "
asked this man, and then immediately answered his own question
by saying, " The chief is right ; I say the chief is correct. The *mara*
that stand are the *mara* of the Ariki . . ." and more to the same effect.
Public opinion was all in the same direction. Everyone said practically the same thing. " The chief says ' They are *mara* of the clan,'
but the clan says ' They are *mara* of the chief.' " It was agreed that
all *mara* are at the discretion of the chief, and that no one should go
and dig without his permission. " They have behaved badly ; the
mara which stand obey the chief " was another general formulation
of the situation. On such occasions there is always discussion of
the rights and wrongs of the case, and public opinion by no means
always sides with the man of rank. This time, however, there was
no doubt about it ; it was all on the side of the chief against the
culprits, since it was held that through pure stupidity and negligence
they had flown in the face of general practice. It may be asked why
Pa Faitoka should have acted thus contrary to established custom.
This was the question I put to my informants, and none could give
a very specific answer. The truth seemed to be that being a man
of strong personality and rather headstrong, he thought to carry off
his high-handed action by virtue of his close relationship and friendliness with the chief. He discovered his mistake too late. The
instance here quoted demonstrated to me very clearly how supreme
in the last resort is the power of a chief in Tikopia. If he tells a man
to go to the woods, or to sea, he must obey. There is no other
refuge for him. As the natives put it, " If the Ariki has become
angry with him, where shall he go ? "

The strength of the chief's position in this case is indicated even
more clearly when it is realized that at the same time as his action
was justified his character itself was being criticized. Pa Fenuatara

after commenting as already mentioned went on to make some pointed remarks about the chief himself. " The chief is good, but his throat is bad," he said ; " the Ariki is bad," arguing that he was of a surly disposition, rarely smiled or cracked a joke, and altogether was a somewhat awkward customer—all of which is quite true. He was to be contrasted with his father, a very pleasant character. This personal depreciation, however, merely acted as a foil to the approval of the chief's action in resenting what he interpreted as a slight upon his authority and a disregard of his territorial overlordship.

The interest of the chief in the land held by members of his clan is acknowledged and maintained from time to time by gifts of food to him. These take place on various occasions, in connection with sacred canoes or houses, visits of ceremony or assistance at any of the chief's public affairs. The food is an indirect, not direct recompense to the chief for his tacit permission of occupation. Chieftainship carries with it certain specific privileges. If one chief is going through the orchard of another he may take areca nut of either the *kaula* or *fuariki* type, or green coconuts as he wishes. As the natives say, such orchards are called " the places of the chiefs," that is, the property of one is held to belong to all. This is really an expression of the solidarity of the group of chiefs, not an indication of true communal ownership. Proof of this is that the chief does not take ordinary food in such circumstances. At the present time the Ariki Kafika is living in Sukumarae on land which is Taumako property. The natives say " the land is the ground of the Ariki Taumako, who allowed the Ariki Kafika to settle on it." And in explanation of this they continue, " In Tikopia here the chiefly houses have the name given to them of ' one house.' They are not a house through having married into each other and formed a body of kinsfolk (*kano a paito*) ; they are one from of old." Actually this attribution of kinship unity does not rest upon a real common origin, but upon an identification of interests on the one hand and intermarriage on the other. It is a factor of great convenience in the social order for the chiefs to be counted as a single group ; the invocation of the kinship principle clothes the class unity in the fiction of a more fundamental social validity.

If an Ariki happens to be passing with a companion through the orchard of a commoner—whether of his own or of another clan— and the latter sees him, he will take some green food and present it, to be carried by the follower. If the Ariki is alone this will not be done, since it is *tapu* for him to shoulder burdens. On one occasion when I was journeying with the Ariki Kafika from Uta over the steep and stony passage in the hill crest to Rofaea he was presented with some coconuts en route. Because of his *tapu* the job of carrying them was deputed to me. Sooner than appear churlish I complied—a proceeding which will be doubtless very shocking to those who hold strong views on the position of dark-skinned peoples.

Areca is one of the things which a chief can demand in the orchard of anyone where he happens to be. The stock formulation is : " areca-nut stands in the orchard of a commoner but it is called the areca-nut of the chief ; it is there to supply the betel chewing of the chief." If a bunch of areca nut is plucked in an orchard at the request of a chief, then the first nut plucked from the lowest bunch is handed to the chief to test along with the particular bunch selected. This is an act of courtesy to give him an indication of the general quality of the produce of the tree ; it is a bunch some distance up the trunk that is usually presented to him as being softer.

The measure of control which a chief has over the lands of his clan is of course a potential source of friction. Normally relations between them are of an equable character. When I was in Tikopia there was some slight feeling, however, on account of the actions, real or alleged, of the Ariki Tafua. He was the father of a numerous family of sons, each of whom was rearing his own offspring. He was alleged to have said that the clan should consist only of his sons and their families, and to have endeavoured to secure this by the exercise of black magic, of which he was acknowledged to be a master. It was said that some of his near relatives, even his brothers, died as the result, as well as other members of his clan. His method was to lay a curse (*tautuku*) on various places in the wood, so that people who went to them were stricken with illness. Some died, others abandoned their orchards to the chief. For instance, the allied house of Fenutapu left their grounds on Maunafaea, which now rests entirely in charge of the chief. Others of the clan also, including the father and brother of Pae Sao, died, and he himself was saved only through the power of his own deity. Such is the opinion of the people at large. It was impossible, of course, to verify this by questioning the old man himself. Some colour was given to his general attitude, however, by the fact that he caused two areas which had been previously used as communal gardens to be planted in coconut palms. In effect he blocked the access of his people to land which really belonged to his family. He had a perfect ostensible right to treat it as he wished, but his people had been in the habit of resorting there whenever they wanted an extra patch of taro ground. His action was resented a little by his clan, not because it was a usurpation of their territory, but because it did not show quite that sympathy with them which their chief should continually exercise. The Ariki Kafika commented on the situation from this point of view.

A commoner, however, has a measure of redress in the face of such encroachment. When the chief once enters into an orchard and begins to take food from it, then those in occupation abandon it to him—as in the case of Mauŋafaea. But if at a later date the original owner wants to resume possession, then he will make a gift of food, go to the chief, crawl to his side, press his nose to his knee and make his request. If the chief is sympathetic—and sensitiveness to public opinion will generally dictate such a response—he will say, " Go and clear your orchard and plant food for yourself and your children."

The statement that the lands of the clan are really those of the chief can thus be reversed. Without a following the chief could not work them ; nor would he gain by continual encroachment and oppression. Supported in all public affairs by the food contributions of his clan members, it would be distinctly against his best interests to restrict their sources of supply very greatly. Tikopia is not like some African communities, where a man can leave a harsh chief and attach himself to another of a milder disposition, but the power of the chief, absolute though it is in theory, is continually held in check in the interests of his people. In matters of land ownership the position of either party is defined by a system of rights and obligations, delicately adjusted and widely spread out through the various social institutions. If space allowed, a detailed analysis of a common form of statement would reveal the forces at work. A portion of ground was described thus : " The *vao* of the Ariki Taumako, the *mara* in Savero. As it stands it obeys the chief, but all the crowd of his clan go to it." Here is indicated that sphere of reciprocal relations, of titular ownership and actual use, which enters into so much of the Tikopia social economy. One important aspect of the suzerainty of the chiefs over the land is that it tends to mitigate the force of disputes between members of the same clan at least. He says to the disputants, " Abandon your fighting that you are carrying on there. Plant food properly for the two of you in my ground." The words " my ground " are not empty of significance. For if the men persist in their quarrel the chief will send a message, " Go the pair of you to your own place wherever it may be ; go away from my ground." In fact, they have no ground then to resort to ; their alternative is the ocean, so they capitulate. It may be noted that the chief usually intervenes only when there seems no prospect of an immediate settlement.

This analysis of the rights of a chief must not obscure the fact that normally each orchard is held by the members of a house and that they are the only people who work therein.

DISTRIBUTION OF LAND AMONG INDIVIDUALS

The property of the various families and clans is distributed fairly indiscriminately throughout the island, which would present, if a map were drawn in colour, a kind of patchwork effect. Plan III is a rough sketch (not to scale) showing the ownership of orchards in Uta. This district, somewhat over half a mile in length, may be termed the heart of Tikopia; it is the ancient home of the three principal clans, contains their most sacred buildings and is the scene of the most important ceremonies for the whole island. Each orchard bears a name, either that of the house which owns it or that of one of its subsidiary components, and that name is usually borne by the building (marked on the Plan) which stands near the lake shore and is the temple of the kinship group. Possession of the property in each case is validated by traditional associations, part clearly historical, part mythological; these do not take the form of a specific tale which is narrated as proof of title, but comprise a series of incidents which are interwoven into the general theme of the emergence of Tikopia society in its present state. The title to these orchards in Uta is never questioned, though there may be sometimes dispute about exact boundaries, as in the case of Maniva and Vaisakiri mentioned below; the traditional background is so well known to responsible people. But the existence and repetition of this body of current lore does serve to maintain and perpetuate the distribution of land; it is the primitive counterpart of a Record Office in which parchment has not yet replaced the memory of men.

A detailed account of the historical background to land ownership will be given elsewhere;[1] here a brief reference to a few instances must suffice.

The Plan shows how the orchards of Kafika lie in the centre of Uta, flanked by those of Taumako and Tafua. This is explained in terms of ancestral residence two centuries or more ago, when the temples of the clans were dwelling-houses of the chiefs as well, and they and their people were penned in Uta by the folk of ŋa Raveŋa to the north and those of ŋa Faea to the south. Then came the slaughter of ŋa Raveŋa, in which Taumako played a leading part, and which led to the acquisition of land in Te Roro and the adjacent part of Uta by them, and to the settling of Faŋarere under Kafika protection in the centre. The later possession of Vaisakiri by Faŋarere

---

[1] *History and Traditions of Tikopia.*

PLAN III

DISTRIBUTION OF ORCHARDS IN UTA

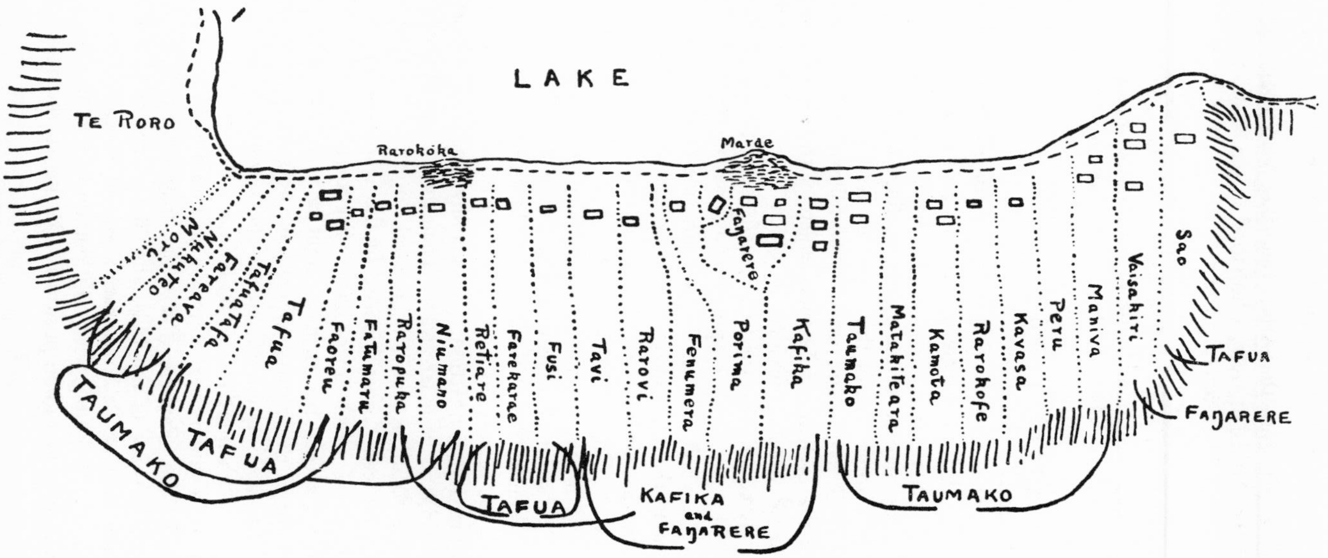

LAKE

Te Roro

Rarokoka

Marae

Fagarere

Sao
Vaisahiri
Maniva
Peru
Kavasa
Rarohofe
Kamota
Matakiteara
Taumako
Kafika
Porima
Fenumera
Rarovi
Tavi
Fusi
Farekarae
Retiare
Niumano
Raropuka
Fatumaru
Faoreu
Tafua
Tafua Tafa
Fateava
Nukuteo
Moru

TAFUA
FAGARERE

TAUMAKO

KAFIKA and FAGARERE

TAFUA

TAFUA

TAUMAKO

was due to a gift from the Ariki Taumako, who took pity on the poverty of the Ariki Faŋarere, who stood in the relation of mother's brother to him.   The present possession of Sao by a house of Tafua is consequent on the arrival of an immigrant from Uvea and his adoption by the chief and a god of Tafua.   As the result of a Tongan invasion the autochthonous house of Sao had been exterminated, and the Ariki Taumako, who had been mainly responsible in repelling the Tongans, occupied the orchard.   At the request of the chief of Tafua, however, he relinquished it to the immigrant, who refounded the ancient house.

So the story runs, the occupation and use of each orchard by a kinship group being a material, visible expression of a complex history and mythology.

An account may be given of the holdings of a few well-known people to give some idea of the resources available.   Pa Fetauta, for example, describes his land interests as follows :—Inland from his dwelling is the orchard of Fetauta, which, with that of Marinoa, is really a single holding divided in olden times.   Their areas are approximately equal.   To the first named goes Pa Fetauta and to the second Pa Motuaŋi, each keeping to his own portion.   Then there is Foŋapae, a whole hill on the western side of the lake, which is split up among the different household groups of sa Marinoa.   " Our one house works our hill, each goes to his orchard, each goes then to his usual place.   One does not entrench on the orchard of another. " This territory, it may be noted, was acquired after the expulsion of ŋa Faea.   The original orchard of this group is Rakau in Te Roro. This, as Pa Fetauta says, " has been abandoned in recent times " ;   he has left it to be planted by Pa Torokiŋa, who is a relative of his by an ancient marriage connection.   This family is near, almost next door to the ground, and he is far away.   Then there is another orchard to which he goes, Murirarovaki ; it lies on the north side of Vai Matautu.

The neutral term " goes " is used by the Tikopia with much more than the force of merely an ordinary visit to an orchard.   It represents not only access, but claim to right of access and utilization of produce.   But in this society, where joint possession is so common, it avoids that connotation of exclusiveness which is given by our word " owns " when used by an individual.

Pa Taitai, a commoner of moderate means, has five orchards : Aroaro in Rakisu, Pankere (" a white man's name ") in Rotoaia, Foŋaroro and Aŋina in the hills, and Matori not far from Rakisu. Variari, now held by Pa Roŋomatini, was given to this man by Pa Taitai's father.   Pa Taitai, with only one brother, a bachelor and not likely to marry, is in a good position.   But he has the name of being somewhat of a spendthrift. A member of the house of Tafua said to me, " Yes ! he has plenty of orchards, but he has not plenty of coconut —he has plenty of coconut, but he does not make good food. I think he drinks nuts every day. Some people, who let their coconuts ripen, have good food—*poke taro*, *susua taro*, *ŋarueŋa futi*—every day. Pa Taitai has good food one day and not the next."

This statement expresses the general principle of Tikopia economy, that care should be exercised in the consumption of green coconut, as the most profitable use of the nut is obtained by allowing it to mature and converting its flesh into cream.

The Ariki Faŋarere has six orchards, Faŋarere and Vaisakiri in Uta, Uaro in Raveŋa, Saupono in Rotoaia, Te Roro in Namo, and Tapukuru in Mauŋa. In addition there is Saravau, which is a *mara* where the clan come and plant.

With this rather meagre allowance may be contrasted the territory of the Ariki Tafua. He controls Tafua and Fusi in Uta, Tasimauri in Raveŋa, Paiu in Potimua, Vaimanini and Rarokafika in Mauŋafaea, as also Rofenua, Paka, and a portion of Tiare. The last-named pair are the *mara taro*, which have been now planted in coconuts. At the back of his dwelling Motuapi he has an orchard and another Ruafao lies a little distance inland. Nearby also is Varuko to which Pa Raŋifuri goes. In Rotoaia is Tuakamali, a portion of which belongs to Nau Nitini. Pa Nitini eats in Tiare as well as the chief. There are again a number of orchards in Namo, which are looked after by Pa Niutao, a relative. Two other areas, Matavai and Raŋikofe, were formerly the property of another branch of the family, but since the males have died out the chief goes to them also. In addition there are four other orchards, Aramera, Nanona, Sekeraŋa, and Matavio, which the chief handed over to his younger brother, Pa Maevetau, because their father was dead. This man also utilizes part of the orchard Fusi.

The holdings of the chief on Mauŋafaea now comprise practically the whole of that slope of the mountain-side. With regard to the two orchards of the Raŋikofe branch, it was said that if the chief wished them to be handed back to the heirs on his death, this would be done, but if he wished them to pass to his own sons, it would be quite legitimate. To take one more example, that of Pa Nitini, a man allied to the house of Tafua but of no particular eminence. He takes food from the following orchards : Tiare (a portion), Sekeraŋi, and Manoŋafau in Mauŋafaea, and Mesara in Rotoaia, all of which came from his father, Pu Paiu. These he shares with his two brothers, and the Ariki Tafua does not go to them. From his wife he has the use of three others, a portion of Tuakamali in Rotoaia, Parekareka in Mauŋafaea, and Te Aravaka in Sapei. This latter is where he now lives. Another orchard, Te Vaitai in Te Roro, was abandoned by Pa Nitini in favour of his brother Pa Naroko (now deceased) whose children have also several orchards in Namo.

Examination of these cases of property holding indicates several principles at work. Although the orchards of any family or individual may be scattered freely over the island, there is a tendency for them to be correlated with residence. Those in a remote district are often left for relatives to work, so that in a generation or two they are apt to pass from one branch of a house to another. It is evident also that the territory of a house is not held in purely undifferentiated communal ownership. Even between brothers there may be a division of the sources of food supply. Then there is the custom whereby a man has access to lands through his wife. We have to consider therefore of what nature is the interest of an individual in the lands of his family, and the rights of a woman in land.

LAND RIGHTS WITHIN THE " HOUSE "

In the broadest sense each orchard belongs to a *paito*, but investigation always shows that by arrangement one branch only, a single household or a group of households, resorts to it. I went one day with the Ariki Kafika on to the plateau of Mauŋa, where many of the lands of his clan lie. We entered the orchard of Veruveru which, in the ghostly sense, belongs to a Kafika chief who was lost at sea on his way to Anuta ; now he lives in the ocean as a powerful deity of the clan. In the evening people seated in the orchard inland hear the spirits whooping down near the sea. If the people are seated near the sea they hear the voices of the spirits up the hillside inland. The dead chief and his people—spirits of the sea—are getting their food from the orchard. The orchard is also inhabited by a deity Pu Veruveru who is its guardian. Once upon a time he was a man and a cannibal. So much for the supernatural aspects of the situation.

At the present time the orchard is divided into sections. The Ariki Kafika takes food from one portion, Pa Tarairaki from another, and Pa Siamano from a third. Each of the latter has about a quarter of the ground and the Ariki a half. The division was made at the instance of Pa Mapusaŋa, the father of Pa Tarairaki. " All of us used to eat from the one orchard," said the chief, " but he cut it up after the birth of his sons." Between the area of the chief and that of the others a couple of chestnut trees serve as boundary. It may be noted that on entering the orchard the old man said to me, " the orchard of us, of Pa Tarairaki." Here, as always, there was a clear distinction between the interests of group and of individual. The land is described in terms of either according to the demand of the situation. Where it is a question of reckoning the wealth of a house, then the generic term " ours " is used. But when definition of specific interests is needed, it is given with a wealth of detail—a description accurate to a minute degree.

The general principle followed is to divide either the ground in each orchard or to allot the separate orchards between the sons in a family after the death of their father. As Pa Vainunu said, " look at me and Pe Paoari. Each has his dwelling and each has the mouth of his oven, because the father of the two of us is dead." The " mouth of the oven " is a figurative expression for source of food supply, that is, orchard. The case is similar with the families of Taumako, Avakofe and Vaŋatau. The heads of these three households were brothers—the eldest, the former Ariki Taumako, now being dead—but now that their children have married and themselves have children old enough to take part in the work of the orchards and gardens, these lands have been allotted among them. So also with the houses of Maneve and Resiake. They eat " in the middle of the house," as the phrase is, that is, they go freely to each other's dwellings for meals, but they do not take food for meals from one another's gardens. Each group has its own land. The separation began with the children of Pu Maneve and Pu Resiake, who were brothers.

Brothers with young families of children generally use the same orchard—as with Pae Sao and Pa Niata. The latter, the younger of the two brothers, obeys the instructions of his senior. He mentions to him that he is going to get coconut or other products from their property ; the latter agrees or makes alternative suggestions. This applies to trees, perennial plants and shrubs. In the case of taro or other annual each brother has his own plots, which he goes and digs whenever he wishes. The ground alone is common to both, but the crop is the property of the brother who has cleared the ground and planted it. If Pae Sao should want some taro, and for any reason has none of his own available, he goes and asks his brother to dig some from his plot. As a rule this is done not for immediate household needs, but to fulfil some ritual obligation.

Control over the lands held jointly by several brothers is very much at the discretion of the eldest. Their father may leave specific instructions to this effect before his death. According to Pa Fenuatara he expected the Ariki Kafika to advise him much as follows : " My father will not divide the orchards among us, he will leave it according to my will. Such will be his words, ' As you dwell here, behave well to your brothers. You eat from your single food basis. I do not know about your children who will come after you; if your children behave badly, then their orchards must be divided.' " The same principles of mutual deference to each other and to the interests of the family as a whole, with some greater measure of respect for the eldest son, which mark the usual conduct of affairs in Tikopia operate between close relatives in the domain of landholding as well.

The division of the joint property of a " house," it may be noted, is effected as a matter of social facility, not as a means of increasing productive power. There is no advantage to be gained from greater specialization, no more economic efficiency, except only to a slight extent where an orchard is handed over to another group on account of its distance from the residence of the former owners. The primary factor involved is the desire to obviate divergence of personal interests; it is recognized that the larger the group concerned the greater the chance of clash between its members. The formation of new kinship groups by the process of fission is accompanied by, and in fact expressed in, terms of a splitting-up of the economic resources of the parent group.

WOMEN AND LAND

Women occupy a peculiar position in regard to the holding of land in Tikopia. They have an interest in the lands of their father and this interest they pass on to their own children, but the inheritance goes no further than this. Strictly speaking, it is not inheritance, for the death of the mother obliterates the claim. It can be best described as an interest only in the land and not a clear title to it; the land is held in perpetuity in the male line. The situation is analogous to the position of the *tama fafine* (distaff line) in regard to the *tama tane* (male line) in Samoa, though it is not clear from the work of Margaret Mead and others just where in that community the interest through the female stops.[1]

Before a woman is married of course she takes food with her father's household, so needs no special rights. On her marriage her *tofi* is divided off from the lands of her father's family by her male relatives. The allotment is made to her only at the time of her marriage and is not determined in advance. As always in Tikopia this gift to her is made with an eye to the prosperity of her children. It may be regarded as one item in the series of gifts which *tuatina* make to their *tama tapu*. After her marriage the woman ceases to

[1] Mead, *Social Organization of Manu'a*, 18, 70-2.

take food from the lands of her father and brothers and they do not go on to her land. If food is absolutely lacking on her side of the hedge, then she may " jump over," as the phrase is, to their portion and take what is necessary. To this no objection is made because, as it is said, " they are of the one fruit." The woman regards this special land as hers in distinction from the orchards of her husband. She may say to him : " I think I shall go and gather food for us from my own orchard." Normally of course the husband resorts to his wife's land—as for example in the case of Pa Nitini mentioned above—without formality, and when they are reckoning the household wealth the orchards of both are considered together. This marriage settlement, as it may be called, goes with the woman in the rare event of divorce. The orchard of the woman remains alienated from her father's family only for the duration of her life. When she dies, it will revert to them again. There are, however, certain exceptions to this rule. When the daughter of a chief marries an immigrant, who is naturally landless in Tikopia, or another man whom the chief particularly favours, the chief may give his daughter as dowry an orchard or so, with the specific provision that it is to remain in the possession of her descendants, and not to be handed back on her death. It may be noted, though, that this does not invalidate the general principle, since in succeeding generations the land continues to pass down in the male line. As examples of this may be mentioned the orchard of Somosomo, which passed to the family of Fenutapu on the marriage of a daughter of Tanakiforau, Ariki Kafika ; and that of Fareava, which was handed over with his second daughter on her marriage into the house of Fatumaru. In earlier years the orchard of Rakau was handed over by Pu Veka when his daughter married Toaki and founded the house of Marinoa, and Matorokiŋa by Tuisifo to the ancestor of Torokinga in similar style. Generations ago Farerava, son of Rifu, Ariki Taumako, had an orchard of this name, Farerava. After his death, without descendants, it reverted to the house of the Taumako chiefs, but on the marriage of Nau Mataŋi, mother of the present Pa Raŋifau, they handed the orchard over to this family. The woman was from Anuta and her father asked the Ariki Taumako that she be given ground in Tikopia, hence the orchard was handed over to her and her descendants. Again the house of Tiu, descendants of Pakisiva, eldest brother of Farerava, held land for six generations. The last representatives were three unmarried men and a woman who married into the house of Reŋaru. After the extinction of the male side of the line the orchards reverted to the chief of Taumako, who takes food there nowadays.

While children remain unmarried they use their mother's land.

On their marriage, however, they will relinquish this interest and take food only in the orchards of their father and in the orchards of the person each has married. For example, when Nau Rarokau took a husband she was given an orchard near Vai Teputa by her house. While her son Pa Taitai remained unmarried he used to go there either with his mother or alone to get food, but on his marriage he began to " rest " (*manava*), that is, to leave the orchard to his mother's brother. His resources were limited by this act, but on the other hand they expanded by the use of the orchard received from his wife, so that the net result was much the same. Nau Rarokau herself, however, continues to utilize the orchard for the family benefit during her life, after which time it will revert finally and definitely to the house of her brother and his sons. A father will say to his son on his marriage, " You will go to the orchards of your wife and your children. Now let it be finished as concerns those from your mother and mother's brother." The native attitude is that such a man " has rested because he has married away into another house." If the land is not abandoned by a man on his marriage, then it usually is when his mother dies. On her death the son hands the land over to her house " because its origin is different. The orchard of the woman which came with her stands only while she is living. When she dies it will be given back to the places of her kindred," the natives say. But there are exceptions to this.

Not always does a person take advantage of the facilities offered through the maternal connection. Pa Motuaŋi, for example, the son of the sister of the Ariki Tafua, said to me, " the chief invited me to eat from his lands but I objected because my brothers have married throughout and their children are many." By his " brothers " he meant his cousins, the chief's sons, who, as we have already seen, threaten to enlarge the chiefly house of Tafua to unwonted size.

The marriage settlement is apparently not universal in Tikopia. It is said that if a man is very poor he will not invite his daughter to utilize any of the family land. This must be rare and I have no cases.

Another example will illustrate the working of the native system of land tenure in respect of the principles set out above. Tauŋarakau is a bachelor in a branch of the great Raropuka house. His orchards are three. There is Saupe, he shares with the son of his *masikitaŋa*, Pa Mauŋakena. The two of them only take food from it. Then there is Foŋataku, a hill above the lake on which each branch of the house has its own orchard. He has his own section to which he alone goes, and his cousins have theirs. Lastly, there is Fakaete, which he shares with the sons of his father's brother Pa Reŋaru. The position is this. He told me, " both my fathers married and then divided their orchards ; my father went then to Saupe while my father in Reŋaru went to Foŋataku." By his "father in Reŋaru" he meant of course his father's brother. As regards Foŋataku, Pa Raŋimarepe, if told by his brother Pa Reŋaru, used to go and get coconuts and other foods from the orchard. He could on his own account go and plant taro there and when it was mature take it out. But unless specially directed he could not plant enduring trees or take the fruits of such. That is, his brother was the real owner and he had only the ordinary privileges of a relative. Tauŋarakau shares the orchard of Saupe with Pa Mauŋakena because the latter's mother, Nau Paka, was a sister in a classificatory sense of Tauŋarakau's father. She was from the house of Saupe, a branch of that of Raropuka, and Tauŋarakau said, "when my aunt dies the orchard will stand in my name alone, I alone shall go there and Pa Mauŋakena will abide."

So far the assumption has been made in our description that the reversion of an orchard takes place without friction. This, however, is not always the case. Quarrels are quite frequent, since the rule is not absolute, and on the death of his mother a man may want to keep the orchard for himself, especially if she has no close male relatives living. Not long ago there was a quarrel between Pa Porima and Pa Raropuka over this. The mother of the latter was from Sukumarae, a house allied to that of Porima, and he wanted to remain and take food from her land. Pa Porima told him to go but he refused, and an argument ensued. This developed into a fight in which each side threw stones at the other. When the supply was exhausted they went for more ; no one was hit but there was much dodging. Then Pa Porima took a knife and rushed at Pa Raropuka ; he was held back by a crowd of men, who grasped his wrists and arms and tried to wrest away the knife, while Nau Paiu held it across her breast. The struggle went on for some hours, it was said. Pa Porima kept on telling the men to take away their hands that he might give the knife properly to Nau Paiu. It should be remembered here that a married woman is an object of respect in Tikopia ; she must not be harmed. Her presence in the fight, therefore, immobilized Pa Porima. However, the men would not do as he requested. Hence he refused to give up the knife, fearing lest he would be laughed at, and people would say that it had been wrested from his hand. At last, during the afternoon, the hands of the men were lifted off and he courteously relinquished the weapon to Nau Paiu. At this moment appeared the party of reinforcement, the Ariki Kafika, Pa Teva and many others, yelling as they came. At their head was Nau Kafika, and as she appeared the opposition, who were of Faea, disappeared. When the party came up Pa Porima showed himself at his house to let them see that he was not injured. After a lot of talk the matter was allowed to rest. But sa Faea did not return to the orchard. Here the position was complicated by the old district feud, but the situation is by no means rare.

During my stay in Tikopia the houses of Fetu and of Mataioa, both offshoots originally of Taumako stock, went to fight about an orchard Foŋasapa in Mauŋa. Of old the ground belonged to the family of Nuŋa which has now died out. They were a branch of the house of Maniva, as also is Fetu. After their demise the house of Turau entered into possession of the orchard, Nau Turau being a daughter of Nuŋa. Later Pa Fetu, as a representative of the original male side, came also and the two houses planted food therein side by side. The house of Turau, however, who were first in the field, objected after a while and cut down bananas and other things planted by Pa Fetu. He retaliated and destroyed food which they had planted. This act is a kind of final insult and invitation to war. The interest of the house of Mataioa, who took up the quarrel, comes through Nau Manono, wife of one of their young men, who, as the daughter of Nau Turau, went and cleared brushwood and planted in the debated ground. The land did not come to her as her dowry, but she went on her own initiative, thus challenging the reversion to the male side of the house. Each protagonist was supported by other houses. Curiously enough the main group of Maniva went to aid not Pa Fetu but the house of Mataioa, the reason being that the mother of Pa Maniva came from that house. They are known to be a house of quarrelsome kind, torn by petty feuds. Pa Raŋituifo and others went to assist Pa Fetu. The Ariki Taumako sat at home and did not interfere, although the orchard was under his control. It was said by public opinion that the house of Fetu was in the right since they were of Maniva, the original owners. Because the woman of whose dowry the orchard formed a part was dead, the orchard should revert to the Maniva representative. But, it was argued too, the house of Turau and their active representatives in Mataioa had also right on their side, since they had been in possession for a long time and had planted much food. Here, as in other communities, utilization tends to give prescriptive right in cases of debatable ownership. The whole village of Taumako went in full force to help in the fight. The result when I first heard of it was uncertain. The suggestion was made by Mataioa that the orchard be handed over to Rimakoroa, eldest son of the Ariki Taumako, and that both sides cease from resorting to it if no agreement could be arrived at. This was in accordance with ancient custom : " when commoners eat in the place of the chief and fight, then they speak thus that someone of the chiefly family should go and eat there instead."

After all, the fight did not eventuate. There was a lot of accusation and denial about the cutting down of food plants and some hard lying, but no material results. Finally, it was agreed by both parties to continue in joint occupation of the land. There was, however, a sequel. Some days afterwards the house of Mataioa began to make thatch for a sail, announcing their intention of going off to sea in consequence of the quarrel. They considered that they had been badly treated, that their dignity had suffered and this was their dramatic method of seeking rehabilitation. Their preparations were made, but before any canoes were put into the water a messenger came from their chief ordering them to desist. This was ignored. A succession of runners followed all through the morning until at last, about midday, they ceased to get ready and to declare their firmness of purpose. In their turn they went to the Ariki in his dwelling of Motuata and crawling to him thus publicly abandoned the projected suicide trip. They afterwards sent a compensatory gift to the chief for having flouted his emissaries in the first place.

BOUNDARY DISPUTES

Arguments not over the actual ownership of orchards but over their precise boundaries are also fairly frequent. I witnessed one such between people of Maniva and of Faŋarere. I went one morning to Raveŋa and found Potu sa Taumako almost empty of men. They had gone to Uta to fight with sa Faŋarere, it was said, with knives and axes. Accordingly I went over there. When I arrived the two groups of people were sitting separately, each in its own orchard. No actual fighting took place, but by the accounts of eye-witnesses, one man had pranced around with a club in warlike gestures and a couple of others had pulled each other about. There was quite a crowd of people, thirty or so a side, including a number of children. As usual there were the few irreconcilables who wanted to fight it out at once, but they received very little encouragement from the others. On this occasion the pacific attitude of Taumako was, to a large extent, due to the presence of the Ariki Faŋarere in the other orchard, which had a distinctly quietening effect. Standing among them I heard frequent admonitions of " Don't talk like that! The chief is there." The cause of the dispute was an ancient boundary stone set in the ground, which it was said had been shifted by one side and moved back again by the other. Pa Raŋateatua, son of the Faŋarere chief, had planted *pulaka* in what was alleged by the house of Maniva

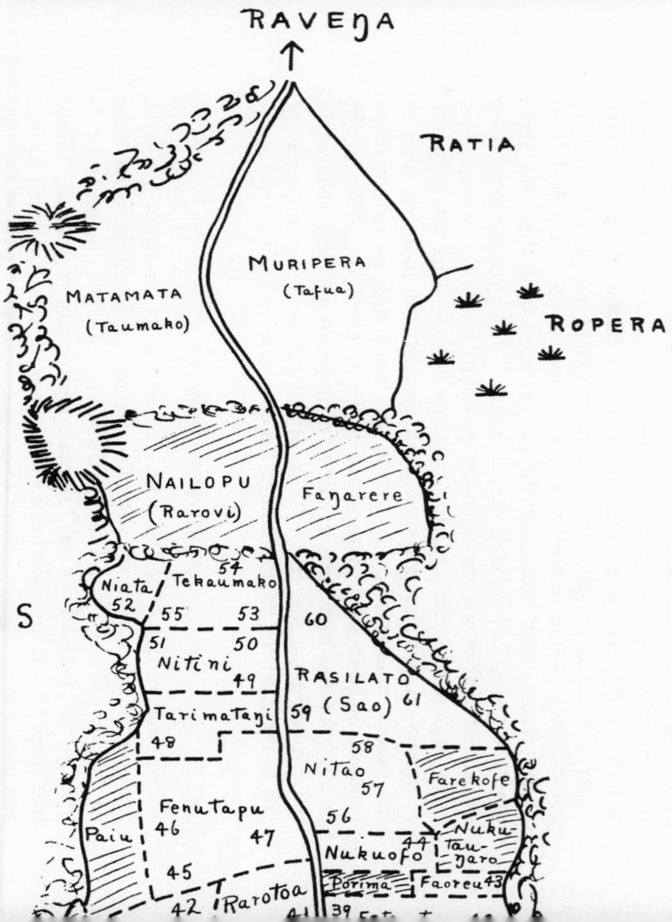

ROUGH PLAN
OF
TARO
GARDENS
IN
RAKISU

1. IV. 1929

RAVEJA

RATIA

ROPERA

MURIPERA
(Tafua)

MATAMATA
(Taumako)

NAILOPU
(Rarovi)

Fajarere

60

RASILATO
(Sao) 61

Niata
Tekaumako 54

55   53

52   51   50

Niteni
49

Tarimatagi

48

FenuTapu
46

45

42 Rarotoa

41

39

58

NiTao

57

56

Farekofe

Nuku
Tau 43

Nukuofo   gato
Nukuo

Forima   Faorea

Paiu
47

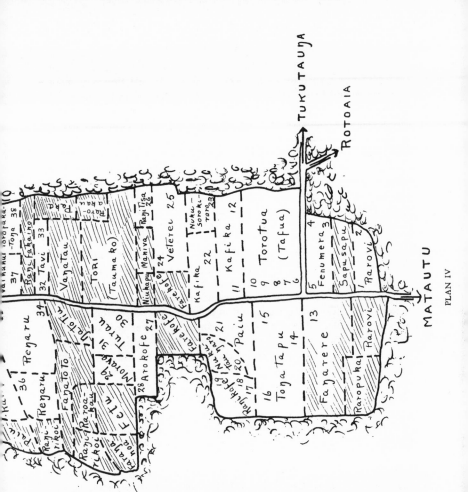

PLAN IV

Map labels (rotated):

TUKUTAUŊA

ROTOAIA

MATAUTU

Vai hahui torotuna—10
37 · 1-Toŋa 38
Ranjaraŋo 33
32 Tavi 33
Vaŋatau
TORI (Taumaro)
Niukapu Maniva Raŋi Tisa 26
Fakekofe 24
Veletet 25
Nuku-soroki-toro 23
Kafika 22
11 Kafika 12
10 Torotua 9 (Tafua)
8 7 6
5 Fenumera 3
Sapusapu 2
Rarovi 1

34 Reŋaru
36 Reŋaru
Raŋu-Reŋaru
Raju-Raroa-tiroa
Fanotoa
Tirou
Totou
Feilu
Motovo 29
Turou 31
30
Arokofe 27
28
Fakakofe
Marae-kofe
Namori
20 Paiu 21
18 19
17
16 Toŋa Tapu 14 15
13 Fajarere
Raropuka
Rarovi

to be their territory; this was denied. A coconut palm on the boundary was also claimed by both parties. At one time a woman of Faŋarere and Nau Tarikitoŋa (sister of Pa Maniva) had made some sort of arrangement, but this had not lasted. After much talk on this occasion, a couple of men of Faŋarere came to the boundary where the crowd of Taumako folk were standing amidst the banana and *pulaka* plantations and a wordy and acrimonious discussion began. Curses of " May your fathers eat filth " were frequently hurled at the other side. The stone was moved several times until both parties were satisfied, and the crowd then dispersed. In this final settlement Mairuŋa, son of Pa Maniva, took a prominent part. His supporters had waited for him to come, since he was one of the principal representatives, and as the chief was present in the other party, they wanted authoritative backing. In the end it was he who indicated the place at which it would be good to set the stone.

If a dispute between houses of a clan threatens to become really serious, then the chief may intervene and send both parties away from the ground, announcing his intention to enter into possession himself. This is quite justifiable in native eyes, since he is overlord, and in the last resort all his people hold their lands at his discretion. Even the warning of such a possibility is usually enough to induce the rival claimants to compose their differences. Between groups in different clans, however, no such course is possible, and the feud may smoulder for a long time, until radical action causes one side to yield. The Ariki Tafua was involved in such a case some years ago. It concerned the boundary between Kafika and Tafua ground in the swamp of Tavi. Pa Fenuatara went there one day and found that the stone which marked the division had been moved and put into the middle of the swamp. He put it back. Later he was very ill, and he blamed the Ariki Tafua, who he said, had been standing in the swamp, unperceived by him, and had bewitched him. After a period of very serious sickness he was cured by being carried to the same chief for treatment. At the same time Pa Raŋimaseke, of the house of Tavi, was standing in the swamp too, and alleged that he heard the speech of the Ariki as he laid the curse upon Pa Fenuatara; the old chief saw him and cursed him aloud by his adze-gods (of peculiarly malignant power). " I left my work in the swamp," said Pa Raŋimaseke, " and came and stood at the side of my house. Then I called on my ancestress, Pufine i Tavi, and was well." But Pa Fenuatara was in ignorance, hence his illness.

OWNERSHIP CONDITIONED BY USE OF THE SOIL

More indication may now be given of the way in which an orchard is used by a group of people who have a common interest in it. Unfortunately I did not make a plan of an orchard of any one family, giving the location of the plots of taro, etc., which would illustrate the general principle. But the facts derived from much individual enquiry are clear enough. The more permanent resources of the piece of ground are at the disposal of all; the head of the group exercises authority in case of abuse. Seasonal products, as taro or yams, are planted by individual members in any vacant area of the orchard and are controlled by the planter, though application to draw upon them may be freely made by the others, and will be granted. Soon after I had arrived in Tikopia I went one day with Te Raŋiata to an orchard of his family. With us went Seteraki, his brother's son, and there we found Arikimata, his brother. The orchard as a whole belonged to the Ariki Tafua, but being an old man he had left it to his sons to work. Most of its food resources were joint property without restraint. If any of them wanted coconuts, bananas, wild yams, bark for cloth, he came and took what he required without asking permission of anyone. I asked what would happen if he took too much. The answer was, " It would not matter." As frequently is the case with early enquiries in field-work, the question was invalid from the start : " too much " implies excess over requirements, and when these are determined only by hunger or by ceremonial needs, there is little incentive for the amount taken to be too great. There is the possibility of preservation of food by an individual, as the storage of coconuts in an enclosure (*ruwa*), but this would not affect his position greatly, as the stock would be available for general family utilization. The limited scope of exchange of food for other goods, too, gives small incentive for the accumulation of wealth upon a food basis. Little personal advantage is to be derived from utilizing the product of the common land in excess of one's co-sharers.

In the orchard a patch of yams stood in one corner, planted by Arikimata. These were to be dug by him at the proper time, and would not be touched by any of his brothers. If they should be required for family needs, as for a funeral feast, or a present, then his permission would be obtained in family conclave. Arikimata had also put a *tapu* sign of coconut leaf on the stems of certain palms ; he did not want the fruit touched, since he wished to have some dry nuts for the making of *vatia* pudding. Again his interests were respected. If Raŋiata wanted coconuts badly, then he might climb the palms and take some, but would make a point of going to his brother's house and telling him afterwards. The reply is usually " E laui," " It is well." As will be seen later, much of the economic life of the Tikopia is managed on this principle of utilization and subsequent announcement to the owner. While in the orchard we drank the milk of green coconuts. They were husked by Arikimata who carefully piled the husks in a heap, rind outside ; this is partly in deference to the tutelary deity of the coconut, but is also a sign to the other owners of a lawful use of the property. Thieves, being in haste, usually leave the debris scattered about. Old barkcloth trees are cut as required. If one of the brothers should plant some, however, then they will not be taken without advising the planter. The person who wants them goes to the planter or his wife and asks permission to fell the trees. Later he goes and gives coconuts, bark-cloth or some other small equivalent. Such are the principles on which family ownership of land is managed in Tikopia.

Partly owing to the wide extensions of the kinship system, however, and partly to the workings of the rules of etiquette and reciprocity, these principles have a wider application. In certain spheres, notably some kinds of food, the differentiation between permanent ownership and use at will is much wider than in our own society. The cardinal points of the Tikopia system are : a definite link of a special and enduring kind between specified areas of ground and persons or groups of persons ; wide rights of temporary utilization of the products of the ground by any other person without asking *prior* permission ; verbal acknowledgment of the special link *afterwards* by the user, accompanied often by a material gift.

For instance, I went one day with Pa Reŋaru to examine his plantation of tobacco at Tufenua. Below us lay an orchard where coconut palms stood, the property of his brother-in-law, Pa Nukuariki. Pa Reŋaru climbed a tree and took one of the green nuts for our refreshment, explaining that his sister was married to this man. Later, when we had drunk, he said to me, " Let us go and announce to him the coconuts that have been plucked by the two of us." This is the ordinary custom. If a man is thirsty, he takes a coconut from an orchard which he happens to be passing, then later goes and informs the owner, who gives his approval. If he did not advise the owner that would be stealing ; if the owner did not approve of his action that would be churlishness of an extreme kind. If the owner does not want his palms touched, then he binds sago fronds (or coconut fronds) around the stems ; no one but a thief—or a close relative—will then meddle with them. In the case of a few coconuts no recompense is made to the owner, since they are plentiful, and are in continual fruit. The only obligation laid upon the person who takes them is to make a point of advising the owner. It is not enough to wait until one sees him abroad a few days later, though if one happens to meet him in the path on the way home that is sufficient. On this occasion it happened that we later saw a son of Pa Nukuariki standing on the beach. Pa Reŋaru told him what we had done, that we had taken one green nut for our own use and dry nuts for the children who accompanied us. The lad answered politely, " It is good to pluck coconuts for our friend." There are no very rigid rules ; an easy application of common sense governs the situation.

Much the same is the case with breadfruit. A passer-by may see a ripe breadfruit in an orchard and take it. This is legitimate, and the owner, seeing it gone, will not object. The reason is that breadfruit once ripe soon rots, and its crop does not stay long on the tree. It is termed a *tama forau*, a voyaging child, a visitor ; after a month or so it is gone. But it is an important food of the people. And in this case the man, having taken his breadfruit, goes to his house, makes his oven and compounds a pudding, a portion of which he carries to the person to whom the fruit belonged. This is *te fakaara*, the acknowledgment. Such conduct is not permissible with other foods, as dry coconuts and with bananas—this is theft. The difference, it is said, lies in the fact that they fruit constantly, and with them there is no waste. Breadfruit in full crop may fall and rot, but not so these other foodstuffs. The same restriction applies to taro, yams and pulaka.

A special variety of this general principle applies to the large areas of open ground where taro planting takes place in quantity. These are split up into a number of plots owned by houses and family-sections of houses. The custom is that any man who wants to plant in the ground of another is at liberty to do so, even without asking permission. I was a little taken aback when I first heard this. I was talking to Pa Niukapu one evening in front of my house when he pointed out to me a patch of ground that he had cleared two days before on a hillside half a mile away. I presumed that it was his own land ? No. Then it was his wife's ? No. A near relative's ? No, it was someone quite different. He had asked permission, of course ? No. Then he proceeded to explain that this was a custom of Tikopia. One plants taro somewhere, waits until it is mature, and then goes and removes it ; one does not go to steal the crops of another, one goes only to get one's taro. Later one makes a present in return for the use of the soil. Asked why he wanted to plant taro in another man's orchard, Pa Niukapu answered, " My wish, simply." He liked the look of the place for growing taro.

It is interesting in this connection to consult the accompanying Plan IV (not drawn to scale) of the taro gardens in Rakisu, as they were in the planting season of April 1929. The names indicate the houses of the owners of the ground, the numbers the owners of the taro planted there. It will be seen that while there is a considerable degree of coincidence, there are also many people who have made use of the ground of others, and that this has gone beyond the bounds of clan affiliation. The term *vao* applied to such planting ground refers primarily to the low scrub which grows on such land when it is left fallow. Each division of such a field is called *te tarutaru*, and is marked off from others by *tuakoi* of stones. Thus there is the *tarutaru* of sa Rarovi, the *tarutaru* of sa Faŋarere etc., rights over the land which remain unchanged from season to season. These are the owners of the soil. Within each division stand patches of taro, belonging to various households, or even to individuals, such as unmarried men. These are spoken of as, for instance, "*a taro sa Tauŋa,*" "*a keri sa Tauŋa,*" "*te vao sa Tauŋa,*" that is referring simply to the growth of cultivation there. From season to season these attributions change, as people select different sites for their crops. If ground is plentiful, then even young bachelors may have separate plantings of this kind ; otherwise each household plants as an entity. Where separate persons plant, no other member of the household presumes to take the crop from the patch of another. In such case each person brings his own " sets " for planting, that is, tops of taro cut close to the tuber. A man may get assistance from others of his relatives (*kano a paito*) if he wishes ; this is quite commonly done. Thus in the apparently communal planting of the house of Tafua each little household did its own work, but Pa Nukunefu had his brothers-in-law Pa Teva and Koroamaŋoni working for him.

When a person plants for himself in the ground of another, it is common to get permission first ; owners who have been anticipated in their desire for a particular piece of their own ground say that it is " correct " (*e tonu*) to do so. Unless under exceptional circumstances this is granted. But to go and dig straightway on the ground of another is also done frequently, and brings no rebuke. If a man wishes to reserve his land, then he sets up a coconut frond on a stick as a sign of *tapu*. No one will then interfere. But if a man wants very much to plant in that particular spot, he will go and ask the owner's permission ; this is rarely refused. Between chiefs little ceremony is used. The Ariki Kafika said, " The chief who wishes the ground of another chief comes, does not advise him, but begins to

PLANTERS OF TARO (see Plan IV)

(Planters indicated by numbers on Plan, owners of soil by house-names)

1. Pa Tauŋa	31. Pa Fenuturaki
2. tama i Paka	32. Ariki Kafika
3. Pa Nopu	33. Pa Saukirima
4. Pa Raŋimakini	34. sa Nukuariki
5. paito i Nukutauŋaru	35. Pa Reŋaru
6. Pa Faoreu	36. Pa Rarofara
7. Pa Motuaŋi	37. Pa Vainunu
8. Pa Nukunefu	38. sa Torofakatoŋa
9. Pa Raŋifuri	39. sa Fetauta
10. Ariki Tafua and	40. Pa Foŋamuna
Pa Mukava	41. sa Rarotoa
11. paito i Tafua	42. Pa Nukutauo
12. tama i Sautapu	43. Pa Fenuafara
13. Tamuriunu	44. Pa Vaimatini
14. Pa Morotai	45. Pa Toŋarutu
15. Pa Tokerau	46. Pa Taraniuo
16. Pa Raŋifatua	47. Kavarauniu
17. Pa Nukuomanu	48. Pa Nukutauriri
18. Pa Mauŋakena	49. Pa Raŋitafuri
19. Vaniaraŋa	50. Pa Nukusaumako
20. sa Nukutauŋaru	51. Firoriki
21. paito i Paiu	52. Pa Niata
22. sa Kafika	53. Pa Farekofe
23. Nukusorokiraro	54. Pa Tapuŋa
24. Pa Taitai	55. Nau Maraŋaone
25. sa Veterei	56. Pa Raŋifakauvia
26. Tiforau	57. Pa Fareata
27. Pae Orokofe	58. Pa Tekaupena
28. Pa Raŋimatere	59. Pa Nukureŋa
29. Pa Nukuva	60. Pa Niata
30. sa Faitoka	61. Fakasarakau

NOTES.—The dark patches on the Plan represent plots not cultivated that season. The names of the owners of the taro are reproduced as given me. Some are married men (*Pa* —), some married couples (*sa* —), some a group of kinsfolk (*paito i* —), some unmarried men or women (names without prefix). Since the data were given to me by men, it is probable that in a number of cases they omitted to mention that in the actual planting the wives assisted their husbands. But this is immaterial, since the ownership and use is joint in such case.

clear." This happened in the season mentioned above. Reference to the Plan will show that Kafika land was planted by the family of the Tafua chief, although they had a considerable area of their own land vacant at the time. And they did not even notify the Ariki Kafika that they were going to utilize his ground. This he took as a matter of course.

Sometimes this elastic interpretation of rights over land is a cause of irritation. Pa Taramoa came back one evening quite angry because he went to clear in the ground of sa Tavi and found Pa Sauki-rima in possession, having already cleared the patch he wanted. He began to clear at the side of the old man's plot, but said that he felt ashamed; he had been driven off. Evidently the old man had been rather curt with him. Pa Raŋimaseke, representative of the house of Tavi, who was present when I heard the tale, said that he was angry, since Pa Saukirima had been given permission not by him, the "root" of the family, but by Pa Raŋifakaino, his *mana*, but not directly in authority.

The main reason that sa Tafua took Kafika ground was that on their own the vegetation was not grown enough to postulate a good crop. They were engaged in specially extensive planting on account of the proposed feast of the Ariki Tafua, and a large number of sa Faea followed their chief in Rakisu, clearing, digging and planting taro for several weeks. Only a few of sa Raveŋa were there, for they objected to the state of the *mara*, saying that the *vao*, the covering vegetation, was not high enough for them. Sa Faea could not afford to be particular, since this was practically the only *mara* available to them, two others, Paka and Tiare, having been planted in coconut at the instance of the old chief, as mentioned earlier. Sa Raveŋa, having plenty of good taro ground, could pick and choose their garden sites.

Some acknowledgment for the use of planting ground is usually made in the form of a basket of raw or of cooked taro. This gift is never omitted when a man makes use of a portion of ground directly controlled by a chief, of either his own or another clan. "He goes to present the taro, be it raw or cooked, to the chief, because he has cultivated in the *mara* of the chief."

A person usually has four or more plots of taro in the ground at once, but if he is a *mafi*, an industrious fellow, he will have as many as ten plots or so. The crop is taken from one or two only at a time, so that when these are exhausted others will be ready. Planting goes on fairly regularly throughout the year. In Rakisu the plots are apt to be smaller than elsewhere, "since people go to the ground," that is, they like it.

The traditional method of utilizing garden land in Tikopia raises several questions in regard to possible competition among those desirous of planting. Such a system of comparatively free access can obviously obtain only in a society where there is no great land shortage. In Tikopia again, the soil is, broadly speaking, of the same general fertility throughout the island, so that there is no considerable quantity of " marginal land." One of the most important factors governing choice of planting site is the state of the undergrowth there, and it is this more than anything else which makes people resort to the land of others from time to time, instead of keeping within their own property. Competition for particular plots is not very intense, and the recognition of heavy calls impending upon his food resources is usually sufficient to drive a man to begin to plant early in the season when there is a good quantity of appropriate land available. The power of selective restriction given by the *tapu* sign means also that in case of need an individual owner can put a temporary barrier against the community interest operating in his property. As in other spheres, the actual operation of the principles of individual and group interest in land is governed by the code of avoidance of excess. A person who attempted to keep his land always for himself, or who systematically exploited the best land of others, would gradually incur opprobrium which would hamper his activities in other directions where co-operation was essential. Even in the case of a chief this tends to be an important factor.

The difference in custom between freedom of access to garden land and restrictions in the case of orchards, it is suggested, can be correlated with the difference in the nature of the crops in each. Where the crop is comparatively impermanent, resting in the ground only a season, the owner of the ground is not seriously hampered by being deprived of the use of it. But in the case of coconut palms, bread-fruit trees, paper mulberry trees, Canarium almond and other fruit trees, which stand for a generation or more, the inconvenience to the owner of the soil would be far more manifest.

Occasionally the owner of an orchard desires to block all access to it; this is usually the result of irritation at theft or damage done. Thus soon after the young people of Faea started playing *fukau*—a kind of hide-and-seek—at night, one man barred all the paths to his piece of ground with branches. Another time Pa Motuata, in anger at some of his bark-cloth tree spars having been appropriated without permission, cut a couple of trees and blocked the main path to Uta. His action was respected for a while, though the Ariki Kafika commmented on it adversely. " It is the path of gods and of chiefs ; no one may block it." Then he added,

" But if a man wants spars why doesn't he go and cut them in his own orchard ? "

Ownership of the lake and the foreshore is not as clear-cut as in the case of land. The lake is regarded as the property of the four chiefs, jointly ; it is " The Water of the Chiefs." The Ariki Kafika as the senior of these has the leading right therein, and he complained to me rather wryly that when a white man from a European vessel went duck-shooting there his permission had not been first obtained, nor had any of the bag been presented to him as a token of his suzerainty. But he hardly expected white people to know and observe the Tikopia rules of good manners. Use of the lake in the ordinary way is free to all ; canoes traverse it without restraint, and nets for *kiokio* are set in any part, without any explicit requirement of donation of part of the catch. But as a rule, after a succession of hauls the fisherman takes along a gift to his chief.

The reef is not vested in any specific ownership, but tacitly the area of it fronting a village is worked by the local people. Some families have erected *fota*, converging lines of stones to assist them in their netting of fish, and they have a proprietary interest in these. Though other people are not debarred from using these fish-corrals, the folk who maintain them expect some acknowledgment to be made.

A few words on the transfer of land may be given in conclusion. This is not common, but may occur for two reasons—the gift by a chief or other man of rank, or seizure by violence. Cases of both have been given in the preceding chapter, but a couple more may be given here.

In ancient times the orchard Veruveru belonged to sa Raropuka. But the mother of Tanakiforau, who was then an infant, came there to clear ground and laid him on a large stone. Then came a man of Raropuka, Kapukona by name, who seeing the babe pushed him off, saying, " What are you doing here ? Go to your own ground," that is to Penusisi, which lies on the hillside below. The babe cried, and the mother came up and upbraided the man. Tanakiforau as he grew older kept this incident in mind, and when he was a man came and ate in the orchard—as the native expression is—displacing sa Raropuka. It has remained in the possession of his descendants ever since.

Not long ago the orchard of Tio belonged to Pa Nukutauŋaru of Tafua. Then came the carrying-off of Nau Nukunefu of Avakofe by the house of Tafua. The result was a struggle between Tafua and Taumako in which the girl's brother, Pa Teva, seized bow and arrows and shot Pa Raropupua, who later died. Pa Teva then put a *tapu* sign of young coconut fronds on trees in the orchard of Tio, in Raveŋa, and forbade any of Tafua to enter.   He said, " I am going to eat here."   Hence though at the present time the land belongs in theory to the Ariki Tafua, it is no longer in use by his clan, and will in all likelihood be lost to them.

It will have become clear in the course of this chapter how far the Tikopia system of land ownership depends upon kinship, and how far it is independent of such ties.   A summary of the position of an ordinary married man as regards land would point to his direct interest in certain orchards associated with his house, undifferentiated in respect of coconuts and other trees, individually differentiated in respect of patches of taro and the like planted by himself ; to his reversionary interest in other orchards or portions of orchards held by women of his house, but which will return to him or his heirs when they die ; to his indirect interest, also of a reversionary kind, in still other orchards now in possession of different branches of his house, but possibly returning to himself or his descendants if all the male members of those branches die off ; to a direct but terminable interest in the orchards to which his wife has access, and he with her during her lifetime—his interest in his mother's having ceased at his marriage ; to his direct interest in plots of planting ground held under the same conditions as the orchards ; to his direct interest in certain patches of taro he has planted, growing on ground to which he has no further claim.   In addition there is the potential interest he has in any ground in the island suitable for planting.   Against this must be set off the perpetual lien which his chief has upon his land and its products, and the obligations he owes to repay others for the use of their ground, or to permit them the use of his own ground and his coconuts, bread-fruit and areca nut at discretion.   It is then obvious that in Tikopia " ownership " cannot mean exclusive right of use, occupation or control ; as used for convenience in ordinary description it must signify simply primary and more permanent rights of utilization as against secondary and less permanent rights.   In this sense only one may talk as I have done, of one man " owning " the soil and another " using " it to plant taro for a season.

It would be well if some such similar definition of rights in land were made in all native communities before European administration began to codify the native system and consent to alienation from the natives.[1]

---

[1] Some time ago Professor Malinowski laid down the lines of such analysis. *v.* his " Primitive Economics of the Trobriand Islanders," *Economic Journal*, XXXI, 1921, 1-16 ; " Practical Anthropology," *Africa*, II, 1929, 29-32 ; *Coral Gardens and Their Magic*, 1935, I, Chs. XI and XII.   *v.* also the present writer's *Primitive Economics of the New Zealand Maori*, Chapter XI.   As a telling example of the way

A system of ownership of land is a mechanism of social stability ; it gives a relation of a consistent character between the individuals of a society and the source from which they draw their material goods. In primitive society, as in civilized, there is no anarchy : rules govern the resort of individuals to the land, however elastic they may be. Difficulties which arise owing to the opposition of interests are settled in Tikopia largely through the agency of the clan organization, expressed in the final event through the fiat of the clan chief. When it is a question of inter-clan opposition there is a difficulty, since in the absence of any unified authority there is no final court of appeal. Chaos is prevented, however, partly by the collective position of the chiefs, who in a sense form a privileged class, and are respected even outside the bounds of the group which each of them rules ; and partly by the general network of social obligations, which cause a land question to be speedily transferred to a wider sphere and settled with reference to other principles of relationship and co-operation.

Inequalities in the possession of land exist, and are perpetuated by the system of inheritance, backed by the supernatural sanctions of ancestral interest. Differential wealth in this is almost bound to occur because of the differential increase in family membership, with the consequent splitting-up of territory. But there are no " landless natives " in Tikopia.

The data given in this chapter have been sufficient to show that the system of land tenure in this community can be hardly classed as of the " communistic order," despite the tendency to a broad equation of rights of usage and personal wants. The strong differentiation of family holdings on a basis of ancestral claim, the exercise of the right of restraint by *tapu* without the necessity of proving need, the gift of acknowledgment for use of garden land, the reprobation of theft of crops from individuals—all these elements are antagonistic to a realistic as to an ideal communism.

in which premature fixation of what is imagined to be the native system of land tenure harms native interests, see Lucy Mair, *An African People in the Twentieth Century*, 1934, 154-172.

CHAPTER XI

A MODERN POPULATION PROBLEM

THE small size of the island of Tikopia and its isolation has meant that for generations past the maintenance of an adequate relation between quantity of land and population has been a problem of fundamental importance in the economy of these natives. In olden days they appear to have attained a rough equilibrium, and kept it by various mechanisms of adjustment ; in recent years this has tended to be upset as a result of contact with European civilization.

According to Dillon the population of Tikopia in the early years of the nineteenth century was in an anomalous state. The number of females was " at least treble that of the males." [1] This discrepancy he attributed to artificial means, alleging that all males except the first two were strangled at birth, the reason assigned by the natives being to prevent an undue increase of population. The Englishmen found on the island by Dumont D'Urville denied this, Gaimard speaks of the number of children in a family as varying from three to eight, while John Maresere, eighty years later, stated that the family was limited in size to four, any number beyond this being buried alive as a rule.[2] Moreover in contradistinction to Dillon, he said that girls rather than boys were destroyed. Durrad, who lived for two months on the island and was a careful observer, stated that the people had large families and that there was an excess of males over females. All these statements cannot be made to tally, and one has therefore either to postulate startling and violent changes in the nature of the policy of Tikopia family life, or to regard certain of the observations as less reliable than others. The latter seems to me to be the preferable hypothesis. Before arriving in the island I had set down for investigation such matters as the proportion of the sexes in the extant population, the proportion of the sexes in the children born (if possible to ascertain), the number of children in a family, the possible existence of methods of infanticide and their differential application, and if any methods of abortion and of prevention of conception were known and used. Most of these questions I was later able to answer, but as might be expected, information as to the numbers and proportion of the sexes of all the children born could not be obtained in any form complete enough for accuracy.

The utter worthlessness of casual observation derived from the stay of a day or so which the *Southern Cross* and other vessels make was demonstrated by a statement which I received as a serious ex-

---

[1] P. Dillon, *Narrative* . . ., etc., II, 134.
[2] Rivers, *H.M.S.*, I, 352.

planation from an engineer on the way down to the island. He said that he believed that large numbers of the boys were *castrated* soon after birth, and alleged that he had ripped off the waistcloth of three and found this to be the case. Hence he accounted for their great stature—almost a legend among white people—and their general mild nature. This, as I noted with some scepticism at the time, would account for restriction of population, but not for a differential sex ratio. Moreover, the effects should be perceptible in families without children, if such lads afterwards married. The statement, as might be imagined, I found later to be entirely without foundation, but it is true that the Tikopia do endeavour to control their population in ways that are hardly less striking.

Let us first consider some of the data empirically established.

SOME STATISTICS IN TIKOPIA

In 1929 I took a census of the house by house variety. The method was to set down the name of every dwelling in sequence from a given point and then fill in the names of all the individuals ordinarily resident therein, with the aid of good informants. The results were checked from my own personal knowledge of households. The enquiries incidental to the recording of genealogies and drawing of village plans on other occasions provided a further means of verification. The population of the island at that time was 1281 persons. Its approximate distribution is as under :

		Males	Females	Totals
(i) Children and adolescents	.	338	249	587
(ii) Adult to middle-aged .	.	249	250	499
(iii) Above middle age	.	100	95	195
Total	.	687	594	1281

The divisions of course are approximate on the basis of observation and comparison. In terms of age they would correspond roughly to : (i) under eighteen ; (ii) eighteen to forty ; (iii) over forty. Allocations made on the basis of personal judgment of this kind are of course apt to be fallacious. In this case, however, a useful index was provided by the residence in Tikopia of the Reverend Durrad in 1910. It was easily ascertained in many cases whether persons classified were B.D. or A.D.—before or after Durrad. By a comparison of memories, persons in the early groups could be placed within about five years. This kind of technique would obviously not appeal to a statistician dealing with civilized communities, but it was the only one applicable to a society which is entirely ignorant of written record and where age in years is regarded as of no importance.

In the figures above the socially reproductive age for both sexes has been taken as eighteen to forty years ; if, as is perhaps more accurate, the period had been taken as twenty to forty-five years for men and eighteen to forty for women, the figure in group (ii) remains practically the same. In either case the socially reproductive males represent about 36 per cent. of the total male population and the socially reproductive females about 42 per cent. of the total female population. These figures are, however, not of great value ; to determine the effectively reproductive group of either sex would involve a careful elimination of the number of bachelors, spinsters, widowed persons and barren couples, which the quality of the evidence hardly justifies. At the time of my census the marriage grouping in (ii) and (iii) was as under :

	Males	*Females*	
Unmarried	117	101	Group (ii) 18-40
Married	132	149	
Unmarried	15	19	Group (iii) over 40
Married	85	76	

Owing to bachelorhood and spinsterhood being a recognized social norm, especially for junior members of a family, it would be difficult to say just what the group of unmarried persons represents in terms of potential reproduction.

I do not attempt to draw inferences of any subtle kind from figures with such a large potential error. What is, however, noteworthy, particularly in view of the past history of the Polynesian people, is that the numbers of the Tikopia seem to be not declining, but stable or even increasing. During my stay on the island, amounting to a full year, there were 60 births, according to my records and to native data supplied me, of which 27 were of males and 33 of females. Five of the children were stillborn and one died a fortnight after birth. During the same period there were only 21 deaths (including those of the infants mentioned above).[1]

[1] It may be noted that the figure of 21 deaths is probably somewhat lower than in a normal year. As pointed out to me by Dr Kuzcynski this figure, compared with the total population, would give an average expectation of life of about sixty years for each individual, which is certainly too high for probability. The period of my stay happened to be a favourable year from the point of view of crops and absence of epidemics. (This facilitated my work greatly, since I was regarded as a person free from malevolent intention and not an object of enmity to the gods.)

The number of living children per individual family is approximately 3·5. This figure, which is fairly high, is the average of about eighty recent families, i.e. where the majority of the offspring were still not adult. General fertility appears good, and there are very few barren couples.

The comparison between births and deaths in the period July 1928-July 1929 may not be entirely exact, owing to the fact that there may have been a few still-births which I failed to record. These would lower the ratio slightly, but would not affect greatly the general position, which is that the factors of fertility are much more than keeping pace with those of morbidity. There is no reason to think that this condition has not been characteristic for a number of years past.

It is of interest to consider in this connection the correlation suggested by Pitt-Rivers [1] to the effect that a stable or increasing population exhibits a tendency to produce a surplusage of mature women over men. In Tikopia the situation is somewhat complex. During my year of observation the number of female children born was slightly in excess of that of male children. But the number of adults of socially reproductive age was approximately equal for both sexes, and the number of juvenile and adolescent males was very considerably in excess of that of females of this age-period. I am at a loss to account for this great preponderance of young males. Differential infanticide in favour of males during the last two decades might account for it to some extent, though native statements do not support this. A heavy mortality rate through losses at sea might explain the smaller proportion of adult males. But the causes are not at all clear. At all events, in a population which is certainly not declining, there will be for some considerable time a marked surplus of males in the total group. [2]

FACTORS OF MORBIDITY

The evident tendency of the Tikopia population to increase is due in the first place to the absence of any very pronounced factors of morbidity. The health of the islanders is remarkable, especially by contrast to that of the Melanesian folk in Santa Cruz and the Solomons. There is no malaria, hardly any framboesia, and though not having made a proper medical survey I am not in a position to speak with certainty, there appears to be very little endemic disease.

[1] G. H. Pitt-Rivers, *Clash of Cultures*, 1927, 246 *et seq.*
[2] A series of figures obtained in Tikopia by Mr B. E. Crawfurd in 1933 and given in the Appendix (p. 600) supports in general the demographic conclusions expressed in this chapter.

There are plenty of mosquitoes on the island, active by day and by night, and I suspected some of being *Anopheles*, but if so, they were not infected. I took no quinine after the first month I was there, and though frequently bitten, had no fever. I observed none in the natives. They recognize chill as an ailment (*te makariri*, the coldness), but it is not of a malarial order. Elephantiasis appears to be entirely absent. I could not test for hookworm. Of tubercular affection there were a few symptoms. Pa Nukutauvia died while I was in Tikopia of what was apparently this disease, and some time before a young man " Mikail " of the Tafua family had also died from similar causes. Both these men had been to the mission school in Vureas. Pa Paiu was ill for a few weeks with glandular swellings of the neck, which later burst, after which he recovered.

Ulcerations are common. When slight they are known as *maŋeo*, and are usually produced by infection in coral scratches. They yield easily to treatment with strong tincture of iodine. When an ulcer is more serious it is known as *tona*, and when the condition is chronic over a considerable area it is known as *para*. There were about half a dozen serious cases when I was there, each with a history of a number of years. The Ariki Faŋarere had a foot affected ; Tikarima a hand and arm badly swollen ; a woman had two legs ulcerated ; Pa Nukuomanu an arm, and Nau Raroakau one leg. In the last two cases some response was obtained to a single injection of novo-arsenobillon, but a cracked syringe-barrel stopped the treatment. The eldest son of Pa Farekofe, an ardent cultivator, was so badly affected in the arm and chest that he lived away from other people in a hut in an orchard, and took no part at all in the social and ceremonial life. I did not even meet him. That this affection is not a recent introduction is shown by the case of the Ariki Kafika Pepe, seven generations ago, who abdicated because of his physical condition. Framboesial lesions in young children are comparatively common, particularly around mouth and anus, but clear up entirely in later life. Large tertiary ulcers are rare.

Ringworm (*kaifariki*) is plentiful. It is regarded as an unpleasant affliction, and a young person who has it may be taunted by members of the opposite sex. It responds to applications of chrysophanic acid in vaseline, but is apt to prove obdurate in long-established cases. Pa Fenuatara, who had a patch on his buttocks, was very keen to get rid of it. And the Ariki Kafika said to me, " Son, have you no sympathy for your brother, Taupure (his youngest boy), to give him the *sinu kaifariki* to cleanse his skin ? " The lad's body was practically covered with ringworm.

The standard of personal cleanliness of the Tikopia is very high.

They bathe several times a day, particularly in the early morning, after the work of preparing the oven, and in the evening. Hands alone are hardly ever washed ; ablutions consist in the laving or immersion of the whole body. Their sanitation is not so good as their personal hygiene. Their water supply should be uncontaminated, coming as it does from the hills which though cultivated are not in residence. I used the water unboiled and unfiltered during my stay. The natural functions of the people are usually performed on the open beach, mostly at morning and evening. This gives relief from the mosquitoes which always haunt the bush. During the manufacture of turmeric all the people engaged are compelled by ritual regulation to defecate in the sea itself. With the chewing of betel spitting is periodic, and the habit is to spit either at the base of the thatch wall of the house, or under a floor-mat, the border of which is lifted for the purpose. This habit, innocuous in the ordinary way, becomes dangerous with the increase of European contact, since any infection introduced tends to spread very rapidly by such means.

From time to time epidemics occur, brought, as the natives themselves realize clearly, by foreign vessels. The generic native term for epidemic disease is *maki* or *makimaki*, and they distinguish such types as *tare*, cough or common cold, *tiko toto*, blood excretion (dysentery). Measles, influenza and other complaints have been introduced in this way, and usually rage with extreme virulence. There is the very strongest possible case for a ship carrying an infection of any kind not to touch at the island. The Tikopia, ignorant of the germ theory of disease, believe that an epidemic is due to the malignancy of those in control of the vessel. They associate it also to some extent with the blowing of the ship's whistle, so that the captain of the *Southern Cross*, at their request, abstained from the usual practice when weighing anchor. The onset and disappearance of a wave of common colds which followed the visit of the ship when I was set down on the island was a perfect illustration of the spread of an infection. It was gone in about a month, and did not recur again during my whole stay. To the rarity of calls of ships from the outside world is largely due the maintenance of the splendid health of this physically fine people.

Accident must be included also in the factors of morbidity. A fall from a tree or a cliff, a wound from a garfish, drowning—several children and even adults have been lost thus in recent times—account for a few deaths, while infant malnutrition produces others. Semi-deliberate factors will be discussed later.

A pleasing feature to one acquainted with the heavy mortality among the young people of the Melanesian islands to the west is that in Tikopia it is practically only as weakly infants or as old folk that people die. According to the natives the commonest cause of death in olden times was the functional decay of old age. The only death of a young person during my stay was that of Pa Nukutauvia, aforementioned, an illustration of the general thesis that removal from their home has been deleterious to the Tikopia.

MECHANISMS OF POPULATION CONTROL

It can be safely said that until recent years the population of Tikopia was normally in a state of equilibrium with its food supply. From time to time the natural check of famine seems to have been operative. Drought, *te oŋe*, occurs at intervals, and would be expected to affect the morbidity rate to some extent by lowering the resistance of the people, particularly that of young children, by compelling a general resort to less nutritious foods. A case is cited from the last severe drought when Pa Nukumaro, younger brother of the present Ariki Faŋarere, went off to sea with two of his sons to perish rapidly there, instead of by slow starvation on shore.

The relation of population to natural resources is not expressed in purely individual terms, but in terms of family equilibrium. The division of the land is on a " house " basis, and the older men, the responsible heads of the house, exercise a considerable amount of control over the number of relatives and descendants who will share the land. For this purpose there are several mechanisms available.

Celibacy.—The younger male members of a family, especially if it is not a rich one in lands, are expected to remain single. The head of the house may issue an injunction to them to refrain from marriage on the grounds that the offspring of their elder brothers will occupy all the food resources at command. Extra-marital satisfaction is not denied these men, but their sex activities rarely result in children. Deference to family interests is strong, and the choice of celibacy is quite often voluntary.

Prevention of Conception.—By the method of *coitus interruptus* sex gratification is obtained by these natives without resulting in conception. This applies to unmarried people, and is used also by the married in order to limit their families. Details are given in Chapter XIV.

Abortion.—This is not common, but is sometimes practised by unmarried girls who desire to avoid giving birth. Married women do not practise it ; they have no need.

Checks on population of a more radical order comprise infanticide, sea-voyaging and war.

Infanticide.—The face of an unwanted child is turned down at birth and it is allowed to smother. This lies at the discretion of the father, and the motivating factor is said to be primarily the comparison with potential food supplies, though in some cases bastardy may be responsible. By some informants it was held that female infanticide is no more common than male infanticide, but by others it was stated " the work of the woman is to plait mats and fill the waterbottles, and when one or two girls have been born that is enough! But men go out and catch fish and do other work." On the other hand it was admitted by these same people that male children, if they marry, cause division of land which may lead to fighting.

The incidence of infanticide varies considerably from one family to another, in some a preponderance of girl children being actually preferred. Again, it is common for a father to ignore the suggestion of the midwife or other old woman present and allow the child to live, from pity or affection for it.

Sea-voyaging.—The practice of men, especially the young and unmarried, of setting out on overseas voyages tends to reduce their numbers very considerably, since so many of them are lost. The genealogies I collected gave evidence of the diminution of the male population thus effected in the last few generations.

War.—When the pressure of population on the land becomes severe the last resort is to drive out a section of the people. This has happened twice already in the history of Tikopia, and the possibility of some similar action being necessary in the future has recently been discussed. The separation is possible on a vertical or on a horizontal plane—the members of one clan or district might be expelled, or those of the lower stratum of the society. The chiefly families might, for example, drive out the commoner families.

EUROPEAN CONTACT CAUSES A UNIQUE PROBLEM

As the result of European contact these checks are no longer operative to the same extent as formerly. Fear of the Government forbids the overt expulsion of any considerable section of the people, and though it has not yet occurred, the time can be foreseen when the Government may forbid the emigration of the young men in canoes, as has been done in other parts of Polynesia.

The other checks are also affected. Owing to the attitude of the mission towards extra-marital sex relations, celibacy is being virtually discouraged. The Tikopia young man, unused to the foreign ideal of pre-nuptial chastity, " sins " and is forced by indignant mission teachers to marry the girl, or is cast out of church for a

time.   As a celibate, not expecting to take a wife, and obeying his
father's injunction, he is careful not to cause his mistress to conceive ;
as a married man he does not exercise the same restraint and produces
children.   Abortion and infanticide are frowned upon likewise by
the mission, though both are surreptitiously practised, even by folk
closely in touch with the church.

The result is that the former equilibrium is being upset, and there
is a threat of congestion of population on the lands of many families.
This has been counteracted to some extent by the adoption of European
tools and the introduction of new foodstuffs, but the temporary
expansion of resources thus induced seems now to have ceased, and
intensive cultivation has a limit.   Moreover, there has been a tendency
to plant more crops in the woods, with the result that the reservoir of
supplies which these afforded in time of drought has been diminished.
Among the more thoughtful natives, as the chiefs and other men of
rank, there is a very real fear for the adequacy of the food supply.
They are honestly perplexed to find the solution, though because of
their comparative wealth in land the matter is not such a pressing
one for them as for their people.   At the present time there is no
acute pressure, nor may there be for another generation ; but if the
present rate of increases continues, it will surely come, and in case of
hurricane or drought, there is no possibility of imports from outside.

What are the remedies for this situation ?   The most obvious
would seem to be the adoption of improved means of utilizing the
soil.   Something might be done along these lines, particularly in the
direction of the introduction of new plants, but any radical change
would have to rely on entirely new methods of agriculture.   This
would involve such a disturbance in the social life of the people that it is
difficult to predict its effects.   It might be argued that a solution could
be found in migration.   But the removal of a section of the people to
another island would involve subjecting them to considerable risks
from novel diseases, the effects of which upon individuals have proved
fatal only too often in the past.   And apart from the probable decima-
tion of those who moved, the shock to the resident section would
be severe, in a community where the members are so closely bound
together by economic, religious and kinship ties.   The natives themselves strongly object to the idea of migration—" to go away and see
other lands, yes, that is good ; but to go and not return to Tikopia,
that is bad, we should die."   A wider sex education and the issue
of a plentiful supply of contraceptives would meet the case to some
extent, but is not practicable for economic reasons alone, even could
the natives adapt themselves to the mechanics of the operation, and
Europeans to the idea of its introduction.

The really regrettable feature of the situation is that but for the moral preconceptions of the interpreters of the Christian religion the old checks would act in a perfectly satisfactory manner. A celibacy in which chastity was not enforced, and a discreet infanticide, would serve to maintain the population in equilibrium, and would be in accord with the feeling of the people themselves. An appeal was actually made to me by one of the leading men of Tikopia that on my return to Tulagi I should persuade the Government to pass a law enjoining infanticide after a married pair had had four or five children, in order that the food supply might not be overburdened. I pointed out to him that Europeans have an unconquerable repugnance to the taking of human life, even when it has not really begun to participate in the community, and declined to press the Government in the matter. But I felt then, as I do now, the injustice of enforcing our European moral attitudes on a people who before our arrival had worked out a satisfactory adjustment to the population problem—particularly when we can offer them no adequate solution to the maladjustment which we thus create.

The commercial interest of Tikopia is negligible ; its people interfere in no way with the life of those in the other islands of the territory. They are contented with their own institutions, comparatively free from disease, and are a peaceful, hospitable and law-abiding folk, with a religious system which does no violence to our basic concepts. It might be thought then, that here, if anywhere, was a case for minimum interference, for allowing the community to maintain its adjustment to its peculiar specialized environment. It might be thought that the so-called sanctity of human life is not an end in itself, but the means to an end, to the preservation of society. And just as in a civilized community in time of war, civil disturbance or action against crime, life is taken to preserve life, so in Tikopia infants just born might be allowed to have their faces turned down, and to be debarred from the world which they have merely glimpsed, in order that the economic equilibrium might be preserved, and the society maintain its balanced existence. This is the argument which a dispassionate sociologist may put forward, when he sees the harmony of life of the Tikopia disturbed, their social and economic equilibrium threatened, entirely against their will. In doing so he ignores of course the thirst of our pseudo-Christian culture to make other people conform to our standards, irrespective of the effect of what that conformity may mean.

CHAPTER XII

FIRING THE OVENS OF YOUTH

THE structional ramifications of a kinship system become more intelligible when traced through the series of stages which mark the maturing life of a person. But what the textbooks call "the life history of the individual" is most unsatisfactory for inclusion in a systematic arrangement of the general institutional scheme of a culture. It is a study of data from another point of view—a diachronic as opposed to a synchronic attitude. From the methodological standpoint too it is not the life history of any single individual that is described, but portions of the behaviour of a number of individuals that are assembled and generalized. But an adequate record in this field is hardly possible, and the following two chapters are frankly given as the result of a process of abstraction due to the fragmentary nature of the material.

The major portion of this book has been given over to a study of the anatomy of kinship—the analysis of it as an articulated system, with emphasis on the structural relationships involved. Now it may be considered functioning in two of the most dramatic types of institution which regulate the lives of the Tikopia : initiation and marriage.

The object, in this present chapter especially, is to show how a society takes charge of its members—like raw material in a factory they come from the furnace, are gripped by different pieces of complicated machinery, are beaten, cut, rolled, twisted, reheated to make an implement fit for social use. Almost literally these are processes which some savage communities utilize to shape their young people to their ends. But society is not a set of machines, and one defect of the analogy is shown by the fact that when the time comes for the defunct individual to be thrown on to the social rubbish-heap, the panoply of ritual with which this is done is perhaps even greater than at any time during his active life.

An account of the complex ceremonies connected with the birth of a Tikopia infant had to be omitted from this volume for lack of space.[1] In earlier chapters the life of a child in a household among its kinsfolk has been depicted in some detail, and it is convenient to include a few observations here on some of the ceremonial events of later childhood before proceeding to consider the major rite of initiation.

---

[1] It is hoped to publish this in the *Journal of the Polynesian Society*.

SOME EXPERIENCES OF CHILDHOOD

When the child is of some size, having learned to run and play in independent fashion, the septum of its nose and the lobes of its ears are bored. This may take place at any time from the age of three or four years onwards. The operation is performed by the mother or another member of the family, and " it has no activities," that is, there are no ceremonies connected with it. " It does not hurt," said the lads whom I asked. Little rolls of leaf are kept in the orifices until the wounds have healed; afterwards tortoiseshell rings or larger leaf rolls are inserted on festive occasions. One does not see in Tikopia, however, the enormous dangling ear lobes which are so common in the Melanesian islands to the west. To some extent this may be due to the fact that though the Tikopia find in a pierced ear lobe a convenient slot to hold a pipe, the folds of their bark-cloth waist-belts provide pockets in which more bulky articles may be stowed. The boring operation of the ears is termed *fakautiuti te tariŋa*, an ordinary descriptive phrase.

The first wearing of clothes comes some considerable time later, and consists in the donning of a tiny scrap of bark-cloth just large enough to fasten in place, and often discarded. It is said that now-adays children are provided with clothing much earlier than was formerly the case. On this occasion the mother's brother may pre-pare a gift of food and take it to his *tama tapu*, when it is reciprocated, but the occasion is not one for much ceremony.

An event of considerable importance to a boy is his first experience of torchlight fishing in a canoe. This is known as the *mataki ramaŋa*, the initial torch-expedition. Since a considerable portion of his life's work is to be spent in this occupation it is but natural that the entry of the boy into this manly pursuit should be celebrated. He is about ten years old when he takes part in such an expedition for the first time. His duties consist simply in paddling as a member of the crew; he is not given charge of torch or net, nor is he specially inducted into their use. He is a *koromata*, novice.

The following day the *puŋaumu*, the " kindling of the ovens," takes place. Food is prepared by the lad's parents, he is smeared by one of the household with turmeric on breast, neck, and sides of the face, and his relatives assemble to wail over him. These are signs that an event of social significance has occurred. In the evening the lad goes to the house of one of his mother's brothers—usually the true maternal uncle—and there more turmeric is put on him. He is presented with a *maro*, a ceremonial bundle consisting of a mat and some ordinary bark-cloth topped with a piece of the orange kind.

He is also a given a basket of food. These items are carried to the house of his parents and reciprocated the same day. If the boy is an "adhering child," then it is his adoptive parents who conduct the affair. When Rakeivave went out for the first time it was under the guidance of his *mana* Pa Taramoa; it was his grandfather the Ariki Kafika who smeared the turmeric on him, and the oven was prepared in Teve. His own father Pa Fenuatara took no part at all in the proceedings. But it was arranged that the boy should go out with his own father the next night. Parental interest followed closely on the heels of custom.

Usually the details of the boy's first trip are settled beforehand, and one member of the crew, frequently though not necessarily a close relative, makes himself responsible for the novice. This does not always happen. From the village where I was staying a lad went out unknown to his parents, who of course made the appropriate exchanges the next day.

A *maro* is also given from the household of the parents to each member of the crew of the canoe—a basket of food topped with a piece of bark-cloth. This custom obtains only when the crew is composed of men who are not very close kinsfolk. When the crew are *kano a paito* of the lad, then no such presentation is made. It is recognized, for instance, that when Soakimaru, young son of the Ariki Taumako, makes his initial trip the Ariki, Pa Teva, Pa Tarikitoŋa and others of the immediate group of kin will go, since they are all experienced fishermen (*tautai*). Moreover, there are plenty of canoes available for them. If a family has no canoe of its own, then the boy will have to go elsewhere, and the *maro* will be made to the crew. It is said that if one man of a crew is not of the *kano a paito*, then the presentation will be made to all because of him.

Girls, too, sometimes take part in such an expedition, and when they go out for the first time the same ceremony takes place.

On the day after his trip the boy appears rather shy and proud; he is distinguished from his companions by the orange pigment, which seems to make him self-conscious and rob him of his customary ease. He goes abroad much as usual in the intervals left to him from the ceremonies.

The novitiate ceremony which takes place when the lad goes for the first time to Marae in Uta to participate in the sacred dances has been mentioned already. His entry into the ceremonies which form the heart of the Tikopia religious system is made under the safeguards of kinship.[1] This, however, does not occur until after his initiation.

---

[1] A full description of the entry of the *koromata* into Marae will be given in *Work of the Gods*.

The ceremony in connection with another novitiate, the *koromata* in the sightseeing circuit of the hills cannot be described here. It is an affair of young people, not children.

This has shown briefly some of the structural features around which so much of the later life of the child is built, and indicates the importance of the respective roles of the father's household on the one hand and that of the immediate mother's brother on the other in all the more formal social events in which the child has to take part. This same theme will emerge in the following chapters too, but combined with other institutional motifs to form a more complex arrangement.

ASPECTS OF PRIMITIVE INITIATION

Anthropology has applied the name of initiation rites to a number of different types of ceremony, on the one hand those which admit to a secret society, an age grade, a medicine lodge or a club, and on the other those which facilitate or emphasize the passage of a person from one social state to another, as from adolescence to manhood. The former may be termed rites of specific initiation, the latter rites of general initiation. The rites of specific initiation have an obvious practical intent—they allow the privileges of the group concerned to be guarded and prepare the novice for absorption into the group as a responsible member who will reflect its character and objects. The exclusion of non-initiates, the terrifying of the novice, the submission of him to ordeals, the disclosure of secrets, the investiture with insignia have a very definite and immediate aim.

The role of rites of general initiation is not so obvious. From one point of view they apply the same principles on a broader scale, induction being not into a particular section of society, but into the social life as a whole. They form part of the general formal preparation of a person for the full exercise of the normal responsibilities of membership of the society, a milestone on the road of progress through manhood or womanhood. Here comes the stress laid upon the need for change in the way of life, the abandonment of non-initiates, the dramatization of re-birth, the trials of hardihood, the education in matters of sex and in tribal lore, the permission to marry or to undertake other weighty and dangerous enterprises. It can hardly be doubted that there is some correlation between such features of initiation and the obligations which confront a person as a mature member of a society. But the correlation is by no means exact. There are many aspects of initiation which do not allow it to be viewed as a simple cultural response to the need for preparation for a place in the social life of the community. This need is presumably universal, but the rites themselves are not. They have a capricious distribution. They are practised by one tribe and not by another; in communities where they do exist the rites for women are often but a pale reflection of those of the men, or such provision may be the perquisite of males alone. Again, some features of initiation are difficult to relate to any scheme of fundamental cultural needs; they are there as elements in the ritual, but they find no ready explanation as a contribution to the social efficiency of the maturing individual.

An adequate sociological study of rites of general initiation must meet these difficulties. It must be prepared to analyse more carefully the precise role which these rites play in the social life of each community where they exist, to describe not merely the geographical distribution, but also the social conditions of the peoples who do not possess them, and to try and find a way through that thorny field of enquiry, the discrimination between the sexes in this ritual sphere. It must also be prepared to examine the reaction which the initiation ceremonies produce in the person who is the focus of them, as distinct from their basic function for the society as a whole. This distinction between immediate and ultimate effects is of primary importance. It may well be for example that the fundamental value of initiation ritual may be the sacralization of a crisis of life, the standardization by society of the psychological changes occurring at puberty, the provision of a set of norms of conduct which by their obligatory character help to tide over the period of crisis. But at the same time an examination of the conduct of the individual concerned may show that in him it is a response to values arising from within the institution itself, that he acts in conformity to emotions generated by the immediate local situation, and that this situation is for him but dimly the outcome of a prior emotional tension. To put the point somewhat crudely— for society the crisis in the life of the individual may produce initiation rites; for the individual the subjection to initiation rites may produce the crisis, or at least bring it to a head.

An analysis on these points bears upon the general theoretical explanations advanced to account for the existence of these rites. As different aspects of the ceremonial have been considered it has been pointed out how they emphasize the social value of the individual to his community, how they facilitate his transition from youth to adult life, fortifying him at a time of crucial physiological, psychological and social change, how they ritualize and surround with a sacramental aura this period of stress. Again it has been shown how they serve more immediate practical ends as in acting as an educational influence, or in particular cases in insuring adequate food supply for the community which practises them.

Any definitive study of the ceremonial of initiation is possible only upon a broad comparative basis. But before this can be done more adequate specific studies are needed which will describe the procedure carefully, not merely as regards technique and sequence of operations, but also indicating the actual native attitude towards the various elements of ritual. The observer's theoretical explanations should be separated from the account of the actual happening and the elements regarded as vital by the people should be made clear.

The initiation ritual of Tikopia is described from this point of view.

Initiation in Tikopia consists in essentials of an operation akin to circumcision ; it is practised upon young males, a few only at a time, and is accompanied by the distribution of huge quantities of food and gifts, regulated upon the basis of kinship to the initiates. A similar ritual, but on the economic side only, is sometimes performed for girls.

The specific name for the ceremony is *rau taŋata* in the case of the boys and *rau fafine* in that of girls. The basic equivalents of these terms might be given as " male leaf " and " female leaf " respectively, but it is difficult to see the force of this translation. Their use appears to be direct and not metaphorical. They are the principal names (*matua iŋoa*). More generally, however, the comprehensive term *puŋaumu* is used to cover both. This means literally " the kindling of the ovens," and refers to the firing of the fuel in the cooking-places for the preparation of the food, which is one of the major features of the occasion. There is, however, a definite ritual significance attached to the name ; it is used in this plural form to designate ceremonies connected with injury or death of a person. At the conclusion of the ordinary sequence of funeral observances two ovens are utilized for the special preparation of food in houses frequented by the deceased ; one is kindled for a person who has suffered injury from the slip of a knife, a fall from a tree or cliff, or the penetration of a fish spine at sea. So also for a lad on whom an operation is performed. The native conception is to show by practical means sympathy (*arofa*) for a person who has suffered injury, and the oven comes therefore to be a symbol of social damage and the attempt at its repair. In the ordinary way of conversation the expressions " his oven-kindling has been performed " or " his oven has been kindled " mean that this person referred to has passed through the initiation ritual ; it is only in a specific context that they would refer to a case of sickness, injury or death, though the expressions used are identical.

THE OPERATION OF SUPERINCISION IN TIKOPIA

The actual operation consists in a longitudinal slitting of the upper surface of the anterior portion of the prepuce, and is thus not circumcision. A similar operation elsewhere has been termed by Rivers *incision*, by Gifford *supercision*, and by Te Rangi Hiroa *super-incision*,[1] a term which I have adopted here; it is analogous with subincision. The operation is performed by a man who is known to be skilled at the task; his special kinship qualifications for the post are described later. There is no special class of such men, but one who is noted for particular ability may be referred to as a *tufuŋa marama*—freely rendered " an expert clear as day." Ordinarily he is termed *te tufuŋa kaukau taŋata*, the expert in the incision of persons. The term *kaukau* is a polite equivalent of *sere*, to cut, which is not used in the presence of *tautau pariki*, or of a mixed audience where the proprieties are being observed. Afirua drew forth mingled laughter and scolding from a group of girls by using the latter word deliberately in describing what was going to happen to a lad.

The technique of the operation is simple. A small stick known as the *afa*—the same term is used for a net gauge—is whittled, about five inches long, elliptical in cross-section and about half an inch in greater diameter. This is pushed down the top of the penis underneath the prepuce (*e fauru atu ko te rakau*), and the skin is then stretched to make it as thin as possible over the wood and gathered down on either side. " It is smoothed out that the path of the knife may be thin," as it is said. The expert then cuts straight down the top of the foreskin towards the tip, carefully, lest he diverge to one side and " cut wrongly," thereby severing the *uka* (vein or sinew). I have been told that a line is sometimes traced first with charcoal to guide the eye of the expert, but I did not observe it done in practice. The cut is made from far back on the penis, as much as two inches, and the stick is levered up hard at this moment, while considerable pressure is exerted by the fingers to keep the skin pushed down on either side. After the cut is made it is parted completely with the thumbnails and the skin is folded back in two flaps. A strip of soft barkcloth, freshly torn off, about two feet long and half an inch wide is then wound round the prepuce and the penis itself, so that the lips of the wound are kept apart.

Nowadays the operation is performed with a razor blade, but in olden times it was done with the sharp shell of a bivalve known as the *kasi*. Then it is said the ceremony took place at a much later

---

[1] Rivers, *H.M.S.*, I, 292; II, 432 *et seq.*; Gifford, *Tongan Society*, 187; Te Rangi Hiroa, *Mangaian Society*, 89.

age—when the beard of the youth began to grow—as otherwise he would not be able to bear the pain. Naturally the incision was much more difficult to make cleanly and quickly in those circumstances. There is a special vocabulary to describe the facility of response of the flesh to the tool. *E sere ŋauŋau*, " it cuts toughly " is said if the operation is difficult, and synonyms for this are *maŋuŋuŋu* and *mapāpā fefea*. The external skin of the prepuce is termed the *raukiri moko*, literally the " lizard skin " ; the interior surface facing the glans, " the skin inside " as the natives call it, is known as *tenea mero*, " the red thing." Of an operation that is complete at one cut, the *raukiri moko* and *tenea mero* both being severed, it is said *ku pipi tasi*. But when the former is severed at the first cut and the latter at the second then it is said *ku pipi rua*. *Tasi* and *rua* are the numerals one and two respectively. For a boy who is *sere ŋauŋau*, who cuts with difficulty, it will take five or six incisions to complete the operation, and this is described in corresponding fashion.

It is interesting to note that such cases of difficulty may be ascribed to extraneous causes, namely, breach of *tapu*. Boys who have not been incised are forbidden to eat the flesh of certain shell-fish as the clam (*toki*), green-snail (*maro alili*) and *nisiore* (a species of ? *Purpura*). These things are gristly and are supposed to induce a like condition of toughness in the prepuce at the operation. " It is difficult because the lad has been accustomed to eat wrongly ; things here, and things there, he has eaten of them." But if the operation is easily performed then people say, " That is a lad of listening ears." He has heeded the advice of his elders and has not partaken of the prohibited things. This *tapu* of food provides an avenue of explanation for the expert whose fingers have not proved so swift and sure as might be expected. A troublesome operation is blamed on the boy himself, who is not usually in a position to deny the accusation, and whose denial in any case is hardly likely to be believed. Previous interference by a woman may also be blamed (*v. infra*).

There may be of course purely mechanical difficulties in the way of an easy incision. The penis of a small boy is apt to prove troublesome, particularly if he is very much afraid, when it becomes retracted. When it is very small (*e miŋi*) the end of it is grasped by the expert and pulled to dilate it and render the operation possible. Advice again to the lad before the operation may embody some similar instruction for his own attention. Care has to be taken too that when several lads are incised at the same time the *afa*, which is used as the basis of the cutting, is small enough to fit each. At the incision of the boys of Nukuafua their mother's brother, Pa Koroatu, who was the principal expert, showed the stick to the elder lad and

asked him if it were of a suitable size for the penis of the younger.
The boy laughed at this, but was reproved and told to answer properly ;
he replied in the affirmative.

It was said to me by the men that the boy feels no pain at the time
of the operation—he feels the movement of the knife, but it does not
hurt.   Nevertheless Seuku and Munakina confided to me afterwards
that the actual cutting had hurt very much, and that the sound of
the flesh breaking was not nice.   Once the operation was over, they
said, the wound itself was not very painful.   Whatever his sufferings
may be, however, the boy is much afraid.   This fear is appreciated
by those in charge of the operation and they are sympathetic about it.
The boy knows vaguely what he has to face but he tends to exaggerate
its danger.   " He thinks he is going to be struck lifeless," as it was
put.   In their preliminary discussions the operator and his assistants
stress the need for care, speed and steadiness of hand, that the lad
may not be wounded unnecessarily.   And the tenderness of the organ
concerned is emphasized.   " It is our death indeed—in the genitals."
Every effort is made to avoid inflicting needless pain, and to calm the
fears of the lad.   The tie of kinship is here both a stimulus and an
aid.   On the one hand it makes for more consideration on the part
of operators and on the other the initiate places more trust in them
than if they were not akin to him.   They exhort him to be strong,
cheer him with the thought that it is brief, and appeal to his pride.
" Fakamate i a roŋo a taŋata," they say to him, " go to death under
the reputation of men," meaning " Do not cry out, suffer in silence
as becomes a man, lest the women laugh at you."   And as the expert
his mother's brother makes the incision he may call out to the lad,
" Fakatoa ! iramutu ! "   " Be strong ! Nephew ! "   At one incision
of which I was witness much advice of this kind was given.   One
man said to the boys cheeringly, " Is it felt ? No ! It is not felt."
Another gave them a word of caution to remember when they should
be carried out from the house to be operated upon.   " Do not wince
from the wailing that is going on ; do not look at it ; one looks only
at the ceiling of the house."   Thus are they advised and heartened
up ; there is no attempt made to terrify them or to inflict upon them
any pain beyond what is unavoidable.

The operation is then in no sense designed as an ordeal to try
their manly fortitude, or to accustom them to the bearing of pain.
To the Tikopia the modification of the sexual organ is its primary
aim, and these other aspects are definitely minimized as far as possible.
The ready adoption of what may be called labour-saving devices in
other Polynesian communities as they have acquired European
materials such as steel or glass leads to the conclusion that the same

GENEALOGY VII (a)

ILLUSTRATING THE PRINCIPAL RELATIONSHIPS
AT THE INITIATION OF MUNAKINA AND SEUKU

(Compare Gen. III)

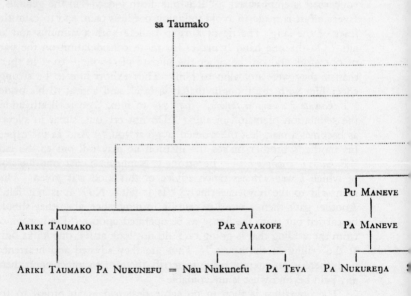

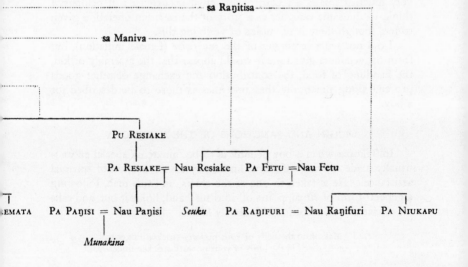

sa Raŋitisa

sa Maniva

Pu Resiake

Pa Resiake = Nau Resiake   Pa Fetu = Nau Fetu

ᴇᴍᴀᴛᴀ   Pa Paŋisi = Nau Paŋisi   Seuku   Pa Raŋifuri = Nau Raŋifuri   Pa Niukapu

Munakina

attitude obtains there also. In Tonga, for example, the operation formerly done as in Tikopia is now performed by competent medical practitioners in the local hospital at Nukualofa.[1] In the general theory of initiation, then, the physical operation is not to be simply explained in all cases as a method of trying the courage of the initiate. In Anuta the operation is said to be that of circumcision, the foreskin being cut completely round and thrown away. This is done when the boy is in full adolescence, much later than in Tikopia. He is taken to the woods by his *tuatina* and the operation performed, while he shrieks with the pain. Then he is taken back to the house and the oven is kindled.

No operation is performed upon females in Tikopia. When I described to a group of men such operations as are performed among certain African tribes, they expressed disapproval : " It is not good," they said. On the other hand I was told that in former times in Tikopia an operation, perhaps clitoridectomy, did take place upon two women who died. This then put a stop to the practice of incision of females : " The female was cut and died ; but when the male was cut he lived, and so, observing that the female was dead, it was abandoned, and men only were operated upon." Personally, I doubt very much if this is a record of an actual occurrence : it belongs, I think, to the same category as a story of the cæsarian operation given to me, though there is no means of verifying this.

I did not see a ceremony of the *rau fafine* (female initiation), but from the accounts given me it would appear that the assembly of kin, the handling of food, the contribution and exchange of other goods proceed along practically the same lines as those to be described for a boy.

ORIGIN AND SANCTIONS OF THE CEREMONY

In Tikopia when a boy of rank is to be initiated a special effort is usually made to ward off fear from him by the invocation of spiritual assistance. He is taken to one of the chiefs, and this man, following a general form of ritual, pours oil into his hand, holds it out, and calls on his familiar, the spirit of his chiefly father. He says :

> Here ǀ Make firm the belly of your poverty-stricken finger-nail,
> Enter you to dwell in the heart of your poverty-stricken finger-nail.

He then rubs his oil-filled palm on the lad's breast in the region of the diaphragm, and according to the natives, the latter becomes filled with spiritual courage and his fright disappears. The term

[1] Gifford, *loc. cit.*

"poverty-stricken finger-nail" is one of pitying contempt used of themselves by men when speaking to gods to excite their sympathy. Kava is then made by the chief.

The reference to supernatural powers brings us to the consideration of the origin of the institution. It may be said at once that no evidence is available which throws any real light on this subject. Comparison with other areas of Polynesia as far afield as the Tuamotu group shows that there are decided affinities in practice ; but what are local features of parallel development, what are survivals of elements disappeared elsewhere, it seems impossible to say. Certainly, however, the institution appears to be of great antiquity in Tikopia, since its origination is attributed to one of the premier clan gods, that of Tafua. In days of old, it is said, he had the operation performed upon himself—but whether he carried it out personally, or induced another deity to do it for him, is not known.

The incident is commemorated in an ancient bawdy song of the type known as *feuku*, the special feature of which is the open mention of the sexual organs (see Chapter XIV). The song, given me by Pa Raŋifuri, runs :

> *Ka toku ure ka sesere*
> *Ka tau iŋoa mo te fofine toko*
>
> *Fai raŋiraŋi*
> *To ko te ua.*
>
> Now my penis will be cut
> There will be a linked name for the unmarried women
>
> Let there be a disturbance of the skies
> Let the rain fall.

The "linked name" is a synonym for the penis in its appropriate conjunction. The song thus lays down that the precedent to sexual intercourse is the operation of superincision.

The deity of Tafua is in control of rain, and the ceremony performed upon his sacred body, it is held, was of sufficient potency to disturb the skies and cause the rain to fall. The ceremony had *manu*, supernatural efficacy. This it still possesses since it is a repetition, a "following after," as the Tikopia say, of that invented by the god himself. Such imitation of his deeds gives him satisfaction. Of old, then, before Tafua became Christian, when the sun had shone for a long time and no rain had fallen, a rite would be performed upon a boy chosen for the purpose to "*sakiri manu*," to seek for power, that is, to induce the rain to fall. "Folk looked at the sun which had shone, thereupon they made speech to perform a superincision that the rain might fall." There was then a definite magical value in the ceremony.

When a boy of rank of the deity's own clan, Tafua, was superincised in former days, a ceremonial offering was made to the deity. This was known as the *epa*, a term applied to a small pandanus leaf mat used in ritual. When all the presents were being folded towards the end of the ceremony, a single mat was chosen, food of the special type known as the *roi* was made, and both were carried to Tafua, the clan temple. There the mat was laid out by the chief and libations of kava were poured to the gods. Later the *epa* was hung up in the sacred house and left there until another superincision ceremony. Then, probably rotten by this time, it was replaced by the new offering. The continuity of the gift had to be maintained. If a very long time passed without an incision being performed, and the old *epa* began to decay, it was carefully wrapped up lest it fall to pieces. There had always to be one such offering there as an acknowledgment to the god of the interest taken in this ritual of his. For sons of the chiefly family the *epa* was always brought, but in the case of commoners the father of the boy was allowed to use his own discretion. If he said, as he probably would, " When my son is done, the *epa* will be conveyed," then his wishes would be respected by the group of people responsible.

In native belief, then, the ceremonies of initiation are the continued reproduction of a model supplied in the dim past by a supernatural person, who, amid his other activities, is still proud enough of his creation to approve of its perpetuation and reward its perpetuators accordingly. The Tikopia hold that imitation, if not the most sincere, is certainly the most lucrative form of flattery. This ascription of initiation to a supernatural origin finds no highly developed expression in the ceremonies. There is no instruction of the initiates in the myth, as is common in Australia, and apart from the obscene song, which is sung in other contexts altogether, the only formalized token of the connection is the mat hung in the temple. There is not space here to follow out the significance of symbols, to explain how a rotting article of simple workmanship, a tenuous link at best, can anchor the ritual to its religious base. Nor can we discuss the role of group privilege and explain how it is that the offering of the symbol by one clan only is adequate to serve the whole community—even nowadays when the majority of that clan have formally adopted Christianity. It will have been noted that there is no developed tale of the origins of the initiation, simply a bare statement that it was performed by a certain person, with certain consequences. This suffices, however, to tie the ritual as at present performed in place in the complex scheme of Tikopia institutions. Normally this background of origins receives no attention from the participants on the stage ; only now and again is it given some scrutiny, particularly to see that the link remains intact.

If we search for the sanctions which lie behind the performance of the operation of superincision, we find first of all a deep respect for traditional procedure. This finds expression in the average man in a reliance upon precedent as a justification for his state, in a sensitiveness to public feeling, and a fear of ridicule. A social distinction between the initiated and the uninitiated males is drawn in theory and also fairly well in fact, the latter being debarred from participation in certain formal gatherings, and liable to embarrassment on informal occasions. Thus when the lad Katoarara was about to attend the dance in Marae, his father, anticipating possible criticism, said, " It is quite proper that he should go. His oven has been kindled," meaning that as an incised person he could participate with the adults freely. No such lad would ever be stopped, no matter how young. On the other hand, an uninitiated lad would probably be barred. If a group of youths are sitting on the beach and a small boy approaches, they say to him in irony, " Come ! Come, but what will you come for among the cut penes ? " and indulge in other jests at his expense. The older a boy gets the more acute does his position become in this respect ; he is always liable to be the subject of jokes so long as he remains uncised. A person on whom the operation has not been performed is said by a jesting metaphor to be *mata seŋi*, blind-eyed, and with this epithet he is apt to be taunted, openly by the boys of his own age, and covertly by the girls. If he passes by a group of these and hears their laughter directed at him, then he guesses the matter of their amusement and feels much ashamed.

The great reason that natives give for compliance with the custom is the *ruma*, the notoriety that is entailed by its omission. One cannot judge of the force of this directly as far as the adult males of the island are concerned, for every one of them has been superincised. But the Motlav mission teacher is said not to have had the operation performed upon him, and in consequence is the subject of sly remarks between the natives—in his absence. Children have actually said to his children in moments of anger, " Go and incise your father " ; the thought of such abuse being possibly applied to himself would be enough to upset the equilibrium of any Tikopia. The teacher's own son, it may be noted, was incised during my stay. My servant, Vahihaloa, coming from Luaŋiua, was not incised in any way, and this was a matter for much rough joking at the time of one ceremony, the men, amid great laughter, threatening to seize him and include him in the list. Examples of this attitude are not altogether wanting in the case of the Tikopia themselves, for largely on economic grounds some lads have to wait a long time before they go through the ceremony. If a father is lazy or poor, and careless of the reputation of his son, he may fail from season to season to make the necessary preparations for extra food supplies, and so the boy's immaturity drags on, a butt for the ridicule of others and an object of his own shame. Such was one of my own retainers, a lad past puberty, whose boon companions sometimes teased him. He was ashamed and mingled laughter and curses in reply to his tormentors. In sober moments it was agreed by responsible people that it was bad of the father not to make adequate provision for the boy's ritual, and in this case it was ascribed to laziness, though it was admitted that his cultivations and orchards were small. It is for this reason that the sons of a commoner are often incised at the same time as those of a man of rank; they are " stuck on " (*fakapikitia*) to the latter, as the natives say, so that some of the economic burden may be borne by the man of wealth. But if a commoner is an industrious fellow, he will for the sake of his own pride make the *puŋaumu* for his son himself.

INITIATION IN RELATION TO PUBERTY AND ECONOMICS

Consideration of the economic factor has shown that the ceremony is not performed at a fixed time in a boy's life. It is calculated to take place as a rule before puberty, and the majority of lads are incised some few years in advance of this time. It is difficult to give any precise data, but it is probably accurate enough to say that the operation is usually performed between the ages of nine and fourteen, the majority of the initiates being on the immature side, where there is no risk of ridicule.

While the ceremony bears some relation to the physiological maturity of the individual, it is not essentially bound to this. Its emphasis lies particularly on the change from one social state to another; it is not a puberty rite but a maturity rite. The conferring of social privilege rather than assisting at a specific time of organic development is the keynote of the institution. The physiological and psychological disturbances of puberty are left to look after themselves; they may come later or earlier, and in any case it is only their external manifestations that are noted for correlation, and then merely incidentally. We must distinguish clearly between any fundamental function which the institution of initiation may have in standardizing the situations of puberty, and the value assigned to it by the people themselves as index of a social rather than a biological change.

The lack of correlation of the initiation ceremony with puberty in Tikopia is emphasized further by the rarity of its performance for female children, in whom presumably the changes at this stage are at least as disturbing as in the males. The much greater frequency of initiation for males has to be correlated with the general position of the sexes in the social life; it is on a par with the tendency for the major items of ritual and the principal spheres of authority to be concentrated in the hands of the men. It is not possible to examine the basic sociological reasons for this sex dichotomy here, but the suggestion may be made that it is associated with the more passive role of women in child-bearing and nursing, which gives scope for and to some extent demands a male assertiveness.

The more general description at the end of this chapter indicates how the description of the initiation ceremony as a " transition rite " or *rite de passage* gives only a very partial idea of its importance and effects.

Most important in Tikopia initiation is the economic side of the proceedings. The actual operation occupies only about two minutes; the handling of food and valuables attendant upon it may take five days or more, and the preparation of them many months of work. Immediately after my arrival in Tikopia, the incision of Munakina, which was not due for over a fortnight, was mentioned to me, and I was told how the family of Pa Paŋisi were making bark-cloth, and how the chiefs were collecting food, mats, sinnet cord and bark-cloth to give as presents. My informants said that the pile of coconuts would be as big as my house, and their eyes dilated as they spoke of the quantities of food to be brought in. It was pointed out that the large scale of the preparations was on account of the rank of Nau Paŋisi, who was well connected among the Taumako clan.

Every social event of any interest in this community has its economic accompaniment, and in some cases it is difficult to decide which is the primary element, the ostensible act or its setting. The bulk of the initiation procedure consists in the accumulation of vast quantities of food and their dissipation, the presentation and the exchange of large numbers of pandanus leaf mats, pieces of bark-cloth and coils of sinnet cord. The occasion is one not so much for the display of wealth as its distribution, and the principle of reciprocity, ultimate or immediate, is the guide. The economic factor in a sense is the pivot of the ceremony, since it determines the time at which it shall be held, and its duration, and provides the material symbol of participation for those who attend. Moreover it is correct to say that the bulk of the interest is concentrated on the arrangement and appropriate passage of food and property. In an examination of essentials, however, it soon becomes clear that the economic exchanges are based almost wholly upon kinship relations and that here in fact is one of the primary elements in the situation.

Normally only kindred or neighbours attend a Tikopia initiation. The *kano a paito* of the initiate assembles and the members contribute in various ways by their services and their property. There is a formal separation between the group of the father of the lad, headed by his father or father's brother, and that of his mother headed by his senior mother's brother. The divisions are known as the *fare matua* and *fare tuatina* respectively, or more simply as *fai matua* and *fai tuatina*, "those who perform" these functions. Apart from them in the formal classification are the *fai soko*, the cooks, whose position has been explained in Chapter IX, and their children, the *tama tapu* of the *fai matua*. For practical purposes these last two sections are grouped together, since virtually the same families are affected by the transfer of the goods.

It will be noted how the bond between maternal uncles and sacred children is continually maintained. The initiate, as the centre of interest, is in the charge of his mother's kindred, but his father and other relatives on the paternal side have a duty to the children of women of their own house, since they themselves are distributing property. A *tama tapu* thus scores in both directions—on his own account as the pivot of the ceremony, and on account of ceremonies performed for people in his mother's brother's family.

FOOD GATHERING AND OTHER PREPARATIONS

Ceremonies of superincision are not very frequent in Tikopia. The last one which occurred before my arrival was about twelve months previously, and the one which was performed shortly before I left was being talked about ten months before it actually took place. For economy several lads are generally incised together, and this is a bond of interest between them for the rest of their lives. Grown-up men will mention casually, in talking of someone, "We had our ovens fired together."

I saw two such ceremonies in Tikopia; the first was that of Munakina, son of Pa Paŋisi, the mission teacher, and Seuku, son of Pa Fetu. This took place soon after my arrival. It was somewhat anomalous in form, since Pa Paŋisi had no relatives of his own there and consequently the *fai matua* of Munakina were drawn from the mother's relatives. The second was the initiation of two brothers of Nukuafua house, and Samako, a lad of Nukuone. This took place towards the end of my stay. The following account is primarily based on it, but reference to the first ceremony is given by way of confirmation or contrast. In both ceremonies Christians and heathens took part indiscriminately, as they normally do in affairs that are not overtly religious.

Mention of the anomalous form is necessary for two reasons. The field-worker often has a tendency to gloss over the fact that a ceremony is not performed according to the ideal arrangement; imperceptibly to himself he tries to stress the symmetry of the affair, to bring out those aspects of it which he regards as most typical, a dangerous habit in the event of later comparative work being done in the same area. Again, the shifts which the natives themselves resort to in order to meet anomalous circumstances are of sociological relevance, as showing the flexibility of the social structure, its weakness and strength.

The length of time occupied nowadays according to the native count is three days, which refers to the actual ceremonial; to this must be added at least one initial day for arrangements. Less than a generation ago an extra immediate day was the rule, making five in all. The specific enlargement of the ceremony sometimes adopted by wealthy men of rank for their sons may take up to eight days to complete. The natives themselves use days as a basis of calculation. Each section of the ceremony is alloted to one day, and speed in finishing any particular section does not prompt any alteration of the general programme.

The most important person at the initiation ceremony apart from the initiate himself is the *tuatina maori*, the true brother of the boy's mother. When there are several, then the eldest takes the chief position. He it is who directs the major activities of the ceremonies and in particular is entitled to invite the *tuatina* of less close relationship. They are known as *te kerekere*, literally "the dirty ones." No one not invited by him or by the mother of the boy will come. The clear distinction drawn between the *tuatina maori* (or, as he is called, the *matua tuatina*, the senior mother's brother) and the *tuatina fakatafatafa* illustrates once again how within the classificatory relationship the individual specification is made on personal grounds. The natives themselves carefully explain the difference to a stranger. There is a very definite distinction too in actual behaviour. The *tuatina maori* issues the invitation, is recognized as the head of the ceremony, and appeal is made to him for decision on disputed points. In the distribution of gifts he receives the most important. He may or may not support the boy during the operation—it lies at his choice, but no distant *tuatina* will do so without permission. " He does not rush foolishly, he goes and listens to the senior *tuatina* to speak. This man may say, ' You go and nurse in your arms our nephew ; I am going to sit among the *kerekere*.' " For such support the distant relative will receive a large gift, but in no case is the *tuatina maori* neglected ; he will still receive the lion's share or at least one equal to that of the principal performers.

Some time before the event is to occur it is made known to the relatives concerned that they may hold themselves in readiness, and also have the requisite food materials, pandanus mats and the like available. For a day or two before—three days in the case of Munakina—the village in the early morning is set ringing with the steady beat of wooden pounder on slab as the women of the households prepare the bark-cloth for the girdles and blankets which play such an important part as gifts. The house where the major portion of the ceremonial takes place is got ready, and if a large crowd is expected, provision is made for the overflow. For Munakina such a vast number of relatives was expected to attend that the father threw two houses into one by removing end walls and bridging the gap with an extension roof (*v.* Plate X). The making of the thatch for this was a special task which does not normally come within the scope of the ceremonial arrangements. New floor-mats had to be plaited from coconut fronds to replace those which were old and dirty. This occupied mother and daughters for three days.

Such domestic preparations cause a stir in the immediate neighbourhood of the household of the initiate, but other families are also affected through their kinship ties. At various times during the few days preceding the ceremony the lad who is to be the object of it is invited by relatives to go to their dwellings. There, after being given food to eat, he is smeared on breast, neck, shoulders, and sides of the face and perhaps upper arms also, with the brilliant vermilion pigment of turmeric and coconut oil, which glistens like fresh blood on the skin. This was done to Munakina four days before the actual rite of incision. At the same time he is invested with a new waist garment of bark-cloth. This little action is done by the female relatives of some of the men who will take a leading part in the ceremony itself, and is in effect a mark of honour paid to the boy. The ordinary reason given is that it is done from *arofa*, affection, in view of the coming trial which he is to undergo. It is a spontaneous gesture, done without any solicitation on the part of the parents, though they know that some one of the kindred is fairly sure to do it. The investiture with the new waist-cloth and the daubing on of the red odoriferous pigment has of course the effect of singling the lad out for public attention, and he becomes for the next few days an object of considerable interest to the small children of the village and a marked individual among his playmates. The ceremony itself, the one great event of a boy's life, is also enhanced in importance thereby. It is not *tapu* to speak of it to him in advance.

The general group of kin is also affected in another way. Affairs of moment in the life of a person, particularly if a suspicion of danger be attached to them, are signalized by the chanting of formal songs of the *fuataŋa* type. His kindred thus display their sympathy. It is customary before an superincision ceremony to practise a number of songs so as to avoid confusion on the occasion. Some of these are old songs specially selected, others are newly composed by relatives who are gifted in this way and wish to express their affection for their child. The aim of the practice is to render the singers as near word perfect as possible ; the air presents no difficulties, being of a well-known type. Examples of *fuataŋa* have been given in Chapter VIII ; some of those sung at initiation are set down in their context later. Song practice usually takes place in a house in the evening or on a wet afternoon. For Munakina the song practice was conducted at various times by Fakasiŋetevasa, Pa Niukaso and Pa Tekaumata, his *tuatina*, who were among the composers.

I spent one evening lying down in the house listening. Seven men were actually singing, while the rest of the household listened or slept. The composer repeated the words of each stanza of his song twice and then they were sung. Fakasiŋetevasa lay down on the broad of his back and sang, resting on the legs of a friend. The latter occasionally chimed in with a falsetto rendering, correctly harmonized. Sometimes a woman sang a few phrases too, but otherwise it was left to the men. The interior of the house was dark, except for the light from a small fire which shone on the bare bodies of the men squatting in a rough circle, and picking out their manes of tawny hair and a necklet of white frangipanni flowers worn by one of them.

The greater part of the energies of the kinsfolk, however, is now directed to the collection of food for the ceremony. This may occupy several days, the amount of time spent depending on the number of people expected, the labour available, and the situation of the orchards or gardens. Taro and yams are dug, green coconuts and breadfruit plucked, bunches of bananas cut, and the whole piled in an immense wall of food outside the eaves of the house of the boy's father, or the building which is the focus of the ritual. Mature dry coconuts are taken out of store and slung in pairs or quadrupled on tall branched stakes nearby, while sprouting nuts are lashed together in bundles. Coconuts in profusion are necessary to give that touch of delicacy and distinction to the mundane solidity of the tubers and breadfruit. And on the day before the ceremonies begin in earnest, the menfolk of the family, aided by fellow-villagers or visiting kin, take out a large seine net and drag the reef for a mile or so in the hope of securing some fish as a *bonne bouche*. Their wives and other female relatives go out with their scoop nets in the usual way when the tide is low. The mass of food thus accumulated is known as the *aŋa*, a term which is applied to all such piles, whether for initiation, marriage, or a chief's feast. One glance at it is enough to tell why the natives lay such stress on the economic factor as the final determinant of the time when a boy shall be initiated. Taro, as always, is the mainstay of the supplies. By no means all of it, however, comes from the father's own cultivations ; even though he be a very wealthy man he cannot support the strain unaided. Various kinsfolk help him in this with contributions from their own resources, even when as maternal relatives of the boy they will be later in the position of recipients of food and gifts from him. At the time of the initiation of Samako, one of his mother's brothers, Taitaimata, had a patch of taro planted in the ground of the Tafua family. He said to his brothers, " Let us go and make a *fiuri* for ourselves for the firing of the oven," i.e. to carry a food contribution to the ceremony, which they did. The attitude taken up is quite consistent from the native point of view. It is argued that the father of the boy has heavy obligations to meet, and that therefore it is the duty of his brothers-in-law to assist him. That these same men as the mother's brothers of the initiate receive food presents from the father which may well include some of the substance of their own gifts is not recognized as a conflicting factor. Each obligation is treated on its own merits. This represents an appreciation of a kinship tie *per se* as distinct from the net effect of the economic transactions entailed by it, and undoubtedly tends to strengthen the links of community interest.

The collection of the great pile of food is described in the words *te aŋa e tokonaki*. It involves the labour of a considerable number of people in co-operation. I paid a visit to a field of taro when the work for the ceremony of Munakina was being done. The ground belonged to the Ariki Taumako but had been planted by Pa Paŋisi. He had said, " Pa Taumako, I want to plant this land with taro for the initiation of your nephew." To this the chief agreed. The taro was planted in January and dug in the following August. This account describes the scene as I noted it at the time.

Men, women and children are assembled together, each taking some share, however small, in the task. Some of the men dig with pointed sticks, levering the taro roots out of the ground, from the surface of which other hands have already cleared away the encumbering weeds. Children gather up the plants as they are thrown out and carry them off to be got ready. Some are treated by stripping off the dead leaves at the base of the stem, scraping the tuber with a knife or rubbing off the dirt and rootlets with the fingers, and then cutting off the top leaves and tying them up in bundles. From others the tops are saved for planting by cutting them off at the base of the stem, and the tubers are then put into baskets roughly plaited on the spot from fresh fronds of coconut. These are lined with *karapusi* or other large leaves gathered from the border of the field. The folk assemble on the scene early, thereby avoiding the heat of the day, and by the time that the sun is fairly up over the top of the mountain, under the shadow of which the field lies, there are fifty-five people assembled. By this time, after three hours of daylight, the digging is nearly done, and the major part of the work consists in the cleansing of the tubers, packing them in the baskets as these are prepared, and carrying them off home. The women bear their loads with straps on the back, the men by a pole on the shoulder. The work in the field is by no means treated as drudgery ; there is frequent discussion of the quantities of taro and details of organization by the boy's father and mother's immediate relatives, who have to take matters seriously, but the whole scene is animated by talking and laughing, by the frequent wanderings of people from one group to another, and the actual labour is interspersed by halts for the chewing of betel. A few very young children are not pressed into service and their play further enlivens the gathering.

The scene is by no means devoid of the picturesque. The field is part of a general cultivation in the small open plain of Rakisu, hemmed in on three sides by orchards, with the feathery palm fronds and fingered leaves of breadfruit against the sky and a thick growth of hibiscus and other bushes beneath as a wall against intrusion. On the fourth side rises the steep slope of the mountain with scattered gardens and orchards hanging on to its side till they disappear over the crest. In the field itself the down-drooping velvet-surfaced leaves of the taro form a level sea of foliage, through which people go on hidden paths as if wading, their brown bodies striking a pleasing note of contrast to the general dark green. A few hundred yards away from the scene of activity one can drink in the peace of the morning—the apparent variety of colour tone in the leaves as the sunlight strikes the infinity of facets they offer to the observer, the calm of foliage unstirred by a breath of wind, the continuous murmur, rising only occasionally to a low roar, of the distant surf breaking on the reef. It is a contrast to the busy life of the human group so near at hand. On approach one is plunged into a turmoil of chatter and shrill laughter, of crude jokes bandied to and fro, of the vigorous activity of restless bodies, earth-stained limbs, and tossing manes of bronzed hair. The sweat of work, nails filled with grime, soiled garments and the crimson saliva spat out from betel-chewing arouse for the moment a repulsion against this defilement. But the mood of detachment soon passes, one remembers that in this island the works of nature and of man merge easily, and in a flash one is caught up again into the details of organization of a task which for the natives themselves is the cardinal interest of the day.

After the return of the working party from the fields some of the household set to and prepare the oven, since it is their obligation to feed their assistants. This hospitality is described as *te umu tapa manava faoa faifekau*, "the belly-filling oven of the working crowd." The number of people to be fed may be so great that the oven has to be divided, so the natives say, that is, the cooking of the food is split up among several different houses. The giving of help at such a time by placing one's oven and one's labour at disposal is one of the services which neighbours usually render each other. At the initiation of Samako and the brothers in Nukuafua the oven had to be divided into four, so large was the crowd assembled for the collection of the *aŋa*.

THE DAY OF THE OPERATION

The day following that on which the bulk of the food is gathered is the crucial point of the ceremony as far as the initiate is concerned, for then occurs the physical operation which is the ostensible basis of the whole affair.

In the early morning wailing begins near the lad's house, a token of conventional feeling for him who has to suffer pain this day and from whom blood will flow. The songs are *fuataŋa* of the child and of the voyage ; dirges for the dead are not chanted. The songs are interspersed by long drawn-out howls of a high pitch—the *aue* of sympathy, affection and mourning which, whatever be the real emotions of the person wailing, sound like the cries of a being in misery and utter despair. The wailing is done in sections by the people who attend. Sa Raveŋa, sa Namo and other groups each take up a dirge as another group finishes, so that there is a continuous stream of chanting. Sometimes the sound drops to a low drone, sometimes it rises to a full-throated roar, and every now and again comes the vibrating cadence of the *aue*. When the wailing for Munakina was in progress one old man of Raveŋa began by being apparently broken by sobs ; tears were streaming down his cheeks, his head had sunk on his arms which were resting on his knees, and in a choked voice he raised the opening words of a song, which was then taken up by stronger-throated members of his party. Other people in the house remained quite unmoved. A few were quietly plaiting sinnet cord ; the mother of the boy was chewing betel, and the father was busy calculating his prospective outlay in mats and bark-cloth, counting on his fingers and talking in low tones to one of his helpers. Interspersed between songs came cries from various kinsfolk, " *Aue toku iramutu* ! " " Alas ! my nephew ! " and similar phrases. Some women cut themselves on the forehead with knives and tore the corners of their mouths so that the blood trickled down. The section of Sa Faea came to wail in a body after they had prepared food for the oven. About a dozen men were pressed close together, leaning on one another and sobbing, almost bellowing the words of their dirge, tearing at their cheeks with gouging finger-nails. Tears streamed from their eyes and mucus from their noses, which was removed at the end of the song with their waist-cloth flaps. They beat their breasts with thumps of the clenched fist, deliberate blows which thudded through the house. On the outskirts crouched the women with bowed heads, taking their share in diminished fashion in the general frenzy. Near by people were talking in low tones, smiling at one another, smoking or chewing betel. Once the wailing of a section is finished its members regain composure almost at once. This reinforces one's feeling that the formal aspect of the mourning is much stronger than the emotional—particularly nowadays when the substitution of razor blades for shell has facilitated the operation and presumably lessened the risk of serious injury.

Here are three of the dirges composed and sung on this occasion. The first is the work of Seremata, and purports to be a lament for someone who has left on a voyage.

I would be busy then with the voyage
I would leap aboard to be borne aloft,
For my namesake is carried on the journey

Fetch then to the sea your canoe
Fetch with it the paddle while I sit
To weep wildly at the trail of foam

> I weep for my necklet
> Who has leapt aboard the vessel
> For us two the mutual sight
> On that day alone.

The " necklet " is of course his dear friend, and signifies here the
lad about to undergo the initiation rite.

Another song is a composition of Fakasiŋetevasa in honour of
the boy's father, lauding his generosity in the distribution of goods.

> Friend ! borne over the land, friend !
> The father of the Tikopia
>
> Your wealth of goods has been distributed to Raveŋa
> It has entered into Namo on the lake-shore
>
> It is scattered around, friend, and stands in the west
> Till it strikes the lowlands of Faea
>
> We shall go and eat of your meals from the vessel
> The praiseworthy man, how we gather around him.

The last of the trio is a song made by Pa Tekaumata on the
same theme. In it he mentions his relationship of classificatory
grandparent to Munakina.

> I go to my grandchild and to Father here
> Lo ! the completeness of your wealth on which we feast
>
> Your *house* standing there has been broken
> For the Tikopia are *plenty*
>
> O, my Father, entering from Namo
> My friend the softest of men dwells here
>
> It was his wish also that I should enter Taone
> To my niece and my grandchildren.

The words marked were rendered by the composer in English—
or his adaption thereof, *ausi* and *pelenti*—as a demonstration of his
knowledge, which comprises perhaps fifty words in all, learnt from
other Tikopia who had been abroad. The large scale on which this
ceremony was carried out elicited a number of comments of an admiring
and sympathetic kind towards the father of Munakina.

In the early part of the morning various female relatives of the lad
smear him with turmeric and provide him with a new waist-cloth as
before. Munakina, for instance, was thus furnished by his *nana*,
Nau Nukunefu ; after he had retired behind a tree to put on the

garment she took up the old one and tied it round her neck. By about half-past eight in the morning he had already changed his waist-cloth three times in this way.

Great activity is displayed in the preparation of food, which proceeds around the cook-house at the same time as the wailing goes on inside and around the dwelling-house. For the ceremony of Munakina the cook-house underwent alteration, the sides being bodily lifted up and supported by new beams about six feet above the ground. The hut was thus converted from an ordinary low gable-roof to an almost flat-roofed shelter with room to walk underneath. All through the early hours of the morning there was a continual train of people bringing provisions. In half an hour I saw three men each with a pole on which hung a dozen sprouting coconuts, five women from Raveŋa with back-loads of taro, a man with a large bunch of bananas followed by two others similarly burdened, and then nineteen people from Raveŋa with various kinds of food. These last halted just before they debouched on to the open space at Putafe and formed up in single file to give a touch of formality to their entrance. Then came six women from Rofaea with back-loads of bananas and taro and about a dozen people from Namo, two with large pole-loads of dry coconuts, two with large bunches of bananas, one with a mass of *pulaka*, and others with various types of food. By the side of the dwelling-house there finally stretched a long wall of baskets of taro, five deep, comprising about two hundred in all, with about thirty baskets of yams, a dozen bunches of bananas, and much *pulaka*. Around several poles were strung huge clusters of coconuts in a solid mass about seven or eight feet high (*v.* Plate X). A diagram of the same is given in Plan V.

The grating of taro, the kneading of *masi*, the peeling of bananas goes on apace, and after some time a succession of whoops from the taro scrapers announces that 100 packets of grated taro have been prepared. A little while afterwards the oven which has been burning is violently attacked by a dozen or so people, some with long sticks raking out the flaming wood and spreading the stones, others holding shields of branches of thick green leaves to protect them from the heat and the glare. At their first uncovering the stones are red hot. The food is put in and the oven covered, orders flying briskly to and fro between the crowd. In charge of the oven is Pa Nukunefu, his elder brother Pa Raŋifuri being present, but not very active on account of his recent emergence from mourning. But the premier gift to the cooks goes to him just the same. Everyone outside the house has now a rest from work. Inside the continuous wailing goes on, changing in pitch as newcomers take up the song. This oven made

UNDER THE KNIFE

Fakasinetevasa is operating on a boy of Nukuafua, whose anxious look is clear. At the side a woman bows her head.

AROUND THE OVEN

People are taking out the cooked food, wrapping it up in leaves and stowing it in baskets for carriage to the homes of kinfolk.

at the house of the boy's parents is called the *umu pariki* or *umu furuŋa kere*, that is, it is associated with the operation. It is designed to feed the *fai tuatina*.

The second oven later in the day is termed *te umu fora o a koroa,* " the oven for the spreading of valuables."

Meanwhile the *umu fai tuatina* is being prepared by the mother's brothers of the boy. It is made either at the house of the principal

PLAN V

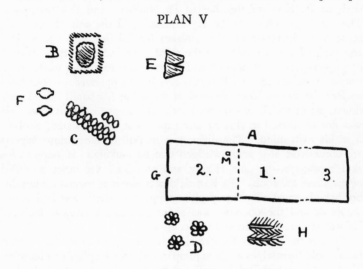

SCENE OF AN INITIATION CEREMONY

A . . . house	G . . . main doorway
B . . . oven-house	H . . . scene of operation
C . . . food accumulated	M . . . mother of initiate
D . . . coconuts on poles	1. . . . people of Faea
E . . . women preparing food	2. . . . people of Raveŋa
F . . . men grating taro	3. . . . people of Namo

tuatina or at the place designated by him. When it is ready the initiate is invited, fed, and carried from there by his mother's brothers to the scene of the operation. With him is taken a basket of food for the *fai matua*.

For the initiation of Samako, Pa Niukapu, the leader of the *fai tuatina,* instructs the oven to be made in Apotau, an orchard of his in Rofaea about half a mile from the lad's house. Thither some of the *tuatina* go while others remain at the house of the parents to assist as cooks (*soko*). The food to be made at Apotau is *sua*, sago pudding made with hot stones. This food is selected because it can be made so quickly. One of the men says, "to-morrow is the day of food, to-day is the day of the ceremony; let us make it quickly." Vaitere, son of Pa Niukapu, is sent as messenger from the *tuatina* to invite the boys to come. After some time they walk in covered with turmeric and conspicuous in their new waist-cloths. In the interval the *tuatina* have been discussing various aspects of the ceremony. They decide who is to operate on each lad. It is arranged that the operators shall be Pa Koroatu, brother of Pa Niukapu, and Fakasiŋetevasa. There are three boys to be superincised, and the pair of operators settle that whichever of them finishes his lad first will "jump in" and perform the operation on the third. The advisability is stressed of gripping the boys rapidly, and many observations are made about points of technique. Pa Koroatu says he has operated on four boys so far; he has his own method of steadying his hands; he kneels down, places his elbows on his knees, and keeps his hands low. He was not instructed in this by any expert but, so he stated, evolved it in his own mind. The differences in skill of the various experts are canvassed; it is acknowledged that Pa Nukutauo is alone in his skill nowadays—he cuts cleanly and at once. Of other so-called *tufuŋa* some are fools. Pa Raŋiriaki was about to operate when his brother observed that the *afa*, the supporting stick, was laid under the penis and the operator was about to make a circular incision. He was at once grabbed and thrust aside.

Such is the habit of the occasion, it was explained to me. Other *tuatina* hold themselves ready to jump in and take the place of a bungler. If a man is not skilled he will cut his fingers and wound the lad. Hardly any expert, it appears, is free from nervousness; his hand shakes, since he is timorous "at cutting the body of man." Of olden days it was *tapu* for the *tuatina maori* to touch the lad. He sat in the house and did not go out; the expert had to be a distant mother's brother. Formerly when there were no razors, there was more demand for skilled performers and more care was taken to seek experts.

Some enquiry and comment is made also between the *tuatina* about the attendance of people at the ceremony. Pa Koroatu asks if no one from Roŋoifo has come. He is told no. "Why not?" he asks. "Sa Nukuone went to their marriage feast." Feeling is strong that attendance at any important ceremony of one social group demands reciprocity. The *fai tuatina* discuss also whether they shall go and wail first before attending to the boys. The motion is rejected. "What?" says someone, "a death, is it?" After the boys arrive they are advised how to act and are then heartened up by being told that they will not feel the operation. Finally they are ordered:

" go to your mothers, go and change." This is a command to go and be invested with still other new waist-cloths by their uncles' wives.

After being fed the boys are carried on the backs of their *tuatina* from Apotau to Nukuafua, accompanied by the women and the inevitable group of inquisitive children. When they arrive at the house of the parents they are set down and the *tuatina* squat outside the house on the *mata paito* side. This is the special distinguishing mark of persons in the relationship of mother's kin, the official sign which separates them from the father's kin on this occasion. There are of course borderline cases. These are decided ultimately by the mother of the initiate. If she sees one of her *kave* sitting in the house she says, " Tell that one to go outside," that is, to join the other *tuatina*. This is a mark of honour and not of disgrace ; it is a compliment and carries also some economic benefit. The ostensible reason given for the action of the mother is her desire that the crowd around the child at the time of the operation should be thick, that the child should be well supported. If she does not see a solid group around her boy she thinks that her child may have been left to lie on the ground. This in a community where personal bodily support in time of stress is regarded as so important would of course be disgraceful. Actually there is never any danger of such lack of attention. Father's sisters rank as fathers at this time and are part of the *fai matua*. *Nana taka*, sisters of the mother, go outside the house with the *fai tuatina*. Later they go and sleep at the feet of the boy, a ritual act which is *tapu* to his father's sisters. It is *tapu* for sisters of the boy to go outside.

Immediately the boys enter the house a general wailing begins, not in the form of a song, but in long drawn-out sounds of *aue*. The lads are seated on fine mats inside the door. String after string of beads is put on them by their female relatives and their father, and perhaps a bonito hook, a valued ornament. They are also dressed in still other new wide waist-cloths by female relatives—all of whom are married or old ; the young unmarried are outside. When the boys have been re-clad a mourning song is raised in which the father takes a principal part. He may also press his nose to that of each lad.

The lads are now carried out for the operation. They are seized by *tuatina* and taken this time in the man's arms. For the moment there is general confusion, from which the rising wail of the dirge breaks out with renewed force. Outside there is a rush of children to see what is happening, and a hurly-burly in which orders are shouted back and forth and people swirl around the immediate performers, who have to push their way through the crowd. At both the ceremonies I witnessed I was left to fend for myself at this moment, and had great difficulty in making observations and taking photographs. The press of men, usually so ready to make way, ignored me in the concentration of their interest on the lads (*v.* Plates XI). Some coconut leaves are laid down and on them sit *tuatina*, one to each initiate, to hold the boy in his arms. These are the *taŋata me*, " the men on whom the boys sleep," and they are important. The operation is then performed as described. In every case I observed that the hand of the operator was trembling, and it was quite evident that there was considerable emotional stress in the men immediately concerned. At the moment the cut is made the man who is supporting the boy covers the lad's eyes with his hand.

All the boys that I saw bore the operation well; they quite clearly blanched a little just after the cutting, but did not show any great signs of pain or weakness. Sometimes, it is stated, they are in a fainting condition afterwards—they wilt and want to sleep, but from this they are roused by their relatives. This condition is known as *fakavao*. Crying of the boy during the operation is bad. It makes the *fai matua* ashamed and the father of the boy angry. If he suspects that it is not fear but injury that prompts the sound, or if he hears from the talk outside that the boy has been badly handled, he grabs up a club or any other weapon nearest to hand and rushes out to strike the *tuatina*. In the cases I observed, however, none of the boys made a sound.

While the operation is being performed the women outside sit with bowed heads, not looking at the scene, but crying gently. As soon as it is over and the wound is bandaged the boy is made to stand, the waist-cloth he is wearing is removed once again, and he dons a new one. In this he is assisted by the mother's sisters (*nana taka*) and by the wives of his mother's brothers (*tuatina*) who have brought the fresh garment. The beads and bonito hook hung on the boy by his father are dropped from his neck and arms—these go to the close *tuatina*. He presses noses with his *tuatina* and *nana* and is then carried or led back into the house while a mourning song is raised again. One might think it would now be a song of rejoicing, but this is not so; its mood is governed by the wound that has been inflicted. Inside, after a few moments, the lad is girdled with a fresh length of bark-cloth or calico; this time it is put around his waist without the removal of the one he wears. This ceaseless changing of garments has the object of allowing his female relatives to show their affection for the initiate by wearing around their necks the garments they

remove. In effect also an interchange of bark-cloth takes place
thereby on a wide scale. The incision of Munakina took place over
a sheet of bark-cloth, and when it was done the sheet was not thrown
away but taken by an " unmarried mother " of his and hung round
her neck. When he has been re-clad the boy goes first to his father
and they press noses, and then goes from one relative to another
around the house, doing the same. As he greets each person that
one ceases his mourning song.

Outside there is peace. When the operation was over Pa Niukapu said, " Our work is good, let us sit and chew betel first." So
they sat and chewed betel with a satisfied air before rising to enter
again into the round of ceremonies. There is a definite release of
tension at this point.

The first act in the series of economic transactions now takes
place. Immediately the boys enter the house coils of sinnet cord
and paddles are pushed out from beneath the eaves to the *tuatina*.
Food from the oven of the morning is brought up too and laid outside for them. In this case Pa Niukapu and others protested and
ordered a portion to be divided off for the parents of the boys. The
paddles and sinnet cord are apportioned by the principal mother's
brother—Pa Niukapu in this case. He takes the coils of cord, about
twenty in number, with a paddle, a cylinder of turmeric, and some
fish-hooks. To the more important relatives he offers a choice ; to
the more distant he hands out a particular item. He insists that each
person shall go away with his or her sinnet cord. Women are
frustrated in their efforts to hand over to others coils they have been
given. " Each of you speak for a coil of sinnet for herself," said
Nau Niukapu to the women near her. It is intended that each
person of the *fai tuatina* shall receive a gift. He or she goes home,
observes it closely, and next day returns with a coil of identical type
which is handed in to the father of the boy as a return gift. In
each case the binding cord of the coil is different—fish-line, hibiscus,
a strip of *rau fara, raupurou, siri futi*, a piece of net or a hank of grass.
This enables the authorship of each coil to be known and reciprocity
to be made exact by the boy's father, through whose hands the property passes. The sinnet and paddles are the only goods reciprocated.
Fish-hooks are given free. At the initiation of Munakina, Seremata,
at the instance of the father, the mission teacher, proceeded to give
out two fish-hooks to each person of the general crowd who had
witnessed the ceremony outside. This was liberality to gain a reputation. Sometimes a man will refuse to go outside in order not
to increase the liability of the father ; those who stay inside get no
presents. So Raŋiata told me that when requested by Pa Paŋisi to

join the *fai tuatina*, he did not do so. " This man," he said, " had to
give away plenty of things already."

After partaking of a little food the boy is taken away by the
tuatina who performed the operation, into the woods or down by
the sea, and instructed how to care for his wound. Leaves of the
kamika plant are rubbed in the hands till the juice comes and this is
then allowed to drop upon the cut ; the *tuatina* shows the lad how to
do this, and how to tie up his penis. The lad dresses the cut himself
afterwards for about a month till it is healed—though I was told by
one man that the bandage is taken off in about five days. He is told
not to go and play in the interval, and is usually too sore to do so
for some time.

"SPREADING THE PROPERTY"

The most important event of the day, from the economic point
of view, is the presentation of mats and bark-cloth, which is known
as the *foraŋā koroa*, " spreading of the property." Each family which
attends the ceremony brings its present, which is then unfolded in
the middle of the house, with an announcement in the name of the
donor. First of all the mats of pandanus are handed in, the recipient
being a man who sits in the centre of the house, spreads them and
calls out the name in which each is donated. Usually he has an
assistant to help him in dealing with them and to prompt him with
the names. The father of the boy does not take this position of
master of ceremonies ; it is assigned to a close relative. The announcement is made with a flourish and in a loud voice. " *Ia !* the mat of
Nau Resiake ! " etc., the mats being given in the name of women.
From all sides they come in, and are spread in a rapidly growing pile
on the floor. Mats from *tama tapu* of the house are laid crosswise on
the pile, thus enabling them to be distinguished from those of the
fai matua ; it is a point of etiquette that in the redistribution such
special mats should not be returned to their donors.

All eyes are directed on the heap, and people listen to the recital
of the list of donors, amid casual conversation and discussion of betel.
Not much comment is passed on the great diversity of mats, but
occasionally a whispered observation is made on a poor specimen,
or on one left unfinished. This last sometimes occurs, since a mat
takes several months to plait, and other calls may have depleted the
family stock. The wealth of chiefly families is shown, *inter alia*, by
their large stocks of mats. One woman remarked, looking at the
pile, " The backs of the women are aching with the plaiting." She
also remarked to me later that the householders usually kept an eye

on the gifts because some women were apt to sneak a piece of bark-cloth during the night.

When the donations are finished the pile is counted carefully ; the announcer at the initiation of Munakina tallied his count by notching with his thumb the bark of the post by which he was sitting. The initial number of mats was forty-one on this occasion ; there were as always some late-comers in addition.

Then comes the handing in and unfolding of bark-cloth blankets, *mami*. These are donated in the names of men, though the women of the family do most of the work of manufacture. They are announced as before, and counted at the end. At the ceremony for Munakina there were fifty-two pieces at the initial count, and eighty at that of Samako and his fellows. After the first few pieces have been laid on the pile of mats, the initiates are ordered to go and lie down there. With smiles they do so, and are then covered by the other pieces ; they take it as rather a joke and peep out from the side. The men who are spreading out the cloths take no notice of them, but keep piling the gifts on top. This is the formal " putting of the boys to sleep," as in the case of a woman who has given birth, a ceremonial invalidism to stimulate recovery.

The bark-cloths are announced thus: *"Ia! fakakafu Pu Faŋarere,"* " Here ! blanket of Pu Faŋarere," etc. After a time the announcers get tired of proclaiming each gift in the name of a particular individual. " Father and mother of Totiare ; names of houses ; the separate naming is finished," called Pa Niukapu when officiating at the ceremony of Nukuone (Text S. 7). It is the custom when several pieces of cloth are presented from a single family, as is quite usual, to have them announced under the names of different children, so associating them individually with the affair. This of course takes time, hence the brevity of Pa Niukapu towards the end of the afternoon. " Blanket of brothers of Rarotoŋa," " Blanket of house of Koroatu all together," and so on.

By this time most of the *fai tuatina* have gone home with their portions of food, and their sinnet ; only the immediate mother's brothers remain to help in the ceremonial. An hour or two before evening food is brought in from the " oven of the spreading of property," kindled immediately after the operation was performed, and all those in the house eat. The boys have to remain under their coverings during the meal, but are allowed to emerge soon afterwards and to take food.

From each family represented at the ceremony gifts should be made and announced. On the occasion mentioned Pa Raŋifuri went to Rofaea with a pandanus mat and some bark-cloth to contribute to

the pile.   They were handed in by his daughter Aumamata to another
woman in the house.   When the presents were unfolded, through
some mistake they were not announced under his name.   He listened
but there was no mention of a mat from his house.   A couple of
blankets were called out as being his, but actually these were contributed by Pa Niukapu who put his brother-in-law's name to them
because he did not hear that name announced.   The next day Pa
Raŋifuri gave another set of presents to his daughter to take in order
that his name might be properly announced.   There was no mistake
the second time !   This little incident illustrates how, in the case of
a man of rank, the contributions sent on a public occasion have as
part of their function the maintenance of his position.

MODERN CHANGES IN PROGRAMME

Formerly the ceremonies of superincision occupied four days.
The programme was as follows :

> First day—*Kaukau ŋa taŋata*, Incising the boys.
> Second day—*Foraŋa koroa*, Spreading the property.
> Third day—*Umu lasi*, The great oven.
> Fourth day—*Fetuŋa koroa*, Folding the property.

A few years after the coming of Christianity the ritual of the
second day was combined with that of the first, so that, as described
above, the mats and bark-cloth are laid out soon after the incision of
the lads.   There was no special reason for the change beyond the
fact that the mission teachers expressed the wish that some of the ceremony should be omitted.   It was not a question of conflict of religious
belief ; there were no *atua* involved.   The alteration was started by
the leaders of the missionary party saying that they would make the
ceremony for their sons in one day only, having the operation performed and all the gifts completed.   Their object seems to have been
simply to emphasize the difference between their converted state and
that of the majority of the people.   Actually it was two or three
mission teachers alone who desired the change.   A number of in-
fluential Christians, among them Pa Raŋifuri, regarded the proposal
with distaste.   They objected, their principal point being that it was
bad to spread out the mats and then take them away without letting
the boys sleep on them for a night.   It was said to me, " What !
Shan't the boy sleep on the mats ?   To put him to sleep and then
to snatch them away at once again—no !   It is bad ! "   This and
similar remarks were made to me during the initiation in Rofaea,

when Christians and heathen sitting together all expressed their disapproval of this unwarranted compression of an important set of ceremonies, innocuous even by Christian principle. The mats and other property are regarded as " the sign of the kindling of the boy's oven," " marks of distinction of the boy." The gist of the native argument is that since these things have been brought to do him honour, the boy must sleep on them as an acknowledgment. If removed immediately they do not fulfil their ostensible purpose of providing a bed for him, and in addition it is really a slight on the folk who have taken the trouble to prepare for the ceremony, to attend, and to make the presents. The people assembled in the house spoke quite strongly about this attempt to rob them of a great part of one of their most characteristic ceremonies. There were no mission teachers in the building at the time.

A compromise was finally reached on three days, which is the present length of the affair. The non-Christian folk of Raveŋa have also now adopted the three-day programme : " they have taken the one path," it was explained. The close kinship connection between people of the two districts probably has made conformity advisable. In contrast to the undiscriminating condemnation of a harmless set of practices by the mission teachers in order to show their superiority, there stands out the tolerant attitude of the heathen, with their conciliatory yielding to Christian prejudice.

" THE GREAT OVEN "

The boys sleep on their unwonted bed through the night with a group of relatives lying at their feet. In the early morning they go out to make their toilet, return and again lie down and are covered over. They remain there, asleep or awake, while the people in the house talk and the oven is made outside. This is the day of food, and the time of the participants in the ceremony is divided between energetic work around the oven and long periods of sitting in the house while the food cooks. Now is the time when domestic occupations are followed and when conversation is desired. All the men indoors are engaged in rolling coconut fibre, in plaiting sinnet cord, or in net-making. From time to time conversation lapses and then there are calls for someone to start a discussion or to begin a story. " To sit in silence is bad," the people say. It gives an unsociable feeling, and unsociability is one of the cardinal sins of Tikopia society. For those who have gathered together betel materials are provided by the householder. Long narratives of fishing, or sea-voyaging, and traditional tales of gods and men are told on such occasions. A visitor is very welcome because he brings news of what is happening elsewhere in the island.

The first food of the day is known as *Te Afi*, " The Fire." This is simply a few clusters of green bananas and several yams roasted at the fire and brought in in a basket as a snack for the resident *kano a paito*. The boys are wakened to partake of this. Sometimes the other people refuse, preferring to wait. Three ovens are made on this day. The first is the *umu ararafaŋa*, " the oven of waking," which is made in the morning and uncovered about midday. The first product of this is called *a loŋi o a tama*, " kits of the boys." It consists of a good *fakapuke* pudding, and despite its name is really a basket (*popora*) with two large packages of food. It is brought in on the *tuaumu* side of the house, since it is designed for the boys, together with their mother's sisters and the wives of their *tuatina*, who have slept during the night at their feet. The lads eat a little of the food and then hand it over to these women who eat and then carry away the remainder to their own dwelling. This is their perquisite. The rest of the food from this oven is brought in bowls and pushed to the body of *tuatina*. In explaining to me the allotment of the food Pa Niukaso speculated on the reason for this division, and, laughing, gave his opinion that it was done so that the women might have the best share.

The bulk of the day's food is contained in the *umu lasi*, " the great oven," which absorbs a large proportion of the wall of supplies accumulated. This oven does not remain covered for a long time. It is immaterial if the food is taken out in a half-cooked state, since it is intended primarily for presentation to all those who have come to the ceremony, and they take it away to their homes and cook it up again. A small amount of well-cooked food is separated off and put into a kit to feed the lads. The last food of the day is the *umu afiafi*, the " evening oven," which is to provide an ordinary meal for the resident *kano a paito* alone.

Here are a few details of the proceedings at the initiation of Munakina and Seuku. Early in the morning the boys have been about the village, walking slowly, but not stiffly, with the aid of spears used as staves. A couple of hours after sunrise they are smeared with turmeric by a woman of their household (*parasi te tama kura*, or *parasi te tama fou*. The expression *tama kura* conveys the idea of the lad as an object of value ; *tama fou* indicates his changed status—" the new child "). The lads are then made to lie down on the pile of mats and bark-cloth, and are covered over. But they rarely lie still as ordered ; they sit up and chatter. Meanwhile preparations for the feast have kept a number of people busy. On one side of the cook-house eleven women from Rofaea are scraping taro. The same number from Matautu are similarly engaged close by, and a dozen more are in another group. Two women are kneading breadfruit *masi* and putting it into packets, one is kneading taro *masi*, two are preparing yams, two men are grating taro for puddings, ten men are skinning bananas. Around the wall of the cook-house sit eight cooks watching the fire on which the stones have been piled. From time to time a man fans the oven fire. Pa Nukunefu, married to a sister of the principal *tuatina*, is directing operations as chief cook. He walks about giving a word here and there in supervision. Children as usual are sitting about close to their mothers or running around in play. About 9 a.m. the high-pitched yell is heard announcing that a hundred packets of taro have been reached by the graters. About ten o'clock the oven-stones are spread and the food put in. An hour later the preparation of coconut cream is in hand, while inside the house there is a large crowd of people talking, smoking, chewing betel, or sleeping. The size of the oven can be gauged from the fact that six men are at work expressing the coconut cream. The oven is uncovered at midday.

On this occasion five baskets each containing pudding and cooked tubers are filled from the oven first and carried off, one to each chief and one to Pa Rarovi, who is present in the house. This gift is known as the *fakaariki*, and is made every time a man of rank performs some really important ceremony. It lies at the discretion of the donor. In addition to the basket, bundles of raw taro, dry coconuts and sprouting coconuts are sent as well. The custom is for the gift to be borne to the chief by a man from another clan than his own. It is not correct for a man of the same clan to take it, as this might give an impression of intra-group selfishness.

The ordinary people in the house are served with food about 2 p.m. A couple of hours later a second batch is apportioned out; this is from the great oven. By now about one third of the *aŋa*, " wall of food," remains for to-morrow, though most of the coconuts are still on the poles. The food of this day is for the general crowd, that of the last day for the *tuatina* and operators in particular. On this night there is still a crowd in the initiation house. About half-past nine I took a walk through the village. It was a starry night with few clouds and a blustery wind from the east. Down by Rofaea moved three or four torches of belated fishermen. People were singing in the house of Pa Paŋisi, and Munakina and Seuku were asleep on their mat bed.

THE DAY OF GIFTS

On the morrow, the concluding day, the boys are made to rise early and the gifts which formed their bedding are folded up. The mats and bark-cloth are to be redistributed by the father of the initiate, particularly in the form of *maro*, bundles of a formal kind. The principal persons who must be honoured are the cooks, the *tama tapu* of the house, and the *tuatina* of various grades.

The gifts to *soko* and *tama tapu* are sent off early in the morning before the oven is prepared. They really fall into the one category, since the *tama tapu* are the offspring of the *soko*. They are known collectively as " folk of the oven border," that is, people who act as cooks in virtue of themselves or their fathers. At the initiation of Samako and the lads of Nukuafua there were fifteen such *maro*. The first four went to the Ariki Tafua and his three sons Pa Raŋifuri, Pa Nukunefu and Pa Mukava, since Nau Tafua was from Marinoa, the stem family of Nukuafua. The chief, of course, did not work at the oven—he did not even go to the ceremony—but received his present just the same. Pa Raŋifuri did not assist either but sat in the house and left the work to his brothers. A gift was sent to the Ariki Faŋarere because his wives were from Totiare, of which house Nukuone is a component. Others went to Pa Avakofe the younger, and to Pa Taitai, since their mothers were from Faraŋanoa ; to Pa Mataŋi, married to the sister of Pa Nukuafua ; to Pa Fetu and Pa Fenuatu, married to sisters of Pa Nukuone ; to Pa Fenutapu, married to the daughter of Pa Nukuone. Other gifts went to Pa Fenuanefu, who had married the daughter of Pa Mataŋa, the dead brother of Pa Totiare ; Pa Raŋifatua, whose father married the father's sister of Pa Nukuafua ; and Pa Mauŋakena, married to the sister of Pa Nukuafua, who in turn had married his " sister " (cf. p. 231). Pa Mauŋakena was thus a *tuatina* and a *soko*. He abandoned the former status on this occasion and went not on *mata paito*, but to help at the oven.

The gifts to the cooks in reciprocity for their services consist each of a pandanus mat, not usually of the best quality, a bark-cloth blanket, and some other pieces of lesser value. At the initiation of Munakina, of the eight cooks who received these goods, two only, the sons of the Ariki Tafua, were presented with mats bearing the decorative border. If the *fare tuatina* had been less, said Pa Raŋifuri, then the gift to the cooks would have been two mats and two bark-cloth sheets each instead of one. The former used to be the rate of payment. The large mats used as the basis for the more important gifts at initiation, marriage and funerals are known as *taka-furiŋa*. Two such which I received before I left Tikopia came from the households of the Ariki Kafika and Fenuafuti; they had been obtained by them at the initiation ceremony of a lad of the Porima family in return for services as cooks. The mats had been woven by Nau Porima.

The preparation of the oven and the arrangement of the remainder of the gifts now begin. There are four types of *maro* to be considered at this juncture :

1. The *maro* of the experts. These consist of a pandanus mat each, a sheet of bark-cloth, and up to ten lesser pieces, including one dyed with turmeric (*marotafi*). To this is added a coil of sinnet cord or a bonito hook or a cylinder of turmeric pigment. This is a special gift to each expert over and above the standard *maro* and is known as the *fanofano rima*, "the cleansing of the hands." This represents a kind of formal solution of his act of drawing blood from the lad, though it is not regarded as being in any sense a ritual purification.

2. The *maro* of the *tapakau* (floor-mats). These are the gifts to the *taŋata me*, that is, the men who supported the boys in their arms. They are of standard type but good quality.

3. The *maro* of the near mother's brothers. These are presented when the true mother's brother is not included in either of the former categories. These three classes are grouped together under the head of *matua maro*, "principal gifts."

4. The *maro* of the *kerekere*, that is, the distant relatives of mother's brother status. The gifts made to them are of more simple quality than the others. They get no mats, one bark-cloth blanket, and a few other pieces.

The initiative is taken by the different people of the *fai matua* group. The principal *maro* are first disposed of. One can soon hear people say, "Experts and floor-mats are finished. Don't bother to count the principal *maro*, they are completed." These principal *maro* are by custom made up by the near relatives of the recipients. For example, that of the principal mother's brother is made up by the father of the lad. The basis of each *maro* is a pandanus mat. This is taken from the pile contributed two days before and without regard to who may have been the original donor. Thus, as I noticed, a mat brought by a member of the Nukuone house was included in a *maro* made by Nukuafua without any observation being passed. The best mats are selected for the principal *maro* and no one may know or care who handed them in. The only point made is to see that the contributions from *tama tapu* are not returned to them.

Much discussion goes on about the arrangements, and there is a great deal of alteration made in the composition of each gift until finally a completely satisfactory set is ready. When most of the *maro* have been prepared, a count is made to find out which are finished and which remain to be made. Questions are put : " Where is the *maro* of so-and-so ? " An answer is given perhaps, " O ! It's awfully good—great is the fineness of that *maro*," or " There remain yet some pieces of bark-cloth to be added."

The principle upon which the *maro* are composed is very interesting. They are gradually built up by a process of mutual assistance, but no matter how many people have contributed to any single bundle, this is conveyed by one person only to the recipient, and any return gift that is made for it will be presented to him. It may be kept by him alone or a part given to his assistant, just as he wishes. This principle applies particularly to initiation ceremonies ; in other cases the return gift is shared. A man comes in the morning with the property he contributes. If he has a complete *maro* already made up, then this may often be allowed to stand, but if a piece of bark-cloth is required to complete another *maro*, then one may be plucked from the former with no objection made by the man who has brought it. The valuables are handed in to be put at the disposal of the group of kindred ; they form a common stock. Generally a person has an idea of whom he wants to make a *maro* for, so when he comes with his mat or his bark-cloth blanket, these are used to form the basis, other bark-cloth is taken from other contributions, and the whole arranged to make a satisfactory present. Then it will probably be given over to the person who provided the basic items.

The technical term to arrange a *maro*, that is, make a bundle with mat at the bottom, half a dozen pieces of folded bark-cloth neatly end to end above and topped off by a final piece often of better quality or turmeric dyed, is *faite*. A person is said " to seek a *maro* " (*sakiri*) if he adds a piece of bark-cloth to it. In this case no return is obtained either from the person who gets the *maro* or from the principal contributor to it. The actual addition of the piece of bark-cloth is known as *tatao*, which describes the action of laying on top, covering, pressing down. Pa Raŋifuri said in the course of the arrangements, " Act according to your own ideas, you women ; if you want to cover (*tatao*), cover, but if not, then don't " (Text S. 12.) The expression *te maro o te tufuŋa ku tao*, " the gift of the expert has been covered," means that it has been enhanced by the addition of extra bark-cloth above the standard number. Another term of importance is that referring to the allotment or " tagging " of *maro*. When one has been set aside, destined for a particular person, then it is said to be " eaten " (*kaina*). Hence one hears such references as " it has not yet been eaten," meaning that though made up, its destination is not yet determined.

Though the *maro* are in principle a gift from the whole body of kindred, the actual presentation is done on a strictly personal basis. Each *maro* is carried at the end of the day by a wife or sister of the person who is regarded as responsible for it to the person for whom it is destined. The *maro* is reciprocated directly to the donor. There is no need for the recipient to ask to whom he must make the return gift; he hands it over direct to the woman who has acted as carrier. Discussion as to who shall be responsible for the *maro* of various people is frequent. Some of the *fai matua* have their preference before coming; some speak up and nominate their " opposite number "; some, through diffidence or dissatisfaction, hang back and at the last have *maro* almost thrust upon them.

A few excerpts from the conversation while the arrangements are in hand will show the method of organization by discussion. Some one calls, " There remains Afirua." The answer comes, " It stands in sa Fenuatu." " O ! There it has been lifted." In other words, it will be seen to by this household, and the questioner is satisfied. Some one remarks with a sigh of relief, " There now, Potu i Korokoro has been lifted completely—that is the last one there." The demand is made, " Why don't you count up your *maro* exactly ? " or again, " Why don't you count them first from the *mato paito* end ? " that is, beginning with the more important relatives. The query as to who is looking after so-and-so is frequently made and answered, either by " It is being arranged by brother and sister in —," or " He is not yet disposed of." Pa Raŋifuri takes an important part at Rofaea. He calls for a count, asks after certain *maro*, and stimulates the laggards. He wants to know about the *maro* at one end of the house; he is told that they are all eaten. " *Maro* eaten only—that is the way to speak." Then he turns to the women who are still hanging back, " You are sitting in your own minds," he says to them, meaning that they must have their own ideas as to what they want to do, and it is time they declared them. The question arises as to whether *maro* shall be given to such of the *fai tuatina* who did not go outside at the time of the operation but stayed in the house. Pa Raŋifuri utters the principle that one who goes outside does so at his choice—his *maro* will be made; one who stays in the house does so at his choice—he leaves it to the *kano a paito* to decide if they will give him a *maro* or not. In other words the latter has no claim. This is approved by all in the house. It is in fact the recognized basis of the system, but at Rofaea the *tuatina* who stayed inside all had *maro* given to them— as an act of grace.

The criterion of exit from the house at the critical moment is a

GENEALOGY VII (b)

ILLUSTRATING THE PRINCIPAL RELATIONSHIPS AT
THE INITIATION OF SAMAKO ETC. AT NUKUAFUA

(Compare Gen. III and V)

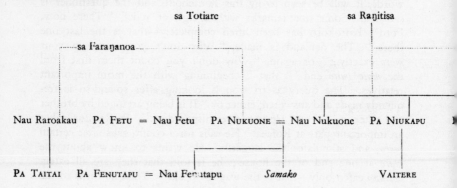

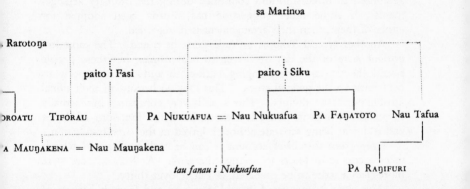

useful one, since many people belong both to *fai tuatina* and *fai matua*. Where their status is more or less equal on both sides they usually decide modestly to stay inside ; frequently they are told by the boy's father to go out, and if they do so then their *maro* are given.   Since one can have two relationships at the one time, but not be in two places simultaneously, the fact of exit automatically separates the categories.   In order that the *maro* shall be adequate, the *fare tuatina* are counted by the simple process of asking who were outside on *mata paito*.   The close observation which the natives generally keep on persons makes this method very accurate.

A useful mechanism for dealing with cases of dual kinship status is provided by the custom of *feuviake*.   When a family belongs to *fai matua* as well as *fai tuatina*, it may arrange with another family in a similar position to exchange *maro*.   This was done by sa Nukumo-sokoia and sa Nukurotoi at Rofaea.   The effect is to put less strain on the resources of the father of the boy.   Such a proposed change is submitted to discussion and confirmed during the ordinary arrange-ments.   If some other suggestion has already been adopted for either of them, then their arrangement is disregarded.

Another typical Tikopia attitude must be noted.   The most im-portant *maro* of the day are given to near *tuatina*, but these people attend the preparations bringing bark-cloth and other property to contribute to the general stock.   This they do because of their affinal kinship with the donors.   This sounds very confusing, but actually in practice works in perfectly clear fashion, the functions of donor and recipient being separate although linked in the same transaction.

Even from this brief account it can be well understood why it takes a couple of hours to arrange the *maro*.   At Rofaea there were more than a score to be prepared, at Putafe over thirty.

The oven is uncovered in mid-afternoon and from it baskets of food are set out to accompany the *maro*.   Normally a basket goes with each.   If a person gets two *maro*, then he receives also two baskets of food, and makes two return gifts.   Sometimes *maro* are *fakafeuaki*, that is, one is superimposed on another.   This is seen by the fact of the head of one *maro*, that is, the folds of the cloth, being above the tail, that is, the loose ends, of the other.   In such case only one basket of food is sent, but since the *maro* is really a double one, though there is only one pile for convenience of carriage, two return gifts are made by the recipient.

The return gift for a *maro* is represented as lying at the discretion of the recipient.   If he likes what he receives, the natives say, then he goes to his store, takes a coil of sinnet cord and hands it to the bearer of the *maro*, to convey to the donor.   In actual practice no one would risk the loss of reputation by omitting to make a return. Here, as elsewhere, the reciprocal gift is termed *te fakapenu*, or more shortly *te penu*.

The events at the house Koroatu in the afternoon will illustrate the mechanism of the process. Pa Koroatu, a younger brother of Pa Niukapu, has a *maro* brought to him by Pa Nukuafua, since he was the principal operator on this man's sons. The oven is made in the house and opened after the *maro* is brought. Three kits are filled, one large one for the eldest and the other two for the younger lads. At the command of the *tuatina* they carry their kits and set them before their parents, who later take the food home. Deprecatory talk begins all round; Pa Nukuafua says, "Why have you made two kits for the brothers? One would be enough." "O, it is their mark of honour, it is good." The kits contain fish which have been obtained by members of the household who went out on logs beyond the reef— a cold undertaking in this windy weather. Again Pa Nukuafua speaks: "Why did you go simply to be chilled?" and so on, which evokes the usual polite reply. Complimentary references are made to the food being well cooked, and people invite each other to continue to eat. Areca nut and tobacco is given to the bearers of the *maro*. There is much talk as to the allocation of the *maro*, and all the details are reviewed, of how some people fought, of how others were piqued, of what so-and-so said to so-and-so, of what return gifts have been made—all at great length and with never tiring interest. Pa Nukuafua, talking of the *maro* made to Tofiariki of Tekaumata, said that thinking of the lad he had a mat in reserve; when some person would come to declare his intention of making this *maro* he would ask if he had a mat, and if not, would hand over the one set aside. Such personal thoughtfulness is common and tends to modify considerably the formal structure of the system of presentations. The propriety of certain people having received *maro* is also questioned on the grounds of the claim being slight—their brothers having been already provided for, for instance. Finally Pa Nukuafua and his party rise to go. Pa Koroatu takes down from a shelf a coil of sinnet: "Put your hand to this length of sinnet here," says he. "Let it stay there, let it stay there, brother-in-law, I tell you" (Text S. 9). The former repeats his offer, a coil to tie up the other's canoe with, he says. The latter objects and carries his point. The sinnet is finally given to a woman from Raveŋa who has brought another *maro*. This incident shows the informality which regulates the act of presentation. The return gift is not invariable, but lies at the discretion of the persons concerned. In this case the close relationship between the pair allows the normal procedure to be waived.

The return gift is not always sinnet. Sometimes it is supplemented by sprouting coconuts or nowadays by fish-hooks or a pipe. If the *maro* of a man is large and contains a mat and eight or ten pieces of bark-cloth, he will then repay it with sinnet. But if it is smaller, he may give yams or a couple of shell arm-rings as a return. My own return gifts—since I received *maro* as a titular mother's brother—were made with calico, a fact which caused some people to say laughingly that all the *kano a paito* fought in order to " lift " my present. Calico to the Tikopia is the equivalent of *mami*, the bark-cloth sheet or blanket, and is greatly appreciated. When the *maro* was brought for his son, Pa Tekaumata went to his stock of bark-cloth, took one piece and gave it to the woman who brought the pile. The *tama tapu* make a different recompense. A day or so after they receive their *maro* each, assisted by his family, cooks food, fills a basket, and takes it to the house of the father of the lads. This food is termed *te vai kira*, and is the *fakaara o a koroa*, the return for the valuables.

Independently of the *maro*, sinnet is brought by various members of the *fai matua*, and is not presented to specific individuals but is given to the father of the boy. He hands the collection over to the principal operator who distributes it as he thinks fit. A good coil is given to the principal mother's brother, who is under no actual obligation to give a return payment. If he keeps it (*tuku mori*), then no objection will be raised by the original donor. He has presented it from *arofa* to his " child." But if the good coil is given to one of the *kerekere*, then the donor will say, " Make sure that he reciprocates it with a decent coil." He wants a return present because the distant *tuatina* has not the same status.

Apart from the ordinary *maro* composed in the house of initiation, members of the *fai matua* may make individual *maro* for members of the *fai tuatina*. In such a case if a man of the latter is ignorant that such a special gift is to be made for him, he will probably hand over a coil of sinnet when it arrives. But he also may wish to give a special *maro* to a member of the *fai matua*. In such a case he brings it with him to the house where all are prepared, and when he hears that a presentation is to be made to him he says, " That is the man to whom my *maro* will be given." Then no *fakapenu* is given ; the exchange of *maro* completes the transaction.

So far the ceremony has been described as if the act of exchange was the sole factor, without reference to the condition of the parties to it. One qualification, however, exists : the Tikopia, while allowing gift and return gift to be made between persons living close to each other, prefer that the body of exchange should pass as far as possible between persons in different villages, or still better, in different districts. At the initiation of Munakina and Seuku, the absence of father's relatives for the former meant that for symmetry the relatives of his mother were split into two parties. This was done primarily on the basis of district affiliation, Sa Faea being opposed to Sa Raveŋa. The decision to divide the relatives illustrates the fundamental place that a symmetrical exchange on such occasion holds in the Tikopia cultural patterns. If the parties concerned come from different districts and without special reason an exchange is initiated between those in the same district, then this is not regarded by public opinion as good. If the exchange takes place between members of the same family, then it is even worse; the expression is *paito fai taŋa*, which colloquially translated means : " family pouching it for themselves." The conventional statement is : " It is good to give to another family," or " it is good to give to another place."

On theoretical grounds one can see the function of such an attitude. One of the primary effects of a system of gift exchange is that it provides a concrete means of social linkage. If such exchange is permitted to take place between members of the same small kinship group, or immediate neighbours, at the expense of others more distant, either in kinship or residence, then a social advantage is lost. The association of meanness with intra-familial presentation of a formal character helps then to maintain the efficacy of the system.

Apart from expressing judgment as to the propriety of a particular item of exchange, the Tikopia also take into consideration the individual response. A man is described as *taŋata laui* or *taŋata pariki*, good or bad, according to the quality of the things he gives.

On the day of the presentation the initiates, smeared with turmeric and carrying spear staves in their hands, start their round of visits to their *tuatina*. Their sleeping mats are sent on ahead of them. They go first to the house of the principal operator, stay there a couple of days, and their bedclothes are then collected by the woman of another *tuatina*. There is no definite order of precedence followed in issuing the invitations.

When Seuku and Munakina came from Raŋirikoi to Raroakau, Nau Raroakau woke up everyone in the early morning saying, " Get up ! the bed-mats of the two boys have come." The lads were given a place in the centre of the house and food was given them. At every meal during their stay they were given by far the biggest portions. A special pudding was prepared, and it was explained to me that if there had been fish, they would have received it in preference to any of the ordinary household. After their first meal they were told to lie down and sleep. They answered that they wanted to walk about. "All right," said their hosts, "but if you are hungry, come back here and eat."

On this occasion there was a disturbance of the normal order of events. Munakina and Seuku quarrelled, and the former hit the latter on the head with a stick. He fled crying to the house, snatched up his bed-mat and left, saying that he was going home. The sister of Pa Taitai ran after him and took the mat back, but he refused to return. He spent the night at his father's home. In the morning a man came to the door of Raroakau and called out, "Munakina, Seuku, wake up," while his wife entered to take their mats. She was told the circumstances by the people and carried off the mat as the principal thing. Seuku came back the same day and was directed to go to his new host. No great fuss was made by anyone over this; Seuku was a *tuatina* (classificatory mother's brother) of Munakina, so their quarrel was not especially offensive.

The economic aspect of the visiting is extremely important. In each case the food is made at the house of the *tuatina* and presented to the parents; this is the *fakaoatea*. It is reciprocated in due course. The parents in their turn make another food gift to the *tuatina*; this is the *fakatavaŋa*, which is reciprocated in turn. Nowadays the double gift and return gift are made only in Raveŋa; in Faea the *fakatavaŋa* alone takes place, in accordance with the attitude of the mission teachers mentioned above. Since the travelling of the boys lasts for a period of two months or so—to cover all their *tuatina*— the economic strain upon the parents' household is severe. It might be argued that the relaxation of custom would provide a welcome relief. But despite their grumblings about the work involved, the folk of Raveŋa are not eager to abandon their extra labour. In any case the reciprocity in the making of food means that it is the constancy of obligation and not the economic loss that is at issue.

The round of visits made by the boys to their mother's brothers' homes has for ostensible object the honouring of the lads and their parents and the display of kinship ties. Apart from this the effect of it in widening the social horizon of the boys must be important. In the ordinary domestic life of the houses where they stay, they are treated with ceremony, and though they are ordered about as younger relatives they are relieved from work. They are given more latitude than usual, and it would be strange if they did not feel that their personality is of more consequence than before. Moreover they make social contacts of more than a perfunctory order with some kinsfolk with whom previously they have been on less intimate terms. In a sense their peregrinations from house to house are their introduction to society. A child, whether boy or girl, pursuing such a round of visits is termed a *tama kura*. This is an honorific expression, the word *kura* being used " because its body is red." [1]

THE CEREMONY FOR BOYS OF RANK

A more elaborate version of the initiation ceremony is sometimes adopted by families of greater wealth, who are as a rule families of rank. I received accounts of this from several informants in which some of the details differed. One account gave the period as eight days. The *fai tuatina*, it was said, stop for some days in their house while food and valuables are sent to them by the *fai matua*. Later the feast is prepared at the house of the latter and all go there where the ceremony is performed. The other account received from Pae Sao and others gave the period as five days. This perhaps did not include the extra days of residence of the *tuatina* before the collection of the feast. The *aŋa* is much larger than in the ordinary case, and an important food is the banana. The ceremony is so arranged that quantities of bananas ripen on the successive days. It is possible that the use of the ripe banana links this more elaborate ritual with the Atua i Kafika, since this fruit is associated with him on certain important religious occasions. I omitted, however, to enquire on this point. According to Pae Sao, the boy is sent for by a messenger who gashes his forehead as he comes, and is carried to the house of the principal mother's brother. The operation is performed and he sleeps there. Meanwhile the wailing goes on in the house of the parents.

This form of ceremony is known as the *fakatuatina*, a name which emphasizes the importance of the role of the mother's brother. The ordinary initiation is termed *fakavao*, which may refer to the fainting condition it sometimes induces. (The *vao* is uncultivated planting land overgrown with grass and weeds ; I have no evidence to relate this to the name of the ceremony.)

The last *fakatuatina* held in Raveŋa was made for Pa Veterei, Pa Tarikitoŋa and Pa Mataŋi, of the houses of Avakofe and Raŋifau. In Faea the last was held for the elder brother of the present Pa Mauŋa-kena of the house of Fasi. These were a generation ago.

In some of its most salient features the ceremony of initiation in Tikopia belongs to a more general class of institution. The assembly of kin ; the division of them into two groups on the basis of paternal and maternal affiliation ; the complex series of exchanges which take place between them ; the lack of any immediate economic utility in

[1] Cf. *kura* in Maori, signifying red, as also a valued object, usually of a red colour (Williams' *Dictionary*, and T. G. Hammond, *Story of Aotea*, 1924, 211-215) ; and the *maro 'ura* of Tahiti. *Mero* is the ordinary Tikopia word for red.

these exchanges ; and the tendency to associate the parties with different residential groupings all fall into place either as factors of distinction or as integrating mechanisms in the general social structure.

BASIC FUNCTIONS OF INITIATION RITUAL

It remains now to be seen whether these data provide any points of vantage from which to survey the broad field of initiation rites in general. In Tikopia and in other areas of Polynesia, this institution for the treatment of adolescents is decidedly atypical. There is no secrecy about its methods, no seclusion of the initiates, few or no food taboos to observe, and those which exist refer to comparatively unimportant substances, no expressed tests of manhood and indeed a positive attempt at mitigation of physical pain, no instruction of a moral order. And yet despite the omission of what in many areas of Africa, Australia and Melanesia would be regarded as essential elements of the procedure, it can I think be shown that the fundamental aspects of the institution are the same. Some of the elements of Tikopia initiation may be considered from this general standpoint and compared with elements elsewhere.

The apparent focal point of the ceremony is the operation performed. Here is a situation in which a small bodily incision, comparatively trifling in itself and of no particular utility, is treated as the centre of an elaborate series of activities. The opinion put forward by Schurtz [1] that there is a hygienic motive in many of these practices is supported by no good evidence. It is true that circumcision properly so-called may have a hygienic value, but this is not great and may be discounted as representing the native point of view ; other forms of operation on the sexual organ have not even this justification. Nor does the most competent investigation allow to subincision a contraceptive motive or effect. The Tikopia practice subscribes to neither of these explanations, nor does it yield to the argument of the possible increase of pleasure in sex intercourse, particularly on the part of women. The attitude of Tikopia women, so one gathers, is that of derision at a person who has not undergone the customary operation, not of irritation at deprivation of enjoyment. By custom the women may prefer superincised persons, but certainly there seems to have been little difficulty on the part of the few natives from other islands, who have resided there in times past, in obtaining wives. I have never heard of the unincised state as tending in any way to place a barrier before sexual relations, though it is conceivable that a girl might refuse a man to whom she was not particularly attracted

[1] Schurtz, *Altersklassen und Männerbünde*, 1902, 97.

with scorn at his condition. In other words it is regarded primarily as a social disability, not as a sexual one.

If the bodily operation cannot be explained on grounds of practical value, what then is its place in the initiation scheme ? It is apt to be described as an ordeal, as if it had the ostensible purpose of trying the courage of the initiate. In some cases this may be so, but often the trial of hardihood is a separate item in the ceremonial, and the operation acts in this fashion only incidentally. Its real meaning is usually to confer the appropriate material token of distinction upon the individual who has been the subject of the qualifying ritual. Among primitive non-literate peoples for whom a written diploma is an impossibility, an unalterable bodily mark, a pattern of scars, a mutilation, of a kind which no person is likely to attempt to perform on himself, is an excellent means of classification. Tribal distinction is in practice frequently made by the recognition of such bodily markings. The operation has often also the effect of characterizing the lad as sexually mature, and of marking the organ principally concerned in the change.

Such operations usually cause pain, but this is not to say that they imply an act planned to inflict it. The Tikopia for one are tender-hearted and try to minimize the pain as much as possible. The answer to the problem as to why operations which are painful are performed lies in the consideration of a complex set of factors—the impressive effect of using the body as a tablet to be engraved, the ritual value attaching to the flow of human blood—these may be important beside the factor of hardihood. Then there is also the consideration as to why certain parts of the body should be selected for mutilation. This is, a question which demands for a reply the correlation of factors of sexual interest and display, personal privacy, the force of tradition, facility of self-performance, and the like.

The persistence of the operation in the customary form is ultimately dependent on the institutional framework of which it forms a part. Here are the values maintained, not in external considerations. Superincision in Tikopia continues to be performed in that precise manner because the social pattern demands it and uses ridicule as its sanction.

The ceremonies of initiation cannot then be explained as the outcome of the particular operation of superincision ; this must be explained in terms of the ritual as a whole from which it derives its justification. This is an illustration of the general thesis that any institution tends to create and perpetuate its own scheme of values, dictating conformity to them from its fundamental efficacy in the culture as a whole. These values themselves are often of no integral moment for the social well-being ; save only in so far as they contribute to the maintenance of an existing institution.

One of the basic functions of the initiation ritual emerges from the examination of its relation to education. The value of these ceremonies as a factor in primitive education cannot be denied, if by education is meant the process of adapting an individual to the community in which he is to live, inducing him to accept its discipline and norms of conduct. But of explicit instruction in tribal lore and manners there is usually, I think, less than is imagined, and what is given is by no means a primary feature of the institution. In Australia, it is true, totemic myths are taught at this time, and as in Africa, certain moral rules are inculcated. Frequently a little sex knowledge of a rough and ready kind is imparted, but this is apt to possess a purely formal value, since the lad is often cognisant already of such facts as the result of practical experiment. In Polynesia there is hardly any of this teaching, and in Melanesia it is perfunctory.

I may be underestimating the importance of this feature, but the insistence on the educative aspect of initiation comes, I fancy, from the attempt to justify rites which on first observation were described as being cruel, barbarous, degraded and meriting abolition. When it was learnt, as in Australia, that moral and religious instruction was imparted at this time, this was grasped as an argument in favour, and sometimes exaggerated.

There is no need to appeal to this. Even in Tikopia, where all formal instruction is absent, the initiation ritual is still of great consequence to every boy in shaping his relation to other persons in the community, and thus helping to fit him for his future life. It is the implicit rather than the explicit factors which are of weight here. The suppression of the individual, the disregard of his normal freedom of choice and action is important. In ordinary life he can obey or disobey ; at initiation he must submit. He is taken in hand by his elders, treated by them as an object, carried about, gripped in strong arms, and forced to undergo an operation from which he shrinks. His submission is taken for granted, and it would be strange if at this time he did not become aware of the power of traditional procedure, made manifest in the personalities of his social environment. On the other hand he is elevated into a position of importance ; he is the focus of attention. He is smeared with turmeric, adorned, fed with choice foods, wailed over and caressed, and later treated as an honoured guest in many households. Here again it would be strange if he did not realize something of his position, and attribute to himself significance in the social scheme. At the one stroke he is made aware of his situation in the community, of

AT REST AFTER THE OPERATION

The *tuaina* are sitting by the eaves of the house; Pa Niukapu, their leader, is on the right.

THE INITIATES ABROAD

Bedaubed with bright-red turmeric and carrying a spear as stave, they pay a round of visits to their *tuatina*.

his dependence upon others and subordination to them as a group, and of his unique personal value to them. A new status is conferred upon him, and his maturity becomes patent to him in that, for example, he is now admitted to participation in adult assemblies and is no longer specifically forbidden sex intercourse. And the attainment of his status is borne upon him in a form of presentation which, however imperfect and exaggerated, is nevertheless exceedingly forceful and dramatic.

The mechanism by which this is accomplished is of the utmost importance, and yet it has often been left out of sight in descriptive accounts as well as in theoretical analyses. In initiation in Tikopia, at every turn the procedure is in the hands of kinsfolk of the initiate— kinship gives the title to attendance, is responsible for the main divisions of the crowd, underlies care of the ovens, support of the initiate, performance of the operation, presentation and distribution of food and valuables. At the critical moment the mother's brother says, " Be strong, nephew ! " and throughout, the lad, frightened at the unknown terrors which lie ahead, is assured of safety by the knowledge that he is in the hands of his kin, led by his mother's brother, who since his earliest childhood has been his comforter, protector and friend. We have no need then to describe the integrative role of initiation in terms of merely vague amorphous group relationship. The linkage is with kinsfolk, the nearest being most prominent. To these people it is most appropriate for him to be closely welded, since he will be depending on them throughout his future life.

Every initiation is not primarily the work of kinsfolk ; in some societies it is essentially performed on the novices by the persons already initiated. But it is probably true to say that in every community there is a division of kindred, often of a very complicated kind, for the exercise of ceremonial functions at initiation. Most frequent is a demarcation of father's and mother's kin. The recognition of such divisions, with their interacting, even reciprocal roles appears to be most important for the induction of a person into maturity. Entry into adult life involves the realization of social obligations and the assumption of responsibility for meeting them. What initiation does is to set a time on the way to manhood—often only approximately the time when the parallel physiological changes are due to take place—and by bringing the person into formal and explicit relation with his kindred, confronts him with some of his basic social ties, reaffirms them and thus makes patent to him his status against the days when he will have to adopt them in earnest.

CHAPTER XIII

MARRIAGE BY CAPTURE

MARRIAGE in Tikopia involves a great change for both man and woman. On the part of the woman it means abandoning all sexual freedom, committing herself to bearing children, obeying in many things the dictates of her husband and his relatives, and leaving her father's house to take up residence in another's. On the other hand it means having a house of which she is entitled to call herself the mistress, a man on whom she can depend for economic co-operation, and a safe and legalized sexual cohabitation. Marriage is looked upon as emancipation, because it enables a woman to exercise authority in a sphere of her own. Since there is mutual deference between husband and wife, marriage by explicit social custom means freedom not servitude for her. Young women in song sometimes assert their intention of scorning marriage, but there is in Tikopia no other career which offers any real social advantages. The type of spirit mediumship which obtains does not sufficiently differentiate its practitioners from the general body of people to provide women with any great inducement to pursue it as their sole vocation.

For a man the change is superficially not so great ; in reality it is no less deep than that of the woman. In native theory he can still pursue a course of sexual freedom, but in practice he seems to find either that a wife satisfies his desires or that his adventurous inclinations are best sacrificed for the sake of domestic harmony. He remains in close contact with his father's home, but as a rule a new house is built for himself and his wife. Most important of all, formerly he could live with a minimum of effort as a subsidiary and not as a principal in economic affairs ; he did not need to accumulate much property, but could borrow from his married brothers ; he was free to wander from house to house and to spend his evenings in dancing and games with the young men and the girls. Now he must be restrained ; he is barred by custom from joining the young people on the beach, he must make or collect tools for himself and under her pressure, for his wife also ; he has an immediate responsibility to work with his wife and provide for her and the children.

This sacrifice of freedom is the greatest drawback to marriage in the eyes of the Tikopia youth, just as the security of a house of her own is the greatest inducement to it for a girl. The natives recognize a clear difference of attitude between the sexes in this respect. The girls desire marriage, the young men try to evade it. This leads to conflict of interests, some recrimination, serious as well as feigned, and certain ingenious devices on the part of young women to accomplish their desires.

THE DECISION TO MARRY

The initial features of marriage in Tikopia depend upon whether the union results from an association of sweethearts or whether the woman is snatched away without previous warning. The crystallization of the relationship of lovers into a permanent legal union has been described in the foregoing chapter. The reasons there mentioned which induce the man to carry off the woman were his desire for her or his conformity to custom once he has made her pregnant. The conditions precedent to marriage may now be described in greater detail.

The resolve of the man to take a wife may be guided to a very considerable extent by the quantity of food available in the orchards of his family. " Proportionate to the plenitude of the food will they two join," say the Tikopia. They stress the importance of this economic provision not for the upkeep of the wife but for the ritual exchanges which virtually seal the union. If, for example, there has recently been a funeral or an initiation in the family, a young man is hardly likely to take a bride unless great pressure be brought to bear on him, and his relatives will object strongly when they hear of his intention. But sometimes the relatives of the man may urge him to marry. The son of a chief, for instance, is pressed by the *kano a paito* to take a wife, and in advance they prepare large cultivations and quantities of mats and bark-cloth in the hope that the event will take place. They keep an eye on his sexual adventures and plan accordingly. Kavakiua told me with great glee that Rimakoroa, heir of the Ariki Taumako, was going to his mistress—in the native phrase —and that the family were planting taro in expectation of the marriage.

Where marriage is the result of compulsion the reason is usually the pregnancy of the woman. Sometimes, though, this may be merely simulated in order that she may gain a husband. Details of a case which occurred during my stay show the conflicting personal interests at work beneath the surface of the customary legal mechanism which represents wedlock in Tikopia.

The news came that Nau Vatere had become pregnant. She was the second wife of Pa Nukusorokiraro, but the pair having no child, she separated from him and went to live with her mother. Then she visited the house of Tereata into which her sister had married before. There, so the gossip went, she had relations with Sauakipure, a son of the house, and became with child by him. The report came that the night before she had gone to live with her lover ; the man did not want to marry her, but having been baptized, his resistance was overcome by the arguments of the mission teachers. The former husband, it was said, objected to the match. He made *te makau*, that is, he seized a weapon and went out to demonstrate his anger as a protest. The lover went out to meet him with a club, but there were no casualties. After that her husband made no further move. " He sits there, but he objects ; his mind is bad."

Later came other news ; the lover's married brother had previously menaced the woman with an adze in an inquisition to find out who was responsible for her condition. The man in the meantime had taken to the woods. Later the marriage actually took place in spite of his objections. But a little while afterwards there was a great furore ; he had taken a canoe and gone off to sea with the intention of committing suicide rather than consenting to live with an unwelcome wife. All trace of him was lost, and public sympathy, which at first had been decidedly against him, now turned in his favour. A typical initial comment was that of Pa Raŋateatua : " If he objects to her he shouldn't have gone to her. To be sure ! " The Ariki Taumako happened to be sitting in my house when the news of the man's flight came, brought by the chief's son. His first words were, " May his father eat filth ! My one transport canoe has been taken ! " Then a little later, hearing that the man's family were wailing, he said, " I am not angry about my canoe ; I object only because its outrigger is bad." Then later he went on to commiserate with the man. (Some of his remarks are given in the original in Chapter VII, Text S. 16.)

The crowning touch to this situation was given when it was discovered that the woman was not pregnant after all—" merely her plumpness " as it was rather cynically remarked. However the worst did not occur. After three days of privation at sea, burnt almost black by constant exposure to the sun, the much abused man turned up again. After a formal ceremony of reconciliation with his chief, he returned home and appeared to settle down quite comfortably with the woman. I did not learn whether he had even had relations with her before their marriage, but opinion seemed to be that this was so. Apparently such cases of attempted victimization—looking at it from the male point of view—or clinching of the relationship, as no doubt it appears to the woman—do not seem to be very uncommon.

Marriage by elopement is nowadays the most common mode. When a man makes his decision, he grasps the woman by the wrist and leads her to his house. The more dramatic method of bringing home the bride is the *tuku pouri*, the leaving in darkness. This is when the woman is seized without previous discussion with her ; it is in fact a form of marriage by capture. On this a few general observations may first be made.

There was such a mixture of sadism and romanticism in the theory of marriage by capture as expounded by the classical anthropologist that it is little wonder it has now been abandoned or relegated to a minor position in the catalogue of the various ways of securing a mate. The popular press still talks glibly of the savage who goes courting with a club instead of a nosegay of flowers, but the modern scientist, acquainted at first hand with native marriage customs, finds the picture ludicrous. He gives a different interpretation of the facts which have lent colour to the legend.

The older theories regarded marriage by capture as an institution characteristic of primitive man in a former social state. The custom which exists among many native peoples of to-day of making a pretended capture of the bride, the violence of the struggle being more feigned than real, they held to be a survival from this prior stage of society. A process of ossification of the marriage custom was imagined, resulting in the retention of the form when the meaning and the need for it had been lost. But it is a commonplace of modern anthropology that the explanation of the form of an institution is to be sought first of all in its immediate context, and that important forms of social behaviour such as marriage exist in relation to some present need. In considering the curious marriage custom of the Tikopia there is no need to have resort to any reconstruction of an obsolete state of their society.

A distinction is drawn by Crawley between marriage by capture proper, formal capture and connubial capture. The first of these he describes as an affair between hostile tribes, and is careful to point out that this could never have been really a mode of marriage but only a method of procuring a wife. The marital bond to be effective demands something in the nature of a legal contract between all the parties concerned, and this is not present in marriage by capture (in Crawley's sense) any more than in highway robbery or piracy. It is always of merely sporadic occurrence. It is connubial capture and formal capture that he gives as the legalized forms of marriage, and these are in no way either survivals from marriage by capture proper or expressions of it. They are practised with the consent of the community which indeed plays its part within the ritual. In connubial capture the husband to be has to pursue his wife and overcome her resistance, sometimes abetted by his kindred and opposed by hers, sometimes not. In formal capture the tussle for the person of the bride is conducted between the families concerned, but is largely pretence, victory being assured to the groom's party after a suitable display of violence on both sides. Formal capture is the ceremonial, idealized type of an institution, while connubial capture is the practical non-ceremonial type. Both, says Crawley, are a natural expression of normal human feelings. These feelings Crawley interprets as being fundamentally based upon a physiological shrinking of the woman from the act of union, a shrinking which has to be neutralized and overcome by a ceremonial use of force, half make-believe and half real. Furthermore, he stresses very strongly his view that the bride is borne off, primarily, not from her family and kin but from her sex. In Crawley's general approach he looks for the explanation of custom in its relation to the other existing behaviour of the people. This method of interpretation is in line with the modern attitude. On specific points, however, the psychological trend of his argument is not borne out by the data. The woman herself so far from exhibiting any shrinkage is often an eager consenting party to the union; it is her relatives alone who raise the objection and who have to be mastered. Moreover, as Marett has pointed out, in most communities where formal capture of the bride takes place, the males of her family offer resistance as well as the females. In these respects the thesis now generally held, that the pretence of conflict is really a dramatization, a ritual and legal expression of the transfer of the woman from one group to the other, is more acceptable.[1]

The marriage institutions of Tikopia bear upon these theories. Here is a form of real abduction of the bride, an abduction which is of special interest since it takes place not between hostile tribes or clans but between groups normally in an amicable state of cooperation in the one community.

An examination of some of the conditions precedent to marriage in Tikopia gives an indication of the form which the institution has assumed. The patrilocal residence of the married pair means a loss of the ordinary services of the wife to the household in which she was brought up. This loss and even the potentiality of it is resented by her parents, and in particular by her father. Whether this resentment is to be correlated with the father's special affection for his daughter or not, it is difficult to say. The Tikopia themselves put his objection on an economic basis. The result is that the parents of the girl are usually quite ignorant of her love affairs and remain so until she has actually been carried off in marriage. The first they hear of it is on the morning after she has gone to her husband's house, when the news runs around the island that " a married pair have joined together." It is difficult to say how far this tradition of parental ignorance is actually borne out. On first thoughts it would seem as if the parents must have previous knowledge of their daughter's intentions. Against this must be remembered the " respect " situation between parents

---

[1] Crawley, *The Mystic Rose*, 4th ed. 1932, 318-336. Cf. Marett, *Sacraments of Simple Folk*, 1933, 86-89.

and children which tends to eliminate discussion of intimate personal affairs ; and the almost complete division between the unmarried and the married in matters of recreation and sex. The girl herself and her companions are therefore not likely to inform her parents of her intrigue, and it is only through such relatives as a bachelor brother of her mother's that knowledge might come to them. If the father hears that she is planning to leave home, he reproaches her and is likely to beat her. It is very probable then that what the Tikopia say about parental ignorance is usually quite true. There is also of course the pressure of tradition on the other hand which would tend to make the parents feign lack of knowledge if they did happen to gain some ink-ling of the situation. Whatever be the actual knowledge of the girl's parents it cannot be great, and the whole character of the act of taking the bride to her husband's home is one of secrecy and haste. There is nothing at all in the way of matchmaking between families, and none of those preliminary conversations and visits from emissaries which form such an important part of the ceremony among African tribes.

The fear of the father's anger seems to be a very real factor in blocking marriage. Pae Avakofe told me himself that his sisters never married through dread of their father's anger. A very excep-tional case is presented by the historical incident of the marriage of Te Ikarua. She was a great beauty and the daughter of the Ariki Taumako, Faisina. She took her fate into her own hands, and, it is said, told her father, " I do not desire the chiefly faces ; I desire only to look on my *kave* Tarakofe." Her father, ashamed at the avowal of this preference for her cousin, pulled his bark-cloth blanket over his face with a curse, " May your father eat filth." Her parents made no opposition to the match, since if they angered her she would pro-bably have swum off to sea and have been drowned. Such is the explanation given by her descendants. She was evidently a girl of strong character.

Since the union of bride and groom occurs without the knowledge of the woman's family, who would stop it if they could, it takes place at night. The man's family on the other hand, who receive the pair and initiate preparations for the ritual to follow, are likely to be apprised of it. Moreover, it is with them that the future wife will be living and working. Therefore, if a man is wise, he will announce his intentions to his parents beforehand and ask their advice about his choice. This is frequently done, particularly by young men of rank who recognize their responsibilities. If a young man brings his wife home without previous announcement, the parents accept the matter with the best grace they can. If they refused to receive her, then presumably the suicide of the pair would be their last resort.

This, however, is hypothetical; I know of no cases in which the *fait accompli* has been rejected and the woman sent back to her people. The fact of going to her lover's house with him and being received there constitutes the all-important step which converts her from a mistress into a wife. To stifle an attempt at marriage, the economic sanction of withholding food from the pair, such as is employed by the girl's family in the Trobriands, is not exercised in Tikopia by the man's parents.[1]

This is an instance of the curious docility which the Tikopia show in situations affecting personal pride, a docility and a respect for personality for which psychological explanation is probably needed. This passive attitude can be correlated to some extent with the high degree of sensitiveness of the people to personal affront and the quick resort to attempted suicide as a means of protest and self-justification. The separation of culture from history and race psychology is an extremely difficult task—admitting that there is such a thing as race psychology. It is a task for which the anthropologist is unfitted, and his contribution towards it lies only in refining his cultural analysis to the point at which an inexplicable residue of behaviour remains. Though he can correlate this element with other items of culture, he cannot explain why it should be present any more than any other of a number of alternatives.

I did not find evidence to corroborate Rivers's statement that the father's sister in Tikopia has the deciding voice in the choice of her nephew's bride.[2] She is frequently consulted as a member of the family and her opinion carries considerable weight, but I did not hear anything to suggest that if she forbade a match it would be given up.

There are several complications which may occur before the bride is brought to her husband's house. The young man may not want to marry. The delights of freedom, of "strolling among the unmarried (*tafau i te taka*)," may appeal to him far more than settling down to a staid responsible existence with a wife. But his parents and relatives, particularly if he be the eldest son of a chief, may want him to marry. They urge him to select someone. Of old a man waited until his beard had encircled his face; nowadays he may marry when he has "set up his hair," that is, has allowed it to grow long. A son of a chief is pressed to marry when young. But the people do not speak to him too strongly on the matter lest he be piqued, take a canoe and go off to sea. For the same reason his father, even if he knows the young man is contemplating marriage, will not mention the matter to him lest he become ashamed. Thus Kavakiua told me

[1] Malinowski, *Sexual Life of Savages*, 1929, 71 *et seq.*
[2] Rivers, *H.M.S.*, I, 308.

that he heard Rimakoroa wanted to get married, but he was not going to speak to him himself because he was the lad's *mana*, in this case his father's first cousin. It is left to other more distantly related people of the clan to suggest to him that he should take a wife.

The choice of the young man may not accord with that of his elders when he makes it known to them. He is led by his desire, they by more sober considerations. Since they will have to live with his wife, they want someone who will be industrious and good tempered ; a woman who will not have a bitter tongue or who will not sulk—in the expressive native phrase, one who will not " turn her back upon the relatives and eat her food alone, facing the wall of the house." In answer to my question why a certain woman had never married, Pa Fenuatara replied, " She is a fine girl, but her lips are awful, scolding lips ; now look at her features, they're extremely sharp." [1] Parents may find other grounds of objection to their son's mistress in her youth, or her gluttony. So they discuss the matter with him, voice their objections and indicate their own preference.

In discussing the case mentioned above, Pa Fenuatara said, " Now in this land, when a man wishes a woman like that, his relatives (*kano a paito*) object. They speak to him, ' Your mind is made up for the woman, but we object, our faces frown at the woman.' Now when the relatives object to her, they make up their minds in a different direction ; they look out for whom may be good and make up their minds. Then the man listens to them. When a man goes to a woman and after some time desires that the two of them come (to his house), he comes and puts the matter before his parents. He comes and says to them, ' We two shall come on this night.' Then when his parents say they object to the woman, he hammers away at them ; he will not agree, and he pleads to be allowed to marry his own woman. ' I object to the ideas you have formed. My own wish among women is one, this one here that I go to.' Now if the relatives do not like the woman their faces cloud over. They don't inform him. The relatives rise and go to fetch a wife ; they go to their own desire and reject the woman of the man. The idea of fetching women is formed in that way, it has root in the elders."

The fetching of the woman is a form of capture. There are three reasons which may lead to the capture of the bride in Tikopia : the desire of a man for a woman who refuses his advances ; the wish of a family to get their son married when he objects to making a choice ; or their wish to anticipate his own selection and secure a more suitable mate for him. In the first case the man himself is cognizant of the affair

---

[1] It is interesting to notice that the same correlation between sharp features and a scolding tongue is made by the Tikopia as by ourselves.

and probably plays an active part in it ; in the others he is ignorant.
But the procedure is essentially the same in each case.   The custom
is called *tukuŋa nofine*, carrying off a wife, and is sometimes described
as *tuku pouri*, carrying off in the dark.   This latter expression refers
to the ignorance of the woman and her relatives.

THE CAPTURE OF THE BRIDE

The practice of abducting a woman with the aid of a party and
taking her blindly to a bridegroom is characteristic mainly of chiefly
families.   The reason seems to be that it is only these families who
are strong enough to bear the brunt of the struggle that ensues.   It
is a question not only of physical violence, but also of authority.
The " assembly of wife carriers " consists mainly of the brothers,
cousins, father's brothers and equivalent relatives of the bridegroom.
They gather together secretly and go to seize the girl of their choice.
The correct thing is to take her from her father's house.   In this case
it is said, " The woman has been sped from the path of chiefs ; it is
good," or again, " Her invitation has been issued from the centre of
the house."   If on the other hand, as sometimes happens, she is
snatched from her work in the fields or as she is walking along the path,
it is said, " She has gone in the path of orphan children."   The phrase
used for this is *tuku fakakaka* or *sau fakakaka*, meaning to take secretly,
furtively, not in the proper style.   This is bad.   In such a case the
father or brother of the woman will later upbraid the man who has
taken her.   " Why did you take her furtively from the middle of the
path ?   Why didn't you come into the middle of the house here to
take your married woman ? "   The resentment aroused is very keen,
and the struggle, which must then take place around the man's house,
is much more severe.   In the case of the abduction of Nau Nukunefu,
for instance, a man was shot with an arrow and died later.

Where the capture is done in correct style the group of men
proceed to the woman's house.   If it is the families of two chiefs who
are concerned, then these two leaders sit down and converse amicably
together, while their respective parties fight.   This is consonant with
the Tikopia respect for chiefs, which will not allow them to be mal-
treated or even handled.   A messenger has previously announced the
arrival of the raiding party, or else someone has seen them and rushed
on ahead to give warning.   The leader of the wife-seekers says in
formal fashion, " I have come for a cultivator for myself."

The father of the girl answers, " Go then to the rich people
to seek a cultivator for yourself ; why have you come to the
poor ? "

The leader replies, " O, no ! I am going with my married woman."

" No. I object to my daughter being taken."

Then the leader of the wife-seizing party gets up, grasps the girl, who weeps, and bears her off. Both sides rise and join in and a struggle ensues. The woman is held back by her brothers and is pulled to and fro. It is etiquette for the capturing party to occupy themselves not so much with the resisting of assault as with the endeavour to carry off the girl. As a man approaches her, one of her brothers grips him by the hair : " Go away ! " " Pull, friend," he replies, " that is my grass "—meaning that it does not matter if some of it is torn out. An alternative reply is, " Grub away, friend, it's my grass," referring to the practice of clearing out weeds from a cultivation. Retaliation for a blow is not usual. Occasionally a man who is the *taina* or *mana* of another may strike him back ; in such case the elders soothe the contestants. When a man of the ravishing party is hit, he tries to placate his assailant with some such words as, " Don't do that, friend ; calm your mind and let our married woman be carried off." The major part of the struggle consists in pulling and hauling each other about. When people are describing the custom they take great interest in going into details of what happens. They tell with gusto how folk are struck with clubs and bones are broken. But the amount of actual damage inflicted does not seem to be great where the orthodox procedure has been carried out. The correct thing is for some of the ravishers to crawl to the relatives of the woman and not to fight them, to suffer blows and hair-pulling while the rest carry off the girl.

After a long struggle the party of the man, being the stronger, usually succeeds in bearing the girl away. As she approaches another village where her relatives live, they turn out with clubs and spears and put up at least a show of a second fight. Sometimes the ravishing party is not strong enough and their attempt fails. Then they will have to retire ignominiously, to be laughed at by the whole island until a second party of sufficient strength has been assembled and has taken her. Sometimes again, in the interval, the woman may have run to the house of a chief or a *maru* and taken shelter there. In such event she may be left undisturbed. But if the party is strong, then it will make a gift of atonement to the chief, enter his house, crawl to him and remove the woman. No resistance is made by the chief's people. The chief himself gives a few loud whoops as a matter of form to save his face, since his house has been entered without invitation. This is acknowledged to be pure pretence ; it is said by the natives to come in the category of *fakamatamata laui*, making his face good.

There are then certain rules of the game in this abduction of the bride. These, however, are not to be taken as an indication that the capture is a mere formality. It comes as a complete surprise to the girl's relatives and usually to her also. What the etiquette of the proceedings does is to soften the asperities of the blow once it has fallen ; if free retaliation by the capturing party were allowed, then a real feud might easily arise. They have the girl, so it is only fair that they should put up with a little pain to get her. This, a fair rendering of the native point of view, is eminently sensible in such a small community where the strain of internecine warfare would be extremely severe.

When the woman has been carried off without warning, while she is out of doors, her kinsfolk assemble and follow the ravishers to their destination. There something like a real battle rages. Some men sit inside, holding the girl, others defend the house without. Here people are sometimes seriously hurt.

The case of Nau Nukunefu illustrates the bad feeling that is engendered when a woman is not taken in the orthodox way. Conversely, of course, there is a tendency for the usual courtesies to be disregarded in abducting a woman from a family with whom relations are already not too good. This was the case with the chiefly families of Tafua and Taumako. Tupaki (now Pa Nukunefu), one of the sons of the former chief, had as his mistress the daughter of Pae Avakofe. He met her one day in an orchard, grasped her wrist and said, " Let the two of us go to my house." She seemed to consent, then suddenly screamed and began to struggle. Tupaki cursed her, grabbed her in his arms and began to carry her off. In this he was assisted by some of his brothers who ran up. She was taken back to Matautu, and there came a strong force of sa Taumako to fight with sa Tafua. In the struggle several people were injured, among them Pa Raropupua. He was shot by Pa Teva, who loosed off a sheaf of arrows at random at a group of people who were running for shelter into the trees. From this wound the man later died. Such was the ferocity of sa Taumako that they recovered the girl and bore her back in triumph to Ravena.

This was naturally a great blow to the prestige of the Ariki Tafua and his sons. A night or two later, as they were sitting disconsolate in their house Motuapi, they heard sounds of something scratching at the thatch of the door. They called out, but there was no reply. What was it, a man or a ghost ? At last someone dragged aside the door and in crawled the girl. She rushed to her lover and clasped him round the knees—much to everyone's astonishment and, for a moment, to their dismay. Then they learnt that she had come alone round the reef from Ravena. She had been out torchlight fishing with her companions and in the darkness had managed to slip away. She was received, and the pair settled down together. When sa Taumako learnt of her escape, they made no further effort to recover her. By returning of her own volition she had cut away the ground from beneath their feet. Such was the account given me.

The screaming of the girl in the first instance was simply an attempt to save her reputation. A woman of rank should be borne off to her husband in the grand style and not meekly accompany him. This *cause célèbre*, though for some time it accentuated the existing feud between the two chiefly groups and their districts, has eventually proved to be a distinct force in drawing them together through a constant meeting of both sides in carrying out the economic obligations attendant on the marriage.

So far we have not considered the position of the two main participants in a marriage of this kind. The woman thus rudely torn from her home weeps, partly no doubt from excitement, but partly also from fright. Often she is in ignorance of her destination, and the prospect of being confronted with a husband with whom previously she has had no intimacy of relationship must be disturbing. The attitude of the man varies. If this is the woman of his choice, then of course he is satisfied. But in many cases the bride is forced upon him by surprise ; his relatives may have said to one another, " Let us go and bring back that one as our married woman, but reject the person to whom he goes. The one for whom he pleads—what sort of a mind has she ? She is one who will turn her back on his relatives." (The question as to the mind of the woman is not an enquiry as to her intelligence, but as to her good nature.) When the woman is brought to the house and the man comes home, he may object strongly to this wife who has been " set down for him in the dark," as it is put. He seizes a stick or a club and beats the roof of the house in his anger, yelling out his disapproval in high-pitched whoops and cursing vigorously in excretory phrases. When the bride sees this demonstration on the part of her groom, not unnaturally shame is added to her fear and she weeps the more. At last the hubbub subsides and everyone settles down for the night.

The actual token of the acceptance of the woman as the bride is the smearing of her head with turmeric by women of the man's family, his mother and sisters. The purport of this is to single her out as having special status at the moment. I know of no cases where, when she has once been brought to the house, the turmeric has not been put upon her. The acceptance of a woman once she has entered the dwelling is probably linked with the general Tikopia attitude of respect towards a married woman. It is significant that the bride is referred to as *fafine avaŋa* (married woman) from the first moment of her abduction from her father's house. It is doubtless intended to convey that it is a " woman for marrying " that is wanted, but the term is the same as that used after her marriage. Apart from the turmeric, which is plastered on her head and breast, the bride is girt with a piece of orange bark-cloth as a belt around her skirt. This is the sign of a newly-married woman.

Nowadays the custom of *tukuŋa nofine* has been largely given up owing to the practice of Christianity by some of the people. No cases occurred when I was in Tikopia ; the marriages that took place were by elopement. I have reason to believe that it was intended to take a bride for Rimakoroa in the elaborate style, but unfortunately a drought towards the end of my stay kept the food supplies low and prevented any possibility of the marriage. Many of the younger benedicts of to-day had their wives seized for them—Pa Nukunefu, Pa Raŋifuri, the Ariki Taumako, for example.

The last named was married to the daughter of Pa Niumano. It was not announced to him beforehand ; his relatives took the decision. The woman was carried off in the night. The affair was described to me by one of the participants, his cousin Pa Teva. The ravishing party assembled after a *kava* ceremony in the canoe-yard of sa Taumako ; when they had made up their minds whom they wanted, they informed the old chief, his father. Then they went to Namo, where the people were gathered together making turmeric. They moved hastily because they were in competition with sa Tafua, who wished to abduct the girl for Pa Raŋifuri. When the party arrived the girl ran and hid in the woods, and they had to seek her. When they found her there was a great struggle, both sides hitting out freely until they were exhausted. Then the folk of Namo watched the girl being carried off without daring to utter a word. When the abductors reached Asaŋa, the residence of her mother's brother, he came out and made a show of fight, but they crawled to him and were allowed to proceed. When morning came they made the appropriate gifts. On this occasion they said that the woman was very frightened, since she did not know to whom she was being taken.

ATONEMENT AND RECIPROCITY

Once the woman has been taken to the house of her husband and her relatives have accepted the fact, the marriage ritual follows precisely the same course in the case of an elopement as in an abduction. Both in fact, as Crawley points out, are methods of getting hold of the person of the bride and do not constitute in any essential fashion part of the wedding ceremony.

Several marriages after elopement took place while I was in Tikopia. I attended two, that of Sauakipure and Nau Vatere in Te Roro, which was an abridgment of the normal ritual (see later), and that of sa Roŋoifo, which followed the ordinary course. I have used the latter as illustration in describing the sequence of events.

THE PLACATING GIFT

It is not surprising to find that the act of obtaining forcible possession of the bride is followed by a show of compensation. Early in the morning afterwards the relatives of the husband bear a gift to the house of the woman's father. If the woman is taken before mid-day, then the gift is taken the same afternoon. If the girl be of high rank, for example the brother's daughter of a chief, then the gift is made to the chief as the head of her kinship group, and not to her father. Since it is in fact made to the ramage from which the girl is taken, there is always a tendency to send it to the house of the senior representative. The gift, in the case of commoners, consists of one wooden bowl and one coil of sinnet cord. Between families of rank a *pa tu maŋa*, that is, a bonito hook with barb attached, is sent as well. If a girl of rank has been carried off by a family of commoners and the head of it has such a hook, he will send it. No food is taken. Occasionally a paddle may be added—one is said to have been given for the marriage of the Ariki Taumako.

This gift is called *te malai*, a name which gives an indication of its function. *Malai* is a general term applied to the gift which a man takes to a chief in atonement for any offence he has committed against him. It is by way of compensation for the violence offered to his rank and dignity. In the present case, the gift is the compensation given to the girl's family for taking away their daughter from them. It is made after an elopement, just as after a more violent abduction. A crowd of ten to twenty people go with the gift, married women as well as men; it is said that if an unmarried girl went she would be taken and kept by the other family. The bringers of the *malai* go and crawl to the male relatives of the woman. As they come to the door of the house, they try and lift up the floor-mats and crawl underneath them to the side of the girl's father. The family will have already been apprised of their approach and will have posted a man at the doorway. If he is versed in such matters, he will press down the edge of the mat so that they cannot submit themselves to this indignity. Particular care is taken when, as is frequently the case, the son of a chief, or a *maru*, is among the party of atonement. Here again a more general system of etiquette regulates the immediate behaviour. As the men advance, crawling either over or under the floor-mats, they are struck by the girl's relatives on the head and back, their hair is pulled, they are pushed and beaten. The women also fight among themselves. With chiefly families there is much more fierceness displayed than with commoners.

On the occasion of the carrying-off of the woman who is now Nau Raŋifuri, the *malai* was brought to the Ariki Taumako. Pa Resiake had the honour of receiving the visitors first. He came out from his house Tuaraŋi—afterwards my home—and, armed with a club, stood in the path. On came the atoning party bearing their gifts, an enormous man in the lead. He advanced and called out in the conventional propitiatory formula, " I eat ten times your excrement, Pa Resiake," and knelt to press his nose to the other man's knee. A thrust with the butt of the weapon and he was sent spinning yards away. " Who was the man who broke M.....'s arm," Pa Resiake shouted. The offender came forward and knelt, to meet a similar fate. The rest were allowed to press their noses to his knee. They then proceeded to the house of the chief. On their way they were molested by the young men of the village, who pulled the wooden bowl off the shoulder of the man who was carrying it and hacked at it. However, it was picked up again and taken along. The visitors were prevented from crawling under the floor-mats, but had to run the gauntlet above. The men of Taumako were lined in two ranks along the centre of the house, their chief at the far end. The visitors attempted to crawl down the lane, but had their hair pulled and were so pounded with fists that the breath was knocked out of their bodies and they fell exhausted. Not one reached the side of the chief by his own efforts. The present Ariki Tafua (then not yet chief, but known as Pa Raŋifuri) was assisted to get there, as also Pa Korokoro. It is the custom that if a man wins through and reaches the chief to press nose to his knee, then the fray stops. It is said " a man has entered to the chief, the shelter of commoners " (*taŋata ku uru ki te ariki, te maru ŋa fakaarofa*). It is *tapu* to strike a man when he is thus near a chief ; if it were done the chief would be angry. It is the custom also for no resistance to be made by the atoning party.

In the case mentioned above the rest of the men were revived by the women of the other side. This is the function of women on such an occasion, the natives say, to restore the men who have fainted or have become exhausted under the rough treatment. This does not bear out Crawley's theory that it is the bride's own sex that show the most animosity to the ravishers. It is actually the reverse.

An amusing sidelight on the position of people of rank in Tikopia is given by the statement of a commoner to me. He said, " When the atoning party comes, the sons of chiefs in it are beaten only by sons of chiefs. We do not strike them, lest they rise up and strike us back, and we have to go off to sea."

After the *malai* has been delivered and its representatives have pressed noses to the chief's knee, the party returns home. They do not wait to be fed as in most cases of visiting.

The girl who became Nau Roŋoifo eloped from Potu sa Taumako one night with her lover of the Niumano house of Namo. Part of the *malai* was taken early in the morning to the houses of the Ariki Taumako, Pa Motuata and Pa Tarikitoŋa. Three people went to the first, two to the second and one to the third, in each case crawling to the man, pressing noses with him and announcing the marriage. The woman was of the house of Vaikava, of ŋatotiu, and these were preliminary announcements out of deference to the three branches of the chiefly house of the clan to which the woman belonged. The actual *malai* gift was taken in a crowd of about twenty people to Pa ŋatotiu. Pa Saukirima and others crawled into the house and pressed their noses to the knee or to the face of the girl's guardian. Pa Sauki-rima, as an important elder, was lifted up before he could reach the other man's knee and they greeted each other face to face. By these little acts of personal discrimination, so simple in performance and so difficult to describe briefly, the Tikopia sense of etiquette and subtle differentiation of rank is made evident. The elderly woman in Vaikava with whom the girl had been living, angry that she had gone, seized a billet of wood and struck at the women of the party. They pushed and pinched a little and then separated, the men not interfering. There was no maltreatment of the male section of the visitors.

THE "OVEN OF JOINING"

The importance of food in the ceremonial life of the Tikopia has already been demonstrated. Hardly any ritual affair is complete without the making of an oven. The first item in the marriage ceremony after the atoning gift is " the oven of joining." It is de-scribed as *te umu tanakiaŋa* or *te umu tanaki*. It is made the morning after the girl has been taken to her husband's house, and as the name indicates, it represents the initial celebration for the pair who have entered into the bonds of marriage. Just as the smearing with tur-meric is in a way the formal acceptance of the bride by the man's people, so the preparation of this oven is the formal proclamation of the union. It is an affair entirely of the husband's family, the food not being sent away to any other household.

It is described also as the *umu fakapariki*, " the oven of the woman who will be embraced in the night," or " the oven of the husband who is going to his wife." This is an indication of another aspect of its function—it prefaces the first formal consummation of the union. If the pair have been sweethearts before, then they probably have had intercourse already, but especially if the bride has been reft from her family without collusion on her part, then she may be unwilling to receive her husband. From Pa Fenuatara I received a description of what happens in such a case. He said : " The oven of joining is made in the daytime, and when night comes on the land the husband goes to his wife. But when he has had his wife left in darkness for him (abducted) and the woman does not desire him, then when the man goes to stay by her side, she turns her face to the wall and presents her back to him. But she does not stay alone, she is surrounded by the relatives and held down lest she run. The man, too, goes to hold his wife down. Now when the oven of joining has been made and the land is dark, the band of brothers of the man come and sit at the side of the married pair. They sit and sit there until the relatives of the household are asleep. They then speak to the man. They do not speak aloud lest the woman hear, but they nudge him gently to go to his wife. His brothers grip the woman. When she sees the man has risen to come to her, she too rises to fly. But she is gripped by the brothers of the man and pulled down, made to lie down. They grip her arms and press upon her, they grasp also her legs and pull them apart. The woman shrieks, but as she shrieks someone grips her and blocks her mouth. While her legs are held down her belt is unwound, and the man enters her. How the woman kicks ! (the native word *taparaki* really expresses the sound made by the knocking of her limbs on the dry coconut matting). Such are the customs of this land, customs of the *tuku pouri*, the abduction, when both parties are ignorant. Now the woman does not object ; the man has arrived there ; the woman objects only before the man has reached her, when the two of them have not embraced before." The woman is not ashamed the next day, it is said, since only the *fare taina* of the man, his band of brothers, were there to see. If the woman does not object to intercourse with her husband on this night, then they do not assist him ; they are there simply to see that she does not run, and to help in overcoming her resistance.

This marital rape must not be interpreted as in any sense a communal affair. The husband is the only one to have intercourse with the woman, and any suggestion otherwise is repugnant to these people. There is nothing to suggest either that the aversion of the woman is feigned; her resistance to a strange man is quite comprehensible. This is still another piece of evidence for the reality of her abduction.

At this initial stage of the marriage the virginity of the bride is a matter of some moment. In the first place, if the husband has had any hand in the selection of the woman who has been abducted, he will probably have chosen one whom he believes not to have had intercourse with other men already. " In this land, if a man is sensible, and hears that a woman is going with another man, he does not wish to marry her." This is perhaps an ideal statement, because in the case of many marriages I learned that the woman had been the mistress of someone else before. The evaluation of virginity has been discussed in the preceding chapter.

At the time of the oven of joining some of the young people who have been associates of the married pair sometimes go and dance at the wedding. This is not to honour the married pair, but to slander them in humorous style. They are vilified in song for having deserted the ranks of the *taka*, for having given up their freedom and the joys of the bachelor state.[1] At the marriage of Pa Roŋoifo some of the bachelors of the woman's village and of Raveŋa formed a party to go and *tauaŋutu*. The reason was that some time before the girl had been one of the leaders in a dance party directed against the bachelors, and had *sava*, that is, had performed a kind of *pas seul* with characteristic movements of the outstretched arms. This was part of a conventional declaration of her contempt of men and marriage. So when she took a husband the young men had their chance for revenge. Kavakiua said, " A girl who wishes to marry will not *tauaŋutu*." This is an exaggeration, of course, but the incompatibility of the two attitudes lays her open to scorn-songs. The young men came and danced around the house, singing some improvised compositions. They were not scolded or driven off by the relatives, as sometimes happens. The girl was not especially ashamed or angry; though she did not laugh, she just looked cross.

One incident was significant. A young man, Pokia, started with the party, but fell out on the way. He was ashamed because the girl had been his mistress—" he had carried tobacco to her." Later she had deserted him for the lover who became her husband.

---

[1] This approximates in feeling to the beating of tin cans when a newly married couple return home—a custom followed in country districts by the British of the Antipodes.

Here are the songs that were sung on this occasion :

> *Tafito :* Where are the experts of the dance
> I look and look for them
>
> *Kupu :* Ie ! Wail the cry
> The stupid woman

This is a song composed by Pa Niuaru. It mocks the woman for having married, and calls for dancers to come and display their derision. Another song used the common metaphor of eating *soi*, which is applied to a person who marries or who desires the love of a near relative. The *soi* in its raw state is extremely bitter ; it is rendered mild only by steeping it in the waters of the lake.

> *Tafito :* Your *soi* will be steeped for you
> Left in Tai it will be steeped
> Carried to the Siku
> The Siku there in Raveŋa
>
> *Kupu :* Observe the land crab of the woods
> It eats *soi* and is rejected.

Here the metaphor of the bitter fruit is applied to the actions of the girl, and is carried consistently throughout the song. The reference to Tai and to the *siku*, the shelf in the lake, are simply inserted for the sake of euphony. And just as the crab (it is said) is rendered unfit for food because it eats *soi*, so the woman is rendered unfit for the company of others by her union. In actual fact in the present case the woman had not married a close relative ; the song was used as a general taunt without specific reference. The next song is of the *feuku* type, frankly outspoken.

> *Tafito :* One hears that it is small
> The vulva worked through
> With which you have copulated
> And made ejaculation.
>
> *Kupu :* The desire of man
> Interferes, interferes with me
> The rat-trap sprung
> No longer stirs.

This is a song of the women, and must have been sung on this occasion because of its general bawdy reference, which would be rather embarrassing to the married couple. The theme of the song is that a man goes to a woman, has intercourse with her and the act of ejaculation completed, rises to go. Once the rat-trap has sprung it does not move again. This is a jeer by women at the inability of men to return immediately after detumescence to the satisfaction of their desire.

THE FEAST

One of the most important events of a marriage is the *aŋa*, the enormous mass of food accumulated by the bridegroom's family and utilized as presents and as meals. This is similar in form and in function to the *aŋa* at the initiation of a boy, the treatment of which has already been described. Families of rank always collect this mass of food, but commoner families may use their own discretion. If a family is wealthy, it makes the *aŋa*; if not, then the oven of joining alone is made. For the marriage of sa Raŋoifo it was made, since not only was the house wealthy, but the bridegroom was the *muaki tama*, the eldest son. In such a case his *kano a paito* come to his aid. With families of commoners the *aŋa* may be delayed until some time after the marriage in order to give them time to accumulate supplies. With chiefly families it is different, since they always have some stocks of food in hand.

At the marriage of sa Roŋoifo the assembling of the food took place on the same day as the oven of joining. The relatives came in with their loads of taro, *pulaka*, bananas and yams and put them in a heap outside the house. The married couple were sitting within. The organization was in charge of members of the bridegroom's own family. They gave directions to the party who went out to get supplies, " Go and dig the yams in such and such a place," " Cut the bunch of bananas which is ready in such a place," and so on. All day there was a busy scene, people assembling from all parts of the island. Nau Taumako, a daughter of the family, brought a contribution from her household. Her husband, the chief, did not come as cook, but was represented by Rimakoroa. For ceremonies of commoners chiefs do not attend, but send their sons instead.

The next day came the preparation of the main feast. There was an atmosphere of activity and excitement through Raveŋa and Namo, focussed on the two households of ŋatotiu and Roŋoifo. In the former the work in connection with the mats (*meŋa*) (see below) was toward, in the latter the work of the *aŋa*. As always there were people closely related to both families, and they had to decide which they would assist. So, going along the path with other people one heard the question, " Are you going to the *meŋa* or to the *aŋa* ? " Men and women had different parts of the work to do. The women scraped taro and peeled bananas, the men grated them up and chopped *pulaka* and breadfruit. There were two groups—that for the preliminary

GENEALOGY VIII

ILLUSTRATING THE PRINCIPAL RELATIONSHIPS
AT THE MARRIAGE OF SA ROŊOIFO

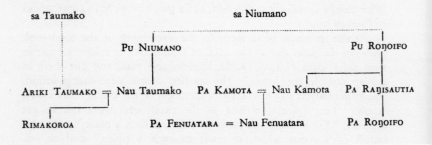

NOTE.—For reasons of space some names mentioned in the descriptive account have been omitted.

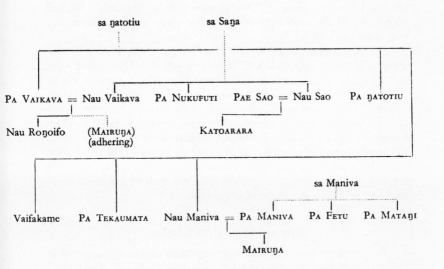

preparation of the raw food and that for the grating of it. At the
latter about ten men were engaged, with boys to assist them. Graters
had been borrowed from other villages up and down the coast, as
the custom is. As in the case of initiation, there is a distinction
between the cooks who come by virtue of their wives being daughters
of the family and those who come because their wives are *tama tapu*
of the family. The former are *soko fai matua*, the latter *soko fai
tuatina*. Pa Fenuatara was in the latter category, his wife being from
the house of Kamota, and her mother being from Niumano. This
extension of the category of cooks as far as the husbands of one's
nieces in the female line is to be correlated with the extent of the labour
power demanded at such a feast.

On this occasion an incident occurred which is typical of the keen
sense of dignity possessed by Tikopia of rank. I saw after a time that
Pa Fenuatara was missing from the group of workers, and enquired
for him. I was told, " Perhaps he is annoyed that the oven was
kindled before he came." This appeared to be the case. He had
withdrawn in dudgeon because the other cooks had not waited for
him, a man of premier rank.

The first oven of the day is the " oven of awakening " (*umu
ararafaŋa*). This provides food for the workers. The second oven
is " the great oven " (*umu lasi*), the food from which is taken wholly
to the house of the woman's family. The third oven is the " oven
of mats " (*umu o a meŋa*), which is made in the evening after the receipt
of gifts from the bride's family. The food from it is taken to them
by the groom's people. From the midday oven a gift is made to
the chief of the bride's clan. It is called *te monotaŋa*, the usual term
for a food gift to a chief, customary on any occasion of note. It
consists of a large basket of cooked food, a bunch of sprouting coconuts and perhaps some sticks of sugar-cane.

THE BARTER OF THE BRIDE

The economics of the marriage ceremony are as complicated as
those of initiation or of mourning. In addition to the transference
of large quantities of food, valuables of several kinds also pass to
and fro. The principal element transferred from the bridegroom's
house is what is known as *te koroa*. Ordinarily this term simply
means property, but as is the Tikopia habit, the generic term has also
a specific connotation. It consists of a set of wooden bowls and coils
of sinnet, with paddles tied to them. These gifts are plainly termed
" the payment for the woman " (*te tauvi o te fafine*), the native word
applying to situations of ordinary exchange. The description does

not mean of course that the woman is really bought.   As the material in earlier chapters has made perfectly clear, a wife in Tikopia is a free agent, in no sense the property of her husband to a greater degree than he is hers.   This set of gifts represents a kind of formal equivalent to her family for the loss of her services.   She goes to live with her husband's people, and these gifts make a show of reimbursement to her family.   The fact that it is formal rather than actual barter is shown by the size of the later return present, which to a large extent repays what the groom's people give.

Bowls and sinnet are assembled in the house of the head of the groom's family, contributions being brought by kinsfolk with value in rough proportion to their closeness of relationship.   There is the usual long discussion as to what items shall be presented to certain people of the other group.   At the marriage of sa Roŋoifo there were a large number of people to be thus accommodated, and Pa Saukirima, an old man wise in such matters, said to Pa Faiaki, who was rather impetuously putting forward the claims of various men, " Don't raise their names, brother.   Sit down and be quiet.   There are a lot of people to be thought of."   (Text S. 6.)

The goods are divided into three sets :

> *te koroa te ariki*—goods of the chief.
> *te koroa fai matua*—parental goods.
> *te koroa fai tuatina*—mother's brother's goods.

The present for the chief is sent because the woman is of his clan and has been contributing to his welfare.   It is very carefully chosen. If the *malai* has already been carried to him, then the *koroa* is " bound to his son."   At the marriage referred to a similar gift to that of the chief was sent to Pa Tarikitoŋa because of his rank in the clan.   Ten other sets of property were allotted to other men of the *fai matua* group.   The accompanying genealogy (Genealogy VIII) shows the principal relations involved on this occasion.   Gifts were made to :

1. Ariki Taumako } (the chiefly brothers).
2. Pa Tarikitoŋa }
3. Pa Tekaumata (father's brother of the girl).
4. Pa Vaikava (father of the girl ; this went to the aunt of the girl and to Mairuŋa, her *kave*, since in reality her father was dead).
5. Pa ŋatotiu (father's brother).
6. Pae Sao.
7. Pa Farekofe.
8. Pa Porima.   (These last three men got gifts through their wives, who were sisters of the bride's mother.   They were therefore " fathers " of hers.)
9. Pa Maniva.
10. Pa Fetu.

11. Pa Mataŋi. (These three men are the chief representatives of the branches of the house of Maniva, the members of which are the "cooks of the house of ŋatotiu" on account of a former marriage. In comment on the presentation of gifts from the house of the bridegroom to these folk whose linkage is with the house of the bride, it was said, "Cooks in this land are never rejected.)

12. Pa Raŋituifo. (The reason for sending him property was that he was the representative of the house of Fatumaru, and each of the principal groups of the clan was remembered, however tenuous their claims by kinship might be. The head of the house to which Roŋoifo belonged was Pa Niumano, and he was also senior elder to the Ariki Taumako. He regarded it as consistent with his dignity therefore to assume the burden of the marriage gifts and to distribute them through all the principal families of the clan, to which both bride and bridegroom belonged.)

13. Pa Nukufuti.

14. Pa Panapa.

15. Pa Siamano. (These three men were of the *fai tuatina* group. The *tafito* or foundation of them was Pa Nukufuti, the mother of the bride having been his true sister. Pa Panapa and also Pa Kamota are of the same house, sa Saŋa. The former received a present, but the latter did not have one allotted to him since his wife was the sister of the bridegroom's father. He therefore came as cook to the bridegroom's group, in obedience to his nearer tie. Pa Siamano was included because his mother was the father's sister of Pa Nukufuti. The special reason for sending a gift to him was that he was living in the house of his dead mother's brother (the father of Pa Nukufuti) in the village of Asaŋa.)

This is the complete list of the people to whom *koroa* were sent from the bridegroom's group. It shows on the one hand the complexity and wide range of the kinship ties involved, and on the other the differentiation made on the basis of individual circumstances. Again it demonstrates how the active recognition of kinship may be correlated with the situation of rank and wealth.

The arrangements for the distribution of the property follow much the same course as has been described for the ceremony of initiation. The goods are set out on *mata paito*, the technical term used being *vero*, the most common meaning of which is to lower down. Here it can be best translated as to orientate towards. As each set of goods is placed in position, it is announced clearly, "*Ia!* The property of . . ." This is done that there may be no mistake, that the people in the house may know clearly the destination of each gift. Various persons from the group of cooks are selected to carry the bowls and cord to the houses of the recipients, and instructions are given according to circumstances. In the case of Pae Sao, for instance, it was arranged that the gift should be carried to his house and put there. If he happened to be helping his neighbour Pa ŋatotiu, then the carrier was to go next door and anounce: "The property of Pae Sao has been stood in his dwelling." If, on the other hand, he happened to be in Asaŋa helping his brother-in-law Pa Nukufuti, then someone would tell him there what had been done. Such arranging demands a great deal of discussion, argument and contradiction, but this is the means by which the organization works.

The number of people for whom provision is made in this way varies according to the wealth and discretion of the heads of the bridegroom's family. The parents and true mother's brothers of the bride, as well as the chief of her clan, are sure to be included, but for less immediate relatives it is often a matter of uncertainty. A man does not know if a gift is going to be made to him or not until the moment of distribution. If in such circumstances he finds himself in the list of recipients his pleasure, the natives say, is great. "A man of the clan has waited and waited, and there! his face has been lifted up, his reputation has been uncovered; that is handsome." The factor which is most operative here is the compliment paid to a person's individuality by singling him out for this attention. Hence it is as if a cloak has been removed from his reputation, allowing it to be seen in public. The bent head, the token of modesty and shame, can be converted into the uplifted face, assured of meeting the eyes of others since the name of the owner has been remembered. This aspect of the matter marks two general points—the elasticity that convention allows in the interpretation of kinship obligations, and the subtle linkage between kinship and personal status given by translating recognition of kinship ties into terms of public reputation. The selection of a person as the recipient of gifts on the basis of kinship is both an index of his public worth and an increment to it.

The *koroa* are carried off in the late afternoon with parcels of food from the *aŋa*. The time of departure depends on that at which the cooks have arrived in the morning and also on the efficiency of the people in charge. Some of the sets of *koroa* may be delivered in a batch if several of the recipients are known to be in the same house. One of the cooks then steps forward and announces the destination of each package. "The property of So-and-so. . . ." After the distribution is over he may recite a formula known as the *oriori*, a conventional utterance of abasement:

I eat ten times your excrement.

According to his wish, too, he may go and press noses with the principal people in the house, though this polite gesture is not essential.

The Gift of the Mats.—On the same day as the property is presented from the groom's people the relatives of the bride make gifts in return. These are spoken of under the collective name of *meŋa* (pandanus mats). Three types of gifts are involved here. From the house of the parents of the girl and from that of her immediate mother's brother come large mats, one from each, which are known as the *matua meŋa* (principal mats). The family of the girl present also another large mat known as the *uruŋa*. The ordinary translation of this term is head-rest or pillow, but in this case the name is applied metaphorically; this mat is kept in the house of the newly married couple as the property of the bride. In addition several other mats and a large pile of bark-cloth sheets and girdles are contributed by various members of the *fai matua* and *fai tuatina* group associated with the bride. There may be eight or more mats altogether. The gifts of the *fai matua* are made into one packet and those of the *fai tuatina* into another and they are carried separately. If the marriage is an affair of chiefly houses, then a chief makes his *meŋa* separate from those of commoners in the parent category. People of Namo will make a separate package from those of Raveŋa etc. also. The cooks associated with the *fai matua* group assist it by contributions of bark-cloth; they have received their share of the *koroa*. The cooks associated with the bridegroom's family, however, do not help to make up the *koroa*; a great deal of the burden of the *aŋa* has fallen on them, unlike the cooks of the woman's family. This is an illustration of one of the principles which animate the fulfilment of kinship obligations in Tikopia—that the contributions should be considered as part of a series, and that services and rewards between different sections should be roughly equivalent.

The *meŋa* are brought from the house of the bride's people by two women, one of whom carries the contribution of the *fai matua* group and the other of the *fai tuatina*.

Their arrival is watched for very keenly and announced to the bride and others. It is a dramatic moment. As the first woman comes close to the house she slips off the bands which have kept the load on her back. The bride runs to her, goes down on her knees, throws her arms round her waist and begins to wail. It is their first meeting since she has left her father's house. The woman gives her a blow with her fist, then sinks down and pillowing her head on the girl's back begins to wail too. Such was the scene as I saw it, illustrated in the photograph (Plate XIV). The wailing, which takes the form of a dirge, goes on for some time, until the second woman comes up. When I saw it, she arrived on the scene rather too early and was told to wait a little. Then the same little drama is enacted. The blow and the weeping are customary, but the women, who are the girl's *nana*, are said to be really angry because of her flight. One of those I saw looked distinctly annoyed, and there appeared to be some feeling of irritation. The natives say that the unexpected departure of the bride does mean tension between the two families.

After the bundles have been set down they are opened by representatives of the groom's family and the contents apportioned among the contributors to the *koroa*. The *matua meŋa* go to people who have given particular help. Again, if a man has suffered injury in the capture of the bride, he will be remembered by giving him a mat. The *uruŋa* only is kept as the bed-mat of the bride. Mats and bark-cloth form thus an equivalent in exchange for bowls and sinnet, though each presentation is viewed by the natives as being independent. The women who bring the *meŋa* are given a coil of sinnet each from the stock of the groom's father for their trouble. This gift they do not reciprocate, but take home without more ado. It is termed "the return-gift of the mat-carrying women."

The *aŋa*, which comprises an immense quantity of food, is not repaid directly. It is said "The *aŋa* is not reciprocated; that is its purchase, the mats which are brought." There is in addition a certain small amount of food made by the family of the bride and presented to that of the groom.

SUBSIDIARY GIFTS AND EXCHANGES

The aspect of the marriage ceremony which bulks largest is the transaction involving the giving of food of the *aŋa*, the *koroa* and the *meŋa*. There are, however, a number of other transactions, some of which assume the character of patent exchanges, others of which are more in the nature of unreciprocated gifts, and which do not involve the participation of the same large number of people as in the former instances.

Fakatara.—On the day on which the woman is carried off, or on the next day, if the distance is great, the sisters of the bridegroom bring bark-cloth sheets and girdles. The former are skirts for the new wife, the latter waist-cloths for the husband. The gift is termed *a fakatara*, meaning literally those things which cause to undo or change the clothing. In other words they are substitute garments. This is a gift, customary in form, but representing the goodwill of the women to their new sister-in-law and to their brother. No return gift is made to it. The origin of the *fakatara* gift is given in the sacred myth, the Kai Tapu, which is the most important tale of the doings of the gods. In this the sisters of one of the gods brought along two *rei*, neck-ornaments, in a kit. The story is that these were the *fakatara* of old and that nowadays they have been replaced by bark-cloth.

Faiteŋakoroa.—When the two women come with their bundles of *meŋa* on their backs, each carries under her arm a number of pieces of bark-cloth. They are " *a fakamaru faite ki a potu mami* " (waist-cloths set upon little bark-cloth sheets). The term *faite* refers to the custom of laying one piece of cloth on top of another to form a bundle. Hence the name of this gift—" the piling up of property." The pieces of bark-cloth have been given by various women of the bride's house to be handed over to the sisters of the bridegroom. The carrier takes one from beneath her arm and hands it over. " Your property which has been bound to you from . . ." The women then wail together. When they have finished each of the sisters of the man goes and fetches a coil of sinnet or a string of beads and hands it over as a reciprocal gift for the female relative of the bride. It is not a material point if the donors of bark-cloth are *nana* of the bride or her sisters. Before the gifts are brought each is designated by the donor as being for some particular woman in the groom's household— " the property of the daughter in . . ." Nothing is given without this indication. Some women may receive two such gifts or more and reciprocate them accordingly.

Te Umu Ririuŋa.—On the day after the *aŋa* all the people go out and catch fish. Food is prepared in the house of the bride's parents and also at the house of the man, and the two sets are exchanged. This food is termed the *umu ririuŋa*, the fishing-oven, the verb *ririu* describing the action of catching fish with the hand-net used by women. In olden days the food prepared at the house of the bride's parents was carried down to the shore and the fishing party ate there. The food from the bridegroom's house was carried straight to that of the bride.

Te Fanoŋa.—The next item in the series of reciprocal presentations is the *fanoŋa*. This consists of food prepared at the bridegroom's house and carried to the house of the bride's parents. This used to take place a couple of days after the *umu ririuŋa*. In the interval the new wife was supposed not to eat. " She fasts for her parents," it is said. This is to be understood as abstention from ordinary meals, but not from nourishment altogether. The existence of such a convention is further evidence of the affection that dutiful daughters are expected to bear towards their parents. Nowadays the *fanoŋa* is not prepared on separate days, but consists of a gift of food divided off from the main body of the *aŋa*.

The *fanoŋa*, which consists of one or more very large baskets, is extremely heavy. It is carried by the bride, who is assisted by some other women, and it may be a severe tax on their strength. People say, " when the woman arrives, she is completely exhausted from the burden of the *fanoŋa*." Some women date backaches and various strains from the carrying of this burden.

The reciprocal gift is made the next day. Early in the afternoon the oven is ready and a large mass of food is sent over to the bridegroom's household. This is termed the *toŋoi* of the *fanoŋa*, its equivalent gift, and is distributed among the relatives of the bridegroom, who then disperse to their own houses. Later in the afternoon the bride herself returns to her husband bearing the *taŋa* (in ordinary speech this is the name of the little basket in which people keep betel or other small effects ; its ceremonial meaning is difficult to relate to this). The *taŋa* is a single basket set aside from the oven, and it is intended to provide food for the actual household of the bridegroom. Sometimes two *fanoŋa* have been sent—one to the parents and one to the mother's brother of the bride. Then two *taŋa* are sent back in addition to the two repayments of the *toŋoi*.

HUSBAND AND WIFE AFTER THE WEDDING

The description of the economic exchanges may be interrupted here in order to consider the position of the newly married pair. The act of consummation and the songs of scorn by young people have already been discussed, but there are certain other aspects to be considered, apart from these more dramatic episodes. The position of the newly married pair at this time is one of some embarrassment. They are the centre of attention, the object of the very elaborate ceremonies that have taken place around them, and yet, except in a few particulars, they are not allowed to participate. They remain inactive, and appear shy and uneasy ; they sit together in a corner of the house and move very little. The bride especially appears bashful.

Apart from the wave of social interest directed upon them by the fact of their union, the bride and her groom may have another reason for embarrassment. The evaluation of virginity in Tikopia has already been discussed. If the bride has been really abducted or has eloped before the man has had access to her, then the consummation of the marriage gives a test of her physical condition. If he finds his wife a virgin, then he rejoices. " The man exults that the woman is his ; he has acquired the woman." In former times he might dip his finger in the blood and smear it like turmeric on his forehead ; nowadays a white *tiare* blossom, barely unfolding its petals, will be stuck in the hair above his brow. So adorned he walks around outside his house in the morning, swaggering in the possession of the treasure that no other man has touched. " The *tiare* has not opened —a bud ; it is compared to the woman."

Another custom is also associated with this. In the morning one of the female relatives of the bridegroom, as the wife of his mother's brother, takes the skirt which the bride has worn during the night, washes it in the sea till it is free of the stains it has received and hangs it up ostentatiously on one of the beams of the house. This also bears witness to all comers that the bride has a good name.

If the husband finds his wife a virgin it is said, " *Ku taka ko na roŋo*," meaning that his reputation is increased, but if she has been deflorated before, it is said, " There is no reputation for him." This bears out the point previously made that the evaluation of chastity in Tikopia is in the interests of the man and not of the woman.

If a girl is brought to a man and they have not known each other before marriage, but on having intercourse he finds her not a virgin, then he may issue a formal protest. On the day of the *fanoŋa*, when the large basket is ready to be carried to the house of the woman's parents, he takes the edge of it and breaks it in two. It is then carried off. When the parents see the broken top of the basket, they are greatly ashamed. " They quiver in shame because their daughter has gone in a bad state, she has no reputation." The husband appears to take no other action, such as beating his wife, and there is no other organized procedure available. If the girl is not a virgin because her husband has been her lover prior to marriage, then nothing at all is said about it.

There are many cases of course where the groom knows the futility of expecting to be the first to possess his bride. I have the impression that it is usually at the marriages of people of rank, which attract much more attention than those of commoners and are more frequently preceded by abduction of the girl, that the tokens of virginity are most often sought and most frequently displayed.

A small ceremony takes place when the oven of joining has to be uncovered. When the food is cooked the bride is led by the hand by a woman of her husband's household out to the cookhouse to take the top off the oven. When I saw her she did not look at the crowd gathered around, but kept her head downcast as she went and performed the task. This represents the formal initiation into the economic life of her new home. Tending the oven is an important part of every wife's work, and her induction into it by her husband's female relatives is a conventional token of the co-operation that must henceforth exist between them.

A touching incident of the meal of the oven of joining is the attendance of a number of young bachelors and girls, who gather in a corner near the married couple and eat from the same basket as they. This is termed the *kai fakamavae ma te taka*, the food of parting from the unmarried state ; it is a farewell meal. It is curious how much sentiment the Tikopia expend on the entry into marriage. The freedom and the gaiety of bachelor days appeal to them greatly, this particularly perhaps because of the limited opportunities for amusement which offer when they have once taken on matrimonial obligations.

Another parting feast of much the same kind is known as the *pureŋa*. I did not observe one of these, but was told that it takes place before marriage. A crowd of young men and girls meet together bringing food and betel material. The occasion is said to be the approaching marriage of a young man, but it is difficult to see how this could be known much in advance. I have the impression that the initiative is taken either by a young man who is contemplating marriage himself or who suspects it of someone else. The young people eat together, drink coconut milk and chew betel with a great amount of talk. They may also sing and wail together over their approaching separation. " Great is the wailing of the unmarried ; he has dwelt in the path of married men ; he has dwelt in the path leading to old age ; but the unmarried stand apart."

The bride's first visit to her parents' home again takes place with the *fanoŋa*. She goes into the house and wails together with the members of her family, then she sleeps the night with them and returns the next day to her husband with the *taŋa*. While she is staying with her people she is instructed by them in the correct behaviour to her husband's relatives. " You treat properly the *kano a paito* of your man," they say to her ; " do not spread evil talk about them lest we do not wish to go near you ; do not turn away from his people ; speak smoothly to them," and so on.

Before going back to her husband's house, the bride changes her garments for others supplied by her mother or one of her other relatives. The new clothing in which she was dressed before leaving her husband's home is discarded and remains as the property of the woman who supplies these fresh garments. If the bride's father or other close patrilineal relative is a ritual elder, then he may put a leaf circlet of cordyline round her neck and recite a formula over her to insure her health and prosperity. Pa ŋatotiu did so for the girl from Vaikava and for her companions.

The preparation of the food in return for the *fanoŋa* means a very busy day for the parents of the woman and their relatives. This is particularly the case if, as at the Roŋoifo marriage, the food is sent on the same day as the mats. When it was ready at ŋatotiu the tide was high and a search was made for canoes to carry the food over the lake. But by this time evening was drawing near and all the available craft had gone out to set nets. There was great irritation on the part of the people who had been getting the baskets ready. Some went off to search for canoes, others on various pretexts slipped away to their houses and left a conscientious few to fulminate. At last Pa Niata went off to Namo to bring back a vessel. It was one of the few occasions on which I had seen the organization of a ceremony break down. Generally it was sustained at the cost of much discussion and running about. This time there was a long wait, distressing to the people in charge who did not know how they would be able to fulfil their obligations. At last Pa Niata returned reporting that no canoe could be got. Pa Teputa in Namo would not let his go and the two of them had fought about it—verbally only I gathered. But Pa Niata was a man of action. He grabbed a pole, got hold of another man, and off they went bearing the food between them. It meant wading nearly breast high amid the waves round the point of Foŋo te Koro. From Pa Tekaumata he drew the complimentary expression, " Now that one there is the single sensible person." Then another couple of men were scraped up. Pa Rarovai was cursed vigorously for going off to sleep in a house near by. Someone was sent to rouse him, but he refused to budge, and was cursed again. At last the canoe of Pa Fetu came and the remainder of the food was carried down by men and women to it. The bride and her companions were keen to go too ; they were told by the rest of the people to wait, but they insisted. At last as it was almost dusk the canoe got away with its heavy load.

Kete.—About the third day after the *fanoŋa* food is prepared again in the household of the husband and carried to the parents of the bride. It is divided by them among the *fenua fai meŋa*, the folk who contributed to the gift of mats. The food is termed *te kete*, a name signifying ordinarily a kit. As usual this is a euphemism, since in fact it is a very large basket of provisions. On this occasion the bride usually does not go to visit her people, unless she has previously not paid a call on her *tuatina*. The *kete* is reciprocated by the bride's people on the following day, and in association with this return present goes a mass of uncooked food—taro, bread-fruit, etc. This latter is known as the *fakasaraŋaumu*. This may perhaps best be translated as " causing to set aside the ovens." It is said that the name is given with the idea that the food which has been gathered by the husband's relatives for their oven will be set on one side (*sara*) on the arrival of the gift of provisions from the wife's family. This raw food is in turn reciprocated by the husband's people on the following day or soon after by a present of cooked food.

The above is a summary of the gifts made at the marriage of sa Roŋoifo. I was given an account earlier of a transaction known as the *fakasaŋa*, which is apparently an alternative name for the *kete*. It was stated that a couple of days after the *taŋa* a gift of food is made by the husband's family to the bride's family, on the grounds that the *aŋa* has not been yet properly completed. It is said, " The *aŋa* is still being made—it has not been finished nicely—the *muna* of the newly married pair is not yet finished." *Muna* as a verb means to speak, to talk, and here refers to the general discussion of the marriage, the publicity that attends it. Here the idea is made fairly explicit that the ceremony demands public recognition, that its efficacy depends to some extent upon a sufficient amount of talk about it being in the mouths of people at large.

Now comes a pause of ten days or so—some say only until the tenth day after marriage. A basket of food is prepared by the husband's family and presented to the family of the bride. This is also called *te kete*. Usually the food is kept in the house of the woman's parents and eaten by her family and immediate relatives alone. After the marriage of sa Roŋoifo five *kete* were made on this occasion, thus giving an index to the wealth of the husband's family. One was sent to the Ariki Taumako, another to Pa ŋatotiu, others to Pa Tekaumata and Pa Maniva, while one was also sent to the woman's maternal uncle, Pa Nukufuti. With the second *kete* arrives the bride. When the family assembles to eat, the woman's father says, " Go and invite our son-in-law," thus for the first time taking official cognizance of his existence. The man comes and crawls to each important member of the family in turn, presses his nose to their knee and is greeted by them. There is no display of anger or impoliteness on their part ; he stands now in a relation of constraint to them ; they are all *tautau pariki* (see Chapter IX). The married pair sleep in the house of the wife's father for a couple of nights, assist in the work of the family, and then return home upon invitation from the husband's kin.

The term *kete* is used for the food gifts of sa Taumako. In Kafika and Tafua the gift is termed *loŋi*, which ordinarily applies to a domestic food kit. Besides the present of food taken to the woman's family, there are in the case of a woman married from sa Kafika four other baskets, one given to the Ariki Kafika, one to Pa Rarovi, one to Pa Tavi, and one to the Ariki Faŋarere. When the woman is of Tafua three other baskets are sent off, one to the chief, one to Pa Saukirima and one to Nau lasi—the last being the official title of the eldest daughter

of the chief of Tafua. The basis of these gifts is of a religious order ;
they are connected with the Female Deity.[1] Futhermore, an annual
gift of the same type is made during ceremonies of the sacred season.
The union of a pair in Tikopia, though not consecrated by religious
formulæ, has nevertheless a religious sanction. This does not
operate to prevent husband and wife from severing their partnership
by divorce, but it does tend to perpetuate economic and social relations between the kinship group of the man and the widest kinship
unit of the wife, her clan.

Fakatavaŋa.—A couple of days after the last *kete* has been presented and the young people have been living with the woman's family,
the household of the husband prepare the oven and carry a basket of
food to the other house as a gift to pave the way for an invitation to
the pair to return home. An alternative name for this gift of invitation is *sakiriaŋa*, which means " searching." The married pair are
" sought " by their relatives. This gift is of course reciprocated from
the house of the wife's father, and with the return presents go the
husband and wife.

The visit of the husband to his wife's people marks the beginning
of a co-operation with them which will go all through his life. The
visit and its ceremony serve to revive social relations which have been
threatened, in fact even temporarily broken by the abduction or elopement of the woman. As described earlier, the natives themselves
regard the visit as the first move in smoothing over the awkward
situation of strain which has existed during the previous few
days.

According to Rivers [2] intermediate cases of residence between
patrilocal and matrilocal forms occur when a man goes to live for a
time at his wife's home. He goes on to say : " Sometimes, as in the
island of Tikopia, the visit to the wife's home is of so short a duration
that it is probably only a survival of a former condition of matrilocal
marriage." This hypothesis, based upon a cursory knowledge of
the Tikopia institutions, seems purely gratuitous. Our analysis has
shown that this initial visit can be explained perfectly well in terms of
revival of amicable relations, and inauguration of economic co-operation which is to be a regular feature of the relationship. The visit is
certainly conventional, but its function is clear enough, and is realized
by the people themselves. Why then should it be necessary to postulate an antecedent condition of which there exists no other trace at the
present time in order to explain it ?

[1] See *Rank and Religion.* A full description of the ritual offerings of food
subsequent to marriage will be given in *Work of the Gods.*
[2] W. H. R. Rivers, article, " Marriage," Hastings' *Encyclopedia.*

ABBREVIATED MARRIAGE EXCHANGES

There are occasions when the complete list of ceremonial exchanges is not carried out. The comparative poverty of the groups involved may cause a curtailment, but as a rule this is in the quantity of the goods exchanged rather than in the number of exchanges. The circumstance which does lead to abbreviation of the ceremonies is either the close kinship of the parties or the previous passage of goods owing to a former marriage.

On the day I landed in Tikopia a marriage took place, but caused very little social stir—partly because of the arrival of the *Southern Cross*. The parties were of the same *kano a paito*, both being members of the house of Faŋarere. The woman incidentally was the man's classificatory daughter. The marriage took place rather suddenly, as the child was big in the mother's belly. Because of the close relationship of the parties, the usual exchange of *koroa* and *meŋa* did not occur. This shows the importance of the group element in the union. Where the groups are not separate entities, there is not the same need for an intricate system of exchange to bind their members together.

On the marriage of Nau Vatere to Sauakipure the *aŋa* was made, but the *malai* and *meŋa*, together with the *koroa*, were omitted. The native reason advanced for this was that in the first place the woman had been married already and therefore the equivalent had already been paid, and secondly, that her sister had been married previously into the same family. At first there was some uncertainty about the *malai*, but in the end it was not taken. The *aŋa* was not carried to the house of the woman's people, but was distributed on the spot. Hence no reciprocal gift of food was made from the woman's family. From the morning oven of the *aŋa* two baskets were filled and, with some bundles of sprouting coconuts, were carried to the Ariki Tafua in Faea. The rest of the food from this oven was consumed by the workers present, and the second oven of the day was distributed among the man's *kano a paito*, also in default of any *meŋa* from the woman's house. The reason advanced for not making the *meŋa* twice is that it is prohibited by the Female Deity, the tutelary goddess of women. This is given also as the sanction against the remarriage of widows—it is not proper that the wedding gifts should be made twice.

Ceremonies of marriage do not imply then a mere blind following of traditional precedent. Their primary object is to give a sanction for the union of two persons, but in their normal form they involve also the union of two groups, and in theory the woman is translated thereby from the maiden state. When these normal conditions are not operative, then the ceremony is modified accordingly. Custom and tradition are not such rigid monitors in primitive life as they are often represented.

An extension to the custom of securing a bride by capture is that termed *feurufaki*, entering into each other. It consists in substance of the exchange of women, a bride being abducted in return from the family of the former ravishers. This custom is particularly common among chiefly families—perhaps because they feel that their prestige demands it. The wife of the present Ariki Kafika was taken from the family of Vaisaikiri with the usual fighting. A little while later the people of Tekava, an allied house, took the sister of the Ariki, thus squaring the account. It is said that the women are exchanged (*tauvi*), though this does not seem to lessen the amount of struggling involved. In the second case, however, the people admit the justice of the abduction.

POLYGYNY, ADULTERY, AND DIVORCE

Polygyny is a custom which is quite in favour with the Tikopia, though at the present time the influence of Christianity has diminished its incidence. The genealogical records show how practically every man of rank had more than one wife. The grandfather of the present Ariki Kafika had six, and then by report was not content, but used to roam the island at night in search of amorous adventure. Before the adoption of Christianity the present Ariki Tafua had two wives, the second of whom, Nau Nukuarofa, he put away by the direction of the mission teacher. Pa Fenuaturaki had also two wives, one of whom, Nau Terara, he sent back with her daughter to her parents' house. Nau Moroŋomua, once a polygynous wife of Pa Tauŋa, lives in the same village as her former husband, sharing a house with her brother, while her young son continues to live with his father. Nowadays Pa Nukura has two wives and lives with both, as also do Pa Ropeaukena and Pa Fenuaone. In Raveŋa too lives Nau Sapusapu with her sons, her husband's two brothers and a son of one of these, her husband having taken a second wife and gone to live in Faea, changing his name at the same time to Pa Matinimua. This name is shared by his second wife. In a polygynous marriage each wife has her own house-name, whether she has a separate dwelling or not. Practice varies in the latter respect. One of the wives, usually the first married, bears the same house-name as her husband, and where there is any question of rank she is the senior. The Tikopia have not the custom which obtained among some other Polynesian people of granting seniority to a later wife on the basis of her rank from her father's house. Normally in Tikopia the polygynous wives are regarded as of equal status, and in fact since each is supported in ceremonial affairs by her own relatives, such a marriage represents two separate unions with the man entering into both. The slight differentiation of rank is seen mainly on ritual occasions when it is the first wife who performs any particular ceremonial. In the cases above mentioned, it is the second wives who have been put away.

The major reason for polygyny is said to be the sexual desire of the man. Sometimes if his wife's sister comes to help in the nursing of their child, he has relations with her and takes her as a second wife. The norm of conduct whereby sex relations outside marriage are tacitly regarded as permissible to a husband, but not to a wife, means that facilities are provided which sometimes lead to polygynous unions. Polyandry on the other hand does not exist in Tikopia and adultery by a woman is taken much more seriously.

The story of the love affair and marriage of Pa Fenuatara, as he told it to me himself, illustrates very well a number of the points that have been raised in the course of this chapter—the conflict between love and respect for parents, the force of desire and the expression of jealousy and wounded feeling.

Before his marriage Pa Fenuatara had relations with the girl who is now Nau Tauraro. She was quite young at the time. He wanted to marry her, but his parents objected, saying that she was only a girl and not fit for marriage. The girl desired him very much and he her, but he gave in to the wishes of his parents and went to another woman. Later he brought this mistress home as his wife. On the day of his marriage a dramatic incident occurred. Another old flame of his, who had been the object of a transitory passion, rushed up, grasped him round the knees and refused to release him. Angrily he threatened to stick a knife into her throat, but without avail. She had no shame—so he said—coming like that before the whole group of relatives on his wedding day. He refused to accept her and his wife too objected. But finally such was her persistence that she was allowed to remain, and the three of them lived together in the one house. After a time his objection to this arrangement and the friction which arose from it grew so strong that he left his family and went to live in Faea. His father was annoyed and sent his real wife to bring him back. He induced her to stay with him there. Thus they were until the Ariki sent another messenger, and this time his son returned. He declared, however, that being ashamed of all this upset, and not desiring the woman, he was going to put off to sea and die. When this reached the woman's ears she left and returned to her own family. Since then she has married happily, her husband being Pa Raŋimatere. This episode had evidently left a deep im-

PA FENUATARA IN THE GARDENS
Summoned from his digging to be photographed, he has his hair bound back
for work. On his chest is hung a bonito hook as an ornament, and he has a
European leather belt around his waist, partly for support, and partly for display.

pression on Pa Fenuatara ; he stressed the strength of the woman's passion and his embarrassment in trying to cope with it.

After his marriage and return to his home, he still had thoughts of his former love. She and his wife quarrelled and fought whenever they met ; the girl insisted on coming to the house and there was always a scene when she did. One night when Nau Fenuatara was sleeping soundly, he got up and went out to the girl, who had been looking for him. The pair went to her house and there had intercourse. His wife woke up, and finding her husband missing, rushed out in great excitement and began to spread the news wildly from house to house. She searched but could not find him. At last he came back to find her waiting for him. Then there was a grand scene. He explained his absence by saying that he had been in quite another place, with a group of men, talking. But he said, " I simply lied ; she knew." Later the girl married, but things are not happy between her and her husband, even though they have children. And between her and Pa Fenuatara there is no pleasant feeling. If they meet in the path the girl greets him only with bad words. She consigns him to evil deities : " Husband of a she-devil, where are you going," she asks him angrily. And he jokingly pays her back in kind. " May your father eat filth ; I excrete in your gullet." He steps aside from the path to let her pass. She takes this attitude since she thinks that he rejected her ; he should have taken her to his house as his wife.

Even in his own home he does not find rest. " We two who dwell here," he said slowly, " things are not right with us." His wife is extremely jealous of him. If a girl comes and sits down beside him, he is angrily scolded for it afterwards ; if he jokes with another woman, it is a subject for reproach. So nowadays no unmarried girl comes to Taramoa his house ; they know. Only his immediate relatives, his cousins and sister visit them. " But I am not angry. I know it is because she desires me and objects to herself and another dwelling together," he said philosophically.

I knew that this calm attitude of his was true, for I had seen him often bear her reproaches. This story is illuminating as an illustration of Tikopia attitudes, and it indicates the imperfections in the functioning of the marriage mechanism. There are elements of tragedy in the lives of these three people. Pa Fenuatara and the girl cannot forget. To hear him speak, to see the expression on his face makes it evident that it is a painful subject with him still. And I do not forget the deep, thoughtful tones in which he said of the girl and her husband, " They two dwell, it is not good." The system of marriage in Tikopia, though it usually secures the external conformity of the people who are caught up in it, leaves much room for maladjustment. The practice of carrying off the bride or of a man bringing home a woman who meets his parents' wishes does prevent obvious unsuitable marriages from being contracted. But it frequently involves a rude disturbance of former sentiments, a wrenching apart of bonds, leaving wounds which never properly heal.

The term used for a polygynous marriage is *te nofo*. Literally this means "the dwelling"; it is really an abridged expression for "dwelling doubly" (*nofo fakarua*). A man who desires a polygynous household is described as *taŋata fia fai nofo*, literally "a man wishing to make a dwelling," the polygyny being implied.

Affection for a former mistress is apparently not unusual as a stimulus to polygyny. After a man has settled down with the wife of his parents' desire, his mind may not have broken free from the woman to whom he went formerly. As he sleeps with his new wife, he says to her, "Don't you object. I am going to bring back my own wife. You are the wish of the relatives." Then perhaps the wife says, "It is well. Go you and bring her hither. I too desire that we should dwell, the two of us." But if the wife objects and wants to stay alone, she says, "O no. If you go and bring her here I shall cut her throat." And she shows her knife, "Look you here at the knife which will cut the two of you." Then it is said the husband desists from his intent.

The choice of unmarried women falls sometimes upon married men for their husbands. It is alleged that in such case it is the desire for marriage as such that animates them; they cannot find bachelors who will consent to settle down. People talk thus to a woman who wants to marry a man who has already a wife : "Now this one here, you are running to go to him, but when you go will the house belong to you ? You will go and live at the back of the post." "The back of the post (*tuapou*)" is a simile for the status of a second wife. She sits there while the first wife, the principal wife (*matua fafine*), has her seat in the front of the post (*aroipou*). Her relatives say to the first wife, who may be inclined to make a scene when the second wife comes, "You sit quiet; your own house which stands obeys you; we also obey you." This advice is both a reassurance and a spur, confirming her in her position and admonishing her not to be supplanted.

The general convention in Tikopia is that a married woman is sacred, and that she does not commit adultery. Here is a typical answer to a question on the matter : "A woman who has gone to the sanctifying, that is, a married woman who goes, she has become sacred; a man does not go to the wife of another." "A married woman indeed, great is her weight." It is true that cases of adultery appear to be comparatively rare, and the restrictions of marital fidelity stand in some contrast to the freedom of pre-marital love-making.

But adultery does take place, and people can be got to admit it if the discussion is pursued. Its origin they say is the custom of sweethearting. A man and his mistress are associated until some other man comes and carries her off as his wife. If then later on the woman meets her former lover by accident in the forest, she may consent to have intercourse with him. After they have copulated the man gives her a load of food, helps her to tie it on and each of them goes away. " But when the woman returns, she does not speak of it, she hides it ; the man also does not speak." When she comes home, she lies to her husband, saying that the food is from their orchard, though it is in reality the gift of her paramour.

Some women accede to the demand of their former lovers, others object. The woman objects because the man did not carry her to his house and marry her. She says to him if he makes advances, " Do not come and touch me ; if you do I will make it known ; go and find another woman ; I am married."

Such encounters though they may result in casual sex intercourse do not as a rule mean a regular intrigue. A man who has relations with a married woman is said to go and " make sport with her," or alternatively, " he makes sport with the face of the man whom she has married."

One of the best-known cases of adultery in recent years was that of the first wife of Pa Ropeaukena. News came that he was planning to take a second wife, and his first one objected. In protest she fled with another man. She and an old lover of hers, Tamataŋi, went off together to the woods in Faea and lived there for some time. The *tau*, the search party, in warlike mood, went over from Raveŋa, but the couple were missing. So they broke down the man's house and went to look for the lovers. These evaded discovery for some days (according to one account for the best part of a month). They lived in caves and woodland huts, hiding to avoid observation. They had many narrow escapes. Once the man hid the woman under a pile of coconut husks while he went up a chestnut tree to escape from the observation of Pa Nukunefu. The latter plucked some coconuts and planting a stake among the debris where the woman lay, literally husked the nuts over her body. Another time the man bent down leaves backwards and forwards over the woman and himself so that they were hidden while a member of the searching party was feeling among the undergrowth for them. The aggrieved husband went armed with bow and arrows, and as the natives say, " If he had found them, they would not have lived." During their flight the couple continued to have sex relations, and in fact the woman became pregnant. Later she bore a son, the eldest of her family. During this time the man returned to Fare and called on the Ariki Tafua, and his brother Pa Maevetau, who were his *tuatina*. He took a pair of old waist-cloths of theirs and hung them round his neck. This was to enlist their sympathy and to obtain leave for the food he was taking from the orchards of Faea. He said to them that he was returning. " I am going to my land the woods." In spite of protests he went back in the early morning, unseen by anyone. His success in hiding himself and his companion is attributed to the fact of his having acquired the magic of the *rau rakau* in the south where he had worked on a plantation, whereby he blinded the eyes of the searching party and others, befogging them. (The Tikopia believe that in the New Hebrides the natives possess magic of a very powerful kind which operates through the medium of leaves, *rau rakau*.)

At length the pair returned after being sought by fresh parties of people almost every day, without success. Considering the small size of the island and the way in which people normally travel all over it to their cultivations, this evasion is a remarkable feat. On their return the man was kept in Faea and the woman was taken back to her husband by a party from Tafua. She was brought into the house where she fell like a log and lay there while her husband insulted her and struck her. Wounds were made on her head and body. Nau Tafua, Pa Ranifuri and the others sat there and watched but did not interfere. Their presence however prevented any extreme ill-treatment. Ultimately the second wife came and they all settled down together quietly enough.

Adultery of a man with a woman who was not previously his mistress also occurs and may even take place in her dwelling-house. When the husband has gone fishing for the night or is away for some other reason, then the lover comes and the pair have intercourse. If the husband finds out he will make some show at least of killing or wounding the adulterous pair. If they meet in the path her husband and the lover will probably fight. " They will fight to the death and will not fight for life," the natives say, meaning it will be a severe struggle and not a pretence.

One case which excited a considerable amount of scandal took place during my stay. News came one evening that there had been a quarrel between the house of Rarofara and that of Ronotaono. The first account was that a child of the latter had been struck by Kapolo, a half-witted lad of the former. This boy was then struck severely by Pa Ronotaono. Hearing the news the brothers of Rarofara abandoned their fishing, came back armed with stones and pelted the house of the other. Then they waited with more stones to throw at him when he came out. The quarrel that day was ended by the action of Pa Raŋifuri, who sent a messenger to say that if they did not cease he would come out to them, and then in colloquial phrase, "there would be something doing." Later Pa Roŋotaono emerged, and abandoning the state of seclusion that he was keeping on account of his dead son, went off to Tufenua and returned after dark. A later version of this incident set it in a different perspective. It appeared that the fight really occurred over the adultery of Nau Rarofara, the sister of Pa Roŋotaono. She had been having relations with Fopeni, her husband's brother, and when her husband asked her whence came her latest pregnancy, she threatened to strike him, so he desisted. Pa Roŋotaono struck his sister one blow on the neck and would have continued to beat her if she had not escaped into the house. He told the story to the Ariki Kafika the same night when he brought him a food gift in exchange for a mourning contribution. He said that two children of Nau Rarofara were those of Fopeni and with the third she was now pregnant. On one occasion the pair were discovered under a tree; also the man was going constantly to her house. It was from the Ariki Kafika that I got these details. No action was taken by the husband, and presumably the intrigue continued. This, however, is unusual.

There is no actual system of technical divorce in Tikopia. But a separation may occur and the woman returns to her house. This may be on the grounds of childlessness or incompatibility, as well as adultery. For instance, Sia was married, but his wife had relations with another man, so he discarded her. In a dance-song which he composed some time after, he referred to women as *atua kai taŋata* (man-eating devils). But when a woman lives apart from her husband he expects her to remain chaste, and if she takes a lover he is angry, as in any ordinary case of adultery. He may come and demonstrate before the other man's house. The result depends on the temper of the parties concerned. If the lover and the wife decide to join forces, then her act of going to live with him, ratified by the usual economic exchanges, is a marriage. There is no formal ceremony of divorce, nor any moral attitude on the part of the community towards remarriage.

The following case, which occurred some time before I arrived in Tikopia and which was told me by Pa Raŋifuri, illustrates these points. Pa Fenutapu had a wife and an "adhering child" living with them, a girl from the house of Nopu, of Faŋarere clan. His wife bore him a succession of girls. At last, with the approval of the wife, Pa Fenutapu had intercourse with the girl and lived with her openly until she became pregnant. His sisters could not stand the sight of the pair of them together and used to turn their backs on the girl. Pa Fenutapu tried his best to win them over, but without success. The girl bore the desired male child (now Pa Repetoŋa) and then went back to her family in Nopu. There the eldest son of the Ariki Faŋarere, at that time hardly more than a boy, conceived an affection for her, they lived together and were married. The woman, apparently at least ten years older than the man, afterwards bore him a child. Later Pa Fenutapu himself had a son by his first wife—this child now being the man known as Pa Fenutapu, after his father's death. But on the day of the marriage, that is, when the woman first went to live in her lover's house, Pa Fenutapu was very angry. Pa Raŋifuri happened to be going with a load of food to the Ariki Faŋarere that day, but was stopped by Pa Fenutapu, who was a relative of his. " Where are you going ? " " To the Ariki Faŋarere." " No food shall be carried to that house to-day ! " He had been on the point of seizing a club and rushing off to demonstrate in anger before the offender's dwelling, but was calmed down by Pa Raŋifuri.

THE THEORY OF PRIMITIVE MARRIAGE

In anthropological textbooks a distinction is usually drawn between different forms of the marriage ceremony which are supposed to be mutually exclusive. Lowie for example includes marriage by capture as one of the forms which lack even the semblance of compensation ; [1] and the securing of brides by the exchange of women is generally regarded as being alternative to the custom of marriage by purchase. The material from Tikopia seems to show that what we have to consider is not so much a number of different *forms* of marriage as a number of *elements*, several of which may be present in the institution at the one time. In Tikopia there may be a very real wrenching away of the bride from her father and her kinsfolk, but this does not prevent gifts from being made later in compensation, and explicitly termed " the purchase of the woman." Here then we have two of what have been regarded as essentially opposed elements linked together. Furthermore, when a woman has been abducted from a group, her relatives sometimes even up the score by later taking a bride for one of their sons from the family of the abductors. Material compensation and the normal exchanges take place in both cases.

In Tikopia the function of each of these elements can be clearly

[1] *Primitive Society*, 1920, 23.

seen. The capture of the woman—or the quiet elopement with her
which is the alternative—has the effect of securing her in circumvention
of the forbidding attitude of her parents.   This of course would be
necessary only in a society where fathers by convention are even
more opposed to suitors than were our Victorian grandsires.   Moreover, the bearing-off of a bride is to be correlated with other social
institutions such as patrilocal residence, which involves her future
co-operation with her husband's group.   It can then have a directly
practical significance—the man's relatives combine against his wishes
to secure a woman of suitable character to live with them.   It is to
be correlated also with the deference of children to their parents, which
is the Tikopia social norm.   A sudden wrench is needed to break the
girl's obedience to her father.   On the other hand the capture of the
bride, while overthrowing the sway of one parent, offers an instrument
of domination to the other.   " Marriage is long, love is fleeting," is
an epitome of the attitude of the man's father and his relatives, and this
custom allows them to force upon their son a woman of the quality
they desire.

But marriage by capture in Tikopia is governed by rules which
have the effect of ameliorating the offence that it gives.   An important
mechanism is the linkage of it with compensation, from which it
need not logically be divorced.   If the capture were from a hostile
community, no mechanism of adjustment would be necessary.   But
since it takes place in a small community from a group with whom
normally relations are friendly, with whom there is co-operation and
even some degree of kinship, some method of restoring the social
equilibrium is required.   Towards this the initial present, made with
all the forms of humble apology and abasement, is orientated, and the
ensuing series of gifts and counter-gifts, enforced upon the two groups
by tradition and public opinion, binds them together more and more
firmly.

With the succession of gifts goes an increase in cordiality ; punishment is succeeded by friendly treatment ; the bride pays a visit to
her parents and is allowed to return, until finally after a decent interval
the actual focus of the offence, in the person of the bridegroom, is
received and his new status accepted.   Here again correlated social
norms give support ; the respect enjoined between affinal relatives is
a barrier against untoward incidents.   Unless the father is prepared
to break all the strictest canons of decorum, he cannot behave rudely
to his son-in-law.

Thus we have in Tikopia a form of marriage which utilizes real
capture as one of its mechanisms, and this not as a survival from a
more primitive condition but as a custom which fits closely into the

other existing institutions of the people. Different societies have each their own mechanisms for dealing with the problem of transferring the major allegiance of a woman from her parents to her husband. It is probable that with the extension of European and Christian influence in Tikopia the difficulties inherent in this transference will have to be overcome in a less dramatic and dangerous way than at present.

CHAPTER XIV
KINSHIP AND SOCIAL STABILITY

TIKOPIA kinship has been treated in this volume from several points of view. First the local grouping of the people has been analysed in order to isolate the basic kinship unit, which has been empirically ascertained to be the family, and the position of this in terms of household arrangements has been defined. Then the relationships between the component members of the family have been examined, to show how the recognized genealogical ties emerge in concrete behaviour in situations of production and consumption of food, education, bodily contacts, conversation and other minutiae of domestic life. The enquiry has been pushed out further along the same lines to cover the relationships between members of the family and those of associated units, whether linked by consanguinity or marriage. Again, the corporate activities of these individuals regarded from the point of view of their aggregation in specified larger groups has been described. All this has represented a kind of dissection of the anatomy of the society, viewing the kinship links as part of the skeletal structure giving the society its form; to this has been added a consideration of the linguistic factor in such relationships, which by implementing and making effective action between individuals, is like part of the musculature of the society. The angle of approach has then been changed again, and analysis has been made of the relationship of individuals and groups of individuals to their economic resources in land, of their reactions to the biological factor of sex endowment, of the crystallization of them around any single one of their number who is at such critical stages in his social development as represented by initiation or marriage. This, to continue the analogy, is like investigating aspects of the physiology of the society. The biological parallel cannot be taken as exact; it does not imply that a society can be studied as a unitary organism, but it is a convenient way of characterizing the examination of the morphology and functioning of a diffused phenomenon such as kinship. Explanation of the recognition of the crude fact of the connection of persons through sex union and birth involves tracing out a series of relationships through the whole fabric of the social life.

Methodologically, it would have been of interest to have given a systematic analysis of kinship as revealed in the life of a single Tikopia; for this I have not sufficient documentation, but space would not have allowed of the presentation of the data, even had it been available.

The general principles on which my study of Tikopia society was based have, I hope, become evident in the course of the book. The test of a method lies in the direct presentation of the results obtained through it rather than in elaborate argument about it. But a few of the cardinal points may be summarily restated.

I have tried to make the generalizations given empirical, based on material actually observed, and have used the statements of informants as an index to the kind of formulation commonly produced by natives on these topics rather than as evidence for what actually occurs. I have tried to reduce assumptions to a minimum, and in particular to discuss what the Tikopia do rather than what they think or feel. In the psychological field, more than anywhere else in the study of un-civilized people, unverifiable postulates are apt to be introduced so subtly that they pass unnoticed by the ordinary reader, and no attempt to justify them is made, or even to admit that they are present. Kin-ship behaviour and not kinship sentiment is the study of the anthro-pologist. Where he uses such terms as sentiment, emotion, feeling, where he describes the workings of the mind of an individual, it should be understood that such characterizations are merely short-hand symbols for a complex system of small observable and observed actions in each case.

In another direction I have concerned my analysis not with the needs of Tikopia society, but with the activities of its members. There are, it is true, certain fundamental conditions to which a society, in the persons of the individuals who compose it, must con-form if it is to maintain its existence. There must be restraints of some kind, for example, on the taking of human life within the society ; there must be some facilities for economic co-operation and sex union among the members. But the direct interpretation of all the institu-tions of a single society, in terms of the basic human needs of its members, is difficult in the absence of a wide series of comparative studies in different societies which will discuss the problem of varia-tion of an institution against its social background in each case, and deal with the absence of the institution in any particular community. The needs of a human being in society are traditionally dictated and are an inference from his observed activities. What I have en-deavoured to do in the case of the Tikopia is to analyse the reper-cussions of the acts of individuals, to show how they are integrated into sets of behaviour each with a guiding theme, and to make clear the relationship of these themes to one another. In concrete illustration, it has been shown how the avoidance of the use of names and oaths between brothers-in-law bears upon the system of economic co-opera-tion socially enjoined between them, and how this co-operation is related to the assistance afforded to a boy by his mother's brother at initiation. How far the practice of initiation is itself a response to the fundamental problem of the adaptation of the adolescent to life in society is another matter.

THE MEANING OF KINSHIP

Kinship is fundamentally a re-interpretation in social terms of the facts of procreation and regularized sex union. The complex series of social relationships formed on this basis comprises activity of a residential, an economic, a political, a juridical, a linguistic order, and constitutes a system of primary integration in the society. A scientific definition of a kinship tie between individuals means not only a specification of the genealogical bond between them and the linguistic term used to denote that bond, but a classification of their behaviour in many aspects of their life.

The fact that there is no society without a kinship system of some kind means that in the first place there is overt allowance made for sentiments generated by parturition, sex union and common residence (to put it at its lowest, even where male procreation is not understood) ; in the second place that these physical phenomena provide a simple base, easily recognizable and usually unchallengeable, on which other necessary social relationships may be erected. Moreover, the kinship tie is permanent until death—unless diverted by the fiction of adoption.   In small societies such as Tikopia, then, it can be readily grasped why kinship is at the root of much of the social structure.

In Tikopia the following are some of the spheres into which kinship enters as an articulating principle.   It is the basis of association in the small residential units, the households ; it is the acknowledged bond between the members of the major named groups of the society ; it provides the link with elders and in part with chiefs, who exercise political and religious functions for these groups and for the society as a whole ; it is the overt principle regulating the ownership and suzerainty of land. Kinship provides terms of address and reference, thus giving a linguistic bridge between individuals ; it is the common basis of assistance in cooking and primary economic co-operation ; it stands behind a great series of duties, privileges, taboos, avoidances ; it proscribes certain types of sex union and marriage ; it is the basis for the assemblage of members of the society on the birth, initiation, sickness or death of anyone. Enshrined in tradition, it bulks largely in the accounts of the origins of present-day social groups and the distribution of territory among them ; projected into the realm of the spirit-heavens it gives the basis for approach to ancestors and gods, and is used as the key to the interpretation of the disordered behaviour of individuals in a state of dissociation.

The Tikopia expressly rely on ties of kinship to explain the existence of relationships in all these fields. The recognition and the utilization of kinship ties in this manner undeniably makes for external conformity to social rules. The general acknowledgment of the validity of the kinship bond, in conjunction with the classificatory system of reckoning kin, for instance, is of great utility in cases of difficulty in complying with economic obligations ; the mobility of the system, the principle of representation, allows of easy substitution and a kinsman slips into the place of the one who is missing. The society is of course not without its elements of friction, some of which are directly associated with the kinship system : the change in the balance of authority between father and eldest son ; the assertion of interests between the eldest and his younger brothers ; the abduction of women from their families in marriage ; the division of lands among branches of a kinship group. Here the pattern is such as often to produce a situation of strain. In other spheres such as the feuds between the geographical districts, the rift between Christian and heathen, the differential wealth of ramages and clans, the separation in rank between chiefly and commoner families, the ties of kinship act sometimes as a factor of reconciliation, sometimes as one of perpetuation of the conflict. The privileges and obligations of the religious system of the people act in similar style.

Evaluation of a society in terms of the cultural efficiency of its institutions is difficult, if only because some elements of every institution appear to provide for more successful adaptation than others. But on the whole it can be said of the kinship system of the Tikopia that its bonds serve as channels of communication for the members of the society, as a framework for economic and social co-operation, and as a factor of stability in throwing a recognized bridge between differences of material interest.

THE PLASTICITY OF POLYNESIAN KINSHIP

In conclusion a brief review may be given of the general nature of Polynesian kinship grouping.

These societies have each different mechanisms for solving the problem of social existence for their individual members on a group basis. To speak of Polynesian societies as patrilineal in character, with the joint family as the kinship group, is to view them in distant perspective. Beyond the nuclear group of the individual family the fundamental common unit is of a ramifying or branching type with the tendency to split up and form new units as its size increases. There is formal utilization of the patrilineal principle for the transmission of membership of the group, but the matrilineal tie is used either formally or informally in each society to fix the social position of an individual and to give him certain material advantages. The extent to which recognition of the tie through the mother is incorporated into the scheme of social institutions, particularly into principles of group membership, is to be correlated especially with variations in the economic structure of the community.

Descent in Polynesia, that is, membership of a named kinship group, is not reckoned everywhere in terms of unilateral consanguinity, but is conditioned to a large extent by residence. For instance, the strict patriliny of the tiny island of Tikopia may be certainly correlated with a patrilocal form of marriage and settlement; the ambilaterality of the Maori and the mechanism of absorption through residence from the female into the male side of the house in Samoa and Tonga are correlates of the greater tendency to uxorilocal settlement at marriage. As this matrilocal residence gives the offspring of the marriage a position in the kinship group of their mother, and thus for one generation allows the operation of matrilineal descent. This factor of residence is reinforced very strongly by the need for personal labour as a basis for economic support. The bond of blood forms the plastic social material on which the conditions of residence and labour operate to produce the particular social form—the " patrilineal " system of descent. The system of land tenure has also to be considered as one of the conditioning factors of the mode of descent.

From our analysis it is difficult to see the kinship institutions of Polynesia arranged in a developmental series such as would be in accordance with their diffusion from a common centre. The great variety of custom and the practical impossibility of deciding whether a variation is an adaptation to local geographical conditions, to some specific local circumstance (as a state of hostility), or to influence from another community enables us to throw very little light on the history of Polynesian institutions. Certain features which appear to be common to the whole area may be regarded as basic or characteristic. These include the branching or ramage type of kinship unit, a strong emphasis on the patrilineal transmission of group interests coupled with a readiness to admit interest through the mother, particularly when facilitated by abnormal residential conditions. A formal expression of this position is given linguistically and socially by the explicit separation of descendants in the male line from those in the female line ; brother and sister, the point of departure, are in some societies (but not in all) given specific terminological distinction by the children of the other. Polynesian societies display too an easy adaptation of their institutions, a plasticity which must have been of advantage to the people when reorganizing after a struggle with the severe conditions of ocean voyaging over such a vast area with its tiny and scattered island groups. The custom of adoption, current in one form or another in all these communities, is evidence of the adaptibility of family life to social needs. Through all this the individual family remains the nucleus of the community life. It loses members to other groups, becomes swollen by accretions from outside, it enlarges and divides, but it has an enduring vitality. It is the basis of economic co-operation, the centre of religious worship, the model for political organization.

This general plasticity is not the same in all Polynesian societies. Some display a firmness in their morphology, a tendency to impose barriers upon the filtration of individuals from one social group to another, and to demarcate clearly the various social units. In Tikopia patrilineal descent and succession are definite ; in the Gilberts marriage is prescribed outside the clan. Such elements of rigidity appear to be most marked in small communities with relatively dense population, and there is a possibility that this is not an accidental association. I am of the opinion that the relation of population to size of territory is a more important factor in influencing the character of social institutions than is usually recognized. Some attention to demography in fact should be the concern of every social anthropologist.

A few specific institutional correlations have been suggested in the course of this chapter. They are essentially of a tentative nature, particularly in view of the paucity of available data. In many cases it seems as if the variations in the form of an institution have been dictated, not by some fundamental cultural need but by institutional efflorescence or the association under conditions now irrecoverable, of individuals from different cultural groups.

A PRACTICAL CASE FOR A STUDY OF KINSHIP

The conclusions drawn in this chapter may seem to have little practical application. They may, however, add some necessary emphasis to the need for recognition as a matter of policy of the fundamental place of kinship in the life of Polynesian people. Many of the difficulties of the administration of Western Samoa, for example, lie in the fact that economic interests are mainly controlled by kin groups and not by individuals. Since the coming of European civilization to the Maori, the increase in the facility of communication has meant a lessening of the residence qualification for land ownership and consequently a greater diversity of landholding, individuals having interests of varying proportion in many parts of the country. The economic difficulties have recently led to a process of consolidation successfully carried through by government officers with due attention to native customs. But if the practice of allowing interest in the land through the mother is to be retained then this will involve a splitting of the present consolidated blocks and in a few generations the same process will have to be begun again. The alternative is that patrilineal inheritance or disposition by will, or inheritance purely on the basis of residence, shall be followed in lieu of the former native practice, and there are signs that a unilateral principle of land transmission of this order is tending to replace the old bilateral system. Though compelled by circumstances to adopt this innovation natives are apt to view it with regret, since the tie with the mother's group, which is of sentimental as well as of economic interest to them, is thereby weakened. The implications of such a change were probably not envisaged by the authors of the consolidation scheme. This example, which illustrates the interaction of economic circumstances and kinship structure, stresses the desirability of understanding the kinship of a people before proceeding to a change in economic policy.

A last word may be said about one practical aspect of anthropological study. In revulsion from the mere folklorist attitude of antiquarian anthropology, science of to-day is in danger of being caught up by practical interests and made to serve them, to the neglect of its own problems. Social anthropology should be concerned with understanding how human beings behave in social groups, not with trying to make them behave in any particular way by assisting an administrative policy or a proselytizing campaign to achieve its aims more easily. The scientist gives generalizations regarding the nature of the working of institutions ; it is not his duty to affix ethical values to them, nor by conniving at such an ethical evaluation to pave the way for their modification. Missionary, government officer and mine manager are free to use anthropological methods and results in their own interests, but they have no right to demand as a service that anthropology should become their handmaid. Nor can the standards which they invoke—" civilization," " humanity," " justice," " the sanctity of human life," " Christianity," " freedom of the individual," " law and order "—be regarded as binding ; the claim of absolute validity that is usually made for them too often springs from ignorance, from an emotional philanthropy, from the lack of any clear analysis of the implications of the course of action proposed, and from confusion with the universal of what is in reality a set of moral ideas produced by particular economic and social circumstances.

This is not to say that the scientist himself may not have his own personal predilections, based on his upbringing and social environment, his temperamental disposition, his aesthetic values. He may regard the culture of a primitive, half-naked set of people in an island of the Solomons as a pleasant way of life, giving expression to the individuality of its members in ways alien to western civilization ; he may regard it as something he would like to see endure, and he may strive to preserve it in the face of ignorance and prejudice, pointing out the probable results of interference with ancient customs. This he does as a man ; his attitude is part of his personal equation to life, but it is not implicit in his scientific study. The greatest need of the social sciences to-day is for a more refined methodology, as objective and dispassionate as possible, in which, while the assumptions due to the conditioning and personal interest of the investigator must influence his findings, that bias shall be consciously faced, the possibility of other initial assumptions be realized and allowance be made for the implications of each in the course of the analysis.

APPENDIX

While this book was in the press Mr B. E. Crawfurd, formerly District Officer at Vanikoro, kindly made available to me the results of a census which he took by a head-count in Tikopia in May 1933. A summary of his figures is as follows :—

	Males	Female	Total
Under (approx.) 16 years . .	384	286	670
Over (approx.) 16 years, single .	126	99	225
,, ,, ,, married .	187	188	375
,, ,, ,, widowed .	25	28	53
Totals . .	722	601	1323

Comparison with my figures for 1929 shows that there has been an increase in the Tikopia population of approximately forty persons, or about 3 per cent., in four years. It appears, as I suggested in Chapter XII, that 1929 was an exceptional year, and moreover, on re-checking my census against my genealogies, I appear to have omitted from the former a family of four or five persons—that of Pa Faiaki. But, despite this, the growth of population in the interval has evidently been considerable. Mr Crawfurd's data also corroborate mine with regard to the large excess of young males over young females—well over a hundred, which is remarkable in such a small community, and strongly suggests artificial selection by infanticide, though the natives themselves do not admit that this has a general trend.

INDEX

Abortion, 373

Adoption: "adhering child," 190-3

Adultery, 119, 471-7

Affinal kinship, 230-1, (*v. also tautau pariki*)

Afu, 218-9, 329

Age factor, 263, 275

Albinism, 16-17

Ancestors, names, 87-88
attitude on incest, 287-90
common to all clans, 319

Anuta, 20n., 34, 303, 312

Aŋa feast, 398, 453, 460-61, 469

Areca 270, 339-40

Ariki, v. Chiefs

Arofa, 151-2, 173, 382, 408

Atua, v. Religion

Authority, father and son, 165-6
in *paito,* 313
of chief, 336

Avoidance of *mata paito,* 78-79
of personal names, 122, 144, 169, 187-8, 195, 196, 261-5
between affinal kin, 261-78
theory, 276-8

Bark-cloth, 396, 402, 408-9, 461-2

Bathing, *v.* Washing

Best, Elsdon, 293n., 327n.

Betel chewing, 267, 409 (*v.* Areca)

Brachycephaly, 14-15

Breach of custom, 188, 262-3, 274

Brothers, relations between, 128, 166-9, 173-8, 217, 239
song, 257-61
and sisters, 178-85, 209-12, 337 (*v.* Incest)

Brothers-in-law, 204, 261-3, 273, 398 (*v.* Cooks)

Burial, 78, 202, 206
of ancestors, 87-88

Canoes, 132, 436, 466

Cats, 33

Census, 368, 489

Chiefs, 86, 176, 221, 238, 273, 303-4, 440, 442, 444-5, 447, 448, 453, 467, 470
fakaariki, 415
kinship with each other, Ch. VI, 318-19
and commoners, 312, 341, 352-3

and land tenure, 333-42

and wealth, 313-16
Ariki Kafika, 47, 48, 122, 124, 160, 308, 315, 335
home life, 91-92, 194, 195
residence, 108
kin ties, 202
Ariki Tafua, 46, 47, 48, 58, 69, 75, 200, 205, 216-17, 308, 340
cooks to, 260
lands, 345, 354
in initiation, 390
Ariki Taumako, 44, 63, 238, 240, 339, 436, 447

Children, behaviour, 270
position in household, 127, 165-7
treatment of young child, 126-34
gatherings of, 131-2
work of, 137
sentiment for parents, 156-9
obligations to parents, 163-73
as factor of linkage, 257-8

Christianity, *v.* Religion

Civilization, adjustment of Tikopia to, Ch. II
names from, 85

Clan (*kainaŋa*), 59, 61, 75, 316-28
numerical strength, 321
and village grouping, Table I, 64-69
distribution of Tafua, 68-69

Classificatory kin, *v.* Kinship

Climate, 30

Clothing, 378, 461, 465 (*v.* Bark-cloth)

Codrington, 76n., 265n., 298n.

Colour problem, 295-7

Communication with outside world, 18-21, 32-36

Comparison with other Polynesian societies, *v.* Polynesian, Maori, etc.

Constraint of conduct, *v. Tautau pariki,* Avoidance

Cooking, *v.* Food

Cooks by kinship, 259-61, 394, 403, 415, 416, 454

Counting, 411

Crawley, E., 437-8, 446, 448

Cross-cousin, 207-9, 220, 249, 285-6

Culture contact, Ch. II, 85, 269, 272, 274, 374-5, 412-13

Cursing, 268-75

Daily life, 51-55